AMERICA'S STORY

A Spiritual Journey

Miles Huntley Hodges

An Abridged Version of the Three-Volume Series:
America - The Covenant Nation

Copyright © 2021 Miles Huntley Hodges

All right reserved. No part of this book may be used or reproduced by any means, graphic, electronic, or mechanical, including photocopying, recording, taping or by any information storage retrieval system without the written permission of the author except in the case of brief quotations embodied in critical articles and reviews.

ISBN: 978-1-7376413-4-6 (soft copy)
ISBN: 978-1-7376413-5-3 (hard copy)
ISBN: 978-1-7376413-6-0 (laminate copy)
ISBN: 978-1-7376413-7-7 (e-copy)

Library of Congress Control Number: 2021915168

thecovenantnation.com

CONTENTS

PREFACE   1
    THE RISE AND FALL OF SOCIETIES
    THE PARABLE OF THE FOUR GENERATIONS
    THE CHRISTIAN COMPONENT IN THE DYNAMIC
    THE PURPOSE AND CHARACTER OF THIS STUDY

1. AMERICA'S MORAL-SPIRITUAL INHERITANCE   12
    WESTERN CULTURE AND THE WORLD
    JEWISH, GREEK AND ROMAN CULTURAL CONTRIBUTIONS
    CHRISTIANITY
    THE BREAKUP OF CHRISTENDOM
    THE IMPACT OF THE WARS OF RELIGION ON ENGLAND

2. GETTING STARTED IN AMERICA   47
    THE EARLIEST ATTEMPTS AT EUROPEAN SETTLEMENT IN AMERICA
    ESTABLISHING AN ENGLISH SETTLEMENT IN VIRGINIA
    THE ENGLISH SETTLEMENT OF NEW ENGLAND
    THE FOUNDING OF THE ENGLISH PROPRIETARY COLONIES

3. INDEPENDENCE – AND THE NEW REPUBLIC   69
    THE COLONIES MATURE, AND WANDER SPIRITUALLY
    THE AMERICAN "GREAT AWAKENING" OF THE MID-1700s
    THE WAR TO CONFIRM AMERICAN INDEPENDENCE (1775-1783)
    THE YOUNG AMERICAN REPUBLIC
    THE AMERICAN AND FRENCH "REVOLUTIONS" COMPARED

4. THE AMERICAN REPUBLIC GETS UP AND RUNNING   101
    LEADERSHIP SHAPES THE CHARACTER OF THE REPUBLIC
    GROWING SECTIONAL TENSIONS
    MADISON AND THE WAR OF 1812
    EXPANSION
    THE AMERICAN ECONOMIC DYNAMIC AT THIS TIME
    AMERICA'S ONGOING SPIRITUAL DEVELOPMENT

5. CIVIL WAR (1861-1865) AND RECOVERY   136
    GATHERING STORM CLOUDS
    SECESSION AND WAR (1861-1865)
    AMERICA RECOVERS (1865-1880)
    THE BATTLE FOR THE WEST RESUMES

6. AMERICA COMES OF AGE   159
AMERICA DEVELOPS AS AN INDUSTRIAL POWER
NATIONAL POLITICS DURING THE LATE 1800s
THE CULTURAL-SPIRITUAL CHALLENGES OF THE INDUSTRIAL AGE
THE RATIONALIZING OF WESTERN CULTURE
AMERICAN PROGRESSIVISM
AMERICA CULTIVATES NEW SOCIAL FORMULAS
AMERICAN CHRISTIANITY RESPONDS

7. AMERICA ENTERS THE WORLD STAGE   203
AMERICA IN THE AGE OF NATIONAL IMPERIALISM
AMERICA ENTERS WORLD WAR ONE
THE "ROARING TWENTIES"
THE GREAT DEPRESSION

8. WORLD WAR TWO AND THE START OF THE COLD WAR   238
WORLD WAR TWO (1937-1945)
THE STARTUP OF THE COLD WAR
THE WAR IN KOREA (1950-1953)

9. MIDDLE-CLASS AMERICA TRIUMPHANT   270
AMERICAN POST-WAR REBOUND
HOWEVER – THE COLD WAR HITS HOME
EISENHOWER'S AMERICA
THE COLD WAR TAKES ON A NEW QUALITY
THE BRIEF KENNEDY ERA (1961-1963)

10. AMERICA SHIFTS TO THE HUMANIST LEFT   302
JOHNSON – AND "DEMOCRACY FROM ABOVE"
THE SECULARIZING OF AMERICAN CULTURE
THE "REVOLUTION OF RISING EXPECTATIONS"
THE PRESIDENT'S WORSENING WAR IN VIETNAM
THE WORLD GOES ON ELSEWHERE
THE BOOMER COMES OF AGE
1968: THE *ANNUS HORRIBILIS* (THE "HORRIBLE YEAR")
CLOSING THE TURBULENT 1960s

11. THE 1970s: AMERICA DIVIDED   337
NIXON ... AND VIETNAM
NIXON'S CHAOTIC SECOND PRESIDENTIAL TERM
THE BRIEF FORD PRESIDENCY (1974-1977)
THE CARTER ONE-TERM PRESIDENCY
THE FRACTURING OF AMERICA'S TRADITIONAL SOCIAL-MORAL ORDER

12. THE WORLD'S SOLE SUPERPOWER   367
REAGAN ENTERS THE WHITE HOUSE
REAGAN GETS TOUGH
THE AMERICAN ECONOMY STRUGGLES FORWARD

    MAJOR DEVELOPMENTS IN FOREIGN POLICY
    THE IRAN-CONTRA AFFAIR
    THE ONE-TERM PRESIDENCY OF GEORGE H. W. BUSH
    FOREIGN AFFAIRS DURING THE BUSH, Sr. PRESIDENCY
    THE BOOMER BILL CLINTON TAKES THE WHITE HOUSE
    DOMESTIC POLITICS DURING THE CLINTON YEARS
    CLINTON AND THE WORLD
    PARTICULAR EVENTS SHAKE THE COUNTRY DEEPLY IN THE 90s
    SOCIAL DEVELOPMENTS DURING THE REAGAN-BUSH-CLINTON YEARS

13. AMERICA STUMBLES   409
    BUSH, Jr. TAKES COMMAND
    THE HUNT FOR THE 9/11 JIHADISTS .. AND BUSH'S NATION-BUILDING
    ECONOMIC CATASTROPHE (2008)
    THE FEDERAL COURTS AS AMERICA'S SUPREME LAW-MAKING BODIES

14. OBAMA STRIVES TO "CHANGE" AMERICA   428
    THE 2008 NATIONAL ELECTION
    OBAMA'S PROGRAM OF DEEP SOCIAL AND CULTURAL CHANGE
    THE OBAMA ECONOMY
    OBAMA'S FOREIGN POLICY

15. INTO THE AGE OF TRUMP   455
    TRUMP, AND THE MEDIA KINGMAKERS
    AMERICA AND THE WORLD IN THE AGE OF TRUMP
    THE CHAOTIC 2020 ELECTIONS

16. BIDEN TAKES COMMAND   482
    "UNITY"?
    THE MAKING OF JOE BIDEN
    INTO THE "BIDEN ERA"

17. THE LESSONS OF HISTORY   492
    THE TWO AMERICAS
    THE TWO SOCIETIES DURING COLONIAL TIMES
    WHY THIS MATTER OF GOD IS SO IMPORTANT
    HUMAN REASON VERSUS GODLY OR DIVINE REASON
    THE ROLE OF PERSONAL AND SOCIAL MORALS IN GUIDING A SOCIETY
    LEADERSHIP IS KEY TO A SOCIETY'S MORAL ORDER
    GOD'S HAND IN HUMAN HISTORY
    INSPIRING THE WORLD RATHER THAN TRYING TO FIX IT
    DEFENDING WESTERN/CHRISTIAN CIVILIZATION
    A CALL TO RENEW THE COVENANT WITH GOD THROUGH JESUS CHRIST

BIBLIOGRAPHY   524

INDEX   550

PREFACE

* * *

THE RISE AND FALL OF SOCIETIES

The larger, three-volume study, entitled *America – the Covenant Nation*,* has been brought together in these pages as a somewhat summarized version, not as detailed, but with all the major ideas and key points of the larger study presented here nonetheless. You may indeed consult the larger study if you are interested in going deeper into these matters.

This work is the result of years of personal study that began back in the early 1960s when I was a student at the University of Geneva in Switzerland. This was a period when America dominated so much of the world that it was natural for Americans to believe that everything about American politics and culture was the proper model for that larger world. But I found myself in Geneva not only in deep company with students from all around the world – an eye-opening experience in that alone – but also in closest friendship with a group of young Germans, friends going at life on the basis of a start on life amidst a rain of American and British bombs on their homes and neighborhoods, and then growing up watching their parents deal with a world that had for a brief time seen great glory, and then the most humiliating of defeats. Listening to them I got a vivid picture of what it was as a people to go through the proverbial rise and fall of a society. It was a very condensed but very vivid example of how history itself works over the long run – and in the case of the Germans in the short run.

But in their coping power, my German friends also showed me a resiliency that made me realize that there was an amazing dynamic to life operating deeper than merely the one providing generous material blessings to Middle American life. I certainly continued to enjoy those blessings of Middle American life. But from that point on, I would continue

---

America, The Covenant Nation – A Christian Perspective, Bloomington, Indiana, 2020, in three volumes: (1) *Securing America's Covenant with God: From America's Foundations in the Early 1600s – To America's Post-Civil War Recovery in the late 1800s*; (2) *America's Rise to Greatness under God's Covenant: From the Late 1880s to the end of the 1950s*; and (3) *The Dismissing of America's Covenant with God: From the Early 1960s to the Present*. See thecovenantnation.com for details.

on in my journey in life with a keen understanding that there were also other ways to go at that life, some of them quite awesome – but also some of them quite terrible. And getting an early taste of this strange dynamic, I wanted very much to dig deeper into the cause of that dynamic, the forces that made for social success – and for catastrophic failure.

After graduating from the University of Illinois in 1963 I moved on to Georgetown to do masters and doctoral studies. It was a great place to learn the lessons of a tough political "Realism" or *Realpolitik*,* both at the university and by working part-time in the Washington bureaucracy itself (Peace Corps Headquarters and the World Health Organization's regional headquarters). And it being the 1960s – the age when the Kennedy dream died and Johnson attempted to replace that dream with massive bureaucratic action designed to bring into being the Great Society at home and a democratic Vietnam abroad – I got to see another example of the rise and fall of a grand social dynamic.†

Indeed, in August of 1968, I left behind me an angry, violent, and highly self-destructive America – which I got to experience up very, very close in the rioting, pillaging and burning going on around me in Washington – to head off overland in a VW "squareback" from Belgium to Nepal and back (via France, Italy, Greece, Turkey, Iran, Afghanistan, Pakistan and India) and then ultimately to find myself in much quieter surroundings in Belgium to do my doctoral research (that is, after working nine months for IBM as a programmer/ analyst in their Brussels office).

Here in Brussels I continued my search into the dynamics of a deeply divided society – Belgium struggling with the problem of being comprised of two distinct and frequently mutually antagonistic cultural groups: the French-speaking South and the Flemish (Dutch) speaking North. But it was

---

*A German term referring to "Political Realism," popularized by Prussian Chancellor Otto von Bismarck, who in the 1870s used all the political tricks in the book to finally bring together a single or united German nation, one drawn from the multitudes of smaller German states formerly making up a deeply divided German society.

†Also, in my first years at Georgetown I researched and assembled a 250-page master's thesis on the social-political dynamics going on at the time in South Africa, noting that the actual dynamics of that country had little to do with the Black-White dynamics unfolding at the time within America itself, something that Americans looking at South Africa had seemingly little ability to understand. I predicted that South Africa was not going to go the way of the Euro retreat taking place at the time in the rest of Africa, but that the social situation would remain unchanged for at least this present generation At the time I was accused (by some, though not by my thesis supervisor who liked my work very much and encouraged me to stay on for doctoral studies) of being a "Fascist." But I was simply analyzing the social-political dynamics, not offering ideological advice.

the end of 1960s and the beginning of the 1970s, and Belgium was finding a higher cause for its existence: serving as the political center of a rising United Europe, relocated to Belgium thanks to French President de Gaulle who tried to undercut the European-unity momentum when it first located itself in France! I saw clearly how a higher social cause, such as was developing in Belgium, has the amazing power to bring people together to greater social strength. A friend of mine, Newt Gingrich – who was also doing his doctoral research in Brussels at the same time – would spend lunches and much of the afternoons discussing with me what it would take to bring a deeply divided America back to a similar sense of unity.

Upon returning to the States, I got a job as an assistant professor in the political science department at the University of South Alabama, set up an international studies program at the university, and then proceeded to teach young people what I had already observed up close about social dynamics, both at home and abroad.

And naturally the one question that kept coming up from my students was what I thought about the status of America itself in this matter of the rise and fall of a society – especially as America at the time was finding itself going through another national trauma, as a Democratic Congress was doing its best to cripple and take down a Republican White House. This question dug especially deeply because I had made it a key point to emphasize the importance of the role that the national leader had in shaping the moral foundations of any society. And America at that time seemed to be caught up in a major battle over that very issue.

* * *

THE PARABLE OF THE FOUR GENERATIONS

In answer to those student questions I told them a story, a parable about a society as it developed across four generations – a narrative that seemed to summarize all of this political, social, cultural and spiritual dynamic that goes into the rise and decline of any society. It is the story of four generations of a leading, guiding, governing family – and of the society they are supposed to be directing, and that society's rise and fall across those four generations. It is a tale well worth retelling here as we dig into the question of America's own social dynamics.

The First Generation. In this story, a small society forms around the mastery or leadership of a very strong-willed individual, a young man who climbs out of very tough – actually brutal – circumstances. And in overcoming those circumstances he achieves a self-discipline in the face of dangerous challenges, one which so strongly impresses a gathering circle of young warriors that he is able to turn this group into a similarly disciplined band of conquerors. The warrior-leader is very generous to those who would follow his lead bravely, against even the most dangerous of challenges. But he could also be equally unforgiving of those who would fail to live up to his very precise warrior code or his high expectations of a very brave performance in carrying out the warrior duties of those who would dare join him.

But what drives this leader is not just some hunger to force others under his direction for the sheer joy of it. That can come to certain people as a big ego-high. But usually that same urge will blind and ultimately destroy such wannabe leaders. No, what drives this First-Generation leader is vision, a higher vision or sense of call that comes from some source other than the approval of the immediate world around him. It comes typically from a sense, even at a very early age, that Heaven itself has a special commission for this young man to build a society that will serve the greater will of Heaven, God, Providence, Allah, Zeus, Tian – or whatever name is given to this Higher Power. It is the ability of our young warrior to keep his eyes on this higher call that allows him not to fall victim to the flattery of those who would try to use him for their own personal gain. He is immune to such human willfulness. Thus such vision – with its call to bold action as well as an unshakable resolve to keep himself and others under the inflexible moral discipline required to see that vision come to reality together – makes him the powerful leader that he is.

He also occupies a special place in history because his arrival on the social scene is timed with developments well beyond his own political-social designs. In fact, he himself is no such political-social designer. Instead, he is an individual fully capable of taking on fearsome challenges immediately in front of him as they arise to confront him on an almost daily basis. He does not design life, like some lofty intellectual working at a desk and living in a bubble of beautiful ideals and wonderfully rational plans designed to achieve utopia. His world is tough, messy, and unpredictable. But he is fearsomely brave as he pursues this political-social call placed on him by the very power of Heaven. He resolves simply to keep moving forward, even in the face of the most discouraging circumstances.

And thus it is that this man of valor is able to inspire others to join him on this path of overcoming – and ultimately this path of social conquest. He is thus able through sheer doggedness to produce social greatness.*

---

*Certainly both Washington and Lincoln are perfect examples of this kind of leadership. So also was the largely unacknowledged true Founder of Anglo-American society (at least the New England version), John Winthrop. And this category should also include Hamilton, a fiercely brave soul who took up the

And in our parable, that conquest would include even the great civilization just over the next mountain range, a civilization that is in deep trouble because it is no longer led by such powerful leaders as our First-Generation founder. This once-great civilization has fallen into deep moral decay, one that inevitably comes along with the rise to power of the Fourth and final Generation. This civilization finds itself caught at this point in time in the throes of social collapse. It is ripe for conquest by some kind of rising power outside itself. And that is where the First-Generation leader finds himself and his men headed in history.

Timing is, of course, also key to success in history.

The Second Generation. The son (the Second Generation) of the original founder-warrior will also have grown up in tough circumstances, though only because of the disciplined social environment established by his father, not because of a threatening political world immediately around him. By the time he is a rising young man, much of that has already been cleared away by his father's early successes. However, the father's grand vision, in which he understood rather clearly the ultimate destiny of his small but growing society, has had the father over the years preparing his son to take up the responsibilities that one day will be passed on to him. The First-Generation father therefore has had his Second-Generation son train and join him in battle, learning the responsibilities of leadership. There is, after all, a world to be conquered by both of them, father and son.

And that conquered world one day will need to be administered by a competent ruler. But it will fall to the son, not the father, to be just that individual. Anticipating this, the father perhaps will have, early along the way, sent his son off to live and study for a number of years within that larger civilization, one that is destined to be ruled by his own rising dynasty. This certainly occurred in the case of Philip II of Macedon, when he sent his son Alexander off to Greece to study under Aristotle. As a result, the son will know and understand the ways of the larger world that one day will be his responsibility to rule.

The son will also know of the Heavenly Commission upon which his society was originally founded by his father, though perhaps only secondarily, through what his father has told him about it. The son will respect that Higher Power and will take its ruling principles into account in his governance. But he will also be shaped by his knowledge of the political codes and moral rules of the society he is about to inherit, its wise counselors, its civilized ways. All of this will come as a blend of the

---

unloved responsibility of getting the new Republic started up on very strong financial foundations. These people carried America forward in its development through the most challenging of times.

son's own vision and self-discipline. He is more the person of Reason, like the civilized world he has come to know, than of dangerous risk-taking, something required by the social conditions his father grew up in.

Typically, the era of the Second Generation will be understood by historians as constituting the political height of that society or civilization, the one created or restored through the conquering efforts of the First Generation, and the considerable administrative talents of the Second Generation.*

The Third Generation. The grandson/son of the two preceding generations will be personally familiar only with life as lived within the palace that he was raised in. He will know well the stories of the great valor of his grandfather, although such knowledge will have more the nature of folklore than reality to him. He will see and experience directly the blessings of his father's well-administered social-legal order. It certainly will have already benefitted the son greatly. And thus he will be entirely devoted to the idea of completing and securing the full development of that perfect social order. He will spend his time in his royal chambers working on that perfect design, working closely with his highly-educated advisors on the specifics of a proposed legal order he wants them to put into place by royal decree.†

Along with the proposed legal order, his own vision typically will include the perfecting or beautifying of the visible features of the civilization he has inherited: the beautification of the palace dwellings; the building of magnificent homes for his huge administrative staff; the upgrading of the public places such as the all-important central market and the houses of worship; the development of public parks and places of leisure (mostly for the privileged urban classes).

Of course all of this will come at a great cost, especially to those least able to fend off the tax collectors, who fleece the poorer classes to pay for these extravagant projects, projects which will bring little or no benefit to the lower social orders. Restlessness and even occasional revolt will from time to time upset this utopian social order that Generation Three is attempting to put into place. And our ruler will be uncomprehending as to

---

*Both Roosevelts, Truman, Eisenhower, and Kennedy would certainly fall somewhere in this category, in the way they worked to maintain and utilize American social power in the face of huge social challenges. Nixon, Reagan, and Bush Sr. probably also belong in this category.

†American examples of this would be Jefferson, Wilson, and Johnson (LBJ), all of whom sought to perfect American society (and even the world in some cases) through highly-planned or rational social redesign. Franklin Roosevelt, Carter and Clinton seemed to have started out this way, but thankfully were forced back into a Second-Generation profile when unyielding Reality struck!

why such turmoil is accompanying his efforts to perfect his people's world. But that is because he lives largely in a social-intellectual-moral bubble of his own making. He is far removed from the hard realities of the larger world around him. Most importantly, he has lost touch with those he is expected to govern. He no longer relates to his people as a moral compass or spiritual guide for them. Trouble brews.

The Fourth Generation. Having grown up in a world of total privilege, surrounded by flattering supporters looking to be brought into that world of privilege, our Fourth-Generation leader will have lost touch completely with the hard realities facing his society, the challenges that as society's governing authority he is expected to address and solve. But he lives in a world of massive disinformation (who would dare to contradict the presuppositions of the Great Ruler). He is clueless as to his responsibilities.

Not only is there a total loss of dedicated discipline to his governance, there is not even any particular direction to it. He is a person of no particular vision, except to hang on to all the entitlements coming his way as Great Ruler. He is bored, listless, and dangerous, not only to those immediately around him but also to himself. Thus he is also a great danger to the society he is expected to lead. He indulges in every known diversion possible, being able (he believes) to afford them all: gambling, drugs and alcohol, sex (in various ways), wild spending sprees (for nothing in particular), cruel games (including the torture of individuals he does not particularly care for), and so on.

And as for the general moral order of the society he is supposed to be leading, it now finds itself in a state of collapse. Hungry gangs wander the streets, violating persons and property as they see the urge to do so. It is dangerous for women and children to go to market for the day's needs, or even to enter the streets at all. Extortionists come around to exact the price of protection on the defenseless people. The social order is simply collapsing. And as for the people's affection for their government, its Great Ruler in particular, there is none. They wish him dead, and would support anyone inclined to cause that to happen.

And that brings us back to the First Generation, for that is where such help is to come from. And thus the cycle begins all over again.

✷ ✷ ✷

THE CHRISTIAN COMPONENT IN THE DYNAMIC

At the time (the 1970s and early 1980s) I was strictly a classic political Realist, rather cynical in my view of political policy-making, legal "reasoning" and intellectual Idealism. Such Realism did not necessarily make for a happy place.

And the economic mess that America fell into at the very end of the 1970s (and into the first years of the 1980s) did not help my mood any. I myself was trapped in a number of investments that, with Federal Reserve President Paul Volcker's astonishingly high interest rate strategy, I knew of no escape. This proved to be too much Realism for me. And it all led me to find refuge from my many social responsibilities by abandoning them – and then even hiding myself away from that world, working in a friend's back office as a simple clerk for a year, while attempting to figure out which direction in life was actually up – and not down!

And in the midst of all this, God showed up, actually in the way Christ was shown to me in the unexpected care Christian friends extended to me in all my confusion.

Actually, Christianity itself was not new to me. But this particular expression of that Christianity was! I had been raised a Christian, had gone off to college to prepare for the Presbyterian ministry, but had a Bible professor (who committed suicide that same year) completely cut away my young faith with his attempt to make the Bible itself more "Realistic." It obviously had not worked for him. And it certainly did not work for me!

Now years later, in coming back to the Christian faith, I did not need to abandon my Realism – for my understanding of human nature itself did not change any, nor did it need to change. I did not need to escape into some kind of idealized Humanism (in which some intellectuals seem to find some degree of religious salvation). Social and political reality was not going to go away.

But I came to realize – as had so many Americans before me – that there was a force in life much higher than man himself in charge of outcomes in this universe. I knew that Albert Einstein, Erwin Schrödinger, Niels Bohr, John Polkinghorne and other famous scientists operated from this same assumption. And I soon found myself operating from that perspective as well. And thus off to Princeton Seminary I went to study the matter further.

My "Realism" continued to be operative for me even while I immersed myself in the world of Princetonian academics, by doing prison volunteer work and then starting up a street ministry of my own to the homeless of nearby Trenton. Here I got to experience first-hand the redemptive power of Christian truth, a truth that needed no clever intellectual argument to justify.* It was true simply because it worked – right there in real life. I

---

*Reason, posing itself as absolute Truth, tends generally to be presented merely from the point of view of personal or social self-interest! This hardly qualifies as "Truth" in itself. Even at six years of age my granddaughter could offer the most sophisticated reasoning in rebuttal to her mom's command "It's time for bed."

continued that ministry for over four years, even after graduating from seminary and remaining in the area as a construction worker.

When I finally got a call as a Presbyterian pastor, I found myself mixing Biblical teachings with actual examples drawn from the social narrative of both America and the larger world, all of which I knew intimately. And while pastoring, I taught courses on the subject as well. And eventually a website (newgeneva.org) was assembled where all this material was laid out. Thus the foundations of this huge writing project (of which this volume is an abridged version) first began to be assembled.

I knew full well that God has long worked redemptively not just with individuals but with whole societies. And this has been true not just anciently – as with old Israel, whose narrative of divine social redemption constitutes the Christian Old Testament – but also on an ongoing basis. Yes, the same God is active among us as a people, as a society, even today.

And that understanding was certainly there in a strong way back in the early 1600s. That was what brought the Calvinist Separatists and Puritans to New England, to build in the New World a society that operated out of that same understanding. New England society was a covenant society, a people covenanted (contracted) to be a people of God – to serve him, and thus be served by him. And it worked. It worked fabulously. It made America (at least the northern and middle portions of the American colonies) a very unique society.

Finally, after a dozen years of pastoring, I was led back to classroom teaching, to a Christian high school this time – where, over the years, I got to teach all of my four children (and their friends) American history and social dynamics, on the basis of this very understanding: America's grand covenant with God.

During these years these ideas got clarified, reformulated for a younger audience, and expanded considerably (the enormous pictorial portion is still to be found online at spiritualpilgrim.net). Then after eighteen years of such teaching, I finally "retired" to put this work into print – the three-volume series completed in the second half of 2019 and first months of 2020. And now the condensed or "abridged" version is finally available.

✱ ✱ ✱

THE PURPOSE AND CHARACTER OF THIS STUDY

Recovering the Christian Covenant with God. So what we have here is the narrative of a people, the American people, going at life by way of a special covenant relationship with God. They do not always live up to that commitment – distracted by waves of "enlightenment" in which some

Americans have supposed that they could control life their own way without God's instructions. But they are a people revitalized by divine interventions (the "Great Awakenings") when God remembers his covenant with America and restores its spiritual character, usually in anticipation of an enormous life-and-death challenge that the nation will soon be facing and will need enormous spiritual strength to take on successfully. And so, like Israel of old, it is the narrative of a "covenant people" living and serving God himself, as a "City on a Hill," a "Light to the Nations," showing the world how ordinary people can do extraordinary things when they work closely with the God who presides over the universe.

The power of the Christian narrative. One of the things I learned in seminary was the power of a society's narrative itself, the way it shapes social identity and purpose. Indeed, Christianity is itself built on the power of such a narrative, found in our Bible. The Biblical narrative has long shaped Western society. And it certainly was critical to the birth of the American nation in the early 1600s, and key to its development over the next several centuries.

I was deeply impressed by how Judaism built itself entirely on its own narrative, and how that Jewish experience also shaped the way Christianity would understand its character and role in life. While other civilizations conducted worship by having priests sacrifice animals (sometimes even people) at alters located at huge temples (the Jews at one point did that as well, just with animals, of course!), the Jews learned to approach God also – and more importantly – simply through prayer, reflection, and study, of God's ways, and of the ways of those Jews and Israelites of earlier generations revealed through their well-recorded social experience (Scripture) which demonstrated by the example of those who went before them how best to work with God in daily life itself – not to mention in times of wars and enormous social crises. So the Jews developed Godly worship simply through devoting themselves to the task of learning from Scripture, gathering weekly to study and learn from such social narrative.

Indeed! Looking to such social narrative for guidance was a very unique way to go before God – one that worked very well for the Jews, certainly at least as well as having priests slaughter animals at the Temple.

And it was this habit that was picked up by Christianity in its formative years (also as an oppressed people), as Christians gathered locally (home or underground "churches") to worship and attend to the instructions or sermons of their elders or pastors. And it proved so powerful that eventually Christianity would take Roman society by storm! But we will have more to say about this in the pages that follow.

But anyway, that was real Christianity. And I understood very clearly its power and its vital importance in the founding and development of American society, unfortunately an understanding that is being lost as America turns away from such "superstitious" doings to follow the more "reasonable" path of Secular-Humanism, a religion established by the Liberal political Left, and the federal courts – quite in violation of a very Christian Constitution that is supposed to be protecting the people's powers to shape and direct their own society, like the ancient Christians – and the Jews before them.

The moral role of leaders. I am also (as my four-generation parable illustrates clearly) a great believer in the enormous power and social role played by the very special people of society: their leaders. Usually leadership comes from a society's governing officials. But it frequently comes also from others who step into the picture to give society critical guidance. The Reverend Dr. Martin Luther King, Jr., for instance, would qualify as the second type: not a government official, but one whose leadership had a huge impact in moving America off in a much grander direction.

Leaders set the moral-spiritual example before the people, helping them to understand the best way to go at life's challenges. Modern social science sees them as planners and managers. I see them as inspirers, people who do not need to dictate to others, but simply show others the way through personal example.

Thus I tend to give America's historical leaders very special coverage in this narrative, especially in the matter of what it was precisely that made them the leaders they happened to be. This is not only to give insightful information to those who want to know more about those who left such a major mark on American society, it is, as with all personal testimony, to inspire the reader to try to follow a similar path in life themselves. That is, after all, how true leaders (not dictators) lead: by inspiring others with their own personal example!

Taking up the narrative. And so we begin our journey, taking up the American narrative or story – learning not just the facts of history but, even more importantly, the ways of society itself: its social dynamics.

Indeed, let us now begin that journey into America's great social narrative, its grand history, so as to know how to deal more effectively with the challenges before us today.

CHAPTER ONE

AMERICA'S MORAL-SPIRITUAL INHERITANCE

* * *

WESTERN CULTURE AND THE WORLD

America was not founded outside of some kind of larger social context. In fact, quite the opposite was the case. Although America seemed to have been built "from scratch" beginning in the early 1600s, it did so with a full understanding of the cultural legacy it had inherited from the motherland back in England, and England's own larger European context. In fact, it was deeply motivated by the desire to build in America a much purer form of exactly that very social inheritance, especially in the setting up of New England.

That social inheritance was not universal, but was – in the setting of the larger world and its many different civilizations – quite unique. And that very uniqueness is what we will be looking at in this chapter.

The heart of the "Western" social ethic. Westerners, unless they have lived and worked substantially in other non-Western cultures, tend to suppose that what they understand to be true about life is something of a "universal" for all humankind. This is hardly the case. In fact, this naïve supposition has been the source of major problems for Westerners – and for America in particular, ever since it took leadership of Western civilization after World War Two.

Because of its development via the Jewish, Greek and Roman experience – synthesized beautifully in the Christian religion – Westerners see life as shaped by deep personal involvement of adventuresome individuals. Western individualism is in fact a key component of Western civilization, found in everything from capitalism, to Darwinism, to Humanism, to modern science, to democracy (and much more). But it is summed up most perfectly in Christianity, which, through the teachings and example of Jesus, makes the bold assumption that we all are potentially sons and daughters of God Himself, divinely empowered individuals able to take on life personally because of this empowerment. There are huge moral and spiritual responsibilities placed on the shoulders of those who rise to this understanding, which could be (even should be) any of us. But we have the wise guidance of holy scripture to help us make the right choices in taking up freely these personal responsibilities.

Of course this understanding allows the option of not following such divine guidance, because Westerners are not God's puppets, but instead fully free agents. Indeed it is God Himself who ordained our human nature, wanting us to choose freely to join him in celebrating His awesome Creation. If we did not have the option not to do so, it would cheat the decision to actually do so of its real significance.

Westerners, especially recent scientists such as Einstein, Schrödinger, Bohr, Polkinghorne, etc. in fact have made it quite clear that human life exists in the midst of this universal vastness specifically for this purpose: to join the Creator of it all in celebrating with Him (Einstein's "Herr Gott" or "Lord God") the beauty of it all. As far as we know, we are the only part of Creation that is fully aware of its own existence! This indeed is the very purpose of quite conscious or "awake" human life itself.

And thus it is that we freely design societies that allow the people themselves to use this special human talent to observe, to learn, to design even their own lives, as they themselves personally choose to do so. Personal "freedom" that allows this dynamic to flourish thus comes to be a Western value of supreme importance.

Of course, freedom raises its own problems, because there is at the same time a primal instinct in humans to want to control the world we live in, to remove its obstacles, its complexities, in order to make it more understandable, more predictable, more manageable. And that includes the world of others, because other people can become quite problematic for us. Dominance, even dictatorship, is a possible result of such human impulse. But supposedly, this is why we have Scripture to warn us, to guide us, to keep us within workable social boundaries. Otherwise either pure chaos or pure dictatorship would come of the full use of absolute human freedom. And there are plenty of examples of this in human history, especially in Western history. And some of these are quite recent, in fact even very operative among us today.

The Hindu social ethic. Other cultures have gone at life in ways quite different from this Western pattern. For instance, Hinduism, which has long dominated the Indian sub-continent, sees life resulting from what we Westerners might term "fate." All of life is shaped by a cumulative record of actions, good and bad, that result from our behavior. In fact it is this record that shapes our destiny, not just in this life but in lives to come – just as the present has been shaped by the record of human action in previous lives. And how do we come to understand the source of our personal fate? It is clearly shaped by the social position we found ourselves born to. We take on a new life as members of a particular sub-caste or jati (India has thousands of just such different social groups or jatis), a community shaped by very clear rules that will determine our social record (and how well or poorly we perform accordingly), and whether we advance or retreat over the flow of many rebirths to a higher or lower social status.

This is a quite compelling social system. There is no room for personal negotiation, no opportunity for an individual to come up against some very serious cosmic judgments that lie beyond his or her control. You must obey, or you suffer.

Interestingly you can build a very strong social order on just such an approach to life. The rules of Hinduism are so fixed that Indian society needs no dictator to make the whole thing work. Social responsibility is completely that of the individual Hindu – to obey and prosper – or otherwise suffer, if not in this life at least in the lives to come.

When Americans look at India, they see "democracy" in action, or at least that is what they think they are seeing. India indeed has governing institutions quite familiar to Westerners – part of the British inheritance, which Gandhi, the "father" of modern India, himself disliked intensely! He himself as a young man tried very hard to become "English," to escape the fate of being Hindu. But he found that his brown skin was very much a problem in this endeavor to enter fully (in high social standing) in English society. He eventually turned bitterly against things English, but could not bring himself to support the Indian caste system on which Indian society rested.

In the end, India came under the industrial modernizer Nehru (and his family) and India managed to move into a world that accepted some of the Western legacy, while keeping the Hindu legacy still intact. Tragically however, it took the slaughter of hundreds of thousands of Indians (including Gandhi himself) to make the transition (1947-1948). But India seems to enjoy a quite workable system today.

Buddhist Asia. Buddhism was born in India centuries before even Christ entered the picture, as something of a reaction to the inflexible social restrictions of Hinduism. Buddha, as an Indian prince-turned-guru (teacher or prophet), tried to create a social system that would be fairer to those who suffered the most socially, economically and politically from the rigidness of the Hindu system. He failed in this socio-political enterprise. However he did end up discovering a way of escaping the rigid Indian caste system, by simply quieting, even deadening, one's concerns over life's many obstacles.

He discovered that a deep spiritual passivity would not only remove the frustrations of this life, but in letting go of the hold of the Hindu social ethic, offer even freedom from the problem of having to be reborn, of having to have another go at life in order to improve a person's place in the scheme of life! No more rebirths meant freedom or Nirvana. But Buddha's Nirvana was a freedom that resulted not from activity (Western style) but from passivity.

For a while (several centuries) Buddhism spread widely across India. But theological splits within the religious community, plus the determination of the Hindu priests or Brahmans to retake control of Indian life slowly drove Buddhism from its homeland in India. But by then it had spread eastward into Southeast Asia (Burma, Thailand, Cambodia, Vietnam, etc.), into Nepal and Tibet, and ultimately into China, Korea and Japan.

Buddhism provided spiritual comfort to the masses of farmers or peasants across the land as they dealt with the many challenges of nature, of insects, disease, floods, droughts, and raiders and plunderers, all of which so often made life very difficult. This tendency toward passivity also made it easier for certain warlords to take command over their region, some even becoming emperors, rulers able to offer protection against the larger threats to local life. And out of this arrangement, life in Asia could take on civilized ways, as long as emperors were able to carry off their responsibilities and as long as the challenges did not become overwhelming (which they could indeed become from time to time).

Democracy was not what the people wanted, or even understood. They simply expected that those that took responsibility for life's larger issues (ones that Buddhism could not take on personally) would do their job. And if so, then Heaven itself would bless the people and the land. They did not ask to be part of the decisional structure. That was the role of the rulers. But they did have their expectations that their world would be served wisely and well by those in charge.

Basically this is what guides China today. This is also what Johnson was up against in Vietnam in the 1960s when he tried to encourage the South Vietnamese to take up the responsibilities of democracy, democracy conducted in the same manner that Americans supposedly governed their lives. But Johnson was working entirely outside of the Asian (largely Buddhist) social context, and had no idea at the time of how problematic that would be for him and his grand plans. For instance, when in the early 1960s Buddhist monks took to the streets to protest against outside intrusions into their culture – one monk even burning himself to death – they were not clamoring for democracy, nor for Communism. They just wanted everyone to go away and let them get back to the kind of life they well understood.

Islam. Islam is a first-cousin of Christianity, but forged out of a very different social metal than the deeply Westernized Christianity. Muhammad was completely fascinated by Christianity, and thought of himself as actually someone operating along the lines of the Judeo-Christian prophets. But he was Semitic in mentality, meaning, he saw life as a tightly structured social realm. Social authority was necessarily very strict (the desert environment in which he lived offered little room for social error), and very hierarchical. In fact, Islam conveys the meaning not of freedom, but of submission, submission to those standing in authority above you. A son obeyed his father, a father obeyed his clan chief, who in turn obeyed his prince, who in turn obeyed God. And there was also a strong element of religious authority in the mix. In fact, Muhammad's successors (caliphs) carried in their all-important political-social governance both secular and theological authority.

Thus to a true Muslim, all this talk of Westerners about personal freedom seems to derive from Satan himself, for such freedom would, in the thinking of a typical Muslim, be entirely disruptive of the Muslim social order. Indeed, the efforts of Westerners to get the Islamic world to take on Western democratic ways is about as appealing to "true" Muslims as, for instance, Communism is to most Americans. It's just not going to happen. The Muslim world has its own ways of governance – patterns established long ago – and still dictated by the commands of the Qur'an (Islam's holy book), a grand work derived from the supposedly divinely-inspired pronouncements of Muhammad – and thus not negotiable! Period.

* * *

JEWISH, GREEK AND ROMAN CULTURAL CONTRIBUTIONS

As with all cultures, Western or Christian culture is a unique blend of various contributing sub-cultures, ones however which combined around the idea of the importance of the sovereignty of the individual. This is partly a Jewish idea, partly a Greek idea, and partly a Roman idea, into which Jesus came to sum up the idea of the sovereign individual. Each of these sub-cultures helped to develop that key idea. And so it would profit us greatly in coming to an understanding of the deeper character of our Western civilization if we took a closer look at each of these contributing sub-cultures. And it is most logical to start with the earliest, and in a way the most determinative, of these ancient sources: Judaism.

The Jewish contribution to Western culture. Anciently, Israel (of which the Jews were the southern-most of the 12 tribes) at one point went at life pretty much like all the other nations of the day. Their capital city, Jerusalem, possessed not only royal palaces but also a Temple, where – under the leadership of the Levitical priests – they performed animal sacrifices in worshiping their god Yahweh.

But in becoming a rich and successful people, the Israelites soon fell away from their devotion to Yahweh, who then abandoned them to the folly of their own political planning and operating. They became reckless in their messing with the growing powers of the Egyptian Empire to the south of them and the Assyrian Empire to the East of them. If they had been wise, they would have stayed out of the growing struggles between these two neighboring empires, for this was not God's plan for them. And they had prophets who warned them of the dangers of such foolish involvement in the larger political battles going on at the time. Eventually Israel got itself in trouble with Assyria, and the cruel Assyrians marched ten of the twelve tribes of Israel off to captivity, where they scattered the Israelites among the peoples of their empire, and soon much of the Israelite identity simply dissolved, never to recover again.

However, the Southern Israelite kingdom, basically made up of the tribe of Judah (thus the Jews) had more wisely stayed out of these political doings, and Assyria left them alone. But such wisdom did not pass on (as so often happens) to a new generation of Jews, who got mixed up in the struggles between Egypt and the newly rising power of Babylon, which had just succeeded in overthrowing Assyrian power. Finally now it was the Jews turn – at least their leading citizens – to be carted off to Babylon.

But by the grace of God, the Babylonians let the Jews at least remain together as a community in captivity. Thus the Jewish identity was not lost. But still, as a people's religion defined the very nature of their societies back then (and still today) they were in a bit of a quandary. The Babylonians would not let them build in Babylon a temple to their god Yahweh (the one in Jerusalem in fact had just been torn down by the Babylonians), and thus it seemed at first that there would be no way for those relocated to Babylon to hold onto to their unique social identity.

But they did have one very precious item that they could cling to, which would serve to keep them mindful of their existence as a distinct people: their own tribal narrative – a history of their tribal ancestors and their relations with their god Yahweh, a story which reached all the way back to what they understood as the very beginning of humankind itself. There in Babylon incredible religious scholarship would develop under the guidance – not of the (unemployed) temple priests, but instead by religious teachers or rabbis, who collected this far-reaching narrative and turned it into a piece of holy writing, something that the members of the Jewish community could study, meditate on, and be guided by socially. And they could do so wherever they found themselves, even there in Babylon. All they needed was some kind of community center, the synagogue, where they could gather locally on a regular basis (at least weekly on the Sabbath) and hear a teaching – usually some form of commentary on their holy Scriptures – presented by their teachers (rabbis) and elders.

And it was all very democratic, in the way that all young men were expected to demonstrate – as a rite of passage into manhood – the ability to perform this kind of rabbinical Biblical study and teaching. In a way it was an early version of the "priesthood of all believers"!

This also gave the Jews the idea that they served the interests of God in the broader realm of humankind, for they were led now to understand that God was not just a Jewish God, but was the God of all people, Babylonians, Egyptians, and everyone else. And as a special covenant-people of God's own choosing, they had the larger responsibility of bringing their awareness of God's role in life to all the people, non-Jews as well as Jews. Thus they became quite active in Babylonian affairs, as a "people of God," a "Light to the Nations."

Eventually the Persians conquered the Babylonians, and allowed the Jews then to return to their lands in Israel. But most chose to remain behind in Babylon and continue their special lives there (Babylon and then Persia would continue to serve as a key center of Jewish scholarship and religious activity). Those that did return to Jerusalem naturally rebuilt their Temple. However, they did not let go of the Jewish spiritual practices developed during their Babylonian captivity, but instead kept Jewish life active around the local synagogues, under the leadership of the rabbinical scholars. And that would continue all the way down to the time of the Roman Empire, and the arrival of Jesus. In fact, it still continues to this day, wherever the Jews find themselves in this world of ours!

Greek (more specifically, Athenian) "Democracy." "Democracy" is a term used today by Americans to describe what it is that they understand America to be in its very essence – unfortunately not always with the clearest understanding of what is involved with such a concept or social identifier. But it is a powerful idea nonetheless, made somewhat dangerous at times because, unlike the Founders of the American Republic over two hundred years ago who understood the possibilities and dangers both of the idea of democracy, to Americans today it has become something like a religion in itself.

Most Americans know that the idea of democracy was a political legacy given Western Civilization by the ancient Greeks (500s-300s BC). Actually it was practiced widely around the ancient world, and not just in Greece – developed out of the need of tribal peoples, generally everywhere, to consult with clan or household elders whenever an important decision affecting the tribe had to be made: when to hunt, when to go to war, when to make a physical move. It was necessary to get every clan, every household of the tribe on board with the decision – for unity of purpose was essential to the survival of the tribe. Thus democratic consultations would continue until some kind of general agreement was possible prior to taking action with respect to the event in question.

Thus it was that the very ancient or early city-state Athens was quite reliant on the democratic process of holding meetings to discuss common matters – and have an affirmative vote from the participants in order to move things forward.

But when the population of Athens began to grow, participation of all Athenian citizens in such decisions became problematic. There simply were too many people involved to conduct such business in an orderly fashion. Consequently, small groups of people – especially ones that could claim a longer line of Athenian ancestry – would tend to take control, turning themselves into something of a ruling class. And the *xenoi* (foreigners) not born of Athenian ancestry, who were even more numerous than the Athenian citizenry, had no place at all in this process, not to mention the slaves, who outnumbered even the xenoi.

Unsurprisingly, as class distinctions developed, so did class conflicts. Several efforts were made to improve the democratic process (a toughening of political requirements under Draco (thus the term "Draconian," something very brutal as social measures typically go), countered a generation later by Solon – who attempted a fairer distribution of responsibilities and rewards. However, this did not make a huge difference in the Athenian political lineup. Finally, in reaction to Peisistratus' tyrannical rule (a "tyrant" was actually originally a strong-handed defender of the rights of the poor) and the rising danger of mounting Persian power to the East, the popular politician Cleisthenes was led to reform the constitution by simply re-classifying the Athenians into ten residential or neighborhood "tribes" and having these tribal districts represented at the Assembly by citizens chosen by lot. Fair enough! And thus it was that Athens affirmed itself as a "representative" democracy.

For a time this reform, plus the mounting danger of an aggressive Persia taking control in the eastern Greek lands of Ionia, brought unity to the Athenian population, bringing even the Greek city-states to amazing unity under Athenian leadership. It even forced Athens' chief political rival in Greece, Sparta, to cooperate with Athens militarily. And this unity finally allowed the Greeks to defeat the Persians at Marathon (490 BC) and Salamis (480 BC).

From this point on (the mid-400s BC) Athens took on the position as

Greece's leading city-state, particularly when other city-states agreed to send funding to Athens to support the unified Greek defenses of the new Delian League against a resurgent Persia.

And this marked the "Golden Age" of Athens, under the capable political leadership of Pericles (excellent orator, statesman and general) during the period from the mid-400s BC to his death in 429 BC, a time in which Athens was also producing the historical insights of Herodotus (to about 424 BC), the creative works of the dramatists Euripides and Sophocles (to 406 and 405 BC respectively) and the outstanding philosophy of Socrates (to his death in 399 BC).

But moral problems within Athens itself had begun to mount during that same period. Peace had brought not democratic nobility of spirit, but a new greediness, stoked by the political self-interests of a series of leading Assembly speakers, clever Sophists or "wise ones," able to convince – through the most clever use of "reason" – the representatives of the people to do the most unwise, most self-destructive things, merely because it played to the interests of one or another of these "demagogues."

For instance, the demagogues led the Assembly to the decision to use the money sent by the other city-states to Athens for Greek mutual defense instead to simply beautify Athens itself (new buildings, improved streets, grand statuary, etc.), despite the protests raised by its Greek allies. Ultimately these other city-states would look to Sparta to champion their cause against an increasingly greedy Athens, and ugly war resulted.

How stupidly selfish Athenian democracy had become. And the Athenian representatives would also foolishly ostracize (expelling for ten years) Athens' very best military leaders – actions inspired by jealous Assembly speakers. What was this democratic body thinking? All of this helped lead to Athens' ultimate defeat in a series of Peloponnesian Wars (the second half of the 400s BC).

Thankfully Sparta ignored the demands of its city-state allies (Thebes, Corinth and others) to enslave the defeated Athenian population, but resolved instead simply to tear down Athens' city walls, leaving the city defenseless militarily from that point on (404 BC). This was the beginning of the end of Athenian greatness.

But the foolishness of Athens' democratic Assembly did not end there.

In 399 BC, the wisest philosopher of the ancient world, Socrates, was voted the death penalty by the democratic Assembly – because he annoyed Assembly speakers by calling into question the wisdom of their words and behavior.

In sum, democracy Athenian-style had led that society down a very self-destructive road.

Socrates' pupil Plato tried to find a better approach to political wisdom

America's Moral-Spiritual Inheritance

by developing in a key philosophical work, *Politeia* (commonly known by its Latin name, *Republic*) his own idea of what a well-run society should look like. But the success of such a venture depended entirely on the wisdom of the leading politician, not the wisdom of the people (which Plato doubted was obtainable anyway).

This would be the beginning of the tendency of intellectuals to design from their desks beautiful societies, or "utopias" (a Greek word meaning literally "nowhere"!) – built entirely on their own powers of rational planning, and not on the basis of actual human experience (which tends to be not very pretty much of the time).

But Plato would have the rare opportunity as an intellectual to discover how well his ideas actually worked, when he was invited by the young tyrant of Syracuse, Dion, to put his philosophy to work there. The end result when Plato faced political reality was total disaster for Syracuse (20 years of chaos under the social breakdown that his experiment ultimately produced) and Plato's own arrest, imprisonment and sale into slavery, which he was finally purchased out of by a sympathetic fellow philosopher.

Plato's own student, Aristotle, was more cautious in his approach to political design, actually studying historically various patterns of social governance. In his famous works, *Politics*, he stated that on the basis of his research, the measure of good or bad in a society and its government appeared to depend not on the constitutional form of government itself – whether a government was made up of one (as in a monarchy) or a few (as in an aristocracy) or the many (as in a democracy) – that is, not by how many ruled, but by how morally they ruled. A rule of one could be good – or bad – depending on the moral quality of the ruler. A rule of the many could be good – or bad – as for instance a rule by an enlightened citizenry would be considered good, whereas rule by a frenzied mob would most definitely be viewed as some perverse form of popular tyranny. Thus to Aristotle, "good" or "bad" depended not on how many ruled but how well the society was ruled by its own high moral standards. Failure to hold to its foundational standards would soon enough bring any society to ruin.

As we shall see further on in this narrative, the Founding Fathers of the American Constitution (1787) were college men, back when college or university education meant principally a study of the humanities (philosophy, theology, history, law, and the social sciences). Thus they were very aware of both the political history of ancient Greece, and the philosophy of the Greeks, especially Plato and Aristotle. We shall see more of how this influenced deeply their decision as to how to build a new Federal system uniting the thirteen newly independent American states. Full democracy was not their goal. Democracy was included as part of the dynamic. But they attempted to put it under the considerable restraint of a constitutional "checks and balances" system. More about that later.

Alexandrian Greece. While we are on the subject of ancient Greece, it is important to bring into the narrative the role that a single individual, Alexander of Macedon, would play in the development of the ancient world. He was the son of Philip II of Macedon, the latter a strong warrior who many of the Greeks had looked to in order to bring Greece out of the disorder ongoing in that land since the days of the Peloponnesian Wars. Philip, anticipating a permanent (or dynastic) call to Greek governance, prepared to have at his side a son, Alexander, well informed in the ways of the people Philip intended to rule. So he sent Alexander off to study under the very wise Aristotle. But Philip was killed in 336 BC, and his 20-year-old son suddenly found himself at the head of his father's project.

Most amazingly, Alexander proved to be as much a leader as his father. He was able finally to assemble the Greeks into some kind of united community, to take on the powerful Persians directly – in Persian territory itself this time. There would be no more just sitting passively waiting to fend off another Persian assault, as had been the pattern previously. Alexander intended to go at the Persians in their own world.

He first captured the lands bordering the Eastern Mediterranean, including even Egypt. He then swung his army eastward and crushed the Persians' own efforts at self-defense in 331 BC.

But Alexander had a roll going, and kept on conquering, deeper into central Asia, and even down into the Indus River valley. But his soldiers were at this point exhausted and wanted to go home, or at least back to Babylon, the former Persian capital, but now theirs as well. Thus he turned around (however, losing half his men trying to get across the Baluchi Desert). But back in Babylon, Alexander was himself soon to die (323 BC), probably his death resulting simply from sheer exhaustion.

Alexander thus left a huge Greek legacy for his successors to deal with (they ultimately split Alexander's huge empire into a number of smaller empires). And it left a lasting Greek cultural imprint on the entire region, not only in the Eastern Mediterranean but even into the Mesopotamian lands (principally today's Iraq) and large sections of central Asia.

The importance to Americans of this Alexandrian legacy is that Greek culture was so dominant in the times of Jesus and the first century church that all of Christianity's foundational writings were done in Greek, not the local Semitic language (Hebrew and Aramaic) of the lands where Christianity was birthed, or even the Latin of the then-dominant Roman Empire.

The Roman Republic. Actually, America long-identified itself as a republic – not as a democracy. There is a difference. A republic refers simply to the idea of the actual *ownership* of a society – not the particular method by which it goes about the business of being governed. The word "Republic" comes from the ancient Latin *res publica* or "thing of the people." A Republic belongs to no particular ruling dynasty (such as the kings or emperors), no ruling class, no particular tribe, sect or socio-economic group within a society. It belongs to all the people of that society.

And for such an understanding, we Americans are deeply indebted to the Romans, for it is from them that the concept originated. Under the Romans, their government or "republic" was originally designed to be a government not of human wills, whether the will of one person or even the many. The Roman Republic was intended to be a government of laws, a permanent body of rules that would describe the order that all Romans were to live and thrive under – an unshakeable legal order that would continue forward in a precisely-defined way regardless of whatever personalities played their assigned parts in this order. A Republic was intended to be a system of fundamental or unchanging constitutional laws – not a system governed by the whims of human ambition and personal political interest, no matter how "rational" these whims might claim to be. And these laws were supposedly eternally valid, because they found themselves detailed on 12 bronze tablets (450 BC) posted in the Roman Forum (central market and religious center) for all to see. And all Romans knew these laws well.

This was the key to Rome's early success in its expansion across Italy, and then across the Mediterranean world (and Europe north of the Alps as well). Unlike tribes and nations that have a very hard time bringing conquered peoples into their social order as fellow members (choosing instead to enslave them or butcher them on the spot), the Romans offered participation of those they recently conquered in their society as full members, provided they were willing to come under Roman law and live accordingly as Roman citizens. That was not only fair, it was powerfully effective in developing Rome's wide-spread multi-ethnic republic.

And it created a powerfully effective socio-economic order. Given their legalistic mindset, Romans almost instinctively organized the world around them physically and materially as they conquered it, building roads (still standing today in many places) to provide rapid communication, troop movement and ultimately commerce connecting the Roman center to its outlying territories. Wherever they conquered they planted military camps (naturally on a perfectly uniform grid pattern!), which became the heart of new commercial towns which quickly grew up around these garrisons. They cleared the seas of pirates and kept marauding tribal raiders from central and east Europe closed out beyond a well-defended line running from the Rhine River in Germany to the Danube in the Balkan Peninsula. Consequently, the Mediterranean world that Rome had "conquered" experienced an unprecedented peace and prosperity, one that made Rome the very model of civilization itself to millions of people.

The Empire replaces the Republic. But again, such politics – even Republican politics – is not a perfect thing. It involves people. And people can be very messy to work with.

Over time, but particularly during the wars with the Carthaginians (the three Punic Wars from the mid-200 BC to the mid-100s BC), the Roman Senate had become the center of all Roman power. It was a club of old Roman families (the "patricians") joined by a select group of "commoners" (the "plebeians") of recently acquired wealth, which closed its ranks against the rest of the Roman common or plebeian citizenry. In short, the Senate had turned itself into a ruling oligarchy. Meanwhile rising taxes necessitated by ongoing war, and competition from the growing amount of slave labor acquired in these wars, were bringing the more middle-class Roman plebeians to ruin. And yet real Roman power, especially the power of the Roman military, was built on the loyal services of these commoners as citizen-soldiers. Something drastic needed to be done to save Rome from collapse or revolution.

Thus as was the case for Athens, efforts were undertaken by leading Roman citizens to reform the system, opening up bitter debate as to exactly how that was to work. "Reform" invites new forms of reasoning into the older legal order, reasoning which can go most any way, or at least in the way of the most powerful of the social groupings within society. In short, the ancient Roman Constitution proved to be not quite as permanent or unchanging as a body of laws.

Social problems thus merely increased as various identity groups wielded reason against each other as Rome sought to upgrade the now-changing constitution. Tragically, identity politics was overwhelming the constitutional republic.

The Gracci brothers, Tiberius and Gaius, as Tribunes (Rome's political officers representing the interests of the commoner plebeians), attempted reforms in favor of the plebeians (133-121 BC), which were blocked by a jealous Senate. The brothers were either clubbed to death by a mob or forced into suicide in advance of a mob, stirred to action by the Senate.

This brought forward the military leader Marius (108-100 BC) who tried to use his power to clean out the corruption in both the military and the massively expanding Roman bureaucracy. But in the end, he was unable to stop the Roman fall into deeper "Social War." This in turn led General Sulla to march his troops into Rome (a highly illegal act), designed to undercut the plebeian reform party and strengthen the position of the Senate. Thus Rome came under the first of its military dictators (82-79 BC) or "emperors" (from the Latin imperator or military commander).

But the chaos only deepened, especially with Spartacus's slave uprising (73-71 BC). At this point, the Senate looked completely to the Roman military to save Roman society. This resulted in the selection of three generals – Crassus, Caesar and Pompey – to bring Rome back under control. But instead, it simply put Rome through the process of a growing political competition among these three military giants. One last effort was made – by Cicero – to bring Rome back under constitutional rule. But getting nowhere, Cicero retired from politics, the last significant spokesman for Roman Republicanism. Finally, with Caesar coming out on top in the competition among the generals – by marching his troops on Rome in 49 BC – Rome now found itself under full military rule. The Republic had just begun its conversion from Republic to Empire (imperator-ruled).

And it would be Caesar's adopted-son (actually nephew) Octavian "Augustus" Caesar who would complete the conversion, as he tightened up Roman "Republican" society just as a general would tighten the ranks of his army. His absolute hold over Roman society did finally bring about much-needed social order. But it also ended forever the role of the Roman commoners in determining the shape and behavior of their society. Rome was now ruled "from the top down" by a rigidly organized Roman military imperium. The "Republic" now existed in name only.

For a while this looked as if it had been exactly the right development needed by a mighty Rome. And this "for a while" was set in place by indeed a number of very capable Roman emperors – Octavian Caesar, Tiberius, Vespasian, Domitian, Trajan, Hadrian, Antoninus Pius and finally Marcus Aurelius – who governed the Empire during most of the first two centuries of the Christian era.

But from the death of Marcus Aurelius in 180 onward, Rome (or its military legions that actually did the selection of Rome's imperial leadership) seemed unable to come up with talented leadership. To a great extent this was caused by the deep infighting that went on among the legions as one or another legion would promote its own general as Rome's new emperor. The situation got so bad that in a 50-year period (running from 235 to 285), constant overthrow or assassinations of emperors (25 in total!) going on within the higher ranks of the military caused Rome to tumble into deep moral corruption and social chaos. And thus did Rome begin its fall from greatness – to the status of its Republic being no more than a fond memory, actually a tragic memory.

CHRISTIANITY

The critical importance of America's own Christian roots. But, of all the different social legacies that went into shaping American society – Jewish, Greek, Roman and, Christianity – it has been the last of this list, Christianity, that served ultimately as the foundational element of American society.

It was Christianity and its accompanying social order that birthed and then developed English America politically, economically, socially, etc. – serving as America's moral-spiritual foundations on which a new American society was built, even many generations before the establishment of the American Federal Republic in 1787.

America was not just suddenly founded with the writing of its Republican Constitution that particular year – or even with its Declaration of Independence a bit earlier in the well-known year of 1776. Rather, America was birthed on very strong Christian foundations a whole century and a half earlier, in the early 1600s. Indeed, the moral-spiritual features of Christianity had already served quite a long time as the young nation's social-moral foundations before these key events of the later 1700s came about.

These 150-year-old American religious norms and principles (largely Calvinist in nature) had a tremendous impact on the way that the Fathers or Framers of the 1787 Constitution understood social obligation, and the way that the Framers held personally a deep sense of social right and wrong. Indeed, Christianity had long formed the moral foundations by which, as a free but united people, all Americans knew how to discipline themselves, in order to live in an orderly, cooperative fashion. Living by that Christian moral-spiritual code, Americans needed no dictator (or English king!) to tell them how to live. God's own instructions, found clearly in the Christian Bible, gave them just such guidance.

Christianity provided an unvarying body of personal and social instructions, already thousands of years old, ones in need of no "progressive" updating, such updating as both Athens and Rome went through repeatedly in a desperate attempt to improve their fundamental social orders. Such Athenian and Roman efforts at rational social reform inevitably unleashed greater personal debate, as their leaders found themselves in deep personal disagreement over the direction that such reform should take! And ultimately, those disagreements became very brutal, resulting in the need to call on a dictatorial hand to restore order.

No, the Framers of the Constitution were not social reformers, nor were they dictators, but simply leaders charged with the responsibility of confirming in the creation of a new political order the social-moral-spiritual traditions that had long guided the colonies, traditions that they expected to now guide the thirteen newly-independent states in their quest to

America's Moral-Spiritual Inheritance 27

continue to work together in union as a free people – rather than as political competitors. Anyway, more (much more) about this later!

That same Christianity also continued to give vision and moral guidance to the American Republic for many more generations after its founding in 1787. Indeed, elements of it continue to perform that vital service even today.

But Christianity today also finds itself greatly on the defensive – as numerous Americans of major political influence want to see America made more "progressive," by "separating" (removing) Christianity and its long-standing social-moral principles from the ever-widening jurisdiction of a very "reformist" Federal government or "state" – a "progressive" state which today reaches into every dimension of life in America possible.

Those that now press the issue of "separation of church and state" – claiming that the Constitution itself requires the removal of religion from America's public domain – do not realize (or at least do not want to acknowledge) how deeply Christianity shaped America and its values, importantly including the understanding and motivation of those who first put the Constitution together.* Indeed the whole of Western Civilization as it has come down to us through many, many centuries, is a by-product of the Christian religion.

Of course many of those who want to see Christianity dismissed from public life actually know very little about Christianity itself – believing (without serious investigation into the matter) that it is restrictive in its quest for social order – and presumes a ridiculously superstitious belief in some kind of power or God who exists above the mechanically operating "natural" or material order – a God able to set aside the mechanical and self-running laws of science in order to favor (miraculously) individuals and societies that follow his guidance.

And such critics are partially correct – for Christians (as well as a lot of very highly respected modern scientists!) do believe God to be quite active in the life of this planet – becausethey have personally witnessed events that support this understanding. But of course not everyone has seen such occurrences – or even wanted to see them.

---

*Nor do they understand or admit that their "Secularism" is itself a particular worldview or religion, a religion that through the federal courts they have succeeded in establishing as the only religion allowed to be taught in America's public schools, thus preventing the people from the free exercise of their right to have their children raised in accordance with their own Christian worldview or religion. And ironically, it is the federal courts themselves, the supposed guarantors of last resort of America's constitutional freedoms, not Congress, that has been used by the Secularists to dismiss the guarantees of the freedom of religion promised by the Constitution's First Amendment!

Another piece of confusion that arises when modern Secularists or "Progressives" attack Christianity is that Christianity is treated as if it were some single social phenomenon. But it has, in fact, (politically speaking) been many things, things frequently much opposed to each other – and occasionally – and tragically – even bloody in that opposition.

But apart from the politics that gets into even the Christian religion itself, there have always been a number of key ideas that truly define the faith – and which, if practiced faithfully, indeed give Christian society a high degree of unity, peace, and prosperity. America has long served as an example of just that very possibility.

Jesus – the pathway to the Fathership of God. Jesus the Christ or "Anointed One," as founder of this Christian religion that was so foundational to American birth and development, was something of a Jewish teacher or rabbi – except that he did his teaching out in the open fields as well as in the local synagogues. He preached a call to come to God personally – like coming to your own Father (and thus he spoke of God as "Abba" or "Daddy" in the language of the day) – so familiar in expression that it shocked proper Jews who thought he was not showing respect to Almighty God. He preached not only to proper Jews (who anyway thought that they did not need his advice) but also to the rejects of Jewish society – and even to non-Jews or Gentiles.

In fact that broadness of his spiritual reach was the very heart of his ministry, the demonstration that God as Father was not interested in the various ways that we humans divide the surrounding world into various identity groups, ones to be loved and supported and those to be despised and forcefully rejected. And Jesus's wide-ranging realm of love included not only tax collectors and women of questionable repute (major sinners in the Jewish social scheme), but also foreigners such as a Roman centurion and the despised Samaritans, and even lepers. And he also had a high regard for the importance of children, a group of small beings who had not yet earned the right of high regard or social respect in the thinking of the time (and maybe still even today). Furthermore, he drew into his closest circle of friends people of no greater status than that of fishermen.

In short, Jesus was no practitioner of identity politics. Quite the opposite. His ministry was a clear demonstration of the fact that our Heavenly Father made no such human distinctions in his love of humankind. That was man's own particular failing: to judge others on the basis of where these others stood in the comparative realm of identity politics.

Jesus demonstrates the power of such faith. And just as shocking, Jesus performed signs and wonders or miracles, calming the storms,

America's Moral-Spiritual Inheritance   29

performing deep physical healings even of lepers, raising individuals from death (even as in the case of his friend Lazarus from the grave itself) – all undertaken to drive home his point about the importance of getting into a right relationship with God as Father. With God as personal Father, even the laws of the physical universe must submit to strong human faith.

Of course people of reason (they existed back then no less than they do in today's "scientific" culture) were disbelieving and even hostile to such demonstrations of Jesus's authority, which he assured others was also – through the simple power of faith in God as Father – within their reach as well.

The cross of Jesus Christ. Ultimately the Jewish political authorities had enough of Jesus's threat to their well-structured universe* by way of his miracles and most unusual street ministry, and had him arrested and turned over to the occupying Roman governor of the day, falsely accusing Jesus of encouraging rebellion even against Rome itself – something to get him to be put away by the cruel Roman device of hanging criminals on a wooden cross until they died a slow and agonizing death. And so it came to Jesus.

But then hundreds of his followers were most certain that he returned (briefly, for 40 days or so) from the grave and again taught them his gospel (good news) message before being taken up to Heaven to join the Father at God's right hand – and by doing so, releasing the Holy Spirit to come among the people (on the day of Pentecost) in order to continue the work themselves that Jesus had started.

It is ironic that the Roman device, the cross – that was intended to force the most humiliating death as possible on a criminal – would become itself the very symbol of Christianity. This is because Jesus's death on the cross was understood by his followers to be an act of cosmic significance: the blood sacrifice or sin-offering required by the power of Heaven as the price for entry into eternity. But Jesus himself was without sin, and so the sins he was paying for in his self-sacrifice on the cross were not his own. Instead the sins being paid for by the cross were in fact the sins of the entire range of humanity.

But how could one man's sacrifice be sufficient to pay for the sins of all humankind? Actually, Jesus was ultimately understood to be not just a mere man – but was fully divine – and thus able, as God himself, to offer himself in sacrifice for the sins of the world. A very loving God had, in essence, offered himself through his Son as the payment for the sins of all

---

*Today we would term their well-structured universe as one that was "scientifically ordered." Jesus seemed not be to be limited in his thinking and behavior by such "science."

mankind – at least for those, anyway, that were willing to put themselves under such divine grace and receive, at the foot of Christ's cross, God's full forgiveness. Furthermore, in doing so, they also received a new, powerful life from the hand of God – without being in any way specially deserving of such favor. In this new life they would live by and through the power of God's own Holy Spirit, to help them take on the challenges of life – including even the challenges presented by their own moral frailties. And they would continue to be fully empowered to meet the particular challenges presented to them individually – and jointly (as members of a Christian society) – until they were to draw their last breath, and at that point, when their work on earth was done, join their Heavenly Father in eternal paradise.

Trinitarianism. This idea of a loving Heavenly Father, sacrificing on the cross his own divine Son for the sins of the world, and then empowering those who accepted for themselves this act of divine forgiveness with the gift of God's own Holy Spirit – all of this came together as a key belief system known as Trinitarianism: a single God in three "persons" – Father, Son, and Holy Spirit.

Unitarianism. However, receiving the salvation that God himself lovingly offered by way of Christ's cross turned out not to be such an easy concept to get over to many people – because it is a more natural instinct of man to want to earn his own moral credits himself – as a matter of moral pride. Setting aside that pride and receiving the undeserved saving grace of God himself just was more than most normal egos could handle.

Those that could not or would not rise above the idea of earning moral merits through one's own good works argued that Trinitarianism sounded like merely another version of Dionysian Greek religion or philosophy. Indeed, members of the Roman world who lived in the predominantly Greek cultural areas of the Empire were more able to understand and embrace Trinitarianism. But those of the Semitic world of Syria, Palestine and Arabia, for instance, refused to embrace Trinitarianism because it did not conform well to their cultural understanding of moral behavior and social obligation. But this would also include many German tribes north of the Roman borders, who did come to accept Christianity, but also only of the Unitarian variety

Ultimately, as Unitarian Christians, they understood Jesus as a fully human creature – not another form of God while on earth. To Unitarians, Jesus was a human without sin to be sure, which made him a perfect moral example worthy of complete devotion by others – one indeed so perfect in behavior that at his death he was raised in heaven to sit at the right hand of God as God's favored Son. And as far as the notion of an assisting Holy

Spirit – Unitarianism found no place in its understanding to include such a concept. That was way too Greek for a Semitic or Germanic mind to grasp.

Trinitarianism versus Unitarianism would remain an ideological tension that would reach through the long history of Christianity and its impact on the larger world – even down to today.

The Early Church. In any case, those who early took up the "Way" of Jesus the Christ during the first couple of centuries of the Christian community did so in a rather typical Jewish way – gathering together regularly at least weekly on the "Lord's Day" (Sunday), although largely in secret because it was very dangerous to be a Christian at that time. Here they would recall the sayings of Jesus, pray together, and just in general fellowship as mutual followers of Christ.

Efforts were soon made to bring together for study various narratives about Jesus' life and ministry (the gospels) – plus letters circulated among the various churches written by key Christian leaders advising them on the Christian life, many of these letters written by the Jewish convert, Paul (formerly Saul). Thus was formed the foundations of the Christian New Testament, the second part of the Christian Bible, following the longer Jewish or Old Testament portion of the Bible. Such writing served not only as the central document that described Christian life in the years of Christ and immediately thereafter – but also as a social model instructive for Christians at all times and for all generations.

Intense Roman persecution. During those first few centuries, Christianity was not well accepted, either in its Jewish homeland or in the broader context of the Roman Empire. It was subject to waves of intense Roman persecution – not because of its rather un-Roman religious beliefs (Rome was actually very tolerant of an amazing wide variety of religious beliefs held by their citizens), but because the Christian religion refused to also acknowledge the divinity of the Emperor (emperor worship). This was too drastic a departure from Rome's imperial policies. Thus the Christians were hunted down ruthlessly, and then put to death for their refusal to worship the Emperor. This involved even gruesome public displays of Christian slaughter by wild animals or gladiators, or anything designed to entertain the Roman spectators.

But ironically, Christian martyrdom merely became an even more-powerful social force spreading within the Empire – because of the very quiet bravery of Christian martyrs undergoing such cruel Roman death. Romans grew increasingly impressed with Christianity's ability to give its followers such incredible personal moral and spiritual strength, even in the face of a most terrible death. Christian morality stood out glowingly in high contrast to the obvious moral collapse going on within a darkening Roman Secular/Materialistic imperialist culture.*

The "Romanization" of Christianity: "Christendom." Then Christianity's fortunes – and its very character – changed dramatically when the Roman Emperor Constantine decided in the early 300s not only to accept Christianity for himself, but also to make it the new moral-spiritual foundation of the decaying Roman Empire.

At the time, Christianity was having a huge impact on the Roman Empire, so much so that the Emperor prior to Constantine, Diocletian, had conducted one of the cruelest efforts to eliminate Christianity (thereby supposedly bringing Rome back to good order), but had succeeded no more than the emperors before him. Then when he died, four imperators competed for the position as grand ruler of the Roman Empire.

One of them, Constantine, in 312 received a vision in the night before a crucial battle with a competitor (the latter was equipped with a much larger legion supporting him), a vision that told Constantine to place the chi-rho (Greek symbols representing Christ) on their shields, indicating that they were doing battle for Christ as well as Constantine. And indeed, the victory of Constantine the next day was so impressive that it confirmed for him the critical importance of Christianity, although his familiarity with the religion was rather shallow at the time.

In any case, it would be another ten years before his sole claim to emperorship would be completed. But nonetheless, in conjunction with an imperial ally, Licinius, Constantine the next year (313) issued the Edict of Milan, ending all further persecution of Christianity.

Indeed Constantine even took for himself the title pontifex maximus, making himself also the religious head of the Roman Empire, and as such began to reorganize the Christian religion, Roman style. He called conferences with the bishops or Christian leaders to clear up the clutter of three centuries of unsupervised religious development, by clarifying the doctrines (or "creeds" or "confessions"), deciding which of the considerable body of Christian writings were to be officially authorized as "canonical," and by developing a huge, bureaucratic ecclesiastical (church) structure to supervise the life of this religious community, whose religion had now officially become the moral-spiritual underpinning of Constantine's Empire.

---

*The Roman government's offering of "bread and circuses" to the masses to keep them supportive of a decadent imperial order was a classic case of a ruling elite failing to understand what it is that makes for a vibrant society, one defended willingly even to the point of death by its members. Cheap material rewards offered by a ruling class will never rescue a society whose moral order is failing.

Thus this 4th century Imperial Christianity would look very different from the 1st century Christianity described in the Bible. Besides the whole Christian social order being put under massive Roman bureaucratic supervision, Jesus would be elevated in status to that of *Christus Rex* or Christ the King – friend and colleague of the Roman emperors – the person supposedly authorizing and thus conferring ultimate legitimacy on the Roman emperor then in power. This in effect took Jesus out of the hands (and the hearts) of the common people, forcing them to look elsewhere for personal spiritual support.

This then led to the adoration of Mary, the mother of Jesus. In fact it became her, rather than Jesus, that the common people now generally turned to for emotional support – something along the lines of the very popular Earth Mother worship (Isis, Astarte, Aphrodite, Demeter, etc.) which had just been suppressed by Christian Roman authorities. And along those same lines, certain Christian saints reputed to have special powers in particular areas of life came to replace the pagan deities that people once prayed to for favor in dealing with daily life and its specific challenges.
In short, in becoming Rome's official religion, Christianity got "Romanized."

Religious works vs. divine grace. This Romanization of Christianity would also have a tendency to move Christianity slowly over the centuries towards Unitarianism – as salvation or access to heaven depended less and less on God's grace and the individual's repentance and transformation in being confronted by that grace – and more and more on the powers of the official Roman Church to offer salvation to the Christian faithful. The Church now required regular periodic confessions to a priest (followed up by certain works performed by the penitent sinner as specified by that priest), allowing the person to be qualified to receive the holy sacraments or blessings of the priest in order to help cleanse the sinner of his or her sins. Thus it was that works slowly took the place of Divine grace in the way the Church instructed the faithful concerning the requirements for salvation, and the reward of eternal life.

But Rome declines in the West anyway. Not only did Constantine reshape Roman culture by adopting Christianity as Rome's new moral spiritual foundation, he also moved the political center of the Empire east, from its original base in Italy to a new position at the point where the Black Sea empties into the Aegean Sea (Eastern Mediterranean) – anciently the city of Constantinople (named after him), today's Istanbul, Turkey. He did so to move his operations closer to where the political (or more particularly, military) action was – against the Persians to the East and against the Germanic tribesmen to the North (the Balkan Peninsula) pressing the

Empire from both directions. But this move of the Imperial capital east from Latin-speaking Rome to Greek-speaking Constantinople left the old Italian city of Rome forlorn – pathetically so.

Thus it was that German tribes migrating into central Europe from the Northeast (under pressure from the Asian Huns coming in from further East) found the eastern half of the Roman Empire a solid barrier to expansion. But as they slid westward, they found a very different dynamic: only a very weak Rome trying to hold its own, an easy pickoff.

Indeed, in 410 Visigoth chief Alaric and his Germanic tribal troops breached the walls and plundered the helpless city of Rome. This was then the signal for the Germanic tribes of north central Europe (Goths, Franks, Alemanni, Burgundians, Angles, Saxons, Frisians, Thuringians, Vandals, etc), to invade the western half of the Roman Empire in earnest.

It is important to remember that these Germans came not to destroy Rome but to capture the elegance of the once-famous Rome. But there was very little elegance left to capture at this point. Roman civilization had simply broken down in the West.

Now travel on the Roman roads became dangerous, leading to a decline of commerce and trade. Consequently, urban life decayed and eventually disappeared in most areas of Western Europe. Survival now depended on the ability of the new tribal societies simply to support themselves locally from the bounty of the small farms that became the sole foundation of the Western European economy. Materially an economic, then social, Dark Age fell upon the West.

Christian survival in the West. Nonetheless a series of talented Christian Bishops of Rome, who remained behind in the ancient capital city, continued to command considerable respect within the Western Christian community – and slowly came to be recognized as the head of the Christian Church in the Latin West – eventually gaining the title "Pope," meaning something like Father – but Father (Papa) above all other priestly Fathers! Especially notable among these popes were Leo I (pope, 440-461) and Gregory I (pope, 590-604), who managed to preserve and strengthen what little remained of Roman or Latin moral-cultural order in the West.

Indeed, the church of Rome not only survived the Germanic impact but converted some of the most important tribes to Trinitarian Christianity* and restored the city of Rome to a position of some degree of religious

---

*Some of these tribes, particularly the Goths, were already Christian, though Unitarian or "Arian" thanks to the missionary effort of Ulfilas and the leadership of the Gothic chieftain Fritigern in the 300s; Rome was "Trinitarian" and thus looked on these tribesmen as not yet fully Christian, and thus in the need of conversion.

cultural importance – at least within the West itself.

And there was the British monk, Patrick, who brought Trinitarian Christianity to neighboring Druid Ireland in the early to mid-400s. In Patrick's 30-year mission to the Irish, he established over 300 churches and he baptized over 120 thousand Irishmen. In turn the converted Irish would soon themselves become Christian missionaries to the Germanic and other Celtic tribes to the East of them, most notably: Columba (mid-to-late 500s) to Scotland; Columban (late-500s) to the Burgundians, the Alemanni and Celtic Gauls on the European continent; and Aidan (mid-600s) to the Angles, Mercians and East Saxons of Britain.

And there were other such missionaries, monks and priests who acquitted themselves quite honorably along vital moral-cultural lines, especially once the monastic movement had been disciplined by Benedict (early 500s), whose monastic rule was widely honored throughout the West. These monks were sent out among the Germanic tribes to convert them not only to the Christian religion but also to the Roman Catholic political-religious order that accompanied that religion. In many cases the effort by monks pointed only to the first part of the program: the saving of souls. But the popes had more of the second part of the deal in mind.

Ultimately tribes had to decide where they belonged in the Christian program, on their own as autonomous Christian tribes, or as components of the larger Western Christian or Roman Catholic community. Thus, for instance, in 664, a religious council or "synod" gathered at Whitby (north central England), where the majority of the delegates voted to end the self-supporting religious life in England introduced by the Irish monks who had originally brought Christianity to the kingdom The Synod decided instead to bring the Northumbrian tribe or kingdom within the religious realm (and its particular Latin rites) overseen by the Pope at Rome.

In effect this decision conveyed the idea that the Pope was the ultimate authority, both religious and political, within Western Christendom. Of course tribal kings tended to ignore in practice the moral-legal distinctions of this relationship. But the popes, especially the more active political popes, were very aware of this special entitlement they possessed.

Charlemagne and the European feudal order. Meanwhile, over in Western Europe, in the late 700s a Frankish tribal king, Charles or "Charlemagne" (Charles the Great)* succeeded in conquering nearly all of

---

*He was the grandson of Charles Martel (the "Hammer") who had made his own great place in history by being able to stop the spread of Islam into Europe by defeating Muslim forces at the Battle of Tours (732) in central France. He went on to establish the Carolingian dynasty ruling France, which Charlemagne was soon to head up.

the other Germanic tribes of continental Western Europe.*

Such political power did Charlemagne accumulate for himself that he was able to end the independent existence of these various Germanic tribes, not only forcing a new unity on much of Western Europe but also making himself now the single landowner of Western Europe! The former tribal lands were now his – personally his. And when the Roman Pope certified Charlemagne as Emperor, any moral basis for contesting this development was eliminated.

But this was an enormous reach of territory for a single individual to be governing – as Charlemagne had no vast bureaucracy, civil or military, by which to manage his lands. So, appointments were made by Charlemagne (and his descendants), to certain well-respected supporters or vassals – authorizing them to govern certain areas of his Empire – all in Charlemagne's name of course. These vassals were then permitted to become lords themselves of these assigned territories, appointing their own supporters, their own vassals, to help manage smaller regions within their own appointed land. Completing this ruling class were then numerous warriors or knights who came into full service to the local lords, offering these lords military support and receiving in return the right to share the dining tables and residence in the castles of their lords.

Over a period of time, these feudal responsibilities tended to be passed on from fathers to sons. Thus it was that Europe's ruling class came to be made up only of individuals born to this small group of privileged families. Likewise, those who tended to hold the higher offices in the Church – which authenticated or legitimatized this social arrangement – also were themselves usually drawn from these same families. As far as the rest of the 95% of the population, they remained permanently locked out of entry into this privileged ruling class. Instead, as peasants, they tended the fields and performed the manual labor needed by the local lords and ladies. And this was then the *feudalism* that would govern European life for centuries.

Viking blood added to the mixture. But about the time Charlemagne was bringing Western Europe under this feudal system, attacks were happening along the edges of his vast Empire – and across the way even in the British Isles. Northmen (Normans) or Vikings coming from the Scandinavian North were beginning to conduct horrible raids on Christian Western Europe – stopping cold the cultural advance that had almost got up and running with

---

*The Saxons and Celts of the British Isles excepted, as they continued to lay outside Charlemagne's conquered territory. Likewise, most of Spain also fell outside Charlemagne's realm because it remained under Arab-Berber Muslim control, and would do so in part for the next 700 years.

Charlemagne's social-political revolution. These Viking raids effectively plunged Christian Europe back into the Dark Ages.

However, around the start of the second Christian millennium (ca. 1000 AD) the barbaric attacks of the Vikings or Normans slowed up considerably, giving Europe something of a degree of peace, the first in a long time. Part of this was due to the settling of the Normans within the communities they had once raided ruthlessly – the Vikings or Normans adopting both the local languages and the Christian religion of the people they had overrun – now becoming as dukes or even kings, protectors of those same communities – such as French Normandy, the English Danelaw, eventually England itself (1066), and even places as distant from the North as the Mediterranean island of Sicily.

The Crusades – and encounter with Islam's great wealth. But even with their settling in, the Normans lost none of that energy – though this energy was now tamed and converted to the powerful service of Christian or Western society.

And in 1095 this energy would be called on by the Christian Pope to rescue the Holy Lands from the Muslim Turkish "infidel" who had made Christian pilgrimage to the Holy sites of the East very difficult, if not even impossible. The Normans – but also the Germanic kings and noblemen (as well as multitudes of commoners) – boldly answered the call to go crusading ("to take up the cross") in the Holy Lands of the Mediterranean East.

The Crusades which followed over the next two centuries (1100s and 1200s) in turn inspired two major developments in Christian culture or civilization at the time. First, it involved the outpouring of a renewed religious spirit eager to spread the Christian faith to the Muslim lands of the East. This spirit could be found high and low in Christian society – although the European feudal nobility of kings and princes quickly took the lead in the enterprise.

But secondly, the Crusades brought the rather materially primitive Europeans into direct contact with the East's fabulous wealth, such wealth as Western Europe had not seen since the fall of Rome many centuries earlier. Not surprisingly, the Crusaders themselves wanted to participate in that world of wealth. Some of the Crusader noblemen even settled themselves amidst the wealth of Islam, establishing Norman kingdoms in the recently conquered lands of the Middle East – sort of "going native" – not exactly abandoning their Christian faith, but wanting very much to combine their Christian world with this higher level of Muslim material wealth. But this new hunger for material wealth would include also those crusaders who returned to their kingdoms and principalities in Europe after having fulfilled their pledges to crusade for Christ in the East.

The Franciscans and Dominicans. In the early 1200s a spiritual "awakening" was to come to a young, very wealthy and very brash Francis of Assisi, through both a series of personal hardships and a mystical call to give his life over to serving the poor, as Christ himself exemplified. In fairly short order a much-transformed Francis attracted a large number of other young Italians to such service, forming something of a monastic community, which the Pope then forced him to bring under Roman or papal supervision (lest he be declared a heretic). Out of this the huge Franciscan movement developed, one that would eventually take multitudes of Franciscan monks to all corners of the world, and one that finds Franciscans even today serving the poor both in urban ghettos and rural villages everywhere.

At about the same time (also the early 1200s) another individual, the Spanish priest, Dominic de Guzman, began to train Christian teachers in order to rebuild proper faith in the Church and its Christian ministry. Here too his new monastic movement (with considerable papal support) spread rapidly around Europe, as vast numbers of Dominican monks or "Friars" were sent out to teach and enforce Christian orthodoxy.

The rise of urban Europe. Meanwhile, taking advantage of Europe's awakened consumer or materialist spirit brought on by the crusades were a number of port-cities located strategically along the sea routes that made for easy access to the wealth of the East. Prominent in this regard within the key Mediterranean region were a number of city-states of Italy, not at all feudal domains but instead types of urban republics – the most important being Venice (which actually went on to develop a vast commercial empire linking Europe and the East) – but including importantly also Genoa (another shipping center) and Florence (a banking center situated in the center of the flow of moneyed wealth East and West). But coastal cities of the Atlantic – such as Portugal's Lisbon, Flanders' Antwerp, Bruges, and Ghent and England's London (not on the coast but accessible to the high seas by way of the Thames River) – and the cities of the Hansa League of northern Germany, such as Lübeck, Hamburg and Danzig and the Rhine region such as Cologne also got involved – and also grew quite wealthy from this new East-West trade.

Renaissance Europe. By the 1300s and 1400s, Europe was being stirred by this flow of wealth and power to a vast cultural awakening, later termed the "Renaissance" (French for "rebirth"). God and Christ soon became upstaged in popular interest by simply the life of man himself, and his new-found ability to bring his world seemingly under human mastery. Thus

"Humanism" increasingly became the cultural motif of Renaissance Europe.

A classic example of such Humanism was found in the works of the political analyst, Niccolò Machiavelli. In his early 1500s study, *The Prince*, Machiavelli insightfully described the way for a dictator to bring unity to a conflicted society, through everything from brute force to simple political deception. Humanists would later denounce Machiavelli for his less than elegant depiction of the human spirit. But they would also find it impossible to prove him wrong. In any case, none of this had anything to do with traditional Christianity and its role in European society.

Indeed, traditional Christianity at the time was suffering deeply under the greed and political corruption of the Church, even papal authority itself, such as the very corrupt Pope Alexander VI and his Borgia family which directed the church during the period 1492-1503, in political opposition to the powerful della Rovere family (Pope Julius II, 1503-1513) and the Medici family (Pope Leo X, 1513-1521). The Church had become a matter of constant, sometimes even brutal, politics – and very little spirituality.

* * *

THE BREAKUP OF CHRISTENDOM

Dynastic rivalry. While all this was going on in Rome, the feudal dynasties of the quite rural European interior did not want to be left out of this scramble for wealth and power that was clearly benefiting these rising city-states of Italy, Flanders and other coastal regions. Thus the Portuguese kings of the House of Aviz in the mid and later 1400s sent explorers from coastal Lisbon to look for a direct passage to the wealth of the East by going around Africa – thereby avoiding the expensive Italian and Muslim middlemen of the cross-Mediterranean route.* Not to be outdone by the Portuguese, the Spanish monarchy of Ferdinand and Isabella at the end of the 1400s commissioned the Genoese sailor Christopher Columbus to locate a supposedly more direct route to the wealth of Asia by heading west directly across the Atlantic – presuming that Asia was only a short distance to the West. What a surprise Columbus had when he ran into islands just offshore of a vast landmass whose existence Europeans were completely unaware of. This discovery would ultimately inspire Spanish adventurers to head to this new land (given the name "America") – when rumors of vast quantities of gold were soon verified with the discovery – and plunder – of both Mexico and Peru (early 1500s).

---

*Actually, before even reaching the lands of the East (India principally), the Portuguese had become quite wealthy in acquiring African gold and slaves.

At this point the Spanish Habsburg dynasty (actually originally Dutch) loomed far above all other European dynasties (the Valois of France and the Tudors of England, for example) in wealth and thus also power. Habsburg Spain would in fact continue to dominate Europe totally during the 1500s – thanks to this huge flow to Spain of plundered American wealth in gold and silver.

The call for reform of the Church. However, by the early 1500s, something else was stirring in the hearts of the Europeans – some of them anyway. The personal empowerment in wealth and the opportunity to explore life more deeply during the European Renaissance served to challenge inquiring minds to examine more closely the way European life itself was structured.

Luther. While the Italian scholar and diplomat Machiavelli was exploring the hard realities of this growing power and its impact on European society, the German monk Martin Luther was looking more deeply into this matter of the Christian Church itself in how all this material power had sent the Church far, far away from the original Christian spiritual roots outlined in ancient Scripture (the Bible) – which Luther had been assigned to teach to his fellow Augustinian monks in Germany.

Luther was so bold as to challenge the Church publicly to return to the original ways of Biblical Christianity – which Christians were taking a new interest in (the Bible was just coming into massive publication thanks to the recent invention of the printing press). This was a serious challenge to the traditional authority of the Church – presided over by the Pope but defended also by the ruling dynasties of Europe, pledged to defend that Christian faith – not only against Muslims beyond the Church but against heretics within the Church itself.

Foremost in answering this responsibility as Defender of the Faith was the very wealthy and very powerful Charles of Habsburg, King of Spain, but also Holy Roman Emperor – actually mostly just an honorific position as feudal lord of the Germanic lands of central Europe.

But Luther found support in his challenge to the Roman (or Catholic) Church from a number of princes and dukes of Northern Germany, feudal lords who chafed at Charles of Habsburg's imperial rule over their German lands. And thus, because of that support, Charles was not able to silence this Christian rebel.

But beyond this political break from the Catholic establishment supported by Germany's princes Luther was not willing to go. When German peasants attempted to put their social-political as well as their theological destinies in their own hands, Luther came out in full support of the efforts

America's Moral-Spiritual Inheritance

by the German princes to put down this populist rebellion*, even when the oppression turned extremely violent (approximately 100,000 peasants killed). Luther simply would not go further than theological reform. And thus feudal society dominated by a variety of German princes would remain the status quo for Germany all the way up to the beginning of the 20th century!

Calvin's Geneva. This spirit of rebellion against the Catholic establishment was also picked up by the naturally inquisitive leaders of Europe's rising merchant cities, a highly literate group fully capable of looking on their own into this religious question unleashed by Luther – through a careful reading of the newly printed Bibles that had recently begun to be translated from the Latin into their national languages – something outlawed by the Church, which claimed that only trained priests were qualified to understand the Bible correctly. But the simple reading of Scripture by literate urbanites seemed to refute this priestly claim – supporting Luther's idea of "the priesthood of all believers." The Catholic ("Universal") Church was outraged – but the urbanites were delighted – and hungry for more.

Some two decades after Luther had challenged the Catholic Church, John Calvin wrote a huge work (*Institutes of the Christian Religion* - in Latin in 1536 and French in 1541)† in the hope of convincing French King Francis to support the reform of the "Protestants" – as they were at this point being termed. But the effort merely forced Calvin to have to flee an angry French king. Calvin eventually ended up in Geneva, where he was asked to try to follow up on church reform in Switzerland started out in Zurich by Ulrich Zwingli (who had begun his Swiss Reform Movement at about the same time as Luther's efforts, but who had been soon killed in a religious battle with Swiss Catholics). Geneva's urban leadership wanted Calvin to put his Reform ideals (quite similar to Zwingli's) into operation in this highly independent Swiss city.

On a second attempt, Calvin's Christian theological and social reforms began to take hold in Geneva. And Calvin's Genevan reforms went well beyond Luther's, focused not just on the reform of the Christian doctrine

---

*In his *Wider die Mordischen und Reubischen Rotten der Bawren* [*Against the Robbing Murderous Hordes of Peasants*] (1525) he advises the German princes to take necessary action against the peasants: "Let everyone who can, smite, slay and stab, secretly and publicly, . . . a poisonous, devilish rebel, like one must kill a rabid dog."

†This work underwent numerous editions, increasing in coverage with each new issue, from a single volume of six chapters in 1536 ultimately by 1559 to four volumes of 80 chapters, indicative of his own development as a scholar-teacher.

according to 1st century standards, but also on calling all members of the Genevan community to strive to live and work together even in their daily lives in accordance with the social standards of first-century Christianity, when Christians took on not only society's theological challenges, but also its political, economic and social challenges as well, as a key part of the Christian life.

In this, Calvin also stressed the idea of *equally important service* to society on the part of all of its members, because he understood that all people – although called to different tasks in life – were fully equal in the eyes of God – and thus must be also be treated with equal respect in their mutual service to the community. Even their social leaders were simply servants, not masters of society, elected to office to work in accordance with the will of the community itself.

Calvin's reforms shook the feudal world with this idea of a basic human equality which placed on everyone's shoulders (including the elected officers of the community) the mutual responsibility of seeing that society lived, in all its ways, according to God's Biblical standards. Calvin's reforms consequently directed Christian society to be a community of self-governing individuals, living together in a mutually interdependent manner – powerfully so because their work together was guided and strengthened by the Holy Spirit.

Calvin's Genevan Reformation thus not only put forth Church-shaking "Reformed" theology, it presented an actual demonstration of revolutionary social philosophy in action.

Soon the word spread around Europe as to what was going on in Geneva, and would-be Christian reformers began to flock to Geneva to see what a community attempting to live according to Biblical standards in all its social capacities actually looked like. They came from England to study the Calvinist experiment in Geneva – and returned to their English homeland as "Puritans" – calling for the Church of England (and thus English society as well) to be *purified* in accordance with Biblical standards. They came to Geneva from the Dutch lands of Flanders and Holland and returned to their lands to institute the Dutch Reformed Church; they came from the German lands along the Rhine River and returned to build there the German Reformed Church; they came from France and returned as Huguenots; they came from Scotland and returned as Presbyterians.

The Catholic Counter-Reformation. Finally, a Catholic Church Council was held at the city of Trent where, from 1545 to 1563, efforts were made to answer the Protestant challenge, in particular by tightening up church discipline, both theologically and politically. Besides trying to reinvigorate Catholic spiritualism, the decision was made to hunt down Protestant heretics and force their reconversion, or, alternatively, their exile – or even death – with the Spanish Inquisition (which had already gone after Spanish Jews and Muslims) leading the way.

Also the Society of Jesus, a priestly order of "Jesuits" founded by Ignatius of Loyola just prior to the opening of the Council of Trent, would play a huge role in putting some intellectual discipline behind the old Catholic order, with each Jesuit sworn to a life of simplicity, study, and total loyalty (military style) to the direction of the Roman Pope and to him alone – overriding the demand of the kings and princes to be the dominant authorities in their own realms.

The religious wars. At this point Europe was being deeply shaken as kings and princes of the old Catholic feudal order joined the Roman Church to fight an expansive Protestantism. Leading in this as the supreme Defender of the "True" (Catholic) Faith was Holy Roman Emperor and Spanish King Charles (ruling during the first half of the 1500s) and then his son Philip II (ruling Spain during the second half of the 1500s). They fought Protestantism fiercely, Philip unleashing his mighty armies on his cousins in the Habsburg's Dutch homeland – forcing the southern Dutch, the Flemish, back into the Catholic fold. But try as he might, he could not bring the Calvinist northern Dutch of Holland to the same result.

Meanwhile, French Queen Catherine de Medicis (ruled France from the mid-1500s until her death in 1589) managed to slaughter off the Calvinist Huguenot aristocracy (about half of the aristocracy at that point) at a Paris wedding they were invited to in 1572 – and then proceeded to go after the rest of the French Huguenots (killing tens of thousands in the process), effectively bringing the Calvinist Huguenot Reform to a halt in France.

By the early 1600s, Europe was caught up in full war between Catholics and Protestants, these wars becoming incredibly bloody, especially in the years 1618-1648 (thus termed the "Thirty Years' War"). Finally in 1648, a religiously exhausted Europe came to an agreement (the Treaty of Westphalia) to simply recognize that further bloodying of the continent was not going to change the religious profile any. It was agreed that certain areas would henceforth simply be recognized as fully Catholic and others as fully Protestant. It was time to move on.

✻ ✻ ✻

THE IMPACT OF THE WARS OF RELIGION ON ENGLAND

English religious neutrality under Elizabeth. England, at this time (second half of the 1500s) under the rule of Queen Elizabeth, managed to avoid this turmoil, due to Elizabeth's ambiguous stance on the subject of Catholics and Protestants (she was seemingly sympathetic to both parties to the dispute). However, "The Most-Catholic Defender of the Faith" Philip II, in his failed attempt to send his mighty naval Armada to crush Protestantism in England in 1588, did not help the Catholic cause in England any. He in fact strengthened the Protestant national character of England when his mighty Armada went down to humiliating defeat at the hands of the British sailors, and God's winds which blew the Spanish Armada into a trap it could not escape. From this point onward, English Catholics – fairly or not – would find themselves under suspicion as being less than loyal to their crown and country.

James I. Then when the unmarried "virgin-queen" Elizabeth died in 1603, leaving no heirs of her own to inherit the throne, a cousin, Scottish King James Stuart, was called on to serve also as English King. With James being a "Presbyterian" Protestant, the Calvinist Puritans were hoping to see their sought-after church reforms taken up by the new king. They were to be greatly disappointed. Being now King of England, James was also the head of the Church of England, presiding over its episcopal hierarchy of archbishops, bishops and priests – and James was in no mood to have his ecclesiastical authority challenged by the mostly middle-class and lower-level-gentry Puritans. But at least he learned to tolerate them.

Charles I and the English Civil War. When James died in 1625, his place was taken by his son, Charles I. But Charles had distinct Catholic sympathies – and tensions thus grew between his supporters and the rising group of English Puritans. Many Puritans – by the thousands – chose to simply leave the growing field of conflict in England and head to America (New England principally, but also the islands of the Caribbean) to build a society there according to their Puritan ideals. But those Puritans that remained behind ultimately fell into full rebellion against Charles, producing a very bloody Civil War which pitted their own Puritan "New Model Army" (created in 1645 by the heavily Puritan Parliament) against the king's royal army. Ultimately, in 1649, Charles was defeated and executed, the remaining members of the Stuart family and their Tory supporters fled to continental Europe, and the Puritans took full control of England for the next decade (1649-1660), and governed the country, now operating as a Puritan Republic or Commonwealth.*

England's Puritan Commonwealth ... and the Restoration of the

---

*Actually, the American Puritans kept their distance from the Puritan developments occurring back in England during the mid-1600s.

Stuart monarchy. But England's Puritan Commonwealth, under the strict rule of Oliver Cromwell and his powerful Puritan army, did not find its way into the hearts of the majority of the English. Thus also failing to find a potentially popular leader after Cromwell died in 1658 (his son was proving to be a big disappointment), the decision was finally made by Parliament in 1660 to call the Stuarts from exile – and turn the crown over to Charles I's son, Charles II. Thus the Stuart monarchy was restored in England (the "Restoration").

But the years of parliamentary rule during the Commonwealth had changed considerably the rules of English politics – so much so that the King and his Tory supporters had to proceed carefully in the presence of the strongly Whig Members of Parliament. The party of Whigs, although no longer Puritans by spiritual inclination, were nonetheless certainly Puritan offspring in terms of their quite post-feudal attitudes about government.*

Charles II however was careful to watch his step in dealing with the Whigs – and managed to conduct a fairly successful reign as English (and Scottish) King. But his brother James II, who took over at Charles' death in 1685 – was not so wise. He got caught up in the trendy fashion set by French King Louis XIV, who not only reigned over the most glamorous court in all of Europe, but also set the example of what truly autocratic rule should look like. Trying to imitate that dictatorial style of government in England would ultimately force James II's expulsion from his throne in 1689. Subsequently the Protestant Dutch governor, William of Orange, and his wife (and James' Protestant daughter!), Mary Stuart, were called on by Parliament to take the English throne as joint sovereigns.

The "Glorious Revolution," and the "Human Enlightenment." But Parliament's success in establishing its own dominance in English affairs was not merely a political matter. In also had a tremendous intellectual, moral and spiritual impact on English society and culture. Just as the European continent turned away from divisive religious matters after the mid-1600s, so a similar development occurred in England at the end of the 1600s.

---

*These labels "Whigs" and "Tories" were terms of contempt that one party assigned to the other: Tories, the name for Irish Catholic bandits, assigned to those who stood with their Stuart king and his pro-Catholic sympathies, and Whigs, the name first for Scottish horse thieves and then later for Scottish Presbyterian rebels, eventually assigned to those pressing for a law which would exclude a Catholic from the English or British throne!

Eventually those terms would also be used to describe the groups in America in the 1770s who either supported, as "Patriots," full independence from England (Whigs) or those "Loyalist" colonials who thought it criminal to rebel against their English king (Tories).

Replacing the old religious idea of God controlling all events in life, a new, quite Secular, worldview (ultimately religion) was coming into place, one which instead saw life as operating under rather fixed mechanical laws of "natural" cause and effect. Things just happened the way they did because they were designed by their very nature to operate that way. Thus "natural philosophers" began the study the "nature of things" (or "natural law") in all realms of life, from the physical universe around them to the natural workings of man's society, even the workings of the human mind itself. Consequently, the later 1600s became a time of intense social inquiry – in the quest of an improved natural design of society, one supposedly that would work better than the ones around them that had simply evolved over time through a brutal process of social struggle.

God did not factor into this rising intellectual world except perhaps as its ancient originator. But God no longer was involved – nor needed to be called on – in helping Europe's enlightened natural philosophers engineer and direct what was expected to be a quickly improving world – a world soon to be brought under human mastery in this new "Age of Reason."

Although people still attended church (at least one or the other of its major ceremonies, such as Christmas and Easter, but also weddings and funerals) and still considered themselves Christian, the reality was that Christendom was dead. Western culture by the end of the 1600s had stepped into the natural world of mechanically-operating materialism or Secularism – and its social-moral counterpart, Humanism. Leading the way were a number of famous natural philosophers, but most notably in England at the time, the physicist Isaac Newton and the social/psychological philosopher John Locke. These men would have a huge impact on their times, as significant as the impact that Luther and Calvin had on the previous century.

CHAPTER TWO

GETTING STARTED IN AMERICA

* * *

THE EARLIEST ATTEMPTS AT EUROPEAN SETTLEMENT IN AMERICA

The Spanish colonies. Meanwhile, across the seas in America, the ongoing plundering of American Indian wealth in gold and silver was beginning to slow up for the Spanish. However, as an alternative source of status improvement, extensive landownership in America itself came to be considered as an acceptable substitute – since the acquiring of more land was always the main path to much higher social status within the dominant feudal system. Thus the feudal social pattern was naturally extended to the Spanish lands of the New World as large landed estates or haciendas – similar to the manorial estates back in Europe – were put in place around the Spanish colonies. These haciendas were naturally supported economically by the labors of local Indians bound, like European peasants back in Spain, in lifetime service to the noble Spanish families that took root there.

Also, alongside this feudal landholding system, the Spanish (Catholic) Church, with its religious hierarchy of priests and monks, was put in place in the Spanish colonies to give them a character as close as possible to the culture back in Spain. This was also intended to help the Spanish Habsburg kings keep a close watch over these royal colonies, which ultimately were the king's personally to rule, exploit and protect. In a way also it was to put Catholic priests and Dominican and Franciscan monks on site in America to protect the king's Indian subjects (they were his subjects as well) from the worst of the exploitation by the Spanish lords.

Portuguese Brazil. Likewise the Portuguese established a foothold on the Eastern shores of South America in a region of what would come to be called Brazil – a convenient refueling station for ships heading onward with the trade winds across the Southern Atlantic to Angola in southwestern Africa, and then the tip of South Africa at the Cape, and from there up the African coast to Mozambique, and then to India, and eventually beyond that to the Spice Islands of Southeast Asia (the future Indonesia) – and finally onward as far as China (the port of Macau).

Like Spanish America, Portugal's American colony of Brazil would also develop along feudal social-cultural lines similar to the mother country of Portugal – except that alongside the local Brazilian Indian population, slaves from Africa were brought in to Brazil (much as they were, however, also in the Spanish Caribbean Islands) to constitute the huge class of servant-workers supporting the whole system.

The French and Dutch in North America. The Spanish and Portuguese had shown little interest in North America, although they considered the Atlantic Ocean their private domain and thus blocked efforts of other European powers to explore the New World. But after the Spanish had suffered a number of defeats, the opportunity to explore and secure the riches of the New World (American furs were particularly popular) both the French and the Dutch got into the act.

But the French sent not only explorers (Cartier, 1530s; Champlain, early-1600s; Joliet mid-1600s) to what would eventually become New France (basically Quebec and the Maritime Provinces), they sent Jesuit priests (for instance, Father Marquette, mid-1600s) to claim Indian souls for the Church, not just along the St. Lawrence riverway but well beyond that into the Ohio region and then finally down the Mississippi River, establishing French outposts along the way.

The Dutch meanwhile hired the English explorer Henry Hudson to do some exploring for them along the middle reaches of the North American Atlantic coastal region, where, in 1609, he discovered a river (named after him) which he hoped would provide the greatly hoped-for passage through the Americas to the Pacific Ocean and thus also to the wealth of Asia across that great ocean. Although that plan did not work out, it enabled the Dutch in 1615 to place a trading post (for valuable Beaver pelts) up that river at Fort Nassau (Albany), soon to be joined by another Dutch settlement (1624) at the mouth of that river at Manhattan (New Amsterdam), and also claim the land between these two settlements, which became the basis of New Netherland. Then the Dutch attempted to expand that position further south into what today constitutes New Jersey and Delaware.

✱ ✱ ✱

ESTABLISHING AN ENGLISH SETTLEMENT IN VIRGINIA

The "Lost Colony" at Roanoke. And of course the English had a similar interest in laying claim to territory in the New World. Thus an Elizabethan courtier Sir Walter Raleigh petitioned the Queen to authorize a settlement

Getting Started in America

of English families at a point along what would eventually become North Carolina, in order to enter an English territorial claim to North America. A Roanoke colony of 116 men, women and children was thus settled at this point in 1587 – with promises of continuing support from England. But support did not come immediately – because of the English naval battle with the Spanish Armada the following year. But when a supply ship was able finally to return to the colony, the colony's members were found to be missing. And there were no signs of what might have happened to them. This shock brought to a halt further English thoughts of colonizing America – until a generation later when the irresistible idea of gold lured forth new attempts at planting an English foothold in America.

The Virginia colony at Jamestown. Thus in 1607 another attempt to secure an English position along the North American coast took place, as a English party of three ships and their men (no women this time) – financed by a group of London "Adventurers" (investors) constituting the Virginia Company – arrived in America to begin the search for America's fabled gold. They immediately built a wooden fort on a small island upriver along the banks of one of the wide rivers feeding into the Chesapeake Bay, honoring their English King James by naming the fort Jamestown and the river the James River.

"Gentlemen just do not dirty their hands in common labor." But they had made no plans to work together as a community beyond the building of the fort. Instead they headed out to look for the gold that would make them rich (and status-worthy). Thankfully they had enough food supplies brought with them (or stolen from the local Powhatan tribe) for them to survive the first winter's rigors. But with the arrival of the next summer, no effort was made on their part to grow the food they would need to get through another winter – for, like the conquistadors of Mexico and Peru, they were busy looking for the wealth in gold that would allow them to purchase land rights, which in turn would bring them into the status as "gentlemen." And besides, English gentlemen just simply did not debase themselves by dirtying their hands in common labor. So, no one bothered to grow the food the colony would need to survive.

A big part of the problem was that the colony lacked true leadership, the kind that could get these Englishmen to work together. Captain John Smith led the Council briefly, though he preferred adventure (and gold-hunting) over administrative work, and anyway was wounded and had to return to England in 1609 – returning the colony to a leaderless existence.

Consequently, by the third winter of 1609-1610, they nearly all starved to death (420 of the 480 colonists died). In fact the 60 survivors were in the process of abandoning the Jamestown project when they were intercepted in their departure by the arrival of a new shipment of 150 men and more supplies. The colony survived at that point – only by coming under the discipline of a new director, Lord De La Warr (Delaware).

Indenture. More men (and eventually women) were subsequently brought in – as indentured workers. These were common laborers obliged for seven years to do the physical labor required to support community life, as payment for their passage to America and for the tools and a small allotment of land they would need to get their own lives started up in America when the term of indenture was completed. Finally, under this new dynamic, the Virginia colony began to grow.

Tobacco. Also, it was soon discovered that although no serious amount of gold was to be found in the colony of Virginia, tobacco, brought to Virginia by the enterprising John Rolfe, proved to be a huge seller back in England.* Considerable wealth could be secured simply by growing and shipping back to England this valuable drug. Thus vast acres of land were cleared to make way for this single crop – one vital to the growing Virginia economy.

John Rolfe. Rolfe's passage to America had not been easy. His ship was hit and destroyed by a hurricane, leaving Rolfe, his wife and baby stranded in Bermuda (where both wife and child died). It was here that Rolf discovered the tobacco seed that the Virginia economy would eventually be based on. Finally having a new ship constructed from the wreckage, he made his way to Virginia. Here he met and in 1614 married Chief Powhatan's daughter Pocahontas, bringing some degree of peace between the English and the Powhatan Indians. But two years later in a special trip the two of them made to England to publicize the Virginia venture, Pocahontas died, and Rolfe had to return alone to Virginia. And Rolf would live on only for a half-dozen more years, possibly killed in the Indian uprising of 1622.

Some social-political reforms. Despite the economic boom that came to Virginia, complements of the tobacco trade, changes were needed to attract more settlers to the colony. In 1617 the Company ended its monopoly on land ownership, allowing private ownership.

By 1619 there were ten major plantations in Virginia, mostly along the wide James River. In that year Virginia received a new governor (Lord

---

*Sugar was, at the time, an even vastly more valuable commodity, produced mostly in the Caribbean. But the Virginia climate was too cool for sugar cane to thrive there.

Getting Started in America

Delaware had died on another trip to America) and a new colonial legislative assembly. As part of the plan to encourage settlers to come to Virginia, this assembly was set up to give the settlers their own voice through two elected representatives sent to Jamestown from each of the ten plantations, plus Jamestown itself. Thus in Virginia the idea of representative democracy was first born in America.

Troubles with the Indians. English settlement on what the Indians knew to be their hunting lands had come to anger the Indians greatly. Finally in 1622, the new chief Opechancanough (younger brother of Chief Powhatan) struck the English settlements hard, killing 300 to 400 settlers in a single day*, although Jamestown was spared destruction because of a warning issued by an Indian boy to the inhabitants of the town. But after a year of constant struggle, both sides arrived at a peace agreement (never fully respected by either side however).

Even at the high death rate of the English settlers, the Indians succeeded in killing off only about a third of the English population. And although the Indian loss was numerically lower, that loss represented an even higher percentage of the smaller Indian population.

Then another Indian rebellion broke out in 1644 when Opechancanough struck again, killing another 500 English settlers this time. But Opechancanough was captured and killed, and the Indian rebellion collapsed. In fact the whole episode ended up breaking Indian power throughout the entire Tidewater region.

But the Indians located in the foothills of the Appalachian Mountains to the west were more determined than ever to stop the spread of the English into their lands.

Feudal Virginia. Despite the ongoing problems with the Indians over land ownership, enterprising Virginians began to purchase more land with their tobacco profits – until some of the widely scattered tobacco estates were proving to be quite immense, worked by multitudes of indentured laborers, especially those family estates that lined the wide Rappahannock, York and

---

*One of the myths perpetrated today for various ideological reasons is that of the "gentle Indian." The Indians were warriors, their men used to the rigors of battle over the scarce hunting lands that sustained their tribes. The American Indians could be very cruel, in that they had no use for defeated enemies – who would be just additional mouths to feed should they let them live on (even as slaves) after defeat in battle. Mostly enemies were killed on the spot. Worse, many of the Indians took great delight in watching a captured foe be put through a torturous death. And women and children were not spared, because their battles were always over the matter of which tribe had the right to the land, an all-or-nothing (men, women, children) affair.

James Rivers of the Virginia Tidewater region. For instance, the estate of William Byrd II reached 180,000 acres in size by the early 1700s! These plantations now began to look quite like the great manorial estates back in England. And thus a Virginia aristocracy was beginning to be formed – modeled closely on England's feudal or class-based culture.

The governorship of Sir William Berkeley. Presiding over all this was Virginia governor Sir William Berkeley (first period of service, 1642-1652), the exception to the rule that royal-appointed governors were always anxious to move on to better assignments. Berkeley actually made himself at home in Virginia, developing a plantation there of his own (Green Springs), where he conducted experiments in raising new crops – in an attempt to move Virginia past its one-crop tobacco economy. He also encouraged the members of the Virginia Assembly to act more independently of the royal government in London. And his role in putting down the 1644 Indian uprising gave him strong support among the Virginians.

But with the overthrow of the Stuart Dynasty back in England, he was ultimately removed from service (1653), until the Restoration in 1660, when he was returned to his position as Virginia governor. But at that point the dynamic had changed, with Berkeley now overextended in his duties (he was also a co-proprietor of the new Carolina colony) and not able to deal with the growing problem with the Indians in a way that satisfied the Virginia frontiersmen located to the West where thick forest, rocky soil and, most of all, angry Indians made life extremely tough and unrewarding.

Rural Virginia. Virginia early on would develop essentially as a rural colony, with no real towns developing there – the sole exception being the colony's political capital at Jamestown (later replaced by Williamsburg), where the royal governor had his residence – but which came alive only when a general meeting of the House of Burgesses was being held. Beyond that, there were no business centers or commercial towns needed for the Virginia colony, as each of the major plantations was quite able to conduct all of its shipping business with its customers back in England right there from the plantation's docks along these wide and deep rivers. Urban life thus was not an important feature of southern society.

Christian Virginia. To be sure, there developed in Virginia a typical "Christian" character about the society – for that went right along with being English. Much like in the Catholic Spanish colonies, in Virginia the King's own Church of England was expected to be established as part of the (feudal) political order there. Parishes were laid out as part of the natural ordering of Virginia and attendance at church service was the law of the land – although the law was not really enforced, in part because there were few Anglican (Episcopal) priests sent on assignment to Virginia and in part because the plantations were so widely scattered and sparsely settled that churches were hard to reach. Actually, relatively few were even put in place in Virginia. Anyway, Virginia was not really that much caught up in the religious issues that were keeping old England in constant crisis. Virginia had other things that concerned it more: tobacco – and the land and servants needed to work the tobacco fields, while the Virginia aristocrats conducted their necessary social rounds.

✷ ✷ ✷

THE ENGLISH SETTLEMENT OF NEW ENGLAND

Persecuted "Separatists." Meanwhile another English settlement was in the making – but of a very different nature. It began in the Dutch Netherlands (at Leiden), to which in 1607-1608 a group of English Calvinists of the "Separatist" variety had fled in order to escape the persecution they were experiencing in England. They were labelled "Separatist" because they had given up all hope that the Church of England would ever be reformed to Puritan standards and simply wanted to "separate" themselves from the English Church, something King James felt amounted to treason.

But it had not been an easy time in Leiden for these English "Pilgrims," as only some of them possessed technical skills that could find work there, the rest being simply of a farming background and thus having to take menial jobs just to survive. Also these Pilgrims wanted to retain their English identity, which seemed to hold less importance among their youth, who were taking up the Dutch language and its more libertine ways. And Dutch politics was bringing them under pressure, as the English King James was leaning on the Dutch authorities to suppress the English Separatist communities taking refuge in their land ... at a time that the Dutch needed English support in the face of ongoing Spanish efforts to defeat the Dutch and force them back into Catholicism.

Thus after ten years at Leiden, the Pilgrims knew they had to move on. But to where?

The Plymouth Plantation and the Pilgrims. Finally, the English refugees chose to make that move to North America, despite the horror stories concerning the "dying times" that accompanied all English attempts at settlement there. They had a social ideal as a "Reformed" Christian community to live up to, in America if need be. And they would meet this responsibility no matter what the cost might be. They were like soldiers going off to war, except their war was in service to God, not any king, not any bishop, not any such human authority.

Tragically, these Pilgrims suffered a huge delay in their departure (a leaking ship forced them to return to port, then try again) and consequently they arrived late in the season (November) at a destination in America that proved to be well north above where they were assigned to settle. Also, the prevailing winds that had blown them north of their course prevented them from heading south along the American coast to that intended destination (the Hudson River area). Thus they were stuck there at Cape Cod – just as winter set in upon them.

But they were determined to make the most of this unexpected situation. Thus before they disembarked from their ship, they created a covenant (the *Mayflower Compact*) among themselves, covenanting to work together as a community.* And then they set out to do just that.

But the winter weather they were forced to contend with proved to be a deadly challenge – and tragically in January (1621) a building they had just constructed to shelter their group burned down. At this point death began to ravage their numbers, the community and the crew losing half its members (of the 102 colonists only 47 survived). The dead included 14 of the 16 women in the group. The children tended to survive better than the adults – although now a number of them found themselves to be parentless orphans.

Nonetheless these Pilgrims persisted – and finally that spring they were able to put into place a permanent settlement, a plantation they named "Plymouth."

Friendly relations with the local Wampanoag Indians (including, miraculously, the English-speaking Squanto who showed them how to grow

---

*The Mayflower Compact reads: *In the name of God, Amen. We whose names are underwritten, the loyal subjects of our dread Sovereign Lord King James, by the Grace of God of Great Britain, France and Ireland, King, Defender of the Faith, etc.*

Having undertaken, for the Glory of God and advancement of the Christian Faith and Honour of our King and Country, a Voyage to plant the First Colony in the Northern Parts of Virginia, do by these presents solemnly and mutually in the presence of God and one of another, Covenant and Combine ourselves together into a Civil Body Politic, for our better ordering and preservation and furtherance of the ends aforesaid; and by virtue hereof to enact, constitute and frame such just and equal Laws, Ordinances, Acts, Constitutions and Offices, from time to time, as shall be thought most meet and convenient for the general good of the Colony, unto which we promise all due submission and obedience. In witness whereof we have hereunder subscribed our names at Cape Cod, the 11th of November, in the year of the reign of our Sovereign Lord King James, of England, France and Ireland the eighteenth, and of Scotland the fifty fourth. Anno Domini 1620.

Getting Started in America　　　　　　　　　　　　　　　　　　　　55

corn!) helped immensely. And thus at that first harvest time in New England they were able, with their Indian friends, to celebrate a great Thanksgiving to God for their success. Clearly, they had built a community of Christian faith where they now could freely worship God as they understood he was to be worshiped – without fear of the English authorities. And they prospered, not elegantly like English (or Virginia) nobility, but like the hardworking Protestant commoners they indeed were.

The Puritan Great Migration to Massachusetts (1630-1642). The Pilgrims were soon followed to New England by other settlers, including importantly a Puritan settlement well to the north of Plymouth at Salem. But poor organization and poor leadership almost scuttled the plantation there – and by 1630 most were returning to England, having given up on the venture.

But another attempt was made that same year, one which would be amazingly successful – due to the excellent leadership of John Winthrop and the accompanying leadership team of equally talented and deeply dedicated Puritan pastors and elders. Winthrop himself personally helped finance the migration of the first group of eleven ships carrying some 1000 Puritans from England to the new Massachusetts Bay colony, located in the large harbor region (the future Boston) just south of the Salem site and north of the Plymouth plantation.

In essence this group of Puritans were now also Separatists by the mere fact that as Puritans they were facing heavy opposition from the newly crowned and quite pro-Catholic King Charles who took the throne in 1625 when his father James died. Thus it was that numerous Puritans had finally concluded that it was time to leave England. They thus had applied for a charter to set up a colony of their own in America, King Charles believing that this was simply just another commercial venture like the Virginia Company. But it was not. Not only would the major financial backers be themselves part of this group leaving England for America (1630), but this group was the advance guard of some 20,000 Puritans who would over the next dozen years migrate to New England, in order to establish there the Reformed society that they had previously hoped would take root in England.

The Puritan covenant. Just as this first wave of Massachusetts Bay settlers were about to leave on ships for their new life in America (March 1630), Winthrop delivered one of America's most famous sermons, reminding these Puritans of the Covenant they were taking out with God, he to be their God and they to be his people. In this Covenant, their settlement was to serve as a "City upon a Hill," a "Light to the Nations," demonstrating to the larger world how living under the authority of God in Christ – in close accordance with God's Word in Holy Scripture – could bring human life to great success. He told them:

> Thus stands the cause between God and us. We are entered into covenant with Him for this work. We have taken out a commission. The Lord hath given us leave to draw our own articles. We have professed to enterprise these and those accounts, upon these and those ends. We have hereupon besought Him of favor and blessing. Now if the Lord shall please to hear us, and bring us in peace to the place we desire, then hath He ratified this covenant and sealed our commission, and will expect a strict performance of the articles contained in it; but if we shall neglect the observation of these articles which are the ends we have propounded, and, dissembling with our God, shall fall to embrace this present world and prosecute our carnal intentions, seeking great things for ourselves and our posterity, the Lord will surely break out in wrath against us, and be revenged of such a people, and make us know the price of the breach of such a covenant.
>
> Now the only way to avoid this shipwreck, and to provide for our posterity, is to follow the counsel of Micah, to do justly, to love mercy, to walk humbly with our God. For this end, we must be knit together, in this work, as one man. We must entertain each other in brotherly affection. We must be willing to abridge ourselves of our superfluities, for the supply of others' necessities. We must uphold a familiar commerce together in all meekness, gentleness, patience and liberality. We must delight in each other; make others' conditions our own; rejoice together, mourn together, labor and suffer together, always having before our eyes our commission and community in the work, as members of the same body. So shall we keep the unity of the spirit in the bond of peace. The Lord will be our God, and delight to dwell among us, as His own people, and will command a blessing upon us in all our ways, so that we shall see much more of His wisdom, power, goodness and truth, than formerly we have been acquainted with. We shall find that the God of Israel is among us, when ten of us shall be able to resist a thousand of our enemies; when He shall make us a praise and glory that men shall say of succeeding plantations, "may the Lord make it like that of New England." For we must consider that we shall be as a city upon a hill. The eyes of all people are

upon us. So that if we shall deal falsely with our God in this work we have undertaken, and so cause Him to withdraw His present help from us, we shall be made a story and a by word through the world.

In short, they were going to attempt to do in America what Calvin had achieved in Geneva.

John Winthrop – Puritan New England's Founding Father. Indeed, Winthrop was the "Calvin" to New England, the one above all others who directed the course of Puritan Massachusetts to its success as a grand religious or social experiment, on quite new and untested principles. It was Winthrop's sense of vision and his optimism that kept New England on course. It was Winthrop who helped steer the course of this development between the dangerous rocks of religious fanaticism on the one hand and heavy-handed religious legalism on the other. And as with all true leaders, he did so by setting the example himself of the kind of humble, self-critical behavior needed by all in order to produce the spirit of mutual cooperation that the new society needed in order to thrive. He inspired others to higher behavior – rather than use his social office to dominate and control the behavior of others. And although he sincerely loved those he was responsible for, he was not one in need of their constant approval. Ultimately, he was answerable only to God – as Winthrop reminded his followers that they too were. They were all to live by the counsel of God (prayer and Bible study), and that alone. Winthrop was to them merely an advisor, not their judge. And they loved him for it.

Winthrop was actually nobly born to a father who was a lawyer, landowner, and Cambridge University director, who opened similar doors to John in his development. After graduating from Cambridge, John became Lord of the Manor at Groton and then eventually a member of his father's law firm in London.

John was also profoundly Puritan in his beliefs, relying on his Christian faith to get him through the death of two wives and then the growing problems as a Puritan with the reign of King Charles.

When as a Puritan he was removed from the Court in 1629, he was then free to take the lead in the development of the Massachusetts Bay Company, using his own finances to help assemble the fleet necessary to bring the first 1000 Puritans to America, be willing to face personally the well-known challenges of life in America by leading that voyage himself, and recruit other Puritan pastors to the same risky mission as leaders in the towns and villages that would constitute Puritan New England. And thus it was that America was blessed to have the New England colony come under such splendid leadership. Winthrop was a gift of God to America.

"Democratic" small-town Massachusetts. The Massachusetts Bay Colony would take on a character very, very different from Virginia. The New England soil was rocky and the forests thick – not suitable for huge plantations to develop. Besides, from the very beginning this was never intended to be an economic venture – nor the path to social status. Many of those coming to New England were in fact leaving behind quite respectable social status in order to start a new life in America. And they would be living at a social level fairly equal to everyone else making the trip. Upon arrival they would be assigned plots of land just large enough to support a hardworking family, these land allotments arranged in such a way as to form a small village, centered on a town square equipped with a meeting house which would serve the village as both church and town hall. And each village would have a seminary educated pastor* whose job was to help guide the village as it attempted to live out its new covenant life.

When the available plots of land for a village were fully distributed, then another village, normally to the west, would likewise be surveyed and subdivided into fairly equitable plots of land for distribution to Puritan newcomers. And so the Massachusetts colony slowly spread its way ever westward.

Thus it was that Christian religious refuge – not improved economic status – was the theme that not only brought those Puritans to New England but also became the moral-cultural underpinning of the entire venture. This had very little to do with what was going on way to the south in Virginia.

Rhode Island and Connecticut. The whole enterprise being essentially religious in character, it was natural that questions of religion and society would develop among the leaders of this enterprise themselves. At one point, Roger Williams was forced to leave the Massachusetts colony when he loudly and persistently complained about a number of ways the colony there did not meet his dramatically high idea of proper Puritan standards – first at the Boston church assigned to him, then the Plymouth church, and finally the Salem church. His constant fault-finding with the lack of proper religious purity in Massachusetts (for instance some of the Puritans had failed to repent of the sin of having taken communion in the Church of England back in the home country) threatened greatly the new-born

---

*This is why Harvard College was founded in 1636, only six years after their first arrival in America. They needed pastors faster than what Cambridge University back in England was able to provide them. Note that Virginia would not take similar action until 1693 when the College of William and Mary was established, in part finally to train Anglican priests.

Getting Started in America   59

and still very fragile foundations of the community. Tiring of his tirades, the colony's leaders finally forced him to leave, to start up his own colony elsewhere (Providence, Rhode Island). There he could also put into service his understanding that religion and secular government ought to be treated as separate functions of the colony.

Also Thomas Hooker requested and received leave to establish a colony of his own in the more fertile Connecticut River valley (already being settled by English immigrants) – and there build a community in which also religion and secular government were treated as separate entities.

Finally Williams came to understand the difficulties of leading a new social venture when he ran into his own troubles with the rowdies who moved to his colony to avoid the disciplines of the Massachusetts colony, rowdies who were glad to remind him of his own words spoken earlier about political freedom amidst religious discipline! It was frustrating meeting human expectations and demands. Thus it was that Williams would increasingly look to friendship and counsel with Winthrop over leadership matters. Indeed Winthrop, Williams and Hooker would find that the path of mutual friendship and counsel served each of them very well over the years, as they took their colonies through the various challenges involved in colony-planting and development.

Troubles with Anne Hutchinson. An event involving deep contention over the running of the Massachusetts Bay Colony has today been made by "progressive" or "revisionist" historians into their unique measure of the moral character of that colony – and of Puritanism in general. We are talking about the expulsion from the colony of Anne Hutchinson. What supposedly is highlighted by the revisionists in this event is the "male chauvinism" that directed horribly not just the colony but Puritanism in general.

What is overlooked by such historians was that she was constantly and most loudly undercutting the leadership of this new and fragile colonial venture (the mid-1630s) – although not for the reason that these historians would themselves sympathize with if they would be more honest about the matter. It is claimed that she was expelled simply because she was a woman who dared to organize her own study group (including males as well as females), and to speak her mind so openly.

Actually, women holding such study groups attended by both men and women – and giving strong opinion on various matters – was not the uncommon event these historians pretend it to be. Rather, she was expelled because she loudly and unrelentingly put forth a claim that, through a prophetic voice given her by God himself, she could see clearly that all the pastors of the colony – except her beloved pastor John Cotton – were in fact serving the "anti-Christ," the Devil himself.

In serving as this highly negative prophetess, she had succeeded in gathering a circle of discontented souls (discontented for one reason or another), and thus threatened to split the still-fragile colony into antagonistic factions. Realizing that she was set on destroying the fragile social order holding this colony together, the authorities (including Winthrop) told her that she had to leave the colony. That punishment was mild in comparison to the damage she would have caused the colony if she had been allowed to continue her "prophetic" denunciations of the colony and its social order.

But ironically (and tragically) the curse she had pronounced on the Massachusetts colony at her departure ultimately fell on her and her family instead when, in the Dutch colony to which she eventually moved (she was even moved on from William's Providence Colony in Rhode Island!), they were murdered in an Indian attack.

Relations with the Indians. The Indians that the English encountered were at first quite friendly, even anxious to work with the English settlers in the matter of trade (beaver pelts in exchange for English tools, for instance) and even in the hope of enlisting the English as allies in the on-going tribal conflicts among the Indian tribes themselves. And the English, in turn, were interested in bringing their precious Christian gospel to their Indian neighbors – eventually even creating communities of "Praying Indians" who joined the English in taking up for themselves the Christian faith.

But ultimately tensions would grow between the Indians and the English over the matter of land rights, as English settlers pressed onward into the Indians' hunting lands. The English did not understand that the woods that housed the animals the Indians hunted were not open land just waiting for human settlement and agricultural development. These were well-fought-over tribal properties vital to the survival of the Indian hunting societies. Conflict thus eventually developed.

At first these conflicts tended to be merely local, although still a matter of life and death for those involved. Such was the case of the conflict with the Pequot tribe (1636) which involved both the English and their Indian allies in a war against the Pequot, which step by step became increasingly bloody for both sides as battles raged back and forth. In the end the war basically destroyed the entire tribe – whose members fled, were killed, or were enslaved.

But the bloodiest battle ever fought between the English and the Indians – bloodiest in the long history of Anglo-Indian relations because of the highest percentages of deaths on both sides during this war – took place in 1675-1676 when the once-friendly Wampanoag came under the leadership of an individual known to the English as King Philip – who went on the warpath against the huge Anglo community which now reached

Getting Started in America

deeply into Indian territory (all the way to Springfield in today's Central Massachusetts). A coalition of Indian tribes at first were very successful in the conflict, burning and slaughtering English settlements everywhere – even reaching as far east as the Plymouth settlement at the Cape and the once-friendly Providence, Rhode Island (the latter which the Indians burned to the ground). But in the end the Indians began to receive the worst of the deal, having missed a growing season and facing a hard winter ahead of them. Indians began to surrender as amnesty was offered to those who did – starvation, disease or the possibility of enslavement or slaughter as the alternative. And little by little the war ground to a halt finally by the following August.

This was simply the early stages of a dynamic that was to continue all the way through the 1800s. The land would be fought over, as it had been since time immemorial. The Indians themselves were warriors, because it was vital to them to be able to defend the forests that they hunted for meat – against other Indian tribes seeking the same privilege.

The problem with the arrival of the European to their land was that socially and technologically, the Indians were now hugely outmatched by these new contenders for the privilege of land ownership. The Indians were a people still living at the level of early Neolithic life, whose economic mainstay of hunting and fishing was supplemented only by rudimentary levels of farming. Thus the land could support only very small, widely scattered Indian communities. The Europeans, on the other hand, were commercial farmers, capable of clearing sufficient land to produce farms able to support comparatively huge numbers of individuals. And thus it was that the European intruders into the Indians' traditional hunting grounds would come to vastly outnumber the Indian population of the area.

Ten Europeans for every Indian killed in battle over the land would be required to keep the two different populations in some kind of balance or stalemate. And try as the Indians might, they simply were not capable of reaching such numbers in their wars waged against the intruding Europeans. Besides, the Europeans came well equipped militarily. Indian bows and arrows were serious weapons; but European muskets were just as deadly and more easily brought to skilled use by the European commoner who was less the warrior and more the farmer, but a dangerous foe to the Indian nonetheless. Also, the Indians had so long been adversaries among themselves, tribe against tribe, that it was difficult for them to find the unity necessary to offer joint resistance to the European. Indeed, at first some Indians tribes saw the Europeans as useful allies against their traditional tribal foes.

Thus it was that history was set against the Indian in this contest with the European for the land. It would be a cruel contest, cruel for both sides of the contest. But in the end, it was the destiny of the European to win this all-important battle for the land.

* * *

THE FOUNDING OF THE ENGLISH PROPRIETARY COLONIES

Maryland. At about the time New England was being settled for religious reasons, so was Maryland – except for the opposite reason in the religion category: as a refuge for Catholics wanting to escape Protestant England.

George Calvert (Lord Baltimore), a recent English convert to Catholicism, saw a double opportunity in securing land in America, both as a way to enrich his family fortunes and as a religious refuge for fellow Catholics. In 1629 he petitioned Charles I for a tract of land in which to establish a settlement along the Chesapeake Bay just north of Virginia [he had given up on a similar venture in Newfoundland because it was simply too cold there!] – but died before a land grant was awarded him by the king. His son Cecil then took over the project, receiving a royal charter in 1632 – despite the opposition of the Virginians who claimed the same land as part of their colony.

Calvert needed thousands of settlers to make the colony pay for itself, so he made settlement available also to English Protestants – at first mostly Church of England (non-Puritan) "Anglicans" – who would actually outnumber the Catholics, even from the very beginning. Thus Maryland was always officially a religiously tolerant colony, open to settlement by anyone, regardless of religious affiliation (Catholic, Anglican, ultimately Puritan, and eventually even Quaker).

The venture, beginning with only a couple of hundred English settlers in 1634, started off smoothly, with no starving time or trouble with the local Indians. In the area where the Marylanders first laid out a town (St. Mary's) the local Indians befriended them because they themselves were in need of allies against their own Indian enemies. The Indians sold them the land they first settled and also corn to feed the colony. And soon the rich Maryland soil had the Marylanders producing enough food to easily feed the colony.

And Calvert was quick (1635) to grant his settlers a voice in colonial affairs with an assembly that operated much like the colonial assemblies of Virginia and New England.

Indeed, in most respects Maryland differed very little from its neighboring colony next door (Virginia). Tobacco was the main crop, at first worked by indentured laborers – and then over time by slaves. The colony was dominated by an aristocracy, set up from the outset by the Calverts,

Getting Started in America 63

who gave large land grants to family members and fellow English gentry. This, as in Virginia, created in Maryland a distinct upper class that stood socially far above the common dirt farmers who then came to Maryland as indentured workers.

More proprietary colonies in America resulting from the Stuart Restoration. The Restoration of the Stuart monarchy in 1660 – after the failure of the Puritan political experiment in England itself in the mid-1600s – was accompanied by shows of great gratitude by Charles II son of Charles I (the former who had been beheaded by the English Puritan army in 1649) who simply paid his political debts, or just demonstrated the size of his gratitude, by awarding huge grants of land – full colonies actually – to various noblemen who had supported him during his exile and then his coming to the throne. Berkeley, for instance, who had been dismissed as Virginia governor during the period of the English Puritan Commonwealth, was restored as Virginia's governor. But there were more, many more, acts of royal gratitude.

The Carolina colony – and Shaftesbury as its cultural-spiritual leader. In 1663, soon after his coming to the throne, Charles II granted a group of English noblemen (which included also Berkeley) a huge section of land to the south of Virginia – in theory reaching all the way to Spanish Florida. The land was termed "Carolina" in honor of Charles's father, Charles I (from the old Latin name from which Charles derives, *Carolus*).

Taking the lead in this venture was another outstanding (and unusually virtuous – at a time when being virtuous could be politically very dangerous) Founding Father, Anthony Ashley Cooper, Earl of Shaftesbury. Although nobly born, he was orphaned at an early age, but raised by relatives through the normal noble path, graduating from Oxford and becoming a lawyer and even (at age 18) Member of Parliament. But he was of a cautious nature, rather realistic in his refusal to enter the intense ideological squabbles going on at the time. Originally, he was a supporter of Charles I, until one of Charles's generals plundered a Puritan town that Cooper himself had negotiated peaceful surrender terms – shocking and grieving Cooper deeply – who at this point went into some kind of political retirement. But Cromwell called him back to service as a member of his new Commonwealth's Council of State, where he trod cautiously the path between the contending sides, doing his best to keep the peace among the groups. With Cromwell's death in 1568 Cooper was brought, now as "Lord Ashley," into the small group negotiating the return to the throne of the Stuarts – which brought him huge favor with King Charles II, membership on the king's Privy Council, eventually appointment as Chancellor of the

Exchequer (Treasury, and second most important position on the king's cabinet), and ultimately selection as one of the proprietors of the Carolina colony.

As the individual taking the lead in developing the Carolina colony so as to best serve its settlers, he enlisted the help of the famous English social philosopher and personal friend (and personal in-residence physician), John Locke. He asked Locke to design a legal order for the colony, one that would make it a shining example of a society based on human reason rather than on just religious or political interests (the kinds that were tearing England apart at the time).

Remember, it was the second half of the 1600s and the time of the Enlightenment or "Age of Reason," and "natural philosophers" supposed that they were coming into a full understanding of the precise mechanics of life. Thus supposedly, with some careful investigation into the matter, they could actually construct a social system of a high degree of human perfection, while sitting at their desks simply contemplating the matter! Thus it was that Locke mapped out a Carolina colony in which, among other things, individuals would receive a varying amount of property-rights on the basis of their social status – English philosophers such as Locke being certain that property ownership, as in feudal times, was the key to social stability and efficiency (which indeed, at least in part, it is!).

As it turned out, of course, Locke's design had to be scrapped when reality struck: the varying lay of the land, the varying quality of the soil, and the problems of finding defense against highly resistant Indians, made for a reality which did not submit well to the beautiful plans of "enlightened" Idealism.

As for Ashley (soon to be named as the Earl of Shaftesbury), he continued to find himself in the middle of a very bumpy political world, especially after he played a leading role in creating the Whig Party,* infuriating the arch-royalists – the Tories – in the process. He would be arrested (1681), flee England (1682), and would die in Amsterdam early the following year, because this was one issue he simply could not find the path of political reconciliation to go down.

But as for the Carolina colony that he had given so much of himself to get started on solid ground, it did prosper. The harbor at the Charleston

---

*Shaftesbury and his fellow Whigs precipitated the Exclusion Crisis when in 1679 they introduced into Parliament the Exclusion Bill, in the attempt to block the pro-Catholic James's future accession to the English throne. The Whigs were also demanding that royal authority be placed under the discipline of a written constitution, a shocking idea in the days of royal absolutism. Opposing the Whigs were the Tories, supporters of James and defenders of the doctrine of royal absolutism.

Getting Started in America 65

site proved economically advantageous in its service to the rural hinterland – and individuals of all sorts of cultural background flocked there – including a good number of French Protestants (Calvinist Huguenots) chased out of France when in 1685 King Louis XIV revoked the *Edict of Nantes*, the century-old promise of Protestant rights in France.

Thus Charleston became the South's first true city.

New York. Another such proprietary colony awarded by Charles was New York – part of the former Dutch colony of New Netherland. While the English had earlier been settling the areas of Virginia and New England, the area between these two English regions had been explored and settled in the 1620s by a Dutch commercial company which sent settlers north up the Hudson river and east across the Long Island to trade with the Indians for their wealth in fur – and to develop the region as Dutch territory.

After the Stuart Restoration in 1660, the Dutch and English – though both Protestant – found themselves deeply engaged in commercial wars – and Charles II's brother James, Duke of York, headed the naval command that seized New Netherland from the Dutch in 1664. For his services, Charles granted James proprietary rights to the Dutch colony – as his "New York." However, during subsequent Anglo-Dutch wars, the Dutch colony changed hands between the English and Dutch several times. Finally, in 1674, the colony came permanently into James's hands.

James never visited his American colony, but governed it through a series of appointed governors – and eventually (1683) an elected Assembly. But by and large the New York colony, with strong Dutch Protestant roots and a variety of other ethnic and religious groups present in the colony, was quite diverse in its cultural makeup – giving the colony a very cosmopolitan character virtually from its founding.

New Jersey. What came to be called New Jersey was also part of the Dutch territory awarded to James in 1664. But he turned around and in 1665 awarded sections of this huge feudal estate to personal supporters of his own, George Carteret and Virginia Governor Berkeley's brother John (the Carterets were also involved in the development of the Carolina colony at that same time). Ultimately William Penn also became part of the New Jersey project when Berkeley sold his shares to Penn, who was looking to provide a place of refuge for fellow Quakers (Penn was himself a recent convert to this new and quite unusual version of Christianity). Quakers had come under considerable attack for their peculiar ways (thus the name "Quakers" – for their behavior when they became overcome by the Holy Spirit) – and like the Puritans of New England and Catholics of Maryland, they needed a place of refuge.*

Pennsylvania, and William Penn. The Penn family, besides having offered invaluable military support to Charles, had lent the Stuart kings a vast amount of money in getting the Stuart monarchy restored to power in 1660. An agreement between King Charles II to pay off that debt was finally struck in 1681 when the king's brother James agreed to turn over to William Penn the vast lands west of New Jersey, a land the king himself named Pennsylvania ("Penn's Woods"). Here Penn could expand his Quaker refuge – and build an ideal city, Philadelphia, the city of "Brotherly Love."

However, Quakers were immediately outnumbered by other religious groups (Mennonites, Amish, Puritans, Presbyterians, Catholics, Jews, etc.). But thus it was that Pennsylvania grew as a land offering religious freedom and the opportunity for people to build their own communities as they so desired.

Behind this spiritually welcoming society was the personal sensitivity of the colony's founder, William Penn. As a youth Penn had shown a rather strong philosophical bent, rather than an ambition to perform great military service, of which the family was highly respected (his father was a leading admiral in the royal navy, and also one of the key agents arranging for Charles's return to the throne). But the young Penn had a heart for serving instead the poor, especially those devastated by the return of the Plague in 1665 and the Great Fire of the following year which destroyed most of London, increasing enormously the misery of the poor. This had led Penn to associate himself with the Quakers, who were offering help to exactly those devastated by these tragedies, bringing upon himself an eight-month prison sentence for his Quaker connections (the first of many such prison terms), despite his family's own prominence.

---

*The Quaker movement was started up in the mid-1600s by an English shoemaker and shepherd, George Fox, who did not believe in original sin (nor the need for the atoning death of Jesus on the cross), but instead emphasized the divine favor awaiting any person who simply sought the "inner light" that God had placed in each and every person, letting that inner spirit lead that person to righteousness. Clergy were unneeded in this process, only communal gatherings at which one or another person was moved to speak whenever led to do so by that inner spirit.

This approach to Christianity upset deeply many "normal" Christians, although interestingly Cromwell found himself sympathetic to and thus protective of the Quakers during the reign of his Commonwealth (the 1660s). This was when Penn joined the group. And in America, Providence colony leader Roger Williams accepted this group into his colony, where they soon came to make up half the population – the other half being mostly Baptists (Puritans opposed to the idea of infant baptism, because to the Baptists, baptism signified a quite adult decision to follow Christ).

But two things were to keep Penn's spirits up, despite the considerable political opposition his work brought him. On his death bed, Penn's father acknowledged the remarkable integrity of his son, and told him never to betray what his conscience knew to be true. And secondly, at this point Penn came into enormous wealth, which Penn then put to use to promote the Quaker cause, and thus his involvement in Quaker settlement in the American colonies.

Penn would be one of the few colonial backers to actually come to his colonial holding in America to personally supervise its development, everything from the layout of his precious Philadelphia (built on a grid pattern at the junction of the Schuylkill and Delaware Rivers) to the political order (the Pennsylvania Frame of Government) which would guide the colony down its welcoming path. And he was generous in his offer of financial compensation to the Indians for the land, blessing his colony with peace with the Indians as a result.

But sadly, the colony would not become exactly the utopia Penn had hoped for, as the Quakers could not agree among themselves as to what their religion constituted exactly, and their rivalries ultimately disrupted greatly the Quaker order Penn was trying to achieve. And tragically for the kindly and idealistic William Penn himself, his Pennsylvania proprietorship bankrupted rather than rewarded him financially – largely because he did not have the heart to collect the quitrent owed him by his Pennsylvania tenants, and because his unsuspicious nature blinded him to the fact that his business manager was stealing Penn's earnings. This would cost him time in debtor's prison on multiple occasions, and leave him penniless at his death in 1718 – Penn believing that his venture had been a huge failure.

Equally sadly, he would die not knowing how well his Philadelphia would serve as something of a national spiritual capital, uniting the various American colonies during the dark days (1770s and 1780s) of their struggle to maintain their independence from an overbearing English king. Nor would he know how America would quickly come to honor greatly the integrity in Penn that the country has long understood as the very groundwork of its own existence – and its larger purpose in the world.

Thus it was that Penn's colonial venture contributed greatly to the growing notion that America was a land not of government restriction and social-cultural conformity, but of true opportunity for those willing to come and work hard to build their own world – in full cooperation with others of different political and religious ideals. So he too helped greatly to make America a "City on a Hill," a "Light to the Nations."

Georgia – the last of the major English colonies in America. Georgia, named after England's King George II, was founded in 1732 as a proprietary colony assigned to a group of English philanthropists. Most important among them was General James Oglethorpe, who personally had taken an interest in England's prisons and sought a colony in America that offered debtors a chance to leave prison in order to start a new life and come out of debt. It would also serve as a military colony buffering the Carolinas from Spanish Florida.

Actually very few debtors made their way to the colony – although others came there for numerous reasons, including religious reasons (Georgia too took a very non-restrictive view on this matter of a person's religion).

However Georgia would also follow the Southern trend to build its society on the Virginia model – idealizing the lifestyle of huge rural plantations cultivating tobacco (and other farm products) by companies of African slaves, the whole thing presided over by a small, but highly privileged local aristocracy.

Yet the colony did provide the South its second city after Charleston, an Atlantic port named Savannah – located at the mouth of the Savannah River and well laid out on a beautiful grid pattern.

CHAPTER THREE

INDEPENDENCE – AND THE NEW REPUBLIC

* * *

THE COLONIES MATURE, AND WANDER SPIRITUALLY

Bacon's Rebellion in Virginia (1676). Soon after the Stuart Restoration in 1660, Virginia fell under the spell of a young English aristocrat, Nathaniel Bacon, a recent arrival to Virginia – who was ambitious and had plans of his own to take charge of the Virginia colony. He cultivated the land hunger of landless Poor-White Anglos and the bitterness of Anglo frontiersmen who felt that Governor Berkeley was uninterested in the problems they faced from the fierce Indian wars on the frontier (Berkeley was known to try to keep the peace between the English and the Indians – rather than solve the matter by driving the Indians from their lands).

Then in 1676, in disobeying Berkeley directly by attacking friendly Indians whose land the Anglos wanted, Bacon was arrested and imprisoned, only to have Bacon's supporters break him free – and start a rebellion. Bacon's militia burned Jamestown to the ground. And then suddenly Bacon developed a fever and died, and the rebellion fell apart.

The move from indenture to slavery. The fallout from this incident was that the Virginia aristocrats were so unnerved by the anger of the rebels that they now lost interest in indenture – and moved to use fully slave labor instead – mostly African.

Up until that time Africans had been brought to Virginia largely as indentured workers (like the English, Scots, Germans and others). However, the much more passive Africans tended to stay on – and then their children after them – even generation after generation – because free life on the frontier seemed more dangerous than simply staying on with the masters of the plantations. Thus step by step, Africans and their offspring found themselves locked into a state of total dependency on their masters – which ultimately became outright slavery.

At the same time, the business of the purchase, shipping and sale of African slaves (brought down to the African ports for sale by tribal enemies) was becoming quite extensive, making slavery in America an option in lieu of indenture.

It should be noted that the sale of people as slaves was not a shocking practice at the time, reaching back to the dawn of history – and long practiced not only among Europeans (and Arabs) but also even among the Indian tribes – and as well as the tribes of Africa. Actually, in Virginia slavery as an institution had been recognized as a permissible institution only in 1654. In any case, after Bacon's Rebellion in 1676, the move to slavery was more deliberate (fully defined in the Virginia Slave Code of 1705) on the part of the Virginia aristocracy, as slaves seemingly presented less danger of future rebellion – although not completely, for the fear of that too was always somewhere in the minds of the slave-owners.

The cooling and wandering of the Puritan spirit. Meanwhile, up in New England, Puritan society was following a pattern well described in the Bible as having occurred regularly with the ancient Israelites: a fervently religious generation that looked to God for support in a great struggle for survival, being followed eventually by future generations that fell away from this affection, feeling that they themselves were in full control of their world and no longer in need of the protection or even the counsel of God. This was proving to be exactly the case for Puritan New England as well.

Whereas Williams's Providence Colony and Hooker's Connecticut Colony had built their social orders on the idea that the realm of religion and the realm of politics were to be treated as separate items (mostly so as not to pollute the religious ideals with political corruption) the Massachusetts Colony had insisted that full religious standing as true believers was absolutely necessary to ensure that those who had political or civil responsibilities carried those out in a truly Christian fashion. Thus civil rights and responsibilities were based on a person's ability to demonstrate to the community their full standing as Christians.

However younger generations of Puritans, who found life much less challenging, and thus the need for Puritan discipline not terribly necessary, just simply did not measure up to Puritan standards, both religious and civil, appearing even to be uninterested in achieving such a goal. The colony by the 1660s was thus in a quandary about how to answer this situation of mounting spiritual indifference. Thus the old Puritan leaders came out with the idea of a compromise of sorts, in which "partial" church membership could be offered to the rising generation, sort of an internship in which some civil responsibilities could be offered the individual pending the ability of that person to demonstrate sufficiently full Christian standing, sort of a "Halfway Covenant" with the community and with God.

But over time either the ability to give proof of such merit was just not forthcoming, or simply there was little interest in taking up the challenge coming from the members of the younger generation. In short, the Puritan spirit was cooling and dying. Massachusetts was, like Israel of old, going through a time of spiritual wandering. The younger generation just did not "walk with God" the way the older Puritans had.

Christian "enlightenment." On top of that, towards the end of the 1600s and into the early 1700s, many of the leading intellectual voices in the "Christian" world itself (both back in England and there in the American colonies) were looking more to Human Enlightenment or Human Reason than to God to solve life's problems. Also, Unitarianism, even Deism, was infecting the upper reaches of the English religious hierarchy.

Thus for instance, the very head of the English Church, the Archbishop of Canterbury, John Tillotson, portrayed Jesus not as the atoning sacrifice for sinners but instead as the great moral example that reasonable people would want to follow in order to achieve righteousness. And others, such as the popular author, Matthew Tindal, in his book *Christianity as Old as Creation*, advised Christians not to put much stock in the Bible's stories of miracles and other non-scientific stories, and instead focus on developing the moral instincts that are to be found in all men, and ultimately in all religions.

The Salem witch-scare. This decline of the Puritan spirit did not mean that the colony had been delivered from all serious problems. It is just that as the Puritan spirit had grown legalistic and stale, many of the less intellectually inclined New Englanders tended to look to more primitive religious instincts for spiritual relief, such as a belief in witches and warlocks.

At this point the rocky soil of New England had been overworked by New England's rapidly expanding population – and the deep and dark fear of another Indian attack had not yet left the hearts and minds of the New Englanders. Thus it was very easy for nervous New Englanders to look to the works of the devil and demons as the logical explanation for the recent round of crises hitting the colony.

Very famous today is the Salem witch-scare of 1692-1693 – told as a rebuke to Puritanism, in an effort to show how degrading such religious superstition as Puritanism can be. The only problem with this theory is that this tragic event resulted not from Puritanism – but from the very loss or lack of the original Puritan spirit.

It is indeed a very tragic mark on the social record of New England how the prank of a few schoolgirls turned the town hysterical in fear of witches everywhere – resulting in the execution or just death in prison of some twenty-four people breezily accused of this practice.

The event was finally brought to a halt when the Puritan authorities in Boston stepped in to stop the whole affair – an important detail usually left out of the modern anti-Puritan (or anti-Christian) narrative. Also the larger context of the times is not mentioned – because much of the West, including enlightened France and newly emergent Sweden (which were hardly Puritan) were also caught up in the same witchcraft hysteria at the same time, and to an even greater extent.

This American horror resulted because the guidance of the Christian faith was being put aside for newer, more rational or "reasonable" thinking. But Reason can go in any number of different directions. Witchcraft had its own way of becoming a reasonable assumption about life, as it also seems so today in modern popular culture where interest in witches is considered cool or cute.

* * *

THE AMERICAN "GREAT AWAKENING"* OF THE MID-1700s

By the early years of the 1700s pastors were complaining about their empty churches, Christians entering church doors only to participate in the annual Christmas and Easter celebrations – or even just weddings and funerals when absolutely necessary.

Then without warning, a great wind of spiritual enthusiasm swept through the colonies (also parts of England and continental Europe) in the 1730s and 1740s – which brought forward a number of preachers (such as Theodorus Freylinghuysen, Gilbert Tennent, Jonathan Edwards, and George Whitefield) in support of this new development

Freylinghuysen, Tennent and Edwards. This spiritual "awakening" actually started rather quietly here and there in the colonies, for instance in the Dutch-cultured Raritan Valley region (New Jersey) where, beginning in the 1720s, Dutch Reformed pastor Freylinghuysen preached a form of pietism (similar to the Puritans), calling on his people to examine their lives deeply, and take careful note of where their lives stood in relationship with God in Jesus Christ. In doing so, he was able to reach deeply into the hearts of what soon became a growing congregation, fanning the flames of Christian revival – which others began to take note of.

One of those was the young Presbyterian minister, Gilbert Tennent,

---

*Actually the term "Great Awakening" was not itself used at the time. It was first applied to this event a century later with the publication in 1845 of Joseph Tracey's book, *The Great Awakening: A History of the Revival of Religion in the Time of Edwards and Whitefield*. But it has been known as such ever since.

Independence - And the New Republic

pastoring a church in nearby New Brunswick. Tennent picked up Freylinghuysen's message (the two often preached in each other's pulpits), and Tennent began to have his own impact in bringing a growing number of people to Christ. Something was clearly stirring here.

That same spirit was to reach also into New England, where a young and very scholarly Jonathan Edwards, in taking over his father's pastorate in Northampton (Massachusetts) in 1729, began to take a similar interest in awakening his congregation to the need to look deeply into their lives and see where sin had blinded them and cut them off from God's powerful grace. Calmly, but steadily, he got this message across to his congregation, until by the winter of 1734-1735 it was quite obvious that his message was stirring deeply the hearts of a growing congregation. Clearly a spiritual awakening was underway in Northampton.

George Whitefield. Then the dynamic seemed to begin to stall somewhat, only to get underway again with the arrival of George Whitefield to America at the end of the 1730s. Whitefield would preach a message of spiritual revival which would reach deeply into the hearts of Americans, from Georgia in the South all the way north to Maine.

When Whitefield was a student at Oxford University, he befriended Charles Wesley, who in 1733 invited him to become involved in his brother John's Holy Club, the "Methodists," as they were contemptuously called by fellow students – because of their efforts to discipline themselves to a life of holiness. But try as Whitefield might, he just could not achieve the holiness he craved, and finally crashed spiritually, only then to be filled by a strange new spirit, which he recognized came solely from the grace of God, not from Whitefield's own efforts to be holy. This discovery would stand at the basis of everything Whitefield was to teach and preach from that point on.

Finally ordained to pastor the area of Bristol (England) in 1736, he found that his message of immediate salvation through simple repentance before God was touching the hearts of the British working classes, the way the doctrinal and ritualized pattern of Church of England worship did not. Soon Whitefield had a huge revival ministry going on in England, even in its fields and streets.

But in 1738 he felt called to go to the new colony of Georgia, where, once there, he took a great interest in building an orphanage (his Bethesda Orphanage). Thus after a short stay in Georgia, he returned to England to raise funds for his orphanage project. To raise that money (and bring his listeners to salvation at the same time), he took his preaching wherever he could, to churches, or, as back in England, to the streets and fields if necessary. This very unorthodox method of preaching to the masses gained him a great deal of attention, both positive and negative. Thousands would come out to hear his preaching, falling into tears of repentance and calling for God to retake the lead in their lives.

Now Whitefield undertook to cover the broader reach of the colonies, taking himself to Pennsylvania with the intention of founding an orphanage there in partnership with the Moravians (a large religious group in the rural region north and west of Philadelphia, who founded towns of their own named Bethlehem and Nazareth!). On his way there, he found himself preaching every step of the way – often several sermons a day! Then Tennent and Edwards invited Whitefield to New Jersey and Massachusetts to preach. And thus it was that Whitefield's open-air revival method reached north.*

Most surprisingly, the greatest American sage of the time, Ben Franklin, found himself warmed at least intellectually by this massive religious revival of Whitefield's. In fact, he personally saw to the publishing of forty or more of Whitefield's sermons on the front page of his newspaper, the Pennsylvania Gazette. Indeed, Franklin and Whitefield formed a friendship that lasted the entire span of Whitefield's remaining life (he died in America on a preaching tour in 1770).

Opposition to the "style" of this Awakening. Once again, there were Christians who found all this open-air activity rather un-Christian – because it did not occur in churches with people properly arranged in their pews in front of real pulpits. Also, the idea that everyone should be called to repentance for their sins seemed scandalous for those "proper" Christians who were quite certain that they had nothing serious to repent of. Such repentance was to be directed only to wastrels and scoundrels, not proper Christians. Also there simply was a certain amount of bitter jealousy on the part of frustrated pastors who watched the huge crowds gather in the fields – when they still faced somewhat empty pews on a Sunday morning. It just wasn't right. Eventually even church leaders, or the "Old Light" group began to challenge the theological correctness of the so-called "New Light" revivalists – causing splits to occur within the traditional denominations, especially the Congregationalists of New England and the Presbyterians of the Middle Colonies.

But there was great Divine purpose in this strange event. Yet, with this Great Awakening, God was being faithful to keep his side of the Covenant with America in bringing on this very spirit. And Americans

---

*But at the same time Whitefield never lost interest in orphanage development, continuing to travel back and forth between England and America to promote the development of orphanages (in Georgia and Pennsylvania principally).

were responding, by awakening to their own responsibilities taken on in this covenant with God, responsibilities that would require all the spiritual empowerment that God – and God alone – could, and would, provide.*

God was strengthening the colonists as "Americans," citizens of a budding nation in which its members were well aware of their connectivity with him, through such events as these revivals, ones which reached from the north to the south of Colonial America. This larger sense of social unity and purpose defined them once again as a unique people "called" to take up the old Covenant – to be a Light to the Nations in the way they went at life as born-again Christians.

And also they would need this new spirit, this Divine empowerment, to hold their ground against what the King of England would one day soon be throwing at them to get them back under his total authority as their King. But as a renewed Christian society, they knew fervently that they had "no king but Jesus." They would not be broken by the rising political ambitions of a far-away English king.

✱ ✱ ✱

THE WAR TO CONFIRM AMERICAN INDEPENDENCE (1775-1783)

Growing troubles in America with the monarchy back in England. When the last of the Stuart monarchs (Queen Anne in this case) died in 1714, the English had to go all the way to Germany to find a Protestant relative to take her place as their monarch. But George was thoroughly German, spoke no English, loved to hunt and involve himself in the dynastic disputes on the European continent among Europe's other monarchs – and was content to leave English business affairs to his English Cabinet. And George II (also quite German) who took his father's throne in 1727 operated much the same way in carrying out his duties as king.

Since its very founding, colonial Americans had learned to take care of themselves against Indians, face the challenging natural world around them, and of course take on the even greater challenge of working together to build a stable society. Thus the politics and leadership of England played only a minor role in the life of the colonies. And with the Georges on the throne – busied in things other than the affairs of their American colonies – this independent spirit only anchored itself even more deeply in colonial America.

---

*Thus it was that by the later 1700s, God would frequently be identified as "Providence," or "The Provider," as in "The One Who Provides." They were well aware of how God's provisions worked so well for them.

But things would change drastically when the young George III took the English throne in 1760. He was thoroughly English and thoroughly royal – on the model of the French kings who at the time set the European standard of royal absolutism. According to the theory of royal absolutism, God alone had chosen the peoples' kings – and thus by "Divine Right," kings were to rule in an unquestioned fashion over their lands and people. And to George III that doctrine applied also to his subjects in the American colonies. Trouble began to develop immediately.

Taxes. At this time royal armies were somewhat like private armies financed by the kings' own personal treasuries – treasuries which, given the frequency of the bitter quarrels among the various royal dynasties ruling Europe, were easily drained almost to the point of bankruptcy. This was no less the case for the young English King George III – who, so as to replenish his empty royal treasury, pushed the English Parliament to approve new taxes – including taxes on his English colonies in America. The Americans were very upset, for they had not been consulted on this matter, and had supplied – at their own expense – American militia or "minutemen" (citizen-soldiers normally called quickly to action to ward off an Indian attack) to fight George's French enemies and their Indian allies.

Protests. Protests over the new taxes led George to send British troops to the colonies to protect his tax collectors. This in turn sparked an incident in March of 1770 when a group of Bostonians taunted a small squad of very nervous British soldiers ("Redcoats") who reacted by firing on the crowd, killing three and wounding eight Bostonians (two of whom would die of their wounds). Surprisingly, a relatively unknown lawyer, John Adams, stepped forward to defend the soldiers, bringing considerable notice to him as one who was a definite Patriot, but one dedicated to being totally "just" in his patriotism. The world would see more of John Adams as a result.

George also forced the colonies to stop buying Dutch tea and instead buy the more expensive tea of the British East India Company (the English company was in deep financial troubles). When a group of Bostonians in 1773 dumped a shipment of English tea into their harbor in protest, George was so angry at this insolence on the part of his subjects that he sent royal troops to shut down Boston harbor – and strangle the city economically so as to force its submission to his royal will. And to make sure the citizens of Boston got the point, he forced the Bostonians to house personally the rowdy troops sent to discipline the city.

Then he irritated the colonials further by promising his Indian allies west of the Appalachian Mountains that he would stop Anglos from moving west into their lands; he promised his French subjects in Quebec that he

Independence - And the New Republic 77

would authorize the Catholic faith (and its church officers) full authority not only in Canada, but also in an expanded Quebec province which reached into that same territory to the west of the Appalachian Mountains; and to top that off, he discussed openly the possibility of also placing the American independent or congregational churches under the hierarchical authority of his Church of England officers (archbishop, bishops, etc.). He was quite aware of the religious foundations of the American colonials' independent-mindedness, and wanted that spirit broken.

War breaks out at Lexington and Concord (April 1775). Tensions thus mounted in the colonies, and the king decided to make a move to disarm their colonial militias in order to better secure his position there. In April of 1775, his troops were sent out to seize the military stores at Concord, Massachusetts, but ran into resistance at Lexington – firing on a gathering crowd there, killing eight and wounding ten Americans. His troops then moved on to Concord, where American minutemen were waiting for them. Fighting broke out between the two groups – with the British taking a bad hit. They found the military stores empty and, as it was late, decided simply to head back to Boston. But American minutemen gathered to fire on the returning troops, inflicting heavy casualties on the British in the process. This now gave the appearance of the existence of a full state of war between the colonials and their would-be British masters.

The forming of the Second Continental Congress (May 1775). Thus in May, delegates from the various American colonies met in Philadelphia to form the Second Continental Congress, to coordinate the American response to the British challenge. In the process, they agreed to authorize an American Continental Army, and called on the Virginian George Washington to command it – a smart move designed to improve the likelihood of Virginia agreeing to join the rebellion, which at this point appeared to be mostly a New England rebellion.

This decision of the Continental Congress to authorize a full rebellion against their king was a very brave thing to undertake, for in essence if this action ended in failure, it would mean that these Congressmen would all be hunted down and hanged or shot as traitors. Furthermore, history offered no example of how this kind of action really ever was successful. However, they counted not on historical statistics but on serious aid from God, with whom their ancestors had first covenanted a special relationship, one which they understood had brought them successfully to the present, and would take them successfully into their future.

George Washington. George Washington. The selection of Washington as Commander of the Continental Army was a brilliant move, not only politically in the way that it helped pull Virginia into this dangerous rebellion, it was brilliant in ways that the Continental Congress had as yet no way of knowing. But they had selected someone who was truly a God-send to their cause.

As a young man Washington was typical of someone born to the ranks of Virginia aristocracy. He came of a highly respected family, and was very ambitious, seeking every opportunity to see his social rank improved even further. But he had to work at this matter, which he did, diligently. In being bold in this matter, he would make mistakes, suffer professional setbacks, but learn from the experience. A big part of this was that from very early on, he felt that he was someone – chosen by Providence no less – destined to greatness. And he would rely heavily on that divine hand in his life to move forward in the very competitive game of life.

As the younger brother of a prominent Virginia family, he would not inherit high status, but would have to work at his own advancement in life. And thus Washington took up surveying, and soon found himself called to survey Virginia's land claim on the frontier (which at the time reached all the way into the Ohio Valley). He thus learned a lot about land, and its challenges and possibilities, and added such land to his own holdings. It also made him very knowledgeable about the lay of the frontier, which he would soon be called on to put to good use.

Along the way, Virginia Lieutenant Governor, Robert Dinwiddie became impressed with Washington's frontier work, and put Washington in charge of one of Virginia's four military districts. Actually, Washington's first military engagement against the French in the Ohio region brought "shame" in victory for Washington when his Iroquois allies killed and scalped surrendered French troops*, and his second action at Fort Necessity actually brought him humiliating defeat. Washington thus resigned his position as commander.

But he was called back into service the next year, serving under British General Braddock, but efforts to dislodge the French from the Ohio region once again ending in disaster – General Braddock even losing his life in the contest. Yet Washington held up valiantly in the battle, having two horses shot out from under him and bullets hitting his hat and coat.

This so impressed Dinwiddie (and some of the Indians) that Washington was asked, and agreed, to take command of the much-enlarged Virginia Regiment. But in doing so, he would find his command challenged by another ambitious officer – something that Washington would have to get

---

*Ironically this event became the initiating cause of the French and Indian War (1754-1763), and ultimately even Europe's bigger Seven Year's War!

used to, and learn to get around in order to keep going!

And in his only serious engagement as commander, he was able to finally take French Fort Duquesne in 1758, when the French abandoned it just before his arrival!

The following year he married a very wealthy widow, Martha Custis, and settled himself down as a Virginia "planter," now possessing huge estates worked by hundreds of slaves. Furthermore, being such a planter, he was expected to be active in Virginia political affairs. Thus he was called on to represent Frederick County in the Virginia House of Burgesses. During this time, he began to distinguish himself as a very strong opponent of the effort by the British King and his Tory-dominated Parliament to bring the colonies under royal control, especially the effort to tax the colonies without their consent (supposedly a basic British right belonging to the people). Indeed, working closely with George Mason, Washington was able to bring Virginia to support the boycott of British goods (1769).

Then as tensions mounted, particularly with the British effort to strangle Boston into submission, again working with George Mason, in 1774 he drew up a list of resolves (the "Fairfax Resolves") put forward by the Fairfax Committee that Washington chaired, which called for the creation of a Continental Congress. And when a Continental Congress was actually called into being (autumn of 1774), he was sent off to Philadelphia to represent Virginia. At this point he also took up the challenge of organizing Virginia militias, in anticipation of troubles ahead.

And when a Second Continental Congress was called in May of 1775, Washington headed off to Philadelphia to participate in its doings. Things were looking very serious after the battles at Lexington and Concord. War actually seemed to be unfolding, wanted or not.

And there in Philadelphia, he quickly impressed the Congress, particularly the Massachusetts firebrand Samuel Adams (organizer of the "Boston Tea Party"), and his cousin John Adams. Thus it was that Washington was chosen (over Massachusetts commander John Hancock) to command the new Continental Army.

The Battle of Bunker (and Breed's) Hill (June 1775). Meanwhile, the colonies also began to send aid to Boston – including American militiamen (soon to be termed "Patriots" or "Whigs"), who in June gathered in the heights above Boston at Bunker Hill and Breed's Hill. Here they found themselves armed with cannons and guns seized from Fort Ticonderoga by the troops of Ethan Allen and Benedict Arnold. When English troops were then ordered to dislodge these threatening militiamen, it took several charges and a huge loss of British officers (by American sharp-shooters) to do so. And even then, the American retreat was orderly – taking place only when the Americans ran out of ammunition.

But the next spring (1776), the Americans had resumed their positions above Boston, but with even more cannons – and Washington in place as commander. At this point the English troops, understanding the resolve of these colonials – and the danger of the position they now found themselves in – withdrew from Boston. Along with them went the "Loyalist" or "Tory" (pro-king) colonists who had taken refuge there. They would not attempt a return to Boston during the remainder of what had now become all-out war.

The Declaration of Independence (July 1776). That summer, while the newly self-proclaimed independent states (Massachusetts, Virginia, Pennsylvania, Maryland, Georgia, etc.) busied themselves drafting new constitutions for themselves, their representatives in Philadelphia drafted and adopted a formal Declaration of Independence from England. Its preamble became very well known to Americans over the generations:

> *We hold these truths to be self evident, that all men are created equal, that they are endowed by their Creator with certain unalienable Rights, that among these are Life, Liberty and the pursuit of Happiness.*
>
> *That to secure these rights, Governments are instituted among Men, deriving their just powers from the consent of the governed, That whenever any Form of Government becomes destructive of these ends, it is the Right of the People to alter or to abolish it, and to institute new Government, laying its foundation on such principles and organizing its powers in such form, as to them shall seem most likely to effect their Safety and Happiness.*

Notice that this declaration, originally designed by the young Virginian Thomas Jefferson, makes it clear that Americans were created as equals, with unchanging rights that came from their Creator (God), not some human authority – not a king, not a parliamentary body, not a huge church establishment (such as the King's Church of England).

Then the delegates began work on drafting a new constitution for their Confederation of American States, a structure designed to help them work together in facing the task of securing that independence against the efforts of the British king to force them back into submission.

Serious problems. This was not an easy matter, because the war at that time seemed not to be going well for the American "Patriots." American General Benedict Arnold's efforts over the winter of 1775-1776 to pull

Independence - And the New Republic 81

Canada into the war on the American side had, despite a very valiant (and costly) effort, failed miserably; Washington's attempt in the summer of 1776 to block the British takeover of New York had also failed miserably* (Washington nearly losing his army in the effort); American soldiers were deserting the cause; and other American officers were conspiring behind Washington's back to have him replaced (by themselves of course).

Trenton and Princeton. But on Christmas night of 1776 Washington took his men across the icy Delaware River and marched them ten more miles during a drizzly/snowy night to Trenton (New Jersey) – to catch an unsuspecting German unit of George's Hessian troops off guard and completely rout them – then hold off a British counterattack at nearby Princeton a week later – giving new courage to the American cause.

British failure at Saratoga (September-October 1777). The British responded to this humiliation by putting together a plan to converge on the northern States from different directions and cut off New England from the middle States – thereby hoping to cripple the American rebellion (running strongest in the North). But the various British units failed to connect. British troops coming from Canada turned back when their Indian allies deserted the cause upon hearing that Benedict Arnold was involved as an American commander (despite Arnold's failure to take Quebec, he was well known to be a fearless fighter); another British group was badly mauled in a battle which took place at Bennington; and the group which was supposed to come up from New York City went off on another venture. Thus the main British force under John Burgoyne arrived at Saratoga, and then waited for the others to show up, as Americans gathered under the command of Horatio Gates, and for weeks the two armies sat there facing each other, but doing little. Finally, Arnold disobeyed Gates' order to stand down and instead led his men on an attack, which inspired the rest of the American forces to join the action. And thus it was in October of 1777 that a huge British army of 6,000 men was brought to surrender.

But typical of the politics of the day, in Gates' victory report to the Congress, he failed to mention Arnold's role in the affair, Gates taking full credit for the victory as the "hero of Saratoga."

The French ally with the Americans (February 1778). Nonetheless the victory was real, and majorly significant. With this American victory,

---

*He and his troops managed to escape entrapment and complete destruction by the British only because a thick and long-lasting fog allowed them to escape the Brooklyn Heights across the East River to Manhattan. This was clearly an intervention of God himself, which Washington was well aware of.

French King Louis XVI decided to jump in the fray to do some serious damage to his British rival George III by supporting the American rebellion. Little did Louis realize that he was setting loose forces that would be the undoing of his own rule. In any case, the French help would come to weigh importantly in the outcome of the American War of Independence.

The winter at Valley Forge (1777-1778). Meanwhile, Philadelphia was lost to the British when they marched on the city (October 1777), the Continental Congress fleeing into the Pennsylvanian hinterland, and Washington having to take his troops into winter quarters at nearby Valley Forge, with nothing to show for his effort – except (most importantly) that the British had failed to bring the rebellion to a close.

But the Valley Forge winter would produce a highly disciplined American army – among those who survived the winter's ordeal anyway. 2.500 of his 10,000 troops would die that winter. But the remainder would emerge as a highly disciplined fighting force. Prussian Baron von Steuben's discipline and Washington's own example as a highly disciplined – as well as spiritually disciplined (including daily prayers) – individual served to produce that result with his men. Indeed, the idea of an army at prayer grew right alongside the now well-understood role of physical training (and tightened discipline) caused by the death and dying.

Washington: military insight. Washington understood the nature of the challenge in front of him as few others (if any) did at the time. While other generals typically understood the war between America and Britain as involving simply a battle of armies (ones they themselves commanded), Washington knew most importantly that this war was about a battle of wills, of human resolve, of sheer determination not to quit no matter how grim things looked.

The goal of all war is to make the other side tire of the game first and simply quit. How that was to occur in colonial America with mere militia coming up against experienced and vastly more numerous British troops would entail far more than armies and battles, although they certainly weighed importantly in the matter. But wars are won as a matter of the commanding officer's ability to see things from a much higher perspective than the viewpoint dictated simply by immediate circumstances, which is what lesser souls tend to focus on. True, immediate circumstances had to be answered – as best as possible given the greater weight of military power of the British enemy. But ultimately Washington's job was to keep the courage of the Patriots intact, to keep them focused on victory, while at the same time undercutting the morale of the British (and American Tory or Loyalist) adversaries – until the latter were willing to call it quits.

Independence - And the New Republic

The mindset of a great leader. Here is where leadership – true leadership, the kind that Washington offered America – came into play. And, as is typical of great leaders, although Washington was as sensitive to public opinion as anyone else, ultimately he went to God, not public opinion, to take full measure of his own actions. Washington was a man of very, very deep faith in God, in God's personal call to him to take up such dangerous and often very unrewarding service (materially speaking).

The role God played in Washington's life is well illustrated by a particular example recorded for us in the *Diary and Remembrances* of a Presbyterian Minister Rev. Nathaniel Randolph Snowden, who recorded a conversation he had with Isaac Potts of Valley Forge, Pennsylvania (at whose home Washington was residing that winter):

> *I was riding with him (Mr. Potts) near Valley Forge, where the army lay during the war of the Revolution. Mr. Potts was a Senator in our state and a Whig. I told him I was agreeably surprised to find him a friend to his country as the Quakers were mostly Tories. He said, It was so and I was a rank Tory once, for I never believed that America could proceed against Great Britain whose fleets and armies covered the land and ocean. But something very extraordinary converted me to the good faith.*
>
> *What was that? I inquired. Do you see that woods, and that plain? It was about a quarter of a mile from the place we were riding. There, said he, laid the army of Washington. It was a most distressing time of ye war, and all were for giving up the ship but that one good man. In that woods, pointing to a close in view, I heard a plaintive sound, as of a man at prayer. I tied my horse to a sapling and went quietly into the woods and to my astonishment I saw the great George Washington on his knees alone, with his sword on one side and his cocked hat on the other. He was at Prayer to the God of the Armies, beseeching to interpose with his Divine aid, as it was ye Crisis and the cause of the country, of humanity, and of the world.*
>
> *Such a prayer I never heard from the lips of man. I left him alone praying. I went home and told my wife, I saw a sight and heard today what I never saw or heard before, and just related to her what I had seen and heard and observed. We never thought a man could be a soldier and a Christian, but if there is one in the world, it is Washington. We thought it was the cause of God, and America could prevail.*

This was what gave Washington the power to answer unflinchingly the call to service, one that would morally exhaust others and make them quit.

Tragically, this was the case for Benedict Arnold, who switched sides to the British because after giving the American cause his all, he finally tired of being undercut constantly by other colonial leaders, including fellow American generals.*

Washington too (as all leaders) had his detractors, eager for his job as commanding officer (Gates and Lee for instance). But Washington paid little attention to their maneuverings with the Continental Congress behind his back. He simply stayed focused on the job at hand, the job he had been called to by God. And to God and God alone did he answer.

But Washington's spirit infused his troops (and again, the American people) with the same spirit: to keep moving forward against huge obstacles – and not get lost in a concern with those immediate obstacles – because there was a higher calling to be answered.

He had his men pray with him, to understand that their cause was much bigger than just personal success; it was to preserve the precious independence of their American society, so that America could itself continue to serve God to great purpose. His men were not just soldiers, they were crusaders, crusaders for the world's "little guy," the average person like themselves – average in social status but awesome in action!

Disappointment at Monmouth (June 1778). As an example of the agony that Washington had to constantly overcome, the following June (1778) Washington had skillfully put his army in a position to deliver a crushing blow to the huge British force that had decided to abandon Philadelphia and head back to New York. But his plan was itself brought to near defeat by an arrogant American General Charles Lee, given actual command of the operation (officially second in command, although a constant thorn in Washington's side), who lost courage at the very moment that the action actually got underway. Instead of pushing forward the American advantage dependent on a surprise attack from behind, Lee ordered a retreat, which immediately turned into a panicked rout of the

---

*Arnold had given the Patriot effort his all, and got virtually no support from the politicians at the Continental Congress. Individuals there even had the nerve to complain about his request for troop funding, after Arnold had exhausted all his own personal financial assets to support his men. Finally, his pretty Tory wife, Peggy Shippen, convinced him that he was supporting a cause that was directed by the wrong element, and that instead he should put his effort in supporting the Tories. This he did (to Washington's great distress, for he was the one general Washington had trusted), and would come to regret deeply this decision. He had to live out the rest of his life in Britain, far from his native Connecticut. And in his will, he asked that he be buried in his American, not his British, officer's uniform. Truly sad!

Independence - And the New Republic

American troops. Washington miraculously was able to rally his fleeing troops, and then turn the battle ultimately into at least a military standoff. That night an exhausted British army was able to slip away from an equally exhausted American army. And thus a grand opportunity for the Americans to end things right there had been lost. But at least it enabled Washington to finally get rid of the troublesome Lee. And it made very clear to all that Washington's army was now a serious fighting force.

And actually, this led the British to decide to give up the war in the North and take the battle into the American South.

The war in the South. Had the British attacked the South first, rather than the North, the war may have early gone in the British favor – for pro-British Loyalist or Tory sentiment was much stronger in the South, where many Americans saw no need for the rebellion against their king. In fact many Southerners formed Tory military units to fight American Patriot units in support of the British effort to put down the rebellion. But the British efforts in the South in the first years of the war had been quite timid – and the Patriots not only held off British efforts there but also humiliated the American Tory military units.

Disaster for the American Patriots (December 1778 to September 1780). But at the end of 1778 the British finally decided to go all-out in their offensive in the South, hoping that American Tories would join them in the effort. Mostly they didn't! But huge British units captured the weakly defended Savannah (December 1778); they did the same in Charleston (May 1780) when 14,000 British troops, surrounded, cut off and defeated the 5,000 Americans attempting to defend the city; and then they repeated that success in August at Camden (South Carolina) when incompetent Gates foolishly attacked directly British General Charles Cornwallis' well-disciplined army, and Gates' troops broke and fled – resulting in the loss of another 2,000 American troops. Then in September it was learned that Arnold had changed sides and was now fighting on the British side. At this point the Patriot cause looked as if it were about to go down in defeat.

The war begins to turn in American favor (late 1780 - early 1781). Yet the fortunes of war began to shift dramatically – when in October of 1780 an American Tory unit of about 1,400 was decisively defeated – ending any further ideas of American Southerners joining the British cause. Then the following January (1781) at Cowpens (South Carolina) the famous British cavalry raider Banastre Tarleton was delivered a humiliating defeat (barely escaping with his life).

Cornwallis decided to counter by chasing down the American army under the Southern commander Nathanael Greene – and indeed humiliated him at a battle in March (Guilford Courthouse, South Carolina) – but a humiliation that Greene managed to shake off with his army still intact – leaving the "victor" Cornwallis with the loss of a huge number of troops that Cornwallis could ill afford – something of a Pyrrhic victory!

Yorktown (September-October 1781). Cornwallis badly needed more troops and supplies – and decided to head his army north into Virginia to the port of Yorktown to await reinforcements shipped in to him there by way of the Chesapeake Bay. But he had marched himself into a trap, when Washington slipped his troops from New York (where the British were expecting Washington's attack) to a position surrounding Yorktown – along with General Lafayette's French troops who joined him there. And the French navy was able to defeat the British ships sent to relieve Cornwallis. Thus Cornwallis found himself with nowhere to go and no help on the way. A final assault on his position by the French (led by Lafayette) and the Americans (led by Washington's top assistant, Alexander Hamilton) forced Cornwallis to surrender his 8,000-man army to Washington. This was the event that finally broke the British will to continue the war.

When news reached England of what had happened at Yorktown, British Prime Minister Lord North declared "Oh God, it's all over." And indeed it was. Although British troops still held New York City, the British would undertake no more military ventures in America.

The Treaty of Paris (1783). It took some time for the British and Americans to work out the terms ending the war. But basically, the agreement drawn up in Paris (notably through the efforts of John Adams, Ben Franklin, John Jay, and a few others representing the Americans) acknowledged that the Americans were indeed an independent people, no longer part of the British Empire.

THE YOUNG AMERICAN REPUBLIC

The need for unity. The thirteen colonies were now thirteen independent states, each state able to go about its own business on a fully sovereign basis. And that's where the problems began. Each state wanted to conduct its own diplomacy abroad with the major European powers – and promote its own industries and trade overseas – in competition with the other American states. But these smallish American states were like mere children messing with the big boys of Europe – very liable to get themselves

Independence - And the New Republic

into trouble – and even worse, become tempting targets for sophisticated and highly ambitious European powers to grab them in their ongoing wars for territory, territory, territory. There was no reason to think that the British, given a new opportunity to do so, might not come back across the Atlantic to reclaim their former colonial territories. After all, treaties at that time had very short lives – merely pauses in the on-going game of big-power politics. Just because England had signed a treaty acknowledging American independence did not mean that they weren't able to put it aside at their earliest convenience and retake some – or even all – of their former colonies.

And the American leaders of these newly independent states, men who had just gone through the horrors of achieving their states' independence through bloody battle, were well aware of how the game was played. Something needed to be done to correct the vulnerable position that these new states were in. Somehow, they were going to have to come together as they had during the recent war – as a "United States of America" – or they would be lost. But with the immediate pressure of war removed, the incentive for unity was not as strong – at least in the eyes of those who did not understand the dangers now facing them.

Maintaining domestic tranquility. There was another problem on their minds at this same time: the rebellious spirit affecting soldier-farmers, typified by those in rural Western Massachusetts. American soldiers had returned from the war only to find that their mortgage debts to banks and taxes owed the local and state governments had merely accumulated, to monumental proportions. They received no forgiveness or even reduction of these obligations – or even some kind compromise in being permitted to pay in goods rather than currency, something they just did not have at war's end. They were furious – not yet on the scale of Bacon's Rebellion a century earlier – but headed in that direction (1786-1787). It took Washington, appearing with the Massachusetts militia, to break up the Massachusetts (or Shay's) Rebellion, a task which Washington undoubtedly disliked intensely, but one that had to be done. The newly independent country could not simply let such rebellious behavior infect its budding social order.*

---

*This is not a dynamic understood by American Humanists, who blanche at the thought of having to maintain necessary social order, even if it is a most unpleasant, most unwanted task, which it certainly can be. It is a duty of those responsible for the ultimate order to society (which a society, after all, is exactly that: an institution of human order), a duty that Humanists typically run from. In fact, they will easily turn on those (such as the police) in ideological fury when this dynamic explodes – which it will do from time to time – and blame

The Constitution of the United States of America (summer 1787). At first the general assumption in meeting these challenges was that the Continental Congress would continue after the war, conducting meetings much as it had done during the war. But the Continental Congress quickly demonstrated that with no common enemy looming before it, the Congress had no serious powers of its own to insist on a higher degree of American unity than the feeble effort it was getting at the time. So – the idea came up of reforming the organization, carefully giving it some new powers to restore a degree of American unity and stability among and within the states. Thus in mid-May of 1787, representatives of the various American states gathered in Philadelphia to begin the process of correcting this huge problem (tiny Rhode Island however refused to attend, fearing the loss of its independence to the stronger, larger states).

The immediate challenge: big v. small states. Rhode Island's absence pointed to a major hurdle that those who gathered in Philadelphia had to overcome. The big states (Massachusetts, New York, Pennsylvania, and Virginia principally) understood that they carried the largest responsibility population-wise and finance-wise for these United States – and resented the fact that in the Continental Congress they had no more say in things than did the small states (Vermont, Connecticut, New Jersey, Delaware, etc.), because the states had merely a single vote each. Thus Virginia arrived at the meeting in May with a plan for a bicameral Congress of two legislative houses – similar to the British Parliament with a House of Lords and a House of Commons (the Continental Congress had been unicameral, with only a single legislative house). The Virginia Plan called for varied representation in both houses based on the relative size of the states, the larger states receiving more votes than the smaller states in each house.

And that was exactly what the small states feared – that they would simply be reduced to irrelevance because of their small size. Thus they proposed a unicameral legislature, one with each state, large or small, allotted equal representation (a single vote each), similar to the Continental Congress. However, this legislature would possess stronger powers than the Continental Congress.

Bringing God's guidance into the proceedings. Most amazingly, at a point when the discussions seemed to be going nowhere, Ben Franklin – always the voice of simple, straightforward reason – spoke to the group (June 28), reminding them that these discussions proceeding from the biting logic of mere self-interest were going to take this assembly nowhere.

---

the police, not those burning away at the social order, for the disaster in front of them.

They needed to put their self-serving logic aside and instead consult God through prayer, and draw strength from his guidance – just as had been the case during the war when they began their meetings each day in prayer. Franklin reminded them:

> In this situation of this Assembly, groping as it were in the dark to find political truth, and scarce able to distinguish it when presented to us, how has it happened, Sir, that we have not hitherto once thought of humbly applying to the Father of lights to illuminate our understandings?
>
> In the beginning of the Contest with G. Britain, when we were sensible of danger, we had daily prayer in this room for the divine protection. Our prayers, Sir, were heard, and they were graciously answered. All of us who were engaged in the struggle must have observed frequent instances of a Superintending providence in our favor. To that kind providence we owe this happy opportunity of consulting in peace on the means of establishing our future national felicity. And have we now forgotten that powerful friend?
>
> I have lived, Sir, a long time, and the longer I live, the more convincing proofs I see of this truth – that God governs in the affairs of men. And if a sparrow cannot fall to the ground without his notice, is it probable that an empire can rise without his aid?
>
> We have been assured, Sir, in the sacred writings, that "except the Lord build the House they labour in vain that build it." I firmly believe this; and I also believe that without his concurring aid we shall succeed in this political building no better than the Builders of Babel: We shall be divided by our little partial local interests; our projects will be confounded, and we ourselves shall become a reproach and bye word down to future ages. And what is worse, mankind may hereafter from this unfortunate instance, despair of establishing Governments by Human Wisdom and leave it to chance, war and conquest.
>
> I therefore beg leave to move, that henceforth prayers imploring the assistance of Heaven, and its blessings on our deliberations, be held in this Assembly every morning before we proceed to business, and that one or more of the Clergy of the City be requested to officiate in that service.

Miraculously, Franklin's call for daily prayer seemed to be the point at which things settled down and real progress began to be made in the discussions!

Benjamin Franklin. This Franklin was greatly loved – but not always well understood – because he was intensely complex. That was because he served the world around him in so many different ways in the course of his lifetime. Born in Boston as the last of 17 children!, he was early-on expected to become a pastor, but chose apprenticeship in the publishing business of one of his brothers. But in his teens, he abandoned this duty and ended up in Philadelphia opening his own printing shop, and soon produced not only a local newspaper, The Philadelphia Gazette, but also published annually (1732-1758) the very popular Poor Richard's Almanac – the sales of this book of simple advice making Franklin quite prosperous.

But his huge sense of curiosity about the surrounding world led him also into the world of science, where he became a very well-known expert in the new field of electricity (a very dangerous enterprise, as some were soon to discover!). He then took his learning into the world of higher education, helping to write educational curriculum, and helping to set up a college that would eventually become the University of Pennsylvania.

And he made his way easily into the world of politics, being sent in 1750 to London to represent the interests of the Pennsylvania colonies, which put him in the heart of the rising tensions between the colonies and the British crown. And when in 1775 the Second Continental Congress gathered in Philadelphia, he not only was there to represent Pennsylvania, but was sent by the Congress to Paris to try to bring the French in on the American side of the growing American-British conflict. And there he would remain during the duration of the war, being part of the group that finally negotiated the Paris treaty ending that war. He then returned to the States in time to become part of the Constitutional Convention of 1787.

As a person of enormous importance, he took on the ways not of an aristocrat, but almost something of quite the opposite: a homespun American farmer! His ways were simply theatrics that Franklin employed in his effort to get across to others an understanding of what it was, as an American, that he stood for. But he could, at the same time, come across as a supreme "wise one" – for indeed, he was brilliant, and recognized as such in all those fields of science, politics, education, and just the philosophy of the times.

At a deeper religious level, Franklin seemed at times, notably in his earlier years, to be merely a standard Deist, one who believes in a Creator-God who long ago put all of life into operation, but who now sits back and watches his creation unfold naturally. But Franklin went through many changes in religious thought over the span of his 84-year life – at first very reactive to the intense Puritanism of his parents, then probably indeed something of a Deist, but eventually aware of the importance of a religious spirit that transformed life dramatically (thus his long friendship with

Independence - And the New Republic

Whitefield), and ultimately, as we have just seen, someone who believed that God indeed was very active in the affairs of both individuals and whole societies.

But, in any case, he pursued his Christian faith so removed from dogma that many denominations (ranging from Catholics to Quakers) could have believed that he was, underneath it all, one of them! This was because he lived as he saw Jesus having lived, inspiring a higher morality that brought a deeper happiness to life, despite life's material circumstances.

The Connecticut Compromise (July 1787). Soon after Franklin's intervention in the stalled proceedings of that Convention, Connecticut came up with an idea (July 5th) that both sides could – after yet more debate – agree on. Congress would be made up of two houses. Congress would have a lower house, like the British House of Commons, that would serve more directly as the voice of the people – and thus base the relative size of each state's representation in that house on the size of the states themselves, the larger states having more representatives and thus more votes in this House of Representatives. But Congress would have a second or upper house, a Senate – similar to the British House of Lords – with each of the states having an equal voice of two Senators and thus two votes each, regardless of the size of the states. And to get any real work done, the two houses would have to work together, so that neither of the two houses would have dominant influence in the new government.

This was eventually (July 23rd) agreeable to all the Philadelphia delegates. Thus they were finally able to move on to shape the rest of the new Constitutional order.

At the end of that long, hot summer, they finally (mid-September) had put together a new Federation, a Republic in form – something that looked like it would build that unity among the states they so badly needed. Under the new Federal Republic they would indeed be "the United States of America."

An *alliance* of 13 sovereign States. It is important to note that this Constitution did not set up a new government to rule over the people. Such rule still belonged to the states – and the people themselves (as clearly stated in the 9th and 10th Amendments attached to the new Constitution:

> 9. The enumeration in the Constitution, of certain rights, shall not be construed to deny or disparage others retained by the people.

> 10. The powers not delegated to the United States by the

Constitution, nor prohibited by it to the States, are reserved to the States respectively, or to the people.

Thus instead of a new government over the people, like some kind of monarchy that the world was well familiar with at that time, the new Constitution provided for an *alliance of independent states*, bringing them together in vital areas – most importantly in the realm of foreign affairs – so as to protect them from the ambitions of European empires – and also to protect them from any competitive ambitions among themselves that would weaken and thus make the states more vulnerable to just those hungry empires abroad.

The Federal Congress. This new political order was definitely not a democracy – as it is so often supposed in today's cultural climate. The creators of this Constitution knew too much history to simply turn the federation directly over to the popular will – where "enlightened" demagogues could easily manipulate the gullible masses into doing something really stupid and self-destructive as a society.

The House of Representatives. They did give the people their voice in a House of Representatives – and recognized the particular responsibility of the American citizenry in the realm of finances and economics by making the House of Representatives the house that would originate all legislation of a financial nature – much in the same manner that the British House of Commons worked.

The Senate. But the Constitution also set up the new Senate with the clear intention that it would serve as the voice of the individual states – sort of a check on the popular will driving the House of Representatives. Senators were expected to be senior statesmen chosen by the legislatures of each of the states (as per the Constitution's original provisions in Article I, Section 3*), whom the states esteemed to be the ones to best represent in Congress the interests of the sending states. In other words, Senators were expected to be senior statesmen (like the British Lords), older, wiser, deeply experienced in public affairs. In line with this expectation, the Constitution specified that ratification or approval of all treaties, all ambassadorial appointments and other key areas in the conduct of the foreign policy of the new Federal Union was to be the special responsibility of the Senate – in

---

*The 17th Amendment to the Constitution, put into effect in 1913 at the beginning of the Wilsonian Era, would however "democratize" the choosing of the states' two senators, by taking this responsibility or right from the state governments and awarding it directly to the people, a move that the Framers of the original Constitution would have been strongly opposed to because of their fear of unchecked democracy.

conjunction, of course, with the President who initiated all action in these areas. Also, the confirming of appointments by the President of all Federal judges was to be the matter only of the Senate. Again, this was because a greater dignity and political maturity was expected of the Senate.

The President. As permanent head of the Union, the President had executive responsibilities – to call Congress into session, to address it annually with his estimation or appraisal concerning the State of the Union, and as a permanent officer to see that the laws of Congress were faithfully executed as Congress itself had directed. But he was also to serve somewhat like a king, in sending and receiving diplomats to and from other countries (the states no longer had such foreign policy rights) and he was to serve as the top commanding officer of the army and navy serving the United States. And, rather unanimously convinced that Washington himself would be the one called on to fill that position, the Framers of the Constitution had a fairly clear idea of how this high office would likely shape up – even though Washington himself had given no indication whatsoever that he was interested in that responsibility. But if not Washington, who then? There would be pressure coming at Washington to accept the job.

In any case, the President – functioning as in one who presides rather than rules – would himself be chosen by the states – not by the people. Each state would appoint its own members of the Electoral College, the institution assigned the task of choosing a new President every four years. The number of voting members of the Electoral College allotted each state would be determined by the size of that state's presence in Congress (the total number of their Representatives plus their two Senators – although Congressmen and Senators themselves could not serve as presidential electors). Furthermore, each state was given the right or responsibility of deciding exactly how they would choose those presidential electors (Article II Section 1).

As previously mentioned, the President was to supervise the actual application of the laws of Congress in specific situations facing America. It was not expected that the President would have a great influence in originating the laws. That was supposed to be Congress's job, in doing so representing the will of the sending states (the Senate) and their citizens (the House of Representatives). No, the President was not supposed to be the maker of the laws, only the supporter and enforcer of the laws enacted by Congress.

However, the President's required approval of Congress's new laws was a key part of the whole legislative or law-making process. If the President himself felt for one reason or another that he could not approve a proposed law coming out of Congress, the President could veto that law.

That would not totally stop further progress on the enacting of that law. But it might – or at least it could – slow its passage up considerably, because to get past a presidential veto of a proposed law, Congress would have to make another attempt at its passage – needing not just a simple majority this time, but instead a 2/3 vote in favor of the law so as to actually put a vetoed law in place. That would not be an easy thing to pull off.

In any case, the general idea was that all laws designed to guide the country would have to have the very broadest of political support in order to be operable, and not be simply the will or design of one or another particular interest group. The new Republic was intended to be built on a foundation of national consensus, not on the partisan interest if this social group or that social group – not a king, not a privileged ruling class, not some military or bureaucratic faction, not a particular ethnic group, regional faction or religious sect.

The Supreme Court. Then too, the Constitution briefly provided for a judicial branch of the new Union, the Supreme Court, given the power to see that Congress and the States adhered strictly to the rules of the Constitution when disputes arose (law cases) over the actual functioning of the Federal legal system. These Supreme Court Justices – and the judges serving below then in the lower-level federal Circuit Courts – would be appointed to life-time service by the President (but confirmed by the Senate) – lifetime meaning there was no way to remove them once in place – except under the unlikelihood of them committing some great crime. This gave the Federal judges unlimited power.

Hopefully they would remain neutral in their judgments. But expecting judges not to have distinct political philosophies of their own was/is most unrealistic. The Framers, however, seemed not to be aware of this power possibility because judges in the English legal tradition that they personally were well familiar with actually had only very limited powers.

The Framers in no way anticipated that the Supreme Court would eventually become the one part of the Republic able to dismiss or reshape the nation's laws as it chose to do so – without any further recourse anywhere in the legal system by which such actions could be blocked or reversed. These justices would step by step take on virtually unlimited or total political power, awarding themselves the authority to reshape the Law of the land to read in any form or fashion as they personally saw fit.

In short, these federal judges or justices would eventually make the Supreme Court – not Congress – the supreme legislative authority of the Federal government.

But at the time, this was not even suspected as a possibility.

Independence - And the New Republic

Ratification. Once the Constitution was drawn up it had to be approved or ratified by the states – usually by the calling together of special state conventions for the express purpose of voting on the new Constitution. In some cases, ratification was quick – and in other cases it took a fair amount of time to get the Constitution approved. There were those who opposed this new Constitution ("anti-Federalists"). But through the writings of those who supported and explained carefully the beneficial features of the new Constitution (notably James Madison and Alexander Hamilton and their many newspaper articles later collected as *The Federalist Papers*), the pro-ratification or Federalist group carried the day. The promise to add a number of Amendments to the Constitution (the Bill of Rights comprising the first ten Amendments) – guaranteeing that the new federal system would not be able to take away the rights of the people and the states – also aided in getting the new Constitution ratified.

Thus, two years later, in 1789, the Constitution went into full effect – and the new Republic immediately took up its duties of uniting the states in their encounter with the larger world. America was now officially a Federal Republic.

"A Republic, if you can keep it" (Franklin). When coming out of that long and hot Philadelphia convention of 1787 and asked what it was that the delegates had come up with for America as its new governmental form, Franklin most insightfully replied, "A Republic, if you can keep it."

A Republic, *if you can keep it*, indeed. A major concern at the time was the question of how such a Constitution could hold against the political forces that seem inevitably to drag all political orders eventually into some kind of tyranny (a tyranny of one, of the few or of the many). Those that put the Constitution together were very aware of history and the lessons it taught about the immense difficulties that societies had holding to their original political purposes. Unbounded political ambition had invariably brought societies of the past to tyranny and ultimately self-destruction, repeatedly.

And more recently, in their own lifetimes, they had seen how the lure of power had changed the English monarchy from a distant and largely inactive agency in the life of the Americans – Americans who had therefore developed the very special talent at that time of taking care of life's challenges themselves. However, recently had arisen a very interventionist, even dictatorial king who loved political power so much, and similar to the French kings, supposed that he had the right, even the necessity (by way of his own superior "enlightenment") to rule directly and fully over the American "peasants." But Americans were no peasants. They were very self-sufficient citizens of a quite free land. And they not only intended to keep things that way but were willing to die for such a right, as indeed many – very many – just had.

But they clearly now needed a larger political system of their own, to protect their small, but independent states. But how were they to set this up so that there would be just the right amount of power to provide that protection – but no more than that, lest it stir the ever-human lust for just a little more power here and there, just a little more power to put themselves in greater control of life's outcomes?

In short, how were they to protect themselves from the temptation to turn themselves into little gods, striving to bring their free (but challenging) world under control by some overbearing human agency? This problem had never been solved successfully in the past. Historically aware, they understood very clearly the necessity, but also the dangers, of power. The Greeks had struggled with the issue. The Romans had struggled with the issue. And it had been a source of great controversy during the West's long "Christian" era. Power was a very tricky matter.

Thus they well understood the question in front of them: how was this new venture in government design likely to prove to be any different?

A system of checks and balances. As Madison pointed out in his *Federalist Papers* articles, the system was set up in such a way that cooperation among a number of various branches of government would be required to make the system work at all. And cooperation meant compromise, the necessity of having to give up the desire for total power, in order to employ any power at all. If one of the branches of government (that would include also the member States themselves as part of the branches of this federal union) would start to assume more power for itself (a rather certain possibility) this would stir the indignation of the other branches, which out of a self-serving sense of the relative loss of their own power, would gang up on the usurper of their joint power! A very ingenious system!

Unfortunately, Madison did not give any indication as to how the Supreme Court could likewise be checked – except to wait for vacancies to be filled by new appointments as seats on the court were vacated by death or self-chosen retirement. And Madison had no way of understanding how a U.S. president's Executive Orders (not part of the original constitutional design) could bypass this constitutional system of checks and balances, and become a source of presidential dictatorship.

Yes indeed, power was a very tricky matter!

The very hand of God. But by no means did the Framers of the Constitution rely entirely – or even mostly – on this ingenious mechanical system. They were well aware, just as Franklin had stated, that this whole

Independence - And the New Republic

enterprise would succeed or fail on the key issue of God's (not man's) will. They needed to stay closely in line with the will of God – who after all had given them the victory against royal tyranny in the first place. Otherwise nothing, not even clever mechanics, would protect them from human evil.

As we have already noted, the hand of God in establishing the rights and leading the behavior of American society was made very clear in the opening of the famous Declaration of Independence:

> *We hold these truths to be self-evident, that all men are created equal, that they are endowed by their Creator with certain unalienable Rights, that among these are Life, Liberty and the pursuit of Happiness.*

Thomas Jefferson would expand on this idea a few years later in his *Notes on the State of Virginia* (1781):

> *God who gave us life gave us liberty. And can the liberties of a nation be thought secure when we have removed their only firm basis, a conviction in the minds of the people that these liberties are a gift from God? That they are not to be violated but with His wrath? Indeed I tremble for my country when I reflect that God is just, and that His justice cannot sleep forever.*

Likewise, George Washington stated the case very clearly in the speech he addressed to the nation as he took office in 1789 as America's first President:

> *It would be peculiarly improper to omit, in this first official act, my fervent supplication to that Almighty Being, who rules over the universe, who presides in the councils of nations, and whose providential aids can supply every human defect, that His benediction may consecrate to the liberties and happiness of the people of the United States . . .*
>
> *No people can be bound to acknowledge and adore the Invisible Hand which conducts the affairs of men more than the people of the United States. Every step by which they have advanced to the character of an independent nation seems to have been distinguished by some token of providential agency.*
>
> *. . . [W]e ought to be no less persuaded that the propitious smiles of Heaven can never be expected on a nation that disregards the eternal rules of order and right, which Heaven itself has ordained.*

This was not mere political posturing, Washington's reference to God as the ultimate provider behind America's development and recent success in preserving its independence. It was very serious business – for it rested on a Truth that recent experience had made very, very clear. This was not just religious platitude, designed by Washington to comfort the people with an assurance that he was a proper church-going Christian (which he frequently was not). This was testimony to the reality of politics that all of these quite astute practitioners of politics had come to understand – at a very deep level. The American venture would not fail – as had Athens' and Rome's and Israel's attempts at self-government – as long as it retained a very deep sense of connectedness to God and his hand in the affairs of man.

THE AMERICAN AND FRENCH "REVOLUTIONS" COMPARED

In 1789 – the same year that the American Constitution was ratified and thus in full effect – the French Revolution broke out in Paris, as the French, taking their cues in part from America, attempted their own rebuilding of French government around the popular will. Certainly the experience of the French fighting alongside the Americans in their rebellion against their own king served to inspire the French to look to the possibility of doing the same to their own bankrupt monarchy. And the Americans coming up with a written program (the American Constitution) certainly also gave rise to the French hope that something similar by way of a perfect social design could also become the foundation for a new French government, a Republic, like the American Republic.

But in fact the results at this French effort to undertake something similar to the American program ultimately proved to be quite different for the French than for the Americans – tragically different.

The American effort. The simple fact was that despite the tendency to want to call what the American colonies went through in the 1775-1783 period a "Revolutionary War" – there was nothing very revolutionary as to what actually took place in America at the time. No new social order was put in place. Only political practices of self-government, ones that had long been operative in America (over 150 years by that time), were simply being protected and preserved – against the designs of an English King intending to end such political independence and put "his" colonies completely under his despotic or dictatorial control (the political lust that comes to all people able to assume unlimited power).

Independence - And the New Republic

The American colonies had been self-governing according to carefully written social contracts that birthed these colonies in the 1600s. And now years later in the mid-1770s when they decided to not yield to the King's pressures but to go fully independent instead, they easily and quickly drew up new state constitutions (for Massachusetts, Virginia, Maryland, etc.) outlining the political institutions and procedures that would govern their newly independent states. And then when they gathered some ten years later in 1787 to put together a Union of these newly independent states, they handled quite maturely the political differences that naturally were there, given the various differences in the makeup and cultural traditions of these different American states. They well knew what they were doing – being long experienced in productive governmental reform. They were simply building on that same long experience.

The French effort. That was not the case for the French. Prior to their rebellion against their king in 1789, the French people had absolutely no experience whatsoever in self-rule. They certainly talked about the possibility a lot, especially at the polite gatherings in fashionable French homes of French intellectuals and socialites – where the dreams of political reform were often the central topic under discussion. These enlightened dreamers could come up with the most beautiful of ideas about constructing a more perfect political world. But these were ideas not based on any real experience, but only on the fanciful dreams that these Idealists held about human nature – and the possibilities of marshaling such human nature in order to build a utopian society. In short, they had no idea of what it was they were talking about – as events would soon prove.

Once they succeeded in collapsing the monarchy, they then took on the privileged feudal aristocracy – and then also the French church and its prestigious hierarchy of bishops and priests. But slaughtering off the keepers of the Old Order (the Ancien Régime) did not automatically open the way to the establishment of a stable, working Republic – for French society had no particular moral foundations at this point on which to erect their radically new society. Chaos thus reigned in France – and only got worse when then the intolerant intellectuals (Girondins and Jacobins) then turned on each other as betrayers of the Revolution – because they differed with each other on points of Reason – or just because of intense political jealousy. By 1793-1794 a "Reign of Terror" consumed France, the guillotine busy night and day cutting off the heads of enemy intellectuals. Ultimately no one was in command of the hungry mobs that prowled the streets of Paris – and in a good part of the French countryside.

It finally took the dictatorship of Napoleon Bonaparte (approximately 1799 to 1815) to bring France back to order – mostly by calling on the

Paris mob and fired-up French nationalists of the countryside to join his new French army in its thrust outside of France to "liberate" the rest of Europe from the monarchs whose families had long ruled the continent. This solved the problem of violent discord among the French – but now pitted the highly nationalistic Frenchmen against the kings, barons and commoners of the rest of the European continent (all the way to Russia) – and also the British just offshore to the northwest of France.

The impact on the politics of the Western world. Eventually (1814-1815) Napoleon was defeated by a grand coalition of European monarchs – and the Bourbon monarchy was (briefly) restored in France. But Europe would never be quite the same again with all this nationalism stirred to life – as the English, Spanish, Germans, Italians organized themselves as nations in order to counter aggressive French nationalism. But in finally ending French nationalist domination, this new spirit of nationalism awakened in Europe would not then go away – but merely grow more aggressive – nation by nation – until it resulted in the mindless war of mutual national slaughter which was termed at the time "The Great War," and which we know today as World War One (1914-1918).

Meanwhile a young Republic – fully engaged with challenges of its own over in America – did its best to stay out of all this dynamic that was rattling Europe. In this it would be only partially successful.

But at least the American Republic itself would hopefully remain strong – a system of fixed laws rather than changing personal political wills, which popular governments had the tendency to turn into, such as France had just become, and later, such as the "People's Republics," would become under their "enlightened" Communist dictators.

Indeed, as Franklin put matters: "A Republic, if you can keep it."

CHAPTER FOUR

THE AMERICAN REPUBLIC GETS UP AND RUNNING

* * *

LEADERSHIP SHAPES THE CHARACTER OF THE REPUBLIC

Washington as America's first president. There had never been any question about who would head up the new Republic as its president. George Washington's power of leadership was fabled. He had led the small American army through the darkest of times – by personal example of his own steadiness, his own willingness to sacrifice personally for the cause, his own obvious devotion to the God on whom ultimately all things were dependent. Even during the heated debates that took place constantly the summer that the Constitution was being worked out, Washington had sat there quietly as its presiding officer, his mere presence reminding those present to stay focused on the task before them – not to get caught up in petty rivalry. This is the power of true moral leadership.

But there was nonetheless a big question on people's mind as Washington now took office as the country's President: would he simply serve one four-year term – or, like so many of the colonial leaders, stand repeatedly for reelection, becoming something like President-for-Life – like a European monarch?

Actually, Washington was hoping, after serving his country as military general and then chairman of the Constitutional Convention, to retire to his farm at Mount Vernon – and only rather reluctantly agreed to serve – just one term, he assured them.

A number of very big issues faced him as he took office: the massive indebtedness of the American states resulting from the long war for independence, the uncertainty of where exactly the lines of authority were to be found under the new regime, and where America stood in the constant tension between France and England – which America was not going to be able to avoid getting caught up in.

Alexander Hamilton. The first issue – America's huge money problem

– was handled swiftly by his newly appointed Secretary of the Treasury, Alexander Hamilton – who had served Washington bravely and faithfully during the war.

Hamilton was the classical Realist – born of questionable circumstances in the Caribbean Islands, orphaned at a very young age, but able early on to demonstrate a brilliance of mind that got him a scholarship, allowing him to head off to New York for study at King's College (the future Columbia University), where he prepared himself for a law career. During the rising contention with King George, Hamilton wrote numerous articles in defense of the colonies' rights in opposing the King's ambitions – yet jumped to the personal defense of the college president when an angry mob wanted to take the president down for his Tory loyalties.

When fighting finally broke out, Hamilton undertook the study of military history and tactics, eventually organizing an artillery company of Patriot militia and becoming the unit's captain. His company served bravely in Washington's army – all the way from the near-disaster in New York City to the victories at Trenton and Princeton. Hamilton was courted by various commanding officers to become part of their staff. But he said yes only when it was Washington himself who made the request.

Washington soon came to depend heavily on Hamilton – who seemed to have a well-informed understanding of what to do in various situations, diplomatic as well as military – and let Hamilton himself issue orders to both military and diplomatic officers on his own behalf. And it was Hamilton – much to the deep concern of Washington – who begged for and was finally permitted the dangerous honor of leading the Patriot charge on the last of the British defenses at Yorktown.

After the war Hamilton went back to his law practice, often defending Tories who were having enormous financial, social and personal difficulties in the post-war period. At this point Hamilton took up the study of finance and in 1784 founded the successful Bank of New York. Recognizing his brilliance, but also serious grounding in life's hard realities, the State of New York chose Hamilton to be one of its delegates to the Constitutional Convention. We have also seen that he and Madison wrote most of the articles of the *Federalist Papers*, very insightful commentaries that explained brilliantly why support of the new Constitution was so critically important to the country.

And ultimately it was to Hamilton that Washington once again turned in his quest to have a strong team working with him in his new role as US President. And the country's economic difficulties being the most challenging of the issues facing the country, Washington asked Hamilton to serve as the nation's first Secretary of the Treasury.

Hamilton's debt assumption program – and the "Whiskey Rebellion." As Treasury Secretary, Hamilton decided to have the new Federal government assume all the debts of the states, restoring vital confidence in the country's finances necessary to get the country up and running again – but requiring the imposition of new taxes to pay off these debts. This however caused frustration among many of the Patriot soldiers who had sold their service payments to speculators for a mere fraction of their face value, believing that this was the best that they would ever get out of these payments – only now to see the value abruptly rise – and the speculators being paid off in full by Hamilton's new policies. They felt enormously cheated – especially then when in 1791 they had to face new taxes on their whiskey (whiskey being a major source of income to these farmers) to cover the costs of Hamilton's policies.

A huge rebellion broke out in 1794 among the veterans (the Whiskey Rebellion as it is known in history) and Washington once again regretfully had to send the standing army (with himself in command) to break what was becoming a violent rebellion – in order to make it clear that the new government intended seriously to follow and defend its laws. Whiskey taxes would always remain difficult to collect. But at least the country now understood that they had a strong hand in Washington's command of the new country.

Indeed, Washington made it clear that the federal laws were not up for challenge in the streets. America was not going to let itself become like Revolutionary France (the French Reign of Terror was in full swing at this time). Laws put properly in place under the new constitution would be obeyed. Period.

Thomas Jefferson. As much as Hamilton was the arch-Realist, Thomas Jefferson was the arch-Idealist. Much of that resulted from the fact that they grew up differently – very differently. Whereas Hamilton had to fight for everything that came his way, Jefferson was born to privilege – and found that this carried him forward in life quite nicely. Jefferson was born within the ranks of the Virginia aristocracy, his mother being of the prestigious Randolph family – with young Thomas joining his Randolph cousins in being tutored in the classics of language, literature and science. He continued his studies of the classics at the College of William and Mary, and upon graduation took up the study of law under the prestigious George Wythe. At age 21 he inherited from his father 5,000 acres and 52 slaves, including land where he began his designs for the place of perfect habitation – Monticello – which as a fervent Idealist he would work on for the rest of his life in the attempt to use the powers of reason to bring it to full perfection (which also led him "unreasonable" financial debt!).

As a practicing lawyer he became a delegate to the House of Burgesses (1769-1775) and in 1772 married a cousin, Martha, adding 11,000 acres and 110 more slaves to his estate. With the calling of the Second Continental Congress in 1775, the young aristocrat was sent to represent Virginia. Here he met John Adams – and joined the small committee called on to draft a Declaration of Independence – a task that Adams turned over to Jefferson to initiate. In completing this task, Jefferson would gain for himself great fame, even though much of what he wrote was simply a rephrasing of Locke's philosophy. And – much to Jefferson's deep annoyance – not only was some of his wording amended by the full Congress, about a third of it was rejected because it went overboard in the way that it tried to justify the American revolt.

That same year he was elected to the Virginia House of Delegates and joined the committee designing a new Virginia State Constitution. This gave him the opportunity to advance his agenda of keeping the religious "establishment" out of the affairs of state, in sponsoring a bill entitled, Establishing Religious Freedom. He understandably disliked intensely the dominating role that King George's Episcopalian Church of England had played in Virginia life. However his bill failed to pass in the Virginia House. But two years later he was able to participate in the task of reviewing all the laws of Virginia, thus finally allowing him to recast these laws according to his rather Deist/Humanist worldview (religion).

The next year he was even elected Virginia governor – putting yet more power into his hands as a designer of the perfect legal domain. However, his work was interrupted in 1781 by the attacks in Virginia of the turncoat Benedict Arnold – who burned Richmond to the ground, and sent Jefferson and his government officials scurrying pathetically here and there to avoid capture.*

After the war (in 1784), as a member of the American Confederation's Congress, he chaired the committee that was to plan the development of the Northwest Territories – in which Jefferson outlined nine territories (with very exotic-sounding names!), eventually trimmed down to five territories (with largely Indian names).

But that same year he was sent by the Confederation to join Franklin and Adams in Europe, to secure various diplomatic agreements with England, France, Spain, the Netherlands, etc. At this point Jefferson fell completely in love with the French lifestyle, especially French intellectualism – which was becoming increasingly aggressive at this point. And he came

---

*It was later that year decided by the Virginia Assembly that Jefferson had acted appropriately in taking himself and his officials into hiding in his various plantations. But he had lost such stature that he was not reelected governor.

very close to being an on-site spectator to those events that broke out in July of 1789 – except that, in what was supposed to be a brief return to America for the summer, he was called on by Washington to take the post as America's first Secretary of State. Thus Jefferson had to watch events unfold In Paris from a distance.

But his heart was clearly with the wildly enthusiastic French Revolutionaries. He was certain that – in overthrowing the Old Order of Monarchy, Aristocracy and Church – the Revolution would be bringing France to an Ideal realm of pure Reason.

Jefferson vs. Hamilton. Soon, because of all the political turmoil unleashed by the French Revolution, facing America was the matter of France versus England – and where America would position itself in the midst of the ongoing feud between these two countries. Jefferson, now (at least theoretically) in charge of American diplomacy – was all-out in his support of France – to a point of dangerous blindness when he refused for the longest time to see any injustice in the way the French Revolution was turning itself into a violent, cruel and bloody mess.*

On the other hand – although they had personally fought the English fiercely in their effort to maintain American independence (while Jefferson had spent the war avoiding the English enemy) – Washington and Hamilton understood that England, despite that recent war, was still the more logical American ally.

But this pro-British stance of Washington and Hamilton so infuriated Jefferson that at the end of 1793 he stepped down from Washington's Cabinet – to form an anti-Federalist faction designed to fight Washington, Hamilton and the Federalists.

Now also Madison switched sides and joined Jefferson to develop the new Republican party (led at the time mostly by Virginians – not connected at all with the modern Republican Party!).

Jay's Treaty. The British did not help their case in America by refusing to abandon their forts located to the west across the Appalachian Mountains – and by maintaining their alliances with the American Indians living in that region. But most infuriating to the Americans was the British practice of

---

*When William Short, a Jeffersonian supporter, wrote Jefferson from Paris that mobs had taken over the French Revolution and had even butchered some of their French friends, Jefferson in January of 1793 wrote back a sharp rebuke: "My own affections have been deeply wounded by some of the martyrs to this cause, but rather than it should have failed I would have seen half the earth desolated; were there an Adam and an Eve left in every country, and left free, it would be better than it now is."

stopping American ships and seizing their hardiest sailors, claiming these to be Englishmen avoiding English naval service – when this was seldom the case. Americans protested – and in 1795 sent Supreme Court Chief Justice John Jay to England to try to straighten matters out. Actually, the English were not greatly impressed by American power and Jay returned home with only small concessions – giving Jefferson's Republicans all sorts of opportunity to mock "Jay's Treaty" and attack Washington and the Federalists.

Washington's second – and final – term. When Washington had approached the end of his term in office in 1793, the Federalists had pleaded with him to accept another term, for there was no one else with the stature to oppose the Republicans. He very reluctantly agreed to do so – more than ever determined that this would be his last term of service to the country. As it turned out, it was – as Washington by the end of his second term in office was exhausted by the slander coming from Jefferson's Republicans about how pro-monarchy he and Hamilton were for supporting the English monarchy against the French Republic. Certainly Washington and Hamilton's choice of Britain over France had nothing at all to do with somehow being pro-monarchy – which definitely they were not (it was they, after all – and not Jefferson – who had just put their lives on the line in fighting the British)! The accusation was simply a case of emotionally-charged cheap-shot politics against the Federalists waged by Jefferson's Republicans.

But in any case, Washington's departure thus helped establish the tradition that two terms of service (eight years) was the absolute limit on Presidential service. It would eventually even become a written Constitutional law in 1951 (the 22nd Amendment) – after Roosevelt abused this principle by running for a third and then a fourth term in the 1940s.

John Adams. Washington's Vice President John Adams was barely elected as the next President. Adams was a small man with very big ambitions – but also very measured in the way he worked out the moral lines of events going on around him, and what he expected of himself in response. He was always subject to a battle that raged within between the strict Puritan structuring he underwent growing up – and his desire to prove himself as a man ahead of the times. His father was disappointed that John's Harvard education led not to the ministry but instead to the law – the son seeing in the law a better road to the greatness that he hungered for so deeply.

But his Puritan side would put his law practice under moral restraints that lawyers do not usually worry about. Thus it was that Adams provided the defense in court of the Redcoats who fired on the Boston mob that was assaulting them, potentially putting him in great disfavor with the Bostonians – but instead earning a degree of admiration for his bravery, such that took him several steps down the road of greatness that he sought.

Then speaking and publishing strong defenses of the rights of the colonies to oppose the King's attack on their long-standing ability to govern themselves fully, he put himself out in the lead of the growing movement against the king. This earned him the appointment as a Massachusetts delegate to the First and Second Continental Congresses, the latter which asked him to head up a committee to draft a Declaration of Independence. The fact that he let Jefferson take the initiative rather than he himself in actually providing the original draft – and thus Jefferson gaining fame forever for doing so – would remain for Adams a perpetual torment!

Adams served on a number of committees of Congress over the next years. Then from 1778 onward he was sent back and forth (along with Franklin) to Paris to develop a working alliance with the French. And he too was part of the discussions that produced the Treaty of Paris formally ending the war in 1783. But in the meantime, he had also been working with the Dutch to coordinate with them their role in supporting American independence – and Dutch banks in helping post-war America financially. Then in 1785 he was sent to London as America's first Ambassador to the Court of St. James (as that position has always been known). While there, he contributed his own excellent writings in support of the adoption of the new American Constitution (which, because he was in England at the time, he had no direct part in drawing up).

By this time he was so well known in America that he came in second in the Presidential vote – and thus, by the understanding at the time, the recipient of the position as America's first Vice President. But as Adams would come to discover, it was a position with a title only, and no real political power or importance of any kind. But finally it did put him in position to run for the presidency when Washington stepped down.

And thus in 1796 he was elected President (barely) over his competitor Jefferson – and only when the election was placed in the hands of the House of Representatives because no candidate had a majority of votes. In the House, Hamilton and his Federalist supporters finally decided that they disliked Jefferson more than they disliked Adams! Thus in electing Adams to the presidency, this made runner-up Jefferson the new Vice President – and Hamilton even more greatly disliked by Jefferson and his Republicans. In the end this action in support of Adams put Hamilton on the Republican hate list.*

---

*In 1804, Aaron Burr shot and killed Hamilton in a pistol dual over insulting comments Hamilton had made in letters about Burr as Republican candidate

Adams as President. In any case, with Adams as President, he had to face the fact that it was now the French who were seizing American ships – embarrassing Jefferson and the pro-French Republicans. Hamilton and the Federalists now called for war against the French. It was all that Adams could do to keep tempers cooled down – especially with the "XYZ Affair" that scandalized Americans when Americans were sent to try to solve this problem, but were told they would first have to pay enormous bribes to French agents (self-identified only as X, Y and Z) in order to get discussions going. They refused. Consequently, Americans became even more enraged at hearing of the French behavior.

Then in 1798, Congress passed (and unfortunately Adams signed) the infamous Alien and Sedition Acts, which branded as punishable "traitors" anyone (principally Jefferson's Republicans) who supported France – or who opposed the position of the President or the heavily Federalist Congress. They would be subject to expulsion from the country.

By the next year (1799) it seemed as if America was actually at war with France (the "Quasi War") on the high seas. And with a large sweep of the 1798 congressional elections by the Federalists, the demand for an actual declaration of war was now very strong.

It was at this point the doctrine of "nullification" began to be discussed openly by the Republicans – as they claimed that sovereign rights in the new Federation belonged with the States and the people, not the Federalist-dominated Congress. And any laws that Congress might want to pass (such as the Alien and Sedition Laws) could simply be nullified by a decision of the states. The congressional majority of course ignored the challenge. But the right of nullification by the states of decisions made in the nation's capital would be heard all the way up to the outbreak of the Civil War some 60 years later.

In the end, to avoid war at all costs, Adams sent an envoy to Paris to work out some kind of understanding with the French that could reduce diplomatic tensions. The envoy came back with a treaty in which the French agreed to leave American ships alone – a treaty which Adams signed – understanding that this would hardly satisfy the war-hungry Federalists, nor bring the angry Republicans back to a cooperative spirit in Congress. In fact, he understood that by signing it he was undercutting any chance he had of victory in the elections coming up only a month away. He was right. But it was a brave thing to do – sparing the country from a war it did not need to fight.

One final act of Adams just as he was about to leave office was the

---

to the position of New York governor, comments Hamilton intended to remain private but got printed somehow.

rush to sign some six dozen appointments to positions in the Federal Judiciary – including the all-important appointment as Chief Justice of the Supreme Court the Virginian (but, exceptional for the Virginian group, a very strong Federalist), John Marshall. This action would not only upset the wave of new Republicans voted to Congress – but would put at the head of the American judiciary an individual who in so many ways would rewrite the American Constitution with respect to the role that the Federal Courts would come to play in the nation's political affairs – putting in the hands of the Supreme Court justices powers never intended by the Constitution's original Framers.

Anyway, having completed his service as the country's second president, Adams slipped quietly out of the new capital at Washington, D.C., as America's new president, Jefferson, was sworn into office there.

Jefferson as President (1801-1809). And once in office Jefferson began to undo the Federalist legacy – by removing the land taxes imposed on the farmers – making him very popular in the South and the West – and shifting the source of revenue to customs duties imposed on (largely Northern) imports and exports. He also raised revenue by selling (quite cheaply) Western land to new settlers – another very popular move among Westerners or those headed West – which came at a great cost to the Indians living there of course! Thus Jefferson built the Republican Party into a great political powerhouse.

To Jefferson's great credit,* it was during the early years of his presidency that America purchased from the French the huge Louisiana territory to the West of the Mississippi (the Indians living there not being consulted on this matter, of course) – blocking the possibility of any European power getting there before the Americans – who were spreading westward rapidly. This purchase effectively doubled the land claim of the American nation!

And in great part this bargain purchase had been made possible because American public finances had such a very strong credit rating – due to Hamilton's monetary policies, ones that Jefferson had so recently hated intensely!

---

*Actually, such credit belongs to his envoys sent to France, Livingston and Monroe, who were originally authorized to purchase (for an amount not to exceed $10 million) only the town of New Orleans located near the mouth of the Mississippi River – but who on their own authority answered with an immediate "yes" when Napoleon offered them the entire Louisiana Territory for $15 million. In part this came about so easily for the Americans because Napoleon was short on funding at the time and found American money rather than American land more supportive of his ambitions.

Lewis and Clark explore this new region. What it was that America had exactly come to in this Louisiana Purchase was largely unknown to its new owners. Thus Jefferson commissioned Captain Meriwether Lewis (accompanied by William Clark) and a team of fifty men to explore this new territory (1804-1806).* They followed the Missouri River West, hoping to find a water route to the Pacific. But as winter set in they found themselves bogged down in the Dakotas, and thankfully were able to bring on a French fur trapper and his Indian wife Sacajawea to guide them westward. The next summer they reached the Rocky Mountains, crossed them, and in November finally arrived at the Pacific Ocean. They wintered there, then in early 1806 began their trek back East, arriving in St. Louis as heroes.

To the shores of Tripoli. Further to his credit, Jefferson had the navy tackle the problem of Muslim pirates operating out of the Mediterranean towns of North Africa. Jefferson refused to pay tribute any longer (formerly paid out to release hostages or just prevent attacks on American shipping in the Mediterranean), instead sending American ships in concert with the Italian King of Naples against the pirates. This worked somewhat – but would need the end of the Napoleonic Wars in 1815 before the task could be completed.

Jefferson takes command of American foreign trade. But on the negative side of his political balance sheet, Jefferson imposed an embargo on the sale of American goods to Britain, in response to the ongoing British impressment of American sailors – the logic of this move being that this would deprive the British of vital American goods and bring Britain to its senses. But Jefferson's commercial boycott served only to make America appear to the British to be clearly a French ally – at a time when French dictator Napoleon, who had managed to seize control of nearly all continental Europe, had also placed an embargo on all European trade with Britain – in an effort to collapse the British economy. So England's response to Jefferson's policy was to become more, not less aggressive, against America – at a time that Jefferson had weakened considerably America's own military capabilities.

Then to make things "fairer," Jefferson decided to extend the same restriction against trade with France as well, shutting down pretty much all of America's export business – and nearly collapsing the American economy.

---

*Jefferson would also send out other teams to explore the new territory, including that of Gen. Zebulon Pike who in 1806 ventured as far west as the territory that would become Colorado (who also was captured by the Spanish in the process, but released in 1807!).

The American Republic Gets Up and Running 111

Jefferson cuts back on the navy. To make bad matters even worse, Jefferson then chose to meet the European challenge by not building more warships (frigates), the likes of which had proven themselves so capably in the war with the Barbary states. He figured that not having a fighting navy would help keep Americans from making the mistake of wanting to go to war with either France or Britain.* Instead he chose to build a number of much smaller gunboats. These would not be terribly effective in defending American shipping overseas, but certainly could be used to help prevent the American smuggling that his embargo encouraged.

Thus it was that Jefferson continued to see himself not as a warrior but as "a man of peace" – unable to understand how international power actually works, and consequently leaving America increasingly vulnerable to European power politics abroad – and vengeful Indians at home.

It is also important to note that for one who had been so loud about protecting "states' rights" against the assumption of autocratic power by an uncontrolled government in Washington, Jefferson had no problems personally acting in such an autocratic fashion when he himself was president (imposing his restrictions on American trade and downsizing America's military defenses).

But of course Jefferson was among the most "enlightened" of Americans, and that justified his autocracy (as "enlightenment" always does!).

But thankfully, just as he was about to leave office in 1809, Jefferson somehow awoke finally to the realization of the magnitude of the disaster his economic policies had produced – and he finally repealed his ill-conceived embargo. And the America economy soon revived.

John Marshall – and the empowerment of the Supreme Court. As we have just noted, one of the last things Adams did before he turned the presidency over to Jefferson was to make the last-minute appointment of John Marshall to the position as Chief Justice of the Supreme Court. Marshall would go on to hold that position from 1801 to 1835. This would have a huge impact on the shaping of American government, for Marshall would gradually, case by case, assign to the Supreme Court increasing powers to

---

*Liberal Humanists such as Jefferson have always supposed that it is weapons that cause wars – and thus disarming the people will automatically cut back on the dangers of the people falling into a war with someone else. But in fact self-disarmament – that is, disarmament if not mutual on the part of all contending societies – will merely undercut the ability of a society to protect itself against another society that has come to hold such power that it no longer fears the consequences of its efforts to bully others into submission. Weapons are not the problem. The political-moral intentions of societies are what are critical in matters such as this.

decide which laws of Congress – and the states – were "constitutional" and which were not, and if not (by the Court's own decision on the matter), then that they would not be supported by the judiciary as the law of the land. Or even the Court might decide that the law ought to be interpreted in this or that particular manner – in essence revising (even extensively) the very purpose of such law. As stated before, this would make the Supreme Court, not Congress, the highest legislative body of the land!

Why did the Supreme Court assume such power for itself? Basically because Marshall saw that it was there for the taking – and because no one at the time understood the dynamic and thus did nothing to block this huge assumption of power by the Supreme Court. Eventually because nothing was done, it became simply assumed that the Supreme Court had such constitutional powers. But unlike the rest of the federal system, which was put in place with a number of built-in checks on its various powers, the Supreme Court was originally defined with no known checks on its power.

The presumption was that a long-held Anglo legal ethic would somehow direct the action of the Court. But such an ethic would prove over time susceptible to being interpreted widely and deeply in a number of quite different ways, depending on the personal political or ideological makeup (always well rationalized, as lawyers are indeed trained to do) of the nine members of the court – or even just five of the justices constituting a slight voting majority for any particular case. That's a lot of unrestricted power to put in the hands of a very small group of enlightened individuals!

* * *

GROWING SECTIONAL TENSIONS

Economically speaking, the America South had always functioned as a supplier of raw materials to England: tobacco, dyes and – at first – small amounts of cotton. New England on the other hand had geared its economy largely around the idea of meeting its own needs locally, from agriculture to finished industrial products.

The impact of the industrial revolution. The New England or "Yankee" temperament also made for a lot of industrial creativity – with Samuel Slater in the 1790s for instance setting up first in Rhode Island, then Massachusetts, then Connecticut and New Hampshire, spinning mills which turned cotton into thread – at about the same time that Eli Whitney invented the machine that could do the work of masses of individuals (slaves mostly) in removing the troublesome seeds from cotton balls, revolutionizing the cotton industry in the American South – able now to fill the industrial needs not only of the spinning and weaving factories of Britain, but also similar factories in the American North.

While this vital North-South industrial relationship should have strengthened the ties between these two sections of the country, actually the reverse resulted. While such developments in the North encouraged the ambitious, hard-working and inventive character of Yankee culture, the South tended to see in this economic development the ability to go deeper into its traditional feudal social dream of a leisured gentry standing atop a social order of hard-working slaves – slaves stripped of any ambition or ability to think inventively. To be sure there were plenty of poor Whites in the South found well outside this romantic dream, living desperate lives trying to compete with the huge plantations in the cotton export business. But these poor Whites themselves were caught up in the same Cinderella dream – hoping, even believing, that they too one day would be sitting on their own verandas, sipping Mint Juleps while discussing social affairs and grand ideas.

Over time such an industrial dynamic was pushing the North way ahead of the South in terms of overall economic development. Factories were going up everywhere and infrastructure in the form of major roads, canals, and even the first of the railroads was being laid out everywhere. To be sure, some of this same activity was taking place in the South, but not at nearly the same degree as in the North. Industrial entrepreneurship certainly did occur across the South. But it did not bring the prestige or stir human ambitions and readiness to undertake the hard work to bring about entrepreneurial success the way it did in the North.

Jefferson vs. Hamilton. In some strange ways the growing differences between these two lifestyles were summed up in the personal differences well illustrated in the lives of Hamilton and Jefferson. Jefferson was the very epitome of the Southern gentleman – naturally and gracefully born to noble status, reflected in the way he approached life. Hamilton on the other hand was the type that the Yankee world seemed to symbolize: self-advancing from even the humblest of social beginnings, through incredible self-discipline and hard work – and a resolve to take life head on, no matter what it threw at you. To Hamilton, Jefferson probably represented everything he detested about a social snob – and Hamilton represented to Jefferson the vulgarity of the typical social climber. There really was no meeting point between the two personalities.

But over time, it would be revealed that the same held true for the entire realm of Northern and Southern culture. As neither side was willing to back down in holding such absolutely positive attitudes about itself and equally absolutely negative attitudes about the other, trouble – bloody trouble – lay ahead.

* * *

MADISON AND THE WAR OF 1812
(ACTUALLY 1812-1815)

James Madison. Jefferson's ever-faithful ally James Madison had served as Secretary of State under Jefferson. And with Jefferson's move to leave office after eight years, the Republicans looked to Madison to head up their party – and run for the office of President. The Federalists were easily defeated and Madison entered the White House in 1809 – to head up a nation that was up in arms about a rise in Indian attacks (headed by Tecumseh) – made easier for the Indians because of Jefferson's weakening of the American military.

Madison was a man who learned to compensate for his small stature and frail health by taking on huge intellectual challenges. He started out life as the oldest son of a typical aristocratic tobacco planter-family of Virginia, well-schooled in math, the sciences and classical languages. But he chose to go to the College of New Jersey (the future Princeton University) rather than the College of William and Mary. There he eventually took up even post-graduate studies under the college's president, the Presbyterian minister John Witherspoon – and developed a strong worldview based on the philosophy of the European Enlightenment (with Christian touches here and there!).

Madison eventually became self-taught in the law. But being of an aristocratic background, Madison never felt the need to take up law as a profession. Instead he simply served as a strong supporter of Virginia's political interests locally, and ultimately, with the outbreak of the war in 1775-1776, in the Continental Congress as well. Key to his own future, both in Virginia and in Philadelphia, he found himself working closely with Jefferson.

After the war he continued to pursue his political interests, eventually being the author of the Virginia Plan that got the Constitutional Convention off and running in 1787, at the same time keeping excellent notes of the entire event. And he used his sense of political dynamics to write insightful follow-up articles in defense of the ratification of that new Constitution (his contribution to the *Federalist Papers*). And he authored and supervised the passage in Congress of the Bill of Rights as the first ten amendments to that Constitution.

But he was also empowered by both his very active wife, Dolly and his friend Jefferson, and joined with Jefferson in opposing Hamilton's Federalists because of the way Hamilton was "over-building" (as he and Jefferson now saw things) the power of the central authority through Hamilton's strong economic measures. This was what impelled Madison ultimately to form the Democratic-Republican (or just "Republican") Party, and thus also what led him to be called to serve as Jefferson's Secretary of State during Jefferson's eight years in office (1801-1809).

And now Madison was President of the country, and had to take on the young nation's challenges on his own (with the "First Lady" Dolly's considerable help!).

The young republic goes to war (1812). The biggest problem at the time seemed to be the British, who not only continued their seizure of American ships and crew but also armed Tecumseh's warriors, infuriating the Americans. Indeed, British arrogance had succeeded in stirring a younger American generation among even the Republicans into the status of being "War Hawks" – eager to take on both the Indians and the British – to restore America to peace. Thus finally in June of 1812, under the sway of the Republican War Hawks (led by Henry Clay of Kentucky and John C. Calhoun of South Carolina), Congress declared war on the British.

How they intended to win that war without a navy or an army was not given much thought. At first the Americans made a move on Canada – with the goal in mind of expelling Britain from the last of its American holdings. The results were disastrous for the Americans – being defeated by unwilling Canadians, crushed by encircling British troops at Detroit, and slaughtered by vengeful Indians who set upon surrendered Americans at Fort Dearborn (Chicago).

1813. The next year, an effort in January to retake Detroit ended up with nearly 400 Americans killed in the action and 500 taken away as prisoners – with the rest slaughtered by Indians. In reply, in April a vengeful America attacked the Canadian capital of York (Toronto) and burned and plundered it – inspiring the thoughts of revenge among the British and Canadians. That August "Red Stick" Creek Indians attacked Fort Mims (Alabama) and slaughtered those who had taken refuge there. On the other hand, the Americans authorized the building of six new frigates (the British possessed some 175 such ships!) – which conducted themselves admirably – as well as American "privateers" who did the same. Also, a huge victory came to the Americans in defeating a British army in Ontario and killing the Indian leader Tecumseh – shattering the huge Indian coalition he had put together. This gave much needed courage to the Americans – although it hardly shifted the war in America's favor.

1814. The following year, the war did go in America's favor in the West, when in March, American General Andrew Jackson delivered a smashing blow to the Red Stick Creeks in Mississippi. But it went devastatingly against America in the East when, having defeated and imprisoned Napoleon in Europe, the British felt free to march on the new American capital at Washington, D.C. in August of that year and burn it to the ground – payment for the burning of Canada's capital at York.

The Treaty of Ghent (December 1814). But with Napoleon finally defeated and imprisoned on the Island of Elbe, the British found themselves very tired of all the fighting that had consumed them over the past decade or more. Also, British revenues were running low because of the Napoleonic wars – and now this war with the Americans as well. Likewise, the British now no longer saw the need to grab American sailors to fill their own ranks – a major American grievance against the British. Consequently, both sides were ready for peace. Thus it was that British and American envoys gathered in Ghent (Belgium) to negotiate a peace treaty.

At first the terms that the British were offering the Americans were harsh – and the Americans refused to accept them.

However, fighting still going on back in America now began to turn in the American favor. British efforts in September to take Baltimore failed completely* – and the Americans' naval victory on Lake Champlain (New York) at the same time stopped the British attempt to march on America from the North. Thus before the end of the year, American and British diplomats finally agreed to a peace treaty based on much more equitable terms – largely returning things to the way they were prior to the war.

The Battle of New Orleans (January 1815). But news of the treaty signing had not yet reached either the American forces (under Jackson) or the British forces gathering for a huge battle at New Orleans. But the British attack on the well-defended American position (behind a huge wall of cotton bales) led to a humiliating defeat for the British: 291 British killed, 1262 wounded, and 484 captured or missing – with only 13 Americans killed and 39 wounded.

Although the battle was unnecessary (for it changed none of the peace terms), it fueled a huge sense of national pride among the Americans, made Jackson a national hero, and in a way gave announcement to the

---

*A witness to this British failure at Baltimore's Fort McHenry was Francis Scott Key, who wrote a poem about the flag remaining aloft through the night of heavy British bombardment. The poem was eventually put to music and became the American national anthem, *The Star-Spangled Banner.*

world that America was a rising player in the game of international politics.

* * *

EXPANSION

Florida (1818). The Napoleonic wars (1800-1815) had undercut Spanish power considerably – both in Europe and in America. Not only had independence movements (Mexico, Colombia, Argentina, etc.) developed in Spanish America as a result, but the Seminole Indians in Florida had used this opportunity to conduct raids north into Georgia and Alabama. Now, with the fighting against the British over, General Jackson was thus ordered into action to defend American territory from these Indian raids. But Jackson took this as authorization not merely to block Seminole raids into the American states, but to take the action against the Indians all the way into Spanish Florida (1818). And he ended up not only defeating the Seminoles but laying claim to the whole of Florida as U.S. territory. President James Monroe (the 5th U.S. President and 4th Virginian to hold that office) was embarrassed. But Americans in general were greatly delighted. Spain quickly decided simply to sell Florida to America for $5 million – ending further humiliation for Spain. Now Jackson appeared to be even more of a giant in American eyes.

But economic crisis (1819-1821). The years after the War of 1812 seem so settled and the national spirit running so high that a Boston newspaper in 1817 termed the times they were living in as "The Era of Good Feelings." But those Good Feelings were not destined to last, for in the return of Europe's national soldiers back to their farms and factory jobs, the glory days of American agriculture and industry suddenly came to a crashing end. The demand in Europe for American products disappeared overnight, leaving completely bankrupt the enterprising Americans who had formerly borrowed money to expand their farming and industrial enterprises to meet Europe's high demands during the Napoleonic Wars. But the banks soon joined these businesses in the growing disaster, because instead of having paying customers (interest and principle on the loans to these businesses) they ended up with only the bankrupted property of these businesses in their hands – whose value had dropped away to a mere fraction of what it previously was. The banks did not want worthless business property, they wanted payments on the loans. But that just was not going to happen. Thus the banks also woke up to find themselves bankrupt right along with their former business customers. And no one knew how to come out of this crisis.

In fact, this was all a big mystery, one that would now repeat itself on numerous occasions in the future.* Efforts to put in place commercial, financial or economic rules that might counter these swings in economic fortune would be attempted. But still, for various reasons not always deriving from things that the Americans themselves did, there was usually very little to be done except wait for the shakeout of weaker businesses and the slow return of economic confidence to society – through helpful instruments which would come upon the scene almost as mysteriously as had the earlier causes for the crash.

Slavery serving to intensify "identity politics," and the Missouri Compromise (1820). Then when Missouri applied for statehood in 1819, another brewing controversy boiled over. The five states of the American Northwest Territories (Ohio, Indiana, Illinois, Michigan and Wisconsin) had been admitted into the Union as free (non-slave) states, and Louisiana had recently been added to the roster of slave states, making a political balance of eleven states each, slave and free. Missouri itself was about half and half (the state itself divided mostly north and south) and thus the issue exploded onto the political stage: how was Missouri to be admitted, as slave or free?

In Jefferson's days there had been some vague idea that slavery would soon end itself naturally. Europe was fast moving to outlaw the vile practice, though hardly naturally – as, even there, much bitter debate was involved in Europe's coming to the anti-slavery decision. But in America, as time went on, the South dug in more deeply in defense of the practice, showing no willingness to give it up. By this point it was widely assumed in the South that its economy was totally dependent on slavery. Further, any talk of ending the practice (now coming mostly just from the North) seemed to be an attack on Southern culture itself – a culture which had come to place slavery symbolically at the very heart of its social-cultural identity.

As feeling grew ever hotter over the issue, the "Great Compromiser" Senator Henry Clay of Kentucky offered a solution: to create some kind of line across the country from East to West, with slavery allowable below that line as territories advanced to the status of states – but Missouri (north of that line) being exempted and admitted as a slave state – because now Maine was requesting admission as a free state, thus continuing to preserve the numeric balance. So it was that everyone breathed a huge sigh of relief – believing that they had solved the problem. But in fact, slavery now

---

*1837, 1857, 1873, 1893, 1907, 1919, 1929, 1979 – and more recently, the near national economic meltdown in 2008.

had become a huge political issue clearly defined publicly, separating both North and South.

Social issues, such as the slavery matter, once they get in people's heads (or hearts) as a key social identifier, simply do not go away on their own. Rather they become major social causes for a society, leading its people to do the most extreme (even highly irrational) things. At some point people would even prefer to engage in bloody battle – rather than appear to be retreating on the matter.

Thus it was that the inability to find a "rational" answer to the divisive issue of slavery only made that social division all the deeper and more emotional with time. Finally, there really was no compromise available – as each side became more deeply invested in its own particular stand as the socio-political identity issue dragged on, and on.

The Monroe Doctrine (1823). Despite Spanish efforts to hold onto its American colonies, Mexico moved to full independence (1821), and various others of Spain's American colonies also did so soon thereafter. As a result, Britain was seeing in all this the opportunity to trade with these newly-independent countries in America, something not permissible under the principle of mercantilism, previously in force in Latin America – which allowed only the mother country (Spain or Portugal) to trade with its colonies.

But not looking for another conflict, Britain approached America to see if it was willing to enter an understanding with Britain that would keep any European power (whether Spain or possibly even France) from taking advantage of the infancy of the new Spanish-American regimes to try to draw them back into a Spanish or even a French imperial circle. Britain would provide the muscle (its navy) if America would take the political lead in the matter. And thus in 1823, President Monroe announced in Congress that America would protect the independence of its neighbors to the South (and also the right of Americans to now trade with its southern neighbors as well!).

European monarchs at first laughed at American presumptuousness. But ultimately, they did nothing when they realized that British power stood behind this "Monroe Doctrine."

Adams II. The New England Federalists had not been active supporters of the American effort in the War of 1812 – and paid dearly for this decision by losing so much support that the Federalist Party simply died away soon thereafter. With only one party (Jefferson's Republicans) now in existence, the Republicans then themselves split into a number of contending factions – which in the presidential election of 1824 threw the election to the House of Representatives to decide.

When it chose John Quincy Adams as President (John Adams's son) Jackson was furious, because he had more votes than the others – though not a full majority. It was Clay that had finally thrown his group's votes to Adams, thus electing Adams as the next president.

Thus Jackson sat offstage fuming (especially at Clay) while the younger Adams tried to guide the country – although there were not many issues, because as Secretary of State under Monroe, Adams had taken care of most of the diplomacy problems facing the country (the Executive Branch of government at that time was still pretty much just focused on foreign policy issues anyway.) Indeed, it was actually Adams that had negotiated the agreement that led to the Monroe Doctrine!

But sadly, Adam's quiet (also not very charismatic) presidency did not connect well with the hearts of American commoners – and four years later (1828) Jackson (with the Southerner South Carolina Senator John C. Calhoun as his running mate) finally won the presidency.

Jackson's world (1830s). Although Jackson was something of a Southern aristocrat, he knew how to relate to the interests of the American commoners – especially of those in the rapidly expanding American West and Southwest. Jackson had organized (with considerable help from his political ally, the New Yorker Martin Van Buren) his own political party, which took the name "Democrats." With this development, American politics took on a more earthy, even vulgar, character – as the political interests of rural and frontier America took the political lead in the country's affairs.*

Jackson would become famous for the way he played to the crowds. Indeed, on inauguration day, throngs of very ordinary people attempted to gather to see and hear their hero being sworn in as president, and then join him at the White House for a major reception. Even in through the windows the crowds came, muddy boots and all, stepping on the furniture, knocking over tables, smashing china. Jackson slipped away from the adoring crowd and quietly had dinner with close associates.

In short, Jacksonian democracy was all a grand show, but one for which Jackson himself had no personal interest. He would let Van Buren take care of the political image-making. As for Jackson, he had other

---

*The election of 1828, for instance, had been particularly vulgar in tone, with candidates, or their supporters anyway, hurling coarse insults against each other. In the case of Jackson, it was slander about the legality of his marriage to his wife Rachel, so vicious that it may have been the reason Rachel died of a heart attack in December 1828, shortly after Jackson's presidential victory, but before he was sworn into office. Jackson, understandably, remained forever bitter about this personal tragedy.

things he would rather be doing!

So, the age of elite-led politics was over. The noblemen (Washington, Adams Sr., Jefferson, Madison, Monroe, and Adams, Jr.) who formerly had quietly assumed the presidency in order to serve the nation, would now be replaced by the politically ambitious, who knew how to work the political imagery necessary for getting elected to public office. In this, Van Buren, on behalf of Jackson, was a genius. He understood what it took to appeal to the common voter. He understood the press and its ability to create reality. He knew how to line up voters and get them to the polls, especially in the newly emerging democratic age of the general electorate.

The "spoils system." This was a term coined by New York Senator Marcy in 1828 after Jackson's victory: "To the victor belong the spoils." Politics now seemed to have one goal for those who served: to get reelected. And to achieve that, politicians would need social assets they could give their supporters as payoff for their votes – government jobs mostly, though sometimes just offering a free round of beer on election day would achieve the same result.

Jackson would become a specialist in this spoils system, for instance, undercutting the vital national bank, the Bank of the United States (BUS) – not because he was opposed to national banking, but because he was afraid that his political arch-rival Henry Clay, who sponsored the renewal of the BUS's charter, would put himself in the position of being able to offer all the BUS's jobs (and loans) to his supporters. Thus Jackson saw to it that the federal government's financial operations would be done instead through Jackson's regional and local "pet banks" rather than the national BUS, thus crippling the BUS – and in the process much of the national government's financial powers as well.

De Tocqueville's *Democracy in America*. An individual who put on record his own observations about the peculiar cultural nature of this Jacksonian America was the Frenchman, Alexis de Tocqueville, who recorded his observations in his *Democracy in America* (two volumes, 1835 and 1840). He noted the highly individualistic spirit of the typical American – tending to take on new challenges without ever having completed the old challenges! Americans simply loved to "move on" to America's ever-expanding frontiers (not an option in a France with very fixed and well-filled-in national boundaries). He also noted the deep impact of the Puritan moral legacy (quite different than France's much looser attitudes about sex – yet much stricter attitudes about social status).

And indeed, America was a very different society than the ones back in Europe. It was young, aggressive, and ever-expansive in its social vision.

The Indian removal (1830s). This factor pointed to another political problem that was brewing in those days. Americans looked greedily at Indian lands still located inside an expanding America – in particular the various tribes located principally in Georgia – but also Alabama and Mississippi. When the Georgia governor indicated that his government was going to take action on the matter of relocating the Indians tribes out of Georgia, Jackson decided not to be upstaged by the governor, but to take the lead in the matter himself. Thus it was that Jackson had Congress push through an Indian Removal Act (1830), calling for Indians everywhere to be relocated to the west of the Mississippi River, principally to the Indian territory of Oklahoma.

However, the Cherokee, who had made every effort to adapt themselves to Anglo-American-Christian culture, fought the move by appealing to the Supreme Court – which under Marshall simply nullified the right of both the Cherokee and the State of Georgia to act on this matter – presumably blocking removal – or did it? Anyway, Jackson ignored the Supreme Court's intervention, supposedly inviting Marshall to come and enforce the Supreme Court decision himself personally, if he wanted!

The Indian Removal Act was also opposed by the newly rising party of Whigs (heavily Eastern-industrialist in membership) – who claimed that the removal policy violated Christian principles in every way possible. But opening up these western lands for Anglo settlement also stole from this business class the workers they were counting on to man the machines in their new industries back East.

The Indians themselves resisted this removal as best they could. In Illinois the Sauk and Fox Indians, led by Chief Black Hawk, revolted against the order and had to be put down violently by the Illinois militia (including in its ranks Captain Abraham Lincoln). But one by one the Choctaw (1831), Seminole (1832), Creek (1834), and Chickasaw (1837) were forced to move. The worst removal occurred among some thirteen thousand Cherokee, who in 1838 were first herded into camps in Tennessee and then force-marched westward through a freezing, snowy winter by General Winfield Scott's soldiers. Cold, disease, and starvation took a huge toll in their numbers. Thus many died along this "Trail of Tears," possibly as many as a third of all Indians involved. In all, some 46 thousand Indians were relocated in order to open the way for Anglo-American settlement into these Indian lands.

Texas. Texas was originally a huge but very sparsely settled northern section of New Spain (the latter after 1821 constituting the newly independent "Mexico"). Comanche Indians were such a problem in that region that the

Mexicans decided in 1824 to invite Anglo-Americans to come and settle the area – in the hopes of displacing or at least subduing the Comanches. Stephen Austin had already brought a group of 300 Americans to settle along the Brazos River in 1822 and the idea was to invite other *impresarios* or group organizers to do the same. But by 1830 the flow of Americans into Texas had become so extensive that the Texas region was in danger of becoming thoroughly Americanized – and thus the flow was officially stopped.* But the Texans immediately understood this to be an effort of the Mexican authorities to isolate their huge Anglo community – stirring deep resentment among these new settlers. This mood also found itself developing at a time that Mexico was itself in a state of near civil war between its Centralists and Federalists.

Texas Independence (1836). Thus it was that a group of Texans gathered near Austin to write the Convention of 1832, demanding a lifting of the immigration restrictions – and greater political autonomy for Texas itself. The Mexican Congress attempted to answer some of these demands (even authorizing English as a second language). But this failed to satisfy many of the Texans who were becoming more insistent on total Texas independence. Then in 1835, when a small Mexican force was sent north to subdue this spirit of independence, it met armed resistance at Gonzales – leading Texans to move to set up their own Texas army under the command of Sam Houston. The following year (1836) the Texans moved to decree full independence – as the Republic of Texas.

The new Mexican President Santa Anna responded quickly by sending 4,000 troops north – to crush the approximately 185 Texans taking a stand at the Alamo – killing the Texans almost to the last man. Then Santa Anna brought up more Mexican troops, took on more Texans, defeating them, and then moving them to a prison at Goliad. Then to everyone's shock, he ordered the massacre of the 300 Texan prisoners at Goliad.

The Texans vowed to never forget what Santa Anna's troops had done. "Remember the Alamo" and "Remember Goliad" subsequently became the Texans' battle cry. A month later the Texans had their chance for revenge – smashing the Mexicans at San Jacinto, capturing Santa Anna, and forcing him to sign a peace treaty recognizing the independence of the new Texas Republic (although he would repudiate the treaty once he was back in Mexico).

---

*At the beginning of the migration in 1825 there were only about 3,500 non-Indian settlers in Texas, mostly Hispanic. Less than ten years later that figure was over ten times that size, about 80% of them Americans – with a large number of slaves among them.

At this point a huge question posed itself to the Texans: was their newly independent Texas to remain an independent Republic, possibly expanding itself all the way to the Pacific, or was it more logical simply to prepare Texas to become a new state in the American Union? The matter was soon resolved when Mexico sent troops north to undo Texan independence, pushing the debate in favor of those wanting to join the U.S.

But this then raised the question in the U.S. itself – would Texas be admitted to the Union as slave or free? Debate in Congress on the matter turned heated, as identity politics always does. Meanwhile, President Van Buren was struggling with the great economic Panic of 1837 – and was not looking for more contention to trouble America's political waters.

But South Carolina Senator John C. Calhoun (who in the 1820s had switched from being a strong nationalist to instead being a strong pro-slavery Southerner) had made the admission of Texas as a slave state a matter of high principle for the South. He warned Congress that the Southern states themselves resolved either to stay – or depart from – the Union, depending on how this Texas matter was resolved. Meanwhile, John Quincy Adams had returned to Washington as a member of Congress – and for three weeks led the opposition to Texas' admission to the Union. Ultimately nothing was resolved on the matter, and the issue simply settled into a tense stalemate.

Finally, a number of years later (1845), at the end of his one and only term (another huge economic crisis had hit the nation) President John Tyler, though a Whig, decided to push through a "Lame Duck" Congress* an invitation to Texas to join the "Union" as a new state. Thus the incoming President James Polk would have the honor of overseeing the admission of Texas to the Union as the country's 28th state. At this point, the South was happy, the Whigs moody, but the Mexicans furious.

Manifest Destiny. In the midst of this debate, John L. O'Sullivan, publisher of the *Democratic Review* wrote an article (1845) explaining that it was America's "manifest destiny" to expand itself all the way west to the Pacific Ocean. All sorts of reactions resulted when this term became part of the national political conversation. Eastern Whigs considered it nothing more than a crude excuse for imperialism, although their reaction was in part a result of seeing themselves lose their workers to an opening West. Then there were those who supported the idea whole-heartedly – including importantly Christians, who compared the American westward expansion

---

*When an election has changed the makeup of Congressional representation, but the older members are still in position for a few months to do business before they are replaced by the newly elected representatives.

to the Israelites entering and clearing out the Promised Land to make way for the People of God to develop there. To such Christians, America had the same divine calling on it, and nothing should get in the way of this call.   It was after all, their "manifest destiny."

Of course the Indians and the Mexicans had a very different view on the subject. But ultimately, they were not invited to become part of the conversation. Nonetheless, they did not intend to be left out of the matter.

The Mexican-American War (1846-1848). The new President Polk at first tried to negotiate a settlement with Mexico over the Texas issue, even offering to pay substantially for the acquisition of Texas – as well as other territory all the way to the Pacific. But Mexico itself was in a state of massive political chaos at that time – and the Mexican leaders themselves could not agree on how to respond to Polk's offer.   When the Mexican Centralists finally won against the Mexican Federalists, the answer to Polk was a very loud "No"!

Then Polk responded to the Mexican "No" by moving U.S. troops through Texas – past the Nueces River which the Mexicans had (grudgingly) acknowledged as the southern border of Texas – all the way south to the Rio Grande. To the Mexicans this constituted an all-out act of war – and they sent 2,000 troops north to reclaim their territory. There they overwhelmed a small patrol of 70 American soldiers. A furious Democratic-Party-controlled Congress now responded with a declaration of war (April 1846) – with the Whigs opposing this move.

American General John C. Frémont then led Americans in California to rise up against Mexican authority there as well. Briefly the Californians took up the Bear Flag Revolt (symbolizing California's independence) – but quickly declared themselves as Americans. Then with the help of American General Stephen Kearny joining them from the East, the Californians took San Diego, cutting the Mexicans off from California. The next year (1847) Mexico was forced to recognize its full loss of California.

General Zachary Taylor then took his rag-tag army of volunteers deep into Mexico, where he was met by Santa Anna, who had again seized control of the Mexican government. But a stalemate resulted, broken only when Santa Anna had to leave the battle and head back to Mexico City to protect his political position there. At the same time, American warships were attacking Mexican towns along the shores of the Gulf of Mexico. They then unloaded their Marine troops, who headed west to Mexico City (to the "Halls of Montezuma") – and there delivered a knockout blow to Santa Anna and his troops – leaving American troops in total control of Mexico.

At this point some discussion arose about simply annexing Mexico – though not only did the Whigs fight this, but the idea found little support among most Americans. Consequently, negotiations in January of 1848 resulted simply in an offer of a $15 million payment to Mexico for the acquisition of the land reaching from southern Texas west to California. The payment was a major face-saving move awarded the Mexicans (the Mexicans had not invested very deeply socially in those areas anyway) – and removed the temptation of Mexico to try to retake the region – especially important at a time when America was soon caught up in its own civil war and would have been weakened greatly in any effort to hold onto this territory.

The Oregon Territory. The British and Americans had been able to agree on a Canadian-American border extending westward along the 49th parallel from Minnesota to the Rocky Mountains. But the territory to the west of those mountains was disputed by both Americans and British, the British claiming the Oregon Territory and the Americans claiming the land in the Pacific region north to the Russian border of Alaska. The feelings in America grew increasingly heated over this, with some calling for "Fifty-Four Forty* or Fight." Finally, in 1846 the British and Americans came to an agreement to simply extend the 49th parallel border all the way west to the Pacific (but swinging just south below Vancouver Island). And thus the Oregon Territory came formally into American hands.

Even before the treaty was signed, both Christian missionaries seeking to bring the Indians to Christ and land hungry Americans had begun pouring into Montana, Idaho, and the Pacific Northwest. Starting their trek from Independence Missouri, they followed the Missouri and Platte Rivers west to the Rockies, crossed rivers, mountains, snow and ice before descending down into the lush Oregon territory along the Columbia River. By the time of the 1846 treaty more than 6,000 Americans had already made their way to the Oregon Territory, to begin a new life there.

* * *

THE AMERICAN ECONOMIC DYNAMIC AT THIS TIME

President Jackson's decision in 1833 to withdraw all government deposits from the Bank of the United States – and move them to his "pet banks" located here and there around the country – undercut deeply New England's world of industrial/financial capitalism. But this action found wide approval among Jackson's rural supporters, who generally hated the banking world

---

*The line of latitude which formed the southern border of Russia's Alaska territory.

(most farmers found themselves in debt to banks in order to finance their farming operations). They were hoping that Jackson's stripping the BUS of its powers would make money cheaper (inflating the value of the dollar, making the repayment of their debts less costly to them). The Whigs, however – representing the banking community of the Northeast – demanded tight discipline of the money supply and the value of the dollar.

The national economic crisis of 1837-1840. An economic bubble of prosperity – built on the huge printing of paper money and the pricing of Western land at nearly give-away rates – suddenly burst in 1836 when currency problems back in London forced banks there to have to raise interest rates dramatically – in turn forcing American banks closely connected with the London banks to have to do the same. At the same time Jackson, oddly enough, reversed course on Western land sales – and demanded that payment be made in gold or silver coin rather than paper money – ruining land speculators, who had bought huge amounts of land rights with paper money, now finding potential purchasers of those lands backing away. Also, people began to make a run on banks, demanding that their deposits be refunded in hard currency (gold or silver) – something banks did not themselves possess in their vaults. Suddenly the American economy seemed to crash.

Jackson's Vice President Van Buren, now newly-elected U.S. President, did not cause the crash – but was the one everyone looked to in order to solve the crisis. But the crisis was one of fear, not policy. Paper money simply was not trusted and gold and silver were not easily expanded items. All anyone could do was ride out the panic – and hope that somehow the crisis would resolve itself. But that crisis was still on several years later when in 1840 Van Buren stood for reelection. Slowly a bit of confidence had been returning to the American economy – and businesses and banks were getting back on their feet (somewhat). But the process was too slow for Van Buren not to take the hit for it all.

Consequently the Whig candidate and former war hero (Indian fighter) William Henry Harrison was elected president – although he served in the presidential office only briefly, having caught a bad cold speaking long at his inauguration ceremony and dying a month later. Thus his Vice President John Tyler stepped into the presidency. Now the pro-BUS Whigs commanded the situation – and slowly put the American finances and thus the economy back on a stronger footing.

Lessons about careless handling of the nation's wealth by a government seeking to gain popularity by making wealth appear to come very easy (thus inflating a huge speculative bubble) should have been learned from this experience. But this would not be the last national financial crisis to hit the nation because of unwise government financial policies (the crisis of 2008 being a recent example.)

America's Industrial Revolution. Moving goods from field to factory and Americans always on the go (usually westward) was greatly facilitated by the development of rail and canal transport – those two technologies requiring the development of massive infrastructure (the laying of tracks and the digging of canals) – not to mention the steam power that drove the boats and trains (and factory machinery). But despite the economic setback of the late 1830s, by the early 1840s there were some 1,200 cotton mills in operation (mostly in the Northeast), the Erie Canal was in place with the Baltimore railroad linked to it (actually the Baltimore and Ohio Railroad had its first section in place as early as 1830), the McCormick reaper was harvesting huge wheat harvests, steam boats were making regular runs on the Great Lakes, etc. And by the early 1850s, railroads had reached from the East coast all the way to the Ohio River in the North and the Tennessee River in the South – and soon thereafter all the way to Memphis on the Mississippi River. America at this point was an industrial giant, not yet quite acknowledged by the European powers.

✷ ✷ ✷

AMERICA'S ONGOING SPIRITUAL DEVELOPMENT

America "wanders" again spiritually (early 1800s). For a number of Americans – located especially in the American East – a comfortable small-town life (dependent on an economy other than just agriculture) seemed to have a natural peace and prosperity to it. Not surprisingly, life took on a more "rational" character – stepping the people back from their previous Christian spirituality. Americans, especially among the more leisured classes, found themselves less interested in what God might do in their lives and more interested in what they might achieve for themselves under this more rational social realm clearly emerging around them.

They did not abandon Christianity – because being Christian was understood to be the same as being "civilized." But the authentic faith component was once again disappearing. Its place was being taken by a rational morality – a key part of Enlightenment Humanism – that was sweeping intellectual circles once again, in America as well as in Europe. Such Humanism usually claimed the moral teachings of Scripture, especially the teachings of Jesus, as its Christian foundation. But in the end no such connection was absolutely necessary, for these were supposedly self-evident truths that presumably any rational person would understand as the foundation of any life well lived (French revolutionaries had gone so far as to disdain even this slender Christian connection with their utopian Idealism).

Once again (as in the late 1600s and early 1700s) "Enlightened" Americans of the early 1800s were convinced that Human Reason was vastly superior to the pre-scientific superstitions about life held by Americans who were intellectually unable to shake off the silly old beliefs about people walking on water and raising the dead back to life. Consequently, they were deeply disdainful of those who clung to a religion drawn from a supposedly darker past.

They failed to notice that their new Rational Humanism as a substitute religion was no newer than the story of Adam and Eve's fall in the Garden of Eden, or the long Biblical narrative about the repeated wandering of ancient Israel away from the counsel and discipline of God – and its tragic results. And America itself had already evidenced this same occurrence a century earlier. But they had learned nothing from such historical experience.

Christian Unitarians. Among those moving in this Humanist or Unitarian (or even Deist) direction were a number of Congregationalist pastors – concentrated heavily in the Boston area. In 1825 over a hundred of these pastors – mostly from New England – came together to form the American Unitarian Association – in part to undo the Calvinism that had earlier formed the foundations of the Congregationalist Churches of the region. Their goal was to bring Christianity more in line with the recent discoveries of science – and with simple Humanist logic that found much of the traditional Biblical claims of Christianity and its miraculous powers to be completely unbelievable.

Once again (again as in the late 1600s/early 1700s) the "more-enlightened" Christians were certain that in making these adjustments, they were strengthening the foundations of the Christian religion that underlay a fast-developing American society and culture.

Jefferson's Unitarianism. An individual to figure big in this rising Humanism/Unitarianism was former President Thomas Jefferson. In 1822 Jefferson wrote his friend Dr. Benjamin Waterhouse attacking the foundations of traditional Christianity, pointing out in particular the ancient apologist Athanasius and the more recent Calvin as "false shepherds" and "usurpers of the Christian name"

> *teaching a counter religion made up of the deliria of crazy imaginations, as foreign from Christianity as is that of Mahomet.*

Their blasphemies have driven thinking men into infidelity.

In that same letter Jefferson (who had compiled an updated Bible eliminating all the miracle stories and focusing only on the moral teachings of Scripture) professed that the simple doctrines of Jesus (to love the only God with all one's heart and one's neighbor as oneself) had been perverted by adding Platonizing doctrine (Jefferson did not like Plato very much either) which he claimed – quite incorrectly – was most evident in Calvinist dogma. But he was confident that such dark days of primitive Christianity were becoming a thing only of the past. Thus he states:

> *I rejoice that in this blessed country of free inquiry and belief, which has surrendered its creed and conscience to neither kings nor priests, the genuine doctrine of one only God is reviving, and I trust that there is not a young man now living in the United States who will not die a Unitarian.*

For those living in the comfort of a secure existence, such enlightened Humanism seemed to be beyond all serious question as the true path to knowledge and happiness. This was the true religion of any enlightened person after all.

The Transcendentalists. Another, somewhat later (1840s), example of this development was that of the Transcendentalists – who pursued the quest for God – not through the way of Christ, but rather as a higher order of "pure thought." They sought, through mental discipline, to be broad in their intellectual reach, encompassing a variety of refined efforts to embrace God both in a oneness with nature and a sense of reaching beyond even the natural. They sought to be as fully human as possible, so as to find God as fully as possible. They too tended toward lofty communalism in the hope of reaching beyond the coarse nature of selfishness and sin, to find a more perfect human harmony.

Ralph Waldo Emerson, Henry David Thoreau, and Amos Bronson Alcott (father of novelist Louisa May Alcott) were neighbors in Concord Massachusetts who set the pace of Transcendentalism. Thoreau attempted to find serenity in two years (1845-1847) of relative isolation in the woods at Walden Pond, Alcott in his experimental school in Concord, and Emerson in his many philosophical lectures and writings.

The earthier intelligentsia. But for those less comfortable, where life's dangers were not guaranteed to be manageable, where life could suddenly take a violent turn (hunger, disease, Indian massacre) such Humanist rationality seemed as absurd to hardened Realists as a personal trust in a God of miracles seemed absurd to the Humanists. Indeed, even Nathaniel Hawthorne, who once was a neighbor of the Concord Transcendentalists, eventually became something of an anti-Transcendentalist, tending to delve more into the darkness of the religious ethical issues of his era in his stories *The Scarlet Letter* (1850) and *The House of the Seven Gables* (1851). Likewise, Edgar Allan Poe could be just as abrasive in his dislike of the romantic optimism of Transcendentalism.

The rekindling of America's Christian fires. The highly individualistic but also highly isolated life on the part of those Americans that lived well away from the comforts of the East produced among Westerners a hunger for personal meaning within the context of community – membership in larger society being a rare but well-appreciated commodity. Most frequently this took the form of huge gatherings whenever a local Christian revivalist appeared in the region. Thousands would turn out to spend a week at an improvised encampment listening to an array of preachers, singing and dancing, shouting and fainting, and having a thoroughly good time.

Particularly prominent in this matter were the Baptists and Methodists (the latter a denomination that had only recently come over to America from Wesley's England) – both groups very different in style from the sober worship styles of the Congregationalists of New England, the Presbyterians of the Middle Colonies and the Episcopalians of the South. Unlike the latter groups whose pastors generally came to the pulpit by way of years of college and seminary training, the preachers of this newer group of Christians were simply common folks who received a call from God to take up preaching directly, without having to go through all the formal schooling of the older Christian denominations.

These new preachers fit more closely the democratic mood of the Jacksonian era and were able to relate better to life on the frontier – where they gathered huge numbers of spiritually hungry Americans to their flocks with their frequent open-air preaching.

Asbury – and the frontier revival. Francis Asbury had been one of the two Methodist pastors who had remained behind in colonial America when, at the outbreak of the American rebellion in 1776, Methodism's founder John Wesley called his pastors (part of the Anglican episcopal system and thus answerable to Wesley as their bishop) back to England. But after the war Wesley ordained Asbury as one of his two American superintendents (essentially a Methodist bishop) – and Asbury began to take up revivalist preaching alongside his supervisory duties (1784-1816).

Asbury's travels and preaching on the widening American frontier by becoming himself one of his Methodist "circuit riders" soon became legendary: in the face of cold, heat, hunger and angry Indians, he traveled some 275,000 miles to deliver 16,000 sermons – helping to increase the size of the Methodist denomination from 1,200 to 214,000 members and bringing 700 ordained preachers to join him in this work.

The African Methodist Episcopal (AME) and AME Zion churches. A similar revival was to come among America's free Black population, most notably in urban America, most notably in the American North. In Philadelphia Richard Allen and David Coker (inspired by Asbury) set up a number of new Methodist churches, and were able to call their first national conference in 1816, the startup of another large American denomination. Meanwhile in New York City, James Varick was able to do much the same in bringing an expanding Zion church into the Methodist union. The two Black denominations would compete quite successfully in bringing the free-Black world more widely and intimately into Christianity.

Thus it was that the Methodists – and the independently-operating Baptists – grew to be the most numerous Christian groups in America.

Finney – and the "Second Great Awakening." But some of the Presbyterians also saw the challenge and took up a similar path. But as in the 1740s, this would create a deep division within the denomination between the New School, supporting the revivalist trend, and the Old School, disdainful of the emotionalism of this trend.

Among these Presbyterian New School revivalists was Charles Grandison Finney, who in New York during the mid-1820s to mid-1830s developed a quite precise revival style that others would pattern their own revivals after. Indeed, upstate or rural New York became the scene of wave after wave of revivals such as his – so much so that Finney himself termed the region the "burned-over district."*

A more favorable term for the same event was the Second Great Awakening – actually a period of Christian revival that began slowly after 1790, gathered momentum in the early 1800s, and reached something of a peak in the 1830s and 1840s, slowing down finally in the late 1850s.

Christian-mission societies. But even Old School Christianity had its

---

*Actually much the same level of activity was going on elsewhere, especially along the American frontier to the West. But Finney's "burned over district" did indeed produce some very exceptional religious developments.

own way of contributing to the "awakening" sweeping America. Notable in this regard was the growth of a large number of interdenominational Christian societies that sought to set Christianity to the task of taking on social problems – to provide Christian answers to such issues as poverty, illiteracy, and just plain ignorance of the Christian gospel. Working even across denominational lines (Congregationalist, Presbyterian, Dutch Reformed, Baptist, Methodist, etc.), Christians were very active in forming such groups as The American Bible Society (to help every American family find itself in possession of a Bible), the American Sunday School Union (to develop Biblical literacy among the children of all social classes), the American Tract Society (to put in the hands of everyone the simplest explanation of and call to Christianity), the American Anti-Slavery Society, and the American Temperance League (both fighting particular social evils). These volunteer organizations became a vital part of the American social-cultural dynamic that developed in accompaniment with America's spread across the North American continent.

Christian colleges. From the time of the Puritans' early settlement in America, higher education was a matter of vital necessity, not only in training the pastors who would be expected to lead the Christian communities the Puritans were establishing but also in training others who would be entering such fields as the law, business and finance, and teaching – all vocations greatly vital to the self-sustaining life of their communities. And even the South caught on to the importance of founding new educational institutions. Thus Christian America founded Harvard, Yale, William and Mary, Princeton, Georgetown, New Brunswick and Andover Theological Seminaries – as well as colleges such as Mount Holyoke, designed to give women the same opportunity at a higher education. In fact, in the period between the founding of the colonies and the mid-1800s, over 500 colleges were founded by America's various denominations. This too was a key part of Christian America's larger mission to be a Light to the Nations.

Perfectionism. In any case, behind all this religious "awakening" was something very much of the spirit of the Jacksonian times. Americans had a strong sense of personal destiny – an urgency to accomplish some greater work, to move forward, to fulfill some nobler purpose in life. Life was viewed as a challenge, one faced with many obstacles, many of them deficiencies in the people themselves, personal sins that needed cleansing, that required some act of purification that would clear the way for them to move toward some personal victory. Christian revivals offered exactly just such an opportunity for "getting things right with God."

Millennialism.* Empowering this activity was an abiding sense that history was about to find completion in the form of the second coming of Christ and his final judgment of all people, saints and sinners – a widespread sentiment of the times due in part to the horrible 1837-1841 Depression which undercut severely the American belief that life moved forward along largely logical lines. Surely this grand catastrophe pointed to the ultimate and thus final judgement of God – in the form of the long-awaited coming of Christ as the supreme judge of life on earth.

Consequently, many Americans came easily to the conclusion that they were approaching the millennium described in Scripture (Revelation) in which all must be made perfect in preparation for that coming of Christ. Sinful behavior needed to be corrected, both for society as well as the individual. Perfectionism or social reform was thus urgent. The institution of slavery in particular needed to be abolished – immediately. Alcoholism, which was rampant on the Frontier and in the workshops back East, needed to be curbed. Caring for the poor became a priority. Injustices of whatever variety needed to be addressed – the treatment of women being one of the issues taken up by a new generation of feminists.

Social experiments accompanied this mood – in which varieties of utopian programs were put in place to answer the challenge of the times. Most of these failed miserably. But failure did not seem to discourage others from trying.

William Miller – and the Seventh-Day Adventists. One group (the "Millerites") that survived failure were the followers of the Baptist preacher William Miller, who gathered on hilltops and rooftops in March, again in April and finally in October of 1844 in anticipation of the rapture, when they expected to greet Jesus as he came to earth. A "Great Disappointment" occurred when Jesus failed to show up on schedule, causing his following to break up.

But others picked up Miller's millennial vision, importantly the female

---

*A belief that the coming of Christ will usher in a 1,000-year Golden Age, a long period of time prior to the Day of Judgment, and the establishment of a New Heaven and a New Earth.

Actually, there was something of a big divide within this community of Christian Evangelicals or Millennialists. "Progressive" Christians tended to be "Postmillennialist" in believing that the thousand-year reign of Christ (the Millennium) would come only after a fully successful conversion of the world had taken place, a matter requiring ever greater effort of Christians to bring Christianity and its civilizing qualities to the world. The "Premillennialists" on the other hand believed that only a time of great tribulation (not human progress) would announce the arrival of the Millennium – requiring of the faithful spiritual vigilance, rather than the progressive social works of the Postmillennialists.

prophet and religious writer Ellen G. White, who cultivated a huge group of followers that would eventually take the name "Seventh Day Adventists." They took up perfectionist ways in the avoidance of alcohol, meat, and other foods, advocating instead vegetarianism.* From this group would eventually come such famous breakfast food producers as Kellogg and Post.

Joseph Smith and the Mormons. But perhaps the most amazing phenomenon to come out of the burned-over district of New York during this period were the Mormons or Latter-Day Saints, a group that followed the prophecies and teachings of Joseph Smith. As a teenager (early 1820s) Smith had a number of visions, the most important being a visit by the Angel Moroni, who he claimed directed him to a place where he uncovered a book of golden plates on which were written in some form of "reformed Egyptian" the story of the ancient Jews and of Christ and his visit to America. Using a special technique, he translated what he saw written there by ancient authors (Mormon being chief among them) – which in 1830 Smith published in English translation as the *Book of Mormon*.† That same year he formed his first congregation as the Church of Christ, teaching his followers the new doctrines, and then sending them west to spread the new revelation as "Latter-Day Saints."

Ultimately, like the Puritans of old, Smith wanted to found a community that could live to the high principle of (his version) of the Christian religion – and moved with thousands of followers first to Ohio, then to Missouri, and – being driven from there – he and 8,000 of his followers moved across the Mississippi River back to Illinois. But they ran into trouble with the locals there as well, and in 1844 he and his brother were killed by an angry mob.

Smith's movement splintered into several distinct factions – although Brigham Young was able to take the lead of the largest of these factions – and move them west to Utah (1847) where they could then build their new Zion without upsetting any neighbors. But eventually even there, conflict would erupt from time to time between the Mormons and those who eventually came West to build homes and farms of their own.

---

*Vegetarianism was a common trend among the millennialists, who believed that meat-eating made man a brutal beast.

†The book states that an ancient tribe of Israel had managed to get themselves to the New World, as well as Jesus himself, who appeared to the Indians soon after his Resurrection, producing a period of exceptional peace among the Indians lasting several centuries.

CHAPTER FIVE

CIVIL WAR (1861-1865) AND RECOVERY

✶ ✶ ✶

GATHERING STORM CLOUDS

The Second Great Awakening served to deepen tensions over the matter of slavery – spurring the growth in number of Abolitionists. They sought to have slavery outlawed everywhere within the country, fearing that not to do so would sooner or later bring God's wrath upon the nation. But the Abolitionists of the 1830s and 1840s were way ahead of the rest of the country (not to mention the South) in their thinking about slavery. The country's leaders even passed a gag rule in 1836 preventing anyone from bringing the matter up for discussion in Congress.

Cultural variations. But the deep split dividing the North and the South merely continued to deepen as the years progressed. The two societies headed even further away from each other in terms of everything from economics to social and cultural dynamics, not to mention politics. The South seemed unable to get away from its dependency on cotton farming – that being such a central part of the image of highly idealized life on the Southern plantation. But actually, for most of the poor Whites – not to mention enslaved Blacks – their lives were tough and with virtually no possibility of improving things in any way. Passivity was thus the key to survival in much of the South. But the North was robust, even a bit on the wild side as it attacked life. And it was made even more vibrant with the rapid expansion of the population of the North, both in numbers and in outreach. Thus it was that the South was feeling highly defensive as it found itself being left behind in the country's growth.

Bitter debate over the admission of new states. With Texas knocking at the door for admission to the Union as a new (slave) state, whatever compromise had been achieved in the 1820 Missouri Compromise now became ineffectual, for Texas was a huge addition to the geographical picture of the Union. But then also California wanted admission as a new state.

But much of it too lay below the Mason-Dixon Line, yet would be clearly admitted to the Union as a Free State. Thus tempers flared in Congress as debate dragged on over the westward expansion of the American Union.

Another "compromise" in the face of bitter identity politics. Naturally there developed considerable ire among Southerners when in 1849 California (with key sections well south of Clay's original North-South dividing line) applied for statehood as a free state. But once again Clay stepped forward to offer a compromise, admitting California into the Union. But also, in defining new Western territories as future states – such as Nebraska and New Mexico – he proposed the idea that these states should be allowed to decide for themselves whether they would be slave or free. That seemed fair enough at the time – but in fact merely shifted the controversy to the states themselves, producing in some cases terrible in-fighting (a prelude to the Civil War). To appease the Abolitionists, Clay called on Congress to regulate interstate trade in slaves. But to appease the South, he also directed the North to send back to the South any slaves attempting to escape to the free-state North. So supposedly Clay was offering a balanced program of partial support for both the pro-slavery South and the increasingly Abolitionist North.

Actually, the willingness of moderates to accept this compromise only deepened the bitterness of the growing wings of extremism in both the North and the South. Abolitionists were outraged at the idea of having to send fugitive slaves back to their Southern masters – and Southern radicals began to talk more frequently about simply pulling out of the Union.

Ultimately the Whig Party would pay dearly for its efforts to follow this path of compromise, one which merely deepened the sectional divide within the country. In the 1850 elections the Democratic Party, claiming to bridge this sectional gap, completely routed the Whig position in Congress and in 1852 did the same with the presidency. Democratic Party candidate Franklin Pierce was elected President as a "Northerner of Southern principles." And thus at this point the nation hoped that with a moderate Democrat in the White House, the country could now move on quietly past the slavery issue.

Harriet Beecher Stowe's *Uncle Tom's Cabin*. However, the publication of Harriet Beecher Stowe's *Uncle Tom's Cabin* (1851-1852) would keep the issue in front of the nation, where it would burn American passions deeply. It depicted the suffering and bravery of American slaves so touchingly that the idea of ever sending Blacks that escaped Southern slavery back to the South became virtually unthinkable to a Northerner, thus outraging the South because of the North's unwillingness to obey the law (the Fugitive Slave Act of 1850).

The "Underground Railroad." Then to infuriate the South even more, rumors began to grow about a secret program that was designed to help Blacks escape to the North, or even to Canada. Actually, it was neither underground nor a railroad but instead a series of safe houses along a trail of escape which provided support and guidance for those fortunate enough to break from their bondage. How extensive it was remained a great mystery, the numbers possibly expanded greatly – by the South to stress how terrible this violation of their "property rights" happened to be, and by the North, eager to show how widespread was the support in the North in the freeing of Southern slaves.

Thus it was that the spirit of Abolitionism finally took hold widely of hearts across the North... at the same time that it spurred a growing resolve throughout the South to simply depart from the Union.

Nebraska – and "Bleeding Kansas." Things finally came to full violence with the question of what to do about the fast-developing Western territory of Nebraska – and how it might join the Union, whether slave or free. This matter was so divisive that it split the huge Democratic Party into two contending wings (the Whigs had all but disappeared at this point).

Ultimately the decision was made (1854) to divide the huge territory into two sections, Nebraska to the North and Kansas to the South. They would also repeal the Missouri Compromise which would have automatically made both states free – and instead, according to the new "compromise," let the two new territories themselves decide how they might enter the Union, slave or free. Again, at the time, this sounded like a very good idea, letting the locals rather than Washington make this vital decision. Actually this decision made the situation worse – far, far worse.

For the northern portion or the new Nebraska, this decision presented no particular problem – as it clearly was inhabited by "Free-Soilers" opposed to slavery. But the southern portion or Kansas was another matter – with the inhabitants in the northern part of that territory also Free-Soilers, but the inhabitants to the south supportive of the slave option. Thus the new "compromise" immediately split Kansas itself into two warring factions – with two legislatures (one at Lecompton and one at Topeka) and all sorts of militias supporting one side or the other of the slavery issue (as were almost most all of the Kansas newspapers). And Americans began to rush to Kansas to increase the size (and thus vote) of one side or the other: pro-slavery "Border Ruffians" and anti-slavery "Jayhawkers."

An example of how savage this Kansas rivalry became was in the action in 1856 involving John Brown and his family. He and his sons killed five pro-slavery farmers – in revenge for the sacking of Lawrence by pro-slavery forces. In return, several hundred pro-slavery forces attacked

Civil War (1861-1865) and Recovery

Brown's hometown of Osawatomie, killing two of Brown's sons (and others) and sacking and burning the town.

Thus turning the matter over "democratically" for the citizens of Kansas themselves to decide merely escalated the problem into full-scale guerrilla-style warfare. Killing, looting, burning and ravaging the homes and farms of "Bleeding Kansas" now became common across the territory.

In short, by 1856, the American Civil War had already begun in Kansas.

The election of 1856. With the Whig Party gone, a number of parties – plus factions taking a stand on the slavery issue – took the political stage. The newly formed Republican Party (no connection with Jefferson's earlier Republicans, but forerunners of today's Republicans) basically took up the Whig cause – but could not get together on which candidate should represent the party in the presidential election that year. Ultimately one group nominated General Frémont and another group nominated Millard Fillmore, former President (1850 1853) when General Taylor, who had been elected President in 1848, died a year into his presidency. So also the Democrats found themselves deeply divided and ended up dropping Pierce and choosing Pennsylvanian James Buchanan, when Illinois Senator Stephen Douglas finally threw his vote to Buchanan on the 17th ballot. Buchanan had been away serving as American Ambassador to England and therefore had no record one way or the other about the deep split tearing at the country. Voted to office as President in the 1856 election, President Buchanan would try to stay above the battle – which meant only that the North-South split would deepen as national leadership tried to look away from the growing problem.

The Dred Scott Decision of 1857. Instead, the Supreme Court found itself taking the crisis head on with its decision concerning the return to a Southern master of a former slave, Dred Scott. Scott had accompanied his master to the North, been sold and resold several times – and after a lengthy residence in the North was being forced to return to the South. Scott ultimately (in his first civil suit in 1846) claimed that he (and his wife and daughter) had earned the right to freedom as longtime Northern residents. But after a lengthy process of multiple court hearings on the matter, the Supreme Court, led by pro-slavery Chief Justice Roger B. Taney, in 1857 ruled in favor of his latest master John Sanford, claiming that the Constitution was only intended for Whites and, since slaves were actually property, Congress had no authority to take property away from anyone – nor also had any authority to grant citizenship to Blacks, who were by God's own decree intended to be a race perpetually in service to the Whites.

Southerners were elated by the decision, claiming that under Taney's ruling, slavery could not be forbidden anywhere within the Union, North as well as South. The North on the other hand was furious at the ruling. In all, Taney's decision did not resolve the question – but instead only deepened the bitter feelings separating the American North and South.

It was also a preview of how the Supreme Court would, from time to time (but with increasing frequency), take upon itself the task of deciding exactly how the laws of the nation should be read and understood, in accordance with the various justices' ideological makeup, of course.

The Panic of 1857. The Dred Scott Decision also made it clear that the Western states were now to be brought into the Union as a decision of the people of those states themselves. This in turn meant that fierce battles (like the one going on in Kansas) would most likely result – something most people chose to avoid. Consequently, once again land values in the West collapsed as people backed away from Western land purchases – leaving private investors and banks holding worthless land titles – which in turn caused bank panic and collapse of the world of investment. But this crisis hit almost solely in the North – the South not being really part of the world of financial speculation. The very fact that the South escaped this crisis seemed to Southerners to confirm what they already supposed, namely that the Southern life and culture (slaves and all) was vastly superior to the Northern way of life – and that they were ready to defend that life and culture to the death. And indeed, Southerners would be called on soon to do just that.

Revolt at Harpers Ferry (October 1859). Semi-crazy John Brown (and his remaining sons) decided to spark an event intended to lead to a massive slave uprising in the South – when he and a group of 20 followers raided the U.S. military depot at Harpers Ferry to grab its ammunition and supplies. But ultimately no slave rebellion took place. Instead U.S. Colonel Robert E. Lee surrounded the Brown party – killing ten of the group in the process. Brown and four others were tried and executed for this ill-fated raid. Overall, the call to the slaves to revolt made Brown the very personification of evil that Southerners saw in the North. But in the North, he became something of a hero, serving the greatest of all human causes: freeing the slaves.

Lincoln's election (1860). The determining event in the move of the South to full withdrawal from the Union was the election of Abraham Lincoln to the U.S. Presidency in November of 1860. Two years earlier, in public debates for the position of Illinois Senator conducted between the Democratic Party Congressional leader Stephen Douglas and the new Republican Party's candidate, Abraham Lincoln, the subject had focused heavily on the issue of slavery – with Lincoln taking the much stronger position against slavery. Very impressive was the presentation of this "country boy" Lincoln. However, a Democratic Party majority in the Illinois Assembly ultimately chose Douglas to represent the state in the U.S. Senate. But so impressive was Lincoln in his speech delivered at the Cooper Union (New York City, February 1860) in his stand on not just slavery but a wide range of issues impacting the country, that the Illinois Republicans got fully behind him as candidate for the U.S. presidency. And it took only three ballots at the Republican National Convention that May to put Lincoln ahead of William Seward and Salmon Chase in the selection of that party's presidential candidate. And in November Lincoln was elected as the nation's sixteenth President: 1.87 million votes for Lincoln, 1.38 million for Douglas, 850 thousand for Breckinridge and 589 thousand for a fourth candidate, John Bell – but an absolute majority of the electoral vote, 180 votes for Lincoln to his opponents' combined total of 123 votes.

Abraham Lincoln. This new president was a man shaped by tragedy. He lost his mother at an early age, lived under the direction of a disapproving father, grew up in an environment of tough poverty, and would himself lose two of his children to death, one even while serving in the White House as U.S. president. But he armed himself against depression by a highly developed sense of humor. He also possessed a most singular perspective on life, one that seemed to show up in the stories and tales that constantly shaped his conversations with those around him.

As already noted, he served briefly as a captain in the Illinois militia during the Black Hawk War (1832), gaining some sense of what wars are really all about. However, his venture into the business world (also 1832) did not bring him success. He at that point ran for a position in the Illinois General Assembly, but just did not have the background to impress voters outside of his own precinct. But he was a voracious learner, and decided to teach himself the law, and became an excellent lawyer.

With a second attempt, he was finally elected to serve on the Illinois state legislature (1834-1846). He then went on to serve as a member of the Whig Party in the House of Representatives in Congress (1847-1849), though he had promised to serve in Washington only one term. He thus returned to his law practice in the Illinois state capital at Springfield, presuming that his political career was over.

But his Southern-bred aristocrat (Kentucky) and highly strong-willed wife, Mary Todd, had plans for him other than his political retirement! But he was also touched deeply by the slavery issue – and what it was doing to the country – as the nation fought over the Kansas-Nebraska Act. And thus in 1854 and then again in 1858 he found himself running for the position of U.S. Senator as an Illinois candidate of the newly formed Republican Party. Indeed, in the Republican Party's 1856 national convention, he came in a close second for the nomination as the party's vice-presidential candidate. And thus it was that his national career got up and running.

Now, as newly elected U.S. President, Lincoln had facing him the deepest crisis the country had experienced since its revolt against King George a century earlier. Many Americans wondered how exactly Lincoln would face this explosive issue of slavery and the probable breakup of the Union, issues that so many before him had done everything possible to avoid.

But Lincoln was a man of incredible talent, a talent needed greatly by the nation at this point. Lincoln was steady, strong and very wise in personal character. From the very start, the wisdom of Lincoln was evidenced in the way he shaped his new presidential administration, by bringing onto his cabinet his strongest political rivals[*] – such as William Seward, Salmon Chase and Edward Bates. He knew the importance of uniting all the major pro-Union leaders, in order to take on successfully the huge challenges ahead.

At first these political dignitaries tended to be contemptuous of him and his "country boy" ways![†] But gradually they all (except Chase, whom Lincoln finally moved onward in appointing him Chief Justice of the Supreme Court) came to see Lincoln's true political genius, and moved to full support of him as their president.

✶ ✶ ✶

SECESSION AND WAR (1861-1865)

Almost immediately upon the announcement of the results of the 1860 presidential elections, South Carolina announced that it would be seceding from the Union. Soon Mississippi, Florida, Alabama, Georgia, Louisiana and Texas did the same. In early February (1861) they met in Montgomery

---

[*]Doris Kearns Goodwin termed it *A Team of Rivals* in making it the title of her Simon & Schuster 2005 Pulitzer Prize-winning book.

[†]Seward, supposing Lincoln to be something of a naïve country boy, at first proposed to Lincoln to have him turn all real powers of the presidency over to Seward himself. And then Seward proposed a bizarre foreign policy in dealing with the South, all of which Lincoln politely ignored as he moved steadily ahead with his own policies for dealing with the rising crisis.

(Alabama) and agreed on the creation of a loose Confederation of Southern states – with Jefferson Davis as the provisional Confederation President.

Lincoln – and Davis. In contrast to his new adversary, Jefferson Davis, Lincoln had only his limited war experience in the Black Hawk War, and no formal military training. Davis however was a graduate of West Point and a commanding officer (colonel) in the Mexican-American War. But Lincoln had a keen mind for strategy, a deep insight into the character of others, and an awareness that he needed wise war counsel – which he got from the elderly Winfield Scott and eventually from his war cabinet. And Lincoln thought through objectives better than the majority of the military men serving under him – who tended to think mostly in terms of battle strategies – designed to win battles. Lincoln however thought in terms of war strategies (economics, diplomacy, ideology, morale – as well as military engagements) – designed to win a war.

At the same time, the very looseness of the Confederacy required as a matter of extreme necessity a strong, commanding hand to hold it together. Thus in the struggle of the South to secure its independence militarily, Davis and his administration would have to take on almost unlimited powers.

Lincoln's Christian faith. But there was more to Lincoln than just profound political-social wisdom. Lincoln was a man of deep spiritual character, founded not on human support but instead on Divine support. Like Washington before him, Lincoln was fully aware of the huge trust that had been placed on his shoulders. He knew that thousands, even hundreds of thousands, of young men would die because of the decisions that he himself would have to make. Previous presidents had shrunk back in the face of this growing social division – precisely because of the obvious social costs involved in finally resolving the matter.

Lincoln of course would have his supporters. He would also have his detractors – and not just in the South. He even had this problem at home – a wife who very soon tired of the stress his position placed on their family (she wanted Lincoln just to drop the war effort so that their family could get back to normal).

We cannot say that Lincoln going into office was a man of deep Christian faith. But we can certainly say that as the war progressed, Lincoln found himself turning more and more to the very special support that God provided him during the very dark days of the war (a darkness that lasted almost up until the war's very last days). Ultimately it was his deep faith that kept him going – when others would have quit. His faith, not human support, is what kept his leadership of the country strong during these most trying of times. It was indeed Lincoln's deep Christian faith, even more than his profound political wisdom, that made Lincoln the truly great man that the world would eventually come to appreciate – appreciate as one of America's greatest presidents (some might even say the greatest of all).

Southern or Dixie "nationalism." At the same time, holding the Confederacy together was mostly the powerful ingredient: fear – fear White Southerners had of their rapidly growing Black population (both free and slave). Consequently, the South became an oppressive land – whose laws and cultural vigilance tightened down on society. Free Blacks living in the South soon found themselves under the threat of being forced into slavery. And war fever in the South demanded that any Northern Blacks captured in battle (those not just killed outright), or simply captured as farm workers in the process of the Southern armies advancing across the land, would be carried off into Southern slavery. As both Jeff Davis and his Vice President Alexander Stephens put it, Blacks by their very inferior nature were intended by God to thrive only within the context of eternal servitude to the superior race of Whites. Enslavement of any and all Blacks was actually a necessary part of the advance of civilization. This credo was thus the real glue holding the Confederacy together.

1861: The first shots of battle. In April (1861) Southerners fired on the Federal Fort Sumter located in the harbor at Charleston, South Carolina, a grand act of defiance – ultimately forcing the Federal troops there to surrender when no support was able to reach them from the North. Lincoln now called on the states to take up arms in defense of the Union – Southern states of course refusing. The real question however was how the border states (Maryland, Tennessee, Kentucky, Missouri, etc.) would align themselves. At first even Virginia hesitated, leading Lincoln to call on General Robert E. Lee to head up the Federal or Union army. But when Virginia finally chose join the Confederacy, Lee turned down the request (he would eventually become the South's commanding general). Maryland was about to join the Confederacy – but Lincoln ordered Federal troops to occupy the state – so that the nation's capital at Washington, D.C., did not get cut off from the North. Tennessee soon joined the Confederacy – but Kentucky stayed cautiously neutral. And a deeply divided Missouri simply continued with its own civil war.

The strategies of war. As already pointed out in the section focused on America's war of independence in the 1770s and 1780s, the purpose of war is to get an adversary to stop doing – or even being – what it is that a society pursuing war finds detestable in the thoughts and behavior of that adversary.

For the South, the strategy was quite straight-forward: simply pull out of the Union, and then dare the North to try to do something about it. Were Southerners truly expecting the all-out war that Lincoln called the Union to? Possibly not.

For the North, the war was a much less straight-forward matter. Was it just about preserving the Union? Did it have to involve the highly contentious issue of slavery? Or was it ultimately all about slavery in the first place?

In short, there was by no means unity of purpose in the North, making Lincoln's job extremely difficult. Making Abolition the primary goal would undermine Lincoln's support in certain circles in the North – and likely drive the people (such as the Kentuckians) along the neutral border regions separating the North and the South into the arms of the South. It would also merely strengthen the resolve of the South to fight on. After all, the purpose of the war was to weaken the resolve of the Southern adversary – not harden it.

For the time being, at least in the initial stages of the war, Lincoln kept matters focused merely on breaking the resolve of the Confederate states to secede from the Union – to force them back into Union membership. To do this, he would have to break their ability to hold out against his efforts. His major strategy was simply to close down the Southern economy – by surrounding the entire region by land and sea with his army and navy, cutting off the South's ability to break out of this economic strangulation (the Anaconda Strategy) in order to sell the cotton that its dream-world so completely depended on.

This was going to hurt the textile mills of the North, which depended heavily on the ability to acquire Southern cotton. But that would be merely one of the many costs of war. And Lincoln was aware that this war was going to be costly – very costly – on a number of fronts. But the Union had to be preserved at all costs – or there would be no very good future for any of the states, North or South.

But Lincoln was well aware of the fact that military challenges also stood before him. An invasion of the Southern heartland itself would ultimately be necessary to finally break the Southern will. But here is where he was handicapped. America's best officers tended to be Southern, not Northern – well experienced from recent service in the Mexican-American War. Sadly for Lincoln, his most capable general, Winfield Scott, was growing old and would soon have to be replaced by younger blood. But finding an equally capable replacement would be a trying matter for Lincoln – who would have to go through the less-than-impressive service of a number of commanding officers until finally (roughly two years into the war) he came up with the talent (Grant, Sherman, Thomas, Sheridan and others) capable of handling this enormous military challenge.

Thus at first the North seemed outclassed by the Southern armies. At the first major battle, Bull Run (July 1861, just south of D.C.), the Northern armies were routed – and the good D.C. citizens who had come out to watch the battle as if it were some kind of sporting event, found themselves fleeing back to the safety of the capital (itself well protected by a ring of forts surrounding the city).

By the end of 1861 it became quite apparent that there was going to be no quick end to this growing civil war.

1862: Bloody stalemate. 1862 saw some great but ultimately inconclusive battles fought along the Mississippi River; in the Chesapeake Bay (the battle of the strange armor-clad ships *Monitor* and *Merrimac*); in Eastern Virginia in June and July when the pompous Union General George McClellan proved to be more interested in winning minor battles that advanced his political career than in advancing the North's cause of winning the war; again at Bull Run in August, which ended in something of a bloody stalemate costly to both sides; at Antietam in September when Lee attempted (unsuccessfully) to take the battle to the North into Pennsylvania; and finally in December at Fredericksburg (Virginia) when the Union effort to take a well-defended Confederate position in the cliffs above the town turned into a bloody disaster for the North.

1863: The North begins to dominate. 1863 started out even worse for the North when a second attempt was made in January to take Fredericksburg – ending up just as badly as the December attempt. Meantime, Lincoln was having a very difficult time of it keeping the North in the war.

Resistance to the draft (which both North and South had instituted in order to keep their ranks full) turned violent in New York City when Irish immigrants discovered that in applying for citizenship they had also signed themselves up for the draft – at a time when wealthier Americans could buy their way out of the draft. To the Irish this smacked of the treatment they had received from the English upper class who dominated their lives back in Ireland. They were livid. Troops finally had to be called in to help the police put down the rebellion.

Also, a group labeled "Copperheads," headed up by the politically ambitious Clement Vallandigham, had been working fervently to deepen further an anti-war mood growing in the North. Vallandigham was ultimately forced to escape to Canada. But Lincoln was well aware that this would hardly be the end of the growing anti-war fever infecting the North.

Civil War (1861-1865) and Recovery

Vicksburg and Gettysburg. But finally, two major events broke in clear Northern favor on virtually the same day, the 4th of July, 1863 – the news adding tremendously to the country's (the North's anyway) national holiday! The Rebel (Southern) position along the Mississippi River had been cleared earlier by Union General Ulysses S. Grant – except for the strategic site atop huge cliffs towering over the river at Vicksburg. Grant had been trying since January all sorts of maneuvers to bring down this last Mississippi stronghold – and finally on the 4th of July brought Vicksburg to surrender – and sent the news to Lincoln to give him finally something to cheer about.

But also on that same day ended finally the four-day battle at Gettysburg (Pennsylvania) which had erupted when Union forces stopped Lee's Confederate army in its second attempt to take the war into Union territory (Lee had been hoping to encourage the growing movement in the North of simply quitting the war effort and letting the South go on its way with its slaves). It was a great victory for the North. But once again, the commanding Union General, George Meade, decided to let his troops rest from their exhausting victory – and consequently let an even more exhausted Lee escape to the South – to fight another day. This inevitably led Lincoln to replace Meade with the tireless and relentless Grant.

At this point, with two key victories and a truly strategic Grant at the head of the Union armies, the fortunes of war began to turn decidedly in favor of the North.

Meanwhile Northern and Southern forces clashed repeatedly at the front along the Tennessee River in the middle of the states. The battles began as another Southern offensive – but instead resulted in a very costly stalemate at Chickamauga (September) and a rout of the Southern troops at Chattanooga (November), forcing Southern General Longstreet to have to give up his effort to take Knoxville from the North.

1864: The South under siege. 1864 turned out to be a grand disaster for the South. Grant led Union forces into Virginia – fighting battle after battle against Lee's troops, neither side willing to give up (Grant would not break off his effort to allow his men to rest – except in one instance, which he would regret and learn from not to repeat). Thus Lee was forced constantly to give a bit of ground at each battle in order not to be outflanked and surrounded by Grant's larger forces. Eventually Grant made a wide swing around Lee's forces who were attempting to protect the city of Richmond and instead put the town of Petersburg below Richmond under Union assault. But Petersburg proved quite defiant – and the battle there seemed to settle into a stalemate.

Meanwhile Union General William Tecumseh Sherman was ordered to slice through the middle of the South, starting at the Union position in Tennessee and swinging south from there to Atlanta – which the Union forces were able to take in September after a long summer-time assault on this key city in Georgia. From there they then headed southeast (November-December) to the town of Savannah on Georgia's coast, Sherman's troops cutting a 60-mile wide swath of destruction along the way – in order to break the spirit of Southern resistance.

Lincoln re-elected (November 1864). Lincoln was facing another national election in November that year – quite aware that no president had been reelected since 1832. But the fortunes of war had clearly by election day turned in the North's favor – and Lincoln's Republican Party was quite clear in its political goal: unconditional surrender of the Confederacy and a constitutional amendment abolishing slavery everywhere within the U.S. Thus it was that Lincoln overwhelmingly defeated his Democratic Party opponent, the self-important Union General McClellan.

1865: The Collapse of the South. Once in control of Savannah (Christmas 1864), Sherman turned his army and headed it north through the Carolinas, again burning and pillaging as it went – to arrive at a besieged Petersburg from the south. Very little Southern opposition at this point seemed to block Sherman's path.

Lincoln's 2nd inaugural address (March 1865). At Lincoln's ceremony inaugurating his second term in office, Lincoln presented the nation with an address (found today etched on the north wall of the Lincoln Memorial in D.C.), focusing the entire second half of the speech on the role of God and his judgement in shaping past events and future responsibilities – and thus the necessity of all Americans moving ahead together to bind up the nation's wounds and get on with the larger call by God himself to greater things as a nation.

At first his address surveyed the war experience that the nation had gone through – and God's hand in the matter:

> *If we shall suppose that American Slavery is one of those offences which, in the providence of God, must needs come, but which, having continued through His appointed time, He now wills to remove, and that He gives to both North and South, this terrible war, as the woe due to those by whom the offence came, shall we discern therein any departure from those divine attributes which the believers in a Living God always ascribe to Him?*

Civil War (1861-1865) and Recovery

> *Fondly do we hope – fervently do we pray – that this mighty scourge of war may speedily pass away. Yet, if God wills that it continue, until all the wealth piled by the bond man's two hundred and fifty years of unrequited toil shall be sunk, and until every drop of blood drawn with the lash, shall be paid by another drawn with the sword, as was said three thousand years ago, so still it must be said "the judgments of the Lord, are true and righteous altogether."*

But he then turned to this matter of the task facing the nation, one to which God had called all Americans:

> *With malice toward none; with charity for all; with a firmness in the right, as God gives us to see the right, let us strive on to finish the work we are in; to bind up the nation's wounds; to care for him who shall have borne the battle, and for his widow, and his orphan – to do all which may achieve and cherish a just, and a lasting peace, among ourselves, and with all nations.*

This was another example of how Lincoln had developed the ability to persevere in the face of all this massive uncertainty and risk, simply by trusting that he was merely a servant of God himself. He made very clear his personal understanding that it was up to God – not Lincoln – to bring the true and the good to bear in this covenant nation that God himself had, centuries earlier, called into being.

Indeed, this was the kind of personal wisdom and spiritual strength that few American leaders after Lincoln would be able to match, even on a partial basis, a wisdom and spiritual strength matured out of having to face overwhelming obstacles, a wisdom and spiritual strength that had brought the Union through very, very dark times, to resolve finally a very, very divisive issue. Lincoln was truly a gift of God to the American nation.

April 9th: The collapse of the South's rebellion. While one Union army was smashing South through Alabama (destroying the last of the South's industrial capacity as it went) Lee's army was finding itself overrun in the East at Petersburg, forcing Lee to pull out of both Petersburg and Richmond. Lee was attempting to link up with other Confederate troops trying to escape further South – but instead found himself surrounded at Appomattox. Thus on April 9th, Lee surrendered himself and his army to Grant.

Although this did not mark the official end of the war (local skirmishes would continue for a while longer) – for all practical purposes the war was finally over.

April 14th: The assassination of Lincoln. Lincoln was already at work seeking ways to bring the nation back together – minus slavery. The 13th Amendment to the U.S. Constitution, ending slavery anywhere within the United States, had been ratified by the Senate all the way back in April of 1864 and in the House of Representatives at the end of January, just a few months earlier. It was yet to be submitted to the states – Northern only at that point – for their ratification. But the amendment was expected to be easily approved by the states.

As Lincoln had stated in his 2nd inaugural address, he was indeed looking for ways "to bind up the nation's wounds; . . . to do all which may achieve and cherish a just, and a lasting peace ..." That would not be an easy task, given the level of hatred still smoldering in many Northern hearts – and given the bitterness Southerners felt about their humiliating loss to the Unionists. However, achieving a just and lasting peace was where he was now directing all his efforts.

But success in that endeavor was not to be. On the night of April 14th the actor John Wilkes Booth was able to complete part of his plot to kill Lincoln and Grant while attending together the play Our American Cousin at Ford's Theater in Washington (but Grant had instead left to visit his children in New Jersey) – as well as Vice President Johnson and Secretary of State William Seward at their homes. Lincoln was shot in the back of the head, Booth escaped by leaping from the balcony to the stage and then fleeing the city. Lincoln died early the next morning. Meanwhile Seward was attacked and nearly killed the same night by another of the plotters, who after repeated attempts to stab Seward to death finally fled into the night when confronted by other members of Seward's family. Seward survived.

Booth was found with a co-conspirator in Virginia twelve days later, surrounded and shot. Arrests of other members of the plot soon followed. On July 7, four of the conspirators were hanged.

Taking stock of it all. And so the war was over: the South found itself desolate and the North simultaneously found itself in a condition of profound mourning. The whole thing had been a sad tragedy, pushed to monumental proportions by the inability or unwillingness of American leaders before Lincoln to confront the slavery issue directly.

It finally took not political reason, but war and devastation of monumental proportions to bring this burning issue to a resolution. But so often is this the case. Passion, not reason, plus the mysteries of circumstances seemingly beyond human control, quite frequently bring human crises to a resolution – not pretty, but well resolved.*

Most tragically of all, a Southern bullet had taken the life of the one person who could have healed the nation's wounds and brought the South back to life more quickly than turned out to be the actual case. As it was, that bullet left many in the North without pity for the South and its vast suffering – and left the South itself to begin a process of recovery that would take generations to complete. Such is the irony of history.

* * *

AMERICA RECOVERS (1865-1880)

"Reconstruction." With Lincoln's assassination, Vice President Andrew Johnson stepped into the presidency – hoping to pursue Lincoln's policy of Northern-Southern reconciliation. But he lacked the political leverage that Lincoln commanded – and found himself intensely opposed by the Northern Radicals – who were in no mood for reconciliation. Instead, they wanted the South to pay deeply for its rebellion – and they were intensely focused on demolishing entirely the South's traditional political culture. Johnson found himself vetoing bills coming out of a Congress dominated by the Radicals Thaddeus Stevens and Charles Sumner – only to have his veto overturned by a 2/3 vote in Congress. Then he vetoed the Congressional bill sponsoring the 14th Amendment affirming the legal equality of all Americans – except for Indians and Confederate rebels – forbidding the latter even from holding office anywhere in the U.S. government – or getting compensation for any loss of property (slaves) or even pensions for service in the Confederate army or government.

Johnson's veto of this last bill enraged the Radicals so deeply that Johnson lost all political footing with Congress. And in early 1868 the Radicals voted for his impeachment in the House of Representatives.† Ultimately, he avoided conviction when the Radicals came up one vote short of the 2/3 vote required for full conviction by the Senate. But from this point on, for the remaining two years in office, Johnson was totally

---

*Of the 2.6 million who had enlisted in the Union army and the 1 million in the Confederate army, 364 thousand Union and 260 thousand Confederate soldiers had died, and approximately 400 thousand each of Union and Confederate soldiers had been wounded for their respective causes.

†When he removed Radical Edwin Stanton from his position as Secretary of War, to replace him with Grant, he did so in violation of the 1867 Tenure of Office Act (of dubious Constitutionality!) enacted by Congress specifically to end Johnson's power to remove Lincoln's Cabinet appointments.

powerless in the face of a Radical Congress.

Slaves were already being freed as the Union armies moved through the South – although there really was no place for them to go (except follow the Union armies). With the end of the war the economic picture of the South was so bad that not only did newly freed Blacks have no real opportunity to get themselves established in the New South – but also neither did the Confederate soldiers who had to return to devastated farms – not to mention demolished plantations and pillaged towns and cities.

At first the South was simply governed by Union army officers – and Northern administrators sent South by the Freedmen's Bureau, individuals who arrived with their luggage (carpet bags) not only to take over local government but also to set up and run schools for the newly freed Blacks. This helped the Blacks (somewhat) adjust to their new lives of freedom, but intensified the hatred of poor Whites towards Blacks – as well as towards the Northern "carpetbaggers" whom they detested intensely. Soon local groups such as the Ku Klux Klan began to form up – to defend the traditional South against those attempting to overturn ("reconstruct") Southern culture. Things got very ugly fast.

The Grant presidency (1869-1877). In the 1868 elections the Republicans were quick to nominate war-hero Grant – whereas the Democrats dropped Johnson (the Republican Lincoln had selected the Democrat Johnson as part of his national coalition) and chose New York Governor Horatio Seymour – holding racist views that were not that far away from the views of many Northerners, concerned that Blacks were really not ready for full freedom. The election was actually quite close – and only the ability of Blacks to vote gave Grant enough votes to win the election.

The closeness of the election stirred the Republican majority in Congress to come up with the 15th Amendment making it illegal for a state to deprive a citizen of the right to vote because of "race, color or previous condition of servitude." As a condition for readmission to the Union, the last three holdout Southern states – Texas, Mississippi and Virginia – had to approve both the 14th and 15th Amendments – thus adding the 15th Amendment to the Constitution in 1870.

Scandal. But America was actually ready to move on to new things – or actually old things: making money. Scandals began to erupt in high places because of a new lax attitude concerning society's moral requirements – one of them being the 1869 James Fisk / Jay Gould gold scandal – when these two Wall Street tycoons attempted to acquire the majority of the nation's gold supply, make it scarce and thus more expensive, and consequently reap an enormous reward on the basis of this little ploy. Grant actually

Civil War (1861-1865) and Recovery

broke the Fisk-Gould project by releasing Federal holdings of gold – driving prices back down again.

Grant was actually not to blame for any of this – but there seemed to be no control over this atmosphere of cynical corruption hanging over the nation. Nonetheless people looked to the President for being in charge of the nation – and blamed him for letting this event occur in the first place.

In 1872 another scandal broke out when it was discovered that Federal money authorized to complete the Union Pacific / Central Pacific railroad across the West to San Francisco had been manipulated in a way to enrich a bank, Crédit Mobilier (but no relationship with the French bank of the same name), set up by Union Pacific director Thomas Durant. He was enriching himself and his cronies to the tune of tens of millions of dollars, until the operation was brought to light by the New York newspaper *Sun*, and the scandal caused railroad and bank stock to suddenly drop away. Once again Grant was blamed for having let things get so far out of hand – though he had no direct role in any of it.

Another scandal typical of the times arose out of the operations of the New York political machine, Tammany Hall, controlled by William "Boss" Tweed. Tweed not only controlled the city's immense patronage system but also much of that of the New York state itself, using his position to help Fisk and Gould in another of their schemes, the takeover of the Erie Railroad from another adventuresome individual, Cornelius Vanderbilt (who would develop his own vast economic empire) – through the issuing of fake stock. This would cost the New York taxpayers tens of millions of dollars (some say today as much as 100 million even in 1870 dollars) and made a number of Tammany Hall figures extremely rich.

Nonetheless, Grant survived the scandals – and was reelected to a second term as president in 1872 – just before the huge 1873 financial panic.

The 1873 Panic. Certainly Grant thought he was doing the nation a great favor when he tightened up on the nation's economy by "strengthening" the dollar – by removing readily available silver as a metallic standard for the dollar, leaving only scarce gold as the dollar's basis. This was timed with the collapse of a major brokerage firm, heavily involved in railroad stocks, which in turn brought down the Wall Street Stock Market. Then the economy simply folded in on itself as frightened customers rushed to their banks to withdraw their deposits before the crisis spread to their banks, actually precipitating just exactly that crisis itself. Bank after bank thus failed.

Grant refused to change his gold-only policy, believing the crisis to be only a temporary fluctuation in the economy (which certainly happens from time to time). But with very low liquidity caused by the gold-only strategy, investors were unable to get businesses back up and running – and the 1873 Panic lasted a full five years. And when the 1874 Congressional elections rolled around, the Republicans were driven from power.

The end of Reconstruction. With Democrats coming to power in Congress, the impetus for Southern Reconstruction slowed down greatly – certainly in the South itself where Democrats took control and did what they could to get things back to "normal." Then when the next Presidential elections rolled around (1876), the Republicans distanced themselves from Grant and chose Civil-War hero and post-war Ohio Governor Rutherford B. Hayes as their candidate. The Democrats chose the New York Governor, Samuel J. Tilden, who had become well known because of his crushing of the Tweed machine. The country thus had two good choices going into the election. The vote was so close between these two men that the election had to go to Congress for a final decision. On the basis of a number of compromise promises, Hayes was finally selected.

The Radicals' program of Reconstruction had depended entirely on the ability of a militarily victorious North to impose its Radical policies on the South through continuing military occupation. This policy of imposed "peace and social justice" presumably justified morally the North's program (in the eyes of the Radicals themselves anyway) – but did nothing to lay a moral basis for a post-war South that would of its own be willing to support such imposed changes. Thus when a huge increase in Indian wars in the American West forced U.S. troops to be pulled out of the South and be sent to the West, the Radical program collapsed completely in the South. What took its place was a deep bitterness reigning in the South, White against Black, Southerner against Northerner – a bitterness that would take a full century to finally get past.

* * *

THE BATTLE FOR THE WEST RESUMES

During the Civil War, the Indian Wars intensified – as Federal troops were pulled from the West to fight the Southern Confederacy. The Lakota (Sioux) in Minnesota for instance in 1862 attacked German settlements at New Ulm and Hutchinson, killing several hundred settlers, women and children as well as men – forcing Lincoln to send troops to the region to break Sioux power (arresting and hanging the leaders). Bitterness between Indians and Whites only intensified – leading to an unwarranted attack in late 1864 by Federal troops on a peaceful Cheyenne and Arapaho settlement at Sand

Creek (Colorado), with over a hundred Indians killed in the attack.

In the Southwest there was a huge effort to force Navajo and Apache tribes onto reservations in the bleak Pecos River region – bringing to notice and fame Indian-fighter Kit Carson – who finally broke the will of the Navajo to resist the move. He then in late 1864 turned on the Kiowas and Comanches who had been conducting bloody raids on White settlements in the Texas Panhandle region. At one point he found himself vastly outnumbered by several thousand warriors at the Battle of Adobe Walls (November) and was forced to retreat, but managed to inflict massive casualties on the Indians nonetheless. This battle proved to be a turning point in the Indian wars in the region – greatly undermining the power of the Kiowas and Comanches and ultimately bringing both tribes to sue for peace in 1865.

But alongside Kit Carson, the Indians could provide heroics of their own – such as the Apache raider Geronimo, whose small band of warriors seemed to be active everywhere in the West. Although finally forced onto the Apache reservation by U.S. military, Geronimo broke out several times between 1876 and 1886. Ultimately his name became so well known that he finally was featured in a number of Cowboy-and-Indian shows – even riding horseback in Teddy Roosevelt's inaugural parade in 1905!

Westward Ho! On they came – White men, women and children – by steamer or river barge (as far as the rivers would take them westward), then by wagon train, following trails set out by trail blazing frontiersmen – and then by train as the American railroads pushed West and Southwest deep into Indian lands. They laid claim to railroad land and set up their own farms – and towns to service the fast-growing farming world of the West.

Many came as Mormons, developing communities centered on their City of Zion of Salt Lake City (founded by Young in 1847), but reaching far and wide from Utah into Idaho, Arizona, Nevada, California, Colorado – and even northern Mexico.

The rumors of gold (but also silver and copper) also brought Americans west – though not usually entire families, but instead merely single male fortune hunters. States such as California, Nevada (with its fabulous Comstock Lode), Montana, Idaho and Washington were states particularly sought out by these fortune hunters. Towns would quickly appear wherever mineral sites were discovered, bringing not only the fortune-hunting miners, but also bartenders and prostitutes to keep the miners happy, but also bankers, clergy, and general store operators to bring some degree of American civilization to the towns as well. Then when the mines yielded up all their bounty, everyone moved on to opportunities elsewhere – and another bustling mining town turned into a deserted ghost town.

Cow trails and cattle barons. With the advent of the railroad into the West, new opportunities opened up for the lucrative trade in beef cattle. Thousands of cattle could be herded north out of the grasslands of Texas, through the Indian territory of Oklahoma, to the various railheads of the Kansas Pacific Railroad. For instance in 1867, when the new Chisholm Trail was first laid out, 35,000 head of cattle were brought up from Texas to the railhead at Abilene, Kansas, in that first year alone. The cattle were then herded onto box cars and shipped up to Chicago – or west to Denver for shipment to the Pacific coast. In Chicago the slaughterhouses would be kept busy preparing meat to be shipped up the Great Lakes waterway to the populous Eastern cities.

From the end of the Civil War to the mid-1880s the cattle business boomed, making a lot of cattle barons very rich – and creating a fabled American proto type, the American cowboy.

The end of the era of the great Cattle Kingdoms. But three things would bring this era to a close: the steel plow, the barbed wire fence, and the overgrazing of the cow trails. The grassy plains through which the cattle trails led were covered by a thick undergrowth of tough grass with deep roots, which made the land prohibitively difficult to plow – that was until the steel plow began to come under wide usage (sometime in the 1870s and 1880s). With this invention, homesteaders could now begin to settle the plains, with their plowed fields and domestic animals able to support the lives of their families. To protect their investment, they began to secure their landholdings by the relatively cheap means of the new barbed wire fencing (developed in the mid-1870s).

Now the cattle herds found their paths along their cow trails blocked here and there by these fenced-in homesteads – and trouble began to brew between these two categories of Westerners, the farmer and the cattleman. For years the cattlemen had been allowed freely to graze their herds on the vast Federal lands of the Great Plains (reaching from Texas to the Dakotas). But now homesteaders were rapidly filling these open lands. Little by little the cattle herding business was pushed further westward, increasing the difficulty and costs of the herding itself. And then a very bad winter hit in 1886-1887, with hundreds of thousands of cattle dying – bringing a number of the former cattle kingdoms to ruin.

The rise of the American farmer. In the meantime, American farming was becoming a very big business – the Western farms fully able to feed the Eastern cities which were also growing rapidly in size. Indeed, America began to see huge industrial farms grow in number during the latter part of the 1800s.

At the same time, towns located along the growing number of rail lines crisscrossing the American Great Plains or Midwest began quickly to develop as economic and social centers for the agricultural industry of entire counties. Thus as the farming business boomed, churches, schools, banks, and general stores began to appear in these towns, bringing American civilization to the American West. In many ways this too, along with the cowboy, was fast becoming a major cultural symbol representing the young and fast-growing America.

The Indians' "Last Stand." Things were growing desperate for the declining Indian tribes of the West. The huge buffalo herds that had sustained the Indians' hunting economy were dwindling rapidly in size – thanks to both the Indians' greater killing ability with the new repeating rifles – and the interest of Whites in killing the buffalo simply for sport (sometimes simply from train windows as they passed the buffalo herds). Then there was also the interest in Christian missionaries in bringing the Indians to Christian ways – meaning a cultural and economic lifestyle similar to that of the "Christian world." Reservations were also being chipped away at by land hungry Whites – despite treaties that had guaranteed the land as Indian territory in perpetuity. But events showed quickly that there was no perpetuity when it came to Indian property rights.

Custer's "Last Stand." In 1875 Sioux (or Lakota) Chief Sitting Bull and his tactician Crazy Horse decided it was time to leave the Dakota Reservation to take the offensive against settlers invading the Dakota Black Hills – sacred Sioux land. The next year they were joined by Cheyenne and Arapaho warriors – which in turn brought Civil War Cavalry General Sheridan west to force them back onto their reservations. But the Indians proved quite resistant. And worse for the American troops, a detachment of several hundred soldiers led by Colonel George Custer got itself surrounded by Crazy Horse's warriors – and all were either killed or badly wounded at the Battle of the Little Bighorn (1876).

But instead of breaking the will of the White soldiers, the slaughter of Custer and his men became a rallying cry for the White nation to take revenge. At this point Sitting Bull decided simply to return his people to their Dakota reservation.

One last effort of Indians to clear the land of Whites occurred in 1890, when, getting caught up in the Ghost Dance craze, they came to believe that the performance of this ritual would finally clear the land of the White man – even believing that the wearing of special shirts would make the Indians invulnerable to White man's bullets if it should come to armed conflict. And it soon came to such conflict – in which Sitting Bull was killed along with a dozen of his warriors. Then the 7th cavalry was sent in to impose order, and, at the Wounded Knee Creek, fighting accidentally and tragically broke out – in which possibly 150 to 300 Sioux men, women and children were killed (no one is sure of the count) – along with 25 U.S. soldiers. It would be the last sad such episode in the long-standing feud between the American Indian and the American White. Indeed, the "Indian Problem" had now been solved, definitively.

CHAPTER SIX

AMERICA COMES OF AGE

* * *

AMERICA DEVELOPS AS AN INDUSTRIAL POWER

America's Industrial Revolution. Meanwhile back East, a new social dynamic had been rising within the fast-growing American cities: modern industrialism. This was due in no small part to the Civil War and its lasting effect on the American economy. The war's demand for steel, and the iron ore and coal to make it, and the railroads and barges to ship it, and the financial institutions to fund its initial outlay, and the laborers to work the whole system – had made a deep impact on what was formerly a largely agrarian society.

Although the U.S. government had played a huge role in getting the American railroad industry empowered through its liberal land-grants to railroad companies, non-governmental or private financial operations played a huge role in amassing the funds to streamline the railroad industry and its construction of thousands of miles of rail. And in turn, these rail lines crisscrossing the nation east and west greatly facilitated the movement of raw materials headed east and finished goods headed west, adding greatly to a fast-expanding national economy. And it carried a restless American population to new ventures, helping to keep the American dream very much alive.

And America demonstrated a very inventive genius in the role it played in creating and developing the telegraph and the telephone, helping to keep all this economic dynamic under careful human management. And this helped to connect the nation socially as well, as Americans acquired phone service to keep them in touch with the larger world. By 1893, when Alexander Graham Bell's patent ended, there were 260 thousand American homes with phone service. And then smaller, local companies jumped into the phone business, so that even poorer Americans could now have the luxury of owning a phone.

And, as we will see in the pages that follow, apart from the early railroad ventures during and immediately after the war, the government or state played only a minimal role in the development of this new industrial society – especially as the war and its needs receded from view and the system seemed to run simply under its own dynamics rather than on the basis of popular social political demands.

Nor was God invited to play a role in the development of this new society. Rather, America's Grand Destiny now seemed to be driven forward largely by a small number of individuals who were particularly ambitious and fearless. These highly talented entrepreneurs – "Captains of Industry" they were termed, unless you tended to see them as "Industrial Robber Barons"! – were the driving force behind much of this huge economic expansion.

Indeed, this was a time in which the spirit of Darwinism soared high, for the basic theme of this rising social order was quite Darwinian: progress through survival of the fittest. To the strong belonged the spoils of their conquests. But for those who fell to the wayside in this struggle for survival there would be no tears wept. But the risk of this competitive struggle seemed worth it – at least to some who anticipated striking it rich in this new game of potentially limitless opportunity – if you were willing to play it hard and fast.

In this unfolding economic game played by these industrial/financial giants, fortunes could be made rather quickly – and they could also be lost just as quickly. And these fortunes could become quite awesome – often exceeding the levels of wealth of the European nobility. Indeed, according to a survey done in 1896,* of a total of 12½ million American families in 1890, 125,000 very wealthy families, or 1 percent of the total number of families in America, possessed over 50 percent of America's total family wealth.

And so it was – at least for some Americans – very much a "Gilded Age" (Age of Gold)!

Cornelius Vanderbilt. Early among these "Captains of Industry" was the New Yorker, Cornelius "Commodore" Vanderbilt. As a very competitive individual, he climbed his way out of poverty in the 1810s by operating a ferry boat (thus his nickname "Commodore") between Staten Island and Manhattan, taking on ferrying monopolies in developing that business, until he had secured his own monopolies in the trade (late 1830s). He then branched out from there to own railroads that connected with his ferry lines, in 1847 even taking over a major line running between New York and Boston. Then two years later, with the California gold-rush madness hitting

---

*Charles B. Spahr, *An Essay on the Present Distribution of Wealth in the United States*, New York: T.Y. Crowell & Co.,1896, p. 69

America, he moved into the shipping business on the high seas, attempting even the purchase of land to build a canal across Nicaragua. Instead he was able to build land and water connections between his Atlantic fleet and his Pacific fleet, the latter which took passengers onward to California.

Soon (the 1850s) this energetic entrepreneur took to manufacturing the new steam engines, which he then put to use in his trans-Atlantic shipping business. Then with the onset of the Civil War, he joined in by employing his flagship, the *Vanderbilt*, to hunt down Confederate raiders. After the war he and his son Billy bought up various railroad companies, and united them as the future New York Central Line, and went on to build a huge railroad terminal in Manhattan on 42nd Street, the forerunner of the enormous Grand Central Station.

And so it was that Vanderbilt became the richest monopolist of his days, failing only once against the very corrupt team of Gould and Fisk, who used politically-backed deception to bring one of his enterprises to ruin. Nonetheless he bounced back and at his death was able to leave his heirs a sum of $100 million,* including $1 million (at that time the largest donation ever) for the startup of a university that still bears his name today!

Andrew Carnegie. Another such individual was the Scottish immigrant Andrew Carnegie (came to America in 1848 at age thirteen), who worked his way from an office clerk to the owner of America's largest steel operation in Western Pennsylvania (Pittsburgh). As a young office clerk he impressed his bosses at the Pennsylvania Railroad Company, in everything from how he easily read Morse Code messages to his ideas how the company could operate more efficiently by bringing together under a single corporate structure various operations – from the securing of raw materials, to the manufacture of the machinery needed for the business, to the shipping of the end product.

Eventually he moved on to put these ideas to work under his own initiative, as he got personally involved in Pittsburg's iron industry. Little by little his own business expanded, as he took on engineers to develop the steel industry, and as he branched out into subsidiary operations, such as building the iron bridges needed by the rapidly expanding railroad industry. He even went into the coke/coal energy business, buying up operations needed to feed his own iron and steel plants. By the end of the 1800s, he was producing steel at the rate of 6,000 tons per day.

---

*This would make him the second richest man American in history, ranking only behind Rockefeller. The $100 million would be approximately equivalent to $150 billion in today's dollars. Interestingly, he lived modestly. All the lavish Vanderbilt estates that were built across the American East were actually commissioned later by his descendants.

But ultimately he had to confront the problem that the industrial revolution itself had produced, the low wages of the workers – supposedly necessary in order to maintain the profits required for business expansion. Labor union activity was running very high at the time, and a quite bloody confrontation developed between Carnegie's corporate supervisor, Henry Clay Frick (Carnegie was away in Europe at the time) and the strikers at the huge Homestead Plant. It was soon after this that Carnegie decided simply to retire, and sold his business, the largest corporate transaction ever, for $480 million ($13 billion in today's dollars) to the New York City financier John Pierpont (J.P.) Morgan. Then Carnegie would give most of that wealth away to various charities and social endeavors, and spend the rest of his life traveling.

John Pierpont (J.P.) Morgan. Not an industrial manufacturer nor born in poverty (actually quite the opposite), J.P. Morgan was a money man, providing the necessary financial support that the industrial world would need in order to do business, and that even the U.S. government would need from time to time in order to stay afloat financially. He proved very skillful in buying up financially troubled companies, reorganizing them to a point of profitability in their operations, and then selling them, at a nice profit for himself. But he also would play a huge role in bankrolling the U.S. government – on more than one occasion – when the government found itself in deep trouble, as was the case in the Panic of 1893 which nearly emptied the U.S. gold reserves. Only an operation (which at first President Cleveland balked at) that he undertook brought the U.S. back from disaster. In this he joined with the Rothchild bankers of Paris to sell the government 3.5 million ounces of gold in exchange for thirty-year bonds.

He also, in 1907, stepped in to rescue the American economy again when Wall Street suffered a huge collapse, nearly pulling the U.S. banking industry down with it. Here too, he put together a number of New York banks willing to invest a massive amount in Wall Street in order to revive the stock market. And soon he moved (with President Roosevelt's permission) to take over a major industrial conglomerate that had failed, in order to head off another economic panic in America.

But a rising concern about the role such monopolies were playing in the American economy would lead Congress to take countering action, setting up in 1913 the Federal Reserve, to do the government's own intervention into the functioning of the national economy when it appeared to be heading into a crisis. In a sense, Morgan himself had shown the U.S. government the proper procedure by which to intervene when necessary, contributing greatly to the stability of the U.S. economy, which throughout the 1800s had experienced one speculative crisis after another.

John D. Rockefeller.

Another industrial captain was John D. Rockefeller, who also rose out of tough family circumstances, to go on to be America's richest individual. During the Civil War he and his brother started up a business selling produce to the army, before switching in 1863 in Ohio to join a group manufacturing kerosene from crude oil (home lighting at the time was switching rapidly from whale oil to kerosene). By 1865 the brothers were able to buy out their partners, placing them on a highly profitable monopolistic path. In 1870 he established the Standard Oil Company, and from there went on to buy up one competing oil business after another – until by the end of the 1870s he held a virtual monopoly (at least 90%) in the oil trade, mostly located in Pennsylvania at the time.

Then he took on the Pennsylvania Railroad Company, to force down shipping rates (although he was even then moving to the use of pipelines), soon finding himself involved in a number of Pennsylvania lawsuits (which would soon become a regular feature of his business) opposing his monopolistic practices. But this hardly slowed him down, instead in 1882 setting up the Standard Oil Trust, a huge financial operation aimed at buying up the various state oil companies. But this not only produced a new outcry against his monopolistic policies, it set the example for other ambitious individuals to also go the "trust" route of setting up large holding companies able to swoop in and buy up smaller companies – in most any economic field. Then he moved into international oil operations, then into the field of natural gas, and finally in the refinement of gasoline (previously considered just a wasteful byproduct of kerosene production), just as the world of automobiles (around the year 1900), with their new internal combustion engines, was opening up.

However, by that time, reformers were also very active everywhere calling for laws to be put in place that would correct the growing injustices produced by this change of America from its agricultural lifestyle to the newly growing industrial society and culture. Thus it was that Rockefeller found himself under constant attack from U.S. President Theodore ("Teddy") Roosevelt, wielding the 1890 Sherman Antitrust Act (originally designed to break up workers' unions) wherever he could, and Ida Tarbell, publishing a lengthy exposé on Standard Oil's underhanded business practices – and finally in 1911 with the U.S. Supreme Court handing down the decision that as a monopoly violating the Sherman Act, Standard Oil had to be broken up* – into 34 separate companies (eventually becoming Conoco, Amoco,

---

*Yet Rockefeller remained a significant stockholder in these various companies. And the oil business continued to be personally very profitable for Rockefeller, eventually making Rockefeller the richest man in the world at the time (and by comparison, even still today!)

Chevron, Exxon, Mobil, Sohio, Pennzoil, etc.).

It is hard to appreciate today the idea that Rockefeller never saw what he was doing as evil, but simply something that had to be done in order to move industrial progress forward. And in a very evident sense, he did just that, even if it seemed to change the rules of America's traditional economic game (building a national economy on the basis of a small number of family-run enterprises). He always saw himself as an authentic Christian, teaching Bible at the church he attended, and helping to turn a small Baptist College into the University of Chicago. And he would set up all kinds of charitable operations, helping to create the Central Philippine University in 1905, then founding an outstanding medical research center in New York City, and finally in 1913, establishing the Rockefeller Foundation to support medical research and training – which in 1918 expanded its operations into social research as well.

Thomas Alva Edison. Although Edison would not become one of these financial giants dominating the American economy, he would be one of the American geniuses that drove the American economy forward, to ever-unfolding progress. He started out humbly as a telegraph, then news wire, operator for the Associated Press, at the same time undertaking various experiments in electricity. His inventive spirit led him to go his own way, to relocate to a friend's home in New Jersey – and there develop the stock ticker – and then patent (age 22) the electronic vote counter. His experimenting finally led in 1877 (now age 30) to develop a phonograph made from a tin-foil-wrapped cylinder, so amazing that he was invited to Washington to demonstrate its operation to President Hayes.

And with this he was now a very big-time inventor, developing his own research center (eventually two city-blocks in size), and ultimately perhaps his most significant invention, the light bulb, coming up in 1879 with a successful carbon-filament bulb (lasting 12 hours) – but through more experimentation,* and discovering the use of a bamboo filament, in 1880 produced a bulb that would last 1,200 hours.

At the same time he ventured into the business world in 1878, to market his lights, setting up (with Vanderbilt's and J.P. Morgan's support) the Edison Electric Light Company, soon expanding that (now the Edison Illuminating Company) as New York City's electric utility company – and in so doing, the 110-volt electric system now standard in all of America (a 220-volt system is used in Europe).

The only truly dark cloud in this picture came in his company's

---

*He once commented about his tireless pursuit of new inventions: "I have not failed, I've just found 10,000 ways that won't work"!

America Comes of Age

competition with George Westinghouse over the matter of using direct current (DC: Edison) or alternating current (AC: Westinghouse). Edison not only lost this battle, but was forced by his investors (including J.P. Morgan) out of his company in 1890, which was then reconstituted as an AC company, General Electric – which went on to control three-quarters of the electrical business.

Edison continued his work nonetheless, interested in visual items, everything from the kinetoscope (peep-hole viewer) in 1891 to a movie projector able to cast a film image on a screen in front of a full audience (1896), going on to add a machine able to synchronize sound with the film. This became for him a very prosperous development, as his movie studio went on to produce almost 1,200 short films. And he ventured into other fields as well, the rubber industry, mining, and the x-ray (which he discovered to be very dangerous). He would remain a ball of energy himself, all the way up to his death in 1931.

The automobile and airplane industry. This same spirit of American inventiveness was pushing small-shop experiments in the world of transportation. The horseless carriage or automobile was an item of particular interest, with the idea of steam (at that time driving trains and ships) being employed to drive these personal means of transport. Thus as early as 1878, steam-engine-driven carriages were used in the 200-mile (33 hour) race in Wisconsin between two such vehicles. This same idea was developed by the Stanley twins (Francis and Freelan) who produced over 200 such cars in 1898-1899, making them the leaders in the industry. They went on (1902) to produce the Stanley Steamer – which in 1906 was able to reach 127 miles per hour over a one-mile course at Daytona Beach. This made their automobile quite popular (in 1917 their annual production rate peaked at 500 cars). But by this time the gasoline-powered internal-combustion engine (ICE) was taking over the market, and in 1924 the Stanley brothers were forced to close their business.

It might be easily supposed that the airplane would have been a later development, getting people moving in the air being much trickier than getting them moving along the ground. But in fact the first heavier-than-air flying machines employing the ICE were under development at the same time as the ICE-driven automobile, both heavily dependent on this new technology (a steam engine would never have worked in the air!).

We know that the Wright brothers (Orville and Wilbur) were the first (December 17, 1903) to actually achieve the flight of this new type of airplane (having previously tested over 200 models in a wind-tunnel they created), flying their plane a distance of 852 feet in 59 seconds of flight, just ahead of other inventors about to do the same thing. They would go on to refine and strengthen their airplane, in 1905 flying it 24 miles in just over 39 minutes. And in 1908 the Wright brothers traveled to France to demonstrate the possibilities of the airplane, and encourage its development in Europe. Indeed, the very next year a Frenchman was the first to fly his airplane over the English Channel (and collect a £1,000 reward!) Thus the age of human flight had arrived.

Henry Ford. It's important to introduce Henry Ford at this point, because not only did he promote the automobile industry greatly, he actually at this point in time (the early 1900s) streamlined business operations so outstandingly that it created a sense of industrial efficiency that would touch the entire American industrial world, and, for that matter, the European world as well.

This farm-boy from Michigan took an interest in the family's steam-driven machinery, which led him to become a servicing mechanic for Westinghouse. But he moved on in 1891 to work for the Edison Illuminating Company, becoming a chief engineer by 1893. But he was doing some experimentation of his own on the side, fascinated by the possibilities of the ICE, resulting in his building in 1896 an ICE-driven four-wheeled cycle. Encouraged by Edison (the two would remain close friends, eventually even neighbors, from that point on), he developed his model. And, with some financial backing, in 1899 he formed the Detroit Automobile Company, but which shut down two years later when it did not succeed. But one not to be discouraged easily, he built a stronger model, raced it successfully, and was able to set up a new company in 1901, the Henry Ford Company. But even here he moved on (sold his company, which became the Cadillac Automobile Company), built yet a new model with an even stronger engine (80 horsepower!), had the famous Barney Oldfield race it successfully, and in 1903 was able to open a new business, the Ford Motor Company.

Up to this point, these automobiles were handcrafted, and very expensive for purchasers. And here is where Ford's business genius changed the world of production. His goal was to produce cheaply a simple but effective automobile, one that was affordable by the huge market of Middle-Class Americans. Thus in 1908 he introduced the Model-T Ford, $825 in its initial offering that year, but constantly reduced in price annually, as Ford discovered new efficiencies – not only in production but also in distribution (a system of Ford dealerships located widely). Then when in 1913 he revolutionized production using the moving assembly line – and in 1914 paid his workers the unheard-of $5 per day wage (greatly motivating his work force, who themselves could now afford his cars) – he was able to double the production rate, and sell over 250,000 of his cars (now priced at only $440)! Thanks to Ford, ownership of an automobile was becoming a regular feature of American Middle-Class life.

* * *

NATIONAL POLITICS DURING THE LATE 1800s

Two things stand out rather notably about America's national politics in the latter part of the 1800s. First of all, with the Civil War and Reconstruction over with, there seemed to be little of importance that the federal government found itself doing. The nation's serious dynamics were located in its economic realm, not part of the jurisdiction of the federal government – as the Constitution made very clear. Rather, American economics was driven (as we have just seen) by private individuals, not government officials.

And secondly, this same free spirit driving a virtual economic revolution raised all kinds of new moral-ethical questions. Most importantly, where exactly were the boundaries for the massive self-aggrandizement behind this dynamic? The economic revolution was not only shaking the old American social order to its roots, its lack of any kind of refereeing was producing a huge culture of greed, and what those who still held on to old-fashioned Christian values viewed as sheer corruption.

It has already been noted that the social challenge of widespread corruption had started out in the days of Grant. But the issue merely grew worse with the passing of time. Who or what could be done to keep this economic game America was playing fair to all?

Rutherford B. Hayes (1877-1881). President Hayes attempted to address this problem of corruption, but stirred a lot of political opposition for himself in the process. Ironically, one of his few successes seemed to be in removing Chester A. Arthur from the spoils job at the New York customs-house, infuriating New York boss Conkling in the process. But overall, such anti-corruption action cost Hayes the loss of vital support when it was time for re-election (Grant was even trying again to get the 1880 Republican nomination). And it took 36 ballots before the Republicans finally selected the relatively unknown James Garfield, who then – to the great shock of Hayes – chose Chester Arthur as his running mate (to get the vital support of boss Conkling)!

James A. Garfield (1881). But once in office, Garfield largely ignored the patronage dynamic and instead chose truly qualified individuals for government positions, pitting himself against Conkling, who actually overplayed his hand, turning many New Yorkers against Conkling.

But the patronage issue would soon come to end Garfield's presidency, when an irate office-seeker shot Garfield only a few months into his presidency, and he eventually died, having served only six months as president. The nation was stunned.

Chester A. Arthur (1881-1885). And thus it was that Arthur became president, but ironically, one who would become one of the country's leading anti-corruption reformers! Besides vetoing Congress's patronage bills, he signed into law (1883) the Pendleton Act, which turned an increasing number of civil service appointments over to a Civil Service Commission, charged with making government appointments solely on the basis of proven merit, not patronage.

And then, after finishing out this single term in office, Arthur chose simply to retire (he was suffering from poor health).

Grover Cleveland (1st term: 1885-1889). The election which brought the Democrat Cleveland to the presidency was fought largely over the issue of personal integrity of the candidates, the Republican James Blaine, unfortunately well known for his involvement in the railroad industry spoils system. Cleveland was known as a man of great personal integrity, which the Republicans attempted to undercut with rumors about the unmarried Cleveland having once conceived a child out of wedlock!

In the end, the election was very close, coming down to the electoral vote of New York, when Cleveland had received only a little over a thousand vote majority out of the million votes cast there. And behind that tiny Republican shortfall had been the Republican Mugwumps,* who simply could not bring themselves to support the corrupt Blaine.

And once in office Cleveland resisted as best he could the demand for spoils from fellow Democrats, even reducing the size of the bloated federal bureaucracy (and not just the opposition Republicans in the mix). He moved to strengthen the navy by getting rid of inferior ships built by corrupt contractors. He took back into federal hands western land that the railroads had made no progress in developing. And he cut back government support of farmers and army veterans, which he understood as creating on the part of the recipients a state of dependency rather than personal and social health.

But a huge political issue facing Cleveland was one he could not bring to resolution: the gold versus silver controversy. Supposedly this was

---

*From an old Algonquin term meaning "a person of importance," implying that those who bolted from the party were being ridiculously sanctimonious or morally condescending in refusing to support their party's candidate, Blaine.

simply an economic issue, about which of the two, gold or silver, served best to back the strength of the U.S. dollar. If the matter had been simply that and nothing more, a reasonable policy could have been arrived at. But actually, it really was not just about valuable metal. It was also about the deep social tensions that hit the country as America moved into the industrial age.

Gold was very much less abundant than silver. Being scarce, it was thus much more valuable, therefore a tougher standard supporting the value of the dollar. Bankers and financial creditors, especially the big-money boys back East, pushed hard for the dollar to be based solely on the value of gold alone, requiring banks (including the federal banks) to hold gold as the backing for their printed dollars, making dollars themselves very scarce and thus very valuable. Those supporting the gold standard were termed "Goldbugs."

Silver, on the other hand, was still flowing quite readily out of the West's many silver mines, and thus, ounce for ounce, very much less expensive than gold. Dollars backed in value by abundant silver would themselves therefore be much more abundant. And those that found themselves in debt to banks, such as farmers who lived off of bank loans until harvests came around – and also had financed much of their operations through bank-held mortgages – naturally wanted to repay those loans with the cheapest dollars possible. Thus they were strong "Silverites."

But there was even more to this problem than the matter of the value of the dollar. The gold-versus-silver matter was actually a symbolic or ideological matter* that served to align American politics into bitterly opposing groups. The very wealth of America's rising financial class (mostly back East) was galling to America's struggling farmers, and their impoverished friends and relatives who had given up the struggle and taken poor-paying jobs in the newly developing industrial world. This all seemed so un-American, especially after so many of those who had fought for the Union during the recent Civil War were finding American society seemingly so insensitive to their social plight. It was just not fair.

Cleveland was forced to make his way through this matter, much as presidents before him had been forced to contend with the slavery issue. But like Grant before him, Cleveland ultimately decided that gold served the interests of the nation best, in making for a very strong dollar. He attempted to cut back the use of silver, which put Congressmen representing the Silverite world of the West, the rural Mid-West and the South, in strong

---

*Symbolic or ideological, much as the slavery issue had been earlier that century, even to Southerners who had owned no slaves and to Northerners who had no personal regard for America's Blacks.

opposition to Cleveland.

Then, on top of this issue, there was the one of tariffs, the U.S. government's primary source of income. Here Cleveland took the position in opposition to the high tariffs (over a third of the value of the product itself) that "protected" American industrial production from foreign goods, and was producing an embarrassing surplus in the government's budget. Cleveland's attack on the nation's high tariffs now embittered the up-East side of the East-versus-West or rural-versus-industrial debate, further undercutting Cleveland's political position nationally.

And thus it was that Cleveland failed at his effort to be reelected in 1888. He actually won the popular vote, but narrowly lost the vote of the electoral college, solely by the vote of his home state of New York, which – because of the opposition of Tammany Hall – left him only 600 votes short of winning New York's vote, and thereby the presidential election.

Benjamin Harrison (1889-1893). And thus another Harrison (grandson of the president who died soon after his inauguration) took office in 1889. Harrison reversed the direction taken by Cleveland on the gold-silver matter, working with Ohio Senator John Sherman to put the Sherman Silver Purchase Act of 1890 in place, committing the government to the purchase of a fixed amount of silver. This pleased greatly not only rural America but also the silver mining industry, which was suffering deeply from a sharp price loss because of the oversupply of silver. But this policy would push America in an economic direction that would help produce yet another major economic crisis for the country.

At the same time, Harrison supported yet another effort by Senator Sherman, resulting in the Sherman Anti-Trust Act of 1890. It was designed to break up the huge financial trusts that controlled America's rail, steel, and financial industry. But it would also be used to try to take down the organized labor movement, which was also on the rise at the time.

And to his great credit, Harrison attempted to extend civil rights protection to the American Blacks through the action of his Justice Department. But White juries would simply not follow through by convicting those accused of committing civil rights violations against Blacks, and ultimately even Congress and the Supreme Court backed away from his effort. The Blacks would have to wait – a very long time – to possess the civil rights that all Americans were supposedly entitled to.

Ultimately, what would bring Harrison to a single term as president was the economy, worsening as time went by. One of the causes of a huge economic slowdown was the McKinley Tariff of 1890, sponsored by Ohio Senator (and future president) William McKinley, which raised tariff rates even further, almost up to half of the value of the goods produced,

America Comes of Age

making foreign products virtually impossible to acquire. The idea was that America's high tariff rates would not only protect American industry, but place in American hands the instruments able to force European countries to negotiate a reduction of their own high tariffs against American goods. However the heightened tariffs also made American products so expensive for Americans themselves – including not just the average American consumer but even America's industrial companies – that the American economy began to decline under the load. And thus Harrison had to go into another national election, with Americans in a very grumpy mood.

Cleveland (2nd term: 1893-1897). Thus Cleveland was returned to office, just in time for the Panic of 1893! As with all such "panics," events were set off by rumors and then rapidly mounting fears, initiated this time by the failure of the deeply indebted Philadelphia and Reading Railroad Company, which declared bankruptcy just as Cleveland took office. This, combined with declining global wheat prices (a huge American income earner) caused cautious investors to demand the exchange of bonds they held, for gold, which neither private banks nor the federal treasury held in sufficient amount. Others seeing such a move, tried to do the same, creating the full panic.

Cleveland succeeded in getting Congress to repeal the Sherman Silver Purchase Act, supposing that this would bring strength back to the dollar, and thus the economy. But instead it merely collapsed the shaky silver industry, and soon much of the rest of American industry.* In turn, the unemployment rate went from 3 percent in 1892 to nearly 12 percent in 1893, to over 18 percent in 1894, then in 1895-1898 hanging at the 14 percent figure.

This deepened greatly labor unrest in America, with Jacob Coxey even leading a march of the unemployed on Washington, and the Pullman Company undergoing a very violent strike by its workers (led by the American Socialist Eugene Debs) – which soon led to the spread of such strikes to other railroad companies. By mid-1894, 125 thousand railroad workers were on strike, shutting down the country's vital rail network. This forced Cleveland finally to send federal troops after the strikers, ultimately breaking up the strikes.

But Cleveland was helpless in the face of the broader panic. And this is when in 1895 he finally (after first refusing) took the help of J.P. Morgan in purchasing those 3.5 million ounces of gold in exchange of thirty-year federal bonds. This calmed the panic down somewhat. But still left a lot of

---

*Estimates are that 500 banks and 15 thousand businesses failed during the 1893-1898 years of the Panic.

dark economic issues unresolved.

Thus it was in 1896, at the Democratic National Convention, Cleveland was pushed aside by a fast-rising William Jennings Bryan, who blasted Cleveland's gold policies by rousing the convention with his challenge: "you shall not crucify mankind upon a cross of gold!" Thus it was that Cleveland quietly went off into political retirement as a trustee of Princeton University.

William McKinley (1897-1901) brings the 19th century to a close. Despite Bryan's energetic campaigning around the country with his strong pro-silver platform (actually Bryan's Democratic Party was somewhat divided over the gold-silver issue), the Republicans found themselves led by former Congressman, then Ohio governor, McKinley, who "sat on his front porch" (literally!), while his friend, Mark Hanna, skillfully directed McKinley's campaign, employing all the modern electoral campaign tactics of a well-organized campaign committee conducting endless publicity and a lot of political negotiations with key political figures here and there. And thus it was that McKinley went on to a rather large victory.

As president, McKinley followed the trail expected of him, holding America's high tariffs in place (the 1897 Dingley Tariff) and maintaining his pro-gold position (the 1900 Gold Standard Act).

It would be in the realm of imperialism that McKinley's presidency stood out. But it was also the age of Western imperialism, driving strongly the expansionist urge of all major Western societies. In 1898 he would direct American troops not only to Cuba to help the Cubans secure their independence from Spain, but he would extend that effort to neighboring Puerto Rico, and then all the way to Guam and the Philippines in Asia. And along the way he would seize the Republic of Hawaii as a new U.S. territory.

McKinley would be reelected in the 1900 national election, but go on to serve only six months of that term – when a deranged anarchist shot McKinley at a presidential reception he was hosting at the Pan-American Exposition in Buffalo, New York. This would bring forward to the American presidency his vice-president, Theodore ("Teddy") Roosevelt, an even more dynamic individual in both the socio-economic and foreign-policy realm.

* * *

THE CULTURAL-SPIRITUAL CHALLENGES OF THE INDUSTRIAL AGE

A rapidly growing America. From one perspective, America – as it stepped from the 1800s into the 1900s – was going through an amazing period of development. In only a couple of generations Americans had gone from horseback to automobiles, and even to flight. Electricity lit up not only cities but also homes, news of the larger world arrived almost instantly to an increasingly attentive population, personal phones put people in direct communication with each other across even the miles, and wealth reached down into even the middle classes, who knew that they were living better than kings and queens had lived only a few centuries earlier. All this change was very heady stuff.

Also the American population itself was undergoing very rapid growth in numbers, with accompanying social changes. In the forty-year period between 1870 to 1910 the population went from 38.5 million to 92.3 million, growing by about 25 percent each decade (28 percent by 1880, another 27.6 percent by 1890, and another 21 percent for each of 1900 and 1910). This time period also marked a huge shift in the nation's demography, 10 to 11 million (figures are not exact) Americans moving from farms to America's fast-rising cities, where they were joined by another 25 million immigrants streaming in from Europe.

This movement was not always a happy event, but one normally necessitated by the need to find life-support in a physical or geographic world that itself had expanded none. Things were getting tight. And poverty was an accompanying feature of this tightness or scarcity of opportunity. And things were merely growing worse with time.

The American Labor Movement. Actually, Americans had begun to take action against this mounting socio-economic crisis years earlier, with the founding in 1869 of the organization, Knights of Labor, originally a union of skilled workers, designed to protect their professional positions in the face of the invasion of masses of unskilled workers (farm boys mostly) into their industrial world. But over time it broadened its membership and pushed for specific items, such as the 8-hour working day, reaching nearly 30,000 in membership by 1880, 100,000 by 1884, and 800,000 by 1886, involving around 20% of America's industrial workers.

But then a number of things would bring this organization to rapid decline after that. Its leadership was not skilled in organizational matters. It was heavily Catholic in membership, and drew the opposition of the Catholic hierarchy because of its secretive ways. Also, Chinese laborers were always glad to take the place of the workers when they went on strike for their 8-hour day program. And the organization could not find support within the American press, which depicted it as being merely a group of anarchists. Ultimately, it was most unfairly depicted as the cause of the 1886 Haymarket Square Riot,* undercutting the organization's reputation

---

*At a gathering of workers at Haymarket Square in Chicago who were demanding the eight-hour working day, an unknown person threw a bomb at police who

so badly that by the time of the 1893 Panic it had become only a very small operation. The organizing of American labor was subsequently taken up by the American Federation of Labor (AFL) founded that pivotal year of 1886 by Samuel Gompers as a result of a dispute with the Knights of Labor over competing labor contracts. It united a number of guilds or unions of skilled workers and craftsmen (as opposed to common day laborers) – beginning with the cigar makers' unions. Then as the Knights of Labor faded away during the later 1880s, the AFL held steady, even picking up new members.

Overall, it supported the idea of capitalism, simply attempting to put skilled workers in a better position to take advantage of the huge profits being accumulated in the industrial revolution sweeping America. Also, its political caution, and distinct patriotism* helped bring the U.S. government alongside the AFL in support of its labor program. By 1920, the AFL had grown to nearly four million members.

The American women's or feminist movement. A huge stimulus to a new women's movement spread across America was alcohol, and the devastation it caused in so many American families, as husbands would spend what little earnings they achieved drowning their labor sorrows on payday at the local bar, arriving home tipsy and with most of their earnings gone. And thus the Women's Christian Temperance Union (WCTU) was born in 1874, ultimately striving not for temperance in the drinking of alcohol (a long-standing Christian virtue) but instead for total abstinence (not at all part of the Christian tradition, but soon to be treated as an absolute Christian law).

But the women's movement moved further, to demand for women the right to vote (women's suffrage), at first to give the women the political leverage they would need to perform their all-important task of protecting their families. But then it became increasingly clear to the more active in the women's movement that women should have the same rights as men in all capacities – publicly as well as privately. It was time to end the idea

---

were in the process of dispersing the crowd, killing seven officers and a number of civilians. On the basis of scanty or non-existent evidence seven (mostly German) anarchists were sentenced to death by hanging (a number of them had not even been present at the gathering) for their contribution to the tragedy. Only four were actually hanged, as one committed suicide in jail and the two others had their death sentences commuted to life imprisonment, but were pardoned by the Illinois governor in 1893 who (as did many) considered the trial a total travesty of justice.

*Such political caution and patriotism was clearly demonstrated during World War One, and in its opposition to the more radical (mostly immigrant) labor organizations such as the "Wobblies" (the Industrial Workers of the World) and the more radical Socialist Party.

that the public domain was strictly the man's world. Thus the founding in 1890 of the National American Women Suffrage Association, with long-standing suffragist Susan B. Anthony heading up the organization. But it would take another 30 years of marches and other forms of protest to finally secure the right of women to vote in every American election with the 19th Amendment which went into effect in 1920.*

Trust-Busting. Other Americans found themselves greatly distressed at how America's capacity to create enormous industrial wealth was held in the hands of only a tiny group of Americans – and how industrialism was also degrading so many people to the status of serfs. Americans (and immigrants) were being forced by rising economic circumstances to have to leave the open-air work of farming and submit themselves to lives underground in America's mines and inside the sweatshops of America's factories. The work was grueling, paid little, and – to the horror of Progressivists – was totally dehumanizing. Indeed, alcohol was becoming the sole source of relief of desperate workers – but also the growing cause of the ruin of America's industrial working-class families. Something needed to be done to save America's soul! Thus it was that "trust-busting" would be a key feature of this new spirit stirring Americans to action on numerous fronts.

* * *

THE RATIONALIZING OF WESTERN CULTURE

Europe had been in a state of huge turmoil since the days of Christianity's split into Protestant and Catholic variants back in the 1500s. The early 1600s had seen the European continent turn bloody over this matter. And in significant ways, America had served for so many as a place of refuge, a way of getting away from all this European turmoil.

And yet European descendants now able to count themselves as Americans never really put the European dynamic behind them. Europe seemed always to be a place of deeper social introspection, much more sophisticated social debate. True, as de Tocqueville observed about America, it had its own ideas about life. But many Americans, especially those of a more philosophical nature – found extensively in the social circles of the rising Progressivists – were greatly attracted to the high level of social thought coming from Europe. In fact, it was considered to be the height of sophistication to go off to Europe to study (the reverse was hardly the

---

*Some of the Western states, Wyoming (1869), Utah (1870) Colorado (1893), Idaho (1896), had already taken the lead in this, prior to the end of the 1800s.

case yet!). Thus in so many ways, in the realm of higher thought, America mostly found itself simply responding to European developments that were well underway across the Atlantic.

Europe's grand fascination with Human Reason. Whereas America seemed to be a land of social development through tough encounters with a primitive environment on the part of multitudes of very ordinary people, Europe was a world that prided itself as being based on well-reasoned order, an order maintained by smaller and more select groups of individuals possessing more enlightened minds, found typically at the upper levels of a long-standing feudal order. Thus it was that by the late 1600s, Europe saw itself as having entered an age of "Enlightened Despotism" – that is, strict rule by "enlightened" monarchs and their small circles of equally enlightened advisors.

But of course, the idea of enlightenment was not limited to royal circles. University-educated intellectuals saw themselves in the same light. And with the rise of Europe's material prosperity, clearly in place by the 1700s, this self-understanding included also the rising group of industrial entrepreneurs.

This "Age of Enlightenment" had its origins in the early 1600s, with the rise of "natural philosophy" – something we today term as "science." Very active in this matter were the English Puritans, led by such intellectuals as Francis Bacon, who at the turn into the 1600s celebrated the new discoveries of the workings of the natural world, seeing the hand of an incredibly awesome God in the newly discovered grand designs of nature. Bacon's "science" was treated as almost an act of worship, as it would be for so many of the other Puritans – who, for the same reason (seeing their natural philosophy as a witness to the glory of God), took the lead in England's scientific revolution that broke forth in the 1600s. And much the same was the case for the Puritans' Calvinist cousins over in the Netherlands!

But France seemed to be inspired more by the kind of thinking that René Descartes put forward in the early 1600s, who found in the human mind itself, and its ability to uncover these great new truths, the real object of worship. Human Reason was a kind of god in itself, worthy of grand respect, and of full confidence in its powers to bring eventually all of life – including man's social life – under rational control.

And the rising field of mathematics, inspired by the Englishman Isaac Newton and the German Gottfried Wilhelm Leibniz (later 1600s), seemed merely to confirm such human power. But Newton also followed the English trend of being more empirical in how he saw such human power brought to reality, believing that nothing could be considered as true until it had been observed to actually work in the real world. Furthermore, he disappointed many intellectual purists with his wandering into Christian mysticism later in life.*

John Locke (also the later 1600s) was clearly a leader in the thinking that Human Reason should be able to design ever-better social foundations and norms. And by the same logic, he proposed ways to make human thought itself more disciplined, more powerful, in its operation. And as we have already seen, he was invited to put his theories to work in the new Carolina colony, though the results of his efforts were less than spectacular.

Rousseauian anarchism. The Swiss philosopher Jean-Jacques Rousseau was able to take such "progressive" thinking even down a very revolutionary path, when he came up with the notion (well-received through his publication, *The Social Contract* in 1762) that what was needed to bring the world to true progress was to dismantle the long-standing and quite artificial social structures that Europe had been living under (the *Ancien Régime* or Old Order of feudal Europe). This would allow finally "natural man" to rise to a rather instinctive greatness, something that had been lost under the cloud of too much "civilization."

Indeed, Rousseau gave Humanism virtually a religious quality in the way it made true believers of multitudes of intellectuals, individuals that believed persistently that simply tearing down pre-existing social orders would provide the perfect path to human progress.

Obviously, such Humanists were not believers in the Christian doctrine of "original sin," something that took a very dim view of the idea of man's fundamental "purity." But this doctrine of man's fundamental purity would henceforth stand at the heart of Western Humanism, in the various "anarchist" forms it would take – everything from Communism and Socialism to Wilsonian Democratization.†

---

*No, he had not lost his mind as they claimed, but had simply turned that great mind of his to higher things, things that pure Rationalists or Humanists would never be able to – or be willing to – understand!

†In America, such Rousseauian thought would lead American President Wilson to believe that all that was needed to bring the world to democratic perfection was to destroy old social orders under the command of traditional "autocrats" (such as Germany), and beautiful democracy would then automatically blossom forth. Tragically, he was able to sell this idea to fellow Americans, and led them off to a very bloody and quite pointless war in 1917.
Other American presidents have also taken up the Rousseauian cause, with equally disastrous results: Carter momentarily vis-à-vis the Shah's Iran; Bush, Jr. in post-9/11 Afghanistan and Iraq; and Obama in Egypt, Syria, and Libya, with his contributions to the very violent "Arab Spring" starting up in 2011.

But the flaws of such Rousseauian thinking should have been made very clear in the way it led the French Revolution down the road to its "Reign of Terror" in 1793-1794, a clarity however that seemed to never reach the eyes of Humanist devotees – who simply refused to learn from the actual examples that history itself provides most amply. The doctrine was just simply too appealing intellectually and emotionally to be put aside.

The Hegelian dialectic. However, a German philosopher, Georg Wilhelm Friedrich Hegel took a quite different tack concerning the matter of human progress than had Rousseau, seeing, instead of blissful utopia blossoming out of some primitive return to nature, a world more likely shaped by conflict – by even the necessity of conflict. And Hegel had plenty of evidence of conflict to work with, writing in the years during and after the French Revolution. But he also saw history as a matter of grand divine design, directed by the hand of God itself, a great World Spirit (*Weltgeist*) that used the natural instinct of man, not towards harmony but instead towards competition and conflict, as the driving dynamic that moved history forward.

He claimed that each period in history was the by-product of a conflict between two social tendencies in competition at the time, which in their struggles actually birthed yet a new and higher social form which then took them into the next historical period. He thus saw history as the result of a *dialectical* process, two (*di*) forces giving rise to a new and more progressive third force through their struggles.

And just as Rousseau was to have a huge impact in Europe's mid-to-late 1700s, so too Hegel was to have a similar impact in Europe's 1800s (pretty much the whole century), tending to move European philosophy down the line of thought that it was in the dynamic of the struggle or competition for dominance in life that life itself took its particular shape in history. Both Darwinism and Marxism would be shaped strongly by this line of thought. But so would be even the rising realm of a tribal-like nationalism that was shaking Europe as it moved into the 1800s.

Darwinism. The British themselves had remained very pragmatic in the face of the Rousseauian Idealism going on in continental Europe. The Scotsman David Hume, for instance, made it quite clear that it was most unwise to accept anything as True that had not proved itself on numerous occasions as the way things happened by their very nature. There was no room for fancy speculation on such matters for Hume. Nor for that matter was it the case for the fellow Scotsman Adam Smith, who studied carefully various societies in order to derive what seemed to be the actual rules of economics – published as his famous *Wealth of Nations* (1776), nor for the Irishman Edmund Burke, who took the French Rationalists to task in his

Reflections on the Revolution in France (1790).

But it would be the Englishman, Charles Darwin, who would put in place the idea that serious geological and biological research, such as he conducted during a five-year voyage around the world (1831-1836), was the real source of Truth, one which produced a very different picture of the dynamics of life than Humanism.

In this, he was following up on the earlier works of his own grandfather, Erasmus Darwin, who in his *Zoonomia* (1796) had explain the role of nature's very competitive process, which created slow specie progress through what would eventually come to be termed "natural selection" or – more crudely (thanks to Darwin's colleague, Herbert Spencer) – "survival of the fittest."

This also followed closely the political thoughts of the British Whig Party, supported by rising entrepreneurs, who justified (thanks also to the earlier works of the English clergyman Robert Malthus and the Frenchman Jean-Baptiste Lamarck) their growing economic power, and the social cruelties it created as a side-effect of the industrial revolution that England was experiencing at the time. They justified such social cruelty (casting the weak aside) as being simply nature's own very competitive way in which it achieved real progress historically.

Thus Charles Darwin's contribution was to "prove" this line of thought through his extensive research, finally published in 1859 as *On the Origin of Species*. He then expanded on this idea in his *Descent of Man* (1871), explaining how man himself was not created in full or modern form at the beginning of Creation – such as the Biblical account given in the opening chapters of Genesis states as being the case. Instead, man had evolved very slowly over the ages from a very early primate stage (the famous Darwinian "monkey"), through multiple specie changes, in order to finally become contemporary man.

This seemed to be a very compelling explanation of man's own origins, compelling enough for numerous intellectuals to put aside Biblical notions as completely unscientific, and thus to be disregarded completely. The Christian world was shocked.

Nationalism, as a rising tribal religion. When Napoleon unleashed his fired-up French citizen-soldiers against the professional armies of Europe's monarchs, he ran right over the opposition. But he also fired up the peasants of those countries, when the monarchs had to call on their own people, and not just their private armies, to save their thrones. And with this, a huge spirit of "nationalism" was born, actually unleashed!

And it would be a very emotionally charged force for these monarchs to deal with. With popular participation in the defense of the lands went the demand for participation in the politics of those lands as well. Thus something akin to "democracy" began to stir, something that the monarchs were quite leery of, having watched what such "democracy" had done to France in its 1789 overthrow of the Bourbon monarchy that had long-directed that country.

But it was a time of a kind of a "Romantic" stirring that also accompanied this new political awakening of the European continent's commoners. In Germany, divided into hundreds of small states, the hunger to see an actual German "nation" arise out of the political chaos was deepened by the poetry and writings of such Germans as Johann Gottfried Herder and Johan Wolfgang von Goethe, who, in the 1770s, even prior to the French Revolution, helped birth the *Sturm und Drang* (Storm and Drive) movement pushing for German national development. Indeed, this political-intellectual hunger stirring in Germany ended up, over the course of 1800s, not only bringing to life various revolutionary movements in Germany (such as the partially-successful Revolution of 1848) but also making German scholarship a leading force in a more broad intellectual awakening that reached deep into European society, and made German scholarship one of the leading forces of 19th century Europe.

And eventually this romantic hunger in Germany would find its fulfillment in the skillfully played war with neighboring France in 1870, which stampeded all these smaller German states unto a single German Bund or Federation under the direction of Prussia's brilliant Prince Otto von Bismarck!

In fact, this same thing was happening all across Europe at the time, as everyone, from Norwegians in the North to Italians in the South and Russians in the East to Irish in the West, began their march towards their "national destinies."

But it was more like a revival of the tribalism that Charlemagne's feudalism 1200 years earlier had put an end to, with his feudal restructuring of European society, placing Europe under long-standing ruling classes and their dynastic masters. All of that was changing now.

But where was it headed? And who was managing this unleashed force, so that things did not get out of hand?

Tragically, the "Great War" of 1914-1918 (World War One), which bled Europe of a whole generation of young men, made it clear that no one was really able to bring this national-tribal impulse under some kind of civilized management once it was unleashed. Not even American President Woodrow Wilson, who thought (very incorrectly) that he had the answer to the whole matter.

Marxism/Leninism. Another individual who believed that he had the proper answer to this growing nationalist impulse was Karl Marx, who did not like the lines that nationalism was taking. Like Wilson, who believed that democratic constitutions following the American model (although personally Wilson even preferred the British model) were the proper path to a glorious future, Marx was convinced that it was through a carefully managed industrial-class revolution that the future was best met. And he did his best, Darwin-style (he was a big supporter of Darwin) to prove through his own historical research presented in his 1867 publication, *Das Kapital,* the iron laws of social development, development determined by the dialectic of class conflict – conflict among the various social classes that emerged historically as a result of the deep changes in economic structuring that occurred over the span of history.

And Marx was certain that the recent Industrial Revolution that was clearly unfolding in Europe was the true millennium that others (such as the Christian world, which Marx did not approve of either) saw headed their way in history. To Marx, the rising of the industrial working class or "proletariat" against the grip of the "capitalist" owners of Europe's new industries would bring history to its final developmental stage., sort of putting some kind of completion to all historical development.

Thus was born Marxist Socialism's own quite Romantic offering – actually even something of a religious offering (like Europe's "nationalism" and Wilson's "democracy") to the masses. All they needed to do was to follow Marx's advice, and rise up against their capitalist oppressors. And voilà, then would automatically follow a "natural" movement of modern society into its final, utopian stage – some kind of workers' democracy.

But the Russian intellectual, Vladimir Ilyich Ulyanov, popularly known simply as "Lenin," was not as certain that the Marxist utopia would come into being of its own accord simply through spontaneous revolutionary action on the part of Europe's industrial workers. Especially when it came to Russia – where the industrial revolution had only recently got underway, and thus was hardly "ripe for revolution" – Lenin took up the political line of thought that a workers' revolution was going to need quite a bit of help from political specialists, intellectuals (principally himself and his fellow Bolshevik Party leaders) to take the initiative on the part of the largely undeveloped Russian industrial working class and conduct Marxist revolution for them, in other words, a "people's revolution" carefully directed by this small Leninist group serving as the "vanguard" of the industrial proletariat.

But it would not be until the midst of the Great War, and all of its bloody havoc – and the way it simply broke down all sense of political authority – that Lenin would have the opportunity to put his ideas into action in Russia. And in doing so, he would plunge the country into a civil war lasting into the early 1920s, killing more Russians than had even the terrible war they dropped out of in early 1918 in order to conduct this proletarian revolution.

The world, which finally was able to pull out of the horrible nationalist slaughter of World War One in late 1918, was forced to look on in horror as the bloodletting continued, actually worsening, in Russia. It was all such a sickening – and frightening – sight.

Europe vowed that never again would it allow itself to get caught up in such political hysteria. Nice resolve. Too bad it did not last very long.

AMERICAN PROGRESSIVISM

Meanwhile, over in America, by the time the country reached the point of entering the 20th century, there was something of its own social "Awakening" well underway in the country. The industrial revolution had produced deep changes in America's traditional social profile – some of these changes of a very dark nature. Numerous individuals urged the nation to take on these issues and correct them – helping the county to move forward, to progress. Thus they advocated certain "progressive" social programs, when possible even supported by "progressive" legislation. And so it was that they became identified as "Progressivists."

Their Progressivist Movement took on many social dimensions. Most understandably, Progressivism demanded better working conditions for all laborers. Progressivism also fought to place restrictions on child and women's labor in the factories and mines. Progressivism was also dedicated to the goal of improved public education, especially for the poor living in urban slums. It fought for quality control of foods, especially meats, sold to the public. It pursued a fight for greater protection of the natural environment against the wholesale plunder of the nation's natural resources. And it included the ideas of turning prisons into reformatories that would reform rather than just merely punish offenders of the law.

Progressivism sought to make local government more democratic and more efficient (often contradictory concepts!) by introducing the ideas of popular recall of corrupt public officials, by putting in place the party primary which allowed the voter rather than the city machine to choose the local candidates for public office, and by the idea of hiring a professional city manager who would be "neutral" in the realm of party politics – as if political neutrality itself was truly attainable by those wielding significant social power.

Secular or Humanist Progressivism. Progressivism was not the program of any particular social group – or even political party. The state itself played a rather minimal role in designing Progressivism's many initiatives – although the state did tend to follow up on social initiatives in many cases with legislation solidifying the gains of the Progressivists.

The Church also played a minimal role directly – although to most people, what motivated all of this Progressivism was the Christian spirit of charity for all, especially the poor and downtrodden. And as most Americans at the time considered themselves as "Christian," Progressivism needed no special affirmation as a Christian movement (although the WCTU was very explicitly "Christian").

However, others reacting to the social problems around them were more inspired by a rising Humanism that was once again capturing numerous American hearts. These Humanists were generally professional intellectuals – writers, journalists and educators for instance – who attempted to support those "less fortunate" than themselves.* Their caring generally took the form of calling for social justice through governmental action or legal reform. God's justice played no necessary role in this matter. It was all simply a case of employing human logic – or "social science," as this logic came to be termed.

Such Humanism was very Rousseauian, in that the Humanists had little doubt about the basic goodness of man. They were not at all supporters of the old Christian idea of a person's own "original sin" as the major handicap facing human life. Humanists were convinced that if given the right opportunity, humans would naturally demonstrate an amazing goodness of spirit and action.

To the Humanists, all that stood in the way of bringing such human virtue to light was a corrupt society built on corrupt laws and consequently corrupt social practices. Society needed only to reform the social laws that enabled and encouraged these corrupt practices – and the utopian bliss which Humanists were positive awaited mankind would dramatically appear of its own accord.

Jane Addams. One of these Progressivists was a most amazing woman – who did not follow the tendency of other Progressivists to be rather socially abstract in their Progressivism (working in support of categories of people rather than with distinct individuals) – Jane Addams. She was a woman of enormous personal warmth, achieving amazing social impact through simply that personal warmth of spirit.

With her mother having died when she was only two, she was

---

*As intellectuals, they typically approached life through carefully designed programs – rather than direct or personal involvement with the "victims" of society.

raised by her older sisters and a loving father, a very successful Illinois businessman, who himself then died in 1881, leaving her $50 thousand (roughly $1.23 million in today's dollars). She was thus able to follow a childhood dream of studying medicine in Philadelphia – with the intention of eventually serving the poor, though the dream ended when she had to return to Illinois because, in part, of ongoing back problems acquired when she was a child. But two years later she was able to travel to Europe, and in England became inspired by Toynbee Hall – where, quite exceptionally for the times, various social classes – ranging from aristocrats to the very poor – lived, learned, and worked together. This would become the model for her when she returned to the States and used her money in 1889 to purchase a run-down mansion, the Hull House, in Chicago.

Here too, members of the different social classes* (including different ethnic groups) learned to share their worlds, their dreams, their actual futures, from childhood onward. Hull House included, besides a school, an art museum, a library, and a theater, eventually thirteen separate buildings and a playground. Here Progressivism took on a very distinct, very strong, personal quality.

Later in life, when World War One broke out in Europe in 1914, her strong pacifism led her to be elected chairman of the Women's Peace Party, and the following year also to become a leader in the International Congress of Women – a group trying to find ways to end the war. Sadly, when American President Wilson decided in 1917 that he would be doing everyone a great favor by sending American soldiers to kill Germans in Northern France, her pacifism became viewed as being highly unpatriotic, and she was treated harshly.

After the war she continued her world peace program , and in 1931 she was voted the Nobel Peace Prize by the awards committee virtually unanimously, capping a long career which exemplified in so many ways the very heart of Progressivism. Four years later she died, deeply mourned by the American nation which saw in her only goodness in inspiring hope to the world, much needed at a time when America was going through the Great Depression.

William Jennings Bryan. We have already met Bryan, the Democratic Party's presidential nominee in 1896, who captivated the convention with his "Cross of Gold" speech. He too took up the Progressivist crusade, inspired from an early age when he became a "born-again" Christian, building on that character by study at the Presbyterian Illinois College,

---

*She was able to get a good number of socially prestigious women to roll up their sleeves and join her in her ground-level work among Chicago's poor!

where he developed a strong sense of the need for greater social justice in America. This then led him to law school, and then subsequently the law practice. But he and his wife, Mary (also a lawyer), felt that greater opportunities awaited them in Nebraska, which they moved to in 1887. There he soon became involved in local Democratic Party politics. He was elected and served as a US Congressman, but then lost the Senate election in 1894 when the Republicans took control of the Nebraska legislature.[*]

But Bryan was a restless crusader – and an excellent speaker – who at that point decided to take to the lecture circuit, to press his case for social justice, especially concerning this matter of how the very wealthy lorded it over America's poor. And as the 1893 crisis was understood as being essentially a matter of gold versus silver as the backing of the U.S. dollar, Bryan took on that subject, enthusiastically. And thus it was that in 1896 he was chosen by the Democrats to run for the U.S. Presidency.

He lost the national election that year to McKinley but was renominated four years later – again losing to McKinley. By the time of this second election in 1900, the economy had already picked up, and his social advocacy no longer had the urgency about it that it did four years earlier. He would sit out the 1904 election (which Roosevelt won) but run again four years after that in 1908, this time losing to the Republican candidate, Taft.

Part of Bryan's problem was that he had been clearly an anti-imperialist, at a time when the glories of imperialism were shining brightly, not only in Europe but in America as well. He hated the Darwinism that stood behind this urge, namely the right of the strong to dominate the weak – yea even the necessity of the strong dominating the weak – in order to promote historical "progress." But he was also at the time a Democratic Idealist, believing religiously that bringing the world to democracy, even by military intervention if necessary, would be the one certain way of progressing the world to a state of true justice, true harmony, true peace. Thus he supported America's intervention in the Spanish-American War, drawing criticism from fellow anti-imperialists. In short, he found himself standing politically in the middle on the key issue of imperialism, or basically nowhere special.

But he would still be a major party figure four years later when, at the Democratic Party National Convention of 1912, he finally threw his support to Woodrow Wilson (on the 46th ballot!), and was then rewarded by Wilson when Wilson became president – by being brought on Wilson's cabinet as

---

[*]The election of the U.S. Senators by the American voter (rather than by the state legislatures, in accordance with the U.S. Constitution's Article 1, section 3) would not take place until the passage of the 17th Amendment in 1913.

Secretary of State. But Wilson and Bryan had very different opinions about exactly how America should get involved abroad, especially as Bryan truly wanted America to stay out of World War One, and Wilson favored deeply the "democracies" Britain and France in the contest. Clearly Bryan had moved on past his Democratic Idealism, whereas Wilson was lost in such Idealism. So Bryan resigned his position in June of 1915.

But he did not put his crusading heart aside, especially when he saw Christian morality being undercut by the Darwinist spirit which hit America hard after the war. And thus (as we shall see in a later chapter) he finished out his life defending his faith, in the famous "Scopes Monkey Trial" of 1925.

Theodore (Teddy) Roosevelt. Another major figure in the Progressivist Movement was none other than President Teddy Roosevelt. He too was an individual involved in almost every aspect of Progressivism, including its more militant varieties. Personally, he was himself a militant when it came to a cause, any cause. Like the robber barons – with whom he often battled (when not befriending them) – he was the picture of Darwinian fortitude, pressing, pressing, pressing forward whatever agenda he happened to be involved with.

Roosevelt was well familiar with struggle in life, fighting to overcome asthma – compensating by become a serious athlete (mountain climbing, boxing). But not only was he athletic, he was quite the scholar, editor of the Harvard Advocate, and graduating Phi Beta Kappa and magna cum laude in 1880. He also did research at that time on the War of 1812, which he eventually published (still considered even today as one of the best in print on that war).

He was also quite familiar with personal family loss. His much beloved father had died in 1878 during his second year at Harvard, leaving him deeply stunned. He married four years later in 1882 at age twenty-two, but his wife died two years later in delivering their first child, Alice. Furthermore, his mother had just died in the same house, only eleven hours earlier.

But from all this he came to understand that the only intelligent response to such events in life, no matter how tragic, was never to quit. It was of critical importance to get back on your feet and continue to press forward, more determined than ever not to be defeated. Thus the same year as his wife and mother's deaths (1884) he was also elected to the New York State Assembly and joined the New York National Guard as a second lieutenant.

He rose quickly in public life, headed up the New York delegation to the 1884 Republican Party national convention where he delivered a keynote speech. But, when Democrat Cleveland won the national elections that year, he retired and headed West to become the "Dakota Cowboy." Two years later he would marry in London, Edith, who would provide him five more children. And soon after that he was back in full swing in the world of national politics serving in Washington, D.C. for seven years on the Civil Service Commission, before, as a major reformer, becoming New York City Police Commissioner. Then his next step up was to become Assistant Secretary of the Navy, actually advising President McKinley directly on naval events, not only because he was well informed on the matter but because his boss, the Secretary of the Navy, became quite sick.

But this was not even enough service to satisfy Roosevelt, who resigned his position on the Cabinet and went West in 1898 to form up his own military unit, the Rough Riders (individuals ranging from Eastern socialites to the roughest Western hunters, cowboys and Indians!) to lead off to Cuba and then the famous charge up "San Juan Hill."

With that accomplishment completed, he ran for – and was elected – New York Governor (1899-1901). As such, he strengthened his talents as a serious political reformer, just in time to be brought on as McKinley's running mate in the 1900 national elections. With McKinley's election (his second) Roosevelt was raised from this totally boring job to become U.S. President himself upon McKinley's assassination only 6 months into his new term.

At this point the nation got to see the real reformer in Roosevelt, as he took on "trust-busting" policies to break up the huge concentrations of American wealth in the hands of a very few corporate leaders. But he also signed into law the 1906 Pure Food and Drug Act, along with other legislation designed to oversee the healthiness of the products of both key American industries. And he was very active in getting undeveloped land transformed into national parks, national forests and game preserves.

But Roosevelt committed one huge political fumble, one that would not only impact his own political career, but also the way American politics would develop in the near future. In 1904, as national elections came around, he promised that this second presidential term he was running for would be his last. He would soon enough regret this promise.

Roosevelt's second term was a bit bumpier. The Supreme Court blocked as unconstitutional his effort to establish a national income tax (to make the rich give greater support to the nation's public affairs), and for that matter blocked similar efforts of his to bring American social dynamics under greater national supervision.* But his biggest problem occurred

---

*Indeed, there really was not (not yet anyway) any constitutional warrant for such political activity, as the Framers of the Constitution had been careful to set

when in 1907 a major copper company got greedy and went bankrupt in attempting a monopolistic move on the rest of the copper industry, sending shock waves through the world of American finance. Stock values on Wall Street fell away, numerous state and local banks collapsed, and finally the huge Knickerbocker Trust Company declared bankruptcy. America at this point was in full panic mode. Thus it was that now Roosevelt (like Cleveland before him) turned to J.P. Morgan for help, allowing Morgan to buy out a number of strategic industries facing bankruptcy in order to put them back on their feet. How ironic it was that during his last years in office the strongly anti-monopolist Roosevelt had to turn to one of his targeted monopolies for help!

William Howard Taft. We bring up another Progressivist for close study at this point because he took up exactly at the point when Roosevelt had to make good on his promise and step down from the presidency at the end of his second term. William Howard Taft was Roosevelt's friend, and a logical successor to Roosevelt in the White House in 1908. Once again, the Democrats put Bryan in the running as their presidential candidate, and for the third time he went down to defeat, this time by the Republican candidate Taft.

Whereas Roosevelt was the hyperactive individual, Taft was the more quietly determined reformer, like Roosevelt born of a high-status family (Ohio politics) but a Yale rather than Harvard product. And Taft's interests were more in the field of law, Taft early on hoping to become a federal Justice some day. He was appointed at age 34 (1892) to the position of Sixth Circuit Court judge.

But he was called from the field of law to the world of politics when in 1900 President McKinley asked him to head up a commission to organize a new government for the Philippines (an American war trophy won in the war with Spain). He accepted, serving the Philippines as something like its own governor, with the understanding that in return, McKinley would make him his next appointment to the Supreme Court. But McKinley's assassination ended that promise.

But his close relationship with Roosevelt would take him down the path he would head, all the way up to the U.S. Presidency in 1909. The two served together in Washington on the Civil Service Commission, and in turn Roosevelt in becoming President commissioned Taft to negotiate

---

up a national government of very limited internal or domestic responsibilities, political, economic, or social. Those matters were "reserved" (Constitutional Amendments 9 and 10) to the doings of the states or the American people themselves.

America Comes of Age

with the Vatican the transfer of massive landholdings the Church held in the Philippines, into the hands of the Filipino commoners. Then, oddly enough, Taft turned down an offer to be appointed by Roosevelt to the Supreme Court, but did accept the request to join Roosevelt's cabinet as his Secretary of War (like Taft's father under President Grant), because that position also continued Taft as Philippine administrator (the Philippines were under U.S. "protection" at that point).

Actually at that point Taft had become some kind of personal assistant to Roosevelt, sent on all sorts of missions. So that when Roosevelt ran for election in 1904, he quite naturally asked Taft to be his vice-presidential running mate. Taft accepted, and for the next four years the two would work together very closely.

Then when Roosevelt finished his second term, he kept his promise and stepped out of Washington politics, setting Taft up to take his place. And thus Taft became U.S. President, and an even bigger reformist "trust-buster than Roosevelt.*

But Roosevelt was ever so sorry that he had stepped aside, and as the 1912 elections approached, he tried to get Taft not to run again so that he could run as the Republican candidate. But Taft, now a self-made politician, was not interested in Roosevelt's program, and the two friends parted company, bitterly. Roosevelt was no quitter, and when he narrowly lost the Republican Party's presidential candidacy to Taft, he and his followers withdrew and set up their own Progressive Party, or "Bull Moose" Party, since the new organization was built entirely on the Roosevelt phenomenon.

But splitting the Republican vote meant only one thing: this would open the door to the White House of the Democratic Party candidate, in this case Woodrow Wilson, who otherwise would have had no chance of getting elected.

And the Roosevelt-Taft split would never be repaired. Eventually when the Republicans were returned to power after World War One, President Harding would appoint Taft as chief justice to the Supreme Court, a position Taft would hold until his death in 1930.

Meanwhile Roosevelt would try to get back into the mainstream of national politics, but with no real success at this point. He died just as World War One ended, deeply mourned by the American people.

Their Christian faith. What can we conclude about these key individuals, as to their place in the world of the Christian faith? Roosevelt was of course

---

*In his four years in office, Taft undertook seventy trust-busting cases under the 1890 Sherman Antitrust Act, as compared to Roosevelt's forty such cases during his eight years in office.

a very "practical" man, not given much to the idea of miracles and spiritual insights. But his practicality was well understood by himself and others to be strongly Christian in character. He was deeply shaped by Biblical instruction which he received in ample supply (his father in fact taught Sunday School), understanding how "Christian character" stood at the very foundations of American culture. Indeed, Roosevelt himself stated in a speech in 1901:

> *Every thinking man, when he thinks, realizes what a very large number of people tend to forget, that the teachings of the Bible are so interwoven and entwined with our whole civic and social life that it would be literally – I do not mean figuratively, I mean literally – impossible for us to figure to ourselves what that life would be if these teachings were removed. We would lose almost all the standards by which we now judge both public and private morals; all the standards toward which we, with more or less of resolution, strive to raise ourselves. Almost every man who has by his lifework added to the sum of human achievement of which the race is proud, has based his lifework largely upon the teachings of the Bible, Among the greatest men a disproportionately large number have been diligent and close students of the Bible at first hand.**

Bryan was most evidently a man of very strong Christian interest, much like Roosevelt's understanding that America was built very strongly on the moral foundations of Christianity. We find this same viewpoint in Bryan's closing argument in the famous 1925 Scopes Monkey Trial, in which he contests the claim of Secularists that human science alone was about to bring life on this planet to perfection, Bryan seeing in such Secularism a lack of moral restraint – such as has thus been making warfare even more brutal, to the point that civilization seems able to commit suicide:

> *Science is a magnificent force, but it is not a teacher of morals. It can perfect machinery, but it adds no moral restraints to protect society from the misuse of the machine. It can also build gigantic intellectual ships, but it constructs no moral rudders for the control of storm-tossed human vessel. It not only fails to supply the spiritual element needed but some of its unproven hypotheses rob the ship of its compass and thus endanger its*

---

*Christian F. Reisner, *Roosevelt's Religion*. Cincinnati: The Abingdon Press, 1922, p. 306.

> cargo. In war, science has proven itself an evil genius; it has made war more terrible than it ever was before. Man used to be content to slaughter his fellowmen on a single plane, the earth's surface. Science has taught him to go down into the water and shoot up from below and to go up into the clouds and shoot down from above, thus making the battlefield three times as bloody as it was before; but science does not teach brotherly love. Science has made war so hellish that civilization was about to commit suicide; and now we are told that newly discovered instruments of destruction will make the cruelties of the late war seem trivial in comparison with the cruelties of wars that may come in the future.

He sees only the moral teachings of Jesus as able to solve the problems that face the world.

> If civilization is to be saved from the wreckage threatened by intelligence not consecrated by love, it must be saved by the moral code of the meek and lowly Nazarene. His teachings, and His teachings alone, can solve the problems that vex the heart and perplex the world.

Although in his long statement he ascribes the power of miracles to God, what he is doing here is essentially defending a Christianity of high moral standards, typical of where Christianity stood in so many American minds and hearts those days.

Addams was actually seminary trained, at her father's insistence attending the Rockford Female Seminary. But her dream was in personally helping the poor and rejected (her back problems and her lack of feminine good looks caused her to see herself in that same category), as at least a doctor able to tend to the physical problems of others. We can certainly see strong Christian character in these interests, although she was much more global in her appreciation of people's ability to love and serve others – for her personally almost a matter of natural instinct rather than any particular religious discipline. In short, she never saw herself as standing apart from the realm of Christianity. But by today's standards she would be classed simply as a Humanist.

And for Taft, it is hard to find evidence as to where he stood concerning Christianity. But we know that he was raised in a home in which his father, a member of the Ohio Supreme Court, dissented strongly in the court's 1870 decision upholding the reading of the Bible in public schools. Alfonso Taft took the side of Catholics and Jews in the view that this was simply a way of imposing the Protestant faith on America's youth, and in violation of the most basic of all human rights. He also questioned the accuracy of Biblical translations or the ability of people to understand on their own the meaning of scripture. This does not sound like Taft, Sr., would therefore have been very encouraging of a Biblical upbringing of son William. Again, we would more safely place Taft in the Humanist category.

✶ ✶ ✶

AMERICA CULTIVATES NEW SOCIAL FORMULAS AS IT HEADS INTO THE TWENTIETH CENTURY

"Democracy" as the new social cure-all. By the beginning of the 20th century, Americans had forgotten that the Constitutional Framers of 1787 had created a Republic of precise laws derived from the disciplines and dictates of America's pre-existing and quite long-standing social foundations. Those Framers of the American Constitution had no intentions whatsoever to put in place a newly conceived democracy of popular political wills, wills easily maneuvered this way and that by clever demagogues. The Athenian example had made it clear to the Framers that this was to be carefully avoided.

Under the rules of the Constitution, the people would have their voice in the House of Representatives. But that voice would have to work with – or be checked by – the U.S. Senate, where the states would send their very best "ambassadors" to represent the interests of the various states –individuals chosen by the state legislatures (as per the Constitution itself). The president would likewise be elected by representatives of the states as special electors (not by the American people themselves) and the federal judges would be appointed for life by the president, subject to the confirming vote of the Senate (not the House of Representatives) as would also be diplomats and other executive officers. The United States was intended to be a republic, not a democracy.

But a Rousseauian spirit was overtaking America, much as it had "enlightened" Europe (including Revolutionary France). A very Romantic vision about the basic goodness of man – and the corruption of traditional social orders – seemed to infect the thinking of the West's intellectuals, in America as well as Europe. Of course such Humanism was not new to the West – nor to America, which had gone through waves of such "enlightenment" already several times since its birth three centuries earlier.

Actually, "democracy" was taking its place in American hearts as something of a religion – closely related to the new nationalist thinking that was sweeping hearts away in the Western world . Democracy was a religion that believed as its central article of its faith that "natural" man was by all instincts an angel. According to this Humanist or "democratic" religion, traditional social orders (built on long habit) were keeping that angelic character suppressed, forcing human behavior to become desperate, even criminal. Crime was a by-product of social injustice, not just a matter of breaking the law. Society thus needed to be reformed, its ancient laws changed, new freedoms offered the people, and happiness would finally reign as the angelic potential in man finally revealed itself.

This was quite a different religion than Christianity, which believed in faith in God, not faith in man, as the way that life took on its glory. The Puritans had built their entire social order on that Christian belief.

But now that belief was being replaced be the idea that man himself – not God – would ultimately be the source of such earthly glory. All that was needed was social reform – led importantly by those who knew how to bring the best out of the people themselves. These select reformers would supposedly not be self-interested, scheming demagogues. These would be the ones enlightened by the new ideas and doctrines coming out as the world entered the 20th century, doctrines that surely had "science" to back them up as being the ultimate Truth in life. All now that was needed was to trust fully the Russian Bolsheviks, the German nationalists, the Washington Progressivists, etc. who had the people's best interests at heart as they pushed for deep social reform (even Revolution if need be). These enlightened ones were supposedly working out of the purest and highest of motives as they pushed for mankind's ultimate success. Just ask them.

So forget tradition, change the laws (deeply if need be), and just trust to the wisdom of the reformers – who were advancing (from the loftier heights of their writing desks) their various social theories as "democracy."

John Dewey. America certainly had its own well-known voices of such "democratic" social reform. One such popular voice was that of John Dewey, an American educator whose writings had a huge impact not only in the growing world of educational philosophy – but on the way Americans moved to a more Humanist or "Liberal" understanding of life itself. Like Rousseau, Dewey believed that under all the social structuring that a person goes through in his or her development there is a basic, instinctive goodness in the human design, one that should be allowed to develop apart from society's mere traditions, traditions which included bad social habits built up willy-nilly over the generations. Real human progress necessitated a thorough social house cleaning. And the best way to get that done is through enlightened or Liberal instruction of the youth, who had not yet fallen into the habit of doing things simply because it was the tradition to do things this way or that. The youth represented the best material for building a very progressive future.*

Dewey graduated from the University of Vermont in 1879 and found a job teaching high school in Pennsylvania for two years before returning to Vermont to teach at a primary school there. But he recognized rather immediately that he would rather study the philosophy of education than actually engage in it, in the elementary/secondary classroom at least. Thus he headed off to graduate school (Johns Hopkins University), got his doctorate and then took a teaching position with the University of Michigan's philosophy department. He moved on from there to additional teaching positions, in 1889 becoming chairman of the Department of Philosophy at the University of Chicago (1894), where he began to write and publish his social-educational theories. In 1904 he moved on to Columbia University in New York City, and continued to write even more extensively on education, society, human psychology, and social ethics.

His philosophy was standard Humanist theory: social environment determines human behavior; reform the environment in very practical ways and you will reform human behavior. He also, like so many intellectuals of his generation, believed that democracy was the proper formula for solving society's problems (though critics were quick to point out that he never really explained how democracy was supposed to work in a mass society). He might not have stood out from the intellectual crowd, except that his massive number of publications made him a well-recognized leader in the rising Humanist movement underway in America (he published some 40 books and over 700 articles in his lifetime).

After retiring from Columbia, Dewey continued over the next twenty years to be very active in promoting his Secular (even atheistic) Humanist philosophy, taking a position in 1929 on the board of the Humanist Society of New York, then being one of the composers of the 1933 *Humanist Manifesto*, and an avid writer and lecturer on the subject thereafter.

And he (and his legacy) would continue after him to help direct the country's rising Liberal intellectualism in its battle against America's long-standing moral-spiritual foundations in the Christian faith.

American "Liberalism." This aiming at America's youth seemed like a very good approach to social progress by those who were calling themselves "Liberals." They intended to "liberate" future generations from imperfect,

---

*Enacting deep social change by taking over the education of a future generation is not a new thing. Back in the 1600s, the Jesuits understood quite well the importance of taking charge of the education of the young, in order to build a purer "Catholic" world. And the Chinese dictator Mao Zedong more recently (1960s) undertook deep "cultural revolution" in China the same way.

even "failed," social tradition – to free them up to follow much better social paths, ones laid out for them of course by their enlightened mentors, their Progressive teachers and professors.

But where Liberalism became truly ironic was in the way it looked increasingly to the federal state to take the lead in changing the laws that tradition had put in place. What is interesting is that the word "Liberal" in the European context meant almost the opposite of what it was coming to mean in America. European Liberalism was founded on the fear of an overly aggressive State, one that took on dictatorial powers in order to force its political interests on its subject people. "Liberal" mean to cut back – to "liberate" the people from, not expand – the powers of the state, an idea that the American Framers of the Constitution understood quite well themselves back in the 1780s after having gone through what they had experienced in their recent war of independence against an overbearing British king.

But now American Liberalism proposed to enhance the powers of the federal or national state (just like Lenin's State Socialism) because the federal state was considered by American Liberals as the country's best locus for enlightened power, such as would be able to put into place true social progress (the reformers' own programs, of course).

In Europe such Liberalism would go by the name of Socialism – a term that in America would long remain taboo.* But under the cover of careful labelling, the policies of both American Liberalism and European Socialism actually had/have pretty much the same ambition: to let "enlightened" national authorities take the reins of power (social powers taken away from not only the states of Massachusetts, Ohio, Kansas, etc., but also local town councils, school boards and churches, and even fathers and mothers) if you want to see social progress truly blossom.

Supreme Court Justice Oliver Wendell Holmes, Jr. Adding considerably to this rising "Liberal" attitude was a very scholarly Supreme Court Justice Oliver Wendell Holmes, Jr., whose legal writings and Supreme Court decisions (often in dissent of the Court's majority decisions) would shape strongly this rising understanding of proper political-legal dynamics.

Holmes was a well-born product of a prominent Bostonian family, like his father Harvard educated, close friends with prominent philosopher-writers such as the transcendentalist Emerson and the James brothers, William and Henry, Jr., and something of philosopher-writers themselves,

---

*That is, until Vermont Senator Bernie Sanders came along in the 2010s/2020s and ran a nearly successful campaign for the Democratic Party presidential candidacy in 2016 on a self-proclaimed Socialist platform!

father and son. But it was military duty in the Civil War – Holmes enlisted in 1861 just as he was graduating from Harvard (and just as the war was starting up), seeing action in numerous battles, and suffering also numerous wounds as a result – that would shape his social-legal philosophy deeply. As he would see things, such sacrificial social service opened his eyes to the world of political realism, and thus the need for the legal system to keep up with such realism. Thus he entitled his legal philosophy "Legal Realism."

Appointed by Roosevelt to the Supreme Court in 1902, Holmes quickly proved himself to be strongly opposed to the idea of there being some kind of permanent, universal set of legal standards (especially those designed by an unseen deity) that should serve unchangingly from generation to generations.* He detested such Legal Idealism (or what today would be termed Legal Originalism).

To Holmes, life changed constantly, and so did society's particular challenges. And it was the responsiblity of the law, even the most fundamental law, to keep up with such changes. And how was it to do so? That was the job of politicians, especially court judges, on whose shoulders fell the responsibility of finding true moral legal principles – in the way they were required constantly to make decisions on the basis of multiple facts and evolving social issues. But through dutiful training and actual experience, such wisdom could be expected of those given such responsibility.

In short, it was up to the wiser elements of society (like Holmes himself, for instance) to define, or redefine, even the most fundamental law as they went along. And so the "Liberal" theory of "democracy from above" got a tremendous push from this very notable 20th century legal philosopher.†'

---

*Actually, he had expressed this view quite clearly in an earlier collection of his lectures and legal writing published in book form in 1881 as *The Common Law*.

†Unfortunately, such "Realist" (or Liberal or Progressive) views as Holmes's seem quite ignorant of the fact that there is more to goodness and truth than an individual's – especially a very "enlightened" individual's – own personal inclination to see things as he or she does.

Too much of just such enlightenment was the problem confronting the 55 delegates who gathered in Philadelphia in 1787 to draft a Constitution for the new American Union. Each of the delegates had his own good idea (like Holmes) as to how things should go, and argued endlessly.

Finally, Franklin took them above their own logic, their own reasoning, to have them put their thoughts before God, and also to listen to each other. Then and only then were they able to get past their personal wisdoms to find a higher truth, one requiring them to let go of their personal takes on matters.

What those 55 men finally secured is incredible wisdom, wisdom of a very lasting variety.

The Sixteenth and Seventeenth Amendments to the Constitution (1913). Along with this went also two new Amendments to the American Constitution, changing deeply the way social power had long been shaped in federal America.

The Sixteenth Amendment awarded the federal authorities in Washington the power to tax directly the American people – at the time thought to offer Washington authorities no more than a small supplement to the fees, licenses, etc. that it collected in order to run its operations. There was little understanding at the time that this opened the door for Washington eventually to lay huge taxes on the American people and their economy – in order to run its various programs presumably designed to better America.

The Seventeenth Amendment also involved a huge reshaping of the American Constitution's checks and balances system when it took the selection of senators away from the states and put that matter in the hands of the people. This was clearly a huge step in the direction of "democratizing" American politics, supposedly taking power out of the often-corrupt political machines operating in the state capitals and placing that power, through the people, into the Washington political arena itself – where supposedly the political doings of America's wielders of power could be more closely watched, and checked, by an enlightened citizenry (enlightened largely by the information put forward by a Progressivist Press corps).

Power problems. There was no doubt that the state legislators and governors' offices were frequently the arenas of amazingly corrupt behavior, such as the laws defined and sought to restrict or suppress. But keeping such corruption under control is not an easy task. Power always attracts the interest of people with more active egos, who find it easy enough to get around moral-legal restrictions holding them back in this power-pursuit, because human reason can always find a way to justify virtually anything. But what these two Amendments did was simply to shift the scene of such grand pursuit of power from the individual states, now to the distant offices of the Washington politicians. And guess what? Political corruption naturally moved in that direction as well.

Those that constantly want to reform that wisdom (with their own enlightened ideas of course) threaten to undermine that wonderful legacy. And thus Franklin's statement, "A Republic, if you can keep it." He understood full well the dangers that "wise men" would bring to the American Republic in their efforts to "upgrade" that incredible constitutional achievement. As Franklin knew full well, constant effort to upgrade the famous Roman Republic was what had finally destroyed it.

Worse, handing Washington such new (and potentially limitless) power would mean that the numerous states would find "checking" the power of the central state (which was the big question which the Constitution faced when seeking ratification in 1787-1788) would be nearly impossible at this point. Then who would place the needed checks on such power: the Washington politicians themselves or the national press corps looking for ways to get into the power game itself?

How would America's citizens effectively protect themselves in this move to "democracy," when action "behind the scenes" would be almost impossible to detect from Omaha or Dallas or Denver? Could they trust the press (supposedly the eyes and ears of the people) not to get ideologically involved in the process and thus become part of the problem rather than its solution?

No one raised such questions in the rush to "democratize" America in the early 20th century.

✳ ✳ ✳

AMERICAN CHRISTIANITY RESPONDS

Christianity again undergoing deep debate. At the time, "Christianity" was so deeply imbedded in the idea of America that the ideological developments going on in Europe seemed to have little impact outside of some smaller intellectual circles in America. Even Liberals like Dewey did not at first see themselves as offending Christianity just because he was not working within a deeply Christian worldview. He was simply doing science the way others conducted science in their chemistry or biological labs. What he was doing had nothing to do one way or the other (not at that time however) with Christianity. However, with time, (by the time of the publication of the 1933 *Humanist Manifesto*) Dewey would find himself taking on a more distinctly anti-Christian role. America needed deliverance from not just tradition, "Christian" as such tradition claimed to be, but from the superstition that accompanied it.

But for the time being, for the vast majority of Americans, still sitting regularly in the pews of the American churches, Christian tradition had not yet been shaken by this "higher" intellectual inquiry going on in the rarified atmosphere of America's intellectual circles.

"Science" or "religion"? And yet God himself as "providence" or provider of American blessings was losing much of his place in American hearts. The social dynamic driving the country was seemingly handled quite nicely by the progress that science and technology were achieving. And science worked mechanically, no miracles needed. And judging from the considerable material progress America was experiencing at the time, science was more than adequate as the true sustainer of society and its progress.

At the same time, the bedrock of America's Protestant Christianity – Biblical Scripture as the "Word of God" – had recently come into deep debate, especially in the higher social circles of science and theology. This debate involved an argument between religious "modernism," supporting the role of science and technology, and religious "traditionalism," with its support of divine miracles that had no known scientific basis for their occurrence. Which of these contending positions was a thinking person supposed to support: science (materialism) or religion (mysticism), especially as the Biblical writings themselves raised those very questions?

Christianity attempts a reply. Princeton Seminary had long taken the position under the dominating influence of Charles Hodge (1850s through most of the 1870s) to be unbending in the attitude that every word of Scripture was God-breathed and thus not to be questioned or disputed. In short, Hodge was defending very strongly the principle of the "inerrancy of Biblical Scripture." But he would find his position increasingly challenged as the 1800s moved towards its close.

Meanwhile, another approach to this issue was that of those who simply chose to ignore the debate, and focus on the issue at hand: saving souls. One such individual was Crawford H. Toy, a professor at the Southern Baptist Seminary, who won hearts by simply focusing on the spirit of love that stood at the heart of Christianity – rather than theological doctrine. Unfortunately, even that proved to be too much of a compromise for the otherwise creedless Baptists, whose Convention in 1879 forced him to resign his position at the seminary because he was not taking a sufficiently pro-inerrancy stand.

More successful in this middling approach was Henry Ward Beecher, son of the conservative Presbyterian preacher Lyman Beecher and brother of fellow Abolitionist Harriet Beecher Stowe (author of *Uncle Tom's Cabin*). As a popular pastor and circuit preacher, Beecher sidestepped the controversial intellectual issues of evolution and Biblical reliability, even stating at one point that he saw no problem with the theory of evolution – as long as it understood God to be at the heart of the process. He preached a very upbeat message of love and a willing accommodation to the changing industrial culture developed around the Christian community. And he proved to be quite successful in developing a stable middle-class message in the face of Darwinism's intellectual challenge, all the way up until his death in 1887.

Another individual to take something of a middling approach to the issue of traditional theological correctness and the rising new cultural norm of industrial/scientific Rationalism was Dwight L. Moody, circuit preacher and simple but straightforward evangelist. Moody preached to crowds of mostly middle-class Americans, who were simply trying to make sense of the social changes underway in their once-familiar America. Moody was far from being an intellectual Progressivist with a moral program designed to make the world a better place. Nor did he have any strong views on the burning issues of the Christian seminaries, such as evolution or Biblical inerrancy. He was a classic premillennial who simply looked to Jesus's second coming to clean up the mess that human sin had made of creation. And that approach to life's challenges at the end of the 1800s made sense to thousands of people who flocked to hear what he had to say at his various urban rallies held around the country.

Charles Briggs and Biblical "higher criticism." But towards the end of the century, a thunderstorm broke over Union Theological Seminary's Hebrew scholar Charles Briggs' clear affirmation that text-criticism or literary analysis amply proved among other things that Moses did not actually write the first five books of Scripture but that these writings were the result of the much later collection of at least four different narrative traditions, and that Isaiah did not write the entire work given under his name but that later disciples of the Isaiah school had written the second half of the work.

Although for any who might have understood that the Jewish Scriptures were community narrative (not science), such a revelation should have come as no surprise. Biblical narrative was about finding the path to Truth through divine inspiration, and was not assembled anciently by those with a modern scientific worldview. But Briggs went further, even claiming that the Old Testament was morally inferior to the moral development of modern times.

This so enraged the Presbyterian denomination that in 1893 it not only excommunicated him* but tried to block Briggs' professorial advancement at Union Seminary in New York City. But the seminary refused to dismiss Briggs, and instead the seminary withdrew from the Presbyterian denomination (both Briggs and the seminary joined the more "modernist" Episcopalian denomination).

But Brigg's excommunication hardly caused the controversy to go away. It merely deepened the controversy, as biblical perfection or "infallibility" became one of the essential doctrines, one of the "fundamentals of faith,"

---

*Commentators have noted that part of his difficulty with the denomination occurred in part also because of Briggs' abrasive manner when challenged.

America Comes of Age

proclaimed by a growing group of Christian traditionalists – who eventually took or were assigned the name "Fundamentalists,," derived from the publication, *The Fundamentals*, presenting essays over the period of 1910-1915, written by some 65 theologians of various denominations, essays in support of the idea of the infallible authority of Scripture.

The Social Gospel. But the modernizers or religious "Liberals" were hardly cowed by the Fundmentalists. They had other things to do than argue over the points of Scripture and its infallibility. They even backed away from the idea that Christianity was essentially about saving souls from going to hell because they had not yet been saved. Rather, they were advocates of a "Social Gospel" – which conformed nicely to the Progressivist spirit of the times. For instance, Congregationalist pastor Washington Gladden, Baptist pastor Walter Rauschenbusch, and economist Richard Ely were all active in promoting the idea that Christianity after all was about social and economic justice, helping the poor the way Jesus looked to the needs of the poor.

But once again, looking to material salvation rather than spiritual salvation hardly needed the personal support of God, the guidance of the Biblical word of God, or any kind of Christian spiritual conversion in order to move their program forward. A purely Secular approach to social and economic justice would work just as well.

Spiritual Universalism. But once again, Humanist Rationalism or Secularism hardly met the deeper urges of people to find spiritual connection with the world around them. But some in the Modernist camp simply came up with the attitude that any kind of spirituality would do just fine, something like the Transcendentalists of the early-mid 1800s. Witchcraft was not one of the ideas put forward (at that time). But the spiritual offerings of other religions were – especially the more exotic kinds coming out of the Far East.

Indeed, a number of intellectuals even proposed simply to create some kind of universal religion, combining the moral features of Christianity, Buddhism, etc. Theosophy was just such an example—cultivated outside America by such Humanists as the Russian occultist and author Helena Blavatsky, her British disciple Annie Besant, and the Austrian educator Rudolf Steiner – that was taken up in America by intellectuals seeking to combine science and the mysticism of the world's great religions, as a form of personal development (also very popular later in the 20th century among very self-focused American hippies!). Thus science could continue to pursue fact and Progressive Liberals could pursue through private faith some kind of universal moral code, even some kind of personal mysticism. And so a sort of spiritual "universalism" came into play in certain social circles, especially among the more modern and thus more enlightened of the Westerners (including Americans, though not in the numbers as was the case for Europe).

It is important to note at this point that Islam was not as interesting to such hungry hearts, in part because it was even more fundamentalist in character, and did not conform well to the goal of "personal freedom" sought by Western Liberals. Islam is as hungry for submission to authority as Western modernism is hungry for freedom from just such authority!

The Asuza Street Revival and the AG church. Then into this growing world of enlightened Humanism another Christian revival burst forth – not quite on the order of the two earlier Great Awakenings, but significant nonetheless. Something very strange broke out in Los Angeles in 1906 (something quite similar to what was going on at the same time in Wales in Britain) at a meeting house on Asuza Street.

It started when strange physical healings and "speaking in tongues" broke out at a home – when a Black holiness preacher and guest speaker William J. Seymour was kicked out of church after bringing his Pentecostal message there, and was thus forced to move his ministry to this home. The event soon drew crowds to witness and then participate in this strange behavior, until it became literally an on-going twenty-four-hour-a-day phenomenon. When the crowds collapsed the porch to the house, the revival moved its operations to a Black Apostolic Faith Mission building on Asuza Street, making it quite inter-racial in nature as well as inter-ethnic (Hispanics also attending), even bringing women forward to take leading roles in the revival. Hundreds, then over a thousand individuals would soon be attending the meetings. And thus was formed the Asuza Street Revival.

Healings, speaking in tongues, and almost non-stop preaching took place there, giving rise to the designation of this growing event as "Pentecostalism" because it so resembled the events on that ancient day when a similar spirit formed the foundations of the first Christian community. Individuals of all social backgrounds were touched by a special spiritual power or charisma (thus also becoming considered to be "charismatics") that seemed to drive this whole development.

Eventually the Asuza Street Revival would burn itself out – but not before birthing the Assemblies of God church in 1914, a Pentecostal/charismatic denomination that would continue to grow through the 20th century, its growth continuing even to today, to the point where the denomination has around 370 thousand congregations with over seventy million members worldwide.

CHAPTER SEVEN

AMERICA ENTERS THE WORLD STAGE

* * *

AMERICA IN THE AGE OF NATIONAL IMPERIALISM

American nationalism. Nationalism was not a new thing at all for the Americans – although it took a Civil War to clarify key features of that nationalism. There were a number of European countries that had also earlier developed a similar national spirit – based on the common language of the people – such as the English, Dutch, French and Spanish. This national spirit was a big part of what made these societies so powerful. Americans themselves had encountered these other nationalisms in various ways – merely strengthening their own sense of American nationalism.

But even as Europe entered the second half of the 1800s, there were all sorts of potential nations still striving to join the nationalist ranks: the various German-speaking groups of North-Central Europe, the various Latin-speaking people of the Italian peninsula, the various Slavic-speaking people of Eastern Europe, with Romanians, Hungarians and other "minorities" (such as the widely-scattered Jews) mixed in – all of them either fighting each other for dominance, (such as the German-speaking Prussians versus the German-speaking Austrians) or trying to unify at a higher level (such as the Italian city-states). In these situations, the hunger for national identity often turned out to be a huge source of very bloody social violence – one that would eventually erupt into World War One (1914-1918).

Certainly this can be said of what America went through in its Civil War, fought bitterly to confirm the social-cultural foundations of some kind of America (which the Southern states attempted – but failed – to pull away from). Although the Northern version of America emerged triumphant, it was still going to take considerable effort to give the sense of American nationalism some precision. For instance, where did freed Blacks fit into the picture (there was far from unanimous agreement on this matter even in the North)? What about Southern Whites, especially those who had fought against the North? What about the Indian tribes of the West? What about the Hispanic population in the Southwest?   What about all the Catholics

flowing into Protestant America from Ireland, Poland and Italy?
America's supposed national model was the rural and small-town America of the American interior. But this America was losing out to the rapid growth of urban-industrial America to the East – which was highly diverse in ethnic character – and very different in lifestyle from small-town America. So – who or what was America as a nation at this point?

Directing the matter abroad. Always – the easiest way to resolve the issue of national identity is to find some great mission abroad to bring the various sub-communities together in unity. Foreign wars often prove to be quite useful in this regard. Prussian Chancellor Bismarck successfully carried off this trick in 1870 by drawing the French into a war against the various German states – and letting the Kingdom of Prussia take the German lead in producing a carefully laid out and quite smashing German victory against the French. The net result was a new federated Germany of multiple German states – united under the leadership of the Prussian king – now serving also as the new German Emperor! So it was that the German nation was finally birthed in 1870.

British imperialism. Imperialism abroad (dominating weak societies overseas) is another such means of solidifying national pride. For the British, such imperialism would develop out of the commercial expansion of the various trading companies that began to appear in the 1500s and early 1600s – similar to the Virginia Company that launched English expansion into North America. The English had taken an early interest – along with the Italians, Portuguese and the Dutch – in expanding their business operations eastward, for instance forming the Muscovy Company in 1555 in the search for a Northwest Passage to the wealth of the East – and at least to trade in Russian goods. An even bigger venture was the English East India Company, formed in 1600 to gain the wealth in trade with India and Southeast Asia. In this the Company became deeply involved in the internal political affairs of the Indian subcontinent – the natural competition among India's rajas (princes or kings) inviting English alliances here and there. The English, seeing also the Portuguese, Dutch and then also the French getting involved in India, began to take the attitude that India was their turf – and moved to secure the English presence there all the more tightly.
By the mid-1800s the British were very proud of their ever-expanding Empire – Queen Victoria even taking the title as Empress of India. But it did not stop there. The British were also deeply involved in the "opening of China" – for the highly profitable sale of opium to the vulnerable Chinese. Then in the latter part of the 1800s the British became very active in the

"opening of Africa" – all in the name of bringing the blessings of English industrial and financial culture to primitive Africa – a responsibility the English themselves termed "White Man's burden."

This certainly justified imperialism by giving it a very noble character – if you were inclined to believe that destroying the traditional cultures of non-Westerners in order to introduce "superior" English ways was well worth the cost in disrupted social orders and destroyed lives. But few questioned the supposed nobility of British imperialism – at least not until the Boer War in Africa (1900-1902) in which the British attempt to take over the valuable gold mining in the Boers' (Dutch farmers) state of Transvaal in South Africa proved to be well beyond any moral justification – even in the eyes of the British themselves. Although the British won the war, a widespread moral outrage throughout Europe ultimately forced the British to have to restore the entire region to the control of the Dutch-descendant South African Boers or "Afrikaners."*

French imperialism. Not to be outdone by the English, the French sought a similar imperial status during the mid-1800s under the new French Emperor, Louis Napoleon (Napoleon III), nephew of the famous Napoleon of the earlier 1800s. The French were having a hard time emotionally with the fact that the fabulous French culture - which had during the 1700s and much of the 1800s been a central part of the culture of Europe's ruling classes – was now in decline in the face of rising linguistic nationalism everywhere in Europe (Germanic, Slavic, Italian, Romanian, Hungarian, Greek, etc.). This loss of interest in things French proved to be a major blow to French pride. Consequently, France's imperial mission in the later 1800s seemed to be to compensate for this loss by taking French culture abroad – trying now to plant French culture among the ruling elite in French Indochina (Cochin China or Vietnam, Cambodia and Laos) and at various points along the African coast (Senegal, Guinea, Ivory Coast, etc.). This urge to assert French national pride became especially strong after the national humiliation delivered to France by Bismarck in his successful effort to unite Germany in 1870 with his carefully executed war with France.

And of course, morally speaking, the French found no difficulty in justifying their larger program of imperialism – because by bringing the backward societies of Africa and Southeast Asia into the world of French culture, they were supposedly doing these Africans and Asians a great favor.

America's position on the matter.   Americans however congratulated

---

*These Dutchmen were "Africans" in the same way that Anglos had come to America and become "Americans," both events in America and South Africa first occurring as far back as the 1600s.

themselves on being anti-imperialistic; they supposed themselves to be totally unlike the aggressive powers of Europe. After all, America itself was forged in the latter part of the 1700s out of a huge struggle against the imperialism of English King George III. America's anti-imperialist position had been even clarified to all in America's 1823 Monroe Doctrine – in which America announced boldly its readiness to defend the independence of its fellow American states to the South in Latin America. American national pride was in fact built heavily on the idea that America was destined to help all the world come to a similar national independence – even if it meant coming up against the imperialism of other nations.

But Progressivist America began to take the attitude toward the end of the 1800s that it also had a huge moral duty to help young nations come to real strength as viable democracies – for America increasingly was looking to Secular "Democracy" (not the hand of God) as the source of its own strength as a fast-rising society. Thus America saw itself taking on the obligation not only of helping the peoples of the world to achieve "self-determination" (national independence) but also of helping them develop proper democratic institutions, ones that guaranteed the success of their national birthing.

But ultimately, this paternalistic attitude of having to "help" budding democracies would become for America its own version of imperialism, much like France's cultural mission and Britain's commercial mission – giving moral justification for a lot of uninvited intervention in the affairs of other peoples.

However, democracy-building was not the only moral instrument called on to justify America's increasing involvement abroad. Christian missionary effort was also a big component – as Americans endeavored to bring Christ's salvation to the rest of the world. This did not (thankfully) require normally the accompanying hand of American military, the way the political agenda of democracy-building usually did. Like the French cultural mission abroad – also usually heavily Christian (although the Catholic rather than the Protestant version of Christianity) in many ways – American Protestant missionary activity abroad tended to be met more gracefully by the locals invited to receive the blessings of such a mission.

Then too there was the business angle to the American involvement abroad – fairly similar to the British effort – especially in the way Americans set up profitable businesses to the South in Latin America. These operations "blessed" the Latin locals with jobs – but also involved the policing action of the U.S. Marines when locals were not inclined to feel so blessed by this Yankee intrusion into the centuries-old feudal life of Latin America. But like the British and the French, Americans assured themselves that such involvement was for the good of these "backward" societies.   Thus to

Americans, such noble involvement abroad could not possibly be considered as just another form of imperialism!

American involvement in Japan. Back in the 1500s the Japanese military dictator or Shogun had shut down the extensive missionary activities of the Spanish Catholics in Japan (slaughtering thousands of Japanese Christians in the process) and closed Japan to further European involvement. But in 1852 the American navy was sent to Japan to "open" the country to Western trade and diplomacy – and to return shipwrecked sailors who disappeared when washed ashore in Japan – by blasting its way into Tokyo harbor. The net effect of this was not only to open up Japan to the West, but to shape the decision of the new (1867), young and highly determined Japanese Emperor Meiji to transform Japan itself into an industrial-military power on the Western model – as a means not only of self-defense, but as entry into the international realm as an imperial power by its own right.

The Spanish-American War (1898) in Cuba. America soon had the opportunity to put its "anti-imperialistic" imperialism to work by moving to support the rebellion of Cubans against their Spanish rulers – especially when the U.S. battleship *Maine*, which had come to monitor this activity, mysteriously blew up in Havana Harbor. Outraged Americans rallied to the cause of Cuban independence and joined official and unofficial military groups which traveled to Cuba to join the fight. This would include Roosevelt's Rough Riders. Ultimately, the Spanish were humiliated by the American "assistance" in Cuba – having to call it quits after only a few months of action.

Americans could thus feel proud that their military intervention had helped free from Spanish imperial tyranny their Cuban neighbor to the South. America would continue, of course, to keep a watchful eye over how a "free Cuba" would subsequently develop, economically and socially as well as politically. But of course this type of American paternalism was never viewed as imperialism – except for the few Americans (such as Bryan) who were loud in their pronouncements that all this was indeed nothing other than pure imperialism.

The Philippines. At the same time a similar American action against the Spanish Empire took place in the Philippines, which (like Cuba) had been under Spanish rule for centuries. Here too local Filipinos had been making the move to independence – and here too anti-imperialist Americans showed up to help their Filipino friends secure that independence. But problems between the Americans and Filipinos soon developed when it became apparent that the Americans were planning to put the Philippines under American "protection" – until such time as America itself decided that the Filipinos were ready to take up the democratic responsibilities of self-rule.

Now the Filipinos turned their wrath on the American occupiers – and guerrilla warfare broke out as Filipinos took on these Americans. Finally, in 1903, a compromise was achieved which settled the Filipinos down a bit, by giving the Filipinos limited self-government in the form of a Philippine Assembly, elected by a select section of Philippine society. Eventually (1916) the Filipinos were promised that full independence would come their way soon (but actually not be achieved until thirty years later – after the end of World War Two).

China. China proved to be less able than Japan to fend off growing Western involvement in its national life, not being blessed at the time with the leadership talent able to get China's act together. The Chinese themselves were divided on this matter of Western culture making its way into Chinese society, with many Chinese, especially along its long coastline, rather willing to cooperate along with Western imperialism – even to the point of taking up Western ways (business, education, religion). America was just about as involved as the other Westerners in this opening of China – seeing itself however as some kind of protector of Chinese rights – by declaring in 1899 (again, in conjunction with the British) an "Open Door Policy" which would keep sections of China from becoming the exclusive imperial domain of any single outside country. In other words, all of China would be open to the business of any Westerner (including now the Japanese) – something that gave entrepreneurial Britain and America the assurance that they could continue to conduct business anywhere within the huge Chinese economy. China would not be carved up into smaller colonial holdings like Africa had been.

But traditional Chinese, especially prevalent in the Chinese rural interior (but still found also in the fast-expanding coastal cities), took huge exception to this Western intrusion – and masses of Chinese commoners rose up in violent rebellion not only against the foreigners in their land but also the masses of Chinese who had accommodated themselves to Western Ways. This "Boxer Rebellion" (1899-1901) became very bloody, and required the armies of numerous Western (and Japanese) powers, including American military units, to finally suppress it. But ultimately (again, because of a lack of decisive leadership) this disaster left undetermined the direction China needed to go to bring itself back under order. Unlike Japan, China would remain severely handicapped by this challenge.

Teddy Roosevelt and American foreign policy. As we have just seen,

Roosevelt was very active as U.S. President serving as a strong Progressivist in the way he took on American industrial and financial monopolies. But he was no less active in the realm of foreign policy – loving to play along with the European powers the international power-politics game. For instance, he hosted and helped negotiate the peace talks ending the war between the Russians and Japanese in the Far East (1905). He was a personal participant in the conference in Spain called (1906) to defuse a huge crisis caused by the feud among Germany, Spain and France over the rights to "protect" the still-independent sultanate of Morocco. And he ordered U.S. military assistance in creating the more compliant country of Panama, carved out of Colombia when the Senate of Colombia refused to ratify a treaty recognizing the transfer of canal-building rights from the French to the Americans. And he continued to push forward with the Panama Canal project – staying on top of the project until it was completed in 1914 – even after he had left office. And he loved to display American military power any way he could – even forcing a reluctant Congress to finance a grand display of American naval power, when he sent an American fleet of 16 battleships around the world (1907-1909) – for all the world to see that America was very much up on naval power (at the time considered the key to imperial power).

* * *

AMERICA ENTERS WORLD WAR ONE AS THE CHAMPION OF DEMOCRACY

Wilson - the autocratic intellectual. Then with the election of Woodrow Wilson in 1912, America was to head even more deeply into the realm that glorified democracy, as virtually a civic religion.

Woodrow Wilson was Southern-born (1856), growing up in an aristocratic and originally slave-holding clerical family headed by a father who was a co-founder and ultimately administrator of the Southern breakaway branch of the Presbyterian denomination. As a youth Wilson was sent north to Princeton (still largely Presbyterian in character at the time) and after graduating from Princeton (1879) studied for the doctorate at Johns Hopkins University (1886), went on eventually to be a Princeton professor (1890) – and ultimately the university's president (1902-1910). However, his autocratic (dictatorial) ways did not sit well with the other Princeton professors – who resented deeply his high-handed running of the university. Eventually Wilson decided to move on to the world of politics – when in 1910 the bosses of New Jersey invited him to run for governor (believing that they could then control this idealistic intellectual for their own purposes). But in Wilson's gaining the governorship, the New Jersey bosses found themselves up against a very determined individual – who quickly began to clean house and rid New Jersey of some of its political corruption. This is what got the attention of the Democratic Party, which decided that it needed to steal the Republican Party thunder by appearing to be more Progressive themselves. Thus Wilson got the 1912 Democratic Party nomination – and because of Roosevelt's third-party involvement, thus also the U.S. Presidency.

Wilson's autocratic Humanism dressed up as democracy. Wilson's autocratic style was well illustrated by his doctoral dissertation and his several textbooks he published – which advocated for a stronger central authority presiding over the nation's affairs (he preferred the more centralized British Parliamentary model over the U.S. separation-of-powers model) – believing that social-political reform could take place more quickly and more efficiently under a strong hand at the head of society – certain that this was always the best way to serve democracy – thus democracy supervised by society's "betters" – rather than by the people themselves. This was a view that many Progressive intellectuals were beginning to take at the time, including Lenin, the future Communist leader of Soviet Russia.

1914 – War breaks out in Europe. Meanwhile, by 1914, things were growing darker in Europe, looking with each passing month as if the continent were headed for nationalist war – something that America wanted to have no part of. But true neutrality in the face of European events would prove to be almost impossible for America to maintain.

Conflicting nationalisms. The problem began as a conflict of budding nationalisms arising from the hearts of European commoners who wanted a "place in the sun" for their own people – a voice in their destiny. This was something just recently coming to the common people, as politics began to open up from being merely the business of the aristocratic upper classes of Europe. Consequently, in 1860 the peoples of the Italian peninsula finally got an Italian state and government of their own – as did Germany, ten years later (1870). But other national groups began to demand a similar development of their own nations: Greeks, Bulgarians, Serbs, Czechs, Moravians, Poles, Hungarians, etc. But national boundaries really were not clear (people lived mixed among other people groups) – and ethnic groups found themselves disputing each other over territorial rights. Also, the empires that many of them lived under were themselves multinational (such as the empires of the Ottoman Turks, the Russian Romanovs and the Habsburg Austro-Hungarians) – and in no hurry to see their subject

American Enters the World Stage   211

peoples attain national independence.

The imperialist urge. Then there was the matter of the imperial latecomers (Italy and Germany) who wanted themselves to get into the imperialist game, only to find that the Spanish, English, French, Dutch, and Portuguese got to most of the world ahead of them. There was not much left to build their own imperial greatness on – mostly just pieces of Africa. When Germany tried to grab Morocco, not once (1906) but twice (1913), the Germans came up against the opposition of the English, French and Spanish. They almost came to blows over this. Meanwhile Austria-Hungary, which had lost to Prussia the battle to head up the German nation, was looking for more territory in the direction of the Balkan peninsula, where Turkish power was slipping rapidly – but where local nationalist impulses already had the Greeks, Bulgarians and Serbs fighting over the region. In all, it was a confusing mess.

Treaties – and more treaties. Imperial jealousies had inspired the Russians to offer the Slavic-speaking nations of the Balkans (notably Serbia) protection if culturally-Germanic Austria-Hungary should make a move on them. But Austria-Hungary had countered this arrangement with an arrangement of its own with the new Germany, which promised German aid if Austria-Hungary should come into conflict with Slavic Russia. France, still smarting from the loss of territory to Germany in the Franco-Prussian War (the war in 1870 that marched the many German states into unity behind the leadership of Prussia), was looking for revenge – and decided to ally with the Russians against the Germans. Then there were the British, normally neutral in such matters – usually waiting to see which of the continental powers was on the rise – and then swinging support to the weaker side in order to balance and contain the growth of a rising power in Europe. But they had actually begun to side closely with France as the problems with Germany seemed to grow more threatening.

America stays out. Meanwhile, America stayed far away from all this political intrigue. America had its own hands full dealing with problems that had arisen along the border with the Mexico. Mexico was going through another of its revolutions and had fallen into political chaos.   America's small army under General Pershing was trying to keep the chaos (and Mexican border raiders) from reaching into U.S. territory.

War – and stalemate – on the Western Front. Finally Europe moved to full-scale war when the incident of the assassination of the heir to the Austrian-Hungarian throne in a visit to Serbia failed to achieve diplomatic resolution – and the European powers finally mobilized for war at the beginning of August (1914).

But within a month, those that had happily joined the nationalist cause, expecting to find glory at the finish of a brief conflict, began to realize that this might be a war without any obvious outcome – much less possible victory (France lost over 200,000 men in the first month of the war alone). A stalemate resulted – caused by well-imbedded trenches – and machine guns and barbed wire to defend those trenches – and artillery to empty enemy trenches of human life (until new recruits could be brought in to replace those slaughtered there). The war was headed nowhere – except to the slaughter of hundreds of thousands – then millions – of young European males. And this would continue almost unchanged for the next four years – at least on the Western Front running across Northern France and Western Belgium.

The collapse of Russia on the Eastern Front (1917). Despite the massive size of the Russian army in comparison to numerically smaller Germany army, the Russians made a very poor showing for themselves. Arms were lacking, leadership was lacking – especially when Tsar Nicholas took command away from his cousin (who was doing the best that could have been expected of a very poorly armed military) – making the military effort of the Russians even more pathetic. Worse, families on the home front were going hungry with the men on line rather than in the fields producing crops for the nation. Morale within the army was sagging – and by early 1917 women were in the streets protesting the lack of even basic bread for their families. Having Cossacks gun down these street protesters did not improve the mood any. And when Nicholas (at the front) got news of the growing crisis, he simply abdicated – abandoning further responsibility for the Russian Empire. Who at this moment was expected to take over was not clear. Nonetheless, the Russian Duma (their national legislature) announced that Russia would continue forward in the conflict under a new Provisional Government – also promising a more democratic Russia led by local soldiers and workers councils (Soviets).

Had Russia suddenly become a democracy at this point? Maybe on paper – but hardly so in reality. The people had not been clamoring for democracy. They most likely did not even understand what that meant – and certainly had no idea of the personal responsibilities that accompany democracy. Besides being totally disillusioned with their Russian leadership, they simply were tired of the war, the enormous loss of life for a cause not entirely clear to them – and furious about the huge disruption that the war had brought to the Russian social order.

Tragically, the decision of the new Provisional Government to continue

American Enters the World Stage

the "patriotic war" indicated that it had no earthly idea of what was happening among the Russian people themselves. Thus a huge civil war broke out at home – at the same time that the Russians were trying to hold off the advancing Germans.

America's pseudo-neutrality. From the outset, Americans had theoretically remained neutral – although it quickly turned into a one-sided neutrality (which of course amounts to no neutrality at all). With European men in the trenches in all the countries involved, women were required to look after the farming – when they weren't in the factories making war materiel. This turned out to be a huge boon for the American farmer who found the Europeans hungry for American food products – except that a naval blockade that the British threw around sea access to Germany prevented American (and other countries') farm products from reaching Germany. The Americans complained to the British about this most unfair treatment of their rights as neutrals to ship non-military items to all combatants. But Britain ignored the complaints (starving Germany into submission was a key part of their strategy of war) – and eventually America simply settled into the position of selling food products only to England and France – making enormous profits in the process.

A very hungry Germany developed the U-boat (submarine) to sink the ships blockading their country – and loud complaints arose from the British (and Americans) that somehow this was inhumane (but what part of war is not?) – and way beyond the rules of war (whatever those might happen to be). A major crisis then hit when a German U-boat sank the passenger ship *Lusitania* in 1915 off the Irish coast, killing 1200 people (128 of them American). But the ship was carrying a huge amount of ammunition – and the Germans had issued a warning to passengers about sailing on a boat carrying such items into a war zone patrolled by U-boats.

Reaction of President Wilson to the sinking of the *Lusitania* was one of outrage – although his Secretary of State Bryan was upset at the inability of Wilson to understand that putting American civilians on ships carrying war materiel was also immoral. Bryan ultimately resigned his position when Wilson would not tone down his public reaction.

In any case the Germans called off such attacks for the future – that was until early 1917 when a desperately starving Germany resumed those attacks in order to break the British naval blockade. Once again American shipping to Europe (England and France) found itself in danger.

Wilson decides that it is time for war (April 1917). Wilson had just been re-elected President in the national elections of 1916 – in part on the boast that he had "kept us out of war." But only one month into his second term Wilson abruptly changed his mind – citing in his request for Congress's declaration of war against Germany (and its allies) this resumption of submarine attacks to be the primary cause, blaming the German government for such barbarity that it required America to act to restore the realm of law in the world (as if Britain were behaving any better in respecting the rights of neutrals under international law).

But to add moral weight to this dubious military enterprise, he also stressed how this would advance global democracy – encouraged by how the Russians had just freed themselves from their own autocracy in their recent advance toward democracy. On this matter Wilson waxed eloquent (and amazingly wrong) in his description of how recent events in Russia had finally brought that country into the ranks of the world's "democracies:"

> *Does not every American feel that assurance has been added to our hope for the future peace of the world by the wonderful and heartening things that have been happening within the last few weeks in Russia? Russia was known by those who knew it best to have been always in fact democratic at heart, in all the vital habits of her thought, in all the intimate relationships of her people that spoke their natural instinct, their habitual attitude towards life. The autocracy that crowned the summit of her political structure, long as it had stood and terrible as was the reality of its power, was not in fact Russian in origin, character, or purpose; and now it has been shaken off and the great, generous Russian people have been added in all their naive majesty and might to the forces that are fighting for freedom in the world, for justice, and for peace. Here is a fit partner for a league of honour.*

What he was describing to the American people was pure fiction, devised inside his own Idealistic bubble. It was about as far from reality as a person could dare go.

Ultimately, Wilson sought to bring America into the war as a great moral crusade which all Americans needed to answer – "to make the world safe for democracy." Americans would have this great opportunity to destroy the autocrats who stood in the way of human progress. Bringing them down would free up the world to finally find its way to some kind of Rousseauian bliss, some kind of natural "democracy" based purely on the primal instincts of a truly free people.

So, lots of American young men would soon be going to their deaths to support Wilson's dream of a world of democracy freed from the tyranny of autocracy. Somehow it would all be worth the sacrifice that these young

American Enters the World Stage 215

men would be making (Americans were quite well aware by this time of the slaughter taking place on the European battlefields to which they would be sending their boys). Ah yes – but well worth it, or so said the President.

> There are, it may be, many months of fiery trial and sacrifice ahead of us. It is a fearful thing to lead this great peaceful people into war, into the most terrible and disastrous of all wars, civilization itself seeming to be in the balance. But the right is more precious than peace, and we shall fight for the things which we have always carried nearest our hearts – for democracy, for the right of those who submit to authority to have a voice in their own governments, for the rights and liberties of small nations, for a universal dominion of right by such a concert of free peoples as shall bring peace and safety to all nations and make the world itself at last free. To such a task we can dedicate our lives and our fortunes, everything that we are and everything that we have, with the pride of those who know that the day has come when America is privileged to spend her blood and her might for the principles that gave her birth and happiness and the peace which she has treasured. God helping her, she can do no other.

America's "democratic" allies have a different agenda. Tragically, Wilson's take on the war was not exactly how America's new allies England and France saw the war. At their home front, in their national capitals, they were indeed democracies. But actually, Germany was no less democratic, governed by political institutions very similar to Britain's. And actually, both England and France were empires too, controlling vast domains in Africa and Asia – and with clear intentions of extending their imperial grip into the Muslim Middle East once the Ottoman Turks were knocked out of the way.

But they played along with Wilson. They were certainly glad to get American help in crushing their "autocratic" enemies, and thus played along with Wilson's crusading Idealism. American assistance would likely break the terrible stalemate that had set in on the war and finally bring their side to victory in this long and bloody (and largely pointless) nationalist conflict.

The Americans join the fight. America's involvement in the war was rather brief – and also rather limited in comparison to the long and deep involvement of its French and British allies. At first there was only a very small contribution to be made – and many men to be trained before America was ready to get going (the spring of 1918, approximately a year after the

Declaration of War was issued).

The Russian-German Armistice. In the meantime, Lenin's Communists had seized both the Russian capital Petrograd (St. Petersburg) and the key city Moscow in the unfolding civil war there. Then Lenin's associate Trotsky had signed at the end of 1917 an armistice agreement with Germany taking Russia out of the war, a very popular move with the Russian commoners at the time – although it was actually designed to refocus the country's military powers on helping the Bolsheviks win the Russian civil war (which would continue for several more horrible years). But the Russian-German armistice also allowed the Germans to quickly move their troops from the Eastern to the Western Front in anticipation of the eventual arrival of the Americans in large numbers the next spring.

Thus it was that the Germans put into operation a huge and desperate early spring 1918 offensive on the Western Front, with the goal of overrunning Paris before the Americans could get in position. But that failed. And now the Germans found themselves highly exhausted. And the Americans at that point were beginning to arrive in large numbers – here and there along the middle of the Western battle line.

Wilson's Fourteen Points. In the meantime (January of 1918), Wilson went before Congress to outline what he expected to be the specific terms of the peace that America was fighting to secure. The terms were presented as Fourteen Points, including the end to secret treaties (which Wilson supposed were a major cause of the war in the first place), the guarantee of full freedom of all navigation on the high seas (a major source of American annoyance with both the Germans and the English), the adjustment of territories such as would restore Russia, revive Poland and return to France territory lost to Germany in 1871, the opportunity for independence of the various nations making up the Austro-Hungarian and Turkish Ottoman Empires. But most important (in Wilson's eyes), was the fourteenth: the creation of a general association of nations empowered to defend the political independence and territorial integrity of all states, large or small. This last point was the intellectual foundation for what would become the first truly international diplomatic organization: the League of Nations.

He made it clear that even for the Germans he sought only a fair or equitable peace – though he would negotiate such a peace with only a German delegation representing the majority members of the Reichstag (the German National Assembly) – and not the "military party and the men whose creed is imperial domination." This was a clear indication that America would not deal with the Kaiser but instead with only a German

American Enters the World Stage 217

group representing the broader or democratic interests of the people of Germany.

The Germans are humiliated. The Germans, sick of the war and starving at home, found themselves in rebellion – along the same lines as what had just happened in Russia. But they eventually were able to come under the order of a group of political leaders determined to end the monarchy (as Wilson demanded) and form a German Republic. German Emperor Wilhelm then took himself off to exile in the Netherlands – and a newly assembled German government accepted Wilson's offer of an Armistice (November 1918). They then sent off to Paris (the suburb of Versailles actually) representatives authorized to work out a final peace agreement. At this point the Germans still held on to a fair amount of French and Belgian territory. No enemy had entered Germany itself.

The "Phony Peace." At the peace talks Germany was actually represented by individuals largely unknown to (and thus only weakly supported by) the German people. Consequently, the German negotiating hand turned out to be extremely weak when it came time to outlining a final peace settlement as a follow-up to the Armistice or cease-fire.

Being the Idealistic Humanist that he was, Wilson failed to connect American power with American diplomacy – and thus the English and French took the opportunity to pounce upon the exhausted Germans, to wreak an expensive revenge (including a massive indemnity payment that Germany was in no position to pay) – despite Wilson's protests. What Wilson failed to understand was that probably no English or French politician who failed to bring home to his people some major exaction of retribution against the Germans would have had a political future there. But Wilson had power he could have used to move things more in the direction he wanted to see them go. However, caught up in his world of beautiful ideas, he failed to see the political opportunities he actually possessed in order to direct negotiations along the lines he had desired.

Also Wilson found himself shocked as he discovered that the English and French were not interested at all in assisting him in spreading his idea of the "rights of national self-determination of people everywhere." They were not about to do that because that would have meant having to give up their own multi-ethnic or multinational empires. Indeed, they were even planning to expand their imperial presence by establishing new Arab states carved out of the defeated Turkish Empire, new monarchies placed under French and English "protection."

Also, to Wilson's great distress, things were not doing well in Russia – because not blissful peace and prosperity but instead a violent civil war had accompanied Russia's move to "democracy." And this civil war had Russia's democrats lined up on the same side with the old Russian autocrats (the Whites) in a ferocious battle against a Marxist-Leninist Communist insurrection (the Reds).

Wilson's proposed League of Nations. On the other hand, Wilson was able to get his allies at least to accept his idea of a world assembly (the League of Nations) where he presumed cooler heads could eventually come together once the fever of war had subsided – and then right the wrongs of the abominable peace treaties foisted by the English and French on their defeated enemies.

But ironically, the one country he could not get to sign on to his project was his own, America. The Senate, which is required to approve all treaties, balked at the idea that possibly America would be giving over control of its foreign policy to the new organization. Wilson seemed unable or unwilling to answer their concerns on this matter – and the Senate vote ultimately fell short of the 2/3 approval required for all treaties. Thus the United States did not join Wilson's cherished organization! Wilson was devastated.

The German sense of betrayal. Likewise, the betrayal of Wilson's promise of an equitable peace, to which the Germans thought they were agreeing when they laid down their arms, would become the source of German ideological opportunity for those (Hitler and his Nazis) who sought to exploit this sense of betrayal (*Dolchstoss* or "Stab in the Back"). They would eventually use this opportunity to overthrow Germany's new democracy and institute a *Neuordnung* (New Order) in Germany.

In short, the Peace of 1919 merely set the scene for a return engagement of the nation-versus-nation contest 20 years later in the form of World War Two.

American disillusionment. Ultimately, Americans came quickly to the conclusion that they had been deceived in taking up arms to fight for the cause of democracy. The results of the peace were not at all what Wilson had promised that the sacrifices of the war would produce. Americans quickly became cynical about Wilson's great crusade – and determined never again to be smooth talked into getting involved in a European war.*

---

*This failure of his dream to come true ultimately helped break the spirit of the President himself, and he ended his last couple of years in office as a spiritual and physical invalid (which was never revealed at the time to the public at large).

The 1918 Spanish Flu. Then just to make the mood of America even darker, a massive and deadly case of flu hit the country during the fall of 1918 – just as the war was coming to an end. Americans (like the Europeans) were hit so badly that more than half a million (675,000?) Americans died from this flu (compared to the 53,400 American soldiers dying from combat in World War One). And those it did not kill, it produced permanent effects for approximately a quarter of the US population. In a few short months it lowered life expectancy in the US by 12 years.

* * *
THE "ROARING TWENTIES"

The postwar "Red Scare." Also in this post-war period, a major "Red Scare" gripped America – as it watched Russia, then Germany and Hungary come under angry social revolutionaries willing to engage in bloody class warfare in order to push their social-political agenda forward. A big question thus hit Americans hard: was this infection of political radicalism headed in the direction of America? Part of this fear was based on the fact that almost nothing seemed to have gone the way Americans were promised – throwing doubt into any thought about where the country was headed. And part of it was that immigrants flooding to America from war-torn Europe were of a new variety, coming from Southern and Eastern Europe – many bringing with them their anarchist attitudes about any and all social authority (in part because of the psychological damage inflicted on these people by the war). Also, a bomb destroyed the home of the American Attorney General Mitchell Palmer – who then turned around and had the FBI hunt down suspected anarchists, ultimately arresting thousands in the process. Then another bomb was set off on Wall Street (September 1920) – killing 30 people and injuring 150 others. Americans were outraged – and had a fairly good idea that an Italian anarchist group was behind it, especially when its leader slipped off to Italy immediately afterward.

Eventually things would settle down a bit (a famous case of two Italian anarchists, Sacco and Vanzetti, would drag on for years however). But there would always remain a level of apprehension about the dangers to traditional America brought on by the surge of immigrants to America in the post-war period.

Depression in rural America. With European farmers taken away to the trenches of World War One, Europeans (at least the French and British) became heavily dependent on American farm products. Consequently, during the war the American farmer did very, very well as an agricultural businessman. Thus he borrowed heavily from his local bank to purchase more land and the machinery to work that land. Unknowingly, all this was creating a situation very similar to the one that occurred a century earlier during the Napoleonic Wars, which in the longer run did not go well for the American farmer.

At the end of the war, European soldiers naturally returned to their farms, and the need for American farm products dropped away accordingly – as also did the prices for their products. Thus for example: wheat prices in 1919 were at $2.15 a bushel. The farmers were doing very well! But by the fall of 1920 the price had fallen to $1.44 a bushel. And by 1922 the price was down to 88 cents a bushel! It seemed even at times that the earnings of the American farmer did not meet their production costs. Farming had become a most unprofitable enterprise.

Thus at the same time, the farmers could no longer meet the requirements of the heavy payments to their banks on the loans they had taken out during the good years to buy more land and machinery. Bankruptcy swept through the farming industry when farmers found themselves unable to make those payments. That meant losing their farms and machinery to the banks.

But the banks had no use for seized farms and machinery. Nor could they find customers to buy this property off their hands. Thus the banks, by way of their loans to their farming customers, found themselves having invested way more money in these farms and equipment than they were now worth. And so the banks were now holding "assets" (farms and machinery) in current value far below what they themselves owed their depositors. Thus seeing looming failure facing their banks, panicked depositors made runs on their bank to get their money back before the banks folded. And indeed, fold the banks did, one by one, until there was a mass sweep of bankruptcies through the world of the rural banks.

Now deep misery set in on rural America. In actuality, the Great Depression had set in there ten full years before it was to hit urban America.

But party-time in America's cities. In post-war America a very different picture presented itself in the country's booming cities. During the war the cities had also been the picture of economic wonder, producing all sorts of war goods, including uniforms, rifles, artillery, ammunition, trucks, airplanes, etc. But the money accumulated among the urban entrepreneurs, plus an ever-expanding technology, led easily to a transition to post-war production of cars, radios, home appliances, new housing – to meet the huge demand of a prospering urban society.

Consequently, a sense of new things, a desire to explore and innovate, was felt strongly in urban America – especially among the youth. In part it was because of a hope that the nightmare of the recent past was put behind permanently. In part it was simply the energy that naturally comes from youth – as they find themselves ready to try new things, new clothing styles, new music, new social styles. It was the age of the Charleston (dance), bobbing (girls cutting their hair short), cigarettes (young women and men, both), scantily clad bathing suits – and drinking at the speakeasies.

Thus, while rural America – once the basic symbol of heartland America – was floundering in economic depression, urban America was aglow with prosperity – and a cultural gaiety that merely deepened the hurt of rural America. At a time when immigrants were pouring into American cities, this growing difference between city and country, not just economic but now also cultural – and even spiritual – made rural/small-town Americans all the more resentful of the fact that they were completely cut off from whatever was going on in urban America. Troubles brewed.

Prohibition. Alcoholism was a huge problem in industrial America, especially in the mining and manufacturing towns of America – where wearied laborers drowned their sorrows at the local bars with the week's paycheck – making their problems all the worse. As we have seen, women took up the challenge to begin a huge crusade against alcohol – which went from a call for temperance to an all-out demand to shut down completely the sale of any and all alcoholic beverages. They finally got what they wanted when the 18th Amendment to the U.S. Constitution went into effect in January of 1919 – with the beginning of full enforcement a year later.

At this point it became most un-Christian to indulge in any alcohol usage – at least within Protestant rural and small-town America. But to urban America, not only vastly more secular but also home to numerous immigrant groups (accustomed to having beer, wine, vodka or other alcoholic drinks as part of their everyday diet), this made no sense at all. Prohibition was immediately perceived by urban America as a clamping down on its freedom by a resentful rural America (which indeed it was). Thus the very idea of Prohibition – prohibiting the enjoyment of a drink or two – became the call to counter-action – usually in the form of open defiance of the law.

Speakeasies paid off city cops to look the other way and not raid their businesses – encouraging massive corruption among local law enforcement agents. And the number of urban speakeasies multiplied rapidly – to a number greater than the open bars that had existed prior to Prohibition. And then there were the alcohol entrepreneurs – running booze illegally but very, very profitably – so profitably that various groups or mobs competed violently against each other for the lucrative trade in alcohol. From the point of view of traditional rural/small-town America, the nation was sliding down into a moral cesspool.

The "Lost Generation." Off on another front, for those who had once held the highest hope that Western Civilization was entering the completion of its rise to greatness, the war had come as a massive nightmare, one that they could not shake. Despite the huge rise in the West's material culture after the war, that was not enough to shake the depression of those who felt so deeply about civilization and its offerings. Notable in this regard was a group of American writers who gathered in Paris, this greatest of Western cultural citadels, to try to recover their cultural enthusiasm. Famous American writers such as F. Scott Fitzgerald and Ernest Hemingway gathered there to find intellectual and cultural support. But alas – not even Paris could offer this to what Gertrude Stein – who basically presided over this expatriate group – termed the "Lost Generation." It was very symptomatic of the times. Those who explored deeply the psyche of Western culture were bound to be very disappointed, cynical, even depressed, about what the recent war had done to Western civilization.

The Scopes Monkey Trial (1925). Then there was another matter tearing at 1920s America: a trial going on in Dayton, Tennessee, contesting a Tennessee law that made it illegal to teach Darwinism. The trial was itself a clever scheme of some of the townsfolk to bring an issue to the town that would put it on the map. And indeed it did, as the "Progressivist" American Civil Liberties Union (ACLU) jumped into the action and brought in famous New York lawyer Clarence Darrow to challenge the law.

Certainly there seemed to be something un-American about civil authorities dictating what the people of their state were to believe or not believe. But as it would turn out, this was more than just a matter of protecting the civil liberties of the Tennesseans. This was the point at which "civil liberties" ACLU-style meant rolling back Christian culture in order to make the way for Secular-Humanism to replace that culture as the nation's fundamental worldview or religion. It was the 1920s, after all, and time for the ACLU to "progress" America to a more "scientific" understanding of how life works.

Thus, like Prohibition, this would end up being just another hot-button issue separating traditional or "conservative" (Christian) rural/small-town America from "progressive" (Secular) urban America.

As the trial unfolded, the matter at hand became clearly one of deciding the question as to whether nature was a result of the hand of God in its creation and ongoing life – or whether nature operated simply mechanically according to scientific laws that required no divine hand to make them fully operative. Was God at the heart of all life – or was he just something that unscientific or superstitious people made up to help them cope emotionally with life's challenges?

Of course both sides had already made up their minds on this matter. That's why the law was enacted in the first place, supposedly to protect the traditional Christian worldview. But the opposition arrived on the scene with their own understanding of things well in place, helped immensely by the writings of the very popular Austrian psychiatrist Freud. Freud had already made it clear to many "hip" urban Americans that religion was merely a neurosis or deep urge to fantasize that people resorted to in the face of difficult circumstances.

Thus it was that America watched very closely the debate going on between the old Christian warrior William Jennings Bryan defending Christian traditionalism and his adversary Clarence Darrow doing the same on behalf of Secular Progressivism during that hot Tennessee summer of 1925.

As with most matters of human reason or logic, America's judgement as to which side ultimately won that debate depended on which worldview the observer came at the contest with in the first place. Ultimately the trial solved nothing – but certainly clarified the depth to which America was finding itself divided on the most basic questions of life and its origins – and purpose.

Corruption in high places. Of course, all this 1920s "attitude" would find its way into the nation's politics as well. America's traditionally Christian moral fundamentals found themselves under deep challenge in that very realm.

Consummate nice guy Warren G. Harding, former Ohio Governor and Republican candidate, was elected President in 1920 by the largest majority on record – and brought to his cabinet a number of old Ohio buddies. He was hoping that his advisors would help him manage the federal budget and continue to advance social reforms in favor of American women, immigrants and Blacks. But when it came to the personal behavior of many of these Ohio Gang advisors, Harding seemed to exercise little or no control. The results were embarrassing to the President (it would have been even more embarrassing had he lived a few more years to see his friends get what was due them!) In fact, Harding died as a result of a heart attack he experienced in 1923 following a trip across the country in which he had set out to give answer to the growing rumors about the corruption of his presidential team.

The corruption was rampant: his Secretary of the Interior sold off public lands to private companies – at a great profit to himself personally; his Attorney General was personally involved in this transaction – as well as others – as was perhaps also his deputy who committed suicide (or was murdered?) just as a Senate investigation was closing in on him (and just before Harding's ill-fated trip).

Calvin Coolidge (1923-1929). Upon Harding's death in 1923 his Vice President Calvin Coolidge was automatically elevated to the U.S. presidency. However, to almost the same extreme that Harding was the picture of loose personal standards, Coolidge was the opposite: the picture of authentic Puritan morality – authentic because his family could trace its roots all the way back to the founding of Puritan New England in 1630!

As president, his attitude conformed nicely to the old adage: "the government that governs least governs best." Although he gave personal public support to the quest of Blacks and Indians for improved civil rights, when it came to government programs and spending, he was strongly opposed. He worked to cut back federal spending, balance the budget, and leave the nation's economics to American business, which was doing quite well at the time. Thus in 1924 he was returned to the White House with 54% of the popular vote, despite there being a third party in the race (Progressive Party candidate La Follette).

He finished out his four years in office in 1929 with no major programs of note (he believed that those matters belonged to the states, not the federal government) and no scandals. As there were no major foreign policy issues burning at the time, American foreign policy during his presidency was also quite low key. But that was the way Americans wanted things. They had other things personally to focus on – like getting rich fast.

* * *

THE GREAT DEPRESSION

Hoover takes over (1929). In 1928, as his term approached a close, Coolidge made it clear that he would not take on another term – although many expected him to do so. He was tired and ready to go home. The Republicans thus chose his highly respected Secretary of Commerce, Herbert Hoover as its nominee – who then went on to easily win the Presidency. When Hoover took office in 1929, America was expecting to see the fabulous economic journey that the country found itself embarked on expanded even more. Little did the country realize that the very opposite was soon to occur.

Collapse of the Wall Street Stock Market (October 1929). The business in consumer goods during the years after the war was so hot that huge profits were being made by those investors who had come up with the funds to get these businesses up and running. Such funds were acquired by selling shares of the company's ownership and profits on the open market – to anyone who wanted to get involved in such economic activity. At first it was professional investors who came up with the funds to buy the shares. But eventually American "moms and pops" got involved – sometimes using their life's savings to get in on the very profitable game – sometimes just borrowing money from banks – expecting to be able to soon repay the bank these loans when their holding of stocks quickly increased in value in this hot market. Thus it was that, as the 1920s rolled along, such speculative fever became ever hotter. The market rose and rose – and people saw themselves getting ever richer – on paper at least.

Market saturation. But almost no one was paying attention to what was happening in the real world of economics. "Market saturation" was developing as Americans, towards the end of the 1920s, had mostly bought their cars, radios and home appliances. The sales of the goods produced by America's companies were thus slowing up – and companies were having to cut back production (and let workers go) as well as drop their prices to stimulate new sales. Profits and dividend payments to investors began to dry up – creating concern among some of the more knowledgeable investors. Some of them began to back out of their investments, selling their shares at a somewhat lower price in order to find buyers. Suddenly the value of shares on the stock market stopped climbing – and more people took the step of trying to sell off their shares. This in turn panicked other investors – who rushed to dump their stocks before they lost even more value. Overnight (late October of 1929) the value of stocks on the market fell away – leaving investors bankrupt because they owed banks more money than the stocks were now worth.

Efforts were made to pump some money back into the market and for a while (April 1930) the worst seemed to be over (though by no means did the market return to a point anywhere close to where it had been previously) – then once again it began a slide downward – reaching a point of almost a total loss of all value as of July 1932.

Hoover addresses the crisis. Hoover had absolutely no idea of how to meet this crisis. From his point of view the matter was purely economic in nature – and the federal government had no constitutional role to play in such matters. At first he expected that the market would simply correct itself. This was how capitalism worked. Weak producers were shaken out of the market during such times of crisis – leaving room for stronger producers to move more widely into the market. It was not the government's job to get involved in this dynamic.

But by two years into his presidency, Hoover's Darwinian approach to market economics was clearly not seeing a turn-around in the nation's economy. Unemployment was rampant and people were clamoring for somebody to do something. Churches offered food lines for the unemployed – lines which were becoming longer and longer. But otherwise nothing seemed to be bringing the country out of this catastrophe.

A Communist or Socialist alternative? Much of Europe had fallen into this same state of affairs – Europeans and their banks having themselves become closely connected to the financial world of Wall Street. But Russia – now under the Communist dictator Joseph Stalin and a country which of course was not only not involved in this commercial relationship with capitalist Wall Street, but was its dedicated enemy – seemed to be from all appearances (such as Stalin allowed to be publicized*) doing awesomely well in building hydroelectric dams, steel mills, industrial plants of all varieties (mostly military-related of course) – at a time when America and most of Europe lay hungry and depressed in their state of economic collapse. Some Americans of the more Progressivist variety were even suggesting the need to look to the Soviet or Communist model as a possibility for America at this point.†

Hoover's belated efforts. Finally and belatedly, as the American economy continued to fail to revive (one fourth of American workers were now unemployed), Hoover began to propose government measures to try to help out the worst parts of the economy. The 1932 Emergency Relief and Construction Act attempted to start up public works programs to put the unemployed to work and to provide government-secured capital to help start up industries. But these measures came too late to swing the country back in support of his presidency. Besides, the Democrats smelled political victory in the coming November 1932 elections and were not in a mood to be very cooperative with the Hoover Presidency, which they were

---

*The fact that millions of people in Soviet Russia were dying of hunger, disease or simply exhaustion (multitudes of them in Siberian work camps) – because of Stalin's industrialization program – was carefully hid from the view of the larger world. In fact, idealistic American youth who traveled to Russia to see the Stalinist "wonder" typically never left Russia alive, because they saw what was really going on.

†During the 1950s McCarthy Era witch hunt for possible American Communist sympathizers, those same Americans would come to regret having gone on record making such a recommendation 20 years earlier in the first years of the Depression.

pleased to blame as the cause of the Depression – even accusing Hoover of attempting to introduce Socialism into the economy with his Emergency Act – which ironically would be exactly the path the Democrats would take soon after Roosevelt came to power in 1933!

The Bonus Army. In the upcoming presidential election (1932) there was little chance that Hoover would be re-elected – although his cause was hardly helped by turning U.S. troops on war veterans who had come and camped themselves in Washington that summer in a desperate attempt to get a promised pension or "bonus" due in 1941 paid to them now – even if in a greatly reduced form. They needed that money now. But ultimately they were dispersed – rather brutally.

Roosevelt takes command. In his nomination acceptance speech at the 1932 Democratic Convention, the aristocratic – and always cheerful – Franklin Delano Roosevelt mentioned a "new deal" he would be offering Americans – connecting this promise with the song "Happy Days Are Here Again" to drive home the point. He was all optimism – although he offered no details about what he meant by his "new deal." Probably he himself was not sure what exactly he was going to do – evidenced in his attacks on Hoover's "extravagant spending" in order to buy the country out of the economic crisis. It is ironic because this was the central strategy of what eventually became Roosevelt's New Deal.

Actually at that point, no one was exactly sure of what needed to be done. Capitalism had failed. That much was clear. And Roosevelt had campaigned repeating the understanding that Americans themselves had failed by making "obeisance to Mammon" (worshiping wealth and the providers of such wealth, the capitalists). Roosevelt repeatedly used Christian ideals and language, drawn right out of the Social Gospel, promising that the Democratic Party would do the "Christian thing," unlike the insensitive pro-capitalist Republicans. And in the end, it was an easy win for Roosevelt, who received 57.4 percent of the popular vote to Hoover's 39.7 percent, with the electoral college going 472 for Roosevelt and 52 for Hoover.

In his inauguration speech he delivered not only his famous words "the only thing we have to fear is, fear itself" but went on to continue his attack against capitalism (again using familiar Biblical terminology):

> The money changers have fled from their high seats in the temple of our civilization. We may now restore that temple to the ancient truths. The measure of the restoration lies in the extent to which we apply social values more noble than mere

monetary profit.

He also promised the American people that his administration would now take over the matter, and undertake action, such as capitalism had failed to do, in the face of this national tragedy.

> *I am prepared under my constitutional duty to recommend the measures that a stricken Nation in the midst of a stricken world may require. These measures, or such other measures as the Congress may build out of its experience and wisdom, I shall seek, within my constitutional authority, to bring to speedy adoption.*

In short, Roosevelt's Washington, D.C. – not Wall Street – would bring the country back to health. But this was unprecedented in America. And yes Roosevelt was right to mention "within my constitutional authority" because what he proposed raised all sorts of questions about America's constitutional legacy. What he was proposing sounded very much like what was going on in a number of European countries, such as in Russia under Stalin's state Socialism (his brand of Communism), or in Italy under Mussolini and his Fascists, or in Germany, challenged deeply by Hitler's Nazi or National Socialism. Was America to join the world in a basically state socialist undertaking? But "Socialism" was a taboo word to Americans. Indeed Roosevelt never identified his program as such, but let it be termed the "New Deal." But what exactly did that mean? What were these "measures" that Roosevelt was going to propose to Congress to speedily adopt? America would soon find out.

Franklin Roosevelt – the man himself. Roosevelt was born in 1882 in the Hudson River Valley town of Hyde Park to a very prominent New York family, was raised as an only child in considerable privilege, and was watched over carefully by a doting mother, Sara. As a youth he attended the prestigious Groton Academy in Massachusetts and then went on to Harvard, where he proved to be in the middle ranks of both schools academically.

With the death of his father James at the end of 1900, Roosevelt's mother Sara became even more directly engaged in her son's life (she had even followed him to Boston when he was at Harvard). But Franklin finally found that a relationship which developed in 1902 with Eleanor Roosevelt (Teddys niece and thus a distant cousin of Franklin's) allowed him to free himself considerably from his mother's domineering ways (Sara was very opposed to Franklin's and Eleanor's relationship).

He went on to attend Columbia Law School in New York City, but dropped out after two years when he passed the bar examination, and went on to be a corporate lawyer with a Wall Street law firm.

His relationship with Eleanor meanwhile was quite mixed, the two of them having six children in fairly short order. But he, meanwhile, was involved with other women, most notably her personal secretary, Lucy Mercer. Rather than divorce, they settled on an agreement to continue the marriage, as long as he cut back on his womanizing (which he did not, especially that with Lucy). Meanwhile, Eleanor would busy herself with a number of social-political activities, which brought her public attention by her own right.

The name "Roosevelt" gave him a lot of political leverage. And the Democratic Party was very glad to have him on board, when the name was otherwise associated with the Republican Party, thanks to his uncle Teddy. Thus Franklin became a New York state senator (being a "Progressivist" himself like his uncle), then brought on to Wilson's cabinet as assistant secretary of the navy (also like his uncle), serving as such through the years of World War One. After the war he was selected as the party's vice-presidential candidate, campaigning with Ohio Governor James Cox. But the Republican Harding easily won the 1920 election and so that effort came to nothing for Roosevelt.

Worse, the next year (1921) he contracted polio, leaving him permanently paralyzed from the waist down. A man of iron will, he refused to admit defeat by the disease, and maintained his law practice, while at the same time attempting various therapies. In 1926 he purchased a resort at Warm Springs, Georgia, not only for his own treatment, but for others also afflicted with the disease. He also developed immense upper body strength and the ability to walk (short distances) with the aid of iron braces, often also leaning on the arms of an assistant – so as not to have to appear in public in a wheelchair. Indeed, his disability was well hidden from the public, which knew little about his disability

Thus he continued his career in national politics, intensely determined that his handicap not stand in the way of his desire to go to the top politically. He was a strong supporter of the Tammany Hall political machine, supported Alfred Smith in his race for governor in 1922 and 1924 (which Smith won) and then for U.S. president in 1928 (which Smith lost).

At the same time Smith encouraged and supported Roosevelt's candidacy for New York governor in 1928, which Roosevelt won (twice) making him the state's governor from 1929 to 1932, when he chose to run for the U.S. presidency – easily becoming the Democratic Party's candidate in 1932. And, with the country caught in the depths of the Depression, his win over his Republican opponent Hoover (naturally blamed for the tragedy) was also fairly easy: Roosevelt was elected to the U.S. presidency with one of America's widest margins of victory (14 percent) over his Republican opponent.

He was an ambitious man, yet one who relied heavily on his own Christian faith, for its offerings of personal strength (rather than for its moral standards as a husband!). He had been raised an Episcopalian, and was personally very devoted to his Groton headmaster, the strongly Episcopalian Endicott Peabody, who not only taught him the social responsibilities that fell on the shoulders of the well-born, but presided at Roosevelt's wedding with Eleanor, and then the weddings of their children as well. And Roosevelt's polio served greatly to lead him to find his dependence on powers greater than his own, or of the surrounding society. And he would be quite successful in conveying that same understanding and approach to life in his frequent counsel (his famous fireside chats on radio) to the nation, especially as he took America through the dark days ahead.

Roosevelt's "Brain Trust." And to do that he gathered around himself a team of bright advisors as visionary as he was – university professors and corporate lawyers – soon to be termed his "Brain Trust." Together they were going to pursue a strategy of putting into action a massive set of government programs designed to provide the forward thrust economically that now-failed private capitalism had so recently offered American society. Government investment on a massive scale would presumably do the trick of getting America back to work.

Roosevelt's New Deal. By the time he took office in March of 1933, Roosevelt was ready to go with a full barrage of such programs designed to get the U.S. economy back up and running again. He asked businesses to join his program of setting prices, wages and services at certain levels – rewarded by being able to display a special window sticker indicating cooperation with the program (supposedly encouraging people to shop there). He offered jobs to young family men (ultimately 3 million jobs) working on state lands planting trees and developing the areas as vacation resorts (the Civilian Conservation Corps - CCC). He set up a huge project to bring flood control, fertilizer manufacture, and electricity to the mid-South through the creation of the government corporation, the Tennessee Valley Authority (TVA). He moved to have farmlands taken out of use in order to increase the price of farmers' grains (but making that food now more expensive for everyone else!). And he got Congress to pass the Glass-Steagall Act giving the Federal Government certain controls over the banking industry – including a bank insurance program (Federal Deposit Insurance Corporation - FDIC) offering government insurance for bank deposits lost in bank closures, designed to help put confidence back in

American Enters the World Stage 231

America's banks. Most of this was undertaken in his first "Hundred Days" in office.

But this was just the beginning of Roosevelt's use of the Federal Government to monitor and guide the nation's economy. In 1934 he set up the Securities and Exchange Commission (SEC) to bring some government control over the speculation that crashed Wall Street – and that same year established the Federal Housing Authority (FHA) to monitor and stabilize the mortgage market.* The next year (1935) he even became ever bolder as chief investor in America's infrastructure with his Works Progress Administration (WPA) – building national highways and municipal buildings across the nation, even simply employing artists to beautify public buildings with their artwork. And that same year he established the Social Security System, a government-supervised trust-fund designed to help the elderly provide for themselves in their retirement.

The rise of Intellectual or Secular Humanism. The depth of the crisis that America was forced to face going into the 1930s not only changed dramatically the direction that American government and economics were taking at this point – from free-market economic foundations involving very limited federal government involvement to a government-commanded or state-socialist economy – but also to new directions culturally, intellectually and spiritually as well. All the social certainties that seemed to have been in place during the Coolidge period (in many ways reaching back to the very founding of Puritan New England) seemed to have simply collapsed, disappeared, vanished. It was difficult to believe in anything with any certainty at this point. A huge moral-spiritual vacuum had taken the place of the former national self-confidence – and quite naturally a whole group of individuals we can term as intellectuals stepped into this vacuum to offer their advice as to how America should be getting out of its predicament.

To such "forward-looking" or Progressivist American intellectuals of the early 1930s, everything America had long relied on had failed – clearly so. Capitalism had failed. Limited government of the Republican variety had failed. In the estimation of these intellectuals, even Christianity had failed. It was thus time to consider a new way of going at life, a new world view, a new social program – one designed not only to correct the errors of the past but lead the country to a bright new future. America needed to

---

*Unfortunately much of the regulatory work of the SEC and FHA was cut back by the Bush, Jr. Administration in the opening years of the 2000s – helping produce through the so called "shadow banking system" the subprime mortgage crisis which started in early 2007 and reached the level of a major financial meltdown in September of 2008.

find its way to a new Enlightenment.

The Humanist Manifesto. Thus it was that in the early summer of 1933, self-proclaimed Humanists signed and published a *Humanist Manifesto* that was intended to serve as a call to head the nation in a new direction. And this change of direction needed to be fundamentally thorough – from a change in world views – even a new religion as they themselves termed this new worldview (a religion it was indeed!) – to the particular social programs needed to put the new Humanist religion into place at the heart of the nation. Signatories included John Dewey, a number of other university professors (Tufts, Cornell, Chicago, Illinois, Columbia, Pittsburgh, Michigan), news editors, and numerous Unitarian pastors.

The Manifesto's fifteen affirmations gave very clear explanation that in its Humanism it was intending to bring forward a new religion. "Religious Humanism." For instance, its Eighth Affirmation states:

> *Religious Humanism considers the complete realization of human personality to be the end of man's life and seeks its development and fulfillment in the here and now. This is the explanation of the humanist's social passion.*

It clearly states its new religious beliefs as: no divinely-ordained creation, but simply self-existent creation; man as an evolved natural creature; truth only through scientific study; the end to theistic (God based) religion; social concern and service to replace the self-serving profit motive of capitalism; the need to embrace life rather than flee from it (seeing traditional religion as "escapist" in nature)

Humanism claimed that it was the path to social and mental hygiene and that it discouraged sentimental and unreal hopes and wishful thinking. However, there cannot be a philosophy that has again and again built more unreal hopes and wishful thinking on utopian dreams of a new or revolutionary society founded on human perfection. Instead again and again Humanism has produced horrible failures that have accompanied every such attempt, beginning with the utopian French Revolution and continued with every utopian Marxist or Communist revolution since then. Even German Fascism ("National Socialism") was built on a what the Germans believed to be "reasonable and manly attitudes" dreamed up by a utopian rationalist named Hitler.

Admittedly, the Humanism of 1933 had not yet been permitted to see the worst of utopian Humanism of the Marxist and Fascist variety. But the seeds of disaster were always there if you actually looked closely at the philosophy. But the religious blindness of the Humanists caused them to fail to see that their philosophy was about the furthest thing possible from social and mental hygiene.

Problems with the Supreme Court. Meanwhile, the U.S. Supreme Court was still under the domination of some very conservative justices. They did not agree with the Humanist idea – or the core idea of the Rooseveltian New Deal – namely, that enlightened individuals in governmental service should take over the responsibilities of power because the people themselves obviously were not in a position any more to help themselves. The members of the Supreme Court did not see things Roosevelt's way at all. Thus a number of key programs in Roosevelt's New Deal were shot down in 1935, with the Supreme Court repeatedly declaring them to have no constitutional warrant. Roosevelt's programs fell way beyond what was permitted by the Constitution – even when stretching the interstate commerce clause to its fullest extent possible. His programs were therefore unconstitutional.

Roosevelt was so upset by this personal rebuff by the Supreme Court that in early 1937, just as he began his second term in office, he announced that he intended to introduce to Congress a bill designed to authorize an increase in the number of the Court's justices. The political intent was clear to all: through the presidential power of appointment, he was looking to pack the Court with enough new "Progressive" justices to swing the Supreme Court rulings in his favor. But in this the reaction was very negative – among the American people in general (who looked upon these Federal judges as the very picture of legal purity) – but particularly also within Congress itself, despite its Democratic Party majority. Debate dragged on in Congress – while Roosevelt began to lose rather than gain political ground there.

But in the meantime a switch of votes in the Supreme Court had occurred, with one of the justices changing sides from anti to pro New Deal, and another justice retiring, thus giving Roosevelt the opportunity to make a new appointment. He now had a voting majority without having to pack the Court. Roosevelt backed down on his court-packing scheme. But he had lost a lot of political standing in the process. Many Americans felt that Roosevelt was taking notes from the high-handed ways of the European dictators, Stalin, Hitler and Mussolini. Roosevelt not only had gambled personally and lost in this contest, he had greatly weakened his ability to continue the political reforms he felt the country needed to undergo in order to get back to economic health.

No, the New Deal did not bring America out of the Depression. This event was also timed with another slowdown in the American economy which hit in 1937, resulting in the growth again in the number of unemployed

Americans. Roosevelt had built all the national highways needed by the country, he had put hydroelectric dams wherever there was some logic for doing so, the national parks were completed, etc. The market for federal projects was therefore fully saturated (just like the consumer market of the late 1920s had become) – and there was very little else for the government to undertake by way of projects designed to hire unemployed Americans.

Private industry had not swung back into business with the arrival of the New Deal. No new products to stir the interests of the American private consumer were brought to market during the 1930s. And the stock market that funded such possible industrial growth remained idle – Americans too afraid to get involved there again. And what money the American workers did gain they "put under their mattresses" – meaning, saving rather than spending their scarce dollars – and thus providing no help to the market either.

So, yes – the New Deal put in place some much-needed social or national infrastructure items (highways, dams, national parks, etc.) that private industry would not have offered America. Thus the New Deal was a very good thing economically (although somewhat questionable politically or constitutionally), and helped reduce some of the massive unemployment that America was suffering from – at least for a few years anyway. But ultimately the American economy is shaped not by government decisions (as in Socialist countries) but by what the American people themselves bring to the national economy. And during the latter 1930s, those American people were still too fearful of economic dynamics to risk their small hold on their own personal wealth to buy into an economic rebuild.

The Midwest "Dust Bowl." Then, just to make the 1930s even more horrible, on top of this return to economic depression a massive drought which hit the American Midwest dragged on year after year in the mid-1930s, pulling down even further the farming economies of states ranging from Texas in the south to the Dakotas in the north. With this the American highways were filled with farm families making their way West as best they could, to find some kind of work in the California vegetable fields. These migrants were a very sad-looking lot, reduced to living in cardboard shacks and moving from area to area as the California plantings and harvests came and went.

Thus by 1937 America was again sliding back into economic depression. 1938 was not any better economically – and 1939 saw only a very slight economic recovery.

No, the New Deal had not brought America out of the Depression – as is so often claimed. It would take something else to do that – something very big and quite different, namely, World War Two – and America's entry into that war. But that was still a few years away for America.

Christianity's ongoing struggle with Enlightened Humanism. We have already seen how in the late 1600s / early 1700s Christianity was losing its foundational position in Western society due to the rise of a new age (actually only just another such age) of human Enlightenment. We saw how this humanism revived itself in the comfortable world of America during the early years of the 1800s (the Era of Good Feelings). And now a century later, Christianity found itself again under the challenge of personal faith in God's caring hand versus social management from above by self-enlightened or "scientific" wise ones (Sophists).

And once again prominent voices even inside the Church were calling for a more "rational" faith – one based more on a logical or scientific commitment to seek social morality – or peace and social justice – rather than one based on the personal quest for personal salvation and consequent faith in God's deliverance. Man needed to deliver himself – Jesus's way, of course.

At the heart of this debate (or even fight) was the huge Presbyterian denomination – caught up in a split that started at the turn into the 20th century and only deepened as the denomination headed into the 1930s. At first Christian traditionalists or conservatives seemed to have the upper hand. But bit by bit, the weight of Presbyterian opinion seemed to be clearly swinging away from such Christian conservatism or Fundamentalism in the direction of Christian Humanism, which recast Christianity as basically centered on social progress through programs of social improvement (the Social Gospel). Princeton Seminary professor John Gresham Machen found his conservative views slowly being rejected by the growing trend at Princeton to take the more "Liberal" or Humanist view – until in 1929 he left the seminary and founded Westminster Seminary in nearby Philadelphia. But the tide of Presbyterian Humanism continued to mount – and in 1933 Machen was even excommunicated from the Presbyterian denomination.

Christian Liberals felt that history and time was on their side and that soon all reasonable people would be joining them in their modernizing religious camp (just like Jefferson expected a century earlier!). But sadly, the more churches drifted further and further in this Liberal or Humanist direction, the more they lost their strong, clear voice – once the moral bedrock of American politics. The churches were once again fast making themselves irrelevant. How ironic: it was their claim that by making themselves look more like the world they would enhance their influence in the world's affairs. But in fact the end result was quite the opposite!

In the midst of this religious transition one of America's greatest theologians, H. Richard Niebuhr, so tellingly described what was happening to the message of the American church:

> *A God without wrath brought men without sin into a kingdom without judgment through the ministrations of a Christ without a cross.**

Fifield's Spiritual Mobilization movement. Yet outside of the world of theological academics there was some action underway to get the country back on course with God, and away from an increasing dependence on salvation by social design coming from FDR's Washington experts. Los Angeles Congregational pastor James W. Fifield, Jr. – who had some of the same bold instincts as did once the greatest of the American capitalists – in the mid-1930s founded Spiritual Mobilization, a grass-roots movement dedicated to getting the gospel of personal independence out to the nation through the sermons preached from the pulpits of the movement's extensive pastoral membership. Fifield was able to gain enormous financial backing from key business leaders so as to hold conferences, bring in speakers, and publish materials to enlighten America's clergy as to the role they needed to play in bringing the country out of its drift towards Socialism and back to America's tradition of personal freedom, one that prompted personal initiative and responsibility, and ultimately personal success, something they were certain was mandated by God himself. This broad mix of Christianity with conservative political values during the last half of the 1930s (continuing through the 1940s and into the 1950s) brought thousands of pastors (and hundreds of businessmen) to active support of Spiritual Mobilization.

Vereide's prayer breakfast movement. On another front, and also originating in the American West, was Norwegian-born Methodist minister Abraham Vereide's City Chapel program, bringing businessmen and local political officials (across the broadest religious and political spectrum possible, although basically Protestant in character) to "breakfasts" where extensive prayer would be offered – for the local community, the nation and the world.

Vereide had earlier founded and led the Seattle operations of Goodwill Industries, a company focused on offering employment to those who had such disabilities that they would not likely find employment elsewhere. Vereide proved to be an outstanding organizational leader, building up the Seattle operation to involve tens of thousands of workers and supporters.

---

*Niebuhr, *The Kingdom of God in America* (New York: Harper & Bros., 1937), p. 193.

But gradually he grew disillusioned with the failure of charity to change people's circumstances for the better, and resigned – to look for life's answers elsewhere. He too was a strong believer in personal initiative rather than governmental dependency.

His next direction in life came when he visited San Francisco during the violent longshoremen's strike of 1934, and found himself invited to lead the local businessmen's association in prayer during those dark times. Then when he returned to Seattle (where the strike was also ongoing) he deliberately set up an early morning breakfast prayer meeting at his City Chapel for some of Seattle's business leaders, soon joined as well by some local politicians.

These prayer breakfasts proved so encouraging to Seattle's demoralized business class that they continued their existence year after year, growing all the while. Here too, in the early 1940s, the war would only amplify the sense of need of such prayer gatherings, spreading Vereide's movement from city to city across the nation so that they would eventually become a key part of the American national religious and political scene, eventually including the president's annual Prayer Breakfast, started up in 1952.

America toughens up. The sad irony is that the Great Depression actually came as something of a blessing – for it brought America out of the silliness of the 1920s as well as the foolish intellectual idealism of the early 1930s – and readied America for a very serious challenge that was waiting for the country in the form of the highly aggressive Japanese and German Empires. Had America attempted to answer these dangerous challenges going at them with the attitudes of ten years earlier, America would have been another of those "democratic wimps" that just was unable to muster the self-discipline and determination to go sacrificially into battle. But by the end of the 1930s the Americans had turned themselves into a tough breed, able to face very hard times without quitting.

This is not to say that Americans thought of themselves ready to go into action. Mostly they were quite content to stay out of the drama that was going in Europe – although the Japanese treatment of the Chinese after their invasion of China in 1937 troubled Americans deeply, because there was among Americans a natural tendency to look to the Chinese sympathetically. Eventually that sympathy would be turned to Japanese counter-action – which would finally bring America directly into the global conflict that was well underway as the 1930s headed toward the 1940s.

CHAPTER EIGHT

WORLD WAR TWO AND THE START OF THE COLD WAR

* * *

WORLD WAR TWO (1937-1945)

The steps toward yet another war. In a very tragic way, the "everlasting peace" that Wilson – and his League of Nations after him – attempted to put in place was turning out to be merely a temporary time of truce among the national contenders who had just come out of the Great War – plus some new entrants into the grand contention. The war had resolved nothing with respect to the political for
es unleashed by the nationalist urge that had begun to develop in the latter part of the 1800s. Consequently, there would sadly be yet another go at this battle for national glory.

Italy. Italy's political leaders had disgraced themselves during the war, leading Italy not to glory but to well-publicized humiliation in the contest with the Austro-Hungarian Empire. Admittedly Italy came out on the "winning" side of the war – thanks to its alliance with England and France – but its meager rewards as "victor" did not compensate for what was widely perceived in Italy as incompetence in high places. Thus it was very easy for the highly ambitious newspaper editor Benito Mussolini to ride to national power in 1922 with merely the smallest of political support – as there really was little willpower among the disgraced political leaders to block him.

Mussolini was persistent in his political theatrics, helped by his small band of bully boys, in promoting his idea of a powerful Italian unity or "Fascism" as he termed it, a Fascism that would bring Italy to new glory. He constantly reminded the Italians that they were descendants of the Romans, who had built the greatest of powers – and he kept pushing the idea that Italy was destined to find its way back to such greatness. The Italians quietly nodded their heads in his direction – and then went about their other business. But that did not seem to discourage Mussolini and his dream of national greatness.

Germany. Germany after the war was a total mess – thanks to the "victors" America, Britain and France having stripped the country of its real leadership – in insisting on dealing only with the representatives of a newly "democratic" Germany. Thus possessing a very weak hand in the defense of German interests in the peace negotiations which followed up the November 1918 Armistice, the French were able (among other humiliations delivered to the Germans at the peace talks) to impose on Germany massive "reparations" payments to France, ones that Germany could not begin to afford. This consequently undercut deeply the German affection for their new Weimar Republic – which anyway had from its outset the smell of being merely part of a foreign conspiracy to keep Germany permanently disabled. However eventually (1925) the Germans were able to elevate war hero General Paul von Hindenburg to the Presidency of the Republic – finally giving the Republic some degree of respectability in German eyes.

But another individual of extreme personal ambition, Adolf Hitler, had been slowly constructing his own German version of Mussolini's Fascism. Since the early 1920s he had been busy putting together his own group of bully-boys in order to overthrow the "illegitimate" Weimar Republic. He intended to revisit the whole war thing – and do it right this time. He not only pointed to the "stab in the back" (*Dolchstoss*) by those German peace delegates who had accepted the French and English (and American) treachery and had agreed to the humiliating Versailles settlement – but also the hated Jews who he claimed had sold out Germany in their quest to sully the racial purity of the German race. Tragically, such political garbage sold well to a German population highly frustrated by the chaos that had come to the nation since the end of the war – a chaos deepened with the onset of the global Depression.

True, the Jews seemed to be a part of the problem, in the sense that they had been escaping intense religious persecution in Eastern Europe (especially Russia) in huge numbers, and seeking refuge in Germany – a very natural goal since the Jewish language used in Eastern Europe was an ancient German dialect (Yiddish from the German word Jüdish). And since the Jews had been prevented from investing their wealth in landholding by the governments of East Europe, their wealth was in valuable items such as gold and silver, which proved to be a very moveable source of wealth when they decided to flee their persecution in Eastern Europe. And with that mobile wealth, they were able to set up their own businesses in Germany – or buy up failed German businesses (particularly during these economic hard-times), giving the appearance that it was all a huge Jewish conspiracy to take control of the German economy. At least that's how Hitler played things. And it seemed to make sense to confused and angry "Christian" Germans, people whose political anxieties the rising demagogue Hitler would exploit to the fullest.

By 1933, the German Weimar Republic was deeply divided among various political parties, and Germany's veteran politicians knew how badly they needed the vote of Hitler's numerous Nazi members of the Reichstag – in order to achieve a voting majority required to form and maintain a government. To woo Hitler into cooperation, they even offered him the position as German Chancellor, believing Hitler to be a simple fool that they could easily control. Thus they convinced President Hindenburg to bring Hitler to power that year.

Hitler promised the Germans that if they followed him he would remove the disgrace of the 1919 Versailles Peace and lead Germany to victory. In fact he promised them that he would build for them a German Reich (Empire) – one that would last a thousand years. This clearly meant war – massive war. But the Germans seemed very much more dedicated than the Italians in following the theatrical little man with the funny mustache – right into bloody war if need be. They were quite certain that under his total command of Germany, the nation would finally find its place in the sun.

There were exceptions of course to this grand affection for Hitler, especially among the old German aristocracy – in particular among the officer ranks of the German army. But Hitler's Nazi bully-boys, his State police (the Gestapo) and Hitler's private army, the massive Schutzstaffel (SS), were designed to keep these non-compliant Germans silent.

Soviet Russia. By the end of the 1920s the Russian civil war had finally come to an end. But Lenin had died in 1924 and the leadership question among the top ranks of the Communist Party now directing Russian life had only recently been somewhat resolved in the rise of the mysterious Joseph Stalin and the expulsion from the party of Lenin's close associate Trotsky.

But Stalin was no Communist – in any sense of Marx's (or even Lenin's) idea of what that meant. He was simply another one of those extremely ambitious individuals who used the political chaos that surrounded him to work his way to power – eliminating anyone and everyone who got in his way. He was nothing more than a classic dictator, determined to put his name in history by dragging Soviet Russia out of its traditional agrarian (and Christian) ways – right into the rising world of modern industrialism – and consequently military power. He too was going to right the wrongs of Russian performance in the Great War. And nothing was going to stand in his way – not personal opponents, not cultural conservatism – nothing, absolutely nothing. Thus the death camps of Siberia were soon filled with multitudes of people that he suspected of getting in his way.

Tragically Americans in the early 1930s simply read the label on the Stalinist bottle, the one that read "Communist," and not the ingredients inside. Intellectual leftists excused what little they heard of his abuse of Russian opposition and held up his Communism – or at least some modified or Socialist version of it – as an ideal that America should take a serious look at. After all, Capitalism had clearly failed. What Stalin was doing in Russia to industrialize Russia at a time when American factories sat idle seemed to speak for itself

On the other hand, the word "Communist" scared multitudes of Americans to a point of hysteria. To these Americans, all this talk of Russian Communism seemed to pose an immediate and direct threat to everything that America supposedly stood for. Tragically, the fact was thus missed entirely that what Stalin was doing at that time in Russia had little to do with American political instincts (of any variety) – or even Communism itself. This misunderstanding would eventually come to haunt America.

Britain and France. The "victory" Britain and France had achieved finally after four years of horrible slaughter on the Western front rang very hollow for the ordinary people of England and France who had given so much of themselves in this recent tragedy. They were not quite as cynical as the Italians about the political legacy of the war. But they were not far behind them in their attitudes. Thus the political leaders of those two countries, individuals who were brave enough to offer their services to their countries, understood that they were treading on thin ice when it came to such issues as national destiny. Indeed, they were well aware that what was expected of them was to keep their countries away from all points of imperial or even just national contention – at all costs. Thus they disbanded their military and signed on to grand treaties that promised that they would never ever resort to war again as part of their participation in the new world of global peace.

Of course the rise to the East of Hitler and Stalin made them very uncomfortable – especially the French who realized that Hitler intended to take some form of revenge on their nation. But also, with a huge Communist Party flourishing in their own country, Stalin's program in Soviet Russia stirred great fear in France that Stalin intended to use the Communist connection to undo traditionalist Christian France the way he was clearly undoing traditionalist Christian Russia. So with two – but potentially mutually hostile – forces in the East rising to threaten the peace of France, France itself was uncertain – even deeply divided – as to how to respond to these dangers. Some on the Right saw Communism as the greater danger and advocated active cooperation with Hitler (actually hoping thereby to turn Hitler's ambitions eastward towards Russia). The political Left was vastly more frightened by Hitler, and advocated an alliance with Stalin's Soviet Russia – something along the lines of the alliance that France had with Russia during the Great War – except that they anticipated that under Stalin, Soviet Russia would be much stronger, able to keep Germany in check.

Gandhi's India. Britain – not so immediately threatened by Hitler – had its own problems. Its great Empire was falling apart. Part of this was due to its undercutting of its own national power due to the post-war mood England found itself in. Part of it was due to the antics of another man of ambition – just as theatrical as Mussolini and Hitler and just as driven by the quest for national power as those two men, at a time when Britain itself was deep into its anti-nationalist mood.

The Indian Mohandas Gandhi had started out his political career as a young man who did all the things necessary to rise to a personal greatness within the British Imperial scheme of things. He studied law in London at the prestigious Inner Temple – but found that no matter how hard he tried, his brown Indian skin stood in the way of his acceptance into the elite political company he believed he deserved. He ended up establishing a law practice in British South Africa in 1893, representing the huge Indian community there in their similar quest for improved status within the British Empire. A little over twenty years later (1915 – in the midst of the Great War) he transferred his activities to India itself, got rid of his English attire and took on the appearance of an Indian holy man – and proceeded to call his fellow Indians to do everything possible to end their cooperation with the British occupiers of their nation. His goal was to get the British to "quit India" – to simply go away.

But he was not only opposed to British governance of his country. He was opposed to everything that had come to India via the English presence – including English industrial culture. He now despised everything English – and had some idea that India could return itself to a pre-British Hindu culture of rural simplicity – not realizing that in doing so half of the greatly expanded Indian population would have died from trying to survive amidst his romantic but primitive economy.

Western civilization in trouble. Anyway – by the 1930s the British Empire was collapsing, the French were politically in disarray, and whatever dignity by which the West once impressed the East was fast disappearing. Indeed, Western civilization – with all its logic and cultured ways – was appearing to be something of a joke – not just to Fascist and Nazi Europe but also to an increasingly ambitious Asia.

Japan. Japan was about the only victor in the Great War that truly came out of the war as such – but was nonetheless divided as to how to move forward into the post-war world. Many Japanese were impressed by the "win" of the "democracies" and strongly supported the idea that Japan should move more decisively in that direction. But there were others, especially among the younger members of the Japanese military, who were more impressed by the mocking of such democracy heard coming from the European Fascists. Anyway, a version of Japanese Fascism was easily developed from their own Shinto tradition – one that glorified the military hero. Also, Japanese society was not suffering from the victor's remorse that so crippled the French and English. The Japanese had no reason to be wary of going deeply military. And little by little, by the mid-1930s, they could see Japanese glory awaiting them as they planned to expand their own political influence – even dominance – in Asia.

China. A confused and deeply divided China would be Japan's first victim in its post-war rise to power. Here too, the Chinese were by no means united in their response to the huge cultural impact the Western presence had on their country. Many Chinese, especially those living in the fast-growing commercial cities that lined the Eastern shores of China, were quite at home in taking up Western ways – even the idea that China should become a democratic republic. This is exactly what officially transpired after the war – when Dr. Sun Yat-sen and his Nationalists were able to establish a Chinese Republic on the Western model.

But Dr. Sun died early on (1925) and China found itself struggling since that time to piece itself back together again. In theory Dr. Sun's place was taken by the young military leader, Chiang Kai-shek. But he was having enormous difficulty not only bringing under control the warlords who typically appeared whenever Chinese central power weakened – but also the Chinese Communists. But they too were divided: those who sought a Communist China similar in character to Stalin's Communist Russia, and those who chose to follow the young and highly ambitious Mao Zedong, who wanted to see China restored to some kind of romantic rural communalism (Mao detested urban culture). It was all very confusing to the Chinese as these various groups took each other on – very violently in fact.

The war begins in China (1937). This allowed the Japanese in 1937 to suddenly invade a greatly weakened China, starting from their position in the northern Chinese province of Manchuria – which had been placed under Japanese supervision as part of Japan's reward for their role in the Great War. China was completely unprepared to offer a strong unified resistance to these haughty Japanese invaders, and it cost the Chinese dearly. Tragically for the Chinese, the Japanese were savage in the way they treated the Chinese as they rolled over their towns and cities – rounding up surrendered civilians and simply slaughtering them at the pleasure of the Japanese. Equally tragically for everyone involved, all of this seemed to validate in Japanese eyes their own greatness as a warrior race.

Americans, who had something of a paternal interest in China and its development, were shocked when the stories began to appear in the American media* about what was going on in China. Americans were furious – although there was little that America could realistically do to help China at that point. After returning from the Great War in Europe in 1918/1919 America pretty much, like France and England, had disbanded its military – presuming that this would inspire peace around the world. Thus America could offer no practical relief to the Chinese, at least in the form of military assistance.

But China's Republic under Chiang refused to surrender. Thus the Japanese now found themselves involved in an ongoing struggle with their neighbor. They had captured most of the coastal cities – but were finding it impossible to bring the rest of China, notably the rural interior, to defeat. Thus the war dragged on there.

Chamberlain tries to preserve the peace through "appeasement." While France found itself in a state of major political confusion, Britain had come under the resolute leadership of Neville Chamberlain – who was certain that he knew how to handle Hitler, and keep Britain out of war. He simply looked the other way when Hitler grabbed Germany's neighbor Austria in 1938, thus expanding Hitler's Nazi Reich in doing so. Chamberlain justified Hitler's action as actually a natural thing for all German-speaking people to want to be united as a nation. This then raised the question of the status of the German-speaking Sudetenland located in the newly created Czechoslovakia, the mountainous borderland where the Czech nation had dug in its main defenses. This included 40 well-armed Czech military divisions and all sorts of military emplacements, aimed against a newly created Poland – but also against a possible German expansion as well. Hitler complained about some supposed "mistreatment" of the Sudeten Germans by the Czechs (untrue) and pressed Chamberlain to

---

*Americans were informed of such developments not only by newspapers and pictorial magazines but also by the brief but dramatic movie clips of current events that were shown in the theaters between the main features.

allow Hitler to bring the region into his expanding German nation, leaving the Czechs defenseless. He promised Chamberlain that if he were granted this territory, this would satisfy Germany's quest for national expansion. Chamberlain, who was not choosing to listen to Hitler's other promises (to his own people), bought the argument. And without Czechoslovakia's consent, at a famous meeting in Munich with Hitler in September (1938), Chamberlain agreed not to block Hitler's seizure of the Sudeten borderlands, and leaned on the Czechs to agree to this "peace-preserving" adjustment. Back in England he proclaimed all this to be a great diplomatic victory, pronouncing loudly how in signing this agreement he had saved the world from war.

Then in early 1939, just as Chamberlain was being proposed as the recipient of the famous Nobel Peace Prize, Hitler decided simply to take the rest of the Czech lands by moving his army on into a defenseless Czechoslovakia, actually with some cooperation from the Slovakians who resented the more Western ways of their Czech partners.

At this point an embarrassed Chamberlain issued a threat of war if Hitler were to pull another stunt like that, presumably in the direction of Poland where Germans lived intermixed with the Poles. Hitler however thought the threat to be empty, given his estimation of Chamberlain personally – plus the fact that England had no practical way to come to Poland's aid without having first to get past Germany to do so.

Hitler and Stalin form an alliance. But Stalin was seeing things the same way. He had previously been counting on England and France to help keep Hitler off his back. But to the ever-paranoid Stalin, it appeared that England and France were purposely attempting to direct Hitler's ambitions away from themselves and instead eastwards in the direction of Russia (which probably was indeed the case) – so he decided to reverse the strategy and signed a "pact with the devil" Hitler – promising peace between Germany and Russia. As part of that agreement, they decided that they both would invade Poland and carve the country up between the two of them – giving both countries a bit of Polish buffer territory between them, allowing them then to go about their business elsewhere. As Stalin well understood, that meant sending Hitler off on his quest now westward (towards France) to restore to Germany the borderlands awarded to France at the end of the Great War. He knew of course that this would mean war with France – and probably England. But he was expecting such a war to once again grind down into an endless gridlock among England, France and Germany – taking all pressure away from Russia.

But as far as Hitler was concerned he was not only going to get much of Poland out of the deal, he knew that in the confused state that France found itself in, he could do this time what Germany had been unable to do in 1914 – strike quickly with a highly mobile (trucks and tanks protected by covering aircraft) German army conducting *Blitzkrieg* (Lightning War) through Belgium and northern France and grab Paris before the French could get themselves organized.

World War Two breaks out in Europe (1939). And thus on September 1st, 1939 – only a week after Germany and Russia signed their new "friendship" pact – Hitler's armies invaded Poland. This immediately drew a declaration of war from Chamberlain, who then – along with France – actually did nothing while Germany swallowed up the Western half of Poland within mere weeks. However, no similar declaration of war was issued against Russia when – several weeks after Germany had invaded Poland – Russia then invaded from the East and grabbed the other or Eastern half of Poland. It was all too much for a totally unprepared Britain and France. Poor Poland quickly went down to defeat. However, many Polish soldiers and airmen were able to escape to England – to eventually join with the British in taking on Germany.

The 1939-1940 "Phony War" or *Sitzkrieg*. Despite their declarations of war, the French and British failed to take any action against Germany – letting an opportunity to hit Germany from behind while it was absorbed in swallowing up its half of Poland. About the only serious action in those days came with Winston Churchill's appointment as head of the British navy – and his orders to his fleets to engage wherever possible against the German navy on the high seas. Otherwise nothing was done on the ground. Some in Germany already began to ridicule the "war" with England and France by playing on Hitler's doctrine of *Blitzkrieg*, terming the war in the West a *Sitzkrieg* (sitting war). Others had their own term of contempt for such inaction, calling it a "Phony War."

Meanwhile, after Russia secured its position in Poland, it turned on little Finland – except that the Finns fought back strongly. But the following spring Finland had to give up the fight. The world condemned Stalin's Russia verbally for its aggression – but otherwise did nothing.

Hitler crushes France – and the Battle of Britain begins. Then in May of 1940, after having suddenly and without warning overrun Denmark in April (in one day!) and capturing parts of coastal Norway, Hitler sent his forces crashing through Belgium and into Northern France – splitting the French line in half east and west – and grabbing Paris (June 1940) before the stunned French could get themselves organized against Hitler's armies. In only one month's action France found itself having to surrender – and accept German occupation of Paris and the northern half of the country.

At this point English King George VI replaced the confused Chamberlain with the determined Winston Churchill – who announced to Hitler and the world that England would never quit – until they themselves had achieved victory in this conflict. And the world knew he meant it. But it would be tough going because England stood alone in opposition to Germany. Not even Ireland, only recently granted the right to exit the British Empire, was willing to come to the aid of England.

American neutrality during the early years of the war. Nor for that matter were the Americans going to do so either. American isolationists made it very clear that America was never again going to get involved in Europe's feuds. The country had foolishly been seduced into coming to the aid of the "democracies" Britain and France in 1917 – and would never be so foolish as to repeat such a stupid mistake again. Never!

Yet as in the Great War (now beginning to be termed the First World War – as a Second World War was presently clearly underway), American sympathies were swinging to the British – especially as German bombs were falling constantly over the English cities and countryside. Yet Congress's Neutrality Acts were reconfirmed in 1939 and again in 1940, asserting America's neutrality in this war in Europe.

Lend-Lease. But Roosevelt was trying to help where he could – among other things getting America ready in case the nation was going to have to go to war, instituting in 1940 America's first peacetime draft and increasing dramatically the military budget. Then in March of 1941 he was able to get Congress to pass his Lend-Lease Bill, permitting the sale of war goods to Britain (and also China and soon also Russia) – also then authorizing the exchange of old American destroyers for British land overseas to build American bases on. Then with the first sinking of an American merchant vessel (carrying war goods to England in October of 1941) merchant vessels began to be armed.

The Atlantic Charter. At the same time (August 1941) a conference was quietly held aboard a ship anchored off the Canadian shores in which Roosevelt and Churchill agreed to war goals (*The Atlantic Charter*) – should America be drawn into the war. This was an increasing certainty at this point – as that very summer Hitler had decided foolishly to attack Russia, and the two former "allies," Germany and Russia, were now at war with each other. Indeed, the whole world seemed to be slowly drawn into this war.

Action in Asia. With France's fall to Germany in 1940, the Japanese saw the opportunity to take advantage of French weakness to extend Japanese power to French Indochina – from which they could then advance against China from the south. But that finally (mid-1941) determined America to take action – at least to the extent of cutting off the sale of all military goods, scrap iron and oil to natural-resource-poor Japan (America was the world's leading oil exporter at the time.)

This so infuriated the Japanese military leaders running the country – suffering from the illusions of Japanese greatness, and the supposedly natural weakness of all democracies, including democratic America – that they decided to deliver a huge crippling blow to the American naval fleet anchored at Hawaii. The intended goal was to force America to have to come to Japan begging for whatever terms the Japanese at that point would be willing to offer the humiliated Americans.

Pearl Harbor. And so on December 7th (1941), as planned, they struck the American Pacific fleet anchored at Hawaii, launching a simultaneous attack against the British in Malaya, Singapore, Hong Kong – and ultimately Thailand (the path to an assault on British Burma and India). They also bombed the Dutch airfields in Indonesia, planning to grab the oil fields located there.

And thus it was that America was finally at war – at least in Asia.

Hitler declares war on America. Then a few days later, Hitler (who was already getting bogged down in Russia) decided that there still was glory awaiting Germany in taking on America – and declared war against America. Mussolini's Italy followed suit soon thereafter. So now America was at war – on two fronts, Asia and Europe.

The American lion awakens. But it was just as Japanese General Isoroku Yamamoto, who had studied two years at Harvard, had explained to his fellow officers: Japan's plan stood the danger of awakening a sleeping lion. And so it was. America had been delivered from the social silliness of the 1920s by the hardships of the 1930s – and the early 1940s saw the coming together of a nation of men and women willing to work extremely hard to win this war – in the process, producing what would rightly be called "the Greatest Generation."

There was nothing abstract about this war. It was not some quest to save the world for democracy – or bring the world to some grand utopian peace. It was simply to defeat those who had decided foolishly to go to war against America. America was not in the mood to be defeated – and willing to do whatever was necessary to win this contest.

World War Two and the Startup of the Cold War

Amazingly quickly, idle American industry came alive with war orders – finally bringing the country out of the Great Depression. Not only was there no more unemployment, the sending of masses of young men off to military training created a huge worker shortage – which soon was met by bringing enormous numbers of young women into the factories to take the men's places. The lion was fully awake!

The Philippines. But victory would not be easy. America was strategically in a horrible position at the start of the war. With the Pacific battleship fleet destroyed, America could not bring supplies or reinforcements to its troops stationed in the Philippines, and those Americans troops – and their Filipino allies – would experience the same savagery that the Chinese had suffered at Japanese hands. Sadly, after almost five months of effort to hold out as a surrounded force with no military supplies or even food able to support them, the American and Philippine troops finally surrendered. Consequently, 12,000 American troops – and even more Philippine troops – were marched off to Japanese prison camps, with thousands dying along the way – and even more doing so during their consequent life in those camps.

Midway (June 1942). Fortunately, four American aircraft carriers had been out on a training mission when the Japanese bombed Pearl Harbor and thus had escaped the destruction of the rest of America's Pacific fleet. Furthermore, because America had cracked the Japanese radio code, Americans were aware that the Japanese fleet was headed to seize Midway Island – located in the mid-Pacific halfway between Japan and the West coast of America, a point from which the Japanese could then attack ships coming out of California to rebuild the American naval position at Hawaii.

Not aware of America's knowledge of their movements, the Japanese were caught off guard – and in the resulting Battle of Midway, they lost badly in the contest. The Japanese would never be able to mount such a bold attack against America after that. Indeed, from this point on, Japan would be fighting a purely defensive action in the Pacific against a steadily advancing, greatly rebuilt American Pacific fleet.

North Africa. In the European theater America's contest with Germany (and Italy) was initially centered on North Africa – with America's British allies off in the Eastern portions of North Africa defending the vital Suez Canal in Egypt against the advance of German General Irwin Rommel – and the Americans themselves getting their first experience in battle coming in from the West, from Morocco and Algeria towards Tunisia. Finally able to reach Tunisia – and their first serious confrontation with the Germans – the

Americans did not do well at first. But they learned quickly and soon got themselves together, so that in May of 1942 the Americans and British were able to close forces in Tunisia. What was left of the Germans and Italians pulled out of Africa and headed across to Sicily – but leaving a quarter of a million German and Italian troops behind as prisoners.

Sicily and Italy. British and American troops were intent on delivering a huge blow to the Germans and Italians in Sicily – though it appeared to many that American General George Patton and British General Bernard Montgomery were more interested in winning the contest of who it was that would gain the honor of being the victor of Sicily. In the end (that August) both armies routed the Germans and Italians – but narrowly missed an opportunity to surround their enemies before they made their escape to Southern Italy.

But at this point the Italians were fed up with Mussolini's program and announced a full armistice. The Italians were officially out of the war. But the Germans certainly were not, and consequently they dug into the mountainous interior of Italy to contest the British-American advance up the Italian peninsula, every step of the way. Thus the allied advance against the Germans became very slow – and very bloody. 1942 turned into 1943, which turned into 1944 – and the Allies had made only painfully slow progress. The Americans finally in January of 1944 decided to do an end-run around German lines and launch a surprise landing at Anzio – which however failed to be a surprise when the American commander proved unwilling to move off the beach until he had what he thought were adequate supplies for the mission he was assigned. That incredibly stupid delay gave the Germans ample time to move into position above the Anzio beaches – and the Americans found themselves trapped there. It would not be until five months later that the Americans – after having suffered huge losses – were able to break out of their position at Anzio and continue on their march north.

Then rather than heading straight east across the Italian peninsula, swinging behind the well-entrenched German army – and thus surrounding it and bringing it to defeat – the Americans decided to head north to liberate Rome (June 1945) – a major emotional success but another military blunder of the first order. It allowed the Germans to quickly retreat to a position from which they could then dig in again and thus continue to hold the northern half of Italy under full German control. Again, for the Americans the glory of a single victory (Rome) overrode the greater requirements of war itself.

Stalingrad (1942-1943). Meanwhile on the "Eastern Front," Stalin's troops were under the strictest orders not to retreat from their strategic position against the Germans at the city of Stalingrad, the adjacent Volga River being the last serious position of defense that the Russians could offer against the German expansion. Thus a massive battle was fought there. But the Russian line did hold, a huge German army succeeded in getting itself surrounded when Hitler refused to let those troops retreat from the trap, and now the Russians found themselves able to take to the counter-offensive against a deeply exhausted German army.

France (1944). On the "Western Front," Americans had been gathering in England for what was to be a grand attempt to cross the English Channel with their British, Canadian (and other) allies and secure a position in Western France from which they could then begin to make some kind of advance against the Germans positioned in France. An earlier attempt (August 1942) at Dieppe along the northern Normandy Coast by the British and Canadians (and a small number of Americans) had proved to be a huge disaster – and thus the idea of such a crossing was considered much less than a certain success. Thus both the huge buildup of troops and supplies – and the secrecy (and deception) involved in the operation – in order to keep the Germans unknowing of the where and when of such a crossing.

Finally, on June 5th (1944), the order was given by Allied Commander American General Dwight Eisenhower to make the crossing the next day.

General George Marshall. Interestingly, that announcement should have come from the U.S. Army's Chief of Staff, General George Marshall. Marshall had been the one to organize this massive operation, which required the ability to work not only with prima donna generals but also U.S. Congressmen. Marshall was so effective in his work that when it came time to appoint the individual who would lead the huge event itself, by all rights that honor should have gone to Marshall. But Roosevelt pleaded with Marshall to remain in Washington by his side, because the president depended so heavily on Marshall's advice and support in leading the nation. So, Marshall took a piece of paper, and on it wrote the name of his close friend, Eisenhower, and passed it to the president indicating that Eisenhower would be the one to lead the assault. And he did so, fully aware that history would remember Eisenhower, not Marshall, as the one who carried off this grand event.

Eisenhower was surprised to receive the honor, but performed well, and stepped into history as the war's most memorable general. And on the basis of that fame, eventually Eisenhower became president of the United States. Marshall gave up that honor in order to continue to serve the country, rather than his own personal career. Now there was a truly great man!

But this would not be the last time that the nation would call on the well-deserved reputation of Marshall for wisdom and integrity, in dealing with problems that still lay ahead.

D-Day. When the "D-Day" landing occurred (June 6th), the Germans were spread widely across the French coast – and the surprise landing at the southern French Normandy beaches by a massive allied force was stunningly successful. However, at Omaha Beach the heights of the cliffs and the German entrenchments made the landing one of horrible slaughter of the American troops who first landed there.

Roosevelt's prayer. That night Roosevelt went on the radio to call the American nation to prayer:

> *My fellow Americans: Last night, when I spoke with you about the fall of Rome, I knew at that moment that troops of the United States and our allies were crossing the Channel in another and greater operation. It has come to pass with success thus far.*
>
> *And so, in this poignant hour, I ask you to join with me in prayer:*
>
> *Almighty God: Our sons, pride of our Nation, this day have set upon a mighty endeavor, a struggle to preserve our Republic, our religion, and our civilization, and to set free a suffering humanity.*
>
> *Lead them straight and true; give strength to their arms, stoutness to their hearts, steadfastness in their faith.*
>
> . . .
>
> *Some will never return. Embrace these, Father, and receive them, Thy heroic servants, into Thy kingdom.*
>
> *And for us at home fathers, mothers, children, wives, sisters, and brothers of brave men overseas whose thoughts and prayers are ever with them help us, Almighty God, to rededicate ourselves in renewed faith in Thee in this hour of great sacrifice.*
>
> . . .
>
> *With Thy blessing, we shall prevail over the unholy forces of our enemy. Help us to conquer the apostles of greed and racial arrogancies. Lead us to the saving of our country, and with our sister Nations into a world unity that will spell a sure peace a peace invulnerable to the schemings of unworthy men. And a peace that will let all of men live in freedom, reaping the just rewards of their honest toil.*
>
> *Thy will be done, Almighty God. Amen*

World War Two and the Startup of the Cold War

And thus it was that ultimately the Allies found themselves in a position to begin their advance across France – in the direction of Germany.

The politics of potential victory. Here too the decision was made to direct the Allied effort to liberating the French capital at Paris rather than heading directly towards the Rhine and the German nation lying beyond it. But this was a wise move, for the liberation of Paris occurred just before Hitler's order to utterly destroy Paris could be carried out. On the other hand, although Russia on the opposite or Eastern Front against Germany was still fully involved in simply clearing the German army out of Russia – there was implicit the sense that whoever got to Berlin first, Russia from the East or the British-American allies from the West, the very character of a post-Hitler world would be largely determined by that particular party. So, a bit of a race was on.

Advance against the Japanese in the Pacific. Meanwhile the Allies were advancing against the Japanese on two fronts, one coming in from the East across the Pacific, jumping past some islands but fighting for others – where airbases were already located or could be built – and up from the South, from northern Australia and the eastern islands of Dutch Indonesia.

The Japanese *bushido* code of military honor knew no such thing as surrender, instead calling for suicidal banzai charges against American machine guns when it was apparent that the Japanese soldiers were about to be overrun. The slaughter was terrible, unnerving young American soldiers. Thus the fighting was extremely brutal, as the Allies fought for such islands as Guadalcanal, the Solomon Islands, Tarawa, Kwajalein, Eniwetok. In capturing Guam (August 1944) they now found themselves in a position to bomb Japan itself. Finally they were able to liberate the Philippines (October 1944 to February 1945) and reach Japanese territory itself at Iwo Jima (February 1945), having to kill nearly all of the Japanese forces in the process. And the same held true at Okinawa (April-June 1945).

At the same time the Japanese countered the best they could the huge American naval force gathered against them with suicidal *kamikaze* crashes of young and inexperienced pilots of their explosive-laden planes against those American ships. Only a small percentage were successful, although even then they were able to sink 30 American ships and cripple 300 others. But this was not enough to stop the Allied bombing of Japan, which was now taking place round the clock.

The failed "Market Garden" offensive. As the Allies advanced across France, British General Montgomery stepped forward with a plan to make the much-feared Rhine River crossing into Germany take place in the extreme north (the British sector of the Western Front) – much to the irritation of American General Patton, whose tanks were headed for the Rhine at the very center of Germany's Western border. Montgomery's plan was ultimately approved by the Allies. But it brought Patton's advance to a halt when supplies were thus redirected to the British sector. But ultimately the plan was a dismal failure, with the British losing the element of surprise (the Dutch slowing the Allies' advance by crowding the roads to celebrate with their British liberators), and the Germans were able to detonate the various bridges the Allies would need to cross into Germany.

The Battle of the Bulge. But by this time the winter was coming on – and the advance slowed up considerably – except that the Allies did not know that the Germans had planned a massive breakout at a very quiet part of the Western Front (the forests of Eastern Belgium). In mid-December the Germans launched an all-out effort at air and ground Blitzkrieg against a weakly defended part of the American line, with the intention of grabbing American supplies (especially much needed fuel), and roll all the way to Antwerp to stop the massive unloading of Allied supplies at this vital harbor. However the Americans refused to retreat from the vital central position at the town of Bastogne; they blew up their own supplies to keep them out of German hands; the winter clouds over the battlefields finally cleared, allowing Allied bombers to hit the German troops, and the Germans soon ran out of fuel – bringing their tanks to a complete halt. The "Battle of the Bulge" turned out to be a complete German failure.

The race for Berlin. From this point on it was a race between the British and Americans coming in from the West and the Russians coming across Poland from the East to get to Berlin first. In that, the Russians won quite decisively.*

---

*But along the way, Stalin cleverly ordered a Russian halt of its advance against the Germans as the German retreat brought the action to the center of Poland, and the Poles decided to take this opportunity to rise up against their German occupiers, in order to secure control of their own country prior to the arrival of the Russians. The Germans, in their rage against this Polish insolence, completely destroyed the Polish effort, not to mention historic Warsaw, which now laid in ruins. Thus the Germans achieved for Stalin what the Russian dictator wanted dearly: the complete destruction of the Poles' ability to defend themselves. Once this was accomplished, the Russians then resumed their offensive against the Germans. And Stalin could content himself with the knowledge that in all this, an uncontested position of immense Russian military-political dominance had just been achieved in the very heart of Eastern Europe. And he had let Hitler do that for him!

Yalta. In February of 1945 Roosevelt (soon after being re-elected to his fourth term as American President!) met with Churchill and Stalin at Yalta in the Russian Crimea. Roosevelt was a sick man (the Americans had no idea of how sick he was) – but was trying to arrange for the best post-war outcome possible. Certainly the Big Three (America, Britain and Russia) would be in charge – in particular of occupied post-war Germany. But there were other lands that had fallen within Hitler's Empire that had to be accounted for.

And then there was the question of Japan. Russia thus far had no involvement in what was going on in the East – and Roosevelt wanted the Russians to help bring the war there to a close. It was estimated that at the rate they were making progress against a very resistant (even suicidal) Japan, it was going to take another two years (and huge loss of life) to bring Japan to defeat. Consequently a very generous offer was extended to Russia: if they were to join the Allies in the war against Japan, Russia would be given the right to occupy and supervise the withdrawal of the Japanese from Manchuria until such time as the Chinese were able to take over from them – and they would have the same supervisory rights in Japanese-occupied Korea – at least in the region north of the 38th parallel (America taking the same role south of that line).

Roosevelt's death. Then just as the Americans were making their way rapidly across Germany (mid-April) they were shocked to learn that Roosevelt had suddenly died while on a visit to his health spa in Georgia. Equally shocked was Harry Truman – who as newly elected Vice President had been left out of all previous presidential planning and now had the most unwanted responsibility of taking over American command in this massive war. This war – despite Germany's immanent collapse (and the problems that would certainly follow in Europe) – was expected to drain American society for another couple of years in bringing down Japan.

But Truman quickly stepped up to the enormous responsibility.

Harry S. Truman. Whereas Roosevelt had been the polished aristocrat – the great charmer who seemed to know how to keep people's spirits up in even the darkest of times, Truman immediately came across as someone with personal qualities like those of your uncle – or your neighbor next door. He seemed so average. He was indeed Middle Class – brought up with no special privileges awaiting him, but knowing how to take on very real challenges that had to be met head on rather than be smooth-talked away. He was not a ruling-class, program-man like Roosevelt, but one who related very personally to the world immediately around him.

Born in 1884, Truman had been raised on a 600-acre farm in Missouri, to a father who was active in local Democratic Party politics. Truman's hopes after finishing high school were to attend the U.S. Military Academy at West Point. But his poor eyesight blocked that possibility. He found jobs as a clerk, but after memorizing the eye chart, was able to join the Missouri National Guard as a corporal in an artillery battery! After six years of such service he dropped out (1911), but was quick to rejoin the unit when America went to war in 1917, bringing friends in with him – who in turn elected him as their 1st lieutenant. In the war itself, now as a captain, he proved to be an outstanding officer, converting an unruly artillery company into a very disciplined unit, which in Truman disobeying higher orders to retreat, instead held their position – and destroyed a German artillery unit, thereby saving an American division that would have come under the heavy fire of the German battery. His discipline and leadership resulted in the loss of not a single man in his unit, and their eternal love and support of Truman (which would later factor into his political rise from obscurity).

After the war, he went into business as a co-owner of a men's clothing store, which did not do well. But a war-time friendship with Tom Pendergast, son of the Missouri's Kansas City boss (of the same name) would prove, on the other hand, to work greatly to Truman's favor. In 1926, with Pendergast support, Truman was able to gain the position as his county's presiding judge. This was largely an administrative rather than legal position – although at the time, Truman had taken up the study of law at night school.

Truman so impressed Boss Pendergast with his dedication to his work that Pendergast used his influence to have Truman appointed as director of one of Roosevelt's local New Deal Programs. This would bring Truman in contact with Roosevelt's personal advisor, Harry Hopkins. But ultimately Boss Pendergast decided to run Truman as Missouri's U.S. Senator in the 1934 election, which as a Democrat, Truman won the election handily.

Of course being a Pendergast protegé brought suspicions from fellow U.S. Senators about Truman's integrity. But that reputation would soon pass, as Truman worked very hard at his job, demonstrating to his fellow senators the deep integrity that shaped his world. That same integrity – and his natural suspicion about the "big-money boys" in both the corporate and government world – led him to create (late 1940) and chair a subcommittee of the Senate Committee on Military Affairs, investigating U.S. army bases. Then with America's entry into World War Two a year later, the work of his Truman Committee would soon draw national notice. His committee not only eventually saved the U.S. government from as much as $15 billion in waste but also drew the attention of Time magazine which featured him on its March 1943 cover (the first of many).

Thus it was that Truman's name came up when in 1944 Roosevelt began considering his run for a fourth term as U.S. president. Henry Wallace had been serving as Roosevelt's vice president. But Wallace's virtually Socialist ideals were putting off Democratic Party leaders. And so it was that Roosevelt and his advisors turned to Truman as a candidate as his new running mate (the vice-presidency), not exactly a position, however, expected to have great significance. Nonetheless, with the Democratic Party's 432–99 electoral college win over the Republican Party in the 1944 election, Truman became America's vice president.

But consequently it was also that Truman was soon to become the new U.S. president. Personally, Truman was himself shocked that, with Roosevelt's death only a few months into the new presidential term, such a heavy post-Rooseveltian legacy had suddenly fallen on his shoulders. He was fully aware of the heavy responsibilities of the presidential office, especially during this time of war, and was unsure of the level of support he would receive in having to fulfill those responsibilities. But he was one who had learned to accomplish much, especially when so little was expected of him.

He presented himself immediately before Congress, ending his address with this comment:

> *As I have assumed my heavy duties, I humbly pray Almighty God, in the words of King Soloman: "Give therefore thy servant an understanding heart to judge thy people, that I may discern between good and bad; for who is able to judge this thy so great a people?" I ask only to be a good and faithful servant of my Lord and my people.*

Indeed, Truman would attempt to live up to that enormous responsibility. But actually, few thought at the time that this new and unsought president would be able to meet those standards. Yet despite his common ways (and often even profane language) Truman personally was a man of great personal faith in God and Christ, a man of daily prayer, and highly Biblical in the way he analyzed, categorized and chose critical decisions that fell to him to make. Most of this was of a very private nature, but highly important to the nation that he would have to guide through the political, economic, social and spiritual minefields that awaited America and the world after the collapse of the German and Japanese empires.

Hitler's suicide ends the war in Europe. In any case by early May (1945) Hitler had committed suicide and the German armies were surrendering everywhere. In effect World War Two was over – at least in Europe.

The Potsdam Conference. In late July/early August Truman journeyed to the Berlin suburb of Potsdam to meet with Churchill and Stalin – his first encounter with the latter. He quickly took a much more skeptical assessment of Stalin's reliability than had Roosevelt – the latter who actually had believed that he could charm Stalin into almost any kind of political relationship. Indeed, Roosevelt was actually more suspicious of Churchill's motives than Stalin's with respect to plans for the world's future. However, Truman and Churchill immediately hit it off – both possessing a similar hard Realism in their approach to the world of power and politics.

But unfortunately the British people themselves did not – and in their first election held since before the beginning of the war, the British voters turned Churchill and his Conservative Party out of power and brought to power the Labour Party under Clement Attlee – right in the middle of the Potsdam Conference. What the British had done was to turn to the promise of Socialism in the hope for a happy fix for the economic uncertainties facing their future. What they in fact made certain however was that in choosing the Socialist road (nationalizing all of Britain's key industries) they were going to ruin all possibilities for an early post-war economic recovery.

The bomb. While Truman was at Potsdam, he was given the news (not a surprise to Stalin whose spies had been keeping him abreast of American developments) that the atomic bomb experiment in New Mexico had proven a success. The bomb was horrible beyond belief. Now Truman was faced with a major moral dilemma: to undertake a bold strike to break the will of a resistant Japan – causing Truman to go down in history as ordering the dropping of the most destructive device in history – or just go through the slow death of advancing village by village, killing as they went in order to bring Japan to the same end. Ultimately – understanding not only that this device should shock Japan to some better sense of where things were headed for their country – Truman would also need to have the political leverage that the bomb afforded America in order to make Stalin behave in the post-war era. He realized that he would have to demonstrate to Stalin that America really would dare to explode such a device over an enemy – otherwise it would have absolutely no deterrent effect whatsoever with Stalin.

Thus just a few days after the close of the Potsdam Conference Truman ordered the use of the bomb over the city of Hiroshima (August 6th).

The Soviet Russians jump into the war in the East. Stalin immediately declared war on Japan, suspecting that the war was about to be over – not wanting to miss out on Roosevelt's promise that if the Russians joined the war effort, they would receive those valuable positions in Manchuria

World War Two and the Startup of the Cold War 259

and North Korea. Indeed, a second bomb dropped on the Japanese at Nagasaki three days later (the 9th) brought, on the 15th, the Japanese announcement of its surrender. World War Two was over.

Victory, and its personal costs. Understandably, America was in a very celebrative mood. They had won! They had defeated these two self-presumed "superior" military powers, Germany and Japan.

But of course they also had wounds to lick. Victory had come at a great price. Over 16 million Americans had served in the armed forces. That was a huge portion of that age-group typically called to military service. And that service ultimately led to the deaths of over 400 thousand who served, and another 700 thousand wounded or missing. Consequently, the war touched painfully many families in the most intimate of ways, with the loss of those family members.

But the word "served" extended well beyond even that. In this war, everyone served, in some capacity or other. The "war on the home front" that everyone talked about had brought new avenues of industrial service to women, and even in small ways to children (scrap paper, scrap metal, etc. collections or "drives"). And everyone lived on rationing.

A generation trained to the sense of service or duty. Consequently, emerging from this war was a generation of Americans – to be termed here the "Vets" because they were veterans of this war, and products of wartime social dynamics – shaped deeply at how they engaged life through a deep sense of personal service or duty. But this was not just a matter of American patriotism or service or duty to the nation. That sense of service or duty actually – and most importantly – started in the family, in all sorts of ways. Obviously, this included sons (and some daughters as well) joining the service. But the Depression had already started this idea as the family being the primary or key unit that disciplined individuals with the understanding of the vital importance of mutual service within the family, for the purpose of survival itself. And then, from these very strong family foundations, that sense of duty extended outward, to the local community, its churches, its school boards, its libraries and city halls. Indeed the very peace of the streets and neighborhood was built on this dynamic (crime rates in America were amazingly very, very low in those post-war days). Then this mind-set quite visibly reached to the very idea of national service. America was their country, and they would serve it, die for it, some even saying "right or wrong" (not actually a very good idea!). But ultimately that sense of service or duty reached in the most personal of ways to the heights of heaven, to God himself. Americans would serve God, and ultimately no other. This was now a very, very patriotic, Christian America.

THE STARTUP OF THE COLD WAR

The Cold War in Europe. For Americans the words "the war is over" meant only one thing: the boys are coming home. But for Truman it meant more, much more. Europe was a mess – the kind of mess that Stalin and his Communist affiliates in Western Europe could exploit in order to expand the Communist Empire across all of Europe. This was as big a threat to the world as had been Hitler's effort to build a continental Empire in Europe.

Traditionally it was Britain's role to do the offsetting of a would-be imperial aggressor attempting to overrun all of Europe. But Britain was in no shape, or certainly in no mood, to play that role anymore.

Churchill's "Iron Curtain" speech. As former Prime Minister Churchill pointed out in his "Iron Curtain" speech delivered in Missouri during a visit with Truman in March of 1946, it was up to America to take up Britain's traditional role as defender of the world's peace and freedom. Churchill pointed out that, thanks to Soviet control, an "Iron Curtain" had fallen across the middle of Europe, stretching from the Baltic Sea in the North to the Adriatic Sea in the South. And that behind that curtain, in the Soviet sphere of influence, were the numerous cities and peoples of Eastern Europe. In these societies, small Communist parties had succeeded, thanks to Moscow's increasing control, in gaining such power as to be able to obtain totalitarian control over these cities and peoples.

He also raised the issue of exactly how this situation should be met – especially by the Americans, on whom so much responsibility for the welfare of the civilized world had fallen, reminding the Americans that the Russians admired strength and despised weakness and, although they did not exactly want war, they were certainly desiring the expansion of their power and the influence of their doctrines.

As he had done with his own people during the dark days of World War Two, Churchill was calling now on America to take up the challenge facing the world. For if the West (under American leadership) did not act now in a show of strength, it would clearly be dragged into war a third time in the 20th century. America and Britain needed to stand together to block Stalin's aggressions.

The American press was scandalized that Churchill would speak so brazenly about some dark intentions on the part of our friends the Soviet Russians and their leader "Uncle Joe" Stalin. But these voices of journalistic enlightenment would soon change their tunes – finally recognizing a mounting problem in Europe.

Still, it would take some time to get Americans to see these rising dangers. But thankfully Truman was able more quickly to develop support in Congress, even from the once-isolationist Congressional faction. But he had to proceed cautiously.

Containing Communism. Actually whereas even the U.S. State Department was still caught up in its dream of friendship with the Soviets – one of their members posted in Kiev, George Kennan, answered a request by the U.S. Treasury Department to explain why the Soviets were not planning to work with the new World Bank (IBRD) and the International Monetary Fund (IMF). In his Long Telegram (February 1946) Kennan described in detail the Soviet anti-capitalist (and Russian nationalist) mindset – and called for the "firm and vigilant containment of Russian expansive tendencies."

The report soon became the basis for a larger analytical study of Soviet goals and strategies (September 1946) – intended for the President's eyes only. But the Kennan report itself was so clear in its analysis and call for a strategic response that it was published in the July 1947 edition of *Foreign Affairs* under the authorship of "X." It had the effect not only of helping to awaken America to the need for vigilance against Soviet aggression but it also gave the resultant U.S. policy its identifying label: "Containment" (of Communism).

The Truman Doctrine. In the meantime a problem had developed in the Eastern Mediterranean region: 1) a Communist-inspired rebellion against the restored Greek monarchy – supported mainly by Tito's Communist Yugoslavia to the north of Greece – and 2) Turkey, under intense pressure from Stalin to bring this gateway country guarding the entrance and exit of the Black Sea (where Russia's largest naval port was located) under Soviet mastery – Soviet mastery such as had been happening all across Eastern Europe wherever the Russian Red Army found itself in rather permanent occupation following the expulsion of Hitler's armies from the region.

Truman was intent that neither Greece nor Turkey should fall under such Stalinist domination. Thus in 1947 he went to Congress for funding (which he quickly received) in support of the Truman Doctrine – pledging American support of those countries struggling against efforts to bring them under dictatorial oppression. Neither Soviet Russia nor Communist Yugoslavia were specifically named as the aggressors. But most people knew who was meant. And thus direct military and financial aid was extended to Greece and Turkey as the beginning of the American effort to protect Europe from an expanding Communism.

The Marshall Plan. There were also problems in Western Europe arising from the fact that the war had either completely devastated the economies of these countries or once again had left the countries floundering because of weak and deeply divided leadership – or both. These were the kind of conditions that Communism loved to exploit for its own political advantage. Indeed, the French and Italian Communist Parties were the biggest of the political organizations in those two countries, and becoming more militant as economic conditions did not improve, but in fact clearly were worsening by 1947. And thus Stalin was directing these parties to bring down the "bourgeois" political systems in their countries, supposedly initiating a Marxist or workers' revolution (meaning, expanding Stalin's domination deep into Western Europe).

Thus Truman recognized the urgency of answering the challenges arising in Western Europe. Again (also 1947) Truman requested – and received (1948) – authorization to pour massive amounts of funding in dollar grants to European nations to help them rebuild their industrial and social infrastructure, however as the Europeans themselves saw the need. This included former enemies Italy and Germany as well. All they needed to do was submit plans for funding for the development of a specific project and they would receive American support..

This of course was designed to help remove the social rot that Communism required in order to expand its influence.[*] Needless to say, although there was actually no prohibition against any particular countries from applying, not even Soviet Russia itself, Stalin understood the intent of this program and would not let any of the countries or territories under Red Army control (the Soviet-occupied sector of East Germany, Poland, Romania, Bulgaria) apply – not that they would wish to anyway, as Stalin had been quick to replace the leadership of these countries with personal supporters of his.

More than $12 billion was granted over the next few years (and billions more after that) to Europeans through the European Recovery Program, more popularly known as the Marshall Plan – carefully named after the highly esteemed former Commanding General and now (since January of 1947) Truman's Secretary of State, George Marshall. It was Truman who let Marshall take the lead in publicizing the plan (Marshall's Harvard commencement speech in June of 1947) and who even put Marshall's

---

[*]The results were amazing. Europe recovered and whatever social antagonisms had produced the war in the first place disappeared, the wounds of war were bound up, everyone was cared for, and a just and lasting peace resulted among the nations involved, at least those in West Europe free to participate in the Marshall Plan (free from Stalinist domination).

name on the program rather than his own, knowing that such a request for unprecedented funding (the initial request was for an unheard-of $5.3 billion) would sell better in Congress if it were identified with Marshall rather than with Truman himself!

1948: Czechoslovakia and the Berlin Blockade. In early 1948 Americans were shocked to learn that the leader Jan Masaryk of the pro-Western group in Czechoslovakia had "committed suicide" (actually murdered by Communist-directed police) – as Czech Communists moved to take total control of the country. This came just as Czechoslovakia was thinking of applying for Marshall Plan funding. Thus, because of this event, Czechoslovakia was now clearly found among the ranks of the countries trapped behind the infamous Iron Curtain.

Then that same summer an expansive Stalin made yet another bold move: one designed to drive out the Western powers (America, Britain and France) from their assigned occupational districts of a divided Berlin, the former German capital. Unfortunately, Berlin itself was located within the Soviet or Russian-controlled portion of Germany – and Stalin wanted the Westerners gone so that Russia could have total control over this vital city. But Truman was in no mood to be squeezed out by Soviet aggression. Thus when land routes (rail and highway) linking Berlin with West Germany were shut down for "repair," Truman responded by airlifting West Berlin's needed supplies to the surrounded city – daring Stalin to start a war by shooting one of those planes down. Stalin figured that he need not bother – that Truman would soon tire of this expensive game. But by the next summer the airlift had not only rescued Berlin – but turned it into a grand symbol of Western resolve to protect the Europeans from Soviet aggression. Finally Stalin gave up the game and reopened the land routes to West Berlin.

Truman had won that round in the growing Cold War (no shots fired – but definitely a war of some kind going on!).

Helping Tito. A major shift occurred within the Communist camp when a personal rivalry ultimately developed between Stalin and Yugoslavia's Communist dictator, Marshall Joseph Broz Tito (formerly America's rival in the contest for Greece). Stalin was hugely annoyed that Tito would want to do Communism his own way – and made a move to isolate Tito – and then expel him from membership in Stalin's Communist community – expecting this to undercut completely Tito's position in Yugoslavia. But the move failed – and now (mid-1948) Tito decided to join the nations that were requesting Marshall Plan aid, helping further secure Tito's position at the head of Yugoslavia (this was a popular move among the Yugoslavians).

The realist Truman was more than willing to help his former rival

– for although this did not make Tito an ally in the growing Cold War, it certainly helped contain Stalin's Empire so that it did not reach down through Yugoslavia to the Adriatic and thus also the Mediterranean Sea.

Stalin thus lost big on that move.

NATO. Also damaging to Stalin, the Berlin incident convinced both the Americans and West Europeans (and Canadians) that a peacetime military defense organization was needed – an agreement that an attack on any member would be taken as an attack on them all. Most importantly it bound America to the ongoing military defense of Europe. And thus in 1949 the North Atlantic Treaty Organization (NATO) was born.

Dealing with Japan. The collapse of the Japanese Empire in East Asia presented something of the same problems that the collapse of Hitler's Empire in Europe had presented. Social chaos and civil war were destined to followed the loss of the Japanese imperial structure.

Japan itself posed no particular problems because it had been so thoroughly defeated by American power, and was accordingly so thoroughly occupied by supreme American power. Yet Commanding General Douglas MacArthur had deemed it wise to let the Japanese Emperor continue in office as some kind of unifying symbol – as long as he cooperated with the American occupation. He did – and things went well in Japan.

China goes Communist. In its war with Japan, America had been closely allied with the Chinese Republic and its President Chiang Kai-shek, doing what America could to bring needed supplies to Chiang by way of the treacherous Burma Road. Now that the war was over, China emerged as one of the world's victorious powers, so important that China was awarded one of the five Permanent Seats (along with the United States, Britain, France and Soviet Russia) on the all-important Security Council of the newly created United Nations.

But Americans sensed that Chiang was facing serious difficulties from the huge Chinese peasant army under the command of Communist leader, Mao Tse-Tung (Mao Zedong) – and in late 1945 Truman sent General Marshall to China as a special envoy, to help these two Chinese political factions come together for the post-war tasks ahead (the Cold War had not yet set in – and the word "Communist" had not yet come to have the threatening quality for Americans that in just a couple of years it would quickly take on). But the hatred of these two men for each other was intense – and little by little even any pretense of cooperation between the two ceased to exist. By early 1947 Marshall realized that he was getting nowhere (and Truman needed him in Washington anyway as his new Secretary of State). By that time it was clear that China was headed for a huge civil war between Mao's Communists and Chiang's Nationalists. Ultimately, Soviet Russia would aid Mao – and America would send aid to Chiang, as the issue became another key piece in the growing Cold War.

Tragically, Chiang suffered from the huge political disability (in the eyes of the average Chinese) of having failed to hold off the Japanese on his own merits as Chinese leader – and having to resort to calling on the aid of Chinese warlords – and foreigners (such as Americans) – to carry out his responsibilities. Mao had carefully avoided such alliances during the course of the war – but at the same time had also largely avoided getting directly involved against the Japanese – thus not darkening his political reputation. Furthermore, Chiang's political strength had been in the urban coastal regions of China – largely Japanese-occupied during the war. That loss both strategically and politically would prove ruinous for Chiang. On the other hand, Mao's strength had been based in the peasant countryside – where he presented his brand of Communism (eventually known as Maoism) as some kind of rural populism. He skillfully employed all the rural and agrarian symbols he could in order to make a deep emotional link with peasant China (still smarting from its loss during the Boxer Rebellion). And thus, little by little, Mao was able to expand his hold over the Chinese countryside – until in early 1949 he was able also to overtake the last of Chiang's urban strongholds.

Chiang and what remained of the Nationalist Party (actually a multitude of Chinese) were able to escape to the huge island of Taiwan – and hold out there. America would continue to support Chiang as China's actual president, and do what it could to isolate Mao's China. It would even continuously veto any effort to replace Chiang's representative occupying the powerful China seat on the United Nations Security Council with a Maoist representative. And America would hold to this all the way up until 1972, when Nixon went to Mao's China to finally open diplomatic relations with mainland China.

* * *

THE WAR IN KOREA (1950-1953)

As part of the enticement to Stalin at Yalta to get him involved in what was expected to be a long war with Japan, an arrangement had been made to allow the Soviet Russians to temporarily (no more than five years) occupy the Northern half of the Korean peninsula while America did the same in the southern half (divided at the 38th parallel) – to help the Koreans get back on their feet after a long and brutal Japanese occupation (since 1910).

Presidential elections in Korea. When in 1947 Truman indicated that it was time for the United Nations to hold national elections to unite the two halves and turn over governing authority to the Koreans themselves, Stalin balked, claimed that Korea was not ready for such a turnover of power (knowing full-well that such an election would end Soviet domination in the North and turn a united Korea towards the West). But UN-supervised elections went ahead anyway (July 1948) – but only in the South. The Koreans elected the conservative Syngman Rhee as President (Korean Communists had boycotted the elections). Interestingly, the "un-ready" North a few months later had its own elections – in which the Korean Communist Kim Il-sung was elected North Korean president.*

However, not wishing at that time to add the Korea issue to the growing tensions between Soviet Russia and America, both countries subsequently removed their troops from Korea.

But with the Soviet Russian detonation of its own atomic bomb in 1949, Stalin decided that the strategic dynamic in Korea had shifted greatly in his favor. The looming threat of an American retaliation against a bold Soviet Russian move had now been greatly neutralized with Russia now also possessing the bomb (the Soviet fear of Truman's use of the bomb had in fact been a big factor in restraining the ambitious Stalin in Europe). Also, America had not taken a very active role in the Chinese Civil War – and besides, in a recent speech by Secretary of State Dean Acheson describing America's sphere of vital interests globally, Korea had been omitted from the list.

America had made its international policy clear as merely containing Communism – and Korea had apparently fallen outside the American line of containment. Indeed, Stalin noted that Truman seemed very concerned about South Korean President Rhee moving to unite Korea under his rule by an invasion of the North – starting a major conflict in Asia. Stalin knew that adding an Asian conflict to America's heavy challenges in Europe was very unwanted by Truman – leading Truman to cut back considerably American military support of South Korea in order to discourage Rhee's ambitions. No, America seemed most unlikely to do anything if Kim himself were to pull the same trick – to unite Korea under his rule by force. So Stalin began to make preparations with Kim for a quick grab of the southern half of Korea.

North Korea invades the South. On June 25th (1950), with no prior warning, Kim's North Korean army invaded the South – in the matter of

---

*This marks the beginning of the ongoing rule of the Kim family – father, son, and now today grandson – in the North.

only a few days overrunning an unprepared and totally shocked South Korean army, which had to flee its capital city, Seoul. And within a week the ill-equipped South Korean army had fallen to a fifth of its original size.

At first Truman thought this was a mere Soviet ploy to distract him from events in Europe. But he soon realized the seriousness of Soviet Russia and its puppet Korea being able to occupy the southern region of Korea – just opposite Japan and overlooking the entire South China Sea – where a huge Soviet Russian naval fleet could be stationed. Truman quickly ferried American troops from Japan over to South Korea. But they themselves were hardly a match to the huge and quite well equipped (thanks to the Russians) North Korean army. Back they fell before the advancing North Koreans.

The United Nations responds. In the meantime, Truman moved to make this an international incident – claiming that it was the U.N.'s responsibility to protect the Korean regime that it itself had set up. Thankfully at the time Soviet Russia was boycotting the meetings of the U.N. – angry over the refusal of the other members of the Security Council to let Mao's Chinese government take the China seat now that Chiang had been forced to take refuge in Taiwan. Thus there was no Soviet veto of the Security Council decision to call on U.N. members to construct a United Nations military force to rescue South Korea. British and French soldiers (and others) were sent to Korea as part of the U.N. Peacekeeping force. But basically the U.N. troops (as they called themselves) were mostly Truman's American troops sent to Korea as a "police action" against the North Korean aggressor.

The landing at Inchon. But the North Korean troops were well dug into the huge mountain range that runs down the center of the Korean peninsula. It was like Italy only a few years earlier. Advancing against an enemy well entrenched in mountainous heights was painfully slow. And indeed it was like Italy – in that a decision (as at Anzio) was made to send a force of 75,000 troops ashore at Inchon behind North Korean lines. Except this time (unlike Italy) it worked – brilliantly. General MacArthur gave his troops no rest when they hit shore; immediately he headed them inland – cutting off the North Korean Army's supply line back to the North. Now it was the North Korean Army's turn to panic – and panic turned itself into a full flight of the North Korean army.

Seoul was liberated – and then on October 1st the U.N. troops crossed the 38th parallel and headed into the northern half of the peninsula. Within two weeks they had captured the North Korean capital at Pyongyang. The North Koreans seemed unable to hold back the forces advancing north.

Now it was Mao's turn to get very interested in Korean developments – fearing that this U.N. army might possibly decide to not stop at the border between Korea and China at the Yalu River – and instead roll on into China in order to liberate China from Mao's Communist control. Warnings were sent by Mao for U.N. troops not to approach the Chinese border with Korea at the Yalu River – for China would under no circumstances tolerate such a development.

At this point Truman and MacArthur began to have a major difference of opinion as to how to proceed. Truman urged caution. But MacArthur went before the press to argue about how an invasion of China to cut off Chinese supply bases supporting the North Koreans was a necessity. So who was in charge? The American Constitution makes it clear that the President is the Supreme Commander of all American military forces. But MacArthur (who always loved public attention) was beginning to sound like some kind of Caesar wannabe.

China intervenes. In any case, Mao was not going to wait around to see who won this debate about the American Constitution and on October 25th sent some 200,000 Chinese "volunteer" troops into North Korea against the advancing Americans – conscripted "volunteers" because he did not want to find himself officially at war with the United Nations! Then a bitter winter set in on North Korea and some 30,000 American troops found themselves at one point facing a Chinese army four times their size at the Chosin Reservoir – and 15,000 American casualties resulted (though the Chinese loss was even greater). Americans now began a retreat – back to the 38th parallel. Even briefly Seoul was once again lost to the North Koreans – for about a month before U.N. troops were able to retake the initiative and again liberate Seoul, also once again advancing across the 38th parallel.

Truman fires MacArthur. Meanwhile, MacArthur continued his speculates before the adoring press, this time about the feasibility of using nuclear weapons to defeat the Chinese – even suggesting that the decision should be his rather than the President's. This was for Truman the final straw – and in mid-April (1951) he simply fired a stunned MacArthur. Mighty Caesar had been cut down! Truman was well aware that he would take a lot of flak for firing this self-made American hero. But it needed to be done.*

---

*Because of this action, many Americans came to view MacArthur as a national hero – and Truman as a coward, if not almost a traitor. But a Congressional investigation ultimately concluded that Truman had indeed acted correctly, and that MacArthur (who actually spent all his time in Tokyo) was out of touch with political realities in Korea, as well as in the rest of the world.

Stalemate. Once more a huge Chinese offensive opened up (some 700,000 Chinese troops this time) at about the same time. But after about a month (May 1951), an immoveable front line of battle seemed to set in, a military stalemate that appeared to be rather permanent.

CHAPTER NINE

MIDDLE-CLASS AMERICA TRIUMPHANT

* * *

AMERICAN POST-WAR REBOUND

A swing to the Republican Right after the war. American capitalism had stormed back into existence because of the wartime need for ships, airplanes, tanks, trucks, arms of all sorts, etc. But with the war ending those jobs came to a halt and workers were let go – reviving old anti-capitalist attitudes of the American blue-collar working class – which went on a massive strike (five million workers out) during the 1945-1946 period. Then too the Middle Class or white-collar workforce employed in wartime government offices also faced similar reductions – except that Middle Class America generally expected this to happen – as Middle-Class America in general found bloated government operations distasteful and understood this wartime government work to have been merely temporary.

Indeed, the reaction of the average American voter was not only to expect government cutbacks but also to do something about "unpatriotic" workers' movement (identified closely with distasteful Socialism). All of this resulted in a massive routing of the Roosevelt New Deal Democrats from public office in the post-war elections and the return of the Republican Party to power, massively so. And one of the first things the Republican Party in Congress did (1947) was to pass the Taft-Hartley Bill which put huge restraints on the American Labor Unions' ability to force the unionization of the American worker. Truman vetoed the bill – but it was easily overridden by a 2/3 vote in Congress, thus becoming the law of the land.*

The G.I. Bill. But one piece of the legacy of the Roosevelt years that the Republicans would not touch was the 1944 G.I. Bill – which promised servicemen that after the war they would receive – not a pension or payment – but financial assistance (very low-cost government loans) in

---

*But then Truman himself during the remainder of his presidency would use the Taft-Hartley Act twelve times in his own confrontation with American unions.

heading off to college, buying a house, or starting up a business. In short, the G.I. Bill worked wonders in helping former soldiers move on – and up – in life after the war, avoiding the typical crisis that occurs when soldiers are returned after war to a sagging economy where jobs are scarce and unemployment rampant.

The booming American economy. In fact quite the opposite actually happened with the post-war American economy. Virtually no cars had been produced during the war years and consumers were eager to trade up to a shiny new car, helping the automobile manufacturers quickly shift back to massive automobile production from the manufacture of tanks, trucks, and airplanes that they had converted their operations to during the war. Then there was a huge demand for the new and quite affordable small homes that allowed young American families to leave the multi-generational old homes of traditional America – and move out on their own in the widening world of America.   Military service had introduced young men to the dreamy world of California, the robust world of Texas, etc. – and after the war young Americans eagerly moved West in huge numbers, into fast-growing suburban neighborhoods – arising, however, around not only the newly expanding cities in the West but also in cities everywhere across the country. Consequently, the construction industry boomed – offering plenty of jobs for young men who had returned home from military service.

The Marshall Plan aiding the European recovery also added immensely to the American economy.   Much of Europe's industrial infrastructure had been destroyed by the war – although America's factories had been untouched. Consequently, the Marshall Plan funds mostly made their way back to America in the form of orders for American goods: machinery, trucks and tractors, electronics, etc. In fact, by the year 1950 it would be correct to say that America itself provided fully half of all industrial products being produced worldwide.

The "Baby Boomers." The startup of a family was a matter that young Americans had been forced to put off during the war years. But now, peacetime presented the opportunity for young men and women to make up for that lacking. They rather quickly married in massive numbers – and soon began to produce the next generation. Babies were thus born also in massive numbers in the period of 1946 and after – the beginning of the "Baby Boom." And those babies, soon children (the 1950s) and eventually young adults (by the mid-1960s) would develop into a very distinct generation of Americans, known appropriately as the "Baby Boomers" – and eventually just "Boomers." They would come to rock the nation.

"Entitlement" replaces the sense of service or duty among the Boomers. Tragically, what these young parents seeming were unaware of was that the enormous dignity they found in their lives as Americans was a huge emotional personal payoff that mysteriously came from the life of service or duty, which they had been forced to take in both the Depression and recent war just to survive. Now with peace in the world and America prospering greatly, they saw the "wonderful" possibilities that their Boomer children would never have to undergo such a social burden.

Sadly this adult or Vet generation failed to understand how importantly their approach to life through the taking up of burdensome but necessary service or duty to the surrounding social world was actually behind their also deep sense of both personal and corporate success. Thus they would raise and "bless" their Boomer children – as part of their on-going sense of personal duty – by trying to keep from them the "burden" of such sacrifice, such dutiful service. They would give their children generously and freely all the personal and social payoffs that they themselves in their growing up never had the pleasure to experience.

And in doing so, they believed they were performing a great service to their children. Actually quite the opposite would be the social results.

Consequently, the Boomers would not form this deep sense of personal connection through the path of duty or deep personal service to the surrounding social world. Indeed, they would be amazingly lacking of such social powers. This was because the Boomers would grow up seeing society not as something you are deeply wed to through the personal investment of service or duty. Instead, when they looked out on society it was to see what social entitlements were due them through their social connections, and changing those connections (marriages, jobs, local communities) when they did not see a proper social payoff coming their way. Thus it was that they were largely attached to society only to the extent that society continued to offer a person his or her "entitlements." In short, socially speaking, they were badly "spoiled."

Christian America. A notable thing about post-war middle-class culture was that it was personal and highly relational – rather than dreamily rational or utopian – the kind of world that those who like to direct the lives of others from a position of lofty and rather abstract enlightenment typically live by. The war that Middle America had just been through was neither rational nor abstract. It had *not* been fought on the basis of high and noble ideas (the way Wilson took America into the First World War in the name of "making the world safe for democracy") but more as a sense of simple defense of the America that had been treacherously attacked by Japan and called to war by Hitler's own design. There had been much personal sacrifice involved for Americans. Indeed, this war had been from the beginning very personal.

But going at life on a relational rather than rational basis had been given considerable impetus by the Christianity that informed most Americans at this point – the sense that their personal relationship with God was critical in their ability to go the course – all the way to victory. Americans looked to God rather than to human programs to keep them moving forward. True, there was a Washington government to lead the way. But even there, that lead was more personal, prayerful, spiritually-directed than programmatic. Roosevelt had kept in close touch with the hearts of Americans with his fireside chats and personal prayers – ones that related President, citizen, and God in a very special way – vitally needed to keep things moving ahead, even in the face of huge uncertainties that always accompany war.

Thus Americans came out of the war highly committed to their Christian faith – especially in the way it defined for them the idea of America itself, what it stood for, how it operated – what was to be expected from American life – and what defined the good and the bad in all of this.

Capitalist America. Right along with Christianity came Capitalism as core to Middle America's understanding of life. Certainly the huge industrial war machine led by American capitalists had proven itself. And the continuing economic prosperity that followed the war in terms of the building boom in American housing, the booming automobile industry, and the easy availability of a whole number of domestic or personal consumer items brought capitalism back into favor in the American heart. It was also easy to look across to Europe and see that continent's tendency towards Socialism seemingly serving much less capably than the American capitalist system.

Constitutional America. And America's governmental system clearly had proven its strengths during and after the war – when Washington's immense military and bureaucratic system needed so vitally during the war now was reduced drastically in order to let America return the focus of its political dynamic back to local American life. Here too, with the process of government carried out essentially as a local responsibility – rather than as some imperial institution located in a distant national capital – there was something very constitutional in all this. Americans were proud of their Constitution, considering it to be the perfect model – even for the world – of excellent government.

Over the next twenty years that followed the end of the war in 1945, Christianity, Capitalism, and Constitutionalism (the Three C's) would all come together to form something of a grand cultural blend.

Christian revival. It seemed even that America was undergoing another one of its Great Awakenings. Interestingly, one of the groups taking the initiative in this matter were America's capitalists, now restored to dignity because of the war. They had joined Abraham Vereide even before the war in strongly supporting his prayer-breakfast movement. But now they were joined by Washington senators and congressmen, as a strong sense of Christian responsibility, not just to the country but to the world, called forward an active spirit of American social mission.

And then along with this, there was the young Christian evangelist, Billy Graham, who seemed to be taking the nation by storm as he packed huge coliseums with vast multitudes attending his various crusades, with his month-long 1952 Washington D.C. crusade drawing as many as half a million participants, many of them also representatives and senators from Congress.

So effective was this crusade (well financed by American business leaders) that it led to the call by President Truman (although he generally tended to prefer to keep the matter of religion personal and private) for an annual National Day of Prayer – the first one, captioned "Freedom Under God," to be held that year (1952) on the 4th of July.*

The world of television. Then too, just as the radio revolutionized life in the 1920s, the widespread appearance of the new television (TV) would have the same massive impact on American life from the early 1950s onward. The development of the TV certainly also put a huge boost in the American economy, Americans flocking in vast numbers to the stores to buy this new and most wonderful addition to American homelife. It was like having the movie industry brought into your home. In fact, Hollywood was in a bit of a panic fearing that TV craze would bring down the movie industry (it did not).

But the TV put in front of Americans a clearer picture of a well-modeled world of everything from family life (*The Adventures of Ozzie and Harriet*), cowboy heroes (*Hopalong Cassidy*), comedy (*I Love Lucy*), and classic drama (*The Hallmark Hall of Fame*). Soon it would move on to major sports events (National Football League games) and the latest dance steps for teens (*American Bandstand*). In short it presented a very clear

---

*Actually Truman had several times previously called the nation to prayer, when he found himself facing a number of crises for which he had no easy answers. His unsophisticated but very Biblical and very personal Christian faith drew criticism from more sophisticated and "theologically-informed" voices of the day. But the important fact was that Truman truly looked to God and the Christian world for support in carrying out the responsibilities placed on him by his nation.

Middle-Class America Triumphant 275

definition of the core ideals of Middle-Class American life, something that Americans felt set them apart from – and way ahead of – the rest of the world in terms of modern development.

✱ ✱ ✱
HOWEVER – THE COLD WAR HITS HOME

But all was not sunny in Middle America. As the Cold War developed, and Americans watched country after country in East Europe fall under Russian influence – in most cases by political maneuvering within those countries by Soviet-backed local politicians (that fear even extended to France and Italy after huge Communist uprisings in both countries in 1947 were put down only with much effort) – America began to be concerned about the extent and intent of Communism planted in America itself.

Authoritarianism as the new threat. It seemed as if Americans had fought in the recent war to destroy the authoritarian regimes of Germany, Italy and Japan only to have those threats to the peace and prosperity of the larger world replaced by a new authoritarian regime: Stalin's Soviet Russia. Great concern developed within Middle America that there was some kind of global historical trend that seemed to be pushing civilization in this direction. And that concern increased enormously with the publishing in 1949 of the English author George Orwell's book, *1984*, which portrayed a world in which the very thought process of the world's people had been taken over – thanks to fast-rising modern technology – by "Big Brother."

Panic set in as Americans considered the possibility that this might be happening right there in America, right there under their own eyes, subtly manipulating the thought processes of vulnerable people into authoritarian compliance. That seemed to have been the very pattern of Communism's spread through East Europe. And it seemed to be part of the ideological fires that burned within Western Europe's labor movement as well.

Thus this same concern hit America as it considered its own labor movement – conducting (in the early post-war years) labor strikes and strife that looked way too much like those labor maneuverings that had brought Communism to power in Soviet-dominated Eastern Europe.

And also there were the numerous American intellectuals who, during the great Depression, had loudly identified themselves as strongly anti-Capitalist and pro-Socialist. Where did they stand on such matters today? Where were their loyalties now to be found in this post-war world?

American intellectuals under suspicion. Leading this inquiry into the

Communist involvement in America was the House Un-American Activities Committee (HUAC), conducting Congressional investigations not only into the labor movement and the world of socialist intellectuals but also into the movie industry – which had produced a number of films now considered to have strongly Leftist messages. This would come to include even the U.S. government itself, when accusations came out in 1948 that high-level officials in the Roosevelt Administration had been spying for the Soviets.

This matter turned itself into extensive social paranoia on the part of Middle America, met on the other hand by the scorn and disgust against Middle America on the part of Intellectual America. When actors began to be blacklisted and refused roles in Hollywood's world (ultimately some 300 individuals were blacklisted, including even famous actors), Hollywood protested that this kind of authoritarianism was what America itself was supposed to be combating – not embracing.

Then when senior U.S. Treasury official Harry Dexter White (who was a key figure at the 1944 Bretton Woods Conference setting up the new United Nations) and Alger Hiss (a top State Department advisor at the Yalta meeting designing the post-war world) were accused of being spies for Soviet Russia, America lined itself up into two opposing camps. Intellectuals were convinced that this was only a form of witch-hunting on the part of unenlightened individuals from the American Middle Class – simply resentful of these individuals because of their highly talented backgrounds (the highly educated White, for instance, was a product of Columbia, Stanford and Harvard University educations – and Hiss was a Johns Hopkins University and Harvard Law School Graduate).

Particular resentment by intellectuals was aimed toward the freshman Congressman and HUAC member Richard Nixon, who refused to relent in his investigation of Hiss... which eventually led to the conviction and imprisonment of this polished diplomat – to the dismay of Hiss's fellow intellectuals.*

Also, when suspicions turned towards some of America's scientific community – whom Americans had assumed possessed the highest integrity of all people – the nation was shocked. Intelligence work had cracked the Soviet code and discovered that nuclear scientist Klaus Fuchs was a Soviet spy. He in turn named David Greenglass and Julius and Ethel Rosenberg as spying for the Soviets while helping to develop America's nuclear weapons.

There were others as well, accused and ultimately convicted of spying in the early 1950s, though only Julius and Ethel Rosenberg were executed – despite the huge international call for clemency (they claimed innocence

---

*Actually, in the opening of the Russian archives after the collapse of the Soviet Union in the early 1990s, it was confirmed that in fact both White and Hiss had been spying for Stalin.

to the end).*

McCarthy cultivates a Red Scare. At this point a loud, accusatory voice in the U.S. Senate became even louder, as Senator Joseph McCarthy in early 1950 began whipping up American fury at this "treachery in high places." McCarthy accused (without any specific details) the American diplomatic corps broadly, then the American civilian government in general, and then finally, by 1954, even the US military, of being loaded with Communists who were secretly subverting America. With this, the Red Scare was whipped up so as to turn in every direction.

American intellectuals fight back. The Red Scare hit especially hard America's intellectuals – who were known to have "fancy ideas" about the need for social reform – ideas which seemed overly critical, even unpatriotic, even treasonous, to fiercely patriotic middle-class Vets. The Vets therefore were (with McCarthy's help) easily led to believe that this class of intellectuals formed a conspiratorial group seeking to overthrow the nation and everything it stood for. Needless to say, the intellectuals did all that they could do to fight back – though it had to be done cautiously, very cautiously.

Arthur Miller's play, *The Crucible*. An example of this was when in 1952 playwright Arthur Miller's close friend Elia Kazan, in a hearing before the HUAC, specifically identified eight members of his Group Theater as Communists. Miller was so offended by this betrayal that he responded the next year by writing a play, *The Crucible*. Miller felt that he dared not answer the Communist witch-hunt going on around him at the time directly (that would have been dangerous), but instead, wrote about a similar betrayal when citizens of Salem, Massachusetts, turned on each other during the infamous witch trials of 1692-1693.

In a not-too-subtle way, this challenged deeply not only the mindset of 1950s Middle America, but also even more deeply the very Puritan-Christian cultural foundations that Miller (and numerous intellectuals) were certain was behind this Middle-American paranoia.

Actually, the play would not do well when it first came out. But in the 1960s, when America found itself moving into a whole new cultural realm, the play would finally find a very enthusiastic audience.†

---

*Again, with the fall of the Soviet Union, it was finally revealed that indeed the Rosenbergs (or at least Julius Rosenberg) too had been spying for the Soviets.

†At that point the play became required reading in most high school American literature courses across the country, helping to turn young Americans away from their nation's cultural roots founded deeply in Puritan Christianity.

* * *

EISENHOWER'S AMERICA

The 1952 election. Despite the new 22nd Amendment to the Constitution limiting a person to only two terms of office as president (in reaction to Roosevelt's four terms) – it did allow Truman to run for yet one more term. However his decision to take on the Korean challenge had not warmed American hearts, which factored in his not doing well in the early Democratic Party primaries. Anyway, Truman was worn out and ready to retire, so he backed out of the race. In these same primaries Senator Estes Kefauver of Tennessee had done quite well, running on his reputation as an anti-corruption crusader, particularly in fighting the Mafia and also local political corruption. But the Democratic National Convention (DNC) was still represented mostly by local political machines, hostile to Kefauver. Thus the Democrats pressured Illinois Governor Adlai Stevenson to run as their presidential candidate (he would personally have preferred to run for reelection as Illinois governor rather than U.S. president!).

The Republicans bypassed the very conservative Robert Taft (son of former President Taft) to pick the centrist and popular former General Dwight D. Eisenhower (at that point President of Columbia University) – with the HUAC activist Richard Nixon as his running mate, pleasing the Conservative wing of the party.

Basically, American labor, Southern "Dixiecrats,"* and American intellectuals backed the rather intellectual Stevenson, who distanced himself from the Truman legacy (not doing well at that point) and focused his campaign on attacking Eisenhower for failing to take a strong stance against McCarthy. But Middle America loved everything the war-hero Eisenhower seemed to stand for, and threw its support to him. Ultimately, the election proved to be a solid win for the Republicans in both the Presidential and House elections – with a Republican-Democrat tie in the Senate. The presidential vote had been 55.2 percent for Eisenhower to only 44.3 percent for Stevenson, and the electoral college was even more skewed in favor of Eisenhower, 442 votes for Eisenhower and 89 votes for Stevenson. Eisenhower had managed to gain the majority even in three of the "Solid South" states!

---

*"Dixiecrat" was a label applied to hard-core Southern Democrats, also known as "yellow dog Democrats," because they claimed that they would vote for a yellow dog for elective office before they would ever vote for a Republican. The Republican Party was still identified in the mind of Dixiecrat Southerners as the party of the hated Abraham Lincoln! Dixiecrats were reliable Democratic Party voters under all circumstances.

Dwight D. Eisenhower. The new president was born third of seven boys in Abilene Kansas, to a rigorously religious family. After graduation from high school he worked two years to help finance a brother's college education, then – to the disappointment of his quite pacifist mother – was accepted to the West Point Military Academy, which offered a free education. There he was quite involved with sports, and academically graduated at the middle of a class – one that would go on (because of the Great War) to provide the nation a large number of active officers.

Just prior to America's entry into that war he married (Mamie Doud), and then during the war served at home in various administrative duties (which he became quite good at), becoming deeply frustrated when just as he was finally about to be mobilized for action in France, the Armistice was signed and the fighting in Europe came to a close.

With the long period of peace that followed, he took up both further military study and service as a staff officer in a variety of commands, before being sent to the Philippines in 1935 to serve under General MacArthur, and the following year receive the rank of Lt. Colonel. He returned to the States at the end of 1939 where he again served as a staff officer to various generals, finally attaining the rank of brigadier general in 1941, just prior to America's involvement in World War Two.

Thus far, however, there was nothing notable about his service that suggested he would one day find himself commanding the most important and final phase of a war in Europe. Yet his administrative work and well-recognized strategic mind impressed General Marshall. And his ability to move things forward in the midst of personality clashes was what had him sent to London to take command of operations there, at the time focused on North Africa, Sicily and then Italy.

But as already noted, it was his selection as commander of the crossing of the English Channel and march across France, Belgium and the Netherlands that secured his place in the history books as a battlefield hero. And after the war, Truman brought him on board as his Army Chief of Staff (Marshall had been sent to China to try to work out some kind of cooperation between Chiang and Mao). And thus as the 1948 elections approached, it was also that both the Republican and Democratic Parties courted him as a possible candidate for the U.S. Presidency, something that Eisenhower refused.

Instead, he accepted the offer to become Columbia University's president, a strange calling considering the vast difference in mentalities that existed between the scholarly and quite idealistic professors and the quite pragmatic – and deeply religious – Eisenhower. But Eisenhower was much more the scholar – or at least man of well-thought-through ideals – than the country understood about him at the time. He was very active on the prestigious Council on Foreign Relations and a founder of the American Assembly, an organization designed to bring together leaders from all walks of America life to go over a broad range of political, economic and social issues facing the country. Here Eisenhower developed from a starting point of deep knowledge of military strategy and organization to a quite sophisticated understanding of the broader world of business, economics, and social-cultural matters.

Actually, Eisenhower was vastly much brighter than his Columbia University professors – many of whom disliked Eisenhower intensely – portrayed him before the public, and was learning to cultivate excellent working relations with American business leaders – whom liberal professors also tended to distrust.

In 1950 he was appointed Supreme Commander of the North Atlantic Treaty Organization – nonetheless retaining his position at Columbia until sworn in as U.S. president in January of 1953. This was an important appointment because Eisenhower could generate stronger support in Congress for this peacetime organization and its operations than could Truman, and at the same time could leverage America's European allies to make a deeper material commitment (men and money) so as not to make NATO a strictly American operation.

As a Christian, Eisenhower would prove to be one of the most active of all individuals to occupy the White House in support of the Christian faith and its central role in the life of the nation. He did not come to the White House with much of a Christian testimony and was not even baptized until once in office. However, as president he took up regular Sunday attendance at the New York Avenue Presbyterian Church. And also as president, Eisenhower constantly reaffirmed the importance of all Americans taking up their particular Christian responsibilities (including prayer and regular church attendance) as the nation faced social problems at home and political and economic problems abroad. To Eisenhower's understanding of things, God himself expected no less of America. And Americans seemed glad to take up this very challenge.

Indeed, it would be during his presidency that the words "under God" would be added to the Pledge of Allegiance in 1954, and "In God We Trust" would be confirmed as the nation's motto in 1956.*

Korean Armistice. As already noted, during the 1952 presidential campaign, Eisenhower had distanced himself from the whole McCarthy matter – drawing sharp criticism from Stevenson for Eisenhower's failing

---

*The motto had actually appeared on American coinage since the mid-1800s, although it would not appear on paper money until the 1950s.

Middle-Class America Triumphant 281

to denounce McCarthy's witch hunt. Instead, Eisenhower had focused his campaign on doing something to bring the Korean War to some kind of resolution (the fighting itself had actually subsided substantially since mid-1952). And thus now as US President, Eisenhower worked to get the various parties involved to sign an Armistice (actually not a formal end to the war) – recognizing the rather permanent division of Korea north and south not too far from the original 38th parallel. But this seemed to put the Korean crisis now as a thing of the past. Korean tensions would flare from time to time after that – but leave the line itself intact – even down to today.

There were now two Korean societies, increasingly different in character as they went off developmentally in quite different directions, North Korea to become over time even more "Stalinist" in its political makeup, and South Korea to develop strongly along Western (deeply Americanized) political, economic and social lines.

McCarthy finally brought down. Meanwhile, McCarthy's reckless accusations before his TV audience of "Commies everywhere" had reached into all segments of society – although only on occasion did he actually mention anyone by name. He was on a major fishing expedition to come up with scandal everywhere – in order to keep things focused on him as America's savior. But in early 1954, radio and TV newsman Edward R. Murrow actually did a series on McCarthyism – the first to openly challenge McCarthy. McCarthy's response to Murrow's challenge was not artful – indeed worsening the slowly declining image of the Senator. But what finally would be McCarthy's undoing was his taking on the U.S. Army officer corps before his Senate committee – and before his enormous TV audience – for the Army's harboring of "known Communists." Finally, the lawyer leading the Army's defense launched into an attack on McCarthy's destructive and ill-founded evidence. McCarthy was at a loss for words. His boldness melted away – and what the Americans now saw on TV was a demagogue with no serious political skills, merely a monstrous political gossip with nothing of substance to his agenda. At this point the Senate finally found its courage and voted a motion of censure against McCarthy – almost unprecedented in the history of the U.S. Senate. And although he kept his Senate seat, McCarthy was no longer a person of interest to America. He eventually faded off into alcoholism – and America moved on.

Directives to the Boomer: "Challenge all authority." America would move on. But it had put in place a set of social-moral foundations that would be lasting: the Boomer mindset. So afraid of the Orwellian Big Brother authoritarianism that walked the earth were the Vets that they made the decision that their children were to be taught in such a way that their Boomer offspring would never become victims of authoritarian thought-control – such as they had witnessed among the Hitler youth, and more recently had heard about taking place in Stalinist Russia – where the youth were so brain-washed by the Communist system that they would even turn their parents over to Soviet authorities if they heard them involved in any "anti-revolutionary" conversation.

So, the Vet parents thought themselves to be very wise in teaching their children to challenge all voices, all efforts of anyone, coming at them as "authority." They were to do their own thinking, come at rational choices through using their own natural logic.

Tragically, the Vets had fallen into typical Humanist thinking in presuming that their Boomer children – by way of natural human instinct – would come to hold the same social-spiritual values, and go at life in the same way that they, their Vet parents, did. The Boomers would do so because supposedly these values were instinctive to all humankind, values that anyone thinking freely and clearly on such matters would necessarily come to hold.

On two counts, the Vets (as with all Humanists, ancient as well as modern) would be making a huge mistake in their program. First of all, there was nothing "natural" about how they, the Vets, were raised. Very precise circumstances had made them to be the people they were: the hardships of the Great Depression and the massive sacrifices they made during World War Two. As a distinct generation, they were very reflective of this particular development, willing to sacrifice personal interest in order to serve a higher social good. They had been forced into that moral-spiritual position in order to survive. And in doing so, they came to believe religiously that this was just a natural instinct of all decent people.

As for their highly pampered Boomer offspring, this generation had come to understand life and its dynamics through a very different set of circumstances, and would therefore understand life's "natural" dynamics quite differently – in fact, very differently – than their parents.

And secondly, as Christians, the Vets should have known better than to take up the religious idealism of Secular-Humanism, having been shown repeatedly in long-standing Biblical Scripture – not to mention in the life they had been required to live – that man's instincts are not naturally always so beautiful, and that human Reason does not always bring things forward nobly, but is often simply the tool by which people justify the worst kinds of behavior. As Christians they should have been acutely aware of the fact that original sin – not original goodness – was what spiritually mature humans always ended up having to deal with constantly, especially when that very sinful instinct came from themselves.

Middle-Class America Triumphant

So actually the Vets were themselves "brainwashing" their children, with very interesting but very foolish Humanist Idealism. They were carefully shaping the thought-processes of a rising generation so that when they reached adulthood, they would finally begin to act on this training, training that had taught them to challenge all social authority.

But the only social authority at hand for their Boomer offspring to challenge would be the social authority of the American society and culture that their own parents (and many generations before them) had carefully put in place. By their very training, the Boomers would see themselves called to challenge that authority, especially in the social areas touching closely to home: their jobs, their marriages, their social affiliations, their local communities, even their nation. And being a pampered generation, it was easy for these Boomers to find reasons to challenge those social ties, those social responsibilities, when it involved commitment and sacrifice rather than just social payoff.

And in this crusade against their inherited social world, they would also have the mentoring or support of the alienated intellectuals, who themselves felt that they had good cause to oppose, or even overthrow, the social-cultural world of Middle America. Most importantly, those mentors included "Progressive" professors, under whom the Boomers studied in fast-rising numbers, playwrights making plays and movies encouraging new social attitudes (ones highly shocking to the Vet world!), and young journalist crusaders, etc., that is, any group of people who lived in the world of "progressive" idea-production. They would be quite active in encouraging and ultimately providing moral justification for the new Boomer-think.

Thus things would soon get very strained in America – as Middle America entered the 1960s only to find that everything that it believed in to now be under challenge, deep challenge, by its own offspring!

The Vets' foreign policy idealism. Sadly, the Vets (as well as the generations of Americans after them) also seemed to go at foreign policy along those same Humanist – rather than Christian Realist – lines.

Certainly the intense strain of going to war against Germany and Japan in World War Two – and then against the North Koreans and their Chinese allies in the Korean War – called for some kind of Idealism to get the Vets through the ugliness of it all. Thus they were not merely involved in killing bad people, the enemy. They were serving the much more noble cause of bringing "democracy" to the world. That grand goal seemed to give their efforts much greater stature, grander purpose.

But huge dangers would accompany this idealizing of American foreign policy. For one thing, democracy is not the natural, inevitable outcome for a people when they have suddenly been freed from what Americans understand as nothing more than dictatorship. They should have learned that lesson from World War One when they sent thousands of American boys off to die in the trenches of Northern France, all for the grand purpose of making the world safe for democracy.

They should have learned that lesson at the end of World War Two when they took such a strong stance opposing their Dutch allies – who were determined to regain their 300-year old colony in Indonesia. Instead, America supported a local independence movement there (and thus the old Wilsonian principle of "the rights of self-determination of peoples everywhere," one that supposedly, when implemented, leads automatically to democracy) conducted by a regime set up by the Japanese at the time of their surrender to the Americans in August of 1945. But after the Dutch were chased off (or just slaughtered), this led not to Indonesian democracy but rather to the ruthless 22-year dictatorship of Sukarno!

Americans have great difficulty understanding the dynamics of power – power which most of the time is subtle, not very glorious in its effect, and always tiresome to maintain. Crusades are much more exciting and seemingly so much more noble. But when back in 1794 Washington marched his army into Western Pennsylvania to put down a whiskey rebellion – doing so only to preserve the little sense of political unity that the new Republic was able to muster – there was nothing very noble about the enterprise. Yet it was quite necessary to make that show of power, or the fragile union holding their new Republic together would have simply dissolved away.

Likewise, there was nothing noble that Lincoln was feeling when he sent Union troops into the rebellious Confederacy in order to force the ongoing unity of the United States. It was simply a job that had to be done. And even in World War Two and Korea the actual task was simply to bring down those whose actions threated the social world entrusted into American hands. Nothing about it was very glamorous. But it was all quite necessary.

The same kind of fundamental Realism driving America's actions abroad however cannot be said to have been present in America's entry into World War One. Wilsonian Idealism was the sole motive, and it proved disastrous in the end. And tragically many of the "save the world for democracy" crusades that America as the West's superpower would undertake from the 1960s onward would be just as bad: Cuba, the Congo, Vietnam, Iran, Afghanistan, Iraq, Libya, Syria. Idealistic crusades, though emotionally thrilling (for a little while anyway) are dangerous enterprises, which a great power like America should carefully avoid.

Black and White America. Although about one in ten Americans were classed as Colored (Black) in the 1950s, actually they occupied a rather invisible part of Middle America's world, living either in Black sections of America's major cities or else scattered around the South. And that invisibleness gave them very little voice in American society. True, some had distinguished themselves, such as the Tuskegee Airmen who were sought after as excellent fighter pilots protecting American bombers in their run over Italy during World War Two. And there was the excellent baseball player Jackie Robinson, who broke the color bar when he was brought onto the Brooklyn Dodgers. But these were by far the exception.

But that began to change in the mid-1950s, when an exhausted Black seamstress, Rosa Parks, refused to give up her seat to a White male on a crowded Montgomery (Alabama) bus, and was arrested and fined. But the Montgomery chapter of the National Association for the Advancement of Colored People (NAACP) decided to fight the case. Parks was secretary of the Montgomery chapter of the NAACP, which included also within its local leadership a young pastor who had recently taken a Montgomery pulpit, the Rev. Dr. Martin Luther King, Jr. – who would come to head up a boycott of the town's busses.* Not only would they encourage Blacks to avoid the use of the town's busses, they would fight the $14 fine – as far up the judicial appeals ladder as the case would go – in opposition to the segregation laws designed to keep Blacks in their place.

The Rev. Dr. Martin Luther King, Jr. King was born in Atlanta, Georgia, in 1929, named "Michael" at the time. His father, also Michael, was the pastor of the Ebenezer Baptist Church in Atlanta and his mother, Alberta, was the daughter of the previous pastor of the same church. While on a trip to Germany in 1934, Michael, Sr. was deeply inspired by Luther's reforms, and decided to identify himself with Luther's work by taking Luther's name, and changing the name of his son Michael, Jr. as well – thus both now becoming Martin Luther King. But the family was not only deeply involved in the Baptist ministry, it was also equally involved in the civil rights movement, with the father head of the NAACP chapter in Atlanta, and a radio broadcaster as well, with a widening influence in the region.

Despite his father's social influence, King Jr. had to face the discrimination typical of "Coloreds" in his day and time, for instance, having to go to a school for Blacks while his best friend went to a school for Whites – and having the White boy's parents inform their son that he would have to stop playing with his Colored friend. But King, Sr. taught his son to respond to these hurts not through hate, but through the struggle to love even those who persecuted you, even though they were still to resist strongly the racism behind such cruelty.

---

*The boycott lasted over a year, until the struggling bus company finally put aside the seating restriction.

Typical of a teenager, King, Jr. distanced himself from his father's deep faith, no longer able to identify with the emotional spirit so strong in the Black community – and in his father's church. Instead he devoted himself to scholarly study in history, English and public speaking, and debate – excelling in these areas. At the same time, he still had to face insults from Whites, which infuriated him greatly. Then, even before finishing high school, he went off to attend All-Black Morehouse College*, where his father and his maternal grandfather before him had attended.

It was during these years that he first traveled outside the South, and was surprised to find that the racial discrimination so strong in the South appeared to be relatively absent in the North. The contrast would help him form a strong idea of what he wanted to see happen in his Atlanta homeland. And it was also in these years, in great part due to his deep admiration for his father – and his equally deep appreciation of the role that the Church played in the lives of those struggling against the pain that the world hurled at them – that King, Jr. decided to prepare for the ministry.

Off to Pennsylvania the 19-year-old King, Jr. went, to study at Crozer Seminary, and to become involved as youth pastor in the Calvary Baptist Church nearby, which a family friend, J. Pius Barbour, pastored. During those years (1948-1951), Barbour would become something like a second father to King, Jr. Also during those years he would fall in love with an immigrant German woman and wanted to marry her, except his friends warned him that this would cause problems in both the Black and the White communities, certainly preventing him from finding a church to lead in the South. So he broke off the relationship, leaving another deep hurt in his life.

After graduation from Crozer, King headed off to Boston University to undertake doctoral studies in systematic theology, serving as assistant pastor in the Twelfth Baptist Church in Boston. It was also during his Boston years that he met Coretta Scott, who was attending the New England Conservatory of Music. They dated for about a year and then in early 1953 announced their intentions to marry, which took place in Alabama that June. Then in 1954 they moved to Montgomery, Alabama, for King to pastor the Dexter Avenue Baptist Church. And this is what brought King into the Montgomery bus boycott, and his life (similar to his father's) not merely as a pastor, but as a civil rights activist as well.

A growing call for Black civil rights. The bus boycott dragged on for days, then weeks, then months, gaining national attention in the process.

---

*Many young Blacks had been sent to fight in World War Two and thus the College allowed high school juniors to apply and then enter in what would have been their senior year, in order to maintain a sufficiently large student body.

Meanwhile another Montgomery racial segregation case had made its way all the way to the U.S. Supreme Court, which concluded that Montgomery's laws were in violation of the Fourteenth Amendment.* Now the Southern segregation rules had the full attention of Middle America.

Then the following year (1957) focus turned to Arkansas and its Governor Orville Faubus, who decided to court White votes by calling out the Arkansas National Guard to block the entrance into Little Rock's Central High School of a small number of Blacks (opened to them by the local school board). President Eisenhower then responded by placing Arkansas's National Guardsmen under his command (plus sending members of the 101st Airborne Division to Little Rock) to open the school. But Faubus fought back, closing all public schools the next year and reopening them as "private" schools, excluding the Blacks of course. But the Federal courts then shut that project down, and Faubus left them closed for the rest of the 1958-1959 school year. But bit by bit, multitudes of Americans were growing very tired of such racist behavior on the part of their public officials.

* * *
THE COLD WAR TAKES ON A NEW QUALITY

Soviet Russia's "New Look" under Khrushchev. In 1953 Soviet dictator Stalin suddenly died – apparently just prior to undertaking a new round of Stalinist purges of the Soviet authorities immediately around him. The Soviet Communist Party breathed a sigh of relief and placed a number of more moderate leaders in command of the Soviet Union (and its Empire). Eventually (1956) rising to the top was Nikita Khrushchev – who played the career card of a "Thaw" in the icy relations Russia had with the rest of the world. He was trying to give Soviet Russia a kinder New Look – one especially that would be more appealing to the recently emerging "Third World"† of Asia, Africa and Latin America.

A major ideological battle thus developed in the effort to win the soul of this rising Third World, comprising these "non-aligned," recently-independent, countries emerging out from under generations of European imperial domination.

---

*"No State shall make or enforce any law which shall abridge the privileges or immunities of citizens of the United States; nor shall any State deprive any person of life, liberty, or property, without due process of law; nor deny to any person within its jurisdiction the equal protection of the laws."

†A "third" part of the world supposedly aligned in the ongoing Cold War with neither the Soviet East nor the American West.

America responds. America was still focused on Eastern Europe – hoping that Khrushchev's Thaw might mean a standing down of the intense (and expensive) Cold War rivalry that had been going on there since the end of World War Two. Possibly some of the Soviet "satellite" nations might be able to break free from Soviet domination – much as the Third World was breaking free from English, French, Belgian, Portuguese, etc. domination. Thus, America was keeping an eye not only on developments in Eastern Europe but also developments in the rising Third World.

The 1956 Hungarian Crisis. Apparently, university students in Hungary were also hoping that Khrushchev's New Look indeed meant that Hungary could move out from under Soviet domination, and they began to make demands (street demonstrations) to that effect. Also U.S. Secretary of State John Foster Dulles had been passing the word via the U.S. government's propaganda radio station, Radio Free Europe, assuring Eastern Europeans that America stood with them in their quest for national freedom.

Of course that was not at all what Khrushchev had in mind with his New Look. But when things began to quickly get out of hand in the Hungarian capital of Budapest, he hesitated. What should he do? To bully Hungary back into submission would completely undercut his Third World strategy of wooing these "emerging nations" with Communism's New Look.

Meanwhile China's rising Communist leader Mao began to taunt Khrushchev about his lack of decisiveness. In part this heckling of his fellow Communist by Mao was because Mao saw those times as very opportune for China – not Russia – to take the lead in directing the Third World towards his own Maoist version of Communism (or "Social Democracy," as Communism was frequently labeled by the Communists themselves).

The 1956 Suez Crisis. At precisely the same time (October 1956) that the Hungarian crisis was going very badly for Khrushchev, another crisis was brewing over in Egypt. Egyptian President Gamal Abdel Nasser was making himself a candidate for leadership within the rising Third World – or at least within the politically divided Arab world – becoming president not of Egypt but of the "United Arab Republic" (which however included at the time only the union of Egypt and Syria). His goal was to make his Arab Republic a rising industrial power (in competition with other rising Arab leaders and their countries), except that the oil-rich region of the Arab world (Iraq, Kuwait, Saudi Arabia) had the monetary resources to do so – resources that Egypt lacked totally. Nasser lamented that Egypt (and Syria) were among the few Arab countries devoid of the valuable asset of oil.

Also once-friendly Egyptian relations with the West were souring – not only with the Middle-East "protectors" Britain and France but also with

Middle-Class America Triumphant

America. America, trying to stay out of the growing Israeli-Palestinian conflict, had cut off arms sales to all national players of the Middle East,, turning Nasser to Russia in 1955 to buy arms for his growing military force – a major "no-no" to Americans.

Still, America had been willing to finance a major project of Nasser's – the building of the huge Aswan Dam across the Nile River in order to generate electrical power for an energy-less Egypt. But when in 1956 Nasser recognized Mao's instead of Chiang's government as the official Chinese government, Eisenhower was so annoyed that he cut off the funding for the Aswan Dam project. Thus again, Nasser turned to Russia for help (June 1956) – receiving some, but not enough funding to carry out the project in full.

This is what decided Nasser in July to simply grab the English-run Suez Canal as a revenue producer for Egypt. A major international crisis now erupted.

America lines up with the Russians against the English and French.
America did what it could to get the British (and French) to come to some kind of deal on the matter (perhaps an international authority governing the canal) – but the effort dragged on for a couple of months with no results. Actually, unknown to Eisenhower, the British and French (and Israelis) were secretly working on plans to simply retake the canal by force – and in late October all three countries invaded Egypt and quickly took the canal.

But an international outcry resulted over this bullying of Egypt – embarrassing and ultimately angering Eisenhower – who was trying to score propaganda points with the Third World against the Soviets for their bullying behavior with respect to developments in Hungary going on at exactly the same time. America's allies were behaving no better than the Soviets as far as the Third World – and Eisenhower – were concerned.

Khrushchev crushes the Hungarian Revolt. Worse, because of the political confusion over the Suez Canal grab, Khrushchev finally felt that he had the opportunity to make a bold move to end the Hungarian uprising, in early November sending in 2,500 tanks and 120,000 soldiers to crush the rebellion. The results for Hungary were disastrous, with the Hungarian Army doing its best to fend off this massive invading force. Around 2,500 Hungarians were killed (700 Soviet troops as well), 22,000 Hungarians imprisoned, 350 executed, and about 200,000 chose to flee the country.

There was nothing America could do to help the Hungarians. But America did help Nasser, coming out strongly against its English and French allies (and Israel) for this act of "imperialism" – actually siding with the Soviets in condemning English and French behavior, and forcing them finally to back out of Egypt and let Nasser keep the Suez Canal.

The political fallout for America (and Europe). Supposedly this was done to put America on the right side of the Third World debate – although time quickly revealed that this position had earned America no political credit from the Third World itself. But it did put America definitely on very shaky ground with its English and French allies – as well as Germany – which began to question publicly the idea of America as a reliable ally, especially as a NATO ally.

America had clearly not come to the aid of its NATO allies, France and Britain, in the defense of vital national interests of theirs. But Americans were unable to understand or even acknowledge the confusion and pain they put the English and French through. The English would basically accept silently their huge loss in national standing. The French, soon under General De Gaulle, would not. In fact De Gaulle would make it a point to work with France's old enemy, Germany, in an effort to squeeze America out of Europe's diplomatic affairs. Americans seemed at a loss to understand De Gaulle – whom they grew to dislike intensely.

Sputnik. In October of 1957 the Soviet Russians launched into orbit the first satellite (Sputnik I) – indicating that the Russians possessed the means to deliver virtually unstoppable nuclear weapons – a fact that Americans noted with horror. A month later, the Russians launched into orbit a 7.8-ton Sputnik II – with a dog aboard. This served to intensify the American horror – and shame at having fallen behind in the technological race with the Russians. Finally, at the end of January 1958, America responded with the launching of its own satellite, Explorer I. It helped some to rebuild American confidence – but it certainly did not relieve the fear that with such rocketry available in the Cold War, nuclear war looked more like a possibility than ever.

Rising concern about a post-Imperial Third World. In the latter part of the 1950s, the Cold War contest moved a bit toward the continent of Africa – as the European grip on Europe's African empires began to weaken – and local leaders began to demand national independence from the various French, British, Portuguese and Belgian colonies.

The Algerian Crisis. This move proved tremendously violent in Algeria – which the French considered not a colony but an integral part of France – so violent in fact that in 1958 it brought to power in France, through basically a military coup against the failing Fourth Republic, former French General De Gaulle. The French were hoping that De Gaulle would bring the Algerian crisis to an end, most of the French expecting him to come down hard on the Algerian rebels. Much to everyone's surprise – and to the outrage of three million Frenchmen living in Algeria – he took action in early 1962 by simply agreeing to complete independence for Algeria. To De Gaulle, France had bigger things to do than waste itself on a war with the Arabs of Algeria, a war whose social costs would clearly outweigh greatly any particular social benefits.

Mostly everywhere else in Africa the transition to independence began to occur fairly smoothly as Western-educated African elite began to take the reins of power of their new "nations."

The Congo Crisis. But the situation in the Belgian Congo did not go so smoothly – as the Belgians had been hesitant to prepare a group of Westernized locals to take over the Congo. Thus the Congo fell into confusion as regions and tribes put forward their own leaders, hoping to either take over the Congo, or break sections from it (such as the mineral-rich Katanga Province) in order to produce their own independent country. Ultimately this stirred both Soviet Russian and American interest in seeing things move in the direction of their own particular choosing. But the chaos made even that fairly impossible. Eventually the Congo, with much help from America, came under the dictatorship of General Mobutu – and things settled down.

This would soon be a pattern repeated in other African countries – as "democracy" failed and dictators came to power to bring these African states under some semblance of unity, ancient tribal hatreds within these new states making the task extremely difficult. In general, America decided that further involvement in Africa was not worth the trouble – and let Africa go its own way (with the exception of South Africa, which continued to interest pro-democracy Americans greatly, in the same way that Dutch Indonesia had once interested them).

Cuba: the problem hits closer to home. Although America never admitted it, America's relations with its neighbors to the South in Latin America had much the same quality as Europe's imperial positions in Asia and Africa. America went from a paternalistic instinct to protect its neighbors from the meddling of European powers (the Monroe Doctrine) to a paternalistic interest in seeing its neighbors join America in exemplifying New World Democracy – such as America believed that it itself exemplified.

However such democratic idealism was deeply compromised by the tendency of American businessmen (who generally took the lead in America's relations with its neighbors to the South) to prefer to work with strongmen (dictators, basically) who offered greater possibilities of social stability and economic protection with respect to America's extensive industrial and financial investment in their countries. This certainly was the case in Cuba – where America supported the very corrupt Batista dictatorship – but somewhat ambiguously, due to his embarrassing behavior.

Anti-Batista rebellion broke out in the mid-1950s, and Americans (some of them, anyway) took an interest in the colorful rebel lawyer Fidel Castro, who was leading one of the several anti-Batista groups in Cuba. Finally in 1958, the US government placed an arms embargo on Cuba – weakening Batista's power considerably. Then at the beginning of 1959 Batista fled Cuba – and rebel groups, including Castro's, took over the country. Castro himself soon took control of Cuba – and proceeded to put into action a huge range of socialist policies, confiscating the lands and businesses of the Cuban wealthy in order to pass these assets on to the poorer classes of Cuba. This in turn caused thousands of middle and upper-middle class Cubans to flee to the mountains – then from Cuba itself, many ending up in Florida.

Then when Eisenhower refused to lift the weapons ban to Cuba, Castro (like Nasser before him) went to the Soviets instead for arms, thus putting Cuba at the center of the Cold War. Consequently, Eisenhower ordered an end to the purchase of Cuban sugar and sale of American oil to Cuba. Here too, the Soviets were quite happy to make up the difference – drawing Cuba deeply into the Soviet economic order. Then when American oil refiners in Cuba refused to service Soviet oil, Castro simply grabbed the oil companies – and other key American industries located in Cuba.*

At this point Eisenhower authorized the creation of a liberation army made up of anti-Castro Cuban expatriates. And the CIA, at camps in Honduras and Guatemala, began preparing these troops for an invasion of Cuba. But Eisenhower finished his term in office (January 1961) just a few months prior to the proposed launch date of this invasion.

The U-2 incident. Eisenhower was hoping to finish out his presidency with politics in an upbeat mood – with improved Soviet-American relations pointing to a more peaceful future. The Americans had been permitted to put on an American National Exhibition in Moscow in July of 1959 – and Vice President Nixon met Khrushchev there to discuss (the famous

---

*Americans have a very hard time understanding that when we try to shut down a society's political system by cutting off our relations with that country economically as well as politically, we simply give our enemies opportunity to rush in there and offer themselves as this country's new ally. We have done this repeatedly – recently in Syria, Iran and Venezuela – giving the Chinese and Russians (as well as the Iranians themselves) opportunity to extend their power bases into these same countries.

Kitchen Debate) the differences between American and Soviet society – all conducted in fair humor. A couple of months later (September) Khrushchev returned the favor with a two-week visit to the United States – to underline the policy of "peaceful coexistence" that was supposed to mark the new international mood. And a much larger international conference was even scheduled for mid-May in Paris of the next year (1960) to bring America, Russia, England and France together – as a big step in the advancement of world peace.

But two weeks before the event, Khrushchev announced that an American U-2 reconnaissance plane had just been shot down in a flight over the Soviet Union. This very high-level flight was not a new thing, as U-2 spy planes had been regularly overflying the Soviet Union in an attempt to locate and analyze Soviet nuclear siting and development. Thus why Soviet leader Khrushchev chose to shoot down one of these planes just two weeks prior to the scheduled Paris summit remains a much speculated on mystery. Was Khrushchev feeling himself under too much pressure from Eisenhower to make deep concessions, or from party regulars not to make any concessions in the arms race that the Soviets apparently were winning?

In any case, at the news of the downing, Eisenhower, who understood the damage this would do to his summit hopes – but who also believed that the pilot and his plane shot down at that height would not have survived the attack – claimed that the plane was a weather plane that had inadvertently strayed off course, not a spy plane.

However much to America's shock, the plane did not disintegrate – and the pilot, who parachuted from the plane, was captured alive, and paraded before the world as an example of American perfidy. Not only did the event provide Khrushchev the opportunity to withdraw from the Paris 4-powers summit meeting with Eisenhower, French President De Gaulle and British Prime Minister Macmillan, but Eisenhower's attempt at a coverup gave the Soviets the opportunity to strike a huge propaganda blow against the United States – and the "liar" Eisenhower personally.

* * *

THE BRIEF KENNEDY ERA (1961-1963)

Kennedy's New Frontier. The year 1960 produced America's first televised debate – between Vice President Richard Nixon running as the Republican presidential candidate and John F. Kennedy as the Democratic candidate. At the debate, Nixon looked tired and washed out (he had just come in from a meeting elsewhere and had not taken the time to put on makeup necessary to give a normal appearance in front of the very bright

TV lights) – which set him back considerably in popular estimation. The smaller radio audience thought that Nixon had sounded more impressive than Kennedy – indicative of the way physical appearance before the cameras was going to play a much larger role in American politics from this point on. In the end the election was fairly close – and went to Kennedy.

John F. Kennedy. Kennedy was second of nine children born to the very prosperous and politically active Irish-Catholic family of Kennedys of Boston. His grandfathers on both sides of the family had been very active in Massachusetts politics. And his father, Joseph, Sr. was quite wealthy as a businessmen in real estate, the stock market (wisely getting out just before the crash), Hollywood movie production, and – with the end of Prohibition – the whiskey business. But his father was also very active in Roosevelt's Administration, heading up Roosevelt's new Security and Exchange Commission and then being sent to London as America's ambassador to Great Britain.

In addition to the learning acquired in being a member of this dynamic family, Kennedy attended the prestigious Choate boarding school and then heading off to Harvard, traveling widely at the same time (West Europe, Soviet Russia and the Middle East). And in 1940 he proved himself very well in writing (and publishing) his Harvard senior thesis, Why England Slept, full of insight into English diplomacy in dealing (or not) with Hitler.

Unfortunately he suffered from serious back problems and was able to enter the Naval Reserve only with some intervention by his father, but advanced in the world of naval intelligence in D.C. nonetheless. The when America finally found itself at war, he finally entered the action as a patrol torpedo (PT) boat commander. In one particular action, his boat was sunk by a Japanese destroyer, but he was able to swim the three miles to shore – towing a shipmate with him in the process. Ultimate this left his back so crippled that after another period of active service he had to have extensive hospital treatment, and ultimately dismissal from active service. It was also at this time that he learned that his older brother, Joseph, Jr. had been killed in active duty in Europe.

Kennedy's considerable talent as a political analyst and writer got brought him to cover the Potsdam Conference in in 1945, but also pressure from his father to take over the expected role of a Kennedy to go big in the world of national politics. Thus it was, with considerable family support, he was elected to Congress in 1946, to begin that much-expected political career. And by 1952, it was time to take on the challenge of being a U.S. Senator, which he achieved in defeating Massachusetts veteran politician Henry Cabot Lodge, Jr., rather substantially due to the strong support he received from Massachusetts's large Catholic community.

It was during his Senatorial campaign that he met the very attractive and highly sophisticated Jacqueline Bouvier, who held off his marriage proposal – in order as a journalist to cover Elizabeth's coronation as British Queen. But they married soon thereafter, a major up-East social event!

But family troubles almost ended the upward move: back surgery that almost cost Kennedy his life, and a miscarriage (1955) and stillbirth (1956) that Jacqueline suffered, before she was finally able to give birth (1957) to a healthy child, Caroline. But Kennedy was reelected Senator in 1958, taking him closer to the goal of the U.S. presidency.

Finally, in 1960, he was ready to have a go at the presidency. His only serious opponent was the Senate Majority Leader, Lyndon Johnson. Kennedy went into the nominating convention with the largest number of committed delegates, but knew that he would have to win the nomination itself on the first ballot, or Johnson would most likely maneuver the convention over into his own camp. But it turned out that Kennedy did succeed on that first ballot.

Then (to the great irritation of his brother Bobby, John's campaign manager), Kennedy asked Johnson to become his running mate. It would be a very close race against Republican Vice President Nixon and Kennedy would need the swing vote of the South where Johnson was from, and where Johnson commanded a lot of support. And, in the end, it would become a very fateful decision for the country.

Undoubtedly the biggest issue Kennedy had to face in running against Vice President Nixon was his Catholicism, alarming somewhat quite Protestant America. But he was quick to point out that he was not campaigning on behalf of the Church, and that his Catholicism had not been an issue to anyone back when he served his country in the South Pacific! Actually his religious faith outside of normal Catholic expectations was itself unknown, and would remain unknown. His close associates, including for instance his personal advisor Ted Sorenson, remained unaware of Kennedy's exact position on such matters as heaven and hell and life after death. Certainly Kennedy lived a life of prayer, personal pain as well as political pain being a big part of his life. But that seemed to have no impact on his extensive womanizing (which at the time was considered by the Washington press and Congressional membership to be nobody's business other than the president himself).

The Kennedy presidential victory. In any case, the November (1960) presidential vote was close – very close indeed, with Kennedy gaining 49.7 percent of the vote and Nixon 49.5 percent. The crucial electoral college majority, however, would register as a bigger difference, with Kennedy's 303 votes to Nixon's 219. Kennedy was thus elected as the country's thirty-fifth president.*

In Kennedy's inaugural address to the nation in January of 1961, he challenged America to step up to the call that had long been on America – to be something of a light to the nations, especially in this Cold War Era. He challenged Americans to "ask not what your country can do for you – ask what you can do for your country."

In this matter, however, he had something in mind more along the lines of a cultural challenge rather than a military challenge – and one directed toward the Third World of Asia, Africa and Latin America – the region of the world to which the Cold War had shifted its playing field. He wanted to show a loftier approach that America took toward the world, implying the idea that Soviet Russia proceeded only through bullying others into submission.

The Bay of Pigs catastrophe (April 1961). But almost immediately in taking office Kennedy had his loftier approach challenged – from within the American foreign policy establishment itself – in the form of the well-advanced plans to launch the CIA-trained army of Cuban liberationists onto the beaches of Cuba at the Bay of Pigs in order to overthrow the troublesome Castro. Kennedy was now facing a major dilemma. The invasion would succeed only if it received heavy American military support. But such support would make America appear to be the neighborhood bully that Kennedy assured the world America would no longer be.

As a result, Kennedy pulled back considerably the promised military support for the 1400-man Cuban invasion – which ultimately failed – failed miserably. And despite Kennedy's pull-back, the hand of America was still very clearly evident in this grand catastrophe. And thus the event played beautifully into Soviet Russia's anti-American propaganda campaign.

Kennedy was highly embarrassed – and America looked as if it were under the leadership of a very weak president. Certainly that is how things looked to Soviet Premier Khrushchev.

The Berlin Wall (August 1961). The NATO-supported Western half of the city of Berlin, located entirely within Soviet-dominated East Germany, was a huge Communist sinkhole into which all sorts of Germans wishing to escape Communist East Germany could make their way to the West simply by reaching West Berlin and flying from there to West Germany. The West Berlin opportunity was draining Communist East Germany of vast portions

---

*There were serious questions about how Chicago Mayor Daley brought in the Illinois vote for Kennedy. But Illinois going to Nixon instead of Kennedy would not have changed the ultimate outcome.

Middle-Class America Triumphant

of its more ambitious and better-educated talent, causing something of a cultural crisis in East Germany. And it was also a huge embarrassment in this Cold War cultural contest to see so many citizens of the Communist World desperate to escape to the West.

Consequently, in August of 1961, the Communist East German authorities suddenly threw around West Berlin at first a wall of barbed wire, then concrete bloc, then a perimeter mined with explosives and supervised by machine-guns – shutting down this escape route to the West

The world watched to see what the leader of the Free World would do in response. Would Kennedy's American tanks and bulldozers smash down the wall in defiance of this outrage? In the end Kennedy did nothing – except eventually (June 1963) fly to Berlin and stand in front of the wall to announce to Germany that he was one of them, he was a "Berliner."*
The Germans were politely appreciative – although their appreciation would have been greater if he had actually made a move to knock the wall down. In any case, East Germany (and for that matter all of Eastern Europe) was now fully imprisoned behind the Soviet Russian Iron Curtain.

The Peace Corps. Not forgetting his promise to advance the American cause in the Cold War through new cultural rather than military means, Kennedy set up a volunteer program that would operate as an alternative to military service widely required of America's young men – except this program would also include America's young women as well. These young Americans (drawn from the "Silent Generation" of youth slightly older than the Boomers – culturally closer to the Vets than the Boomers with their strongly patriotic mindset) would sign up as a Peace Corps Volunteer for a two-year term of overseas service in one or another Third World country. They would receive a quick training in the local language and then be sent off to a village to undertake English teaching – or even something as creative as poultry farming (briefly trained in that as well before being sent off!) – to demonstrate the blessings of the American approach to life.†

Thus hundreds of thousands of young American college graduates signed up for this opportunity to show the world the better "American way." And indeed, it was obviously a well-received program abroad – although exactly how deeply it pulled the Third World toward the American way was

---

**Ich bin ein Berliner* – not realizing that his choice of words was such that he was telling the Germans that he was a popular sweet bun (a "Berliner")! What he meant to say was "*Ich bin Berliner.*"

†For their service they would receive the equivalent of a soldier's very low military pay, indicative of the fact that Peace Corps service was an act of patriotic duty rather than a professional government job!

easily questioned. In fact, these idealistic American youth probably learned as much about the blessings of village life of a Third World country as they were able to show the locals the blessings of the American way! Ironically, many Peace Corps volunteers returned to America hungry to continue to live the communal way they discovered abroad. And thus a trend toward the founding of hippie communes got underway in America.

The Cuban Missile Crisis (October 1962). Castro continued to believe (correctly) that it remained a goal of America to remove him from power in Cuba – drawing him even closer to Khrushchev as an anti-American ally. Seeing Kennedy back down from a direct confrontation with Russia in the building of the Berlin Wall, Khrushchev came to the conclusion that a much more forward strategy would result in the same lack of strong response from the weak Kennedy. Thus it was that he was so bold as to propose to Castro to base nuclear-tipped missiles in Cuba – easily able to reach any of the American cities of America's East and Mid-West. Siting such first-strike missiles in Cuba would not only protect Cuba – it would slow even further any American responses to further Soviet moves around the globe – as the risk of a nuclear retaliation would cause the Americans to have to back down in such events. Castro agreed to the idea in the mid-summer of 1962, and work on the Cuban missile sites began soon after.

American U-2 spy planes picked up the activity – and when questioned, the Soviets answered that these sites were designed only for local defense. But the character of the nine bases (of the 40-total planned) distinctly had the same structure as the major missile launch sites located within Russia itself – and American concern began to develop. A cloud cover prevented further observation – until mid-October when spy planes detected the delivery to the launch sites of a number of R-12 medium-range missiles – able to carry nuclear warheads 1200 miles into America. They were not yet operational. American action was required immediately.

The White House staff thus gathered to consider a number of strategies to answer this serious threat coming from Russia and Cuba. Finally, after several days of consideration, Kennedy was ready to move. First he got the Latin American members of the Organization of American States to approve a quarantine of Cuba – not only isolating Cuba but also undercutting drastically Khrushchev's Cold War initiatives in the Western Hemisphere. Then he made a televised announcement as to the nature of the crisis – and sent his ambassador to the United Nations to show the pictures of the Soviet activity in Cuba – making Russia's earlier denials of such activity appear to be the huge lie that it indeed was. But Kennedy gave Khrushchev a way out of the corner he found himself in by offering an exchange: America would remove its missiles in Turkey if Russia would do the same in Cuba.* While Kennedy was awaiting Khrushchev's response, an American naval blockade was placed around Cuba – and the world watched tensely as Russian ships carrying more missiles headed toward that blockade. Finally it was Khrushchev who blinked first and turned his ships around to head them back to Russia. He then accepted Kennedy's compromise offer of an exchange in missile dismantling – much to Castro's fury. And thus it was that the world breathed again. Had the world just come to the brink of a nuclear disaster? Possibly.†

King's appeal to the conscience of the nation. Considering the fact that America was attempting to put itself forward to a rising Third World of Africa, Asia and Latin America as the social model they should be following as the societies of these regions were one by one coming to independence, America's well-known problems in the area of race relations did not present a very nice picture to the outside world. Khrushchev knew this – and the Soviet Russian propaganda machine was quick to pick up on every front-page American news report concerning one after another racial incident in America.

As America headed into the 1960s it was clear that Blacks were becoming much more aware of their rights, and demanding that segregation be brought to an end. And American Northerners, Whites as well as Blacks, were joining the chorus demanding an end to this dark mark on America's national character. Thus sit-ins and protest marches (often joined by Northern Whites) began to break out across the American South. When the ever-active Rev. Dr. King was arrested in Birmingham (Alabama) for conducting a peaceful protest, Northerners were outraged.

Thus King took the issue all the way to the nation's capital on August 28, 1963, where he stood on the steps of the Lincoln memorial in front of hundreds of thousands who had gathered before him (not to mention the millions watching on TV) to appeal to the Americans' better instincts. It was time to change things, to bring the country together across racial lines.

Like Kennedy, King was not asking for the Washington government to

---

*Actually, Kennedy had much earlier brought under consideration the removal of those missiles based in Turkey, fearing that they were more a trip-wire to nuclear war than they were an effective deterrent to just such a war.

†During the intense days of the crisis, an American ship had dropped depth charges in Cuban waters, nearly taking out a Soviet submarine possessing nuclear missiles of its own, a submarine also possessing orders to use them if attacked, but provided that all three levels of command aboard the submarine agreed. Thankfully one of the three refused to agree to the counter strike, and thus the world was spared the horror of a full nuclear exchange, one that once was started might have spun itself into a global nuclear holocaust!

make these changes. He was asking the Americans themselves to do so, after all, this was the American Way. Certainly he wanted developments in the realm of law to occur, particularly those allowing Blacks to enjoy every American's right to vote. But ultimately, he was looking to shape American social dynamics through a change in American hearts, not through the takeover of those dynamics by masses of government officials.

And indeed, his strong appeal to American consciences had its huge impact, shifting the country, including the South, towards the understanding that it was time to bring Blacks into Middle America as equals.

Mounting problems in Vietnam. From the American point of view, things were not going well in the region of the old French Indo-China (Cambodia, Laos and Vietnam). The French finally had given up their colony by way of an agreement worked out in 1954 at Geneva between major parties (including the Soviets and Chinese as well as the French and British). But with the French gone the question immediately developed as to how these newly independent countries would rule themselves. Cambodia came to independence under its old monarchy, Laos was taken over by a 3-way coalition of Leftists, Rightist and Centrists – and Vietnam was divided (supposedly temporarily, like Korea) in half, north and south, pending national elections designed to unite the country under a single regime.

But in Vietnam, only the nationalist but also quite Communist leader Ho Chi Minh seemed to have enough of a following to unite the country. But America was in no hurry to see yet another Asian country come under Communist leadership – and so did what it could to stall the scheduled national elections – and instead turned to support the rule (at least in the South) of the pro-Western Ngo Dinh Diem. Soon America began to take the attitude that the division of North and South was a permanent one. So in Vietnam, America was taking up the role that it accused Russia of playing in Korea: blocking national elections destined not to go its way politically!

But Diem's style was drawing very negative responses from some of the South Vietnamese. Was it because he was so authoritarian in style – or just because he was so pro-Western? Some of the strongest of his opposition was indeed coming from Buddhist monks – who obviously had no interest in promoting Communism – but who were very much opposed to his introduction of Western cultural norms into their formerly Buddhist Vietnam. America and the world, in fact, were shocked when in June of 1963 a Buddhist monk publicly doused himself in gasoline and lit himself on fire in protest against the Diem regime.

This then led to the decision that Diem had to go. A plot developed by the Americans, involving the Vietnamese military's removal of Diem, took place in early November of that year. But Diem – and his powerful brother

– were not merely ousted from power, they were both assassinated. And tragically, no strongly respected national authority was in a position to then step forward and take command of the situation (Americans seemingly unable to understand the problems that inevitably explode when you take down a country's leader!). At this point Vietnam began its slide into anarchy.

Kennedy is assassinated (November 1963). What Kennedy planned to do at that point about the deteriorating situation in Vietnam will never be known – because three weeks later he too was assassinated.

The assassination occurred in Dallas, Texas, on November 22nd during a visit of Kennedy and his wife with the Texas governor, John Connally – in order to repair strained political relations between the two. Riding in an open convertible, both men were shot, Kennedy fatally. The trail led immediately to Lee Harvey Oswald who was arrested – and then he too was assassinated by Jack Ruby a few days later when Oswald was being transferred from the Dallas police to the county sheriff.

America was horrified. How had this happened? Was it all just a private act of a deranged Oswald? He had Communist connections. Were they involved? But Ruby had mob connections. Was the mob involved? Was this all just a huge plot? If so, by whom?

In any case, Americans were not used to having their Presidents shot riding innocently through the streets of America. Such innocence would itself be a victim of the assassination. America was about to enter into a whole new world – right there at home in America.

Kennedy's assassination was the announcement that things were about to change in America – dramatically. And there would be no going back. A certain period or age in America had just come to a close.

CHAPTER TEN

AMERICA SHIFTS TO THE HUMANIST LEFT

* * *

JOHNSON – AND "DEMOCRACY FROM ABOVE"

With the assassination of the young President Kennedy in 1963, Vice President Lyndon Johnson, a quite sophisticated (in his own way) veteran of Capitol Hill politics, now assumed the Presidency. Johnson did not have Kennedy's good looks and cultural polish, nor his personal charisma – and was well aware of the fact. He came from Texas good-old-boy cultural stock – and had worked his way up in Washington power through a lot of self-discipline, long hours of work, and political connections he worked hard at cultivating. He was a behind-the-scenes operator, used to getting things done privately rather than publicly. And he was very, very good at getting things done in Washington. That's why he had advanced all the way to being the most powerful man in the U.S. Senate, before accepting the position under Kennedy as U.S. Vice President.

Now as President, America could expect Johnson to continue to work according to the "Johnson style" – and get things quickly done politically in Washington, things that Kennedy could only have dreamed of someday maybe actually accomplishing. Johnson was a political mover and shaker. And America would indeed be moved and shaken dramatically by Johnson and his government programs.

Lyndon Johnson's political goals outwardly were similar to Kennedy's: a Liberal Democrat who emphasized the importance of American civil rights and also one who understood that Communism was still the greatest threat to America. However, his political approach in addressing these challenges to America would prove to be drastically different.

A major shift in the idea of American government. At the time Johnson stepped into the American presidency, "government" meant the Americans themselves. The Washington, D.C. "state" did not rule. In fact, at the time of Johnson's arrival to power as President, Washington had more the feel of a comfortable Southern town than that of some imperial metropolis. But that would quickly change under Johnson.

In any case, in America the people supposedly ruled. A formal government consisting of the people's representatives existed in Washington solely to service the people and their general will – as the people themselves directed (the power of the voting booth). The economy also belonged to the people and their private businesses. Educational policy belonged to the people and their local school boards. Health care belonged to the people and their doctors.

National government was designed largely to deal with international issues – as had been the intention of the original Framers of the Constitution – and mostly had been the case since then. There was still little sense that the national government in Washington had any important role to play in the nation's domestic affairs.*

Certainly Roosevelt's New Deal stretched the reach of the Washington government well beyond what the Constitution itself authorized (and got in trouble with the Supreme Court over that) – but at the time it seemed well justified in the hearts of most Americans because of the severity of the Great Depression. In any case the New Deal would back down after it ran out of projects to pursue – although it would leave a political legacy among some Democrats – Johnson included – that felt that it was quite legitimate to look to the Washington government (and its bureaucracy) for help in promoting progressive social programming.

And then there was World War Two in which quite obviously the Washington government took the lead in all things, from the fighting overseas to the mobilization of American economic power on the home front. But the end of the war returned things fairly quickly back to the traditional role expected of Washington: lead foreign affairs, yes – take control of America's domestic life, no.

True, there was the huge domestic program, Social Security, a pension fund for the elderly managed by the national government. But in this the Washington government was considered to be only the caretaker of this

---

*The 10th Amendment – the famous Reservation Clause – concludes the Bill of Rights: "The powers not delegated to the United States by the Constitution, nor prohibited by it to the States, are reserved to the States respectively, or to the people." This meant that unless the Constitution had specifically assigned powers to Congress to act in certain matters, all other political activities were reserved to the States and the people, the federal counterbalance of the states checking the powers of the national government – against the tendency of all ruling bodies to want to expand their powers at will. But the 10th Amendment check against the accumulation by the D.C. government of unlimited power would all be put aside as a safeguard during the Johnson years. And the Supreme Court would not challenge Johnson's assumption of unauthorized power the way the Court did with Roosevelt's New Deal.

huge pension fund, not the owner of it. Social Security too belonged to the people.

But this traditional understanding of the proper role of the Washington government would change during the five-plus years of Johnson's presidency – change drastically.

Lyndon Baines Johnson (LBJ) – the man and his making. In an important way, Johnson was still a Roosevelt New Dealer – having early on taken a lead in the world of American politics as a local administrator in Texas of one of Roosevelt's 1930s New Deal programs. Johnson remained forever convinced that letting the Washington Establishment take command of the country's affairs New-Deal style was always the best way of going at the nation's challenges. Nothing would ever change his opinion on that matter.

Part of this Johnson approach to life was undoubtedly shaped by his own personal sensitivities – his concern about the racism he saw around him in Texas, something that deeply distressed him. He had grown up on a farm in the tiny and remote community of Stonewall, Texas, in a condition of poverty and humble social circumstances. He attended public school in nearby Johnson City (named after his own ancestors) and went on to Southwest Texas State Teachers College, intending to become a teacher. He took a year off (1928-1929) to teach Hispanic-American children, touching deeply an old nerve when he found himself in the midst of these children's deep poverty and social discrimination.

But he switched quickly from teaching to politics after only one year of teaching public speaking (!) in Houston (1930-1931), when he became involved in Richard Kleberg's Congressional campaign. With Kleberg's victory in 1931, Johnson followed him to D.C., where he found it almost natural organizing fellow Congressional aides into something of a political fellowship. But he also cultivated personal relationships with key politicians such as Vice President Nance Garner and the powerful Speaker of the House of Representatives, Sam Rayburn, a fellow Texan who took a deep interest in Johnson's political career.

Also interested in Johnson was "Ladybird" Claudia Taylor, also of Texas, but with Alabama aristocratic background as well. The two of them were to meet in D.C. in 1934, and get married only ten weeks later. Both of them were very decisive individuals!

But they were to return to Texas the next year for Johnson to become a key part of Roosevelt's New Deal programming, with Johnson becoming head of the Texas National Youth Administration, most importantly setting up job training programs for Texas youth. And this would dig itself deeply into the Johnson mentality, as the understanding Johnson would hold as to what the proper role of government happened to be. It was there to take care of people in need. Period.

In 1937, financed heavily by his wife, he ran and was elected in a special Congressional election, and would remain a Congressman for the next dozen years. However, with the mounting appearance of a war before them, he joined the U.S. Naval Reserve in 1940. When war finally did break out at the end of 1941, he sought active duty. But Roosevelt instead wanted him to stay on in Washington to look into the matter of how government money was being utilized by American industry to support the American war effort (the same thing Truman was doing in the Senate). And thus Johnson helped create and then head up a key subcommittee of the House Naval Affairs Committee investigating such matters.

After the war Johnson was ready to move on to bigger challenges, and in 1948 ran for the position as U.S. Senator, winning the Democratic Party nomination very narrowly (and very questionably). And thus with Texas still very "Dixiecrat" in political character, running as the Democratic Party's candidate, Johnson easily won also the Senatorial race itself. Now in the Senate, he continued his role looking into government contracts with private industry. This in turn caused him to rise in importance within the Democratic Party itself. And he soon (1951) was chosen to become the Democratic Party Majority Whip (charged with the task on making sure that all Democratic Party members are present for Congressional votes). He lost the position as "majority" whip in 1953 when the Republicans took over Congress and the White House. But instead he was elected by his party as its minority party leader, the youngest person to have achieved such political distinction. And then when in 1954 the Democrats took back control of the Senate, he found himself as Senate majority leader to be one of the most powerful political leaders in D.C.

And what kind of moral-spiritual qualities came with this man of power? Actually, on his mother's side he was the descendant of a number of Baptist pastors. But his father was not deeply interested in such a religious life. But Johnson himself grew up in the Disciples of Christ or "Christian" church, a denomination that tried to rise above Presbyterian, Methodist, Baptist, etc. differences, to become broader in its theological character (which becomes denominational itself in time!). Consequently, although Johnson was non-sectarian in Christian identity, he did indeed enjoy himself in the company of a broad span of Christian pastors, although he seemed to prefer the liturgical character of the Episcopalian and Catholic Churches somewhat. Consequently as president, he would move around from church to church, keeping the press guessing as to where he would show up the next Sunday.

Nonetheless, the one person who meant most to him personally as a Christian pastor or counsellor was Billy Graham – whose contact with Kennedy had been quite minimal. Graham and Johnson became very close over the years of the Johnson presidency. Graham was called on to speak at every one of the presidential prayer breakfasts in those years, and Graham met frequently with the president both in the White House and on Johnson's Texas farm, to pray and offer comfort to a personal friend who was well aware of the troubles his presidency had come to encounter. Johnson even asked him in 1964 as to who he thought would make the best running mate, to which Graham wisely declined to give an answer! Graham stayed with Johnson the president's last night at the White House, and eventually would be called on to conduct Johnson's funeral service (1973). But very little of this close relationship was known outside the inner Johnson social-political circle.

Johnson never saw the need to personally inspire, through his own spiritual qualities, a "Christian America." He did not usually talk about his religion publicly, or bring religion into his public arena. Although he himself personally was a fairly strong Christian, and found himself in personal prayer often over his work, his public working-world was strictly Secular, and would remain that way, even through all the difficulties he would face in trying to lead the nation.

Johnson's Great Society Program. Johnson was fairly quick in getting into action pushing his own Progressive program for America – one unlike Kennedy's (and King's) program that called on the Americans themselves to take up the country's various challenges. Instead Johnson was going to gather in Washington technical experts of all variety – and give them the responsibility of designing a vast array of programs (New Deal style) designed to put the finishing touches on America as a "Great Society." All the Americans themselves had to do was sit back and marvel at what the experts could achieve by way of presenting an expertly-managed America acquire such social perfection that it would knock out the Soviets in the Cold War contest for the hearts of the rising Third World. In short, he had completely reversed Kennedy's challenge, so that it read something like, "ask not what you can do for your country; ask what your country can do for you!" The government was going to take care of you. Expect it.

Thus it was that on May 22, 1964, Johnson took the opportunity, during a graduation address he had been invited by the University of Michigan to deliver, that he announced the particulars of his new Great Society Program. He began by explaining how today

> *we have the opportunity to move not only toward the rich society and the powerful society, but upward to the Great Society.*

America Shifts to the Humanist or Progressivist" Left

He pointed out that it was in three areas in particular that his new program was designed to make improvements in American society: improved urban infrastructure, protection of the natural environment, and improved education of America's youth. Clearly this pointed to massive Washington involvement in the internal affairs of America formerly left in the hands of state and local governments closer to the dynamics of America's towns and cities across the nation. However, he reassured Americans:

> *While our Government has many programs directed at those issues, I do not pretend that we have the full answer to those problems.*
>
> *But I do promise this: We are going to assemble the best thought and the broadest knowledge from all over the world to find those answers for America. I intend to establish working groups to prepare a series of White House conferences and meetings on the cities, on natural beauty, on the quality of education, and on other emerging challenges. And from these meetings and from this inspiration and from these studies we will begin to set our course toward the Great Society.*
>
> *The solution to these problems does not rest on a massive program in Washington, nor can it rely solely on the strained resources of local authority. They require U.S. to create new concepts of cooperation, a creative federalism, between the National Capital and the leaders of local communities.*

"Creative federalism." What Johnson said in that last statement – "The solution to these problems does not rest on a massive program in Washington" was in fact complete fiction – because that was exactly what he had in mind as he developed his new Great Society Program. And his understanding of things in creating "new concepts of cooperation, a creative federalism, between the National Capital and the leaders of local communities" was that the local communities would be expected to follow the lead of Washington as it laid out this concept of "creative federalism." And creative federalism it would be indeed!

He was indicating more accurately what he intended to do in his Great Society Program when he said "We are going to assemble the best thought and the broadest knowledge from all over the world to find those answers for America."

"Democracy from above." Thus it was that Johnson was preparing America to come to the new understanding of "democracy from above." And as such, he was preparing the Democratic Party to reshape itself around that same idea as to what it would henceforth offer America: a better (or Progressive) government from above. This would leave the (conservative) Republican Party to continue to defend the idea that government in American rightly belonged to its people, not the "more-enlightened" Washington experts.

The 1964 Civil Rights Act. There was not much argument in America (angry Southerners and Northern racists excepted) over the issue of whether or not Black civil rights needed "help from above." That was one area of Johnson's Progressivism that had wide support in America. The front-page newspaper photo of the attacks in Alabama on peaceful Black protesters (May 1963) by Birmingham police and their attack dogs – or Birmingham firemen and their fire hoses cruelly aimed at protesters seated along the street – or Alabama Governor Wallace personally blocking the entrance of Black students to the University of Alabama (June 1963) – outraged most Americans – now quite convinced that waiting for the State of Alabama to do the right thing (actually the Constitutional thing) was not going to happen.

Thus in 1964 Johnson was able to persuade Congress to pass a Civil Rights Act (actually originally authored by Kennedy), outlawing the discrimination by way or race, religion, sex or national origin in voting registration, school segregation, employment or hiring, and in public accommodations (restaurants, hotels, etc.)

Much celebration accompanied the signing (July 1964) of this wide-ranging civil rights law. But in fact the new law lacked strong enforcement possibilities – and also it was largely disregarded in the South, where attitudes were widespread that Congress had no right to pass legislation concerning purely domestic matters. Nonetheless, the law did carry enforceable weight in the North, where racist lines still played a role.*

The "War on Poverty." Ultimately, however, the centerpiece of Johnson's Great Society Program was his "War on Poverty" set up in 1964 and directed by the new Office of Economic Opportunity – overseeing such programs as VISTA – sort of a domestic Peace Corps of volunteers directed to help not Third World countries but instead American communities caught in poverty (inner-city neighborhoods, Indian reservations, rural communities) with job training. Then there was the Job Corps, a federal employment program modeled along the lines of Roosevelt's CCC, offering the unemployed jobs in Federal Parks and other Federal lands. Another program was Head Start,

---

*The 1964 Civil Rights Act would continue to serve as the moral foundation for the future expansion of federal involvement in matters of civil rights of an even widening nature: gender, preferred language and sexual orientation, and even the dismissing of the long-held Christian norms in public affairs.

setting up early childhood education, health service and parent training for children in poverty areas of the country, to help prepare the children about to enter elementary schooling. And there were the Community Action Agencies, supporting local programs designed to help people caught in poverty – programs ranging from the local Head Start operations, to food pantries, to utility bill assistance, to other programs local welfare agencies might want to develop.

Although these programs operated at the local level (obviously, because that is where the challenges were to be found) they were overseen by a Washington bureaucracy that exploded in size over the next few years, as multitudes of individuals flocked to the nation's capital to find employment in this massive governmental enterprise.

Vietnam: The domino theory. Meanwhile the long-brewing crisis in Vietnam had taken on growing significance. The necessity of acting boldly in Vietnam as well as at home was thus put forward to the American people by Johnson. In explaining this mounting international challenge facing America as the defender of the Free World, he employed a logical line of argument built on the "domino theory." This theory was that if America did not take a firm stand against aggression in one place in the region and let that nation fall to Communism, then soon the country next door would fall, then the one next to that, and then next to that – like a line of dominoes. The presumption was that Communism was a single-minded force ultimately directed from a single command center: the Kremlin in the Soviet Russian capital at Moscow.

Tragically, the role of nationalism and nationalist varieties within the Communist camp – often in sharp conflict with each other (which Truman wisely exploited) – did not factor into Johnson's presumption of Communism being a single-minded force. Thus arose the conclusion that America needed to take a rigid stand in Vietnam – lest all the countries in Southeast Asia fall to Communism like a line of dominoes.

The Gulf of Tonkin Resolution (August 7, 1964). To get America on board with him on his plans for Vietnam, he put before Congress in August two incidents that were reported as having occurred just days earlier – when two American navy destroyers stationed just off the coast of Vietnam were attacked by Vietnamese torpedo boats. Unknown to America – and Congress – the second attack indeed did not actually occur – and the first attack was likely provoked by attacks of South Vietnamese commandos on the North Vietnamese coast. In any case it served Johnson well enough – so that he was able to get Congress (almost totally unanimously) to award Johnson special war powers to do what he saw fit about the conflict going on in Vietnam. Johnson would use these powers widely – supposedly to stop the domino effect of Asian societies falling to Communism.

The professionalization of the Southeast Asian conflict. Johnson did not see himself as actually calling the nation to war, as had been the case in World War Two and in Korea. He did not want the Vietnam issue to distract the nation from its more important task of putting his Great Society Program in place. Rather, he supposed he could simply assign American military units (already in being) to head to Vietnam, go ashore at various points along its long coast, fan out from there as they took ground from the enemy, and quickly bring the country under American control. It looked quite clear on a map how this was to work. So, no, America was not going to war. It was simply going to involve itself briefly in a "police action," one conducted by America's rather professional army.

In short, American action in Vietnam would be another variety of "democracy from above" – the American soldiers qualifying as the "experts" who would install democracy in Vietnam for the Vietnamese themselves.

The national elections of 1964. Behind much of the speed by which Johnson moved to get his Great Society Program planted – and increased American involvement in Vietnam underway – was Johnson's awareness that it had only been months since he assumed office as President, and now similarly only months before the time he would have to face voters in the November 1964 national elections. He naturally was eager to see himself actually elected by the American people themselves as their President.

Facing him as presidential candidate for the Republicans was Arizona Senator Barry Goldwater – who was so bold as to present himself proudly as a Conservative – even authoring a book in 1960 entitled *The Conscience of a Conservative*. During the 1964 campaign, Goldwater was quick to point out that Johnson's Great Society program amounted to a huge Washington overreach – and a serious danger to American democracy.

But Johnson conducted an effective campaign depicting Goldwater as a dangerous threat to world peace – because Goldwater, in being pushed by the press corps to give an answer to the question, "would you ever resort to the use of atomic weapons if you saw their need in fighting Communism, even in Vietnam," in essence said 'Yes." How could Goldwater have said "no?" That was a politically loaded question, of course. No one wanted to see those weapons ever unleashed. But as Truman himself understood, possessing the weapons – but going on record as unwilling to actually use them – destroyed all the deterrent value that came with possessing them. A leader had to make it clear that he had the guts to use them if necessary.

But the Democratic Party played very big Goldwater's response, in

America Shifts to the Humanist or Progressivist" Left 311

order to heighten the natural fears of the American voter about any form of a nuclear war. The Democrats even broadcast a TV commercial ("Daisy") implying the nuclear devastation that would hit the world if Goldwater were allowed to become President. That stuck in people's mind – more than any other feature of the national elections. Goldwater stood for war. Johnson stood for peace. It was that simple – or so the Democrats convinced the American voters.

Goldwater fought back – pointing out that Johnson's growing focus on Vietnam was devoid of any realistically achievable goal – and would merely end up destroying multitudes of young American soldiers for no particular purpose. But Americans – at the moment – were well convinced that a strong (but conventional) military stand in Vietnam was needed in order to stop the advance of Communism. Even on this point Goldwater could make no headway against Johnson.

As a consequence, the November elections turned out to be a huge disaster for the Republicans – and an equally huge mandate for Johnson and his programs both at home and abroad. Johnson ended up with 61% of the popular vote, to only 38.5% for Goldwater – and with 486 electoral votes to Goldwater's mere 52 electoral votes. Goldwater won the electoral vote of only his own state Arizona (barely)... and the Solid South – which was beginning to switch its loyalty (since the Civil War) from the Democratic Party to now the Republican Party.

The 1965 Voting Rights Act. Then when in March of 1965 Alabama state troopers attacked with tear gas, billy clubs, and whips a nationally televised peaceful protest march from the towns of Selma to Montgomery – led by the Rev. Dr. King himself – the vast majority of Americans were convinced that it was time for the Washington government to step in and enforce Blacks' 15th Amendment voting rights[*], now – not tomorrow or some day in the near future – and by whatever means necessary to enforce the law.

Thus two months later (May of 1965) Johnson was able to get the Senate to approve (77-19) a voters' rights bill – and then in July the House of Representatives to approve the same bill (333-85) – including most certainly the six Black members of the House. He was then able to sign it into law on August 6th – with the Rev. Dr. King at his side at the well-publicized signing. Basically, the law made illegal all the "literacy tests" (having to recite the entire Constitution, for instance) imposed on potential Black voters as a means of keeping them off the voting rolls. Simply as

---

[*]"The right of citizens of the United States to vote shall not be denied or abridged by the United States or by any State on account of race, color, or previous condition of servitude."

American citizens they were fully entitled to vote in all elections. There would be no more qualifying tests allowed.

Under federal supervision, Blacks now began to register in huge numbers. And the South now understood that segregation was about to lose its political grip south of the Mason-Dixon line! Fair enough!

* * *

THE SECULARIZING OF AMERICAN CULTURE

Whereas the Dream that the Rev. Dr. King put before America fit very closely the long-standing tendency of Americans to see themselves as serving as some kind of God-appointed people placed on this earth to be a positive beacon light to the world – Johnson's Great Society made no use whatsoever of the idea that there was anything divine or Godly behind his program. The Great Society did not need to call upon that religious enthusiasm in support of its progressive reforms of American society – because those reforms would be based simply on the logic of social science. In other words, Johnson was intending to take America into yet another period of Human Enlightenment.

The Judicial activism of the Warren Court (1953-1969). The natural tendency of Enlightened Man is to want to put away all thoughts of a Higher Hand in life – or rather, to put themselves in that position instead of looking to a God above to play that role. This is an instinct that reaches way back in the development of human thought and behavior – clearly narrated in the story of Adam and Eve in God's Garden of Eden. This tendency of man to want to gather as much power as possible into his own hands – to play God himself – was the main reason that those who wrote the American Constitution were so very careful to put checks and balances into their Constitution. It was also the reason they added the Bill of Rights – to block the expected ambitions of American politicians wanting to take control of the governmental process guiding America. The writers of the Constitution wanted the powers of government to remain in the hands of the States and the people. Congress, that is, the national government, would be called on to take political action only on those restricted areas carefully outlined by the Constitution.

Needless to say, the Constitution's authors were very concerned as to whether or not such Constitutional boundaries would hold. That's why Ben Franklin issued his famous statement describing the new frame of government: "A Republic – if you can keep it."

We have already seen how John Marshall early on assumed for the

Supreme Court extra-Constitutional powers (powers not awarded by the Constitution itself) in making the "obviously more enlightened" justices of the Supreme Court the ultimate and final voice in what would be considered legal (and thus politically moral) in the doings of American government.

We have seen how those who wrote the *Humanist Manifesto* in 1933 were calling for a new religious culture based not on "sentimental and unreal hopes and wishful thinking" (meaning a belief in a supernatural God and His presiding hand in the affairs of this world) but instead on "reasonable and manly attitudes." The Humanists made it very clear in the Thirteenth Affirmation as to how this was to work:

> *Religious humanism maintains that all associations and institutions exist for the fulfillment of human life. The intelligent evaluation, transformation, control, and direction of such associations and institutions with a view to the enhancement of human life is the purpose and program of humanism. Certainly religious institutions, their ritualistic forms, ecclesiastical methods, and communal activities must be reconstituted as rapidly as experience allows, in order to function effectively in the modern world.*

But Humanism would have to wait until the 1960s to find a way to put in place this great project of "reconstituting" America's religious foundations. And they would do so not by going the democratic route of putting the matter before the American people to decide – that is, put their program to a vote in Congress – but would have their program installed at the heart of American culture by going to the one American institution able to dictate to the rest of the country its particular views on matters: the Supreme Court. Here they would need at the most only five people to see things their way – and force those views on the rest of the nation as now being Constitutional law. Jefferson must have been cheering from his grave!

Engle v. Vitale (1962). In fact the voice of Jefferson would play a huge role in the judicial roll-back of Christianity as the moral-ethical foundation of the American Republic. That is because a letter he wrote back in 1802 mentioned the phrase, "wall of separation" – a wall that he claimed was what the First Amendment was all about when it included the anti-establishment clause in that Amendment. Those very words of Jefferson's (thus by one who had no role whatsoever in drafting either the Constitution or the Bill of Rights) – "wall of separation" – now became themselves Constitutional, according to the to the ever-vigilant ACLU and now also the 6-1 (with two abstentions) Supreme Court decision. Prayers in public schools (going on at this point for the past 3½ centuries) were henceforth unconstitutional because they violated the wall of separation provision, not mentioning however the "non-prohibiting of religion" clause of the First Amendment – that should have stopped abruptly all further Supreme Court action on this matter.

So, the prayer of a public school in New York supposedly violated the wall of separation prescribed by the First Amendment – despite the fact that the prayer was quite generic in its appeal to God – and no children were required to join in. In short, thanks to Jefferson, the ACLU, and the Warren Court, any such appeal to God was now deemed unconstitutional.*

The follow-up. That point would be driven home in two more cases heard before the Supreme Court the following year, *Abington Township School District v. Schempp* (1963) and *Murray v. Curlett* (1963), in which also the reading of the Bible in public school was deemed by the Court to violate the First Amendment's wall of separation.

Actually, the First Amendment makes no mention of a wall of separation:

> *Congress shall make no law respecting an establishment of religion, or prohibiting the free exercise thereof; or abridging the freedom of speech, or of the press; or the right of the people peaceably to assemble, and to petition the Government for a redress of grievances.*

A "wall of separation" is certainly implied here – but it is a wall designed to *protect religion* from the effort of Congress or any other government agency to take control of the people's religion – certainly not to authorize any public officials (such as the Supreme Court Justices) to get in the business of deciding how America is supposed to relate as a matter of religious faith and belief to the challenges of life. The First Amendment clearly states that not only will the State not establish a religion (such as "Religious Humanism") but also quite clearly *take no action "prohibiting the free-exercise" of the people's religion.* But prohibiting the free-

---

*What is ironic – even tragic – is that the organization that claims that it is dedicated to protecting the liberties of the people should be the very organization that in bringing these pieces of anti-Christian litigation to court would be employing very authoritarian methods to get the religious liberties of multitudes, even the majority of the Americans, shut down. And it did so simply because those liberties were at odds with the ACLU's own Secular-Humanist worldview or religion. In this the ACLU was acting the part of a Fascist hit squad rather than the protectors of American liberties.

exercise of the people's religious activity it clearly did in these early 1960s decisions shutting down local prayers and Bible reading – violating the very Constitution that the Supreme Court was supposed to be protecting.

Instead the Court was moving ahead to promote the establishment of Secular Humanism of the variety called for in the 1933 *Humanist Manifesto*. Step by step the Court would over the years continue to move ahead in the direction of removing America's Christian moral-spiritual foundations – in order to replace them with the "non-religion" of Secularism, which is a religion like any other, one promoting a more "enlightened" Humanist (when not also Darwinist) worldview – as the Humanists themselves affirmed in their *Manifesto*.

The new Science of Society. Accompanying this effort to remove Christian moral and spiritual norms from America society was the move to replace all social theory with the Secular wisdom that pure science supposedly afforded. This was not a new thing. America had been through this craze before, in the late 1600s and early 1700s, in the early 1800s, and again in the 1920s. The results disappointed Americans greatly – which brought Americans back to their original Christian faith – usually in preparation for a major challenge which was about to rise and threaten the very existence of their society (the War of Independence, the Civil War, the Great Depression and World War Two). But as America entered the 1960s, times were good (and had been so for a quite long time), a younger generation (the Boomers) that had experienced no particular hardship (in fact amazing plenty instead) was just now beginning to enter adult society – and thus once again the natural human tendency to want to be all the God this new America would need was again on the rise.

There definitely was a strong belief arising that America was about to be able to bring the country to perfection – under the guidance of a rising group of intellectuals (lawyers, economists, sociologists, journalists, dramatists) – who during the 1950s had been placed under suspicion by the Vets, but who were now – with considerable backing by Johnson's Great Society programs – finally able to take their "proper" place at the head of American society.

Playing a major role in this development were the new breed of Behaviorists – psychological and social scientists who were convinced that the scientific method could be properly assigned to human and social research so as to bring forth new insights, new scientific laws, that could better serve as guides on the path to individual and social perfection. The old paths, such as historical analysis long used to find those social patterns that seemed mostly to determine life, needed to be put aside. History had nothing to show a new Behaviorist culture, a new culture that supposed it could find life's answers simply by applying statistical study to personal and social behavior (like studying the behavior of laboratory mice). Of course it would take some time to build up a body of such precise knowledge. But the expectations were that America was about to enter a huge new age of social science – and leave traditional religious faith and old intellectual habits behind.

The secularizing of American Protestantism. And once again a number of leading voices in the American churches came to the conclusion that Christianity would be best served by making major theological and operational adjustments that would put the Christian faith in a better, more scientific light, that is, more "realistic," more mechanistic in approach to the dynamics of life and society.

Had the Church not learned from past efforts to "enlighten" Christianity – that this was not only foolish in the extreme, but left the country lost in confusion about its basic worldviews? But here again, certain pastoral voices were calling for the "de-mythologizing" of Scriptural faith – that is (like Jefferson) getting rid of all the miracle stories about God's intervention in the confused affairs of man. This stripping the Bible of its "superstitions" would supposedly then bring out the essential and most important core of the religion: the moral-ethical teachings of the Judeo-Christian faith.

Of course this left Christianity with nothing to offer the world that Secularism would not also claim to offer: peace and social justice, for example. Younger Americans just did not see the point of signing up with the dwindling Christian community. It seemingly had nothing to offer them that the secular world unfolding before them in the 1960s would not also offer.

Needless to say, by the mid-1960s, once again church attendance – then even church membership – began a decline. This would prove to be a decline that the once-dominant mainline churches would be unable to turn around – despite (or – better yet – because of) major efforts to make themselves more relevant to the evolving culture walking away from them.

Failed efforts at countering this trend. Americans in the pew were shocked by the move of the Supreme Court against Christian practices in play since the founding of the nation itself. A protest naturally went up, picked up by Congressman Frank Becker, who in August of 1963 proposed a constitutional amendment designed to make it very clear that the Constitution in no ways outlaws either prayer or Bible reading in America's schools. The "Becker Amendment" seemed to enjoy widespread support, except it could not seem to get past the careful opposition of the House Judiciary Committee whose chairman, Emanuel Celler, had no intention of releasing the bill for vote before Congress. Finally Celler, when much of the momentum had died down, opened hearings, bringing in not only ACLU lawyers to testify against the bill, but also (interestingly enough) Christian denominational leaders – ones who had made it clear that they did not believe that the Court's decisions had indeed blocked prayer and Bible study, and thus they believed strongly that this amendment was not needed (how unprophetic!). In the end, Celler made sure that his committee took no action, and let the bill die in committee before its members headed home to get ready for the upcoming 1964 national elections.

Thus thanks to Celler, the ACLU, and the Christian "leaders," prayer and consideration of the ancient teachings of the Bible which had guided countless previous generations in bringing their nation to greatness could now be included in the education of America's rising generations only in violation of the Supreme Court's new ruling. This was now the law of the land.

A second attempt to free up prayer and Bible-reading with a constitutional amendment would be made two years later by the Senate's Republican Party Leader Everett Dirksen. But again, he got no assistance from the denominational leaders, including the National Council of Churches – although he was deluged by letters from the laity in strong support of his amendment. But ultimately party lines determined the outcome of the September 1966 vote when only 49 voted in favor (nearly all Republicans and most of the Southern Democrats) and 37 were opposed (all but 3 of them Democrats). Thus failing to get the necessary 2/3rds vote for an amendment proposal, Dirksen's effort came to nothing.

But the vote made the deep ideological split developing within America itself very obvious. Clearly Johnson's Democratic Party was pulling away from Middle America, to head down the Secular (non-Christian, and at times even anti-Christian) road.*

* * *

THE "REVOLUTION OF RISING EXPECTATIONS"

"Affirmative Action." Given the new drive to social perfection unleashed by Johnson's Great Society and by the Behavioral Revolution, it was deemed time to do some compensatory work to reverse the impact of past racial discrimination. The blemish of racism needed to be removed immediately – and thus "affirmative action" was required. Actually, Kennedy had initiated

---

*Still to this day it is not clear why Democrats are so readily opposed to the active role of Judeo-Christianity in the life of the nation.

the idea in March of 1961 with Executive Order 10925 requiring government contractors to take affirmative action to make sure that their employment was done without regard to "race, creed, color or national origin." But in September of 1965, Johnson issued a more expansive and more muscular Executive Order 11246 – requiring contractors to take compensatory action in promoting the full equality of women and racial minorities in their companies – in other words clearly demonstrating a special favoring of them over White males in their hiring and professional advancement – if they wanted to continue to do business with the U.S. government.

The entitlement mentality develops. Non-WASP (White-Anglo-Saxon-Protestant) minorities – such as the Irish, Poles, Italians, Greeks, Jews, etc. – had consistently faced the challenge of making their way forward in America's dominant WASPish culture, against subtle or not-so-subtle discrimination. But they worked hard to succeed – not giving up despite the slow process involved in becoming accepted. And eventually they were able to take their place properly in American culture – even as Middle Class Americans.

But Blacks had been in America since its very founding – and the feeling was that they had waited long enough. They deserved immediate integration. They were entitled to it.

And thus expectations ran high – much, much higher than the culture was going to be able to accommodate such a major cultural shift. Frustration set in almost immediately among the Blacks – actually anger, as the litany of Blacks' long suffering under racism became a theme heard everywhere. And that anger soon enough turned violent. For some Blacks (notably the group of young Black Panthers), the days of King's non-violent protest were thus over.

"Burn, baby, burn." Young Blacks now turned on the system in anger, looting and burning the world immediately around them. In 1965, the Watts section of Los Angeles was looted and burned – with 34 people killed in the accompanying violence. All of this was accompanied by the refrain of "Burn, Baby, Burn" – but also police sirens answering back in refrain as Black Power advocates were carted off to jail, either as self-sacrificing heroes – or dangerous criminals – depending on which side of the ideological divide you found yourself on.

But this was just the beginning. By 1967 Black rage had spread widely across America: In early July, in Newark (New Jersey) the arrest of a Black cab driver turned out young Blacks who looted, firebombed and even engaged in sniper fire at police and firemen trying to bring the city back to order. Eleven people were killed, 600 wounded and whole sections of the

America Shifts to the Humanist or Progressivist" Left 319

city were gutted by fire.

When several days later a pre-scheduled National Unity Conference was held in Newark, the language was one not of unity but of declared war. Black power advocate H. Rap Brown urged the gathering to "wage guerrilla war on the white man." Los Angeles Black Nationalist leader Ron Karenga stated "Everybody knows Whitey's a devil. The question is what to do about it." Moderate Black leaders such as King, Roy Wilkins, and Whitney Young, Jr. avoided the conference.

In late July, violence broke out in Detroit. Learning from Newark, Detroit mayor Cavanagh immediately called in the National Guardsmen. But seven thousand Guardsmen, complete with tanks and armored cars, could not restore order. Michigan Governor George Romney (who was understood to be a potential Republican candidate for the Presidential election in 1968) contacted President Johnson for assistance. Johnson held back until Romney confessed before the public that he had lost control of the situation. Then Johnson sent in US paratroopers to retake the city house by house, block by block – similar to a Vietnam military action. When a week later the troops had brought Detroit back to order, 43 people had been killed and over a thousand injured.

Meanwhile the violence spread to New York City where a 28,000-man police force with experience in riot control restored order to East Harlem after three nights of violence. Two people were killed.

H. Rap Brown had in the meantime moved on to Cambridge, Maryland, and following a Black Power rally there, the town was subjected to looting and arson. Brown was arrested for inciting a riot. As he was led away by FBI agents, Brown challenged: "We'll burn the country down."

***

THE PRESIDENT'S WORSENING WAR IN VIETNAM

Mass confusion in Vietnam. Tragically, it seemed impossible for Americans (including the President – and even his generals) to understand the nature of the political crisis in Vietnam. The Communist enemy wore no uniforms – and in fact was indistinguishable from the people America was trying to save for "democracy." Most of the people America was trying to save were Buddhist, loving neither Communism nor the Western culture that Americans were trying to uphold in Vietnam. Mostly they wanted to be left alone by everyone so that they could peacefully tend their rice fields.

There were of course pro-American Vietnamese, located especially in Saigon and some of the other urban areas of the South. And the *montagnards*, the mountain people who centuries ago had originally inhabited the area but had been driven by invading Vietnamese into the mountains for survival, were big supporters of the American presence. But mostly, the Vietnamese were simply proud nationalists who wanted non-Vietnamese (that would be the Americans), out of their country – along with the Communist guerrilla fighters – armed with guns and supplies coming from the North – who were helping to make life in the South miserable. Saving Vietnam for democracy had little meaning to them.

Thus the goals of America's involvement in Vietnam remained unclear. And the means by reaching these unclear goals were thus equally unclear – especially when it appeared that there were no front lines the soldiers could expand – as the enemy soon reappeared behind American lines once the Americans swept through an area. It was a frustrating war.

So, contrary to Johnson's original expectations, America's strong presence in their country did not bring forth exuberant Vietnamese praising and thanking the Americans for their liberation from Communism. Nor was it something that could be quickly resolved (as Johnson had originally expected). Instead American soldiers found themselves encamped behind barbed wire enclosures, venturing out into the countryside in search of an enemy they could not distinguish from the general population, and getting shot at from behind as well as in front. There were no visible lines of military progression that could be seen on a map – but merely an uneasy occupation of sections of territory here and there which changed hands constantly.

Americans were getting killed without any visible signs of progress, except that Americans seemed to be killing more of them than they were killing of the occupying soldiers – though also there were a whole lot more of them than Americans to be killed. "Them" was not a clear concept – and Americans soon found themselves killing anything that looked suspicious – even whole villages by aerial strafing and bombing. It was an ugly sight – covered in gory detail by a watchful American press.

But watching all this very closely were the young Boomers – now old enough to be drafted into military service.

✳ ✳ ✳

THE WORLD GOES ON ELSEWHERE

What was unusual at the time was how "superpower" America – the leading figure in the NATO European-American military alliance and in fact defender of the "Free World" in general – was so completely wrapped up in the Vietnam issue that America seemed to have no time or interest, and thus played no particular role, in other major international events going on at the time.

De Gaulle attempts to undercut American leadership in Europe. De Gaulle's dislike of the Anglo-Saxon world (British and American) reached all the way back to World War Two, when De Gaulle did not receive the attention he felt he deserved as self-appointed leader of the Free French. Also he suffered from a sense of rejection when after the war the French were not interested in designing a new French republic that would give him the powers and thus prestige he felt he deserved. Thus he went into political retirement – that was up until 1958 when a military coup he directed brought him to power, thanks to the terrible confusion France was experiencing due to the independence movement of Muslim Algerians desirous of taking Algeria out of the French Union. In setting up the new French Fifth Republic De Gaulle finally had the political formula that he wanted by which to govern France.

But De Gaulle had one more political item to attend to: the humiliation of the British and the Americans. First he vetoed the application of the British in 1963 when they finally decided to join the European Economic Community, a deep humiliation indeed. Also he turned on NATO, headquartered in his country, but clearly led by America. In 1959, the year after coming to power in France, De Gaulle pulled his French Mediterranean naval fleet out of NATO and then demanded that the British and Americans remove all their nuclear weapons from the country, a move designed supposedly to bring as much of Europe as possible under the French nuclear umbrella instead of that of his Anglo-Saxon opponents. But the other NATO members were not interested. In 1963 De Gaulle went further and pulled his more strategically important French Atlantic fleet out of NATO, hoping that others would do the same (none did). He then also moved to strengthen diplomatic relations with Mao's China and Soviet Russia, demonstrating France's new "neutrality" in the Cold War. In 1965 he demanded that all French dollar holdings be converted into American gold, and sent the French navy to America to collect that gold. But once again, no other nation joined him in this gold-run designed to collapse the dollar's international status. In 1966 he ordered all foreign troops (mostly American) out of France*, with NATO responding by moving all its operations (including even its civilian headquarters) out of France and north to Belgium, helping Brussels, already the administrative seat of the European Community, become even more the administrative center of West European society!

---

*American Secretary of State Dean Rusk sarcastically asked de Gaulle: did this order to evacuate all U.S. troops from France include the 50,000 American war dead buried in French cemeteries?

In all this, Johnson did nothing, perhaps because there was nothing he could have done about such behavior. De Gaulle was a very determined American opponent. Finally the French themselves had enough of De Gaulle's imperiousness and in 1968, when the French refused to ratify a new constitutional amendment that De Gaulle wanted in order to give himself even more power, he quit, expecting France to fall apart and the French to come on bended knees pleading for his return. They did not, and France moved on quite well without him.

Mao's China. With the collapse of the Chiang government in China (and its transfer to the huge island of Taiwan) America had focused its "China policy" entirely on Taiwan – and had simply ignored developments going on after that in China, which actually helped Mao greatly in securing his Communist hold over mainland China.

But his fellow Communists in China tended to ignore Mao now that Communism was securely in place in their country. After all, Communism was about the modern industrial world, not the world of the traditional peasant countryside – which stood behind Mao and his accomplishments. But Mao was not one to be put aside – and thrust himself forward again as China's savior when he regained political control by offering to show how, under proper direction, Chinese rural society could do industrialism more quickly than its urban society. With his "Great Leap Forward" program, put into effect in 1958, he planned to have China's thousands of tiny villages undertake iron production in their new small smelters. Supposedly the combined effort of all these villages going at this project would make China now a major producer of iron – in Mao's eyes a key indicator of China's move into industrial leadership.

Actually all this did was to produce inferior-grade iron – which had no real industrial use, and take millions of farmers away from their fields where China's food should have been produced. As a consequence, millions of Chinese (anywhere from 20 to 40 million?) began to die – of hunger, of exhaustion, or simply of human discouragement. Finally, Mao had to scrap the Five-Year Plan, even before its full run. It had obviously been an enormous failure.

But again, Mao was not one to be put aside. Thus in 1966 he came forward with another of his moments of grand insight: he would push the Communist Revolution forward in the form of a grand Cultural Revolution, revolutionary ideology planted in the hearts and minds of the more trainable Chinese youth (Mao was finding the adult world less amenable to his "revolutionary" thinking). Indeed not only would he instruct (brainwash basically) China's youth with the thoughts of the Great Leader himself through the reading, reciting and even singing of his words found in Mao's Little Red Book, he would activate that youthful spirit by having it become the vigilant eyes and ears of the Revolution, ferreting out any "anti-Revolutionary" activity – even thought – found in the older Chinese generation. Not only the West's Christianity but also China's traditional Confucianism came under fierce attack, as the youth "liberated" the country from "unprogressive" social norms.

Thus young vigilante "Red Guard" youth took over the schools, the town halls, the local communities themselves, setting up their own judicial councils to try and punish anti-revolutionary activity found still existing in the country.

Consequently, once again Mao simply shut down Chinese society, as schools, businesses and local community operations came to a halt under this new Red Guard regime. Finally, by 1968, even Mao realized that he had gone overboard with his Cultural Revolution, and in 1969 was even forced to call in the Chinese Army to get things back under control!

The Arab-Israeli "Six-Day War" of June 1967. Another event that took place in these years, one that America actually might have been able to direct to fairer results – but basically looked the other way as events unfolded – was a disastrous war conducted between the new state of Israel and its Arab neighbors. Israel had been created in 1948 by masses of Jews, the ones fortunate enough to have escaped death in Hitler's concentration camps, flooding to Palestine, in order to set up a state where they would no longer be bothered by a hostile non-Jewish world. Unfortunately, Palestine was not uninhabited, but instead was fully inhabited – the portion that was not desert anyway – by Arabs, both Christian and Muslim in religion, as well as Jews who also had been part of Palestinian society since time immemorial. And other than the desert, there was nowhere else for these Palestinians to go if the Jews were absolutely determined to take over fully the part of Palestine that could support human life.

Consequently a very ugly battle for the land resulted, one that would be ongoing, not only as long as there were still Palestinians left to contest the Jewish invasion of their homeland but even as long as there were other Arabs in that part of the world outraged in seeing their fellow Arabs in Palestine driven from their homes, farms and businesses.

And that fellow-Arab world included Egypt, right next door to the new Israel, where Egyptian President Nasser was posing himself as the leader not only of Egypt but of all the Arab world, through his newly-created United Arab Republic. And he had as his rallying cry to promote his Arab candidacy the call to do something about the "Jewish problem" in Palestine. Thus not only was he developing a military well beyond any immediate need for Egyptian national defense, he was talking loudly (part of his political campaign) about his intentions to lead the Arab world in delivering Palestine from its occupiers.

But Israel was in not in the mood to wait around to see exactly how he was planning to advance his candidacy, and, without any warning, struck hard at Egypt, fully destroying the Egyptian air force with its planes still on the ground, and thus making it impossible for the Egyptians to offer air cover to their ground troops now facing an advancing Israeli army and it covering air force. It was a slaughter for the Egyptians, as the Israelis rolled quickly all the way up to the Suez Canal – which now found itself shut down as a result of the war.

Then foolishly Jordan and Syria decided to come to the aid of Egypt, and Israel crushed their forces as well, all of this in a mere six days (thus the term "Six-Days War").

This was the event – not that America had any part in it – that brought Americans finally to want to offer full support to Israel in its contest with its Arab neighbors (America had been fairly neutral about this complex matter prior to this). The very one-sidedness of the news coverage of the 1967 Jew-versus-Arab conflict made this rather inevitable (there were not many Arabs running America's news organizations!).

But what was not inevitable – actually quite strange – was the way that Evangelical Christians came out so strongly in favor of Israel against Palestine's Arab population, not realizing what a high percentage of the Palestinian population was Christian. Evangelicals seemed not to understand that chasing Palestinian Christians from the land would not advance the gospel in that part of the world (Israel was not a big supporter of the Christian gospel!). But unlimited Evangelical support for Israel was indeed the case. And indeed it would come to be that way for all the nation, America now dedicated to supporting Israel at all costs (it would have the opportunity to be more proactive in this regard within another five years, with the outbreak of the Yom Kippur or October War of 1973).

The "Prague Spring" and the Czechoslovakian Crisis of 1968. Another major international event that Superpower America did not participate in – or even influence in the smallest way – was a spontaneous uprising of the Czechs in 1968 against the Soviet domination of their country. The Czechs had formerly been very productive members of Europe's industrial world, that was until the country fell into the hands of Soviet-backed Communists in 1948. The Czech economy had done very poorly since then, even in comparison to other subject nations within the Soviet bloc or Empire.

Surprisingly, it was the Czech Communist leader himself, Alexander Dubček, that decided that the country must open itself up to greater personal initiative, that is capitalism itself, in order to get the Czech economy up

America Shifts to the Humanist or Progressivist" Left 325

and running again. But such independent-mindedness, especially from a Communist who was supposed to be getting governing instructions from the Kremlin (Communist headquarters in Moscow) – and from there alone – could be a real danger to the Soviet Empire.

Thus after some efforts to talk the Czechs back from this program – with no results (the Czechs themselves were very enthusiastic about this new "Prague Spring") – in mid-August (1968) Soviet leader Leonid Brezhnev ordered hundreds of thousands (some say as many as half a million) troops and 1200 tanks to roll into Czechoslovakia and put an end to the program.

The world was loud in its denunciations. But ultimately it (along with America) did nothing, and moved on to other matters.

✶ ✶ ✶

THE BOOMER COMES OF AGE

At around this same time, the Boomers were just reaching early adulthood, and eager to become heroes by challenging on all fronts any form of suspicious social authority – something they had been prepared for since their early school years. Unfortunately, the authority at hand to challenge was not some conspiring Communist intruders into American life. That fear had proved groundless. Instead, the only authority that otherwise stood before them available to be challenged by young crusading hearts was their middle-class parents' own highly patriotic political cultural legacy.

Boomer Progressivism. Much had been made publicly about the blemishes afflicting American society – and the need for deep reform. Clearly to the Boomers, the America that their middle-class American parents lauded as the best of all possible worlds was an idea itself that needed to be rejected as foolish – even dangerous – blind patriotism. Thus – with considerable encouragement from the intellectuals who commanded the university classrooms the Boomers attended in increasing numbers – virtually in every aspect of middle-class life that was put before the Boomers as traditional cultural legacy they found some element to be challenged, if indeed not even the whole middle class cultural package to be put aside in the name of serious progress.

"Come together." But this huge emphasis on resisting all forms of social authority did not satisfy the human heart and its natural desire to find its basic identity within some kind of social context. Communalism thus became one of the forms – if not the major form – this instinct took. Boomer communes were first modeled by older members of the Silent Generation who returned from overseas service in the Peace Corps – impacted by the communal life typical of the villages they lived and worked in during their two-year time abroad in Third World countries. Hippie communes thus began to spring up among the Silents – but soon were picked up by the rising Boomer generation as well as an ideal social form.

Hippie communes had very little in common with the American Middle-Class family – but were gatherings where Boomer music, drugs and free sex were readily available. Soon hippie communes became standard as a social prototype chosen by the Boomers in their quest to belong.

The fundamental conformity of Boomer "individualism." Indeed, for a generation raised to resist all social authority and do its own personal thinking, the Boomers turned out to be amazingly conformist – clothing and hair styles – even the swaggering walk – as well as music, topics of social interest and even language styles modeled closely on the personal styles of Joan Baez and Bob Dillon – the coolest of the early Boomer social models (soon to be joined by other Boomer social models such as the Beatles, the Rolling Stones, Janice Joplin, Jimmy Hendrix, etc.). This tendency to conformity included even VW minivans decorated with peace and sex symbols – the minivans themselves symbols of the mobility and rootlessness of Boomer life.

Drugs. Boomers enjoyed indulging in social drugs, ranging from marijuana, to LSD, to heroin. It certainly helped them get in the social mood in their communes. And they enjoyed seeing the shock on the faces of the Vet generation watching this drugged up social development rising among their Boomer children. Drugs were cool. After all, this social trend started out at Harvard, the citadel of American intellectualism, with the LSD experiments of Professor Timothy Leary. And American troops had found marijuana to be very comforting in facing a war that seemed unwinnable – and without any military honors coming their way for their wartime service and sacrifice. So they brought their marijuana habits home to America with them after completing that service.

Drug usage itself became a key element of the Boomer identity. Helping to clarify the pattern was the Beatles music group – making the transition from the innocent *"Love, Love Me Do"* and *"I Want to Hold Your Hand"* (1962) – to the nonsensical *"We All Live in a Yellow Submarine"* (1966) – to the LSD-inspired *"Lucy in the Sky with Diamonds"* (1967).

Protest. Besides drugs, relief from social boredom was offered in what the Boomers had best been prepared for: protest against social injustice –

injustice usually in the form of some aspect of Vet society.

Christianity. The Vet generation's close attachment to Christianity as its fundamental civic religion was not protested. It simply was not taken up as the Boomer religion – through the simple strategy of Boomers just not bothering to attend church.

Feminism. Then there was the cause of feminism. In 1963 Betty Friedan published a book, *The Feminine Mystique*, one that would not only announce the startup of a new round of militant feminism, but serve as the basic Bible of young college-educated women, instructing them as to how to combat the male domination of the professional world.

Marriage and the family (that is, the fundamental institution of Middle-Class America) took a huge hit with Friedan's call to arms. In her book she depicted family life not only as the underpinning of male tyranny but also as terribly stifling of a woman's intellectual abilities. Women needed to find escape from the marriage trap – and discover their real purpose in life in the professional world. Of course they could expect to find sexual discrimination awaiting them there. But this was the point of the book: it was time for women to rise up (like the Blacks) against this world of (male) domination and secure for themselves the right to take as much control of American society as had long been held by men. And thus the battle of the sexes got underway.

Black civil rights. Marching in protest against Southern racism certainly stirred the hearts of young Americans. But it was mostly the older Silents who joined the pastors, professors and journalists who headed to the South to support the social and political rights of Southern Blacks. Boomers would eventually join the ongoing civil rights movement – sort of – at least from a distance. Anyway, by the time the Boomers had emerged on the political stage, the Black militants such as the Black Panthers had taken over the Black civil rights movement – and Whites were not invited to become part of their campaign.

Against President Johnson's war in Vietnam. Boomers did, however, have one great crusade to undertake, one that would put heroic touches to their lives: the need to end the Vietnam War – and the accompanying military draft that was carrying young American males off to a conflict that was deadly – and apparently pointless.

Thus the Boomers were beginning to voice loudly their opposition to "Johnson's war." Why should America's youth be drafted to serve in a distant war whose morality was questionable? Boomers were beginning to identify the motivation behind the entire Vietnam venture war as being simply raw imperialism – American imperialism. This was pure evil: the strong dictating their social-cultural organization to the weak – the very thing the Boomers had been carefully programmed to resist – as heroically as possible.

Thus the Boomers began to do what they had long been trained to do: protest political authority whose actions to them seemed entirely wrong. In 1967 they gathered in mass in front of the Pentagon to call for an end to the war.

The deep split between the Vet and the Boomer generations. The Vet parents were perplexed – even irate. The Vets were an unshakably patriotic group, standing with the government no matter what ("my country right or wrong"). Anyway – wasn't America trying to bring democracy to Vietnam? Did the Boomer youth not see the importance of setting up a viable democracy in South Vietnam – one that would act not only as a barrier against Communist expansion coming from the North – but like America itself, serve as a beacon of light, lighting the way to other countries in the region to find democracy for themselves as well? How in the world could the Boomers be missing the point?

And thus it was that a vicious war of words broke out between the two generations – words mostly of just an emotional rather than truly rational character to them. Indeed, complex concepts such as democracy, imperialism, Fascism, and Communism became mere slogans rallying intense support or opposition rather than actual argument or reasoned debate that the two generations hurled at each other.

Tragically for America, this Boomer-versus-Vet battle produced a generational division that would never find healing – a lack of healing in part due to the involvement in this Boomer crusade by numerous American intellectuals, individuals who understood the Boomers as valuable allies in their own quest for vengeance for the mistreatment they – or at least their older colleagues – had suffered at the hands of the Vets in the 1950s. Thus it was that the causes for this generational split were broad and vague in nature – but at times violent nonetheless.

1968: THE *ANNUS HORRIBILIS* (THE "HORRIBLE YEAR")

Tet (January-February). 1968 was a very pivotal year for the Johnson Administration, because Johnson's Great Society and his Vietnam "police action" were put to the test, and found wanting. At the beginning of 1968,

America Shifts to the Humanist or Progressivist" Left

the "Tet Offensive" of the Communist Viet Cong broke out across South Vietnam, reaching all the way into the supposedly secure capital of Saigon – where even the army guards protecting the American Embassy were shot down. It was a bold move – a desperate one actually on the part of the Viet Cong, one in which they nearly wiped themselves out in the effort. But the American media covering (in gory detail) the disaster there had no way of knowing that. Instead, it was portrayed as a major Viet Cong victory, making Johnson's assurances that America was making great progress in Vietnam appear to be a horrible White House lie.

Consequently, the Viet Cong, with much help from the American press, succeeded in the goal of any war: to make the enemy want to quit. After Tet, that was exactly what many Americans wanted, especially those loudest in these matters. Kids poured out onto the streets, even filling the small park in front of the White House with protesters chanting day and night: "Hey, hey LBJ, how many kids did you kill today?"

Johnson's announcement (March).   Thus in a regular television broadcast, Johnson surprised the country by announcing (this tidbit was not included in the speech handed out to the press previous to its presentation) that he would not be running for reelection that November. The country was shocked. Johnson seemed simply to be bailing out as US President.

King's assassination (April). Then in April came the assassination of Dr. King, who was in Memphis supporting a garbage workers' strike (he had switched to supporting all the poor of America regardless of race).* Blacks responded in what was becoming a rather typical fashion now, going on a rampage plundering neighborhoods and then torching them, in American city after city. Police had to be called in to protect the firemen who were being shot at by the rioters, and afternoon curfews, requiring everyone to be inside their homes, had to be imposed to bring order back to America.

---

*By another one of those strange interventions of what I at the time called *fortuna*, I found myself at the Washington National Cathedral the Sunday before King's assassination (at this point attending more for sentimental than for theological reasons), with King as the featured pastor. He spoke prophetically (as it turned out) about how his focus on Black civil rights was coming to an end, as he took up a new line of work in promoting America's poor, Black and White. He was in fact, planning a Poor People's March on Washington for the next month (May). He was stepping back from the Black Movement – which had been taken over by the Black Panthers, whose brand of politics he did not approve of. Tragically he had no idea of how indeed his work in favor of Black civil rights was coming to an end. And I gave that last prophetic sermon of his much thought that week, as I saw the racial unity that he sought so earnestly go up in the smoke of burning American cities.

It took several days to get things calmed back down again.

This was definitely not how Dr. King would have wanted to be remembered. But this was no longer about Dr. King. This was about Black power, and Black Panther militancy. White man's world needed to be destroyed.

Thus so much for Federal poverty and educational assistance offered by Washington to the Black minority community in order to put the icing on the cake of the Great Society. It all seemed so pointless now.

The hippie takeover of Columbia University (April-May). But White Boomers were not intending to be left out of the action. Thus students took over the offices at Columbia University in New York City in late April – and shut the university down completely, to the anger of those students anticipating graduating soon. Fighting broke out between student groups. Finally, the police were brought in to reopen the university. But it would be a much-changed institution (student applications and alumni financial support would drop away dramatically) as a result.

The Poor People's March on Washington. (May-June). Soon after this, a peaceful demonstration of poor people (of all races) converging on Washington went ahead as scheduled in Mid-May. But without its leader, Dr. King – and because of the heavy downpours which soon turned the encamped demonstrators' tent city into a quagmire of mud – it too seemed all so pointless. The days dragged on through much of June ...and little seemed to have been accomplished through the effort.

The second Kennedy assassination (June). Then in the midst of all this, in early June, Robert Kennedy was assassinated by an Iranian youth, whose motives were never understood. Kennedy was the individual most likely to be the Democratic Party's nominee that November, and thus also most likely to be the next U.S. president. What was going on? Like everything else at the time, it all seemed so pointless.

Rioting at the Democratic National Convention (August). Then there was the Democratic National Convention held in Chicago in August, to find a new candidate for the presidency now that Kennedy was gone. Masses of "Yippies" (militant "hippies") descended on Chicago to protest (what exactly?) and to take on the "pig" police, turning the area around the convention center into a war zone, as police (nearly qualifying as rioters themselves at one point) and Yippies attacked each other, resulting in numerous people (including delegates) getting hurt badly. And the scene inside the convention was just as ugly, with Chicago Mayor Daley cursing the convention speakers, the television crews catching the complete madness with their cameras. Again, it all seemed so pointless.

* * *
CLOSING THE TURBULENT 1960s

The November 1968 elections: Nixon to the White House. The selection of Richard Nixon as the Republican Party's candidate at their National Convention was a huge contrast – by way of the quiet order in which it was conducted. And that atmosphere helped immensely to bring out Vet voters, tired of all the political commotion consuming their country. Thus it was that Nixon won the election, drawing 43.4 percent of the popular vote to the Democratic Party's candidate Senator Hubert Humphrey's 42.7 percent (Third-Party Southern Democrat George Wallace with 13.5 percent), although the electoral college vote was strongly in Nixon's favor 302 to 191 (Wallace with 46).

This was hardly what the Boomer activists and their intellectual mentors wanted. These two social sectors were so ideologically opposed to Middle America at this point that they seemed totally unable to accept the verdict of the vote. How in the world could "Public Enemy Number One" have managed to get himself into the White House? They would do everything possible to nullify his presidency.

The making of Richard Nixon. Nixon was born in 1913 in Whittier, California, a very Quaker community, to a family which was also Quaker. Family tragedy made life hard for young Nixon, a younger brother having died in 1925 and an older brother also badly ill with tuberculosis. In fact, a Harvard Club prize he was awarded because of his excellent grades he was not able to use, because the family could not afford the rest of the Harvard education costs, due to the expense of the older brothers' medical treatments. Thus Nixon attended the local Whittier College, and then, with a substantial scholarship, Duke Law School, graduating summa cum laude ("with highest honors") from the latter in 1937.

However, despite these accomplishments, with his older brother having died in his senior year in college, and with the Depression in full force and law jobs hard to find upon law school graduation, Nixon's Quaker faith was tested in the extreme. From this point on, that faith would remain a very private matter.

In returning home to California to practice law there, he met and two years later (1940) married a local school teacher, Pat Ryan.

Then with America's entry into World War Two, the Nixons moved to

Washington, for him to take a job in the growing D.C. bureaucracy, with him then being able to leave this unloved work to become a lieutenant in the Navy. He would see service in the South Pacific as an administrative officer, serving in that role until 1946, although he would remain in the Naval Reserves, rising in rank over the years, until his retirement as commander in 1966.

In that year 1946, he was urged by the local Republican Party to run for Congress, defeating the Democratic incumbent Jerry Voorhis, and thus beginning his Washington political career. We have already noted his work in Congress with the House Un-American Activities Committee (HUAC), investigating the Communist presence within Washington's own officialdom, automatically making him an enemy of self-identified intellectuals who felt he was unfairly attacking those of their particular social profile. They would never forgive him for what he did in those post-war years. But his work did bring him to the attention of the Republicans who brought him alongside Eisenhower in the 1952 presidential campaign, which the two won, making Nixon now U.S. Vice President. And Eisenhower put him to work doing some travel and diplomacy for him, especially in the effort to cultivate a "thaw" in America's Cold War with Russia.

This put him in position to run as Republican presidential candidate in 1960 when Eisenhower completed his second term as president. And he came very close to defeating the more charismatic Kennedy, but ultimately failed in the effort. He then ran for California governor two years later. But found that California press coverage was very negative, making him furious about the treatment he received by the press.

Then he went into some kind of wilderness years. But he used the time fruitfully to visit the larger world, meet with a grand variety of leaders of other countries, and learn first-hand the more subtle ways of the world – and the politics and cultures that made for such variations.

Nixon's political "Realism." In this, he would become very much a supporter of the idea of Realpolitik, the German term applied to the varied use of diplomacy, bluff – and, when absolutely necessary, very carefully calculated economic and military assault (war) – in reference to the strategies of Prussian Chancellor, Otto von Bismarck, who skillfully used all these techniques to assemble a new German nation in 1870. Thus Nixon found himself replacing his older approach, mostly ideological (which America largely follows in its own domestic and foreign politics), with the subtleties of a chess player, who sees diplomacy as a game of power, and careful power moves in support of a very carefully measured "national interest," rather than all-out crusades for this or that grand political ideal.

And now as president, he would strengthen this approach to his duties

America Shifts to the Humanist or Progressivist" Left 333

in appointing the Harvard professor and political Realist, Dr. Henry Kissinger, as his National Security Advisor, then also as his Secretary of State. And the two of them would go at the international problems facing the country in quite new ways, opening the doors to better relations with both Russia and China, and also re-strategizing America's involvement in Vietnam, something unfortunately that most Americans, including most importantly his dedicated "Liberal" opponents in Congress, in the press, and in the world of academics, would never quite understand. And America (and Southeast Asia) would suffer horribly because of this lack of understanding.

Nixon, the Christian. Nixon's tendency to keep his religious faith private meant that although he definitely knew the Bible well, was a man of prayer, and spent a lot of time before God seeking divine counsel, little of that appeared in public. He even held Sunday worship at the White House itself, calling on pastors of a wide range of faith to lead these services – though clearly his favorite was Norman Vincent Peal of New York City's Marble Collegiate Church. And he was especially close, on a very broad basis, with the evangelist Billy Graham, with whom he met often for prayer and discussion.

But he also understood deeply the role that Christianity has long played in American life. For instance, in his 1972 Thanksgiving Address he emphasized the fact that Puritan founder John Winthrop was most correct in identifying America as God's "city set upon a hill," that it was important to follow the Puritan heritage in being "the light of the world," and that it had always been America's call by God, and source of the country's greatness, to provide spiritual leadership to that world. He also stated that every American president had found cause to turn to God, ultimately leaving office with a very deep religious faith.

Sadly, though Nixon personally was a man of very high moral self-discipline (thanks to his Quaker upbringing), his moral credentials would come to be measured in history solely on the basis of the Watergate scandal, where his paranoia about the public treatment he got from the Leftist Congress and press led him to get involved in an illegal coverup of what some of his subordinates had done quite unnecessarily during his 1972 reelection campaign.

Thus Nixon's personal tragedies continued to follow him, all the way through even his White House years. Thus Nixon is still today not really remembered for all the ways he served his country extremely well as president. It seems instead that he will always be remembered by generations to come as Nixon, the evil president.

The Apollo 11 Moon Landing (July 20, 1969). Actually, in entering office in January of 1969, Nixon was hoping that an event occurring the next summer would give America something positive to rally around: the landing on the moon of two American astronauts – and their moon walk to gather rock samples – and even more amazing, their safe return to the earth a day later. This helped America politically, a little anyway.

But it did at least pretty much close out the space race America had been engaged in since the Russian Sputnik launch back in 1957. America – which had been engaged in this contest through four Presidencies (Eisenhower, Kennedy, Johnson and now Nixon) – had finally won! The Russian opponents would not attempt their own version of the event – something that would have awarded them only a humiliating second-place trophy.

Ted Kennedy and Chappaquiddick (July 18, 1969). But while America was focused on events going on at the moon, another event took place at exactly the same time – an event which would challenge American politics deeply. On the night of July 18th, the car of Senator Ted Kennedy (youngest of the Kennedy brothers) was headed to a small island (Chappaquiddick) when it went off a narrow bridge and turned over in the water. Kennedy was able to get out.

But left inside was a pretty young "Boiler Room Girl" – who had been attending something of a reunion of the former campaign staff of the recently deceased Bobby Kennedy. She was left to either drown or suffocate (trapped in the car possibly for as long as two hours) – no one is quite sure which. In fact the whole incident raised all kinds of questions (why Kennedy got out and she didn't; why she was in the car in the first place; why they were headed in the direction they were going; why he didn't go immediately for help; why he didn't report the incident to the police until the next morning – when they had already discovered her body).

Amazingly, Kennedy got off with merely a suspended sentence (leaving the scene of an accident) – and the matter was soon dropped. Even more amazing, his political career hardly suffered – as not only did the Democratic Party give him a pass on this event, he very soon became the leading moral voice of the Democratic Party in its assault on the "evil president" Nixon.

The Kennedy name had real power – like the European royal dynasties of Habsburgs, Valois, Bourbons, Tudors, Stuarts, Romanovs, etc. Even in democratic America names like Adams and Roosevelt (and eventually Bush and Clinton) had a special power. And in Massachusetts, the name Kennedy would continue to have unchallenged power – all the way up until Senator Ted Kennedy's death in 2009 (still in office at the time).

America Shifts to the Humanist or Progressivist" Left 335

The Manson murders (August 1969). The next month America was shocked to hear of a number of murders undertaken by a California hippie community – murders directed by their sleazy guru, Charles Manson. The very nature of the murders was grossly bloody – and though somewhat ritualistic – generally pointless. The murderers and their leader were soon apprehended. But they too could give no sensible reason for these shocking events.

Was this what typical hippie communal life (also typically dominated by an aggressive Alpha male) was ultimately destined to become? There were no good answers. Anyway, communal life was lessening as the Boomers, moving into the 1970s, now seemed mostly interested in pursuing their own personal careers out there in the professional world.

The Woodstock Music Festival (August 15-17, 1969). In mid-August as many as 400,000 music-loving Boomers descended on an open-air music festival – to listen to an endless array of the musical greats of their day – and to enjoy the basic Boomer lifestyle of drugs and sex (although amazingly restrained on both counts, considering the size of the crowd). In a way it marked the summit point of the 1960s hippie era – unprecedented in the way it pulled a huge amount of talent together – but also a summit that would never be achieved again. It would serve as a lasting symbol of a great age – one that would be looked on nostalgically by the Boomers as they took their places in the adult world.

The "Days of Rage" (October 8-11, 1969). But they would not move into the world of the 1970s by giving up (not immediately anyway) their crusading spirits. In October, the very radical Boomer protest organization, Students for a Democratic Society (SDS) called for a campaign in Chicago they termed "Days of Rage." The rage was aimed in a number of different directions – in part, of course, about the war still underway in Vietnam – but also over the trial of the "Chicago Seven" who had instigated the violent student protests at the Democratic National Convention in Chicago the previous year. They demonstrated their rage by smashing store and car windows as they marched through the city – finally clashing with the police (as they fully intended) with the result of the injury of a number of protesters – and police – and the arrest of many of the protesters. The protests nonetheless continued the next day – and the next – although the numbers involved began to quickly diminish.

The point of it all was never quite clear. But it spoke volumes about the way Boomer youth were so easily mobilized for action, violent action if necessary, in pursuit of some social ideal – any social ideal – as long as it was indeed ideal (meaning: more of the nature of a slogan demanding action than any well-thought-through social policy).

America's new political logic. And even though the street-based protest movements would decline in number in the 1970s (although there would still remain a number of the more professional of the Boomer protesters who would continue to show up for almost any kind of a demonstration, anywhere and for any cause), the crusading spirit of the Boomers would in general continue to impact Boomer ideas of how American politics ought to proceed.

This would show up in the new social-political and even cultural attitudes that would find their way into Congress – where politics would become more and more a matter of bringing ideological opponents down to humiliating public defeat – rather than coming at America's huge challenges, admittedly from different political directions, by seeking authentic social progress through the skilled art of political compromise. Somehow this older but well-proven political style would get lost in the new political atmosphere. The Boomers – and their intellectualist mentors – would much rather conduct crusades against fellow members of society than find ways to move in strong unity in facing the larger problems facing the society as a whole.

As the Beatles' song *Revolution* (1968) put matters so elegantly:

You say you want a revolution,
Well, you know
We all want to change the world

This spirit of radical protest pumped political adrenaline and helped maintain a revolutionary high among the youthful crowd. The Boomers were in no mood to give up what they understood as the meaning of life itself, the purpose of their very existence. And America's Progressivist leaders – in Congress, in the academies, in the press – were always ready to find similar purpose for themselves as sponsors of exactly just such political activism. Consequently, the 1970s (and after) would offer in-your-face testimony to the belief of the Boomers – and their moral mentors (such as Ted Kennedy) – that their loud and aggressive moralizing/crusading political style was the best way to serve the nation's true political interests.

CHAPTER ELEVEN

THE 1970s: AMERICA DIVIDED

* * *

NIXON, AND VIETNAM

Vietnam. During those first years of Nixon's first term as president America would find itself heavily focused on one huge political issue: Vietnam. Johnson's efforts to make Vietnam the showcase of his resolve to block any and all advances by Communism not only had blown up in his face, it had turned the American nation into a deeply divided society – with two American sub-communities feuding bitterly with each other over this issue: the Vets – and their new champion, Nixon – versus their Boomer youth – and the Boomers' champions, the American intellectuals.

The very idea of Vietnam had become a matter of major political crusade – not that both sides wanted different goals. Both sides wanted America out of Vietnam. But the two sides differed greatly – even violently at times – as to the manner of that departure. Vets were hoping that there would be some way to leave behind in Vietnam some measure of accomplishment achieved by all the blood and social agony America had expended in trying to "do the right thing" in Vietnam. But the Boomers wanted out now, yesterday even, and they did not care how an immediate departure would leave Vietnam itself. They were very angry about having been called to do pointless killing in Vietnam and they could see no reason to stay a day longer there. They wanted out now – and any voices calling for any other approach to the problem they were willing to turn out in huge numbers to protest, shout down, and confront violently if need be.

Being able to pull any kind of success out of the Vietnam misadventure would not be easy. But Nixon – who had promised America to "bring the boys home" – would attempt to effect an American departure – yet at the same time leave behind some kind of pro-American legacy. His goal was to force North Vietnam to back away from its support of the South Vietnamese Viet Cong guerrilla fighters – and get Russia and China to back away from their support of North Vietnam – so as to make it more likely that North Vietnam would have to yield to Nixon's game plan.

But first he would have to make it clear that although America would be transferring ground operations over to the South Vietnamese military (the "Vietnamization" of the war), he would continue to offer American air cover – a strategy in which America would hold a distinct advantage over its Vietnamese adversaries. The Viet Cong had used non-uniformed guerrilla fighters in opposing clearly-identified American troops to great military advantage. But America had its own realm of distinct military advantage: air power. And, as a political Realist, Nixon intended to go at the Vietnam challenge using fully that distinct advantage. Thus he immediately ordered a new round of B-52 bombing raids in Vietnam – in anticipation of the withdrawal of 60,000 troops scheduled to take place by the end of that first year (1969) – the first round in the withdrawal of the 550,000 American troops stationed in Vietnam. The plan was for a 15-step troop withdrawal, to be completed by the end of 1972.

But there was still ground-laying to be done in Vietnam at the same time. Peace negotiations between North and South Vietnam had long been dragging on in Paris – a nervous South Vietnam facing a still aggressive North Vietnam. Nixon decided to act – in order to strengthen the position both on the ground and at the peace table by ordering a withering assault (April 1970) on the Ho Chi Minh trail – a military supply route running just inside the Cambodian border next to South Vietnam by which the North brought tons of military supplies south to the Viet Cong. This was something that Johnson had avoided doing, supposedly so as not to drag a neutral Cambodia into the conflict. But Nixon was not slowed up by the fiction of Cambodian neutrality. In any case, the assault was highly successful – and crippled rather severely the Viet Cong effort in the South.

Kent State Massacre (May 1970). Of course to the Boomer crusaders, such strategic matters were of no great interest, or anyway beyond their political comprehension as crusading Idealists. Boomer protests broke out all over the country against Nixon's "expansion" of the war effort in response to this actually quite carefully limited raid into supposedly neutral Cambodia.

Such "Fascist Imperialism" was exactly the enemy that Students for a Democratic Society (SDS) leaders needed to energize their movement – and focus was turned on the campus of Kent State University, where the SDS organized a huge protest, including the burning to the ground of the Reserve Officer Training Corps (ROTC) building on campus. However two days later, when the SDS leaders called for yet a wider protest on the central campus, protesters now found themselves faced by the Ohio National Guard – which had been called out to protect the campus from just such protests. Shots suddenly rang out, and four students were killed and nine wounded – some protesters, some just observers of the event and some just students crossing campus to get to another class. A major tragedy, one that would shake the nation, had just taken place: the Kent State Massacre.

Vietnam Veterans against the War. Even though the American military draw-down in Vietnam was continuing on schedule, it would never be fast enough for some Americans – and in April of 1971 Vietnam Veterans gathered in Washington to protest the war, some even standing on the U.S. Capitol steps and throwing away their military medals as a sign of their disgust at the continuation of the war.

They also were invited to speak before a Democratic Party controlled Congress about their concerns – most notably a young (27) Lieutenant John Kerry, who was brought in by Senator Kennedy to describe the shocking behavior of fellow soldiers in Vietnam – and the depravity of American officers who covered up – even supported – such behavior:

> ... *not isolated incidents but crimes committed on a day to day basis with the full awareness of officers at all levels of command.*

Kerry spared no detail in describing the gruesome behavior – which he personally did not actually witness (he served in Vietnam only four months), which under American law therefore made his testimony mere hearsay:

> *They told the stories at times they had personally raped, cut off ears, cut off heads, taped wires from portable telephones to human genitals and turned up the power, cut off limbs, blown up bodies, randomly shot at civilians, razed villages in fashion reminiscent of Genghis Khan, shot cattle and dogs for fun, poisoned food stocks, and generally ravaged the countryside of South Vietnam in addition to the normal ravage of war, and the normal and very particular ravaging which is done by the applied bombing power of this country.*

This act of "shaming"* his fellow soldiers would not only bring considerable

---

*The "shaming" of America became for the Boomers (and their offspring) a kind of ideological vaccination supposedly protecting them from falling victim to the Fascist disease of patriotism – a disease supposedly rampant among their Vet parents. Being visibly anti-patriotic or as Boomers termed the matter, anti-Fascist – for patriotism and Fascism were the same thing in the Boomer lexicon – Boomers participated eagerly in protest marches, the burning of flags, even the burning down of ROTC buildings, for instance. To them, participation in such group action was a popular way of evidencing just such immunity to "blind

public attention to Kerry but open his way eventually to service as Massachusetts Lieutenant Governor (1983-1985), following that as U.S. Senator (representing Massachusetts, alongside Kennedy), and finally even the Democratic Party presidential candidate in 2004. However the last achievement would be undercut greatly when a number of men who had served in Vietnam came out in protest against Kerry's own service medals, claiming that some were most undeserved – damaging considerably the Kerry campaign. But Kerry would make a grand political comeback when President Obama appointed Kerry as his Secretary of State (during Obama's second presidential term, 2013 through 2016). Such are the enormous social rewards that come from the simple anti-Fascist act of shaming America.

The Pentagon Papers. Another event that same year (1971) pointed to the passion rather than the logic behind the forces working against the President – even as Nixon continued to follow his program of strategic withdrawal from Vietnam. In June *The New York Times* published a long series of full-length articles revealing a secret document (which became known as *The Pentagon Papers*) that had been put together in 1967 at the request of Johnson's Secretary of Defense Robert McNamara – who simply wanted to know the details of exactly how America fell into the Vietnam crisis in the first place. The published document revealed the deception Johnson had engineered – particularly in his manipulating the Gulf of Tonkin incident in order to march Congress and the American people off to a war in Vietnam that Johnson wanted badly (basically to prove himself to be a stronger foreign policy president than Kennedy had been). It also revealed the hand that President Kennedy had in the assassination of South Vietnamese President Diem in 1963.

The nation was shocked – angered actually – by the knowledge that American presidents had played the American people so deceptively – especially Johnson. But oddly enough, the anger – which should have fallen largely on Johnson – was instead cleverly redirected by Nixon's enemies at Nixon himself, who actually had no part whatsoever in the Vietnam deception. Democrats did not bother to point out that most of this scandal was a result of the (bad) political choices of the two previous Democratic presidents, but instead stressed the point that such behavior was a natural outflow of the office of the presidency itself, an office which

---

patriotism" – of manifesting a high degree of personal nobility. Thus Kerry's shaming of his fellow soldiers before Congress stood him out as a person of enormous integrity and nobility. That's how things worked in those days (and generally since then): to be able to shame America in some form or fashion automatically elevated a person to political sainthood.

The 1970s: America Divided

had become intoxicated with its political powers. Thus to the Liberals of the Democratic Party – and its followers in the world of media, higher education, and bureaucratic professionalism – The *Pentagon Papers* clearly underscored the grave dangers to American democracy and American personal liberties posed by the "imperial presidency" – which Nixon clearly exemplified. Certainly therefore, America needed to do something to curb such presidential imperialism – meaning, the ability of Nixon to effectively conduct the office of U.S. presidency. Presidential power needed to be trimmed back – drastically.

Détente – and the full withdrawal of American troops from Vietnam.
Meanwhile, Nixon had been delivering on his promise to pull U.S. troops from Vietnam. By the spring of 1972 he had reduced the number of troops there to only 6,000 – most of these now serving simply as advisors to the South Vietnamese army.

But he had also been busy on the larger world stage – working to improve East-West relations – but also with an eye on helping smooth America's exit from Vietnam. He had sent Kissinger off to China to explore the possibilities of improved Chinese-American relations – a diplomatic initiative helped by the fact that Chairman Mao had been moderated greatly in his political behavior by the grand failure of his Cultural Revolution – allowing the more sensible Chinese Foreign Minister Chou En-lai (Zhou Enlai) to take a stronger hand in shaping Chinese foreign policy. And having once been the militant anti-Communist congressman (in the late 1940s) no one could fault Nixon as being soft on Communism. And thus it was that in February of 1972 Nixon himself flew to China to follow up on the program of improving relations with China. The 25-year American boycott of mainland China had come to an end.

But at the same time Nixon took the same diplomatic line toward Soviet Russia – just three months later (May 1972) flying to Moscow to open talks with Soviet Premier Brezhnev about the possibility of working together to bring the arms race under some kind of control. The reception in Moscow was highly positive.

Actually, Nixon and Kissinger were playing the Realpolitik game – playing to the weaknesses of their Cold War adversaries – knowing full well that China and Russia, though both being Communist nations, were bitter rivals on the stage of world diplomacy. Cutting back on the tensions (popularly termed a *détente**) between America and these two nations would strengthen both Russia's and China's hand in their mutual rivalry. But this assist from America would come at a cost: Nixon intended to link

---

*The French word *détente*, means a relaxing or backing down.

(the policy of "linkage") these improved East-West relations with some kind of understanding that America now expected both countries to back away from their support of Nixon's adversaries in North Vietnam.

Nixon's re-election (November 1972). For the upcoming national elections, the Democratic Party had nominated the professorial senator from North Dakota, George McGovern – loved passionately by the Boomer youth who saw him as crusading hero against the vile Vietnam policy of Richard Nixon (McGovern had in 1970 and 1971 sponsored congressional legislation calling for an immediate termination of all American involvement in Vietnam). However by 1972 the American voters – still largely drawn from the Vet Middle Class – saw Nixon, not McGovern as the true American hero, and in the November election returned Nixon to the White House with the fourth largest majority of all presidential elections.* The Boomers (and their intellectual mentors) were humiliated. Middle America (termed by Nixon as the "Silent Majority") was jubilant.

But all that pro-Nixon enthusiasm did not however alter the makeup of Congress itself – with both the House and Senate remaining under a Democratic Party majority and thus control. Consequently, the battle lines between the Republican White House and the Democratic Congress would merely harden because of the 1972 national elections.

The 1973 Paris Peace Accords. With support for his presidency thus confirmed by the November elections – and some kind of understanding worked out with the Russians and Chinese – Nixon now moved more boldly to bring some kind of acceptable conclusion to the long and painful Vietnam episode. The peace discussions between the North and South Vietnamese representatives meeting in Paris had dragged on long enough – with neither side willing to move to an agreement. Nixon decided it was time to break the stalemate – and proceeded to show a doubting South Vietnam and a sneering North Vietnam that he was serious when he had stated that although American military presence on the ground was coming to a close, America's interest in protecting South Vietnam's integrity through the use of American air power was not. During the next month after the elections, Nixon directed a massive air assault on Vietnam's capital at Hanoi and its major port city of Haiphong. This time the Vietnamese got the message – and in January (1973) both sides came to an agreement about the sovereign rights of each other's government – under the understanding

---

*Nixon received 60.7% and McGovern 37.5% of the popular vote; the electoral college vote went 520 votes for Nixon against a mere 17 votes (14 from the very Liberal Massachusetts and 3 from equally Liberal Washington, D.C.) for McGovern.

The 1970s: America Divided

that America intended fully to enforce the agreement with its own air power if that sovereignty were violated.

While Nixon's enforced peace in Vietnam made great sense in terms of international Realpolitik, it was a policy greatly weakened by one key fact: the Democrats in Congress were in no mood to support Nixon's success in any field of endeavor – and would do everything in their power to embarrass and handicap Nixon's ability to conduct "imperialistic" American foreign policy. This would soon become quite apparent.

* * *

NIXON'S CHAOTIC SECOND PRESIDENTIAL TERM

Watergate: "Dirty tricks." An event that occurred during the summer's presidential election campaign would provide exactly the opportunity to undo the results of the election that had just delivered the humiliating defeat to the Democratic Party in its attempts to capture the presidency. Fairly high-level staff members of Nixon's re-election committee decided it would be a cool (and quite unnecessary)* trick to raid the Democratic Party offices in the Watergate apartment complex in order to plant listening devices – sadly rather typical of the "dirty tricks" that go on with political campaigns. Except that their prank got detected by Watergate security police – and a number of these pranksters were caught and arrested.

Woodward and Bernstein. This event would likely have gone largely unnoticed, except that two young crusading journalists of *The Washington Post*, Bob Woodward and Carl Bernstein, saw a headliner story in this event,

---

*The polls made it quite clear that Nixon was running well ahead of McGovern in the race for the presidency. However, the break-in was perhaps motivated by the hope of finding precise information about Democratic National Chairman Larry O'Brien's connections (if there actually were any) with the incredibly wealthy but highly secretive Howard Hughes. It seems that the Democrats had been feeding information to Nixon through his rather improvident brother Donald that Nixon was going to lose the 1972 campaign because O'Brien had damaging information about Nixon given him by Hughes – including evidence that the gift of $205,000 from Hughes back in 1957 to rescue Donald's failing restaurant business was actually given as a political favor for then Vice President Nixon. Such information – true or not true – would have damaged the 1972 Nixon campaign tremendously. However, the whole thing was likely a hoax. But this was the kind of misinformation that the Democrats were possibly hoping would put Nixon in a self-destructive frenzy. Unfortunately, it was not untypical of the kind of antics that go on in races for political office. But in any case, it did succeed after all (quite ironically) if this is what got the Nixon team to attempt the disastrous Watergate stunt.

one that might reach all the way up to the president himself. And with some inside help from an FBI informant, they began to develop the story into a full-blown presidential scandal.

Congress goes to war. With the beginning of the trials of the culprits in January of 1973, the call went out for a complete Congressional investigation into the affair. Kennedy sponsored a resolution calling for the creation of a select committee of four Democrats and three Republicans to undertake a full investigation of Nixon's re-election committee. Senator Sam Erwin, rather than Kennedy, would however head up this committee – as Kennedy's moral credentials were not themselves all that great – and he had ambitions to run for the 1976 presidential race and did not want the committee to look like it was part of his personal electoral strategy.

Actually, of course, as with everything that goes on in Washington, this was all indeed pure politics. Although Nixon was likely not originally part of the Watergate prank, the committee was hunting for something, anything, that would lead directly to a Nixon involvement that they could then bring him down with.

Nixon paranoia. Nixon did not help his own case – paranoia in dealing with the Democratic Congress and an equally hostile and aggressive press having completely overtaken Nixon at this point. At first Nixon tried to head off the investigation – the very thing that the Democrats would be looking for in their efforts to find impeachable "high crimes and misdemeanors" on the part of the president. Then (April 1973) he fired a number of his staff – merely further conveying the image to the press of Nixon conducting a cover-up.

John Dean. At the same time, Nixon's young Legal Counsel, John Dean, decided at this point that it was wise to switch sides in this political contest and offer himself as a witness before Congress (June 1973) to Nixon's attempted cover-up of the criminal investigation. Dean did not have any actual evidence to offer, other than the assurance that Nixon certainly knew about the Watergate coverup and also tried himself to keep things hidden away. And he suspected that there was taped evidence that would corroborate his story.

Dean was describing a series of taped recordings that Nixon had been making over the years of White House operations – with the intent of eventually using those tapes to help him write and publish his memoirs. Congress wanted to get their hands on those tapes – in order to find actual evidence of an attempted coverup of the investigation. A battle over the tapes ensued.

The "Saturday Night Massacre." Attorney General Elliot Richardson had earlier, in May – in agreement with the House Judiciary Committee – appointed Archibald Cox to look into the Watergate affair. Understandably tensions in the White House grew over Cox's wide-ranging investigation, when it became apparent that Cox was clearly also looking for broader instances of corruption in Nixon's Administration (even the president himself), and was particularly interested in getting his hands on Nixon's tapes. When Cox finally insisted that Nixon had to turn over taped copies of his White House conversations, Nixon refused, offering instead to turn them over to Senator John Stennis to review and summarize. But Cox refused the "compromise." Thus on the night of October 19th, Nixon at that point demanded that Richardson fire Cox. But Richardson refused, and instead resigned. The same would also hold true that same night with Deputy Attorney General William Ruckelshaus – who also resigned rather than carry out the Nixon request. Finally the matter fell to Solicitor General Robert Bork, who complied with the order, firing Cox, though Bork would fairly quickly appoint Leon Jaworski to fill Cox's position.

This event finally began to swing American public opinion in favor of impeaching the president.* But even more importantly, it finally gave the House of Representatives justification for undertaking the process of impeachment when Nixon refused to comply with a congressional subpoena to turn over those tapes.

Vice President Agnew. Then as things seemed to Nixon that they could not possibly grow worse, the Department of Justice came out with an announcement that it was investigating Vice President Agnew for having taken large bribes for government contracts. In October Agnew resigned – and Nixon appointed the popular Michigan Congressman Gerald Ford to replace him. The next month Congress gave a strong vote of confirmation to the widely-admired Ford.

The Arab-Israeli Yom Kippur or October War of 1973. In the midst of all of this turmoil, the world was shocked to hear that on October 6th, the Egyptian Army crossed the Suez Canal to attack Israeli forces holding the East bank of the Canal. Another Arab-Israeli war was underway.

Egyptian President Anwar as-Sadat was hoping to draw the larger world into the Egyptian standoff with the Israelis – because despite the United Nations Resolution 242 calling for Israel to return to its 1967 boundaries, the Israelis had refused to move from their position at the Canal – or for

---

*However, only slightly at the time, with now 44% in favor of impeachment versus 43% opposed, and 13% still undecided.

that matter their control of Syria's Golan Heights or the Palestinian West Bank region. The Israeli explanation was that they would not move until the other part of the Resolution – Arab recognition of Israel's right to exist within certain defined borders – had taken place. No such recognition had been forthcoming from the Arabs. So Israel was not moving.

In the years since the 1967 war, Egyptian President Nasser had died (1970), Sadat had taken the presidency and – with considerable Soviet help – had upgraded the Egyptian military defenses (air and ground) quite considerably. But Sadat's loyalty to the Soviets was rather limited. And he was willing to play a round or two of the Realpolitik game himself – forcing some 20,000 Soviet advisors out of Egypt in July of 1972 in order to keep a free hand in his own doings. He then undertook the holding of huge military exercises – which put the Israelis on edge wondering if Sadat was about to start something. Apparently he was not, and everyone backed down.

But this time, October 6th, he was not just conducting an exercise. It was an actual attack – and timed for the Jewish celebration of Yom Kippur – when the Jews would be more focused on religious celebrations than war (but oddly enough it was also the beginning of Ramadan, the Muslims' month of fasting). At first the Egyptians made huge advances against the Israelis. But the war was costly to both sides. Both sides were losing jet planes, tanks, trucks and soldiers rapidly – and began to look to their military suppliers for help: Israel to America and Egypt to Soviet Russia.
Syria and Jordan joined the conflict, and Israel turned its attention to these less prepared foes – humiliating both countries with swift Israeli counteraction. Then the Israelis began a strong counteroffensive against the Egyptians.

At this point the Arab oil-exporting countries jumped into action – especially when Nixon went to Congress with a request for $2.2 billion in aid to Israel. The Arabs now moved to impose an immediate slowdown in oil sales – putting America's allies in Europe in a very tight spot – but also putting the squeeze on America's energy supplies as well. Very quickly the price of gasoline at the pump went up and up (fourfold), when it was even available.

This in turn brought the United Nations into action, with both America and Russia agreeing to terms for a cease fire – which Israel ignored in its effort to surround and crush the Egyptian Third Army. At this point the Russians threatened to intervene directly if the Israelis did not back down. Thus something of a cease fire came into effect. The war was (more or less) over.

In the end, the real benefactors of this event were the Arab oil exporters – who now found their small populations among the richest in the world. This would work to the great benefit of the regimes governing

The 1970s: America Divided 347

these societies – mostly. But one country that would actually find itself in trouble because of this sudden wealth was Iran. Eventually this would be a key factor bringing down America's most important ally in the Muslim East, the Shah of Iran.

Congress takes over American foreign policy. Meanwhile, Congress was busy attempting to undo the Nixon legacy in American foreign policy – by curtailing the "imperialistic" powers of the American presidency – and restoring American "democracy" by placing foreign policy activity fully in the hands of the Democratic-Party-controlled Congress. In June of 1973 Congress passed the Case-Church Amendment to the government budget bill, preventing the president from providing any kind of direct military aid to Vietnam – aimed particularly at Nixon's use of the threat of air attack to make the North Vietnamese respect the Paris Peace Accords protecting the sovereignty of the South Vietnamese society and government.

Then just to make matters even worse for America's friends in South Vietnam, the following May (1974) Congress turned down a Nixon request for a small amount of additional funding for South Vietnam – to carry that country until June when a new round of funding (supposedly) would be forthcoming. With the huge price hike in energy costs, the South Vietnamese government had run out of money to buy fuel for its military. But Congress gave Nixon (and Vietnam) a flat "no" as its answer to this request. And worse, it announced that as of 1976, South Vietnam would receive no further financial support from America!

What was Congress's thinking on this matter? It already had Nixon pinned against the wall. Russia was still giving serious financial and military backing to North Vietnam. Why would Congress desert America's allies in South Vietnam? What was to be gained by this "anti-imperialist" move?

Obviously Nixon, not the Vietnamese themselves, was the target of this move by Congress. But it would be the Vietnamese who would ultimately pay for this piece of incredibly poor and politically-blinded policy, pay dearly.

Stripping the president of his discretionary spending powers. Much to the annoyance of Congress, Nixon had pledged to cut back on government spending – and was simply refusing to release funding for various programs and projects approved by Congress (to the tune of some $12 billion). But many of these programs were pet programs of Congressional legislators, ones that they liked to remind folks at home about at election time, jobs for the many and favors for the special few that were considered absolutely necessary in order for these Congressmen to remain in office in Washington. Nixon's crippling of this game infuriated them, of course.

Thus in July Congress put into effect the 1974 Congressional Budget and Impoundment Control Act – which required Congress to approve any desire of the president to hold off spending for any part of the national budget. In this they stripped presidential powers that reached all the way back to 1801 during Jefferson's presidency – this too done in the name of promoting democracy.

In addition, Congress set up the Congressional Budget Office (CBO) specifically to see that the president was actually spending the money as Congress directed. But what they inadvertently had done was to set up a budgetary enforcing agency that would end up being just as interested in the curious ways the Congressmen themselves might be using their fiscal powers. Thus Congress's favorite system of political rewards – the "pork barrel" system – found itself as well under detailed scrutiny! Ooops!

Watergate finally brings Nixon to resign (August 1974). During all this time, the Watergate battle continued to focus on Nixon's White House tapes. But the nation was also following closely the trials of the "Watergate burglars" presided over by Washington, D.C. District Court Judge John Sirica, who used his own legal authority to subpoena those tapes. Thus some of the tapes were turned over. It was at this point (November) that it was discovered that some 18 minutes on one of the tapes was missing, blanked out by some unknown source. That in itself fueled even more speculative fire.

Meanwhile Congress (and the press) pushed ahead with its own investigation, in April (1974) subpoenaing those tapes, all of them. Nixon ultimately offered Congress 1200 pages of edited transcripts of those tapes. But this hardly satisfied his accusers. When Nixon again refused to turn the tapes over, Jaworski turned to the Supreme Court, which finally on July 24th (1974) in an 8-0 decision ruled against Nixon's claim that he had executive privilege allowing him to keep those tapes personal and private.

Thus the full array of tapes were finally released on August 5th. And yes, one tape in particular pointed to a discussion that Nixon had with his Chief of Staff H.R. Haldeman soon after the Watergate event – concerning what it was that they needed to do to make a potential scandal go away. With that disclosure Nixon lost all ability to defend himself.

Republicans in Congress were now panicking. Watergate – and just the general political tenor in Washington – had destroyed not only Nixon, but was also undermining the Republican Party's chance of any kind of good results in the Congressional elections coming up that November (indeed, the Republicans would take a big hit that fall). It was quite obvious that Nixon was not going to be able to avoid impeachment by the House. And enough Republicans were considering switching sides so that it appeared most likely that the Senate would find the 2/3rds vote needed to convict. Thus Republican advisors pleaded with Nixon simply to step down.

This he did in going before TV cameras on August 8th.

* * *

THE BRIEF FORD PRESIDENCY (1974-1977)

Thus as Nixon bade farewell, Vice President Gerald Ford took over the U.S. presidency. Ford would be greatly handicapped as president (which was just fine with Congress) – never actually having gone before the American voter to achieve his presidential position. However, it would turn out to be a huge blessing to America that the individual left with the responsibility of getting America past this huge mess was an all-around "good guy," able to pull off one of the greatest feats in American political history, which is to get both his Democrat and Republican colleagues in Congress to like and respect him deeply, at least up to this point.

Ford issues a presidential pardon for Nixon. Certainly the most important task facing Ford as he took office was bringing America past this one issue that had the country so divided that politically speaking it could do nothing to help the nation itself or the surrounding world. Thus after a month of pondering the matter, and then a Sunday morning of worship – and of much prayer on the matter – Ford announced to the press that he was extending a presidential pardon to Nixon. This would exempt Nixon from all charges, all efforts of the those eager to continue their crusade to destroy the imperial president, the evil Richard Nixon.

The Democrats (and some Republicans) were furious. They wanted "social justice" (revenge), not pardon. But there was little they could do at that point. Ford had just taken out of their hands a key political weapon – an extensively dragged-out show trial – that they were counting on to destroy not only Nixon (they wanted him behind bars), but the Republican Party in general, in anticipation of the coming November 1974 elections.

But for the well-being of the country, this was absolutely the right decision. And Ford was able to take this stand because he was a Christian, answering to God first and foremost, and not America's "peace and social justice" warriors. It would cost Ford dearly, to save America from itself. But he did, and America moved forward, amazingly quickly afterwards.*

---

*Forgiveness always comes at a huge price, one that human pride finds very difficult to muster. The human ego instinctively prefers revenge – and has well-developed means by which to rationalize or justify that burning desire. That's why we hire lawyers: to achieve "justice." But forgiveness is the most important of all Christian virtues, powerful in the way it restores broken life, which "justice" seldom achieves. For instance, it was Truman's willingness to

Moral recovery. It had to have inspired Graham and others who had put so much trust in Nixon, and felt so deeply betrayed by Watergate. But ultimately Graham and some others moved on, even rebuilt a relationship with the disgraced former president, and Nixon himself moved on, actually to serve as wise counsel to future presidents and political officials. The social justice warriors, of course, never forgave Nixon, and were able to write that unforgiveness into their history books, even elementary and high school textbooks, ones that would remember Nixon only as that evil president.

But didn't the social justice warriors forgive Ted Kennedy for Chappaquiddick? No, not really. They just simply put it out of their minds and thus avoided having to pay some kind of personal price in the matter. It was simply as if the event never actually happened. That's not forgiveness. That's politics.

Horrifying collapse in Southeast Asia. In the meantime, the situation in South Vietnam was worsening drastically. In early 1975 panic set in among the South Vietnamese soldiers who now saw their cause as lost without further American aid. And at the end of April the world was treated to the spectacle of the last of the American diplomatic mission beating a cowardly retreat from Saigon – with loyal Vietnamese civilians hanging on to the American helicopters in an effort to get out of the country with them. The Communists had completely routed the mighty America in Vietnam. But this also meant that the political status quo in the entire region of Southeast Asia was going to suffer a huge shift.

The Communist "re-education" camps. Now the Communist victors in the South began to march multitudes (possibly as many as a million) of Vietnamese off to "re-education" camps – to cleanse them of the "capitalist" ways they might have picked up in those years working with the Americans. Conditions in these camps were so terrible that huge numbers of them died. And then to make the situation even worse, the new regime seized the small independent farms and local businesses in order to collectivize or bring them under full governmental control – thus crippling further the economy – to the point of human disaster.

---

quickly forgive America's former enemies Japan and Germany that allowed America to bring true peace to a European continent (at least the Western portion) that had known only bitter nationalist rivalry since the beginning of the 20th century, and also Truman's willingness to work with former adversary, Yugoslavian Communist President Tito, that enabled Europe also to keep the Mediterranean realm from being dragged into Stalin's Empire. Forgiveness is a powerful social as well as personal instrument.

The Vietnamese "boat people." Consequently, millions of Vietnamese attempted to flee the country – by any means possible. Some fled across the countryside in an attempt to reach Thailand or Malaysia. Others took to boats – or anything that would float – in the hopes of being picked up by passing Western commercial freighters and thus brought to freedom in the West. Multitudes simply drowned. Many were picked up by pirates and raped and killed or sold into slavery. Even then, if they were somehow able to reach foreign lands in the area (the Philippines, Malaysia, Thailand) they would spend months, even years, waiting to receive refugee status in the West. But ultimately, America took in 800,000 of these refugees – and another 250,000 were settled in Europe or England's Commonwealth countries.

The "Killing Fields" of Cambodia. One place the Vietnamese were not headed for in their escape from Vietnam was next door in Cambodia – for there the situation turned even uglier than was even the case for poor Vietnam. With the withdrawal of the American presence in Vietnam, Communists were also emboldened to end the fiction of Cambodian neutrality and simply take over the country. But this was a different group of Communists – not of the North Vietnamese type – who mostly took their ideological cues from Russia. These were Maoists, termed the "Khmer Rouge"* under their leader Pol Pot, taking their cues from the zany Mao Zedong – who, like him, held some kind of romantic view about the purity of rural life in contrast to the corruptions of urban life (supposedly too Western or capitalist in style). Urban Cambodia thus had to be purged of this evil – with those who had come under its influence either marched off to re-education camps of the Maoist variety – or simply executed on the spot. No one was keeping population statistics at the time – but the best estimates run in the range of 1.5 to 2 million Cambodians died from either execution or exhaustion/starvation – this holocaust discovered when multitudes of "killing fields" of thousands of skeletal remains were later uncovered – discovered when the Vietnamese Communists next door finally sent troops into Communist Cambodia to end the slaughter.†

---

*The French name of the group comes from the fact that a number of the leaders of the Khmer Rouge were Paris-educated intellectuals of the worst kind with their pure and unyielding idealism, idealism that turned them into moral monsters.

†Although both Vietnam and Cambodia were officially Communist as of 1975, the two countries practiced very different forms of "Communism" (actually just ethnic nationalism) and found themselves in conflict along their mutual borders from 1975 onward – with the Cambodian Khmer Rouge actually undertaking several direct attacks on Vietnamese territory. Finally in late December 1978,

The American Bi-Centennial (1976). The year 1976 was supposed to be a year of celebration – for it marked the 200th anniversary of the signing of the *Declaration of Independence* – considered by most Americans as the birth date of the American nation. But there was very little to cheer about. Officially, America put on a happy face. But the spirit behind that face was lacking. Fireworks and grand ceremonies tried to mark the importance of the occasion. But actually, America was feeling low – very low.

✱ ✱ ✱

THE CARTER ONE-TERM PRESIDENCY

The national elections of 1976. The gravely wounded Republican Party decided to stay with Ford as its candidate – despite a strong run at the candidacy by California actor and former governor (1967-1975) Ronald Reagan. The Democrats, however, had no strong front-runner. Kennedy would have been the most logical choice, given the power that the Kennedy name seemed to have among the Democrats. But Chappaquiddick was still too fresh a memory – and would certainly have been brought up as a campaign issue by the Republicans.*

Carter proposes a foreign policy of "morality." The Democratic Party finally nominated as its presidential candidate the one-term former Governor of Georgia (but also the Campaign Chairman of the Democratic National Committee), Jimmy Carter. Outside the inner circle of the Democratic National Committee, he was largely unknown – thus having the appeal of not being a Washington insider – a blessing in the eyes of many Americans. Also, it was hard to fault his record – as he had none foreign policy-wise and very little domestically.

In his public presentations and in the presidential debates with Ford, Carter stressed how it was time for America to find its way back to serving a more moral purpose in the world of domestic and foreign policy. America had too long supported dictators, had conducted foreign policy away from the view of the American people, and was way too reactive in the field of foreign affairs – causing America a huge loss of global respect generally

---

the Communist Vietnamese invaded Communist Cambodia and overthrew the Khmer Rouge government, placing in power a pro-Vietnamese government in the Cambodian capital, Phnom Penh. This finally brought the massacre of the Cambodian population to an end.

*Chappaquiddick somehow never seemed to bother the good people of Massachusetts, who were perhaps a more "forgiving"(or "forgetting") people, especially when it came to the doings of the Kennedys.

The 1970s: America Divided 353

– and in the United Nations in particular. America would do much better presenting a more moral, a more democratic face to the world than had been all too much the case recently. Carter pointed specifically to the Park Chung-hee dictatorship in South Korea – and indicated that he would pull American troops out of Korea if South Korea were not redirected to a more democratic political profile. He mentioned other dictators as well that America had been wrongly supporting (specifically Latin American) – leaving Americans wondering what he would do about all the dictators of the Muslim Middle East – for the region knew no other form of government. Would America also be pulling its support away, for instance, from the Shah of Iran – famous for imprisoning political opponents?

The November election was a very close one, with Ford coming from way behind at the beginning of the contest but moving up quickly on Carter as the election approached. But in the end Carter won with 50.1% of the popular vote to Ford's 48.0% and 297 electoral votes to Ford's 240 electoral votes (the solid support of the American South was a big factor in Carter's win).

James Earl Carter. Carter was born in 1924 to a very non-conformist Plains, Georgia, family, especially with his mother as a very independent-minded political Liberal. From an early age, Carter dreamed of gaining entrance into the U.S. Naval Academy, but had to start his college career in local community colleges, at least for a couple of years before finally being admitted to the Academy. He performed well, and became a nuclear engineer serving in the navy's submarines in the immediate post-World-War-Two era. But in 1953 he would leave the service to return to Plains to take over the family farm when his father died.

But national military service had stirred his interest in political service, and in 1962 he was finally able to run and win a seat in the Georgia State Senate. Then four years later he took on the race for the Georgia governorship, losing out to the arch-segregationist Lester Maddox in the Democratic Party primaries.

This threw his political ambitions into confusion, but at the same time stirred a very strong interest in going deeper in his Christian faith and calling. With the help of his evangelist sister, Ruth Carter Stapleton, he went through another "born again" experience, and then headed North (Pennsylvania and Massachusetts) to do some door-to-door evangelistic work himself, particularly among some poorer Hispanic communities there.

But he eventually returned to Georgia, to take on another run at the governorship (1970). This time he hid his Liberal orientation and let the press speculate on the matter, saying nothing when even the Atlanta media accused him of being a segregationist – when he refused to announce his stand on the race issue. This tactic worked, and in November he was elected governor of the state of Georgia.

And weren't the Georgians surprised when it turned out that he was not at all the segregationist they believed him to be. In fact he was quite the opposite! But he also pushed other political items strongly besides racial equality and aid to the poor: educational reform, governmental restructuring and environmental protection, reflections of his own tendency as an engineer to want to see a high degree of order brought to the state's social activities.

But as his term as governor was limited by Georgia law to a single term, he soon began to look to larger political fields to cultivate. He made no particular impression at the 1972 Democratic Party National Convention. But the next year he did succeed in getting himself appointed to Rockefeller's newly created (and quite prestigious) Trilateral Commission, designed to bring Japan, Western Europe and North America into closer cooperation on a number of fronts. This brought him the notice that he needed to move forward with his plans and dreams. Thus the year after that (1974), he was asked by Democratic Party national chairman Robert Strauss to head up the party's campaign committee, monitoring the 1974 mid-term elections. This of course made him a very familiar figure to a large number of party members. And then when in 1976 he took an early lead in both the New Hampshire and Iowa caucuses, he became quite the political topic. Who was this rising figure from Georgia? There seemed to be almost something magical about his strong political rise.

There was, however, also some concern about his "born again" Christian character, like Kennedy's Catholicism, something that made others (such as the very secular press) rather nervous. But like Kennedy, Carter made it clear that his strong personal faith had nothing to do with the way he intended to approach the very technical issues of environment, health care, education, foreign policy, etc. Those were matters of state, not religion.

Anyway, he gained the party's presidential nomination, and then went on to defeat Ford in that close election.

As president, he stayed away from the topic of religion, although he had made his understanding of the moral principles he intended to follow as president quite clear, basing these however on the peace and social justice norms familiar to the Secular world. He also tried to run a tight ship in terms of administrative discipline, actually a bit too involved directly in administrative details that should have been assigned to staff. But that was the perfectionist engineer in him showing itself.

Nonetheless, despite his promise to keep religion out of his presidential responsibilities (even Billy Graham was rarely seen at the White House),

The 1970s: America Divided 355

private Bible study and Christian spiritual reflection would be a strong part of the Carter presidency, all the way to the end of his four-year presidency. And if nothing else, this certainly helped introduce the nation to the idea of the more evangelical, born-again side of the Christian faith (which was also being pushed forward by the growing charismatic movement of the 1970s and after).

The Panama Canal. Early on as president, a decision of Carter's to offer the Panamanians full possession of the Panama Canal brought bewilderment to Americans – as Carter met with Panamanian military dictator, General Omar Torrijos, to consummate the deal. Where did Carter's scruples about not working with dictators go? And why was Carter giving up such a valuable American asset? Panama as a nation was originally a fiction of American creation, America had paid dearly in dollars and human effort (and loss) in building that canal, and the canal was a strategic necessity in the way it linked America's two sea coasts – and vital to the American navy in its call to protect those coasts.

Supposedly this was done to encourage good-will between America and Latin America. But it merely ended up making America look weak – and in no ways improved the respect or love that the Latin neighbors had for America.

South Korea. Carter also announced a pending withdrawal of American military from South Korea – as he had promised during the campaign. But thankfully some of his own foreign policy team convinced him that this would simply invite another North Korean invasion – and war – similar to what happened in the early 1950s, when America pulled its troops out of South Korea. So Carter backed down on this matter.

Iran. With respect to Shah Mohammed Reza Pahlavi's Iran, here too, Carter's moral-initiative threw confusion into the works. He threatened the Shah with a withdrawal of American support (sale of military items) if the Shah did not undertake a more democratic hand in the governing of Iran. Specifically, he wanted an end to the imprisonment of Iranians (presumably some 3,000 individuals) simply because of their opposition to the Shah's rule. Under such a serious threat, the Shah complied – and released most of these political adversaries.

But again, wise counsel got to Carter – who was reminded about what had been going on in neighboring Afghanistan, when the Shah of Afghanistan was overthrown and a Republic – headed by the Afghan Shah's cousin, Daoud – was declared. The Communists had taken advantage of the chaos – and were a rising threat to the Daoud regime – which put the Soviets in the position to make some very serious trouble in this quite vital part of the world (very close to the Indian Ocean and the path of the West's oil from the oil-rich Persian Gulf region). Iran found itself in a similar situation located where it was (right next to Afghanistan). Carter needed to tread lightly in his "straightening up" of the Shah.

So at the end of 1977, Carter flew off to Europe and India. But that trip included Iran (celebrating New Year's Eve in Tehran) as a demonstration of America's ongoing support of Iran – Carter even publicly praising the Shah's Iran as "an island of stability in one of the more troubled areas of the world."

Understanding that he now had full American support, the Shah moved to arrest again opponents of his regime. But he now found himself facing a new resolve from these opponents – who were able to mobilize street protesters in support of their anti-Shah crusade. Mostly the opponents were young Secularists – indeed looking for an Iranian Republic, and the economic and political advantages they saw in such a republic. But this protest movement also allowed very traditionalist Muslims and their religious leaders to also get into the act – to oppose the Shah's very secular culture itself (proto-Western and pro-American) as the embodiment of pure evil.

Inflation and unemployment. Two major economic factors drove the anger of the protesters. The sudden wealth that had come to Iran as a result of the four-fold increase in oil revenues had the effect of driving the price of available goods also to new heights. But Iranian salaries did not keep up with this increase in consumer prices – angering multitudes of Iranians. For the Iranian farmer, the situation was even worse because the earnings from their harvests were pegged to the price of agricultural products globally (including American agricultural exports) – meaning, they went up barely at all – at the same time that the cost of fuel for their machinery and the cost of their fertilizers rose sharply. In short, the oil bonanza had actually made the Iranian farmer poorer – much poorer.

And there was the problem of the multitudes of young Iranians whose families were able to send them off to study engineering at various universities in the West – thousands of educated young men who subsequently were to discover that Iran's basic oil-driven economy did not need multitudes of engineers. There were no jobs for them as engineers back in Iran.

Mounting protests. Thus it was that the Shah found himself facing mounting bitterness and anger – over matters that he himself had little ability to alter or improve. And prompted by a rising Muslim voice – in particular through the cassettes of sermons sent back from Paris to Iran by the top Muslim cleric, the Ayatollah Ruhollah Khomeini – it seemed clearer and clearer to many Iranians that the Shah had allowed some great evil to come in among the Iranians. And if the Shah was powerless before such evil, then he needed to go.

The Shah flees Iran. As the year 1978 developed, so did the street protests – which by the end of the summer had virtually paralyzed the country – yet somehow grew even worse as the rest of the year unfolded. Finally, the Shah simply fled the country early the next year (mid-January 1979). The streets were immediately filled with cheering crowds at the news of the Shah's departure – for Iran could now move to the status of being a Republic.*

The Islamic Republic. But almost immediately a split began to develop in the anti-Shah ranks – between the modernizing Secularists (Westernized youth) and the arch-traditionalist Muslims, headed up by the Ayatollah Khomeini, who arrived from Paris at the beginning of February – just as the last pro-Shah forces were being crushed. Employing young Muslim zealots (the Revolutionary Guard), the Muslim faction slowly drove the Secular Iranians from power – then suppressed all voices of dissent.

Iran was indeed going to be a Republic – but an Islamic Republic, complete with an elected national Assembly – but presided over ultimately by the Supreme Ruler, the Ayatollah Khomeini.

The Camp David Accords between Egypt and Israel (1978). In November 1977 Egyptian President Sadat surprised the world (including Carter) by flying off to Jerusalem to address the Israeli Knesset about the possibilities of an Egyptian-Israeli peace. Sadat of course had secretly worked out a deal with Israeli Prime Minister Menachem Begin – who was eager to see a split in the Arab ranks (this action would certainly alienate Sadat from the rest of the Arab front) and was willing to negotiate some kind of a deal over Egypt's Sinai Peninsula (still under Israeli occupation) in

---

*Soon after this, I had an Iranian student who had just taken my politics of the Middle East course come to me, all excited about developments in his home country. I didn't want to dampen his enthusiasm. But I did ask him if he was also aware that Muslim traditionalists were just as anxious to gain control over events as were the young Westernized Secularists like himself back in Iran. He hadn't thought of that. A year later he came to me and told me that his parents had written him, and told him to make no plans to return to Iran. Developments back home had turned in a direction under the control of the Muslim hardliners that had made life very dangerous for the Westernized Iranians like themselves. Truly sad.

order to achieve such a political breakthrough.

This move in turn put pressure on Carter to do something to help Sadat bring some kind of fruit from this venture – for all this also put Sadat in trouble with his own people. Thus Carter finally invited both Sadat and Begin to come to the presidential retreat at Camp David (September 1978) – to see what could be worked out. But now Carter put a larger set of interests into the discussions – demanding that the status of the Palestinian lands of the West Bank and the Gaza Strip be included in the deal. Sadat was not all that interested in going beyond retrieving his Sinai territory. But Carter put the pressure on both Sadat and Begin – demanding some kind of reward for the Palestinians as well in the deal. Finally, not wishing to come away empty-handed from the nearly two-weeks-long talks, Begin yielded and agreed on a withdrawal not only from the Sinai but also the Palestinian lands still occupied by the Israelis (Syria's Golan Heights however were left out of the deal).

Even though this finally brought progress in the stalled Israeli-Arab standoff, it would not benefit Sadat very much politically. In fact it would have the opposite result. Egypt was immediately kicked out of the Arab League – and the United Nations announced its deep opposition to the deal – because negotiations had not included the leaders of all the Arab states involved (although such larger involvement would have resulted in a continuing deadlock – in other words, no deal at all). But the Norwegian Nobel Committee was not bothered by this widespread negative reaction – and awarded both Sadat and Begin the 1978 Nobel Peace Prize.*

China. At the same time, China was undergoing deep changes since Mao's death in September of 1976. His domineering wife and three colleagues (the Gang of Four) were arrested, and Deng Xiaoping moved up to take control of China (although Hua Guofeng would serve as the presidential face of China up until 1981). Deng had a very different plan for China than Mao's zany (and lethal) socialism: he wanted to open China up to foreign investment – and full involvement of China in the international marketplace – in order to get China's economy finally up and moving.

Carter certainly wanted to support this new phase and in 1977 sent his National Security Advisor Zbigniew Brzezinski to China to explore the possibilities of upgrading America's Liaison Office (established during Nixon's presidency) to full diplomatic recognition – and exchange of ambassadors. This meant having to agree on the status of Taiwan. Carter subsequently agreed to withdraw all diplomatic recognition (and naval protection) from

---

*Unfortunately, this deal would ultimately cost Sadat his life, when bitter Egyptians assassinated him in 1981 during a military review he was attending.

Taiwan in acknowledging the island's status as merely a part of China. But he did so under the agreement with China that America could continue to trade freely with Taiwan. Thus in January of 1979 Deng flew to Washington to meet with Carter and sign the new diplomatic accords – followed that summer with full diplomatic recognition of Deng's Chinese regime.

Carter and Soviet Premier Brezhnev's SALT II Treaty (1979). At the same time Carter decided to balance his eastward diplomatic offensive by bringing the Soviets into a new arrangement concerning arms limitations. There was growing concern that the SALT (Strategic Arms Limitation Treaty) negotiated in 1972 was not keeping up with the advances in military technology, especially the development of MIRVs – missiles with multiple nuclear warheads – and thus SALT I needed to be upgraded with a SALT II. On the Russians' part, they were also interested in such an agreement, growing nervous about America's new fondness for the Chinese – Russia's major competitor, even opponent. Thus in June of 1979, Carter and Soviet Premier Leonid Brezhnev met in Vienna to sign the new SALT II document.

But Congress balked at the vagueness of the provisions, concerned that the only serious limitations that would come from the treaty would be on the American side. In any case, when then in December the Soviets invaded Afghanistan – even Carter was willing to back away from the agreement. Thus it was never ratified by Congress – although it did remain as something of a diplomatic understanding in continuing Soviet-American talks over the coming years.

Afghanistan. As already mentioned, the Afghan King Zahir Shah had been overthrown in 1973 by his cousin Mohammed Daoud Khan – who attempted to construct something of a modern republic in Afghanistan. At the same time Daoud had attempted to follow a neutral foreign policy in the Cold War – which irritated the Soviets, who considered that part of central Asia standing between themselves and the Indian Ocean as entirely within their sphere of influence (potentially including also Pakistan's largely uninhabited Baluchistan desert along the Indian Ocean just to the south of Afghanistan). Finally, in April of 1978, Communists (under Soviet direction) made their move against Daoud, had him assassinated, and took control of Afghanistan under their leader Nur Mohammad Taraki. Taraki then began to take out anti-Communist (or just Westernized) political opponents, with possibly as many as 27,000 executed over the next year and a half.

But this merely stirred opposition all the more – and a massive rebellion broke out later that same year – involving not only conservative Muslims but also members even of the Afghan army.

Now both the Soviets and the Americans got involved – with Carter sending secret aid to the rebels (not exactly the open diplomacy he promised America!) – and the Soviets having Taraki assassinated (October 1979) and replaced by Hafizullah Amin. But Amin was not servicing Soviet interests adequately either, and the Soviets then had Amin assassinated (December) and replaced by Babrak Karmal – who immediately invited the Soviets to send troops to restore order.

At this point the Soviets were about to discover what Vietnam felt like to the Americans.*

America's further humiliation delivered by Iran. In October of 1979 a very sick Shah of Iran was being considered by Carter for medical treatment in America. When the Iranians got wind of the news, they exploded in anger (or was it just clever manipulation?) and invaded the grounds of the American embassy, seized, bound and blindfolded the staff working there – and paraded them in front of the world's camera – proud to be able to demonstrate such contempt for the American diplomatic staff. And there was no way they were going to release them (except for the Black employees, who were released and sent home).

Finally Carter decided to do something bold – or just desperate – to secure the release of the American captives, when in April of the next year (1980) he sent Special Forces for a surprise raid by night on Tehran to retrieve the 52 Americans being held at the Embassy. But an early landing just inside Iran in preparation for the final assault turned into a disaster when a sandstorm and mechanical failure disabled three helicopters – forcing a cancellation of the operation – but not before another helicopter collided with a C-130 transport plane (killing 8 American troops). Consequently, a very humiliated Carter had to go before the American press to explain the failure of Operation Eagle Claw.

Volcker makes an economic crisis go from bad to terrible. Once again, the world by 1979 was hit with another major energy shortage – and consequent massive rise in energy prices – due to the political chaos in Iran which took Iranian oil out of the global market. Long lines at the gas pumps and inflation everywhere once again afflicted the energy-hungry West – America no less.

Then to make matters worse, the Federal Reserve chief Paul Volcker

---

*Carter ordered the boycott of the Olympic Games held in Moscow in July of 1980 as punishment for the Soviet invasion of Afghanistan. In the end the only ones punished by this decision were the U.S. athletes who had trained for this grand event, but who would now not be participating in the games. Furthermore, when the Olympic Games were held four years later in Los Angeles, the Russians returned the favor by not participating.

got the brainy idea of fighting inflation by driving up the Federal discount rate to 20% – forcing banks, which depended on dollar reserve backing by the Fed, to raise their prime rates offered to their very best industrial/commercial customers at the unheard-of rate of 21.5%.

How Volcker figured this would combat inflation was a mystery – because in order to stay in business, companies now not only had to raise prices to cover their new energy costs – they would have to raise them even more to cover the cost of borrowed capital running at these outrageous interest levels. Thus the only way that Volcker's monetarist policy could have brought down inflation would have been to throw the whole economy into a deep depression – which is exactly what happened. Not only did businesses begin to shut down, but banks financing those businesses soon followed when their customers went bankrupt.

Carter takes the hit. Carter was naturally the target of a very grumpy America – so much so that even "Chappaquiddick Ted" Kennedy decided he had a chance at the Democratic Party nomination – and boldly challenged Carter as an incompetent president. But Volcker intervened and lowered the Fed's discount rate back down again – in time to get the economy back up and moving that summer (1980) – and Carter re-nominated as the Democratic Party presidential candidate. But then Volcker raised the rates back up again (even higher this time) – and threw the economy back into another decline. At that point Carter had virtually no chance of winning the November election.

* * *

THE FRACTURING OF AMERICA'S
TRADITIONAL SOCIAL-MORAL ORDER

The assault on the American family. Since the days of the Puritans, the political foundations of American politics had always been the family – an enormously strong social institution able to carry the heavy responsibilities of truly democratic governance – meaning exactly, governance by the people themselves. The family was represented in the voting for local community officers, from city hall to the school board. The family controlled the nation's economy through the simple device of local demand for goods and the willingness to use family wealth to purchase these goods. It even controlled its religion through the ability to call, by way of a congregation's vote, their own pastors to their pulpits.

Men worked hard in fields, factories and mines to put food on the table. Women represented the family in the larger social context (church work, library work, sewing circles, etc.). And children were raised at an early age to prepare to take up just those same roles.

But now, centuries later, things were changing – dramatically. The call to family duty was being replaced by the call to personal professionalism. Getting married and having a family was put off so as not to interfere with the task of achieving and developing a person's professional status – women as well as men now. Indeed, marriages were no longer lifetime commitments – but instead divorce was becoming rampant (as many as 50% of Boomer marriages were ending in divorce) – thanks in part to the no-fault divorce and the prenuptial agreements where divorce was understood to be a huge possibility even as a man and a woman entered marriage.

Sex was now viewed widely as a matter of recreation – not family responsibility. Consequently, abortions exploded in number as unwanted pregnancies multiplied dramatically in the new age of "free sex."

Also the role of the male became confused – as men were told to back down and let the women advance in the professional world outside the family. Indeed, feminism even took on a distinct anti-male quality – as men were accused of being "male chauvinist pigs" in not letting women advance to full equality with them in the work place. Lesbianism (what woman would come to have any affection at all for a male chauvinist pig?) developed as women fell into each other's arms – and male homosexuality now "came out" in huge public displays as men simply found mutual attraction in each other's company (expressed in a typical male fashion, to be sure).

A classic example of how far America had moved from its 1950s idealization of the American family is summed up in the top-rated TV series *All in the Family* (which ran through the entire 1970s) in which Archie Bunker, the father, is portrayed as the quite ignorant male chauvinist, his wife Edith as the male-dominated (but subtly the one with something of real social sensibility) wife, and two Boomer college-age kids – who pretty much played out the classic Boomer roles. America did not realize that it was laughing at the very institution that had long carried America through hard times as well as good times. The family now seemed overstated, ridiculous at times, and generally an almost pointless accident as a social institution.

The rise of Federal Judicial legislation. Since the early 1960s, "Progressive" organizations such as the American Civil Liberties Union (ACLU) had demonstrated that the Federal Judiciary – rather than Congress – was the place to go to get their programs put in place as national law. A favorable decision required only five individuals of the nine Supreme Court judges in order to get the kinds of laws that the ACLU wanted to see direct

The 1970s: America Divided

the country. That certainly was easier than going through the complicated task of getting multitudes of Congressmen and Senators (ever sensitive to the views and feelings of the American voter) – plus a willing president – to put those laws into full effect.

Desegregation. Thus it was that federal judges – even at the regional level of the federal circuit courts – got into the legislation business. For instance, federal judges took it upon themselves in a number of court cases to design exactly the specific ways that the country was to undertake racial integration (as in the 1969 *U.S. v. Montgomery County Board of Education* decision) – establishing specific racial hiring goals and various bussing programs sending specific numbers of school children to this or that local school district – regardless of the views of the local citizens, even when Black parents showed an interest in sending their children to schools of their own racial character (as in the 1968 *Green v. County School Board*) – all of this supported all the way up to the Supreme Court (the 1971 *Swann v. Charlotte Mecklenburg Board of Education* case). This judicially-decreed program coming from the Supreme Court would naturally survive all political challenges over the next thirty years.*

Abortion. Then there was the matter of abortions – outlawed in the majority of American states. A Texas law prohibiting abortion made its way up to the Supreme Court in 1973 (with others much like it pending) in the case of *Roe v. Wade*. In a 7-2 decision, the Texas law was overthrown, because it (according to the 14th Amendment) deprived a woman of her right to due process. Realizing the highly controversial nature of this ruling, the Supreme Court then set out specific terms by 3-month periods as to when an abortion could occur, with increasingly restrictive standards as the fetus developed into a full child. That was simply legislation!

In any case, feminists were overjoyed – and Christians deeply outraged, for Christianity had always considered life from the moment of inception as belonging to God – neither man nor woman. To them *Roe v. Wade* simply amounted to court-approved murder. But there was little that the Christian world could do. The Supreme Court had made it quite clear on which side of the moral issue it stood (at least the majority of its

---

*Did desegregation equal integration? Not exactly, as the bitter anti-White attitudes of the Black Panthers demonstrated, even as White America was moving strongly to desegregate the country. Desegregation could be done under government authority, no matter what the public feelings were on the matter. But integration requires a change in the human heart, not something that laws can themselves generate. That takes inspiring leadership to develop the necessary changes in human hearts.

members, anyway). And there was no known appeal that Americans could make to block a Supreme-Court-created law.

Christianity in trouble. Right along with the middle-class family, Christianity was finding itself losing status at the heart of American culture – for the two were closely connected. And behind this was again, the Supreme Court and the legal crusaders of the American Left – who wanted to see Christianity gone from all public life. Citing the First Amendment as calling for the separation of church and state, in case after case the Supreme Court had since the early 1960s been invoking the "non-establishment clause" of the Amendment as actually calling for the legal disestablishment of Christianity whenever and wherever it should come into the ever widening realm of the state – meaning, virtually all public life now. Even locally, the state (local schools, town halls, public parks) could not involve itself with the Christian religion in any way – for to do so would be to "establish" it. The fact that this had long been a key part of local life was no longer sufficient reason to allow this to continue. And all of this was done in violation of the protections of religion outlined in the First Amendment which stated clearly that Congress (meaning the part of the Federal system that made its laws, not anticipating that the Supreme Court would take over supreme responsibility in that area) was to "make no law respecting an establishment of religion, or prohibiting the free exercise thereof." But prohibiting the free exercise was exactly what the Supreme Court was doing. How was it that the Supreme Court could not find itself able to defend the very clear wording of the Constitution?

Lemon v. Kurtzman (1971). Worse, the Supreme Court even got into the business of the "establishment of religion" in its 1971 decision in the *Lemon v. Kurtzman* case. Its decision stated that only secular (or basically non-Christian) programming could be part of the local school program. Also, the only material that could be brought into the classroom had to clearly serve a purely secular purpose.

Supposedly secularism was not a religious matter, and therefore the Supreme Court felt it fully within its power to prescribe the Secular Worldview as the only worldview to be presented and worked from in developing the thinking and understanding of America's rising generations. What this small group of "enlightened" lawyers was doing was actually deciding for the rest of the country the quite religious question as to the dynamic source of life. They had made for the country the decision that life was to be understood as being by nature purely secular, that is, mechanical, operating only from a set of natural laws that scientists (social and physical) have discovered – or will soon discover anyway – which direct all existence.

And that sense of life being purely mechanical extended also to all social as well as material dynamics (the Humanist part of Secularism). According to Secular-Humanists, society too operates strictly according to a set of mechanical or "natural" social laws, which "social scientists" are working hard to discover.

And in any case, being purely "mechanical" in view of life and its dynamics, Secularism cannot be considered to be "religious," because religion is only about supernatural or "non-mechanical" causes. Or so the Secularists argued.

Therefore, anything to do with advancing a Christian worldview, being obviously religious in nature, was supposedly forbidden by the Constitution (which part were they actually referring to?). Only Secularism had the right to be established (by the Court itself) as America's fundamental worldview (in other words, religion), the only one to be allowed legal support in America's public life.

Wow! With that Supreme Court decision, the people's right to determine those religious matters themselves, one of their key freedoms – the first one to be mentioned, in fact, in the First Amendment – just got thrown out. Religious orthodoxy was now completely in the hands of the federal judges, the new high priests of Secularism.

The Humanists respond. Of course the American Humanist Association* recognized its opportunity in the *Kurtzman* ruling – but also the dangers. If the original *Humanist Manifesto* (1933) had been brought into the Kurtzman hearings, it would have been very clear that what the Supreme Court was supporting was indeed a religion, not merely some neutral Truth – because the *Manifesto* itself clearly confessed this to be the case in its repeated use of the term "Religious Humanism." Consequently, the organization came out in 1973 with the *Humanist Manifesto II* – in which all the language about Humanism as being a new, more progressive religion was dropped. Humanism was simply pure science, nothing more.

Mainline Christianity in crisis. As the 1970s rolled along it became increasingly apparent that the traditional denominations (Baptist, Methodist, Presbyterian, Lutheran, Episcopal, etc.) were being sustained largely by an ageing Vet generation. Boomers showed little interest in participating in, much less committing themselves to, congregational life.

To try to reverse a persistent decline in numbers, church officials at the national level attempted to design programs that would adjust their

---

*The Humanist Association states in its letterhead: "Good without a God: Advocating progressive values and equality for humanists, atheists, and freethinkers."

denomination's agendas in a way to make them more relevant to the changing culture around them. They proudly took up the causes of "peace and social justice," authorizing special seminars on the subjects – and just in general going on public record in favor of this or that stand (mostly Leftist) similar to the progressivist world around them. "Old-time religion" (personal salvation and gospel missionary work among the unchurched at home and abroad) dropped from the agenda.

But sadly, all this did was make their churches so much like that larger, secular culture that there was very little reason to come into church from that culture – when culture and church offered mostly the same programs. Thus the persistent decline in Mainline Christianity continued.

Sadly, the denominational leaders never caught on to what was actually happening, or were so deeply committed to their religious "Liberalism" that they refused to change course.

The Evangelical – even Charismatic – movement. Yet there seemed to be something of a small "Awakening" among a breed of independent, mostly Pentecostal, churches – that directed Christianity down that "old-time-religion" road. Not only did they bring the message of repentance and God's offering of personal salvation back into focus – but as Pentecostals they engaged in prayerful healings, prophesy and other works of the Spirit (that scared mainline Christians terribly). And pianos, guitars and drums replaced the church organ – and the music became more contemporary in style – helping to bring in even some of the Boomers and their children.

New kinds of leaders – with popular TV ministries – began to come into view – and speakers at renewal events began to take up the preaching circuit. Missionary work became emphasized – supported by real tithing (and not just tipping the offering plate) which now became the norm. And personal testimonies of the work that God had accomplished through this or that individual – sometimes just ordinary members of these churches – filled their time together. Bible studies and family seminars became common.

Did all this start up a new grand revival in America? Was America entering yet another Great Awakening? Not apparently. But the Evangelical agenda certainly slowed down the overall decline of Christianity in America.

But there still remained a lot of work to be done to get America back on its original Christian foundations. America was up against a culture which was swinging rapidly to the Secular, Humanist, not to mention hedonist/narcissist Left.

CHAPTER TWELVE

THE WORLD'S SOLE SUPERPOWER

* * *

REAGAN ENTERS THE WHITE HOUSE

The 1980 presidential election. In the upcoming 1980 national elections, the Republicans nominated as the party's presidential candidate the former actor Ronald Reagan – who however also had a long political career – as once head of the actors' guild and then two terms as governor of California (1967-1975). He had run for the Republican nomination in 1976, taking a tough stance on the Cold War (he was not greatly fond of détente) – but in the end lost out to Ford. In the 1980 convention he competed against and ultimately defeated veteran Washington insider George Bush for the presidential nomination – but ended up asking him to join him on the Republican ticket as vice president. He campaigned on the same tough stance – depicting Carter as just another nice guy.

But the sad state of the economy would ultimately be the cause of a sweeping Reagan victory in the November 1980 elections. Reagan received 50.7% of the popular vote and 489 electoral college votes to Carter's 41% of the popular vote and only 49 electoral college votes, the balance of the popular vote going to third-party candidate John Anderson with 6.7% of the popular vote (but no electoral college votes).

As the last humiliation to Carter, on exactly the day Reagan was being sworn in as the new U.S. president, Iran released the American hostages – and they were on their way home. True, Carter had worked hard for that release. But the fact that it came when it did made it appear that it was done possibly out of fear of the new tough president – at least that is how a lot of Americans read the event.

Reagan – the man, and the Christian. Reagan was born in Illinois in 1911, and raised in several Illinois towns, to an Irish Roman Catholic father, who was a salesman, and a Protestant mother, whose deep religious convictions would have a very strong influence in the way Reagan grew up, and the way he looked at life. In Dixon, where the Reagans finally settled in, Reagan became strongly influenced by his pastor, Ben Hill Cleaver – who would become like a second father to Reagan – and ultimately also Cleaver's daughter, with whom Reagan became engaged, until she moved to Europe and broke the engagement. Although this hurt did not undercut his Christian faith, which remained strongly private, it did end his church attendance, for a very long time.

His youth seemed unexceptional, even at Eureka College where he was merely a "C" student. But his service as a life guard (saving numerous lives), swim team captain, and student body president gave indication that he did not intend to stay "average." And he got that chance to step out in life as a radio sports announcer. And then, on a trip to California covering a game there, he took and passed a screen test – which then opened the door for him to become a bit-player in numerous B-grade Hollywood movies. But he moved up in importance, until his role as the lead actor in the *Knute Rockne* movie (1940) brought him to stardom.

In the meantime, he had entered the Army Reserves (1937) as a second lieutenant, and in early 1942 was activated fully, in the military's Public Relations division, producing everything from military training to war-bond campaign films. And like so many, his military service introduced him to the world of political affairs. Thus in 1947 he ran and was elected as the president of the Screen-Actors Guild.

But it was a very troubled time for the movie industry, due to the political controversies aroused by the post-war Red Scare, and Reagan had to tread lightly, although he himself was strongly anti-Communist in his own political standing. Yet here is where his strong Christian background – and his mother's influence – played a key part in his efforts to bring reconciliation rather than condemnation to all this political dynamic.

Unfortunately, such reconciliation did not work with his wife, actress Jane Wyman, and their 9-year marriage ended in 1949 when she divorced him because of all the political dynamics their lives were caught up in. But he would remarry three years later another actress, Nancy, whom he come to the aid of when she was confused with an actress of the same name, who was identified as a Communist. And though she would never become quite the Christian that he was, they worked closely together in a very harmonious marriage, one that would be a big support to Reagan as he moved forward in life, increasingly of a conservative political nature.

His known conservatism – and national popularity because of his long hosting of the popular TV show, *The General Electric Theater* – led him to be a keynote speaker at the 1964 Republican National Convention and Barry Goldwater supporter. This in turn caused the California Republican committee to ask Reagan to run against Democratic Party Governor Pat Brown in the 1966 gubenatorial election, which Reagan won!

Here his conservatism demonstrated itself in the way he went at the state's finances, and his stand against all the student protests that had rocked the state. This proved to be exactly how the California majority (at that time, anyway) wanted things. And he was reelected governor in 1970.

As he approached the end of his second term as governor, he began to look at the idea of running as the Republican candidate for the U.S. presidency itself. And indeed, in the 1976 race, he became the leading contender against Ford, the latter who however ultimately got the Republican nomination (but lost the presidential race itself to Carter).

That did not seem to slow Reagan up much, and four years later he made another run at this goal, was indeed nominated as presidential candidate by the Republican Party, and ultimately brought to the White House by the American voting public.

As a strongly self-acknowledged Christian (as Carter had also been) Reagan certainly led the nation to wonder where his Christian faith would touch on his political leadership. He had not been a church-going individual, and seldom spoke of his personal faith. But he (much like Eisenhower and Nixon before him) spoke very often about the American nation itself and the vital relationship it had long had with God – and the way that this relationship was so important to the nation's development. And indeed, it would be this sense of America's ties with God that would register itself deeply during his presidency, in numerous ways.

The importance of the Christian religion would even become an important part of his discussions with Gorbachev, in Reagan's efforts to bring Russia out of its Communist camp and into a much freer world – one of peace rather than contention

* * *

REAGAN GETS TOUGH

The air traffic controllers strike. The American economy remained in horrible shape, thanks to persistent inflation, ruinously high interest rates, and high national unemployment. Consequently, America's labor groups were in a very restless mood. But when the members of the Professional Air Traffic Controllers Organization (PATCO) went on strike in August of 1981, Reagan moved strongly against them, claiming that they had no right to shut down America's airports – merely worsening the national economy all the more. He fired some 11,300 strikers, cut back scheduled flights to about 50 percent of the normal rate, and brought in replacements (including military air traffic controllers) to take over those flights.

America was not used to seeing such presidential power – but greatly approved his actions. Ultimately this shattered PATCO – and sent a warning to other unions not to mess with the nation's economy. They didn't!

The Lebanon crisis (1982-1984). In 1982 Reagan decided to answer an appeal for help by the United Nations in pacifying warring groups – stirred to wrath by Israel's attack on Palestinian refugee camps in Lebanon that June. Lebanon was tearing itself apart. Consequently, Reagan sent 800 American troops in August to try to separate the warring parties. But the fighting only grew worse, especially when Christian Lebanese fighters, allied with Israel, surrounded and then slaughtered men, women and children in those same refugee camps – causing America, France and Italy (the bulk of the UN peacekeeping force) to increase their number of soldiers. For a while it looked as if the situation was improving.

But the next year the situation had deteriorated again, especially after Syria decided to intervene in the civil strife in Lebanon and invaded the country – merely increasing the level of chaos there. Then that October a truck-bomb attack on the UN barracks killed 241 American and 58 French soldiers. Now Reagan had a decision to make – pull out – or dig in even more deeply. Ultimately he decided to pull out in early 1984.

Actually, Americans were rather impressed by the ability of the president to admit defeat and go home – rather than what was often the case (such as Vietnam) when leaders would only get themselves and the country caught more deeply in a mess – because they could not admit to a mistake. Americans in fact felt comforted by the knowledge that they had a president of unusual political wisdom operating from the White House.

The U.S. military intervention in Grenada (October 1983). Partly the decision about Lebanon was shaped by events taking place in the Caribbean – when Marxist revolutionaries overthrew the government of the tiny island Republic of Grenada. From Reagan's point of view, this was a totally unacceptable development, especially as Grenada was located on the path leading to the entrance of the Panama Canal. America did not need another opportunity for the Soviets to gain yet another strategic position in the Western hemisphere. Encouraged by other Caribbean governments – which felt themselves vulnerable to the same kind of action – Reagan sent American troops to Grenada – sparking the angry outcries of the "anti-imperialist" wing of American politics (and the world). Even the United Nations was quick to protest the American action. But the American troops moved so quickly (just a few days) to restore the Republic's constitutional government back to power that the American voices of opposition died away quickly. As for the United Nations, Reagan was tiring of its whining – and simply disregarded it – much to the delight of the majority of Americans.

Clearly Reagan was not one to be pushed around by world public opinion. Everyone – including the Soviets – took notice.

* * *

THE AMERICAN ECONOMY STRUGGLES FORWARD

Supply-side economics. Reagan had made a big deal of how he intended to fight the stagflation (economic stagnation and accompanying inflation) with his own approach to the economic crisis (popularly termed "Reaganomics"). He was going to pursue the doctrine of supply-side economics – in short, get industry back up and running so that a more abundant supply of goods would begin to bring prices back to normal.

But how he planned to do that with Volcker's interest rates running so high was a huge mystery. With car loans and mortgages running at such high interest rates, few Americans were willing to purchase either cars or houses. Likewise, businesses could not contemplate their expansion when interest rates demanded by the financial world remained prohibitive. How exactly then was Reagan going to get production or "supply" back up and running again?

Actually, two things would have to happen first. The price of energy would have to come back down to an affordable level. And so would interest rates. But those were matters with two very different causes: Arab-dominated OPEC – and America's "economic czar" Federal Reserve chief Paul Volcker – neither of which seemed to be in a very cooperative mood.

Energy prices. But something was stirring in the energy world. And it was coming from Russia. The Soviet economy was slowing down. Socialism had not brought "workers' paradise" to Russia – and Russian workers were losing interest in the well-being of their economy, with workers' absenteeism rampant at the work place – as well as alcoholism when they did show up. Years of focusing the Russian economy on the military had left the country with little to offer its workers. Russia had no plans to cut back on its military – but needed something extra to provide funding in order to develop something of a private or personal economy. But the only such asset Russia possessed – one that had serious value on the world market – was oil and gas – which Russia was enormously abundant in.

Russia was not a member of OPEC, but followed OPEC pricing closely. But now Russia was going to have to break from that group and drop prices for its petroleum products in order to get them to a hungry market ahead of OPEC. So in 1981 the Soviets lowered their prices. This now put OPEC members in a bind because they would have to do so also – in order not to have all their customers head off to Russia for their oil purchases. But then OPEC's lowering of its prices forced Russia to have to do another round of price reductions – forcing OPEC to do the same thing. Now a price war began to bring energy prices down – dramatically so. Thus the politically designed energy shortage, the primary cause of the global inflation, eventually came to an end – and inflation with it.

Dealing with Volcker. Now Volcker no longer had the excuse of fighting inflation with his monetarist or tight-money strategy. Volcker, as the American economy's supposed savior, did not let up gladly – until Congress threatened to reduce the powers of the Federal Reserve if he did not do so. Thus interest rates finally came down – and the economy finally got up and moving again.

Social Security. One of the issues that had troubled the 1970s and was needing a solution heading into the 1980s was the matter of Americans' Social Security funding. Due to the immense energy-driven inflation that hit during the 1970s, the Cost of Living Allowance (COLA) had to be adjusted to the point that it nearly emptied out the assets of the Social Security Trust Fund. Thus Social Security taxing was increased from 2% to 6.15% of a worker's earning, helping somewhat. Also the rate of increase of the COLA was slowed up.

Then in 1983 it was decided to separate the Social Security Fund from the federal government's general revenue, giving it its own dynamic to be worked with (at this point combining its account with the federal general budget account was actually considered a detriment – not a boost – to the federal budget picture!).

But, provision was made to use now-independent Social Security Funds to "help" the federal government by purchasing the federal government debt – which is supported through the sale of bonds or IOUs to a funding source. And why not the Social Security Trust Fund? That money just sits there. Why not "invest" that money in government bonds? But critics pointed out that should some serious problem arise with the government debt, the people's Trust Fund could be found to be holding only worthless government IOUs. Defenders said that this was highly unlikely (conveniently forgetting the numerous times in the past that the federal government came close to financial failure). Supporters of the deal ultimately won the argument, and thus this indeed became the character of the Trust Fund: a major creditor to the federal government, holding a massive amount of federal government IOUs, at times fully one-half of the huge federal debt.

Reagan's reelection in 1984. The Democrats would certainly understand that they were going to have a hard time running against the very popular Reagan – who was due to run for reelection in 1984. Democrats nominated the former U.S. senator from Minnesota and vice president under Carter, Walter Mondale, as their presidential candidate. In the end, Reagan scored a huge 58.8% of the popular vote and 525 electoral college votes to Mondale's 40.6%, and only 13 electoral college votes: the ever-Democratic-Party supporting three votes of Washington D.C.* – and those of Mondale's home state of Minnesota. The outcome was never in doubt.

* * *

MAJOR DEVELOPMENTS IN FOREIGN POLICY

Muammar Gaddafi. With the exception of Egypt – now under Mubarak but continuing to follow Sadat's same pro-West, even pro-American, foreign policy – the Arab world was as eager as ever to develop Arab nationalism. Israel provided the ever-ready cause behind restless Arab nationalism – with various Arab modernizers such as Muammar Gaddafi of Libya trying to present themselves as the Arab world's best champion. The flamboyant Gaddafi attempted all sorts of programs (his little Green Book of Gaddafi quotations – similar to Mao's little Red Book), from Arab Socialism and then back to Arab Capitalism (Libya was very wealthy in terms of oil reserves) – sometimes quite Secular, sometimes orthodoxly Muslim (in Gaddafi's own unique way). When the Arab world turned out not to be terribly responsive to his attempts at Arab leadership, he then became very "African" – attempting to make himself the leading voice in African affairs taking place to the south of Libya.

But he pushed things too far with Reagan when it was discovered that he was connected to the 1986 Berlin bombing of a discotheque in which a number of American soldiers were killed – and Reagan retaliated by sending patrol boats into waters claimed by Libya (considered by the West as high seas and thus nobody's territory) – which naturally were fired on by Libya – and which Reagan answered by attacking Gaddafi's Presidential Palace.

---

*Ever since Washington, D.C. was given the right to choose its own presidential electors in 1961 (the 23rd Amendment), D.C. has been the strongest Democratic Party supporting constituency in the nation. This is hardly surprising, as the Democratic Party represents perfectly the idea that the Washington bureaucracy should be running the country. In fact it is surprising that there are any Republicans at all in this district! Thus in the most recent national elections, the Democrat Biden received 92.15% of D.C.'s vote, compared to the Republican Trump's 5.4%, a D.C. voting spread identical to that of the 2016 race between Hillary Clinton and Trump.

When the United Nations condemned the attacks, Reagan simply ignored the organization – as did a number of other countries which too were tired of Gaddafi's ventures (principally supporting various terrorist organizations such as the Irish Republican Army and various Moro or Islamic jihadist groups operating in the Philippines). Even the Soviets found themselves backing away from Gaddafi, not wanted to get dragged into an unwanted event.

Anyway, for a while, Gaddafi would be forced to behave – for fear of Reagan's reprisals.

Other militant organizations. But huge problems in the Middle East were coming from a number of other sources, principally the PLO or its subgroup Fatah, plus Hezbollah and Hamas – primarily dedicated to the crippling or even destruction of Israel. But each represented a very different part of the world of Islam. The Palestinian Liberation Organization (PLO) or Fatah had long been the voice of the Palestinians chased out of their homelands by the Jewish migration into Palestine – and was the organization officially sponsored by the Arab League. Defending both Christian and Muslim Arab interests in Palestine, it tended to be mostly Secular in its promotion of Palestinian rights. Hezbollah however was a strongly Muslim voice of the Shi'ites – founded and supported by Iran and numerous Shi'ites among the Lebanese and Syrians – which found itself constantly in competition with the Arab Sunnis. Then Hamas came into being in the later 1980s – upset that the PLO/Fatah was beginning to show a willingness to negotiate a compromise of some kind with the Israelis. Hamas was also more militantly Muslim (Sunni) – rather than merely Secular in character.

The Rapid Decline of the Soviet Empire: Afghanistan. Meanwhile, the Soviets found themselves caught in a quagmire of rising Afghan Muslim and tribal hostility – aroused by the Russian attempt to impose a Communist puppet government in the Afghan capital city, Kabul. Afghan rebels (mujahedin) even looked to the Reagan government for help in ousting the Russian troops occupying their country – finding Reagan very eager to help out. Americans sent the mujahedin all varieties of weapons, including missiles that could easily take out Russian tanks and jets. Consequently, the Soviets found themselves struggling to hang on to any kind of defensive position in the country. Soon anti-war sentiments began to grow among the Russians – including even members of the Russian military.

The rapid turnover in Soviet leadership (1982-1985). This all was taking place at a time when the Russians were having a very hard time getting leadership in place – ever since Brezhnev's death in late 1982.

The World's Sole Superpower

At first a Communist hardliner (supposedly a good match to the equally hardline Reagan) was put in place at the head of the Party in Moscow. But he died only a year later. He in turn was replaced by another individual – who was in no better health – and who also died only a year after that.

Pressure from Reagan. Meanwhile Reagan was pushing and pressuring the Soviets in every way possible. He sensed the Soviet decline and intended to exploit it. He threw down the challenge to Russia in a speech before the British Parliament in 1982 when he called the Soviet Union an "Evil Empire" and predicted its collapse in the near future. Soon thereafter Reagan restored the B1-bomber program that Carter had canceled and armed NATO with Pershing II missiles. In 1983 he announced plans (the Strategic Defense Initiative or SDI) to develop and deploy missiles capable of defending America from a missile attack from any enemy – which Kennedy termed as "reckless Star Wars schemes." It was an expensive program – but one which the Soviets – whose economy was stumbling – would be unable to match. Ultimately, the American people seemed to approve of Reagan's "Star Wars schemes." Once again, Reagan's toughness drew the approval of the majority of Americans.

But in the end, the program would not be needed. The Soviet Empire would soon collapse.

Mikhail Gorbachev. In 1985 the Russians brought to power a younger, more visionary Mikhail Gorbachev – who was looking forward to enacting a number of reforms to liberalize the government and Russian society. He was also hoping to improve relations with America.

Gorbachev introduced a number of liberalizing reforms – known as *glasnost* (more personal freedom for the people), *perestroika* (liberalizing the economic system), and d*emokratizatsiya* (a democratizing of the political system). These reforms were well received both at home and abroad – and led to a number of very friendly meetings between Reagan and Gorbachev – to see how they could finally end the Cold War.

Reagan's challenge. At one point, in June of 1987, when Reagan was visiting Berlin, he issued this challenge as he was speaking at the Brandenburg Gate:

> ... if you truly want peace and liberalization – Mr. Gorbachev, open this gate! Mr. Gorbachev, tear down this wall!

This did not happen right away – but something like it was underway. And Reagan knew so – although he would be one year out of office when this challenge finally was answered with the coming down of the Iron Curtain separating East and West Europe.

China continues self-reform under Deng Xiaoping. While the Soviets were undertaking deep reforms to get their economy up and moving, the Chinese Communists were doing the same thing, except with very different results. At the same time that the reforms crumbled the Soviet social-economic-political order, in China similar reforms were clearly working to strengthened Chinese society – politically in a moderate fashion and economically in a massive fashion.

Part of this was due to the Chinese entrepreneurial instinct being still alive and well in China – especially along its major Eastern cities such as Shanghai, which earlier in the century had been a hub of Chinese industry. But part of it was also due to the very favorable trade protection deals with the West that Deng had secured from the Westerners, the latter anxious to see China move closer to their world of capitalism.

Deng also kept important restraints on the dynamic in order to keep it from getting out of control (as things had developed in Russia), largely through the heavy government subsidizing of this new "independent" industrial dynamic. This heavy government support not only gave huge trading advantages to the Chinese industrialists, it kept them in a very cooperative relationship with the Deng government. Thus the Chinese economy began to boom, annual growth rates averaging 8-10% during most of the 1980s and 1990s.

* * *

THE IRAN-CONTRA AFFAIR

In the meantime a major problem for Reagan exploded at home when in November of 1986 a Lebanese newspaper reported a story about a secret deal to get Iran to intervene to release kidnapped Americans held in the Middle East by Hezbollah – through the sale of various US weapons (via Israel as intermediary) to Iran. At about the same time (October), a CIA plane was shot down by the Nicaraguan Sandinista (strongly Leftist) government, a plane carrying weapons to anti-government troops known as the Contras. One American, Eugene Hasenfus, survived the downing, was arrested by the Nicaraguans and immediately tried – at which point he confessed to the secret shipment of arms to the Contras. Both actions were in violation of very specific legislation (the Bolen Amendment to the Pentagon budget forbidding further help to the Contras) plus the long-standing taboo of paying off kidnappers (even if only indirectly, by way of

Iran's intervention), because it merely encouraged more kidnapping.

The two events occurred at around the time of the 1986 Congressional elections in which the Democrats increased their majority in the House and now took control of the Senate as well – with large majorities in both houses (House: 258 to 177 and Senate 55 to 45).

But even before the new Congress could take its seat, the Iran-Contra Affair (as it came to be known) exploded as a major news item – forcing Reagan in mid-November to go before national television to explain his side of the affair. Two weeks later U.S. Attorney General Edwin Meese admitted that the money from Iran was used to finance the Contra shipments. On that same day Reagan fired Marine Lt. Col. Oliver North – who confessed to being in charge of the whole matter. And on that same day Reagan set up a three-man Presidential Commission, headed up by former Texas Senator John Tower, to look into the matter. In late February of the following year (1987) the Tower Commission delivered its report, outlining the actions of various participants in the whole affair – although it largely excused Reagan as not having much knowledge of the operation.

In March Reagan again went before TV audiences – to apologize for his mishandling of the whole affair – explaining that he was in part trying to help get the release of hostages and in part working with Iranian moderates in trying to improve Iranian-American relations.

But in the meantime (January), the new Democratic Congress set up its own investigative committees – dismissing the Tower Report – obviously looking for more material to bring against the Reagan "imperial presidency." It was Watergate all over again. The hearings ran from early May to early August – again watched closely on TV by the Americans – especially when Lt. Col. North was interviewed. Finally a Joint Committee Report was published in November – with Republican members of the Committee issuing a dissenting Minority Report. Basically Reagan was criticized for not doing his job in staying on top of such matters. However, the Report came up with nothing specific that Congress could charge Reagan with. But even then, that would not be the end of the matter – as further investigations were conducted by a Democrat-controlled Congress all the way into 1991.

At the time, Reagan's popularity dropped dramatically from a two-thirds approval rating to less than half. Yet his approval ratings would soon climb again to pre-Iran-Contra levels as he finished out his presidential term – due to his obvious success with Gorbachev in lowering the tensions of the Cold War.

* * *

THE ONE-TERM PRESIDENCY OF GEORGE H. W. BUSH

The 1988 presidential election pitted Regan's vice president George Bush against the Democratic Party nominee, Massachusetts governor Michael Dukakis. At first Dukakis led in the polls – then Bush began to pull ahead as the elections approached – finally finishing with a large Bush victory, 53.4% of the popular vote to Dukakis's 45.6% – and the Electoral College vote 426 to 111 (the latter, however, did not include Massachusetts!).

George H. W. Bush – the making of the man. Bush was born in 1924 to a very prestigious Connecticut family, his father, Prescott, being a Yale graduate, a World War One artillery officer, a very successful Wall Street investment banker, and then (1952-1963) U.S. Senator representing Connecticut. The son, George, attended the elite Phillips Academy (1937-1942), but upon graduation joined the navy rather than head on to college. After all, at this point America was deeply involved in World War Two.

As a navy pilot, his combat experience included being shot down in the Pacific, but being picked up by a navy ship, one of the lucky survivors of the battle. He soon learned that other downed Americans were captured and executed, even having parts of their bodies eaten by their Japanese captors. This would have a profound spiritual impact on Bush, causing him to wonder why God had spared him.

Just prior to the war's end he married a sweetheart, Barbara Pierce, from his Phillips Academy days, and they would go on to have six children, including George W (or just "W") and Jeb, who would go on to develop their own careers as political notables (Jeb as Florida governor and the younger George as Texas governor and U.S. president).

After his release from service, Bush would head to Yale, graduating in 1948 with distinction, having served as captain of the baseball team, as Phi Beta Kappa, and member of the secret and very prestigious Skull and Bones society. Bush then headed into the business world, notably that of the Texas oil industry rather than the Connecticut financial world he had been born into. He wanted to be "his own man." He quickly rose from oil equipment salesman to owner of his own oil exploration company.

But his father's 1952 run for the senate seat, and his involvement in Eisenhower's presidential campaign brought a strong political line to his work, though he would stay in the oil business into the early 1960s. But he could not avoid attracting the attention of the Texas political parties and he was courted, first by the Democrats and then the Republicans (the latter fitting better his conservative political instincts), and in 1966, he was able to gain a seat in the U.S. House of Representatives, one of the few Republicans to come out of the traditionally "Dixiecrat" South.

Two years later (1968) he came close to being named as Nixon's running mate, though Maryland governor Agnew was chosen because of his

The World's Sole Superpower

strong stand against the Black riots that had shaken the country (Maryland had thus been spared the destruction experienced elsewhere). But Nixon nonetheless appreciated Bush's political potential, and appointed him as the American ambassador to the United Nations – beginning Bush's serious international experience. Then as Watergate was embroiling American politics at home, Nixon convinced Bush to chair the Republican National Committee, now moving Bush front and center in the party's national political dynamics. Then with Nixon's resignation and Ford taking the presidency, Ford asked Bush to head up the U.S. Liaison Office in China, making him something like the American ambassador to China (1974-1975). Then Ford brought Bush back to D.C. to take charge of the C.I.A., which was suffering from serious image-decline due to the strongly Leftist atmosphere blanketing the nation's capital. But he would hold that position only a year, when Carter's election put Bush out of a job. He thus returned to his Texas business world as a Houston banker, and began thinking about a run for the U.S. presidency in the upcoming 1980 race.

And so he undertook to build his support going into the 1980 electoral campaign, but found himself up against the even stronger support running in Reagan's favor. So he backed out of the race, only to have Reagan ask if he would be willing to serve as his running mate. He agreed, worked hard in support of Reagan, and then for the next eight years found himself serving strongly, but quietly, Reagan's presidency. And thus it was an easy thing for the Republicans to ask Bush in 1988 to take over the Reagan legacy as the Republican Party candidate as Reagan approached the end of his second term of office.

Bush as a Christian president. In taking office in January of 1989, Bush (and America in general) found the Christian world rather deeply divided between a rising Evangelical Christianity and a declining Mainline Christianity, the division itself hurting the Christian legacy in America. Bush himself was a member of the very Mainline Episcopal Church, but himself of somewhat an Evangelical nature. Thus the Christian world looked to him to take up the Reagan legacy, and give the nation some spiritual guidance greatly needed by all.

At first he seemed simply to affirm merely the Evangelical side of things, in his public speeches often (in more than 200 speeches) calling on the nation to go to prayer over this or that matter. And like Reagan, Biblical verses and language found their way often into Bush's speeches.

But because of Bush's strong support of the 1992 legislation making it a "hate crime" when behavior was directed against the rights of minorities, notably homosexual rights, Evangelicals (who believe that the straying from divinely ordained sexual norms to be wrong in every way) saw this as a Bush move over to Mainline Christianity's "peace and social justice" agenda – considered by Evangelicals to be no different than the social-political position of the "Liberal" or Secular world.

Thus Bush's effort to appear more "inclusive" in spirit succeeded only in weakening the vital support of Evangelicals in the 1992 elections. Nor did it improve his standing at all with the very sensitive "minorities," which were finding a louder voice in American politics.

* * *

FOREIGN AFFAIRS DURING THE BUSH, Sr. PRESIDENCY

The Lockerbie bombing (December 1988). Perhaps as the result of an effort by Libyan dictator Gaddafi to see what the newly elected American President was made of (would he be tough like Reagan?), at the end of 1988 a Pan Am passenger jet (Flight 103) exploded in the sky over Lockerbie, Scotland – with everyone on board and 11 people on the ground killed. Under the subsequent investigation of the explosion, the trail led back to Libya. But nothing was done immediately to punish Gaddafi.

However long-standing (and already struggling because of earlier security concerns) Pan Am was sued for failing to take security precautions (but Pan Am reminded its opponents that it received hundreds of notices daily about security concerns and had no way to check out each and every one of them), bringing one of America's oldest and largest global airline companies to bankruptcy and extinction.

The breakup of the Soviet Empire in East Europe (1989). Although President Bush had little to do with what was about to break out in the Soviet Empire, events there would form a huge part of America's political focus during the Bush years (January 1989 to January 1993).

Gorbachev's reforms – not surprisingly to those who understand these things – set off another "revolution of rising expectations," which once underway would get way out of Gorbachev's ability to control. The well-announced new freedoms of *glasnost* and *perestroika* were also received in the European satellite countries as some kind of permission to move to the same freedoms in their own countries – first in Poland, then East Germany and Czechoslovakia, etc. – and finally the very repressive Romania. 1989 would be the banner year for this event. Poland had actually been heading down this road since 1980 under what started out as a labor organization: *Solidarność* (Solidarity). It had been suppressed by the Polish military (fearful that it would invite another Soviet invasion) but had survived nonetheless. And now in the new Gorbachev era, it was an

The World's Sole Superpower 381

active participant in Poland's 1989 summer elections – in which Solidarity trounced the Polish Communist Party. Gorbachev made no move to dismiss the election results.

Now began a mad dash of other East European countries to attempt the same kind of national elections – with virtually the same results: the Communists were swept from power and replaced by new national parties. The most dramatic was the event taking place in East Germany – when East Germans began to flood into newly free Czechoslovakia and Hungary ...embarrassing the East German Communist leader Honecker sufficiently so that he stepped down from power. At this point, the East German government simply disintegrated. In November East Germans found themselves free to leave the country – and by Christmas German youths had taken to smashing down (or trying anyway, because it was quite sturdy!) the Berlin Wall.

Only in Romania was the new order met by violence, when Romanian dictator Ceaucescu had his troops attack protesters – until the soldiers actually joined the protesters. In late December he and his wife were arrested and rather immediately executed by a firing squad. The last of the Soviet satellite nations had made their escape from the Soviet Empire.

The Disintegration of the Soviet Union itself (1989-1991). But the momentum did not stop with East Europe. At the same time, minority Soviet Republics (from Estonia, Latvia, etc., on the Baltic Sea, South to Moldova and Ukraine, and East across Asia to the Turkish "stans" of Kazakhstan, Uzbekistan, etc.) were demanding independence from the Soviet Union itself. Even the Russian Federation (headed up by the Moscow Mayor Boris Yeltsin) was calling for independence from the Soviet Union. Gorbachev was quickly losing control of political events over the country that he theoretically still presided over.

So angry were the old Communist hardliners in Gorbachev's own cabinet over his reforms that in August of 1991 they attempted a coup against Gorbachev, which did not go very well – when Yeltsin led angry Russian protesters to virtually imprison the plotters inside the Parliament Building. Thus the coup failed. But in the end, it also undercut Gorbachev's authority so badly that Russia's political leadership seemed simply to have passed on to Yeltsin. And by the end of 1991, the Soviet Union was no more when all of the former Soviet Republics (including even Russia) had declared their national independence.

Tragedy at Tiananmen Square. Chinese youth were watching closely developments in the Soviet Union, and decided that they wanted to go down the same road to full political freedom. In April of 1989 thousands, then tens of thousands, of youth gathered in Beijing's Tiananmen Square to demonstrate support for full release from the Chinese government's political restraints on Chinese society.

At first the Chinese government did nothing, while a bitter debate developed between the hardliners and the appeasers. Finally Deng, seeing social disintegration as the possible result of appeasement, moved toward the side of the hardliners, and the decision was made at the beginning of June to forcibly clear the square of its (possibly a million by this time) youth gathered there.

Thus on the night of June 3-4 the Chinese military was ordered to clear the square, by whatever means necessary. Guns and even tanks were brought into use, resulting in the clearing of the square – but also the death of countless youth in the process. And thus the political movement such as it was (not always clear what exactly it hoped to achieve) came to an end in China.

Bush, in company with the rest of Western leaders, was outraged at the Chinese government's actions. But Bush soon backed off, trying to keep a positive attitude toward Deng's China and its efforts to Westernize, without disintegrating socially like Russia in the process.

The Gulf War or "Desert Storm" (1990-1991). In the meantime, a very big problem had developed in the Middle East when Iraqi dictator Saddam Hussein had his Iraqi army invade and occupy the tiny (but oil rich) neighbor, Kuwait. The whole thing ended up as a huge political miscalculation by Saddam – one that threatened to start up another Arab oil crisis. But Bush was determined to prevent that from happening.

Saddam had been long involved in an Iran-Iraq War (1980-1988) which started up when Saddam attempted to grab ethnically Arab lands located just across the Iraqi border in ethnically Persian Iran (Persian Iran is not Arab in language or culture – though certainly Muslim, although of the dissenting Shi'ite variety, as are most of the Arabs in that part of the Muslim world). But this merely bogged the two countries down in a campaign of vast mutual destruction ...until in 1988 when the United Nations was able to work out a truce between the two countries. At the end of this war Iraq found itself hugely in debt due to the fact that its oil industry had been mostly shut down during that long war.

Then tensions had grown between Iraq and Kuwait, when Iraq accused Kuwait of not only overproducing oil sales (thus keeping prices very low) but also slant-drilling below ground – right into Iraqi oil fields near their border. There was also Iraqi resentment over the very existence of Kuwait in the first place – carved out of former Mesopotamia (Iraq) after World War One – simply to give the British oil company, British Petroleum, an oil source it could continue to control. Also Saddam had the usual Arab desire to play the part of grand leader of the larger Arab world.

On top of this, Saddam thought he had the go-ahead from America via the American Ambassador who seemed to offer only an indifferent response when Saddam told her of his plans to grab Kuwait. Besides, Iraq was something of an American ally – being the third-largest recipient of American foreign aid (especially during the Iran-Iraq War).

Thus when Saddam invaded Kuwait in August of 1990, he was stunned to find himself in trouble with Bush, who demanded that he get his troops out of Kuwait. But at that point Saddam felt he could not do that – for such a retreat would deeply undermine his ever-shaky position as Iraqi dictator.

This was importantly due to the fact that he was a Sunni Arab, supported by the smaller Sunni Arab portion of the Iraqi population, holding tight control over the majority Shi'ite Arab portion of the population, the latter group resenting deeply Saddam and his Sunni Ba'athist Party's dominance in Iraqi political affairs. Thus it was that his position in Iraq was very fragile.

Negotiations between Saddam and Bush dragged on, going nowhere in the process. But in the meantime, Bush was putting together a grand coalition of European and Arab countries (other Arab countries were also afraid of Saddam's ambitions), including Saudi Arabia, which let America use its land as a base to build up a large coalition force there. By mid-January the coalition army was ready to move.

The Iraqi Army and Air Force proved to be no match to the coalition forces which quickly downed and blasted everything Saddam could muster. In the matter of simply a few days, the Iraqi Army was chased from Kuwait. Of course at the first gun shots, the "anti-imperialist" voices of the American Left waxed indignant – but soon were silenced by the stunning success of Bush and his coalition forces.

Then Bush halted his attack on the retreating Iraqis. He had no interest in going any further after Saddam. He had kicked him out of Kuwait. That was as far as he was going to go. Furthermore, he had no desire whatsoever to find himself having to take responsibility for a shattered country of conflicting ethnic groups (60% Shi'ite Arabs, 20% Sunni Arabs, and 20% Sunni Kurds) groups that hated each other and were held together as a society only by the tight grip of the Ba'athist organization that Saddam headed up in Baghdad. No, America was not going to get itself caught up in nation-building. Vietnam had taught President Bush the dangers of such arrogance. America would not be fixing Iraq. To try to do so would be for America to fall into a "quagmire," as Bush's Secretary of Defense Dick Cheney would later (1994) explain the decision.

Troubles in the American economy. In his early years in office, during the horrible economic recession he stepped into, Reagan had lowered taxes in an effort to put money in people's pockets so as to help get the economy back up and moving again. This of course cut Federal tax revenues at a time when Reagan was also trying to rebuild American military strength. Then when the economy began to move, Regan could have – should have – moved toward a balanced budget of government expenditures being matched by government tax receipts – by raising taxes or cutting back on government programming, or both. But Reagan did neither. And as a consequence, the Federal debt grew monumentally, more than tripling over Reagan's eight years in office.

But Bush, in his 1988 presidential campaign – at a time when America was again experiencing a small recession – promised American voters that during his presidency there would be no new taxes: "read my lips – no new taxes." But unemployment brought on by the recession meant that the government was going to be spending more money for federal unemployment benefits – at a time that tax revenues would also be down even further. Thus the deficit continued to climb.

Finally in 1992 – in cooperation with the Democratic Party controlled Congress – a range of tax increases were put in place to slow up the growth in the deficit. But it was a presidential election year – and those increases (plus his promise of "no new taxes") would be played against him by his political opponents (two actually) in the presidential race that year.

Ross Perot. Indeed, the failure of Bush to bring the growing federal deficit under control gave billionaire businessman, Ross Perot, just the right cause he needed to put himself in the running for President as an independent, third-party candidate. He voiced concerns Americans had about this matter or that – sometimes taking a Democrat position, sometimes a Republican position. His rankings in the polls also rose and fell – causing Perot at one point to back out of the race – then reenter again. He even flew off to Vietnam to demonstrate his ability to conduct a new style of diplomacy – only to have the Vietnamese refuse him entry into their country. And – his unusual campaign was heavily financed by his own immense personal fortune.

The 1992 campaign and election. The presidential campaign of 1992 was an amazing balance of all three candidates. In June, polls put Perot at 39% approval, Bush 31% and Clinton (not yet officially the Democratic Party candidate) at 25%. The debates helped Clinton move ahead, the sense of economic slump undercut Bush – and Perot – despite his zaniness – was able to hang on to a respectable size of support.

What was sad for Bush was that the economy was actually picking up again – in fact would go on to one of the longest growth periods in American history. But this was not yet perceived by the American voters. Thus when elections were finally held in November, Clinton came in with 43% of the popular vote, Bush 37.4% and Perot nearly 19%. It is easy to wonder what the results would have been if Perot had not been in the race – hacking away at the Washington Establishment (Bush and company) for its poor economic performance.

But in any case, the electoral college gave Clinton a full majority win with 370 votes to Bush's 168 votes (and Perot, nothing). Clinton would thus be entering the White House the following January (1993).

* * *

THE BOOMER BILL CLINTON TAKES THE WHITE HOUSE

William (Bill) Jefferson Clinton. Clinton was born in Hope Arkansas in 1946, just after the end of World War Two, thus qualifying (even exemplifying) himself as a Boomer. But unlike most Boomers, Clinton's life as a child and youth was anything but normal for the times. His actual father had died just before his birth, and his mother, a rather dramatic individual, remarried four years later to a quiet, not terribly successful, alcoholic – who proved to be abusive of her.

In his family's move (when he was just six) to the most unusual Southern city of Hot Springs, Arkansas, Clinton found himself in the midst of a multi-ethnic (and corrupt: gambling, Mafia, etc.) environment. And with both his parents working, he found himself alone at home much of the time, or on his own exploring the larger world around him. Actually the family housekeeper offered the nurture that his parents did not, and would become a strong influence in his own Christian development.

He even walked by himself regularly to the huge Park Place Baptist Church and became very active in Sunday School there. The contrast between the violence of his step-father (the Clinton surname came from his step-father, not his biological father) and the Christian counsel he found both at church and from the housekeeper – who advised him "live and let live, for God will ultimately take care of all matters" – turned the young Clinton even more closely to God. At age nine he confessed Jesus as Lord of his life and was baptized, an event he claimed was a major part of his personal development. Also the fact that Billy Graham refused to segregate a crusade he once held in his town touched Clinton's heart deeply.

Clinton's need to grow his world himself led him to push himself educationally, take up music (saxophone), and become active in every social circle possible, winning awards and finding himself taking up leadership positions widely. In this he saw himself called by God to make a big difference in the world.

His high academic performance opened his way in 1964 to Georgetown University's School of Foreign Service in Washington, D.C., quickly even there finding leadership, as president of both his freshman and sophomore classes. But he did not follow the 1960s trends, and failed to win that position his senior year (1967-1968), as he was now viewed as too much a part of the "Establishment" that Boomers by this time were in the streets protesting against everywhere – and especially in D.C.

He continued his schooling, the next year (1968-1969) at Oxford University in England as a Rhodes Scholar, and then after that Yale Law School. Here he met the equally scholarly and ambitious Wellesley graduate, Hillary Rodham. The two of them would eventually move to Clinton's home state of Arkansas to practice law, and both become Law School faculty at the University of Arkansas. And in 1976 Hillary would set aside her hesitations and marry Bill Clinton.

His ambition now turned in the direction of public office, and in 1974 he ran for the position as the Democratic candidate for the U.S. House of Representatives, though he proved not to be successful in the venture. But two years later he ran (unopposed) for the position of Arkansas Attorney General, a key stepping stone on his way to the Arkansas governorship. And this he won in 1978, making him the youngest governor in the country.

Not surprisingly, he was a very active "reformer" as governor, taking on tax reform strongly, which upset voters sufficiently for him not to be reelected two years later. But he was the "Comeback Kid," and two years after his defeat, he was reelected on the basis of a more "moderate" platform, having learned how to read the public's interest a bit better. And from that point on, he would be reelected continually, until his run for and election to the U.S. Presidency ten years later. Meanwhile Hillary worked hard on building the couple's family fortunes.*

---

*One of the Clintons' financial ventures, the Whitewater Development Corporation – a vacation properties investment venture undertaken with Jim and Susan McDougal in 1978 – failed badly a few years later. Then in 1992 McDougal's Madison Guarantee Savings and Loan Association was accused by the *New York Times* of illegally granting money from the financially shaky (and ultimately insolvent) Madison Guarantee to the Clinton campaign organization. This raised other questions, such as the possible involvement of McDougal's bank in funding the Whitewater venture as well. Soon accusations about various questionable financial transactions (and Hillary's and her Rose Law Firm's involvement as legal counsel to the McDougals) were raising the matter to the level of major political scandal. And in 1995 – with Clinton in the White House as U.S. president – the U.S. Senate finally set up the Whitewater Committee to

The World's Sole Superpower 387

As governor, Clinton proved to be still a reformer at heart, and poured his efforts into educational reform, his reform programming taking the state from the country's lowest ranking on the testing scale to the most greatly improved in all the nation, drawing him much attention from the nation in the process. This brought him the invitation to offer an opening-night address at the Democratic Party national convention in 1988, now making him indeed a national political figure. At this point, the U.S. presidency itself interested Clinton as a new personal political goal.

He used his talents learned from his rise in Arkansas politics to very carefully pick up support here and there for his candidacy. And in the process, he was able to arrive at the 1992 Democratic National Convention with the key states of Florida, Texas, New York and California committed to his nomination. Thus he easily secured the presidential nomination at the convention itself.

As for his Christian life, not untypical of a self-advancing youth, he had let his churchgoing fall to the wayside during his college years, and in fact would not resume active church attendance until 1980, when he was reelected as Arkansas governor after his first reelection defeat to an active churchgoer. So it certainly helped his political image to now be a churchgoer in his second attempt at reelection. But part of the change was undoubtedly authentic, as he sought God's support in the road that still lay ahead. Indeed, he would draw very close to his Immanuel Baptist Church pastor, W.O. Vaught, all the way up to Vaught's death in 1989.[*]

* * *

DOMESTIC POLITICS DURING THE CLINTON YEARS

"Two presidents for the price of one." Actually America had elected a husband-wife team of Bill and Hillary – proudly declared by Clinton himself when he uttered the famous phrase that a vote for him would amount to "two presidents for the price of one." He fully intended to put Hillary to

---

look into the matter. Ultimately in 1998 (as the public's attention was turning to the Lewinsky-Clinton sex scandal) the Whitewater Special Prosecutor Ken Starr (who was also now investigating the Lewinsky scandal) concluded that there was insufficient evidence in the Whitewater affair to indict the Clintons of any criminal act (although fifteen other people were convicted of various crimes in this matter – including Jim Guy Tucker, Governor of Arkansas) – and the investigation was thus dropped.

[*]Hillary however would remain true to her Methodist upbringing, attending the also Liberal First United Methodist Church in Little Rock, even teaching Sunday School there.

work at the very top of his Administration.

Hillary was born a year after Bill (1947) in a Chicago suburb to a strongly Methodist family, with a father as founder and director of a small textile company and a typical at-home mom. Hillary too proved to be academically talented as well as an active leader in high school. And she, like her family, started out as a political conservative, but was professionally quite ambitious – and very irritated at the roadblocks females experienced on such a road. She went on to all-girls Wellesley College, majoring in political science, and saw her political loyalties shift to the Democratic Party – feeling that the Republicans were not strong enough on their civil rights stands. And then at her graduation, she was called on to address her fellow graduates (Massachusetts Senator Edward Brooke was actually the commencement speaker), receiving a seven-minute standing ovation from fellow graduates for her speech – and bringing her national recognition in the process.

She then went on the Yale Law School, where found herself focused on child care, poverty, and migrant labor issues. And she soon met Bill and the two moved in together in New Haven. She then finally made the decision (after many requests) to follow him to Arkansas to begin his – and her – professional careers, as faculty at the University of Arkansas Law School. And in 1975 they finally married.

But she nonetheless worked hard at keeping their professional lives quite independent of each other, as she took on her own assignments, such as moving to Indianapolis in 1976 to help the Carter presidential campaign. But finally she settled down (somewhat) in joining the Rose Law Firm, a leading Arkansas group, working now more in the business realm, but still active in children's issues as pro bono supplementary work.

National health care reform. He immediately assigned Hillary the task of putting together a new national health program – similar to the ones in Europe – considered highly Socialist in typical American thinking.

Almost immediately things did not go well with this effort. The doctors' national organization, the AMA (American Medical Association), was highly opposed – as was the private insurance industry. Too many people (including lawyers) were getting very rich from the way the health industry worked in America – and were in no mood to see things changed. Thus the idea soon got dropped by Clinton – both Clintons.

Homosexuals in the military. Then Clinton attempted to move down the Boomer path that not only saw nothing amiss about homosexuality but indeed viewed bitterly the lack of sympathy of most of American society to the plight of the homosexual – especially since so many of them had begun to suffer agonizing deaths from the AIDS virus that broke out within their circles in the 1980s. As usual, the U.S. military's chain of command reaching all the way to the White House seemed to be the perfect laboratory to conduct the moral reform of America with respect to its traditionally very negative reaction to homosexuality.

But here too Clinton's effort did not take him very far – when it became clear that American society was not yet ready to undergo such reform. He finally agreed to settle on the principle of "don't ask, don't tell" – actually not a new principle at all. Something like thus understanding had pretty much been policy all along. Homosexuality in the military existed – and was tolerated – as long as it remained "in the closet." The homosexual community (and its Boomer supporters) would thus have to wait – until yet another generation came along – the Gen-Xers and their President Barack Obama – to finally "change"* the official American position on the practice of homosexuality in the military – and in American society in general.

Deficit reduction through the raising of taxes. One area that Clinton did indeed find success was in attacking the problem of the growing federal deficit. In sponsoring the Deficit Reduction Act of 1993, he was able to raise taxes on a wide variety of incomes – which naturally met resistance from those whose taxes would increase. But nonetheless, the bill passed, though only by the slimmest of margins (the Republicans strongly opposed, as well as numerous Democrats). Nonetheless it would have a dramatic impact in bringing the federal budget into balance – even reducing the deficit somewhat.

The Gingrich challenge moves Clinton to the political center (1994). In the House of Representatives, the Congressman (and former university professor) from Georgia, Newt Gingrich, had taken the lead of his party as Minority Whip, and had begun to rebuild the party around a program which he clearly outlined in his publication, *Contract with America*. It called for the classic Republican doctrines of balancing the budget – not by raising taxes but instead by reducing the immense size and cost of the Washington bureaucracy. It also called for the reforming of the welfare programs that had many Americans living off the dole rather than from their earnings from jobs. And it called for a transformation of Congress itself through the infusion of new blood.

And indeed, in the 1994 elections the Republicans came in control of both Houses of Congress – ending the 40-year reign of the Democratic

---

*Actually, reverse the position, now making any visible opposition to homosexuality the new social crime highly punishable under the law.

Party in the House of Representatives – which then would also elevate Gingrich to the powerful position as Speaker of the House.

But this would then lead to a political standoff between the Republican Congress and the Democratic White House – a reversal of the previous political profile of Washington politics. At the heart of this standoff was a federal budget approved by Congress – which followed Gingrich's lines quite closely – and which got vetoed by Clinton (as was the case also with much of the Republican Party's other bills). Finally, a shutdown of the Federal bureaucracy occurred in mid-November (1995) when neither the White House nor Congress would back down with their opposing positions on the budget bill.

But of course, this was portrayed by the press as a result entirely of Gingrich's intransigence – such hardness of heart that Americans were having to go without various governmental services. Clinton's vetoes were not mentioned. The American press – now almost entirely on the Leftist side of the political spectrum – hated Gingrich, depicting him in the worst possible light.

But at this point Clinton was already beginning his move to the political center, sensing the opportunity there to undercut Gingrich – even by taking on some of Gingrich's programs. For instance, after twice vetoing Republican bills calling for reform of the welfare system – offering job training instead of outright monetary grants to individuals – Clinton finally signed on with the program (the Personal Responsibility and Work Opportunity Act of 1996, also known as the Temporary Assistance for Needy Families Act, or TANF) – actually making it appear as if this new approach to unemployment and poverty was his idea! Initially the Democratic Party was very unhappy at this Clinton betrayal. But it certainly was greeted with strong approval by the Americans themselves – and Clinton's move to the center finally was accepted by his party.*

Then there was the matter of a North American Free Trade Agreement (NAFTA) with Canada and Mexico – opening the economic borders with America's neighbors to the north and south. Actually the Agreement had been put together in the last days of the Bush presidency. But it was Clinton who came up against the American labor unions and their Democratic Party voices in Congress when he pushed for Congress's ratification of the NAFTA treaty. But its passage by the Republican Congress actually soon demonstrated that this helped boost the American economy greatly – even for labor union workers!

---

*After at first supporting the concept as an Illinois state senator, Obama, as president, would work to reduce the work requirements of the TANF welfare program.

The World's Sole Superpower 391

Clinton also took up the task of deregulating the banking industry (pleasing the Republicans) at the same time supporting the expansion of low income mortgages through Fannie Mae (FNMA or Federal National Mortgage Association) and Freddie Mac (FHLMC or Federal Home Loan Mortgage Corporation) – government-subsidized lending (pleasing the Democrats), however leaving both lending organizations vulnerable to financial mishap (which would indeed take place disastrously a dozen years into the future).

Consequently, the American economy entered into a long period of growth – some seeing Clinton as the force behind this development, some seeing Gingrich as its author. Actually, it was a bit of both.

Clinton as a Christian president. When in 1993 the Clinton's came to reside in the White House, the two eventually attended together quite regularly the Foundry United Methodist Church located nearby. And Clinton's relationship with Graham deepened, Graham being called on to deliver the benediction at Clinton's inauguration ceremony and the two meeting often for prayer and consultation thereafter.

* * *

CLINTON AND THE WORLD

In the field of foreign affairs Clinton was to demonstrate an instinct for *Realpolitik* – perhaps picked up from his university days at Georgetown, perhaps by learning from the examples set before him by both Reagan and Bush, and certainly learned from his own experience as Arkansas governor when he had to change course in order to make a political comeback after having lost an election to a more populist opponent.

His moves abroad were carefully calculated on the basis of cost versus reward in promoting the American national interest (the central thesis of Political Realism), but also the global interest – thanks to America now being the world's sole superpower.

"Black Hawk down" in Somalia (1993). Somalia would be an early test case. The United Nations looked to America for help in its efforts to get food aid to thousands of civilian victims of a civil war going on in Somalia among various tribal and gang groups, a war that was tearing that country apart. In October of 1993 Clinton ordered an air assault on the group holding the Somali capital of Mogadishu – which did not turn out well when the local citizens shot back – and two Black Hawk helicopters were downed. Clearly such American intervention had little local support from the Somalis (probably too afraid to come up against the gangs).

At this point Clinton's goal became one of simply extracting American troops from Somalia. There would be no further effort to straighten out Somalia. Actually – as with Reagan's failure in Lebanon in his early years as President – Clinton's pullout from Somalia was greeted with respect on the part of those watching the drama unfold there. Clinton had done the right thing – in not letting his ego get the better of him – and admitting failure in the effort. As a Realist he had simply cut costs and moved on.

Haiti intervention (1994). In Haiti, Clinton was faced with another rapidly deteriorating situation as a result of the overthrow by a military junta in 1991 of the elected government of Jean Bertrand Aristide. Deteriorating conditions in that country had set Haitians in huge numbers (tens of thousands) fleeing the country, heading for America by sea – but with many of the overloaded and unseaworthy boats sinking along the way.

In this matter, Clinton was more circumspect because of the Mogadishu mess. In 1994, with full backing from the United Nations – even as he began military preparations for intervention in Haiti – he sent representatives (former President Carter, General Colin Powell of Iraq War fame and Senator Nunn) to Haiti to let the military junta know that the US was getting ready to send troops to their country, and that they had better restore the civilian government of Aristide before these troops landed.

The Haitian military officers ultimately backed down just as some 20,000 troops (mostly the American 82nd Airborne, but including some from other nations) were about to land in Haiti (September 19, 1994) – and in October Aristide returned to power in Haiti – under the protection of US troops sent to Haiti to oversee the transfer of power. The American troops were then soon pulled out.

Clinton came away from this venture looking very presidential.

"No" – to Rwanda (1994). On the other hand, Clinton had to say "no" to a request from the UN to intervene in the slaughter taking place in Rwanda, as Hutu tribesmen and Tutsi tribesmen fell into mutual slaughter – causing virtual genocide – when possibly as many as a million Rwandans (no one knows for sure the actual count) were butchered in the fighting. This was way too big for America to take on. Clinton's "no" was greeted with scorn by fellow Liberals. But Clinton was very wise not to drag America into something that would only tragically drain a huge amount of American blood with little likelihood that it would make much difference in how things worked out among the Hutus and Tutsis.

But "yes" to Bosnia (1995). Ever since Tito died in 1980, it had been a struggle to keep the various ethnic groups making up Yugoslavia together.

The World's Sole Superpower 393

Basically, divisions were getting deeper – and increasingly hostile. Then with the example set in the departure of the East European countries from the Soviet Empire, the various national groupings in Yugoslavia began to declare independence, starting in early 1990 with Croats and Slovenians (basically Roman Catholic rather than Eastern Orthodox like the dominant Serbs). Then Bosnia-Herzegovina declared independence in 1991 – except independence would carry away a huge section of the Serbian population (about a third of the population in Bosnia). At this, the Serbs invaded Bosnia (also about 44% Muslim – with another 17% Croatian), and ethnic and religious tensions exploded. Civil war soon became mere genocide – as, for instance, in the town of Srebrenica when in 1995 some 8,000 Muslim men and boys were executed by Serbs. And the beautiful city of Sarajevo (the site of the Winter Olympic Games of 1984) became a no-man's land and a physical disaster.

Europeans looked on in horror, and began to discuss the possibility of NATO intervening to stop the genocide. At first, Clinton's reaction was shaped by his experience in Somalia. But the situation grew so grim that he agreed to lead NATO airstrikes against Serb positions – at the same time that Croatian and other Muslim nationals engaged ground troops against the Serbs.

Finally, toward the end of 1995, an armistice – followed by peace negotiations at Dayton, Ohio, plus an agreed-on stationing of 60,000 international troops (20,000 of which were American) – brought the region to a nervous peace. At this point a quarter of a million people had been killed and over a million had been made homeless and living in refugee camps. Getting the states of former Yugoslavia back into some kind of order could now begin – although it was not going to happen quickly – and would require the continuation of the stationing of international troops in the region – on a reduced basis, but there in any case as a warning not to start things up again.

In the end this measured response worked the best way possible. There would be no victory parades and no heroic talk. But the job had been done – and again, Clinton looked very presidential!

The Kosovo Crisis (1999). Then ethnic tensions flared up again in the former Yugoslavia – this time in the southern region of Kosovo – pitting a Serbian minority (but backed by Serbian power to the north) against the Albanian-speaking and largely Muslim Kosovar majority. Genocide again became the rule of the day – with a million Kosovars forced to flee their homes or be slaughtered by the invading Serbs (but small Serbian communities here and there suffered as well from groups of Kosovar militia).

Having so recently experienced the Bosnian crisis, NATO was quick to respond this time – with Americans once again involved in heavy air attacks on Serbian positions – including even the Serbian capital at Belgrade. Rather quickly Serbian President Milosevich was forced to yield – and accept another peacekeeping force of 50,000 troops (7,000 of them American). Milosevich was subsequently arrested and brought before the International Court of Justice at The Hague for war crimes – but died in a Dutch prison during his long trial. And the Kosovars erected a large statue of Clinton in their capital of Priština – certainly the hero to many in Kosovo!

The new friendship with the Russians. The Russians, now under Boris Yeltsin, were experiencing something that roughly qualified as democracy – and enjoyed watching the developing friendship between Clinton and Yeltsin. But underneath it all was a Russia that was having a very hard time coping with a world in which the Russians themselves – and not just their government – found themselves responsible for the social rewards that came their way. A few of them (mostly younger) grew quite rich – some through what would qualify in the West as purely criminal behavior. Others just could not figure out how this democracy thing was supposed to work – and found their lives gradually growing poorer and poorer. Life expectancy dropped by a full ten years – and Russia began to look and act like a Third World country. Increasingly, disenchantment with "Russian democracy" mounted in Russia.

The development of the European Union and NATO. For the West, these were very good times. European nations were coming closer together through the European Union – and the new Maastricht Treaty (1992) which pointed to a full unity of European states – through Europe's single currency, the Euro, and through the free movement of workers and industrial products from country to country within the Union (with Britain still a bit standoffish in keeping their Pound rather than the Euro as their currency).

In addition, the military side of this unity, NATO, was looking very good after action in old Yugoslavia – and was also taking on new members from the former Soviet bloc (to the annoyance of Russian hardliners): the new Czech Republic, Hungary and Poland – bringing the total membership in NATO to 19 countries.

Saddam Hussein's Iraq. Ever since the ouster of Saddam from Kuwait, America had kept a close watch on the Iraqi dictator's doings. He had been forced to accept U.N. terms allowing inspectors into his country to confirm that he was keeping his side of the agreement to suspend chemical, biological and nuclear weapons development ("weapons of mass

The World's Sole Superpower 395

destruction" or WMDs). But Clinton was not convinced that the inspections were digging deeply enough. Thus in October of 1988 he signed the Iraq Liberation Act, financing Iraqi opposition to the Saddam regime. Then in December of that year he forced the inspectors out of Iraq in order to conduct four days of missile attacks on Iraq – although they appeared designed more to undercut the Iraqi government than simply take out questionable weapons production sites (mostly military installations and their personnel were targeted).

There was considerable international opposition to Clinton's program this time, not only from outraged Arabs but also from Russia, China and even France – which reacted with a call to end the oil embargo aimed at Iraqi exports. Others loudly accused Clinton of undertaking in this attack merely a diversion away from the spotlight aimed at him because of the scandal of his having sex with a White House intern. But it certainly was also part of Clinton's tough response to the bombing of the American Embassies in East Africa just a few months earlier. He was getting very tired of dealing with rising Arab Islamic radicalism – from any source, whatever that might be.

Dealing with Islamic Jihad. This matter arose from a growing a problem brewing in the Middle East – one that did not necessarily take conventional national lines and thus fairly expected behavior. Muslim fanatics, young and extremely dedicated in their hatred of things Western, were growing in number – in various ways that had little to do with nations or even countries and their governments. These fanatics, *mujahideen* or jihadists – both words formed from the Arabic *jihad*, meaning "struggle" (against evil) – could be found widely around the Middle East (even as far away as the Philippines) – forming here, moving there, so that it was all that Western intelligence agencies (such as the America's CIA, Britain's MI6 or MI5, or Israel's Mossad, etc.) could do to keep up with their activities.

The Taliban. One such group was the Taliban (from *talib*, Arabic for "student") – that had formed originally at various conservative Muslim schools – most notably the one in Pakistan headed by the Mullah Omar. They were found strongly positioned among the Pashtun tribesmen of Northern Pakistan and Southern Afghanistan. This was the group actually helped by America in their effort to oust the Russian Soviet troops from Afghanistan in the 1980s. But now (1994) from a political base in the southern Afghan (Pashtun) city of Kandahar, the Taliban were focused on overthrowing a tribal coalition governing in Kabul – one which the Americans were trying to work with. In 1996 the Taliban advanced on Kabul and drove the coalition from the capital city – the coalition retreating to the north of the country to become the Northern Alliance under the leadership of the Tajik, Ahmed

Shah Massoud. But the regime of the Taliban was so oppressive (they executed thousands of civilian Shi'ites and minority Hazaris – and drove thousands more to the north of the country as refugees) that Americans felt compelled to support Massoud and the Northern Alliance. This in turn brought friction between America on the one hand and its old allies Pakistan and Saudi Arabia on the other – Sunni Muslim states actively supporting the Taliban. Clinton thus had to move cautiously concerning the mounting crisis in Afghanistan.

Al-Qaeda (or more properly al-Qa'ida). Even more ominously for America, another group of Muslim jihadists – al-Qaeda – was being organized by a Saudi Arab, Osama Bin Laden. His anger at the Saudi Royal family for allowing the stationing of *kaffir* (infidel or unbelieving) American troops on holy Arabian soil (Saudi Arabia itself) during the Gulf War of 1991-1992 had led to his expulsion and flight to the Sudan. In the Sudan, his family name (he was the son of a very wealthy Saudi businessman) convinced the Sudanese government to give him permission to set up a training camp there to prepare young Muslims for jihad – until his organization started conducting attacks on Sudan's neighbors – and he was again expelled. This time he moved to Pashtun lands (both in Afghanistan and Pakistan) where his radicalism was well received. From this position, Bin Laden began to organize cells of operatives instructed in the art of suicide bombing against various kaffir targets – all done to the glory of Allah. At the same time al-Qaeda missionaries were sent around the world to various mosques to bring them to al-Qaeda's jihadist vision.

Part of this was also done in competition with Shi'ite Iran – to promote a Sunni lead in the destruction of infidel Western culture – in Europe, in Asia (principally the Philippines), in Africa, and in America.

The 1993 New York World Trade Center bombing. In late February of 1993 a van parked in the garage of the New York Trade Center exploded – with the purpose of collapsing the North Tower against the South Tower and killing the tens of thousands of people working at these immense towers. Instead, it merely destroyed six stories of the building – although it did kill six people and wound thousands of others. Had the van been parked closer to one of the main supports of the North Tower, the bomb might well have succeeded in its evil design.

The attack was supported financially by a Pakistani al-Qaeda member, Khalid Sheikh Mohammed, uncle of the actual organizer of the event, Ramzi Yousef – who would also be the mastermind of the second (and successful) attack on the World Trade Center in September of 2001 (9/11).

The 1993 operation involved a number of mosques in the New York

The World's Sole Superpower 397

metropolitan area, and the arrest of a number of the conspirators gradually followed. From the outset, American investigators were strongly suspicious of the al-Qaeda organization as the source of the enterprise – though no precise connection was established in the investigation. But at this point, al-Qaeda was put at the top of America's list of terrorist organizations.

The attack on American embassies in Tanzania and Kenya (1998). In August of 1998 two American embassies in East Africa were bombed, with hundreds of people killed. This time al-Qaeda's connection (through its Egyptian affiliate, Egyptian Islamic Jihad) was clearly identified as responsible for the bombings. Clinton struck back immediately, with missile strikes on Afghan and Sudanese targets (although the Sudanese site may have been unconnected to the event). Many Arabs cheered the al-Qaeda attack on the embassies – and took to the streets in protest against the American retaliation.

America's relations with significant parts of the Arab Islamic world were clearly reaching a very low point.

* * *

PARTICULAR EVENTS SHAKE THE COUNTRY DEEPLY IN THE 90s

Although the country had settled down greatly since the tumultuous 1960s and 1970s, there were a number of incidents (besides the Twin Towers bombing of 1993) that shook the country, incidents that stood out not because they represented the sweep of new political impulses, but incidents that for unique reasons of their own shattered the American image of prevailing peace and social justice.

The Rodney King incident (1991-1992). A major tragedy hit the nation in 1992 when a court decision in Los Angeles did not go the way Blacks felt that it should, and for the next six days they rioted, plundered and torched the world around them, causing over $1 billion in property damage to some 1,600 businesses (some 40% of them owned by local Korean shopkeepers), a social catastrophe that injured 2,000 and killed 63 people as well.

The incident occurred over the arrest of Rodney King the previous year, whose takedown by police was videoed by someone drawn to the commotion by police sirens and helicopters. The video was submitted to a scandal-hungry press, which repeatedly showed only the last moments when King was beaten to the ground, failing to mention in their report the long chase of his (and two companions) car through the city's streets and failing to show (in the same video) King's repeated efforts to break from the police when finally caught. But the jury that tried the case did have all the contextual information, and acquitted the police.

That was not a decision that the Blacks wanted. So they rioted, urged on by LA Mayor Tom Bradley, expressing his own anger at the jury decision (understandable on the part of a Black mayor, but one disastrous for LA in the way it encouraged the wrong kind of behavior, not to mention disastrous for Bradley's own political career).

Ironically, King eventually sued the city of Los Angeles, and was awarded $3.8 million in compensation (plus $1.7 million for his lawyers). Thus supposedly American justice was served. King would continue to drink and take drugs, was arrested eleven more times, and finally drowned in his own swimming pool years later.

The Ruby Ridge incident (August 1992). A local feud among neighbors in Idaho turned into a major Alcohol, Tobacco and Firearms (ATF) disaster when an angry neighbor – who lost a property claim in court – took revenge on the Weaver family by reporting them to the FBI and Secret Service as having made threats on the life of the President, the Pope and the Idaho governor (pure fabrication by the neighbor), and eager government officials took the bait. The matter was put in the hands of the ATF and they set a trap to bring Randy Weaver into custody, and the event went wrong. Their warrant, deviously place in his hands when Randy Weaver attempted to help ATF agents pretending to be stranded motorists, listed the wrong date for the court appearance. And when he did not show up, ATF agents were sent to arrest him, resulting in months of a standoff when Weaver refused to give himself up. Then when a TV cameraman filming from a helicopter the action accused (quite falsely) the Weavers of having fired on his helicopter, the Feds felt that they finally had the just cause to act directly against Weaver. Thus six Federal Marshalls were sent to raid his home. When Harris, a family friend, and the Weaver's 14-year-old son went out to investigate the family dog's barking, shooting broke out between Harris and the Federal agents and the son was killed – as well as a US Marshall. Then a sniper killed the wife when she went to the door to let Harris back into the house, and for the next twelve days a standoff occurred at the site as agents negotiated Weaver's surrender.
Ultimately the ATF had no case to stand on other than Weaver not originally showing up at court on schedule. Harris was found not guilty of all charges on the basis that he had simply responded to being fired on by an agent who had failed to identify himself before firing. In fact it became clear that the Federal agents had disregarded the Rule of Engagement (ROE) completely.

Ultimately the "Ruby Ridge" episode became famous as a case of government misconduct – books, songs, and even a CBS miniseries was published over the tragedy, and a lawsuit (quite light in terms of the horrible damage to the Weaver family) was brought successfully against the government.

The Waco Siege (February-April 1993). A similar incident of government malfeasance occurred the following year in Waco, Texas, when locals reported to local officials all kinds of misconduct going on at a very secretive commune of Branch Davidians (a break-away millennialist group from the Seventh-Day Adventists). The locals had no evidence of any of the "facts" they were reporting – only rumors which grew more graphic with the retelling. Thus it was that the ATF was once again brought into a local drama in order to bring "justice" to the matter.

Here too a standoff occurred, which the ATF tried to resolve by simply invading the compound, only for a firefight to break out between the two groups. Four federal officers and five Davidians died and more than 20 other federal officials were wounded in the action. Now the matter became truly a war. Water was cut off to the compound and over 900 officers assembled to begin a full-scale attack (including armored tanks), which on April 19th finally took place. In the melee, the compound burst into flames, 76 Davidians (including numerous women and 25 children) died in the blazing inferno (only nine Davidians came out alive from the event).
The trial of the survivors dragged on for years, even reached the Supreme Court, which finally reduced greatly the sentences imposed on the survivors, and the ATF again came away looking very bad as the facts of the whole incident became ever clearer.

The Oklahoma City bombing (April 19, 1995). Two years later on exactly the same date as the Waco disaster, a huge explosion took out the front portion of a federal building in Oklahoma City, killing 168 people (19 of them children at a day-care center located in the building) and injuring some 680 others, and causing property damage reaching blocks away.
Timothy McVeigh and his accomplice Terry Nichols were stopped for a license plate violation, which in the process revealed to police a record of weapons possession – which in turn led the police to realize that these two were the ones who had carried out the explosion.

McVeigh explained his action as revenge for both the Ruby Ridge and Waco disasters caused by federal authorities (the latter determining the date for McVeigh's action). But McVeigh's vigilante act gave him no just cause in the eyes of the jury and he was found guilty (1997) and executed (2001), with Nichols receiving life imprisonment. This in turn prompted Congress to pass the Antiterrorism and Effective Death Penalty Act of 1996, providing for stronger protection at federal facilities.

The O.J. Simpson murder case (1994-1995). Another event which had the potential to shake the country to the core was the trial of O.J. Simpson, accused by Los Angeles authorities of having killed his ex-wife, Nicole and her boyfriend Ron Goldman on the night of June 12, 1994. Evidence, (a bloody glove found at the scene of the crime in front of Nicole's home and a matching bloody glove found at the home of Simpson) immediately pointed to this famous football (and media) celebrity. Thus when the news hit the media, a huge national drama unfolded. At first it looked as if Simpson might take his own life rather than surrender himself. But ultimately, he gave himself up, and the country prepared for a major courtroom media event.

To make the case as "fair" as possible, a predominantly Black jury was chosen, and the defense thus was able to employ the "bad police" defense (the prosecuting attorney was a "genocidal racist"; racist police could have planted the second glove at Simpson's home to make him look guilty). But the racist argument was countered by pointing to the fact that police had been called to the Simpson's home eight times by battered wife Nicole and only the last time was Simpson actually arrested. However the October 3rd (1995) verdict was foreordained. There was no way that a predominantly Black jury was going to find Simpson guilty of the murders.* Thus the hundreds of police (remembering the Rodney King situation), who were ready to deal with a situation that was expected to follow if he were found guilty, were able to stand down.

The Million-Man March (1995). Just two weeks after the Simpson verdict a huge "Million-Man March" on Washington, D.C., was assembled by Black Muslim leader Louis Farrakhan. But it was designed to encourage a very different sense of honor among Black males than simply "burn, baby burn." Behind this event was deep concern that it was Black women who were left with the responsibility of holding the Black family together – in the face of widespread male no-show at the family scene. The March was a call to men to repent of the way they related to the women of their community, to put themselves before God, and take up the family and social responsibilities that should be theirs as men.

The gathering was peaceful and dignified throughout, seemed to please the White world (which actually commented very little about the

---

*Black jury members included even a former member of the Black Panthers – who in the announcement of the verdict, raised the Black Power fist salute to Simpson!

The World's Sole Superpower

event), but did draw some complaints from Black feminists – who did not find anything redemptive about any event that was focused just on men and them alone.

In any case, would this appeal work? Would it restore the Black family (over 70% of Black children lived in homes with only the mother present) – once the bulwark of Black strength through some very terrible times in American history. But to address that issue, America would also have to address the welfare system that rewarded Black families only when an employable male was not present. This was a major financial disincentive facing the Black family. Thus ironically, the effort of the welfare system to help the Black community had only seemed to make things worse.

The "workfare" policy of Gingrich/Clinton was designed to address this situation, but seemed only to give Black women greater talent as members of the work force (a good thing) without addressing the matter of the missing male (a bad thing). In the meantime, young Black males were still being left to enter manhood without any guidance from a loving father at hand to help them make that entry. Gang membership was too often providing such instruction to rising Black males. But that was hardly a good thing.

What could be done to correct this matter? No one seemed to have any good answers. The Million Man March was an excellent step forward – but ultimately seemed to have changed very little over the longer run.

Impeach, impeach, impeach. Clinton's last two years in office were darkened by revelations of an affair he had been having with a young White House intern, Monica Lewinsky. Sex or money in exchange for status and power has not been a particularly new thing in Washington, or for that matter in the world or across the centuries. This does not make it right. There are rules against it. But being powerful tends to cause people to think themselves exempt from such rules. You are just not supposed to get caught.*

Naturally, Clinton denied having the affair. Then the truth of this affair came out, along with a number of other women who testified that they themselves had had the same experience with Clinton along his way to power. Ah-hah!, so he lied about the affair! Certainly lying to Congress about this affair constituted supposedly one of those "high crimes and

---

*A classic example was King David of ancient Israel, who had sex with a man's wife while the husband was off fighting wars for the King. And bitterly ironic, Gingrich, who was leading the impeachment effort against Clinton, was having his own affair with a woman not his wife (but soon to become his third wife) while Clinton was being tried for his sexual "high crimes and misdemeanors"!

misdemeanors" that then allowed the Republicans to begin impeachment hearings against the president.

But the American public was in no mood for such a move against the president, and the November 1998 elections cut back the Republican majority in the House from 21 seats to 12 seats. This in turn caused a Republican revolt against House Speaker Gingrich, who then announced his resignation as Speaker.* Nonetheless, the impeachment hearings continued forward and on December 19th the vote went against Clinton on two counts and in his favor on two other counts (most of the voting along party lines).

Thus the Republicans joined the Democrats in confirming the new political practice of impeaching the President when any opportunity to do so would present itself, a horrible political activity to mix into the "normal" process of Washington politics.

But when the case went to trial in the Senate, the best the Republicans could do was a 50-50 vote on one count and an even worse 45-55 vote on the other, neither coming close to the 2/3s vote needed to convict.

There were some interesting outfalls from all this. First of all, a new email campaign which called itself "moveon.com" mobilized the young "wired" generation during the 1998 electoral campaign to "move on" past this meaningless scandal, the organization then itself "moving on" to become a major Democratic Party campaign support group in future elections.

And most bizarre of all, Clinton ended his last months in office (prior to the end of his term in January of 2001) with one of the highest approval ratings of a president at the end of his term! Indeed, the nation had "moved on."

The Columbine High School Massacre (April 1999). A tragic event became part of the closing of the 20th century when two high school students undertook a long-planned massacre of fellow students at their Columbine High School in Littleton, Colorado. A bomb by which they had planned to blow up the school failed to detonate. But they were fully armed and succeeded in killing twelve students and a teacher, before they turned the guns on themselves and ended their lives when the police arrived on

---

*Gingrich, despite being returned to his House seat by a huge majority in the November 1998 elections, in January of 1999 – when new terms were due to start – announced that he was stepping down from even his position as simply a House member. Actually, this seems to have been the startup of a spiritual journey for Gingrich, from a Secular Realist (we were both of that same moral-spiritual order back when we were frends, both doing our doctoral research in Brussels in the late 1960s) finally developing into to the strong Catholic Christian he is today.

The World's Sole Superpower

the scene. Ultimately, there was no reason given as to their actions, other than the desire to commit a grander murder than had been the case in the Oklahoma City bombing.

This raised the question, would there be more copycat killings (as this one seemed to be), by people who simply wanted to be significant, to be noticed? People do the most horrible things for the worst reasons imaginable, especially when it becomes a trend (like mass rioting, pillaging and ultimately killing). Would America see more of this kind of behavior in the future?

* * *

SOCIAL DEVELOPMENTS DURING THE REAGAN-BUSH-CLINTON YEARS

Overall, America had certainly settled down a lot since the tumultuous days of the 1960s and 1970s. America enjoyed strong, stable, and quite wise presidential leadership during the 1980s and 1990s. But this did not mean that America was a completely harmonious society. Indeed, a number of fundamental social (even spiritual) problems continued to tear at American society – especially as the world of the Vets gradually found itself giving way to the rising world of the Boomers – with a very different set of political expectations accompanying this major cultural shift.

The continuing advance of professionalism. The American family took a huge hit – as personal professionalism as the supreme goal in life replaced the goal of a family and comfortable place in society, characteristic of the way the Vets went at life. The workplace, not the home, was becoming the staging ground for life's most important endeavors.

Increasingly militant feminism. And there – at the workplace – was the biggest of all problems – for feminists anyway because the workplace had long been dominated by men – and women were demanding equal opportunities to rise professionally, much like the men. And when the system seemed not to move fast enough to accommodate these rising expectations – for instance women claiming to have hit a "glass ceiling" – when they seemed unable to rise to the top in their climb professionally – feminism turned increasingly militant. Men were viewed not as partners in life but as the problem, at times even the enemy.

"Progressives" picked up on the challenge and began to call for an end to the subtle ways men were given priority status in American culture. "Inclusive language" was to be employed in all walks of life. One could no longer talk about "man" as the representative of all humanity (such as in "paleolithic man"). Instead of mailman, the term mail-carrier was to be employed. Congressmen became congressional representatives. "Our men" at war were now "our men and women" at war. Gender studies – or more directly, women's studies – were added as major fields of study at numerous colleges and universities across America (no men's studies however). And virtually all men's colleges were forced to go co-ed (men and women students) – though numerous women's colleges chose to remain in that single-sex category.

In the Christian world the change was just as apparent. Women were not only entering the Christian ministry in large numbers but even finally being appointed as Methodist (1980) and Episcopal (1989) bishops. And, following the trend of the culture, the use of "inclusive language" even in Scripture reading, much less sermons and theological studies, became mandatory in many of the mainline denominations.

One of the more radical of developments along the feminist line was the November 1993 Re-Imagining Conference in which over 2000 women – mostly from the traditional mainline denominations – (plus some 80 men) assembled in Minneapolis to consider ways to rid Christianity of male-centered language which supposedly oppresses women – not to mention to end centuries of patriarchy which crushed the souls of women. To strip God of masculine traits such as "our heavenly Father," the conference continuously referred to God as "Sophia," understood as the life-giving female God of Wisdom. And a communion service was held in which milk was substituted for wine as the new sacramental element. Lesbianism was honored (standing ovation) as the successful release from the oppressive male-dominated family system.

Ultimately the conference sparked enormous outrage of such mainline denominations as the Presbyterians and Methodists, whose national officers had originally contributed funding and planning for the conference, so that the movement backed down and no further attempts were made to go further down this road.

The Feminist/Liberal attempt to block the Supreme Court nomination of a conservative Black, Clarence Thomas (1991). Things got explosive when in 1991 Bush had the audacity to nominate as a Supreme Court Justice a Black conservative, Clarence Thomas. The large Democratic Party majority was not in the mood to see political conservatism grow within the Black world and tried to shoot down the nomination, the same way they had four years earlier when they threw full opposition to the appointment of another conservative (but White), Robert Bork.

And just the previous year another Supreme Court appointment by

Bush, that of David Souter, barely got past the full-force opposition of the National Organization of Women, the NAACP and Senators Kennedy and Kerry, because Souter was a known "conservative," and such ideological bias had no place on the Supreme Court (meaning by someone who did not have the Democratic Party's ideological bias!).

Now the Democrats fully intended to block another conservative Supreme Court appointment by "Borking" Thomas (as the resistance action was coming to be termed). Their effort to destroy the character of Thomas was built on the testimony of a Black female, Anita Hill, brought forward to testify about "inappropriate" behavior of Thomas towards Hill when she worked for him as a staff member. But the effort was muddied greatly by the number of women staffers who came forward to testify strongly in favor of Thomas's excellent behavior as their boss, and the fact that Hill had followed Thomas from job to job, and that it was she who seemed to be initiating whatever relationship (which turned out to be not much) that actually existed between the two of them. Thus the effort to "chauvinize" Thomas fell somewhat flat, and eleven Democrats found the way to vote in favor of his appointment, which passed 52 in favor and 48 against (again, with those 11 exceptions and 2 Republicans who opposed Thomas, the vote being along party lines).

Supreme Court appointments were now big political business, since the Court had taken up the responsibility of being the country's chief legislative branch of the federal government.

The "coming out" of gays and lesbians. Feminists were not the only ones attacking the traditional role of the male in American society. The Boomers' social justice instincts turned to a new victim group – the homosexuals or gays who were being hit hard with the deadly plague of the AIDS virus. The source of the problem was clear enough – as was its most obvious solution. But abstinence even in the face of this deadly disease was not going to happen, and now Boomer Liberals or Progressives began to demand that medical research be diverted from traditional pursuits (cancer, for instance) and focus on finding a cure for AIDS, no matter what the cost. Anyone who differed with this sense of urgency received the immediate label as "homophobe" (hating homosexuals) – so discussion or debate was placed out of reach. For that matter all research into the causes of homosexuality was now declared off limits – because it was decided by the social justice crusaders that homosexuals had no more choice about their status than did Blacks – or even women, for that matter. A person was simply born that way. End of discussion.

Indeed, those who came out of the closet to confess their homosexuality were celebrated as the real heroes of the day. Any who did not feel like celebrating this development with them were portrayed in the most negative of ways.

Traditional Christianity of course considered homosexuality to be no less a sin than prostitution, alcohol, drug and gambling addictions, tendencies to physical violence, etc. – human problems that needed addressing – and deliverance from.* But homosexuality was by the 1980s being taken off the list of such sins, even by some Christians.

Soon therapy was being insisted on not on the part of homosexuals seeking to emerge from that status (actually such therapy was now even outlawed in some parts of the country) but instead, on the part of those not ready to accept it as proper behavior. Pro-homosexual "sensitivity sessions" were being required by corporations of their officers, or employees in the field of government and education, and ultimately even of pastors and lay leaders in some Christian denominations.

This gave recognition to the fact that people's attitudes, beliefs and deepest tastes and preferences can be reformulated through careful re-education ("brainwashing" some would call it, as has so often taken place in dictatorial countries) – and that not only was such action allowed in America, it was even required – as long as it went in the "right direction" – that is, in the direction of "political correctness," as some would term the newly enforced cultural dynamic.

The continuing decline of America's traditional Christian denominations. Christianity was losing its membership rapidly during the 1980s and 1990s. For a variety of reasons, Boomers were not interested in church life, either for themselves or in the raising of their children. Morality was viewed as a matter of simple human logic (just as the Vets had unfortunately supposed to be the case with their Boomer children) – which required no special modeling or discipline. Anyway, the public schools could tend to that matter – because that was simply part of what public education was supposedly all about.

Also this issue of homosexuality tore deeply into the unity of the various Protestant denominations, the ones that once had been the foundation of American culture and society. Fierce battles were fought at national conferences on the issue of the ordination of homosexuals, starting

---

*The first-century Christian leader, Paul, in his Letter to the Romans (chapter one, verses 20-32) goes into lengthy discussion about how such male and female sexual perversity is a result of men and women abandoning their knowledge of God ... with the tragic result that God then simply allows them to fall victim to their own very self-destructive sexual lusts. Not surprisingly, therefore, many Christians believed that AIDS was simply the fruit of just such a horrible sexual dynamic.

with the need at first to affirm that no such thing was going to be allowed – only to have that position challenged at each new national gathering – with the pro-homosexual group making slow progress against the traditionalists (older Vets disappearing in numbers with age). Ultimately the decision would go fully in the LGBT direction – splitting the denominations – and causing bitter battles over church properties of those congregations that pulled out of the old denominations because of this issue. Certainly the loss of unity contributed greatly to the increasing emptiness of the old American churches.

Reagan's prayer amendment. And then there was the failed effort of Reagan in 1984 to get Congress to try once again to put into effect a constitutional amendment protecting the right of prayer in the public schools or any other public institution. Reagan cited the Constitutional Framers' own pro-Christian views on the matter. But it was all to no avail. Reagan could not get the necessary two-thirds vote (only 56 in favor with 44 votes opposed, largely along predictable party lines) needed to authorize a referendum on a constitutional amendment proposal. Reagan would try again the next year, but again with no success.

***Edwards v. Aguillard* (1987).** Just to add to the sense of decline of the Christian covenant that had so long carried the country, the Federal Judiciary got into the act again by way of a case that made its way to the Supreme Court. This blow to the Christian faith came in 1987 in the Court's decision in favor of plaintiffs who argued that the teaching of creationism (the universe being created by God) alongside Darwinism (creation as a self-engineered mechanical process moving forward through time on the basis of its own momentum) was disallowed by the 1973 Lemon Test, which stated clearly that only things that served a purely secular purpose – namely the Darwinist worldview – could be taught in the public schools.

During the court hearings, the only scientists that were allowed to testify were ones that affirmed that creationism was not a co-equal science with the secular world view, "science" now meaning only things that operate mechanically, and thus predictably – and consequently subject to full human control, socially as well as materially. Other opinions were not allowed – as this would merely move things down the forbidden religious path.

Thus with this decision, American children could no longer be taught in the public schools that there was intelligent design in the creation of the universe – only a mysterious self-generated creation. Scientists who would have pointed out that statistically the secular viewpoint made no sense at all were not allowed to make their case – not in 1973, not in 1987

– nor repeatedly after that. To the Federal Courts – God did not exist in any meaningful way. Once again, the First Amendment was interpreted to mean not the *freedom of religion*, but instead the *freedom from religion*!

Evangelical or charismatic Christianity continues forward. Only in the area of Evangelical Christianity was real growth still being registered – again, not at the same rate as the decline of the traditional mainline churches, but certainly at a rate strong enough to keep Christian America from sliding into the status of the largely defunct European Church. Many of these churches were part of the breakaway groups that formed new denominations. But most were simply independent churches formed up out of no particular denominational family – or were part of church growth movements that developed so strongly that satellite churches were started up by the mother churches – even in other parts of the country.

Liberals termed these churches as Fundamentalist. But they really were not part of that group at all – any more than they were a part of mainline Christianity. Evangelicals considered both fundamentalist churches and mainline churches as heavily into "works righteousness." They saw fundamentalists as religious legalists – possessing something of the same legalistic spirit as the ancient Pharisees – the very ones who had Jesus put to death because he was not keeping the Jewish Law the way that the Pharisees read the Law. Likewise they saw the focus of the mainline churches on peace and social justice as just more Liberal abstract idealizing of a perfect world, one that would never come to pass through Christian Progressivists' carefully-designed social programs.

Evangelicals continued to focus on sinners (to the Evangelical, that was *all* of us) and the need for repentance, the acceptance of forgiveness by God through nothing more than faith in God's sacrificial gift of Christ's cross (such faith if even only the size of a mustard seed!), and the acceptance of help by the Holy Spirit to live the new life in Christ in power – power to push back the ever-pressing forces of evil.

Evangelical Christianity was/is personal – very personal – personally relational rather than rationally programmatic. It did not happen by taking the right position with respect to the fundamentalists' laws of the Church – nor the Liberals' programs of peace and social justice. It came through getting involved, personally, in a very confused and needy world, needy of personal companionship and a mutual sharing of life's journey. As some would put it, Evangelical Christianity was like one street bum showing another street bum where they could together get some food.

And certainly the world would not soon run out of the need for that kind of Christianity!

CHAPTER THIRTEEN

AMERICA STUMBLES

* * *

BUSH, Jr. TAKES COMMAND

The national election of the year 2000. The Presidential electoral campaign of 2000 seemed to offer America an assurance that the politically mature path it had been on since the grand catastrophe of the 1960s and 1970s would continue. The two Boomer candidates competing against each other both came from political families well known to the American public – both the Bushes and the Gores. The Democratic candidate, Al Gore, had served eight years in the U.S. Senate – before being brought on board in 1993 to serve eight more years as Clinton's Vice President. George Bush (we will call him "Bush, Junior" because he differs from his father, the former President, only in dropping one of his father's middle names) was a newcomer to the national scene, but was in his sixth year serving as Texas governor as of the 2000 national election. Both seemed excellent choices. Indeed, the election was a very close one, Gore actually winning the total popular vote – but losing the electoral vote by only 4 votes. The Florida vote was so close (a mere several hundred votes separating the two candidates) that it went through a long period of recounts – only to have the Supreme Court validate the decision of the Florida Secretary of State (a Republican) that Bush had won that state's electoral vote – and thus the national election.

In keeping with long-standing American political tradition, Gore was gracious in accepting the final decision of the Supreme Court on the vote and stepped aside politely to let Bush take leadership of the nation.

George "W" Bush. Bush, Jr. was, like Bill Clinton, born in 1946, and most certainly qualified as a Boomer, political idealism and all. We already know about his family background, and can safely say that although born of a traditional Connecticut dynasty, he was raised clearly as a Texan, and was most affirmative of that fact.

He not only saw the world as something that needed to be conquered, but also had a tough generation or two to follow – and measure up to in his own development. And it would always leave the haunting question to Bush, Jr., who would be left to wonder if it was on the basis of his own merits, or on the merits of his father and grandfather, that he was experiencing success in life. That's one of the truly tough things that comes with being born to enormous social privilege.

He would of course be raised a Christian, but would have that faith tested deeply early on, when at age seven he had to watch his younger sister die of leukemia. And oddly enough, even his family name could not open the doors for him to study at Houston's prestigious St. John's School. That was hugely disappointing. But ironically, he was instead enrolled in the even more prestigious Phillips Academy up East in Andover, Massachusetts. So, was that God's doing, or was it due to the fact that both his father and grandfather went there as well?

Interestingly, he rather enjoyed being the Texan amidst the polished up-East aristocrats, playing the "good-old-boy" Texan to the hilt! It gave him important social standing, which his mediocre grades did not! He became a leader thereby, and took this social profile along with him when he later (1964) entered Yale University (also a family legacy and certainly responsible for his admission, achieved in spite his poor academic record). And at Yale he kept up the profile as a smoking, drinking, fraternity boy, popular with the girls in the nearby girls' colleges. And certainly not because of his grades, he was even admitted to Yale's prestigious Skull and Bones Society (like his father).

However, he never became truly fascinated with the "polished" up-East world, and returned to Texas in 1968 and joined the Texas Air National Guard (family connections opening the way for him into this highly-sought-after unit).* Then he went through his ten "nomadic years" – as he termed them. But those years included getting an MBA at Harvard Business School (1975), starting up his own oil business on his return to Texas, and then bringing that era to a wonderful conclusion in meeting, and three months later marrying (1977) a former 7th grade classmate, Laura Welch. This began the process of settling him down, especially when in 1982 twin daughters were born.

It was in meeting the traveling evangelist Arthur Blessitt in 1984 – and the following year, Billy Graham – that made Bush's Christianity more

---

*During his 2000 presidential campaign, his joining the Air National Guard was cast simply as a way of avoiding the draft – and dangerous military service, such as his opponent Al Gore had undergone. Maybe. But Bush actually proved himself to be an excellent fighter pilot in training exercises, though he never saw actual active duty.

than a mere church-going formality. In his new "born-again" life, he took up Bible and devotional reading and a life of prayer, and ended his drinking and eventually his smoking. In fact, so immersed in this evangelical world was Bush that, in helping out in his father's presidential campaign (1987), he was assigned the task of developing invaluable liaison work with various American evangelical ministries.

Finally however, he was able (1989) to establish credibility by his own right, investing money from his oil business in the Texas Rangers baseball team, in the process, putting his name out front in Texas public affairs.*

Thus in 1994 he took up the challenge of running for public office as Texas governor (he had failed back in 1978 at a run for Congress) against the Democratic Progressivist and incumbent governor, Ann Richards, a daring thing to do. But it was a big year for the Republicans nationally (thanks to Gingrich) and Bush defeated her soundly, gaining 54.5% of the vote to her 45.9%.

Besides taking a typical Republican stance on such items as cutting taxes, as governor he also presented himself as a "compassionate conservative" (in Boomer-talk, meaning sensitive to the injustices in the world), supporting educational reform, Hispanic community development (he loved to demonstrate his Spanish linguistic abilities), and community action programs through groups set up to work locally on social reform. And here is where his Christian faith played a big role, when he looked especially to "faith-based" groups to take the lead in developing and administering the local social programs.

He did so well at his job that he was reelected four years later – with an even bigger 69% support in the election, the first person in Texas history to win a back-to-back electoral victory as governor!

Now as his second term was coming to a close, he took up the idea of a run for the U.S. presidency. It seemed to be a familiar world, and he felt quite confident that he could win the contest. And what he brought to the field of competing Republican candidates was his own record as a "compassionate conservative" governor, ready to see things run from Washington on much the same basis.

Eventually the Republican field was thinned down to just Bush versus John McCain, a war hero and Arizona senator. The campaign against McCain got ugly. But Bush came out on top in the contest.

Now in taking on his Democratic Party opponent, Al Gore, one of Bush's lines of attack was all the costly and dangerous "nation-building" that the Democrats had involved America in during Clinton's presidency

---

*And becoming a multi-millionaire when he sold his interests in the team nine years later, just prior to his run for the U.S. presidency.

(and – more importantly at the moment – Gore's vice-presidency). *

In the end, probably most of the people who went to the polls to vote for Bush did so because he was the Republican candidate and because he was the son of a well-respected former American president. Otherwise there seemed to be very little differing the two candidates. Both ran as politically experienced "centrists."

The Bush Administration. Bush had appointed a very diverse cabinet, knowingly or unknowingly likely to have conflicting views on strategic issues, especially those concerning foreign affairs.

Chief among the voices that would have a strong impact on the way Bush saw and went after things was actually not an appointee, but his vice president, Dick Cheney. Cheney had served presidents as far back as 1974, rising to be Ford's very youngish chief of staff. He then became a congressman (1978-1988), rising to the ranks as Republican minority whip, before being appointed by the elder Bush as his Secretary of Defense. He then retired to private service in some conservative think tanks before becoming chief executive officer (CEO) of the Haliburton energy giant (1995). Cheney would serve as something of a sounding board for Bush, Jr., Bush meeting with him privately after cabinet meetings to get Cheney's opinion on matters, something Bush valued greatly.

Then there was Donald Rumsfeld, who had also served on Ford's cabinet (Secretary of Defense) and close Cheney associate since then. In fact it was on Cheney's advice that Bush, Jr. appointed him as his own Secretary of Defense. Together, those two would dominate Bush's foreign policy thinking, for better or worse.

True, Bush had a Secretary of State, General Colin Powell, a veteran military advisor as Reagan's National Security Adviser and Bush, Sr's Chairman of the Joint Chiefs of Staff. But knowing the military quite well – its capabilities and its limitations, he typically advised a much more cautious approach to foreign policy matters than did the Cheney-Rumsfeld team.

And allying with Powell was Bush's own National Security Advisor, former Stanford University professor and then university provost, Condoleezza Rice. But the Cheney-Rumsfeld duo did not pay much attention to her, Rumsfeld at times treating her as if she were merely some university grad student offering limited advice on matters.

Then there was George Tenet, Director of the Central Intelligence

---

*But ironically, Clinton's nation-building (in Haiti, Bosnia and Kosovo) had actually been quite cautious and relatively restrained in extent, in stark contrast to what Bush's nation-building (Afghanistan and Iraq) would soon come to be, especially as it became the all-consuming focus of much of Bush's presidency! And the reason why this should be the case was never very clear.

Agency, a carryover from the Clinton Administration (the CIA and its officers were expected to be "non-political"). He too would find himself up against Rumsfeld in taking on the key issue of America's "war on terror."

This would be the team that would have to somehow work together to support its president, as he came to face major foreign policy issues that arose after the 11th of September during his first year in office.

No Child Left Behind. Actually Bush presumed that his real work as a "compassionate conservative" president would be in the realm of domestic affairs, and had taken on the challenge of national education reform with the same zeal that he had done so when Texas governor. But educational policy had long been a state and local matter, not one of Washington's business. But Bush was able to put Republican support behind him (Democratic support was considered to be automatic in such matters) and thus found huge support in Congress for his "No Child Left Behind" (NCLB) Act. This program called for states to undertake standardized testing, and receiving federal financial support if they did so, with the expectation that those testing scores would also improve every year in the process.*

Anyway, Bush was in Florida for a well-publicized visit to a school there, designed to give support to his educational thrust, when an event occurred that would change everything about his presidency.

* * *

THE HUNT FOR 9/11 TERRORISTS, AND BUSH'S NATION-BUILDING†

9/11 and its aftermath. That morning he got the terrible news that deep tragedy had just fallen on New York City's Twin Towers – the tragedy soon amplified by a similar hit on the Pentagon, and also a downed plane in the Pennsylvania countryside.

Four commercial airplanes had been highjacked by al-Qaeda jihadists. Two planes were flown straight into the New York World Trade Center buildings, eventually bringing them down, with 2,600 office workers,

---

*Not surprisingly, over the years, complaints grew that Bush's program had teaching now shaped by the single consideration of improving test scores, making the education process itself very mechanical and not terribly effective in creating truly well-educated youth. In 2015 the program was finally replaced by one supporting the states, as they themselves saw the need for educational reform.

†For a truly in-depth coverage of this section, see my Volume III, *The Dismissing of America's Covenant with God* (Westbow, 2020), pp. 206-232.

police and firefighters dying in the tragedy. Another one was aimed at the Pentagon building, killing 125 officers and workers there. And one flight – alerted via cell phone by spouses that their highjacked plane was undoubtedly headed for a strategic site in Washington, D.C. – was brought down in rural southwestern Pennsylvania by very heroic passengers. All aboard were killed (40 passengers and crew as well as the hijackers). But either the Capitol Building or White House (the probable goals of the hijackers) was spared the fate of the Twin Towers and the Pentagon.

America – and the world – was stunned, though parts of the Muslim world understood the jihadist source of the hit and celebrated this "victory" accordingly.

It is not that the world should have been completely surprised by this event.* A similar attack had happened only eight years earlier. And a key Afghan ally of America's, Massoud, had been assassinated only a couple of days earlier – and the American intelligence community sensed that something big might be about to unfold. But the sharing of intelligence across the many agencies involved in such national intelligence activity was very poor – actually rather competitive, thus the subsequent creation of the Homeland Security Office in order to force better cooperation within the intelligence community.

In any case, it took no time to realize that behind this all was the hand of Osama bin Laden and his al-Qaeda jihadist group. His training camps in Afghanistan were well known to American intelligence, as well as the even more numerous camps located in America's supposed ally Pakistan.

The "Bush Doctrine." Thus on September 20th Bush went before Congress to announce his "Bush Doctrine" – namely that any country harboring such jihadist criminals must give them up, or suffer dire consequences from the Americans. Americans would go after bin Laden and his associates, wherever they might go.

---

*Very, very ironically, in early September of 2001 (as a just-hired history and social studies teacher at a Christian school in Pennsylvania) I was making this introductory point that foreign affairs was not really an option for "Fortress America," despite the huge walls of the Atlantic and Pacific Oceans that it seemed we could hide behind if we chose to do so. I knew that there were enemies abroad intending to bring the battle to America itself, despite those oceanic walls. I cited as the most obvious example Muslim jihadists, America-haters that I pointed out were certainly going to make another attempt on the highly visible and extremely valuable American national symbol, the New York Twin Towers. However, I had no idea that this prophesy would be fulfilled literally the very next day. My students never forgot this act of unintended prophecy. But tragically, I lost two former parishioners in that disaster. Thus this was indeed horribly painful prophecy, something I would hope never to be called on to do again.

At the time, supposedly the search for bin Laden involved only the Taliban group that had overthrown Massoud's Northern Alliance group and taken control of Kabul, the Afghan capital. But clearly the Taliban were in no mood to give up bin Laden and his terrorist organization. To them the al-Qaeda terrorists were heroes, defenders of Muslim integrity.

And so the Americans would have to devise their own way to bring down bin Laden and al-Qaeda. Supposedly this would involve undercover work of CIA operatives – bribing local clan leaders to zero in on bin Laden. But even then, such action would involve some large-scale operations which certainly were going to involve deep conflict with the Taliban.

As it turned out, the Northern Alliance – even with its leader gone – was able to keep itself organized and, with the aid of NATO airpower, ultimately was able to chase the Taliban out of the Afghan capital of Kabul (mid-November) and off into the Afghan Tora Bora mountains. But still, this did not bring bin Laden or al Qaeda to account.

Nation-building in Afghanistan. At this point Bush seemed to see the Afghan picture in much, much bigger terms. With the expulsion of the Taliban from Kabul, Afghanistan supposedly could now be brought into closer alliance with America – by "democratizing" its political habits. The president's wife, Laura Bush even went before the press to talk about how American action in Afghanistan could finally liberate Afghan women from the traditional oppression that they had suffered under for so long.

In short, the Bushes were now focused on "nation-building" in Afghanistan – a much, much bigger process than simply bringing bin Laden to justice.

While such talk impressed many Americans and Westerners, it also impressed many in the Muslim world – except in the very opposite manner. Americans find it virtually impossible to understand that not everyone else in the world goes at life, or even wants to go at life, the way they do. Muslims understand that the good life comes from a universe in which everyone finds a place of submission to the larger order of things, children to their parents, wives to their husbands, families to their elders or community leaders (from tribal sheiks to religious mullahs), regional community leaders to their ruling or presiding princes, amirs, kings and ayatollahs, and all of them ultimately to Allah. The central idea in Islam is "to submit." Muslims are "those who submit."

American (especially Boomer) talk about pursuing full personal freedom from any and all authority shocks Muslims, appearing to them as something very dangerous to human order, to the good life, especially to the pleasure and blessings of Allah himself. Thus when Americans go invading a Muslim country to bring "democracy" as part of a new nation-building venture, this is not destined to work the way Boomers believe it is supposed to. "Freedom of choice" to Muslims means the opportunity to show ever stronger support for those in authority, not infrequently in opposition to other groups seeking to do the same. If this is not handled carefully, such "democratizing" can easily plunge a Muslim society into a horrible state of civil war among local groups that have found no higher personality to unite around. Thus dumping Muslim "dictators" is a very dangerous program in the Muslim world.

And America was soon to discover this. And once again, America would also fail to take note of the actual dynamic – instead simply pushing ever-harder to make their version of social dynamics work in a setting where there was no natural inclination of the people themselves to go the way Americans thought things should go! Therefore, things would get very brutal, very fast.

With the decision to go to full nation-building in Afghanistan the operation was taken out of the hands of the CIA and put under direction of Donald Rumsfeld and his Department of Defense – that is, the American military establishment. But of course the U.S. military was by no means battle-ready at a moment's notice for such an operation, and would need weeks of preparation, during which time bin Laden naturally slipped into the mountains – and then probably back into Pakistan.

And there in Pakistan, where the Americans had no authorization to pursue him, he would be safe from the American military's effort to hunt down him and his organization. Because Pakistan was a supposed American ally, and because it was a nuclear power, and because Pakistan made it very clear that they too would under no terms give bin Landen and al Qaeda over to the Americans, Pakistan was one place – the key place in fact – where the Bush Doctrine did not apply. Thus in terms of political reality, the "Bush Doctrine" had no real meaning.

But in any case, the "democratization" of Afghanistan would supposedly justify any and all American political and military operations in Afghanistan – even if all that ultimately had nothing to do with bringing bin Laden to justice.

This would prove to be a major American foreign policy distraction –along the lines of Johnson's Vietnam program – one which would prove very costly to the Americans, and to the Afghans. And it had strikingly similar qualities to the (failed) Soviet efforts earlier to bring Afghanistan into their political orbit. But Bush took no notice of the dynamics that made his program there look extremely costly – with little real political benefit likely to come from the effort.

But oddly enough, America had the rather substantial assistance of a number of its European NATO allies, in part due to the fact that they too had lost some of their own citizens in the Twin Towers tragedy. But what that had to do with Bush's program of democratizing Afghanistan was just as remote for them as it was for America.

Nation-building in Iraq. What then possessed Bush to turn his attention to Iraq remains to this day an unanswered question. Iraq's President Saddam Hussein was a dictator, a flamboyant self-appointed candidate to become the leader of the entire Arab nation (all the Arab countries of the Middle East), in competition with other such Arab candidates. He used the usual Arab call to unity around the Jewish intrusion into the Arab world in the establishment of Israel and made all kinds of noise in that regard. And he built up his military accordingly in order to present a plausible claim to such candidacy.

But as we have seen, he overstepped himself in Kuwait and he and his army got burned badly. He was put under all sorts of military quarantine which restricted his venturesome ways – though not necessarily his language, used to keep himself "important" in the eyes of his own people. Bush Sr. had not bothered to do more than kick him out of Kuwait, but had gone no further in the matter of hemming in the loud dictator. As his Secretary of Defense Dick Cheney would later explain, to have gone deeper into Iraq would have amounted to entry into a "quagmire." Nothing would be gained – at great expense to everyone concerned.

But Bush Jr. somehow decided that the world would be a better place if Saddam were to just disappear. And it would also offer Iraq the opportunity to go "democratic." That, to Bush, justified the huge enterprise. He was determined to go nation-building in Iraq, no matter what the cost involved.

But Bush's cabinet seemed to be less than unanimous about undertaking this project. However, Dick Cheney, now Bush's Vice President and closest advisor, was changing his tune – and was now fully in favor of jumping into the quagmire. Likewise his Secretary of Defense, Donald Rumsfeld, not only had the U.S. military standing in readiness, but had the perfect candidate in mind, Ahmed Chalabi, to lead Iraq to "democracy." And the U.S. Congress, in October of 2002, not wanting to appear to be unpatriotic, authorized exactly such action in Iraq – by a huge majority: 297-133 in the House and 77-23 in the Senate.*

But unlike his successful efforts in enlisting allies for his Afghan

---

*All but 8 of the 213 Republican congressmen approved the resolution; but 126 of the 208 Democrats did not. In the Senate, all but one of the 49 Republicans voted approval. But so did 29 of the 50 Democrats (one independent voting "no"), those voting in favor including Hillary Clinton, John Kerry and Charles Schumer – who would of course later try to backtrack on that unfortunate decision of theirs.

program, he got very little support from the international community (Britain would however join Bush in this enterprise – at great loss to both Britain and its Prime Minister Tony Blair). At first Bush tried the "Bush Doctrine," claiming Saddam's support for al-Qaeda, and thus candidacy for American retribution. But nobody bought that explanation. Then in September 2002, Bush went before the United Nations General Assembly to put forward the claim that Saddam was violating the international restrictions he had been placed under since his rebuke over Kuwait – that Saddam was secretly developing weapons of mass destruction (WMDs).

The physical evidence in this claim offered by U.S. intelligence was very questionable – and it quickly appeared that the larger world was not buying his story. Ultimately the UN simply decided to send more inspectors into Iraq to see what evidence they themselves could find on this matter.

But when, after months of searching Iraq, the UN inspectors were unable to come up with any such WMD evidence, an anxious Bush saw his case before the court of world opinion weakening rapidly. Thus he made one more effort to win the world to his cause, using the excellent international reputation of his Secretary of State, Colin Powell, to make a hopefully compelling presentation in February of 2003 before the United Nations on this WMD matter. Bush also had an American proposal put before the UN Security Council authorizing action against Saddam. But when it became apparent that France, Russia and Germany were strongly opposed to this, he had the proposal withdrawn.

Bush thus decided that he was going to take out Saddam anyway, no matter what the rest of the world's opinion happened to be on this matter.

Into the quagmire. Thus on March 20th, Rumfeld's military unleashed "Shock and Awe" (very heavy bombing) on the Iraqi capital of Baghdad. Saddam went into hiding and Iraq found itself leaderless as Americans, joined by British (and smaller units of Australian and Polish) military invaded their country. Within a few weeks Iraq found itself delivered over to its new "democratic liberators."

Then the quagmire revealed itself. Looting and ransacking of Baghdad got underway as people scrambled to get what they could of items before the economy shut down. Then the three major ethnic groups that had been held together only by Saddam's tough hand fell into fighting among themselves: the Sunni Kurds in the North, the Sunni Arabs in the West, and the Shi'ite Arab community in the East and South. And the Turks next door – America's long-standing NATO ally – became intensely upset with Bush and his American invaders because Iraqi social breakdown also jeopardized the social order in heavily Kurdish south-eastern Turkey. This would mark the beginning of the Turkish pull-back from its formerly close relationship with America.

Mission accomplished? But Bush ignored these deepening disasters, and on May 1st, arrived by jet aboard a U.S. carrier located offshore from San Diego (not somewhere in the Middle East!), Bush wearing a flight suit, although he himself had not piloted the plane. He changed clothing and then appeared on deck to address the world with a very upbeat speech, with the huge banner "Mission Accomplished" displayed above the deck – in indication of how things supposedly stood on this Iraqi matter.

But at this point nothing except disaster had been accomplished! And that would immediately be worsened even further by Rumsfeld's envoy, Jerry Bremer, sent to administer Iraq as Bremer himself saw the need. In early May, Bremer issued fundamental Orders 1 and 2. The first declared that anyone formerly connected with Saddam's Ba'athist Party (virtually every professional in the country) would be prevented from serving in their former capacity in the "new Iraq." And the second order, issued over the objection of the U.S. military commanders who had called on the service of the Iraqi army to keep some degree of order in the country, was to disband the Iraqi army – to un-employ hundreds of thousands of young men with rifles, and the knowledge of how to use them. So upset was the U.S. military command over this huge political blunder that all of the top generals chose to "retire" – leaving the new military matters in the hands of a very inexperienced American one-star general (actually Rumsfeld would direct overall U.S. military policy from DC anyway).

It was also at this point that anger aimed by the Iraqis against their fellow Iraqi social-cultural opponents now got turned on the occupying Americans and British, especially against the Americans. At this point the real Iraqi war got underway. And it would drag on for years – a true American (and British) quagmire.

Ultimately, Americans never came up with any evidence of Saddam having been developing WMDs. However, Saddam himself was finally captured, sentenced and then executed – for committing crimes no worse than the ones Lincoln had committed in order to preserve the unity of the U.S. against Southern rebels. Then Americans directed those Iraqis willing to take up the task of putting together a new Iraqi constitution – something that supposedly would finally justify this grand misadventure.

But politically speaking, all that would develop from this effort to "democratize" Iraq was to shift power from the Sunni Arab portion (about 20%) of the population, the sector that Saddam had counted on for his political support, to the Shi'ite Arab portion of the population (about 60%), the largest of the social groups and the one that had suffered minority status under Saddam. But oddly enough there was little gratitude from the Shi'ites for their "liberation" by the Americans and the British. Instead they simply took this opportunity for revenge against the Sunnis, and then turned on the Americans and the British when the latter group tried to settle the angry Shi'ite community down. And then there were the non-Arabic Sunni Kurds (another 20%), who had been waiting for decades for Kurdish independence (much to the anger of the Turks next door), the only group that showed some degree of real support of the American presence in Iraq.

Thus exactly how leaderless "democracy" was going to restore social unity in Iraq instead of merely intensifying these deeper social divisions would remain a mystery to Iraq's American and British "liberators." None of the Iraqis had ever even heard of Rumsfeld's presidential candidate Chalabi (!!!) and so coming up with a leader was going to become difficult. Finally (October 2005), under the new constitution, national elections were held (boycotted by most all of the Sunni Arabs) and a Shi'ite, Nouri al-Maliki, was put forward as a leader of a coalition and thus also as prime minister.

But this in no ways settled down the violence that consumed Iraq. In 2006 the situation worsened deeply when some group blew up the al-Askari or Golden Dome in Samarra, one of Shi'ite Islam's most holy sites. Shi'ites turned on Sunni mosques and murdered the imams found there. Soon death squads were roaming the country, especially in the Sunni West where American troops were expected to keep some kind of order (although Rumsfeld was trying to maintain a "small footprint" by keeping U.S. troops mostly restricted to the U.S. military bases in the country).

And wouldn't you know, all this chaos (thanks to Bush) would allow al-Qaeda and other Sunni jihadists finally to make their way to Iraq and begin to base their operations there, a much more strategic location than Afghanistan or Pakistan in making anti-Western mischief throughout the Arab Middle East. Thus it was that the only true "mission accomplished" that occurred in Iraq was the one gained by the anti-American Shi'ites (religious kinsmen of the Iranian Shi'ites next door, Muslims pledged to bring "death to the Great Satan America") in the Iraqi East and South, and the anti-American Sunni jihadists in the West and Northwest of the country.

Political repercussions back home in America. In the 2004 American presidential elections, Bush was able to gain reelection against the Democratic Party candidate, John Kerry – to a great extent because the election got to be not about public policy but about very personal matters. Kerry's Vietnam service record was challenged (unfairly as it turned out) by a group of Vietnam veterans, sinking greatly Kerry's political support. CBS had countered this attack with its own report of service scandal on Bush's part – and then had to repent when it was discovered that the material Dan Rather had been using as "evidence" was a forgery.* While this CBS special was clearly intended to sabotage the Bush candidacy, it actually stirred sympathetic support to the besieged president! Thus it was that, quite exceptionally, Bush was reelected – virtually unheard of at a time when a leader's war was clearly not going well at all.

But the 2006 Congressional elections would hit the Republican hard. They lost their majority in the House to the Democrats and had their position in the Senate reduced further, with also the two Senate independents tending to vote with the Democrats.

It was at this point that Bush got rid of Rumsfeld. He had removed Rumsfeld's cabinet rival Powell back in 2004. But Bush was now reversing course (too late for Powell however) in getting rid of Rumsfeld. But the Republicans were very upset: why hadn't Bush done this before the elections, when it would likely have helped the Republicans considerably?

The 2007 "surge" in Iraq. The situation in Iraq was growing worse, not better through previous (Rumsfeld) policies. And finally, on the basis of a study that Bush took a great interest in, the decision was made to end Rumsfeld's "small footprint" strategy, increase considerably the number of U.S. troops in Iraq and pursue a very aggressive forward strategy, designated as a grand military "surge." Not surprisingly it worked. It impressed the Shi'ite leaders enough that they decided to be more cooperative with the Americans, it allowed the British to back out of an Iraqi mess that had cost Britain's political leadership deeply, and it cut back considerably the operational abilities of the Sunni jihadists in the northwest. And hopefully it gave the Americans (and their private "contractors") the opportunity to do some serious training of the (now mostly Shi'ite) Iraqi army so as to be able to take control. And thus as Bush approached the last months of his presidency in late 2008, he was finally able to begin the drawdown of the American military presence in Iraq.

* * *
ECONOMIC CATASTROPHE (2008)

---

*Scandal rather than serious news filling America's media front-line reporting was not a new thing. Grocery store checkout stations had long been loaded with "newspapers" reporting such things as: "I was raped by a monster from Mars"; "Dog gives birth to a puppy with two heads"; etc. But when the nation's prestige papers began to undertake this same behavior, along with national TV feeding sensationalist "news" to the public 24/7 as simply another form of entertainment, America's news industry became itself a much-degraded American institution. The Walter Cronkite days of CBS were clearly over.

The "easy money" disaster. But at this point, Bush had big problems at home to deal with – actually huge problems, because the American economy was facing a meltdown, such as it had not seen since the early 1980s, and possibly even since the days of the Great Depression. Much of the cause was foolish economic policies undertaken by the Bush Administration when the long economic growth experienced since those early 1980s and extended through the 1990s seemed to lose some steam in the early 2000s. To encourage continuing economic growth, Bush decided to set aside regulations carefully put in place in the early 1930s – regulations designed to protect the American financial world from falling into a speculative bubble, such as the one that burst at the end of the 1920s. And yes, at first it looked as if the new "freeing up" of the world of American finance was giving the American economy the medicine it needed to get up and moving at the pace it had been doing so formerly.

But this was timed with (and part of the cause) of another economic issue developing at the time: the huge growth in the American national debt. It went from 57% of the nation's total economic output per year to 70% of that amount in Bush's eight years in office, actually doubling from $5 trillion to $10 trillion in that same time. So critical had the national debt become that it looked as if merely paying the interest at the normal rate of about 6% on that debt would take up most all of the federal government's discretionary funding (the part that is not already mandated, such as Social Security funding, and thus not accessible for government spending) leaving little funding available for the government's operational programs – including the very, very expensive war in Iraq.

So a simple solution was offered by the Federal Reserve Bank: to lower the Fed's discount rate – that is, the interest rate that the Federal Reserve charges the banking world for the financial backup banks need to conduct their own financial operations (a complete reversal of the high interest rate strategy enacted 30 years earlier by Federal Reserve chief Volcker!). Reducing that rate would also lower greatly the interest rate that the government would have to pay to cover its own enormous (and rapidly growing) debt. And thus it was that the Federal discount rate steadily came down, to a point where by 2008 it was running at the unheard of rate of less than 1%!!!

This cheapening of dollar-financing not only helped the federal government cover its growing debt expenses, and not only did it help America's world of financial capital (the bankers) give a boost in supporting America's world of industrial capital (the producers), it also gave ordinary Americans a major incentive to finance the purchase of a new car (why not an expensive SUV?) or a much nicer and bigger home. With car and house loans running at amazingly low interest rates, why not?

And thus there was a rush to purchase these new goodies – especially in a hungry housing market moving faster than the rate of production (at first anyway) of these items, driving up their prices steadily (the price of a typical house would double over a ten-year period from the mid-1990s to the mid-2000s). Nonetheless, with interest rates so low, and with Americans now believing that financial indebtedness was simply a natural part of American life, Americans jumped into the market anyway – to pick up these items before the prices got any higher.

Banks also jumped into the frenzy, not wanting to be left behind in the buildup of their "assets" (the number of loans and mortgages they were holding), to make themselves rank higher in the numbers game played in the heart of this competitive financial world.

And now, with financial restrictions greatly eased, they could even extend "subprime" home mortgages to borrowers whose actual financial abilities (the ability to continue to make regular payments on loans over a 15 to 30-year period) were at best very shaky. This was most unwise. But the logic was that if the holders of the loan found that they could not continue to make payments, then the house could be sold – and, with the continuing rise in the cost of houses, everyone could even make a bit of a profit in the deal.

But wasn't this cultivating exactly the same philosophy or financial mentality that led America into the grand stock-market crash of 1929?

Market saturation bursts the speculative bubble. Unsurprisingly, once again, market saturation entered the picture. Contractors had jumped at the opportunity to build new homes. Build, build, build. The housing market was hot, very hot.

But by 2006 there appeared a slowdown in the housing market, as contractors were finding a growing number of their new homes were simply sitting there empty, unsold – with little apparent prospect for a purchaser in sight. By 2007 it was quite apparent to all that that they simply had overbuilt housing units well beyond the interests or abilities of the world of home purchasers, even despite these low interest rates. Consequently, there was only one thing to do at that point: reduce prices in order to lure people to buy these unsold homes. But once one contractor did so, thus so did another, and then another. Suddenly the pricing or value of these homes begin to drop – dramatically.

At this point the presumption disappeared that subprime-mortgage holders, unable continue to make house payments, would be able to easily sell off their houses and walk away with a small profit. With the dramatic drop in housing prices, people's mortgage commitments now exceeded the actual market value of their homes. People now found themselves trapped financially, able to escape that trap only by simply walking away from their home, losing whatever they had previously invested in that home, leaving their home now in the hands of the mortgage bank to deal with. And many people began to do just that.

But whereas a borrower could walk away with the loss, a bank could not. The house was the bank's problem now – a huge financial problem now that the market value for that house had fallen well below what the bank itself had originally invested in it by way of the original home loan. The banks too could rid themselves of these liabilities only by trying to sell them off in a very horrendous housing market, involving huge financial losses with each house that they had to unload.

But banks are in the business to make money, not lose money. Thus banks now found themselves in trouble, deep, deep trouble. The speculative house-financing bubble had burst and the results were very, very ugly.

Panic sets in (2008). At first the huge investment bank Bear Sterns was in deep trouble. JP Morgan (supported by a $30 billion federal loan) agreed to buy out Bear Sterns, thus avoiding a catastrophe, and calming down the nervous stock market (for a while anyway). Then by the summer of 2008, America's biggest mortgage companies, the Federal National Mortgage Association (Fannie Mae) and the Federal Home Loan Mortgage Corporation (Freddie Mac)* were on the edge of bankruptcy. Here too the federal government stepped in to offer $100 billion to get these two companies going again. Then in September Lehman Brothers was in similar trouble. But no purchaser could be found to buy out the company, even at a greatly reduced rate. Bankruptcy resulted. Likewise, the stock brokerage company Merrill Lynch and the huge banking company Washington Mutual collapsed. Then the Federal Reserve itself stepped in to bail out ($180 billion) the massive insurance company, American International Group, when the AIG found itself facing bankruptcy.

But the Republicans were ready to let the companies fall into bankruptcy (and restructuring); the Democrats however wanted to save the companies – and thus the jobs of all the workers whose support they depended on politically.

But by this time the stock market was finally in full panic mode. Bush then stepped into the picture in late September, presenting to Congress a request in the form of a $700 billion Troubled Assets Relief Program (TARP), to extend federal loans to troubled companies. The Republicans at

---

*Despite the names, these are not federally-owned or federally-operated mortgage companies, only federally-originated – but definitely privately-run banks, operating like any other mortgage bank.

first balked at this "socialist" idea. But when in response to this "no" the very next day the Dow Jones Stock Market index lost 778 points (the worst single-day drop in the history of the stock market), the Republicans were forced to back down and accept TARP.

But it was not just the housing industry that was behind this crisis. The same was happening in the automobile industry. The "Big Three" Detroit auto manufacturers (Ford, General Motors and Chrysler) were also having big problems selling their cars. Gas prices were running at a high of $4 a gallon, causing a drop in the sales of Detroit's best-selling SUV and pickup trucks (the big money-makers for Detroit). Where there was still any action in the automobile sector it was in the realm of the small sedans – where German and Japanese companies were actually doing quite well, especially with the models manufactured in America by a younger work force (lower salaries and less expensive health and pension benefits required). These foreign companies had over the previous ten years increased their percentage of overall car sales from 30% to 47%. Detroit was falling into deep trouble. And thus it was (again despite Republican resistance) $17 billion of the TARP funds were directed to helping Detroit – with the proviso that the unions would be willing to accept cutbacks on their wages and benefits.

And then Bush left the office as American president. It would be somebody else's job to steer the country through what remained of this economic mess.

* * *

THE COURTS AS AMERICA'S SUPREME LAW-MAKING BODIES

It had not taken the American "progressives" or political "Left" long to figure out that it was not to Congress they were to go, but instead to the federal courts in having their political-cultural-moral-spiritual agenda enforced as the foundational worldview or religion, in opposition to the traditional Christian worldview – one which the "progressives" wanted gone, gone, gone. Congress still responded to the will of the vast majority of the American people, registered in their right to vote in defense of their fundamental values. But Leftists knew that they could have a simple decree by a handful of judges effectively revise the law of the land completely in their ideological favor, and that there was no recourse available to the American people once the lawyers in black robes had decided to favor the "progressive" views of those self-enlightened Leftists. The rulings of the federal judges were the absolute law of the land, Congress notwithstanding.

Newdow heads to court to undercut the Pledge of Allegiance. And thus in the year 2000 Michael Newdow sued the U.S. Congress over the phrase "under God" contained in the Pledge of Allegiance, claiming that this was harmful to his daughter. He naturally went to the 9th Circuit Court (the American West Coast and Hawaii) – where "progressives" knew they could always count on great ideological favor. And indeed the court agreed with Newdow. However, this decision stirred a major reaction, including even in the U.S. Congress. Then the 9th Circuit Court bent over backwards to help Newdow, awarding him custody over his daughter, after the U.S. Supreme Court in 2004 dismissed his case when it was discovered that only his mother, a Christian, originally had such custody – and thus he had no right to present his case. Newdow then tried again in 2005, again getting another 9th Circuit Court decision in his favor. This time the Becket Fund fought both Newdow and the Freedom From Religion Foundation (FFRF) that was supporting Newdow. Newdow went from court to court, fighting case after case not just about the pledge but also the use of prayer and the wording of the presidential oath at presidential inaugurations, both Bush's and Obama's in fact. But he was increasingly finding the decisions not going in his favor.

Judge Jones decides for America its fundamental worldview. But a decision that hit the Christian world hard was the 2005 *Kitzmiller v. Dover Area School District* case. Eleven parents, supported by the ever-vigilant ACLU, took the Dover (Pennsylvania) school district to the federal District Court of Judge John Jones. The plaintiffs complained that a required reading of a short statement – recommending 9th grade students to also take into consideration (on their own, not in class) the Intelligent Design (ID) viewpoint that challenges Darwinism – violated the earlier 1987 *Edwards v. Aguillard* Supreme Court decision. This earlier decision had clearly outlawed the teaching of the doctrine of "creationism," a Christian, and thus not scientifically "Secular," view on the origins of the universe. And Intelligent Design was simply another form of creationism – and thus automatically "unconstitutional."

Judge Jones knew exactly how he wanted the case to turn out and would not let those supporting the ID viewpoint bring in expert witnesses. He simply decreed that ID was merely a sneak attack in favor of creationism – and slapped a $1 million fine on the Dover School Board as a lesson to anyone else who would attempt such "breathtaking inanity" (his words). He intended his case to be a landmark case. And indeed it was in the way it made very clear how the federal courts served as a highly authoritarian instrument by which a small group of people are able not only to impose their view on others, but to leave those others devasted should they dare to resist such authoritarianism. So much for "democracy" and First Amendment Freedoms ("Congress shall make no law respecting an establishment of religion, or prohibiting the free exercise thereof.") This was classic authoritarian prohibiting of the free exercise of the people's religious rights, a prohibition making it not only illegal but highly punishable just to mention that there are other viewpoints than the court-certified and thus "established" Darwinist view concerning the creation of the universe, and in general the court-backed Darwinist or Secular (atheist) worldview on all matters concerning life on this planet.

CHAPTER FOURTEEN

OBAMA STRIVES TO "CHANGE" AMERICA

* * *

THE 2008 NATIONAL ELECTION

The 2008 candidates. Not surprisingly, given the weariness of the Americans over the apparently highly expensive but also highly pointless Bush-led military effort in Iraq, but especially given the state of the nation's economy as the Americans went to vote in November, the Republicans took a huge beating, both in the presidential and congressional elections.

The centrist Republican candidate, Arizona Senator John McCain, did what he could to liven the party's conservative political base by appointing Alaska Governor Sarah Palin as his running mate. But the chemistry was just not there.

He himself was 72 years old – considered at the time to be way too old to be assuming the presidential office. But his family's long history of naval service (his father and grandfather were U.S. Admirals, and he himself was a U.S. Naval Academy graduate in 1958), his bravery as a navy pilot shot down over Hanoi (1967) and one who refused, as a 6-year war prisoner, to offer his captors propaganda advantages in denying his country before cameras,* his continuing service in the navy until 1981, and then Congressional service as an Arizona Representative (1982-1987) and then Senator (since 1987), should have been very compelling reasons to want to put him in the White House.

Thus the American Left (dominant in the news media) had redirected their attacks away from the proven patriot McCain and instead aimed them at Palin, whom they portrayed unceasingly as being merely a "beauty-queen bimbo" (she was in fact no bimbo) and only a single, dangerous heartbeat away from the presidency, because of the incredibly old age of McCain (they would sing a very different tune 12 years later when they were running the 78-year-old Biden for the presidency!).

---

*In his refusal to do so, his torture was worsened. He was however released in 1973 as part of a peace settlement between America and North Vietnam.

Obama Strives to "Change" America

On the other hand, the Democratic Party candidate, Barack Obama, was portrayed in the most glorious of terms by a fawning press – which loved especially his bi-racial origins. And he had the most powerful TV figure of the time, Oprah Winfrey, not only endorse him but put her full weight behind her request for him to run for the presidency, when he had very little national political experience behind him.

Deep "change." But he was such a wonderful living symbol of political dreams, able to speak movingly to the idea that America needed to undergo thorough "change" – in all areas of its national life. This was deeply inspiring to all those Americans who would find it easy to identify themselves as "minorities" – like Obama – and dream the dream that with Obama in office, they would no longer be "victimized" by Middle America. And Obama played the victim card splendidly.

In so many ways he disliked intensely the Middle America that had been at the heart of the founding, development, wartime self-defense, and ultimately grand social success as the sole standing superpower at the end of the 20th century. All that mattered little because – as he saw things – none of that had worked out well enough for him personally, although it certainly did not prevent him from becoming president of the United States! But he was absolutely determined to change whatever he could about Middle America. Middle America was too White, too Anglo, too masculine, and too sexually "straight." He would do everything he could to promote the interests and empowerment of those who did not fit one (or more) of those despised categories, in full support of the minority "victims" of Middle America and its oppressive values.

He would thus end up being the first American president unable to personally identify with, much less exemplify, the heart and soul of what had been since its founding the very cultural heart of America. But in the age of the Boomer and the rising Gen-Xers, this would no longer be a matter of great importance. And thus he would find it easy to change, change deeply, the very identity of America itself, in every way possible.

"Generation X." Indeed, just as McCain was typical of his "Silent" generation, so Barack Obama was typical of his, the Gen-Xers.

The "X" part referred to the way in which this generation, children of Boomers, had no particular ideals, no particular heroes (though something of a fascination with media celebrities), and no particular sense that their lives were going anywhere special. They answered to no particular standards – except the need to prove that they had no such standards – finding that just "fitting in" with fellow members of their generation was standard enough.

Male heroics based on the ideals of male self-discipline passed down traditionally from fathers to sons did not play a major part in their lives, as many of them (especially the 70% of the Blacks of that generation) were raised by single moms. Thus it was that Gen-X males tended to look to their peers to secure their male identities. Not surprisingly those identities were quite fluid and thus also quite shallow, except in the case of taking on very strong sectarian, racial and even gang identities (not uncommon) – identities which had a strong base of anger in them, anger at the larger world where they personally were having a hard time figuring out how to find a respectable way to fit in. Blaming that world became a political centerpiece for them.

And this male social feebleness and lack of direction is also why Gen-X women were found in the 1990s entering the academic and professional worlds in greater numbers than their male counterparts.

Barack Obama. Obama was born in 1961 to two students at the University of Hawaii – a White mother, Ann Dunham, from Kansas and a Black father, Barack Obama, from Kenya, the two marrying just before Barry (the name he went by during his pre-teen years) was born. But soon after his birth, his mother took Barry with her for her studies in Washington State, and his father the next year moved on to study at Harvard. Then, following their divorce in 1964, he returned to Kenya (actually he was already married to a Kenyan woman at the time). Young Barry would see his father only once more, very briefly in 1971 when he was age ten.

His mother returned to Hawaii, married an Indonesian student, Lolo Soetoro, a Muslim by background but quite Western in attitude – at least as long as they were still in the States. But the family moved to Indonesia in 1967 when Barry was six (his step-father worked with American oil companies), where Barry would take up schooling, first at a Catholic school (three years) and then a public school (Islamic, as Indonesia itself was largely Islamic). Actually, this highly varied religious experience did not dig deeply into Barry's life, especially as his mother was something of a self-designed spiritualist.

In 1971 Barry was sent back to Hawaii to live with his White grandparents, joined the next year by his mother, who had returned to Hawaii to finish her doctorate, and his younger half-sister Maya. That fall Barry was able to enter 5th grade at the prestigious Punahou School, thanks to a scholarship – and the hard work of his grandmother, who paid the balance of the costs (his grandfather was retired). Four years later (1975) his mother returned to Indonesia and Barry would continue on at Punahou, finally graduating in 1979 as "Barack," now preferring the more exotic sound of his father's name.

Indeed, although Hawaii was a land of many races, young Barack had found getting a fix on his own identity problematic. As a male, he had grown up with largely only strong-willed women to guide him in his personal development, the male input (again, typical of Gen-Xers anyway) largely lacking. He would idealize his African father*, but receive no actual direction from him on the path of male development. And high school drug use would not help the situation any.

He headed on to California and Occidental College, but two years later, with a scholarship in hand, transferring to the more prestigious Columbia University in New York City – to major in political science. While he was there, he naturally explored that world, in the process discovering the Black cultural world of Harlem to be very inviting. And thus it was that he began to secure his own identity – despite his "White" upbringing – as "Black." And he would eventually become quite purposeful in confirming that particular racial identity. The White world would no longer be his, but instead a highly problematic matter for him.

This process did not happen immediately, but instead developed in stages. At first, upon graduation in 1983, he took a job with a corporation helping businesses invest and operate abroad. But that work did not appeal to him. Then he joined Ralph Nader's campus activist organization, before moving to Chicago (1985) to work with a Catholic organization doing community development work in the cityy – helping to administer a number of developmental programs, including legal support.

Thus he found himself fascinated by the power of law, and after three years in Chicago headed off to Harvard Law School. Here he became a very focused, hard-working law student. Indeed, at the end of his first year he was elected as an editor of *The Harvard Law Review*. The next year he was even elected president and editor-in-chief of the *Review*.

During the two summers between classes, he headed back to Chicago for internships, the first summer (1989) interning under Michelle Robinson, a Princeton University and Harvard Law School graduate, who had joined the firm only the previous year. By the end of the summer they were actually dating (they would marry three years later,in October of 1992).

Upon graduation in 1991 from Harvard Law *summa cum laude* (with highest honors) he returned to Chicago and took a position at the University of Chicago as a Visiting Fellow, also working hard in directing a massive voter-register drive designed to get Blacks on the voting lists. His work in this matter would bring him serious national political attention (as well as his book, *Dreams from My Father*, which he was putting together at the

---

*Expressed beautifully in his *New York Times* best-seller, *Dreams from My Father; A Story of Race and Inheritance*, New York: Crown Publishers, 1995.

same time).

Soon he was appointed to the board of directors of a number of major community development corporations, at the same time that he moved up the ranks as Lecturer at the University of Chicago Law School.

But the death of his mother in 1995 would shake up his world, when uterine cancer forced her to return to the States in early 1995 – to then die that November. Not only had her disease and death been a heartbreaker for Obama, all the hassle to get medical attention and accompanying medical insurance coverage for such treatment had also deepened his despair greatly. It would leave him deeply committed to the idea that something was badly needed to improve such a draining medical system.

The following year (1996) Obama would enter the elective-office world, taking up a vacated seat in the Illinois Senate, then being reelected in 1998 and again in 2002. Meanwhile he had made a run for the U.S. House of Representatives in 2000, but lost that race rather substantially. But he was determined to enter national service, and took on the challenge of a race for the U.S. Senate in 2004 – easily winning the spot as the Democratic Party candidate. And as the election approached, his Republican opponent resigned his candidacy over a sex scandal, opening the door for Obama to an easy win (70% of the state's vote) that November.

Now a U.S. Senator (January 2005) he was assigned to several committees as a junior member, the Senate Foreign Relations Committee being the top of the list in importance, allowing him some considerable travel abroad.

Then Oprah stepped into the picture in September of 2006, finding in Obama everything she longed to see in a political figure, and worked hard at promoting the idea that, although Obama had no serious amount of experience in political administration, he would make a wonderful U.S. president – representing personally all the values that she supported. She put more muscle into the effort, interviewing Obama again the following month, with his wife Michelle also participating. And Oprah pushed Obama's second book, *The Audacity of Hope* to the number one spot on both *The New York Times* and Amazon's bestseller list. And thus it was that Obama became a very serious contender in the 2008 race for the U.S. presidency.

As for the presidential campaign itself, a large field of contenders had narrowed down by early 2008 to only two contenders, Obama and Hillary Clinton.

Along the way a sad event had taken place for Obama, when a sermon delivered by the Chicago pastor Jeremiah Wright was presented in part on the ABC News, showing the Rev. Wright repeatedly cursing America for its failings. Despite the fact that this pastor had served as something like the father that Obama had long needed – for twenty years, in fact – Obama distanced himself not only from the comments, but from the man himself. Indeed, Obama soon went before the nation in a televised address to deliver a speech "A More Perfect Union," in which he explained his negative views on racism, racism of any sorts.

In the end the controversy and his public response probably helped considerably move his candidacy ahead within the Democratic Party primary process. For indeed at this point he pulled ahead in the race, and in June Clinton dropped out. But this had an additional side effect, for in distancing himself from the Rev. Wright, Obama would not find another such pastoral figure to support his spiritual journey as president.

This would merely increase the Secular nature of the leadership flowing from the White House with Obama in place there (January 2009). This was sad for both the Obama family and the nation.

* * *

OBAMA'S PROGRAM OF DEEP SOCIAL AND CULTURAL CHANGE

Supreme Court appointments: "identity politics" in action. This move into a much more Secular world demonstrated itself clearly in two early and very important Supreme Court appointments that Obama made, ones that would aid considerably in Obama's determination to "change" America. Both appointments were of unmarried and childless women, pointing to the degree of support that the traditional American family was likely to get from the all-powerful Supreme Court.

The first appointment (May 2009), that of Sonia Sotomayor, was of a Puerto-Rican-born Hispanic militant who distinguished herself in her college years by leading a movement to force Princeton to hire more teachers of Hispanic background and to offer more courses on Hispanic culture. And her general outlook on life did not change much over the years, offering a comment on things in 2001: "I would hope that a wise Latina woman with the richness of her experiences would more often than not reach a better conclusion than a white male who hasn't lived that life." This was the kind of minority mentality that Obama found so appealing.

A year later Obama was able to make his second appointment, that of Elena Kagan, who had never served as a judge, but had been called out of academia as Dean of the Harvard Law School to first become Obama's Solicitor General – before receiving the Supreme Court appointment (May 2010). She was a strong opponent of "homophobia" and as Harvard Dean had opposed the military's recruiting efforts on campus because of the military's "don't ask, don't tell" policy concerning homosexuality. This too pointed to where the Supreme Court was likely to head things. And she would be the third Jewish member of the nine-member Supreme Court (which at this point included not a single White Protestant male!). Middle America was in for some changes, deep changes.

Obama's own assault on "homophobia." In October of his first year in office, Obama was able to sign into law (thanks to the Democrat-controlled Congress) the Hate Crimes Prevention Act, making any act motivated by a person's antipathy towards homosexuality a "hate crime," and thus subject to a doubling of the penalty for such a crime.

It was at first simply the belief that this law merely protected homosexuals from abuse, not itself authorizing the pro-homosexual world to go on the offensive politically against those who still held the view that homosexual behavior was a serious social problem (as America and most other societies traditionally had viewed things almost eternally). But indeed, this step of the president and Congress would be the first in exactly that direction. And in very short order, from that point forward, any opposition to homosexual activity (even just holding such a "homophobic" opinion) would now be considered the truly serious "social problem."

A year later, Obama took the next step down this same path, but only after the Democratic majority in the House of Representatives had been overturned by that November's Congressional vote (2010). He was quick in response to the Democratic Party setback to run through what was at that point a "lame duck" Congress an amendment to the Small Business Act (?!!) repealing the military's "don't ask; don't tell" policy. It passed, not surprisingly, largely along party lines in both houses (it would have failed passage if it had been put before the new incoming Congress a month later). So this was how Obama was going to "change" America.

Then also in February of the new year (2011) Obama had his Attorney General send a letter to Congress announcing that the Department of Justice would no longer enforce the 1996 Defense of Marriage Act (DOMA). So much for the president's inaugural vow to faithfully enforce the laws of the land! So, "change" thus also now meant that the president could enforce whichever laws he himself personally decided to enforce, and could ignore the others if he chose to do so.

But ultimately it was the Supreme Court, not Congress or the president, that in two steps overturned DOMA as law. In *United States v. Windsor* (June 2013) and *Obergefell v. Hodges* (June 2015), by a 5-against-4 decision, Supreme Court politics first cut down one of the provisions of DOMA and then finally dismissed the whole thing. Thus five lawyers in black robes decided for America what constituted marriage and what did not.* And there was no known way for Congress to get its law back as the law of the land, because those five (which of course included Obama's two court appointees) had made the final decision as to what was national law and what was not. And there exists no known way for Congress, through its own legislative power assigned by the Constitution, to counter the Supreme Court's greater legislative power, one simply assumed by the Court itself.

"Change" now includes the bullying of Christians for failing to hold "politically correct" views on sexuality. It did not take long for the new attitude of Obama's Washington to make its way to the nation's streets. When the president of Chick-fil-A, Dan Cathy, commented in an interview by the Baptist Press in July of 2012 that he held a traditional view on marriage (being ordained by God himself as only between a man and a woman), the attacks against him and his restaurant business were fierce. Chicago mayor (and former Obama chief of staff) Rahm Emmanuel and Chicago Alderman, Proco "Joe" Moreno" announced that they would block the opening of any new Chick-fil-A restaurants in the city. This position was also immediately taken up by Boston mayor Thomas Menino. But this violation of Cathy's right to express an opinion was even too much for the very Liberal ACLU, which joined the voices protesting against such political bullying. Both the Chicago and Boston mayors backtracked from their announcements. But from that point on, Chick-fil-A would find itself constantly in the middle of controversy over this issue of marriage.

Then things ramped up even more the following year (early 2013) when a young couple, the Kleins, owning a small bakery, told one of their customers that they would not be able to bake a wedding cake for her because their Christian beliefs would not allow them to support a lesbian wedding. She would have to go elsewhere for a wedding cake. So hurt was the lesbian couple that they turned the hurt back on the Kleins, filing a complaint with Oregon's Bureau of Labor and Industries. This soon hit the news, which brought protesters stationed outside their bakery, finally forcing the couple to close down their bakery and try to continue their work from their home. But the countering hurt did not end there. In 2015 Oregon authorities hit them with a $135,000 fine (but the Kleins in turn received considerable financial support through the Go Fund Me website – which then got shut down when those managing the website discovered the purpose of the funding!). The decision against the Kleins was appealed in 2017, but went against them – as well as did the appeal all the way to

---

*DOMA had been approved in 1996 with a huge majority vote of 342-65 in the House and 84-14 in the Senate. But, with the encouragement of the Obama administration, it would take only a 5-4 Supreme Court decision to overturn that socially strategic law.

Oregon's Supreme Court (June 2018). Christian "homophobia" was going to be eliminated, by force if necessary.

Racial hostilities fire back up again. An incident that occurred in Florida in early 2012 pointed to how a local event was once again going to become a national matter – and a revival of bitter "identity politics" – especially when the President and his Department of Justice signed onto the matter. A man (of mixed race) George Zimmerman, who was undertaking nighttime community watch (the neighborhood had been hit by a number of burglaries), got into a fight with a young Black, Trayvon Martin, and Martin was shot and killed.

Zimmerman was of enough "whiteness" that the incident, pushed heavily by the national media, was slanted into a new example of White v. Black racism, supported even by Obama, who went on record stating that "if I had a son, he would look like Trayvon" (Obama had only two daughters). Others, such as sports figures and celebrity stars, also signed in on the event, including (naturally) the Reverend Al Sharpton. An online campaign run by "Change.org" gathered over two million signatures calling for Zimmerman's arrest for murder, even before the full evidence in the matter was assembled. It simply had become Black v. White, with Obama himself part of the chorus demanding "justice" – also, even before the matter had been put under the scrutiny of a court trial.

But interestingly, leaders in the Black organization NAACP came out against this very racial hyping – convinced that such heightening of racial tensions served no very good purpose in improving the nation's race relations. Ultimately a jury also found that under the circumstances, Zimmerman, in the struggle, had acted fully within the law and thus was guilty of no crime. Even when Obama's Department of Justice looked into the matter, try as it might, it could not find any grounds for Zimmerman's arrest either. And the effort to cast mixed-race Zimmerman as a racist just could not stand up to the facts of the matter, though it did nothing to satisfy those determined to depict this event as nothing more than White racism in action.

Ultimately, Zimmerman and his family had to leave their homes and go into seclusion as the threats against them mounted (and still continue to this day). Overall, the whole incident heated up the nation to the point that it would take months for America to get past this tragedy.

But that was mild in comparison to what happened across the nation as a result of an event in Ferguson Missouri in August of 2014, when a White policeman, Darren Wilson, shot a Black youth, Michael Brown, in a conflict between the two. Once again, even before the facts of the matter were in, Americans began to take action against "police brutality," especially when undertaken by a White policeman. Protests broke out immediately once the event hit the national news, and soon local pillaging and torching began to take place across the nation. Naturally, the Reverend Sharpton was quick on the scene to cultivate the outrage of Blacks, registered in the refrain "hands up; don't shoot" which Brown's friend had (falsely) claimed Brown had uttered just before being shot.

Most ironically the main theme of the protests that hit the country (including in many college campuses) was "Black Lives Matter." Certainly they do. The death toll of young Blacks in America is a huge national tragedy. But it only seems to matter when a White is involved, which is actually only a small percentage of the time. And why does it not seem to matter when it is a case of Black-on-Black? Those deaths are just as tragic. And yes, their lives matter too.

But that is not how this incident was being developed. Again, this was simply identity politics in action. And also, once again, President Obama quickly signed on to the event, identifying with the young man who died so tragically (Obama certifying that he too had felt the racism that Brown had experienced) , and once again promising to send the Department of Justice, even its Attorney General Eric Holder himself, to look into the matter, to make sure that the local police investigation did not just sweep the matter under the rug (implying that this was what could easily be expected in such events).

However, little by little the actual facts in the case began to come out, though it did not seem to matter much to those committed to defending the "Black Lives Matter" crusade. It seems that Brown was hyped up on PCP, the huge youth had just pushed aside a store clerk who was contesting him over some cigars that Brown was determined to walk out with (caught on a security camera), and then was walking down the middle of the street with his friend Dorian Johnson when officer Wilson pulled up alongside them and told them to move to the curb, an order that Brown was in no mood to obey. A struggle ensued when Brown reached into the car in an attempt to grab Wilson's gun, shots were fired inside the police car, Brown and Johnson then ran off, with Wilson in pursuit – until Brown turned and charged Wilson, and got shot and killed in the process. The "hands up; don't shoot" statement coming from Johnson was countered by observers at the scene who said that Brown had said no such thing, and that officer Wilson was under full assault when Brown was shot and killed. Forensics confirmed the latter account.

And although cleared by the evidence in the case, here too officer Wilson had to leave Ferguson under death threats. And again, try as he might, Holder's Department of Justice also could find no basis for further action against Wilson – although Holder could not pass up the opportunity to deliver a sermon about the deep racial injustice that governed American society, and, being a minority himself, he could feel the pain of America's minorities. In short, Holder was inviting America to pursue its cultural animosities through bitter identity politics, rather than find higher ground to come together over. But that seemed to be the theme of the times, or at least the theme of the Obama Administration (and many of the Congressional Democrats).

The Obama moral-spiritual legacy. Eight years of Obama's "change" indeed left the country just that: deeply changed. In attacking and bringing down Middle or "White" America at every opportunity, he left Middle America bewildered, and Blacks and other self-identified "minorities" very vigilant against any effort of Middle America to reassert itself. Obama (along with the federal courts and the lawsuit-happy ACLU and its associates) had succeeded in branding Middle American social-moral standards as racist, homophobic, sexist, etc., in other words, prohibited by law on every front. But worst of all for America, this same group had finalized the understanding that the Christian religion was prohibited in public everywhere.   Religion could be touched on publicly, but only as long as it was non-specific ("spiritually generic") in nature.

Worse, the legacy was to live on (supported strongly by Obama even out of office) in the form of the refusal of professional athletes to stand in respect during the playing of the national anthem, but to kneel as a sign of protest against all these "isms" that caused minorities to suffer so. This included very well-paid and highly popular football players, who just could not get enough of a social payoff to make them loyal supporters of the very idea of the American nation.

Black lives do matter, greatly. Racism in any form, Black as well as White, serves no one honorably or even profitably. It's a sign of insecurity rather than any serious understanding of life and its challenges. Racism, just like nationalism (English and French killing Germans because, well they're just Germans and need to be killed, or so went the thinking of World War One), simply finds some great source of evil that, in being brought down, will supposedly make life much, much better. So racism in the 1950s and 1960s not only gave Southern poor Whites some sense that fighting the "Black peril" brought some logic to their difficult lives, it in no ways improved the picture, for anyone. Well, anyone except the segregationist politicians who promoted such racism in order to get themselves elected and reelected. And Joe McCarthy did the same thing with the Red Scare, until the shallowness of what he was up to finally got exposed.

There's much the same problem in the way Blacks explode easily over the difficulties they are having gaining the social standing that any person naturally craves. No one can claim that there are no serious problems confronting Black life. That just isn't so. But the problem is very complex, with all kinds of causes behind this issue. Blaming Whites is, of course, the easiest explanation, one that hustling Black politicians at all levels of American society have been exploiting for their own political purposes. But as with all racist responses, this is not likely to bring serious solutions to the social problems facing the Black community.*

The Black murder rate is most disheartening. A government report that came out in 2011, early in the Obama Administration, pointed out that murder constitutes the biggest cause of death of Blacks in the 15-34 age group, almost 40 percent of those deaths (compared to 3.8 percent in the same age group of Whites). Most all of that is Black-on-Black action, though the police are sometimes involved. Actually, police shooting of Whites is twice the number involving Blacks, a tragedy for everyone involved. But nearly all of even those incidents show that the police were doing exactly what they were hired to do, in the line of duty in often very violent neighborhoods. There were tragic exceptions of course, but quite few considering the hundreds of thousands of police serving the country.

In any case, this very serious problem facing America is just not getting the serious attention it needs and deserves, because it has become much too politicized. Again, easy racist answers do not ever offer wisdom in the search for a solution to major social problems.

But thankfully a number of Black public figures have been speaking out about how racism is the wrong approach to the problem, something that racist politicians do not want to hear. But at least this former group is trying to get some serious action underway to improve the lives of young Black males – and Black neighborhoods – caught in a serious social crisis.

* * *

THE OBAMA ECONOMY

Government grants. Obama inherited a national economic mess in

---

*In 1965, as Johnson's Great Society got underway, 25% of Black children were born out of wedlock. That number now runs at 70%.

Even Obama himself in one of his more lucid moments once commented, on Father's Day of 2008 (when running for the presidency), "Children who grow up without a father are five times more likely to live in poverty and commit crime; nine times more likely to drop out of schools, and 20 times more likely to end up in prison. They are more likely to have behavioral problems, or run away from home or become teenage parents themselves. And the foundations of our community are weaker because of it."

coming to office at the beginning of 2009. Bush's emergency loans enacted during his last months in office seemed to slow up the disaster rocking the banking industry. But America's "Big Three" auto manufacturers (General Motors, Ford and Chrysler) were still in deep trouble. And Obama agreed that they would need some additional funding to get through the crisis.

But what he actually called for in taking immediate action on the nation's economic crisis with his $787 billion American Recovery and Reinvestment Act in fact was not loans to help American businesses to get back on their feet but instead a simple giveaway of government funds for expanded unemployment benefits, health care, green energy, education, infrastructure development and various job creation programs.

Again, the Republicans balked at this, seeing the roots of rising Socialism and not just assistance to a hurting corporate world in the program. But the Democrats were delighted. America was back to doing "New Deal" programming like those of Roosevelt and Johnson's administrations. Thus the measure passed quickly in Congress (late January of Obama's first weeks in office), 244-188 in the House and 61-37 in the Senate – almost entirely along Democratic-Republican party lines.

Bankruptcy in the auto industry. As far as the troubled auto industry was concerned, Chrysler was on the verge of bankruptcy – and General Motors was not far behind. In February, an agreement was made with the two companies that in receiving $20 billion in funding, they would close five plants (and 50 thousand jobs) and shut down hundreds of local dealerships. But in April, Chrysler filed for bankruptcy anyway, with Fiat agreeing to gradually come in alongside Chrysler as partner to rebuild the company. Then in June, General Motors also filed for bankruptcy, with the U.S. government taking 60 percent ownership of the company, the Canadian government 12.5 percent and the rest going to the labor unions. The original stockholders (a lot of them members of Middle America) were left out in the cold in the deal.

"Cash for Clunkers." Then Obama put into effect the Car Allowance Rebate System ("Cash for Clunkers") in which the government would offer from $2500 to $4500 towards the purchase of a new car, by turning in gas-guzzling cars (trucks and SUVs mostly) and buying smaller, more fuel-efficient automobiles. Thus since trucks and SUVs were American car companies' big income earners, "Cash for Clunkers" merely served to worsen the situation for the American companies, at the same time benefiting greatly the Japanese, Korean and German car manufacturers making the smaller sedans. Furthermore, almost $1.4 billion in car value was lost over any fuel-efficiency gain, because these "clunkers" exchanged in the deal could not be resold, but instead had to be destroyed, cutting back enormously the number of used cars that poorer Americans looked to for purchase.

The rising national debt. And of course all this government giveaway merely increased enormously the national debt, already doubling from $5 trillion to $10 trillion in Bush's eight years and now rising even more rapidly in these first years of Obama's presidency, with $1.9 trillion added to the figure in 2009 and another $1.7 trillion in 2010. At this point the government deficit was calculated to be about 94 percent of the nation's total productivity, up from the 57 percent figure it stood at when Bush first took office in 2001 and 70 percent when Obama took office in 2009. The government debt, now running close to the full value of the nation's productivity, was a very dangerous economic indicator.

And still it had little impact on the poor showing of the American economy, whose official unemployment rate was rising, from 9.4 percent in 2009 to 9.9 percent in 2010, a figure which would actually have been much higher (around 15.9 percent) if those who simply had given up looking for work altogether (and thus no longer on the books) or were merely able to find part-time work were added into the calculation.

"Obamacare." At the same time, the American medical industry was in crisis mode, although not because the health industry was in financial difficulties, but because ordinary Americans seeking medical help were finding it financially impossible to meet skyrocketing healthcare costs. The American medical industry boasted about the sophistication of the industry itself in comparison to the European healthcare industry. But the fact of the matter was that Europeans could receive rather normal medical care without being thrown into deep debt, whereas for many Americans just a 15-minute visit to the local doctor cost the equivalent of a full day's wages, making medical visits as rare as possible. And costs for a single night's stay in a hospital could easily amount to a several months of a person's income. Worse, problems that required a "lengthy" stay (meaning more than a day or two) in a hospital could run costs up into the $millions.

Of course there was medical insurance to cover those enormous costs. But Insurance companies were not in the charity business and covered expenses by way of very expensive insurance premiums available to the Americans. And those costs were rising rapidly.

And what did these rapidly rising costs have to do with "improvements" in the medical industry? With insurance costs rising 5 to 10 percent annually, did this imply that healthcare was also improving at that rate? What was driving up these costs? And the answer can only be, greed on the part of those involved in the industry – fancy hospitals, high-status doctors, wealthy insurance companies, but probably most of all, medical liability lawyers who were more than happy to bring a client's lawsuit against any doctor who made medical mistakes (doctors are not supposed to make mistakes, even though medical analysis is a highly risky matter). The rewards for the medical "malpractice" industry ran medical costs up into the clouds.

But this meant that the problem was more that of a social or ethical matter than a political or governmental matter. Nonetheless, Obama would attempt to take the problem head-on with his July 2009 1017-page document (which no Congressman had the time or ability to read in its entirety) Affordable Care Act (ACA) – or "Obamacare" as it was popularly termed. Again, Republicans balked at the bill, especially the part that proposed to put a government health plan into effect in competition with the private health insurance companies – Republicans claiming that this would give the government the power to drive those companies out of business and leave the country with only a government or "Socialist" medical program for the country. Also the Congressional Budget Office's analysis revealed that this would run the government deficit up another $1 trillion, minimally (if not even more than that figure). And polls were indicating that the American voters themselves were deeply concerned about what this "change" in the American medical industry would mean to them personally. Democratic Party House Speaker Nancy Pelosi's comment "just trust us" was not very reassuring to the general public.

Thus the fast action on this bill that Obama was hoping for just simply did not happen. By the end of 2009 only the Senate had passed the bill, 60-40 (along party lines), and at that point it was greatly changed, having dropped the government insurance program option. When early the next year (2010) the House finally voted on the measure, it narrowly passed with a 219 to 212 vote. On March 23, Obama was pleased to finally sign his signature Obamacare bill into law.

In the end, although Obama had his law, he forfeited a lot of popular support in the deal. And in the Congressional elections that November, the Democrats lost their majority to the Republicans in the House, the latter picking up 63 seats, the biggest swing in party fortunes since the 1938 election. With Republicans now holding 242 seats to the Democrats' 193 seats, Obama had lost his former position in the House. But this was also when he pushed to overturn the "don't ask' don't tell" rule in the military, before those 242 Republicans could take their seats in January of 2011 and he would no longer have full control of Congress.

The national debt continues to climb. By August of 2011, the government debt was approaching its debt ceiling, preventing the government from borrowing (selling bonds) beyond that figure. But the Republicans were much opposed to simply adjusting upward the debt ceiling, and instead wanted government spending to be brought under reduction in order to bring the budget closer to a balance of income versus spending. It was even proposing a constitutional amendment requiring government spending to stay within the limits of its income.

But all this speculation was making investors very nervous, and even the global stock markets began to take big hits. Worse, Standard & Poor downgraded the U.S. credit rating from a solid AAA to a reduced AA+, the first downgrade since 1919. Ultimately there seemed nothing left for the Republicans to do except to give in to the inevitable: the debt ceiling would have to be raised in order for the government to continue its operations. It repositioned the figure at $14.5 trillion, a new ceiling which government spending quickly reached by the end of the next year (2012).

But at this point increased borrowing had simply become a debtor's habit for the government, and the debt ceiling had to be "temporarily" suspended in 2013, then again in 2014, again in 2015. By the end of Obama's presidency in January of 2017, the national debt had reached the figure of nearly $20 trillion or 104 percent of America's annual productivity – the debt having also doubled, like Bush's administration, in Obama's eight years as president.

* * *

OBAMA'S FOREIGN POLICY

The "New Look." Sounding very much like Jimmy Carter in his first days entering the White House, Obama made it very clear that with himself in the White House a very new look would come to American foreign policy. Towards Russia he offered a "reset" in Russian-American relations and in Cairo he addressed the Muslim world with much the same message, although what this new look would actually entail was by no means clearly outlined. But this new attitude so impressed the Norwegian Nobel Committee that in February (with just a month in office) Obama was nominated for the Nobel Peace Prize, and in fact the final recipient of that honor that October. Many stood in amazement, because he had actually done nothing in particular to deserve such a high honor, other than advocate publicly the kind of Idealism that touched the hearts of the "Liberal" world. But being the head of the world's supreme superpower would require a lot more than nice-sounding language. Obama was about to discover this.

Iraq. In campaigning for the presidency in 2008, Obama had promised that if he were elected president, he would bring American troops home from Iraq. And indeed upon entering the White House, he announced that U.S. combat operations would be ended in Iraq by August of the following year (2010), and the 142,000-troop level there would also be reduced to 30,000-50,000 by that date. Those remaining would serve only as trainers and advisors. And all troops would be gone by the end of 2011. And indeed, he was able to keep to this timetable, having problems only with negotiating an understanding with the new Iraqi government as to the status of American troops remaining as advisors.

Meanwhile Iraqi "democracy" made little headway in resolving the Sunni anger at the loss of power to the Shi'ites. The Nouri al-Maliki government continued to represent the hard-core Shi'ites, despite American efforts to promote the more moderate Ayad Allawi and his party – which had actually gained a slightly larger vote in the March 2010 elections, although both groups were unable to operate without going into coalition with other parties.

Anyway, Obama finally decided to simply leave the Iraqis to their own fate. And as soon as the Americans departed at the end of 2011 al-Maliki issued a warrant for the arrest of the Iraqi Vice President Tariq al-Hashimi (a Sunni), who fled to Kurdistan to avoid arrest. Thus with the American departure, Iraqi politics was now allowed to take a more natural Middle Eastern profile! So much for Bush's extremely expensive "democratic nation-building" in Iraq.

Afghanistan. However when it came to the Bush legacy in Afghanistan, Obama met it with a different strategy, attempting a "surge" there, one that had worked so effectively in 2007 in Iraq. Thus in his first month in the presidency he announced that he intended to deploy an additional 17,000 American troops in Afghanistan.

But increased deployment seemed to take on more the older Vietnam profile than the more recent Iraq profile. Trying to run down the Taliban proved to be pointless, largely because of the Taliban's ability to retreat into Pakistan (where American soldiers dared not go) when the Taliban found itself hard pressed by the American and European troops.

At the same time, America's ally, Afghan President Karzai, saw it wiser to undertake negotiations with the Taliban, shocking Americans who saw in this some kind of betrayal of their alliance with his government. Obviously, those Americans had no idea whatsoever about how Afghan politics worked, and had worked since time immemorial!

Not finding much success in his initial "surge," Obama in December (2009) announced that he would be upping the American military presence in Afghanistan even more, adding another 30,000 troops to the American force there. But facing growing opposition at home, he also announced that he would be bringing all American troops home by the middle of the next year. This strange announcement only emboldened the Taliban even more – who, with the promised departure of Western troops, were willing to wait out all of Obama's back and forth military moves. And it put Karzai in an even tougher position in trying to govern Afghanistan.

Pakistan, and bin Laden's takedown. Meanwhile tensions were rising with America's former ally Pakistan over the protection that the Taliban was finding in that country. And with Wikileaks publishing thousands of classified U.S. documents, it became quite clear to all that America was very upset over the fact that the Pakistani Intelligence Service (ISI) was actively supporting the Taliban.

But in the meantime American intelligence had discovered bin Laden's location in Pakistan (less than a mile away from the Pakistani Military Academy) and on May 2, 2011, sent two Black Hawk helicopters with a dozen Navy SEALS to take out the hated enemy, and then fly bin Laden's body off to the Arabian Sea to dump him there (after appropriate Muslim burial rites!). The Pakistanis were furious about this violation of their country's territorial rights. But there was really little they could do at that point.

And Obama came away from this risky event looking very presidential! And thus also ended a 10-year-old chapter in American life.

NATO troop draw-down in Afghanistan. The draw-down of the Western troops went ahead on schedule, with Obama signing a partnership agreement in 2012 with the Karzai government, promising continuing support despite the withdrawal of the Western or NATO combat troops. Thus at the end of 2014 a formal withdrawal of the NATO troops finally took place, although staying behind (with even official United Nations approval) would be some 17,000 multinational troops, plus "private" or contract soldiers – their purpose being solely to train Afghan government troops. Nonetheless, this departure would be the signal for the Taliban to begin their move to retake villages (and punish villagers) that had cooperated with the Western forces.

The "Arab Spring" breaks out in Tunisia (2011). Part of Obama's "New Look" included his widely watched televised speech "A New Beginning" that he delivered to the Arab world during a visit to Egypt in June of 2009. In that speech, he emphasized his commitment to helping develop a greater spirit of personal freedom, political democracy and economic development in the Middle East, not exactly a novel ideal for Americans, for that had also been part of Bush, Jr's intent in Afghanistan and Iraq. In short, America under Obama would remain in the business of supporting nation-building abroad. Would this work any better than it had for Johnson in Vietnam, Carter in Iran, and Bush, Jr. in Afghanistan and Iraq? Time would soon tell. Troubles in the streets broke out in January of 2011, when Tunisian youth came out in huge numbers to protest a broad number of social issues that had them deeply angered. With this, the "Arab Spring" got underway.

The protest was characterized by much electronic connect through computers and cell phones, and the active involvement of the media in dramatizing the event. By the middle of the month Tunisian President Zine ben Ali had fled the country, and it seemed that the youth had achieved a tremendous political victory, although street action continued all the way up to October, when finally elections were held to appoint those who would write Tunisia's new Constitution.

The Arab Spring comes to Egypt. But the rest of the Arab world was watching events in Tunisia closely. And soon the youth of other Arab states took up the same cause: to overthrow their long-standing governments, in order to replace them with new similarly "progressive" systems. Egypt would be hit hard with this rising mood, as Egyptian youth camped out in Tahrir Square in Cairo with the intentions of outstaying the Egyptian police until the nearly 30-year-long regime of Hosni Mubarak was brought to an end (actually the elderly and very sick Mubarak was preparing his son, Gamal, to take over his position as Egyptian president.)

As the Cairo protest dragged on, Mubarak shut down the internet, but also made some efforts to appease the protesters with changes in the Egyptian government cabinet and the appointment of a Vice President (not part of the Mubarak family!). But this hardly satisfied the protesters, whose numbers gathered in Tahrir Square merely increased (similar to the way things had developed over the days and weeks in Tiananmen Square in Beijing). Seeing huge troubles developing, the Egyptian military finally stepped in and in mid-February arrested Mubarak and took control of the Egyptian government, promising constitutional reforms. But still, the protesters remained encamped in Tahrir Square, their numbers continuing to grow.

Now Egyptians found themselves fighting fellow Egyptians as the days, weeks and then months passed, the level of violence continuing to mount through the summer and into the fall. Sectarian or religious-cultural violence became a key part of the chaos, as, for instance, Coptic Christians (about 10 percent of the population) became objects of Muslim retribution. Also Muslim groups themselves turned on each other, as well as against the more culturally secular of the Egyptians. By the time that elections for the new Constituent Assembly were held in November, Egypt was on the verge of civil war.

But hope ran high that elections under the new Egyptian constitution, held in May the following year (2012), would produce the step of Egypt into the world of democracy that Obama supported so strongly. In those elections, Muslim Brotherhood leader Mohammed Morsi won 51.7 percent of the vote, his Secularist opponent Ahmed Shafik coming close at 48.3 percent. Obama was enthusiastic about the results and congratulated Morsi on this wonderful development. But a wiser Shafik left the country, just before Morsi put out a warrant for his arrest. So much for Third-World democracy.

And the chaotic situation in Egypt did not improve any – "forcing" Morsi to take an ever-stronger or dictatorial hand. The situation grew so bad that finally, with not just Tahrir Square but the very streets of Cairo filled with anti-Morsi protesters, the Egyptian military again stepped in and deposed Morsi, finally bringing Egypt back to order.

Obama was furious over this violation of "democracy." But he could say little about matters in Egypt when another election was held (with Muslim radicals boycotting the election) and former General / now President Sisi gaining huge Egyptian civilian support for his leadership.

Then Syria. Meanwhile by mid-March of 2011, the mood of youthful protest had moved on to Syria, where protesters gathered in Damascus with their own list of demands for political and economic reform. But as in Egypt, the demands became increasingly confusing as they intensified, some wanting more secular reform, others more Islamic reform, but deeply divided as well over whether that should take a Shi'ite or Sunni character. Even more than Egypt, Syria was a complex mix of all sorts of sectarian groups, not only Sunni versus Shiite Muslims, but also Druzes (semi-Muslim), Christians (from various versions of Eastern Orthodox to equally culturally diverse Catholic groups), not to mention long-standing family, clan and tribal loyalties. And of course there were a huge number of simply Secular Syrians, diverse in character as well.

Syrian President Bashar al-Assad was a member of the Alawi sect, part of Shi'ite Islam, but mostly Secular in political character. He and his father before him had been holding this fragile social mix together, at times by forceful means. Actually, at first protests were for simple reforms, not for any end to the Assad presidency. But with time as the protests radicalized, they did indeed take on an anti-Assad position, which merely provoked an equally militant reaction of Assad supporters. It was everything Assad could do to keep the country from falling into bitter civil war.

Then Libya. There was also the matter of Libya, where the "Arab Spring" had hit that country in February. Actually, in Libya the rebellion involved no more than a rivalry between the two chief cultural regions that made up the country, regions that had long competed against each other in that part of North Africa (Libya was assembled as a "nation" by the Italians in the early 1900s by lumping these mutually antagonistic regions into a single colonial holding). Thus the Arab Spring in Libya entailed simply a civil struggle between the groups, one found mostly in the eastern part of the country with its political center in Benghazi and one in the western part of the country with its political base in Tripoli. Libyan President Muammar Gaddafi held this together by building a strong political base in Tripoli, and keeping the country focused on foreign developments – which Gaddafi involved himself in constantly (and rather flamboyantly and recklessly) in order to keep his people distracted.

In the midst of all this confusion, Obama and his NATO allies (notably France) decided that this would be an opportune time to get rid of the very troublesome Gaddafi, and at the same time bring Libya to real democracy. So they called for a no-fly zone over the country (meaning that Gaddafi could not use air power in the defense of his government), and then "enforced" this decision by flying their own missions in Libya to bomb his forces, and to supply his adversaries, most notably the National Transition Council (NTC). And thus with considerable NATO (including American) support, the NTC was able to extend its position in Libya, until Gaddafi was trapped, caught and executed on the spot, all graphically displayed to the world. In Libya, part of the country cheered; part of the country seethed. But Obama felt well content that America and its NATO partners had just led Libya to the right kind of political dynamics.

The chaos worsens in Syria. Meanwhile, back in Syria, there too the international community decided that it needed to get involved in helping return Syria to some kind of social order. Shi'ite Iran decided that it needed to help fellow Shi'ite Assad in crushing the rebellion (which would also bring the reach of Iran all the way up to the Mediterranean Sea). Russia's President Vladimir Putin noticed the same possibility of finding itself usefully stationed in Syria by offering Assad some military assistance (and thus also achieve in the process the long-sought goal of a Russian position in the eastern Mediterranean). And the Turks next door were growing increasingly concerned about the violence spilling over into their country and wanted something done to stop the chaos.

Once again, Obama decided to "help" Syria (like the help offered Libya), demanding in August that Assad step down in order to allow his country to move to actual democracy (like Iraq?). He was even more forceful in threatening Assad with "serious consequences" if he crossed a "red line" in the illegal use of chemical weapons and certain categories of bombs in his efforts to crush the rebellion. But Assad was too busy trying to stop Syria's collapse into complete chaos to pay much attention to Obama's threats, and simply ignored them. An embarrassed Obama ultimately came up with no compelling "consequences" and had to backtrack on his threats, prompting Putin to agree to step into the mess and help "mediate" between Obama and Assad. But instead Putin moved to full support of Assad, at the same time that Obama (in cooperation with the Saudis) began sending arms, even tanks, to one of Assad's Sunni opposition groups.*

But unlike Libya, Obama's intervention did not tip the balance in favor of a "democratic" group able to bring the war to a close by crushing Assad and his supporters. The intervention simply intensified the violence all the more.

Worse, Sunni jihadists who were escaping Shi'ite dominance in Iraq, were able because of the total chaos prevailing in Syria not only to position themselves in the eastern half of the country bordering the Sunni lands of Iraq, but were even able to set up a new caliphate (Sunni Islam's highest religious-political office) as the nucleus of a new jihadist Islamic State, from which they could then cleanse the earth of unbelievers.

As for the vast majority of the Syrians, they now found themselves with only one serious alternative if they were to survive at all: flee to other countries where they could live out at least a very minimal existence in refugee camps, or, if really lucky, possibly escape into Europe. Millions of Syrians now took flight. Syria was no longer a place fit for human habitation, thanks in great part to all the outside "help" the culturally-diverse country was getting.

Yet, with Russian and Iranian help, Assad was surviving. And indeed, both Russia and Iran now found themselves positioned politically in a very strategic location along the Eastern Mediterranean coast. Furthermore, a very violent form of Islam found itself well-based in the wastes of Eastern Syria and Northwestern Iraq, ready to take on the world. And as for America, Obama had succeeded only in making America politically a persona non grata (unwanted personage) in what was left of life back in Syria.

---

*Obama's Saudi allies were of course totally uninterested in seeing Obama-style democracy (whatever that actually meant under the complex cultural circumstances of Syria) put in place in Syria, but instead a strong Sunni government that would replace Assad's Shi'ite Ba'athist government.

Benghazi. Meanwhile now-dysfunctional Libya struggled to contain the mess that followed Gaddafi's downfall. And the next year, 2012, on exactly September 11th, Muslim militants of Ansar al-Shari'a succeeded in attacking and torching the American consulate and the CIA annex located in Benghazi (the capital of the Libyan region Obama had been supporting in the war against Gaddafi), also killing the American Ambassador to Libya, Chris Stevens, and three other Americans.

At first the State Department claimed that this tragedy was the result of a spontaneous uprising of local Muslims – because of a video offensive to Islam that had just come out. But very soon it was revealed that Stevens had previously warned the White House of a mounting danger with Islamic militants in the area, had requested extra security, but had failed to receive it, leaving him and his team totally defenseless. It was clear that this Muslim uprising was not "spontaneous" but instead an action long in development, one which Washington had basically ignored, until it blew up as it did.

With national elections coming up soon (that November) and expectations that the Republicans would run big with the story of the huge blunder, Obama answered by announcing the departure of a number of State Department officials, and that Secretary of State Hillary Clinton would be stepping down at the beginning of 2013, with Senator John Kerry taking over her position.

From this point forward, America simply looked the other way as the situation in Libya deteriorated even further, leading the Libyan army in 2014 finally to move strongly against the militant Muslim groups. But in doing so, while they brought an improvement in the Libyan situation, they also succeeded in driving these militant groups off to Iraq and Syria, where they then added to the strength of the Islamic State or Caliphate seeking to overthrow the governments of Iraq and Syria (and elsewhere).

Growing problems with Putin's Russia. At the beginning of his presidency, in hoping to push a "restart" in Russian-American relations – in part by relaxing the American military posture in Eastern Europe – Obama ordered the abandoning of plans to place a missile shield in Poland (originally planned as a defense of Europe against a feared attack from Iran) as well as radar intercepts that were supposed to be placed in the Czech Republic. Obama claimed that American ship-based interceptors ready for service by 2018 would suffice in providing such security. Russia was delighted at this American step-back in Eastern Europe. But NATO partners Poland and the Czech Republic were left in a state of shock over the matter, wondering exactly what it meant in terms of their own larger security needs (such as against an aggressive Russia).

Then the "restart" would find itself in trouble with political developments

Obama Strives to "Change" America

occurring in Ukraine. This newly-independent Ukrainian Republic (part of the former Soviet Union) was deeply divided culturally and politically between a Ukrainian-speaking majority and a large Russian-speaking minority (the latter located in the eastern provinces of Ukraine). Ethnically, the two groups were close in character, except that politically a bitter division ran deep. From 2007 to 2010 Ukraine possessed a Ukrainian-speaking Prime Minister Yulia Tymoshenko. But in 2010 she narrowly lost the national elections to Russian-speaking Victor Yanukovych, who, in rather typical "Third World" fashion, found cause in 2011 to have Tymoshenko arrested and imprisoned on "corruption" charges, which in turn set off demonstrations and then riots (Arab Spring style!) in the Ukrainian capital, Kiev, action which only grew more violent over time (termed the "Euromaidan Revolution").

By February of 2014 the action was so bad that Yanukovych went into hiding, and Russia's strongman Putin decided that it was time for Russia to act. Obama warned Putin not to get involved or, again, "serious consequences" would result. But by this time Putin had no regard for Obama as a strong leader whose word was to be fully respected. Thus at the end of the month he sent Russian soldiers into eastern Ukraine, wearing no military identifications – and thus termed simply the "little green men!" They seized the joint Ukrainian-Russian military base at Sebastopol in Crimea, turning it into a solely Russian base, and leading Putin to claim the whole of the Crimean Peninsula as now part of Russia. But Putin went no further with respect to the rest of the Russian-speaking sections of Ukraine, which now found themselves living in political limbo.

Obama's "serious consequences" ultimately turned out to be whatever action Obama was able to get America's European allies to take, with France and Germany (not America) leading the 2014-2015 Russian-Ukrainian ceasefire talks, and economic sanctions taken up by both America and Europe in reduced trade with Russia (although Europe, especially Germany, remained heavily dependent on Russia's oil and natural gas exports). In the end, all this changed nothing about the way the situation in Ukraine developed. But it also ended the "restart" of Russian-American relations. Putin's Russia would become much more aggressive in opposing America any way it could at this point.

Growing problems with Xi's China. Twenty years earlier America had invited China into the world of international trade and finance by favoring the struggling Chinese economy with all sorts of exceptions to the rules of the international economic game as played by the veterans of the West. The Chinese currency, the yuan or renminbi, was allowed to be offered at well-below market price in order to give the Chinese trading advantages they would need to get their own market economy up and running. And the results had been phenomenal: around 10 percent annual growth in the Chinese economy as vastly cheaper Chinese goods flooded the world market, improving vastly the Chinese employment picture – at the same time working deep harm on the American producers and their workers, who could not compete with the heavily subsidized Chinese products.*

At the same time, Chinese dollar earning from Chinese trade grew so vast that China was able not only to keep its huge workforce employed and allow the country to purchase scarce resources (such as oil) in which it was lacking, it enabled the Chinese to invest abroad in the production and sale of not only scare resources it needed, but also that the world needed. China was slowly putting itself in a position of market control of various strategic products, as well as bringing a lot of Third World countries into dependency on this Chinese economic "assistance." The West was quickly losing diplomatic as well as economic leverage abroad to the Chinese.

Furthermore, with America running up a huge debt – accelerated greatly under Bush, Jr., but continuing at the same rate under Obama – China was able to purchase huge portions of that American debt, which placed America as a debtor nation even more deeply in a state of dependency on China and its economic policies.

Obama tried to renegotiate the economic relationship with Xi Jinping's Chinese government, especially on this matter of currency subsidies which were resulting in a one-way trade program which had Chinese goods flooding America (and the West) – with no significant amount of trade moving in the opposite direction. Understandably, Xi was not interested in changing the arrangement. And ultimately, short of some serious muscle applied to China – which was not Obama's style – there was little that China would be willing to do to adjust the situation. And so things went.

Then there was this matter of Obama's proudly proclaimed "Pivot to Asia," in which America would shift some of its diplomatic attention to Asia – thus strengthening America's relations with Japan, South Korea, Taiwan, Australia, etc. Obama affirmed that this Pivot was also intended to improve relations with China as well. But Xi did not see things this way, interpreting this as a move merely to put America in a better bargaining position in its relations with China.

Anyway, Xi had his own "pivot" in mind for Asia: his claim that the South China Sea, bordered by many Asian countries, was in fact Chinese territorial waters, not "high seas" as America (and the rest of the world)

---

*Also the fact that the Chinese were refusing to respect international trademark rights and were producing cheap copies of more expensive Western goods – as well as stealing patent information on products brought into being in the West through costly research and development – was producing in the West growing bitterness about Chinese economic policies.

Obama Strives to "Change" America

claimed. To support this claim, Xi ordered the dredging of coral reefs in the Spratly Islands (close to the Philippines) in order to create new islands whose political goal was kept mysterious, until it finally became apparent that these were to be Chinese naval and air bases, positions from which Chinese sovereignty over the entire sea could be enforced.

In 2014 the Philippines challenged China at the Permanent Court of Arbitration at The Hague in the Netherlands, resulting in a decision in the Philippines' favor. But Xi had no interest in bowing to such international authority. To Xi, the South China Sea was Chinese, and it would remain that way.

In 2016 America conducted naval exercises there in order to confirm the South China Sea as international waters. But in the end it did nothing to change the fact that China was fast establishing itself as the dominator of the region. Obama could, of course, have dredged and built his own militarized islands in the area – to enforce the understanding that the area belonged neither to China or anyone else. But in the end, Obama did nothing. The "Pivot to Asia" – like so much of Obama's diplomacy – came with no muscle.

"Improved" relations with the Islamic Republic of Iran. Then there was the matter of Iran, and the distinct possibility that it was attempting to turn itself into a nuclear power. As there was yet in the Middle East no country functioning as a nuclear power (excepting Israel, which might possibly be a nuclear power – although the yes or no concerning that matter has long been held in utmost secrecy) this would put Iran in a hugely dominant position in that part of the world. However, Iran claimed that its extensive nuclear research and development was merely for the production of new energy sources, which, considering the fact that Iran sits on top of huge oil reserves, made little sense.

In any case, since the Iranian Revolution against the Shah in 1979 and the coming to power of the militant Shi'ite Muslim religious party led by the country's ayatollahs, American relations with Iran had been very negative, especially under Iran's constant theme of "death to the Great Satan America." Things would remain tense between Iran and Obama's America, especially with the 2009 reelection of the fiercely conservative Muslim President Mahmoud Ahmadinejad, and the outcry by many (both in and outside of Iran itself) that those elections been conducted very corruptly. Obama thus continued the American boycott of Iran and its oil sales (Iran's almost sole international income earner), because of Ahmadinejad's brutal hand in putting down the demonstrations against him that were rocking Iran at the time.

But in 2013, Iran succeeded in electing a more "moderate" Muslim cleric Hassan Rouhani as the country's president, who indicated that he wanted to explore the possibilities of improving Iranian-American relations. The response of both Obama and the other leaders of the West was highly positive. And in 2015 negotiators (Secretary of State Kerry directing the American team) sat down to work out a deal to reopen (gradually) economic and diplomatic relations with Iran, including the gradual releasing of Iran's frozen bank funds held abroad, provided that Iran place its nuclear development under certain internationally monitored limitations guaranteed to keep this development from producing weapons-grade nuclear material.

In January of 2016, with the signing of the Joint Comprehensive Plan of Action (JCPOA) with Iran, Obama felt he had achieved a great breakthrough in American diplomacy. Many Americans were excited about this development, for it seemed to be a big step in the direction of reducing international tensions (especially with Iran playing an ever-bolder hand in Middle Eastern affairs). But others remained concerned that it left it all too easy for Iran to pull out of the agreement and move to full nuclear military power. Iran was known to have its own moral rules about dealing with the infidel West, and was never to be trusted. Here too, only time would tell which group got things right.

CHAPTER FIFTEEN

INTO THE AGE OF TRUMP

* * *

TRUMP, AND THE MEDIA KINGMAKERS

The media as kingmakers. The 2016 presidential primaries gave rather strong confirmation that the traditional nominating conventions, attended by seasoned politicians assembled to choose from among their ranks the best-qualified candidate for the American presidency, had given way to the new process of selecting presidential candidates by the national media, on the basis of social identity. This was not entirely a new thing, but it was becoming the determining thing. Indeed, this new driving force in American politics reached back to 2007-2008 when TV celebrity Oprah Winfrey helped considerably push the only slightly politically experienced Obama past the well-developed political machine of Hillary Clinton to win the Democratic Party's presidential nomination in 2008.

Thus is was that in this new age of constant (24/7) barrage of entertaining news and media social hype – complements of not only the TV, but also the computer and the smartphone – the media would be the platform from which American leaders would now be selected. All the media needed to do was to shape and ultimately control the political narrative. And that is exactly what they lived for.

The "Trump Style." And it certainly was the case when the 2015-2016 series of televised debates hosted by the various news networks helped push the totally governmentally inexperienced Donald Trump to the head of a huge list of presidential candidates, and thus gain the Republican Party's presidential nomination in 2016. But this media coup Trump carried off all by himself, having served a dozen years as an aggressive TV director and host of the popular TV program, *The Apprentice*. Thus he made up in extensive media experience what he lacked in political office experience, and used that skill to run crudely over his Republican opponents in the primaries.

He was heavily engaged in Twitter in offering ongoing account of the failures of his opponents. Employing a stream of personal insults, he would run roughly over his Republican opponents, issuing such ad hominem phrases as "Little Marco" (Senator Marco Rubio) or "Lyin' Ted" (Senator Ted Cruz). About Republican opponent Florida Governor Jeb Bush, he had this to say:

> Jeb failed as Jeb! He gave up and enlisted Mommy and his brother (who got U.S. into the quicksand of Iraq). Spent $120 million. Weak no chance!

He even needlessly went after former Republican candidate John McCain (thus turning McCain into a dedicated political enemy):

> . . . not a war hero, he's a war hero because he was captured. I like people that weren't captured.

But he kept up this attack also even during the televised debates – when he would offer very audible insulting side comments, drawing the attention of the cameras to himself, away from those whose turn it was to present their case before the viewing audience! And thus it was that he drove his opponents to defeat one by one, and ended up, by the process of such elimination, with the Republican Party's presidential candidacy.

Then he turned on his Democratic Party opponent Hillary Clinton, whom he constantly termed "Crooked Hillary," over the use of her personal email account to transmit Secretary of State messages, some considered top secret.

But the media act did not stop there. He also issued sweeping statements that had virtually no chance of being true, but which, repeated often enough in simple form, took on their own weight, thanks to media coverage, (even if the coverage was trying to be fully negative). Thus Trump keep repeating about how Mexico was going to pay for a greatly expanded wall along America's border with Mexico (which refugees from Central America were breaching in massive numbers). But exactly how was he going to get Mexico to pay for that expansion? He never explained.

The 2015-2016 Democratic Party contest between Hillary Clinton and Bernie Sanders. Over on the Democratic Party side of the presidential contest, Clinton had stepped down from her position as head of the State Department back in February of 2013, allowing her to devote her energies to directing the Clinton Foundation – focused primarily on developing women's rights globally (ah, identity, more identity!). But those years also saw her busy fending off Republican efforts to undercut her politically because of the Benghazi fiasco and the discovery of her use of her private email accounts to send confidential messages, in violation of Department of State policy. Basically she held up well under the accusations. At the same time, she was preparing herself for another run at the U.S. Presidency, gathering massive campaign support and hitting the speaker circuit extensively.

Her only serious opponent within the Democratic Party was the Vermont Senator, Bernie Sanders, an avowed Socialist with all the political instincts Socialism stands for. Actually, the race was intense and Sanders did surprisingly well, indicating how far America had moved away from its traditional Middle-Class cultural roots.* Hillary had tremendous support from major corporate donors (such as the billionaire George Soros), as well as Blacks and Hispanics, and of course, women. Sanders' support came from younger, White, and more small-town Americans, as well as the more independent-leaning of Democrats. But in any case, from a very nearly equal start at the beginning of primary season, Clinton began to pull ahead of Sanders in gaining pledged delegates – and arrived at the Democratic National Convention in Philadelphia in July of 2016 with approximately a 20 percent lead in the delegate count (still, an amazing count in support of the Socialist Sanders), ensuring her the Democratic Party nomination.

The 2016 campaign. Clinton gave indication that she would stand with the changes in American society undertaken by Obama, even protect those from any effort of her opponent, Trump, to reverse those changes, as Trump clearly indicated he would do if elected president. In a sense, the campaign between the two seemed to be a lineup (as a continuation of the Obama social legacy) of Middle America versus America's many minorities, which included not only Blacks and Hispanics, but women, or at least the professional class of women working outside the home who saw themselves as part of that "minority" world. That was a huge segment of the American

---

*Middle-Class Americans were noted for their strong support of the political idea that success in life is achieved through individual initiative and personal responsibility – rather than on the basis of a dependency on the offerings that larger society "owes" individuals as their personal entitlements, entitlements always paid for by someone else. This "something for nothing" or "everything for free" was viewed by Middle-America as the grandest political deception of all offered by ambitious political demagogues. To Middle-America, such Socialism always leads to a horrible condition of personal dependency on the state for whatever favors come to the people – a very destructive undermining of personal freedom, one which also invariably leads to the economic and spiritual collapse of the community, Venezuela being a most horrific recent example. But it is a mentality fundamental to most Latin American politics, and politics in other parts of the world as well.

It never belonged in Christian America, which was the moral-spiritual foundation of this idea of the sovereignty of the individual, and not the state.

population. Thus Hillary was expecting a fairly easy win over Trump.

The Steele dossier. But just to make sure, Clinton campaign operative Marc Elias paid Fusion GPS $1.02 million to dig up dirt on Trump, and Fusion in turn hired for $168 thousand former British MI6 agent Christopher Steele to see if he could find some kind of political connection between Trump and the Russians. Steele obliged the Democrats, coming up with 16 different memos (based on information that Steele later admitted he had taken from a discredited CNN blog). Then in October of 2016 the periodical *Mother Jones* published rumors about the existence of Steele's anti-Trump dossier, which was actually put in the hands of the FBI, US State Department officials, and the office of Senator John McCain – the latter whose office in turn would put the very damaging dossier in the hands of the nation's press on January 10th, only 10 days before Trump's inauguration. While this would have no immediate effect on the election – which Trump had already won handily in the electoral college – this would provide the fuel for efforts immediately to impeach Trump and chase the Democrats' new "public enemy" from the White House.

The election itself. Trump, though indeed crude and vulgar, was no nitwit, and carefully targeted his campaign efforts with an eye on winning the electoral college vote (exactly as the Constitution specifies). And the results on election day (with only about 55 percent of eligible voters turning out to vote), he won 304 electoral votes to Clinton's mere 227 votes. The Democrats were shocked at the result, complaining bitterly about the way the electoral college weighted the vote in favor of Trump, because in the actual popular vote, Trump had won only 63 million votes to Clinton's 65.9 million votes. Thus she "won" the popular vote. Actually she did not. 4.5 million votes went to the Libertarian Party (generally considered a party of the Right) and 1.5 million went to the Green Party (generally considered a party of the Left). If these votes were combined by actual political lineup, the Political Right won 67.5 million votes and the Politically Left won 67.4 million votes! Close, but in any case, not exactly a Hillary victory.

Angry protests about the election results broke out immediately, not only in America but across much of the world. Here too, telecommunications aided considerably in mobilizing this huge outcry. Younger generations of Americans took to the streets announcing "not my president." And women dressed in pink also turned out to make it clear that there was no way they would ever consider Trump their president. And celebrities joined the anti-Trump chorus, some even announcing the possibilities of simply leaving the country, they were so angry.

They were all angry, very angry. Trump personally represented

Into the Age of Trump 459

everything they had come to believe to be the source of great evil in the country: White privilege, toxic masculinity, homophobia and Christian superstition. And, with Trump's slogan "Make America Great Again" (MAGA), it was obvious that Trump intended to undo all the wonderful changes Obama had brought to America. They would fight him over his MAGA program, from protesters in the streets to angry Democrats on Capitol Hill.

Already, Congressional Democrats were calling for Trump's impeachment, even before he had formally taken office. Not only was the new president-elect vulgar and ridiculous, they were claiming that he was a dangerous sociopath. But to impeach him he had to be found guilty of having committed the high crime or misdemeanor of ... ?

The making of Donald Trump. And yes, Trump certainly came across most frequently as vulgar and ridiculous. And he could certainly be very theatrical. That was indeed a key part of his background. But he was a successful venture capitalist, who took on huge investment risks, sometimes failed, but never backed down (except one period of depression in his life), and pushed ever-onward to various goals he had set before himself – big goals. And certainly one of those goals included residency in the White House.

Trump was born in 1946 (just months apart from both Bill Clinton and Bush, Jr.) and came from a family line of successful entrepreneurs, especially his father, who developed a huge housing construction and landowning company in the New York City boroughs of Queens and Brooklyn after World War Two. Trump grew up in a dedicatedly "Middle Class" (despite the family's enormous wealth) Presbyterian home as the fourth of five children (two sisters, one who went on to become a U.S. Circuit Court judge and another to become a Chase Manhattan Bank executive, and two brothers, one a TWA pilot and the other who eventually took over the family's property-management business).

Trump was raised fashionably, eventually entering (8th grade) the New York Military Academy, where he proved to be an outstanding athlete in several sports. Upon graduation in 1964, he started college at Fordham University, then transferring to the Wharton business school at the University of Pennsylvania, to prepare himself to take up the family real estate business. During those years he worked closely with his father in a major apartment complex redevelopment in Cincinnati, Ohio, and then, with $1 million in support from his father upon graduation, took on the challenge of major building construction in New York City (Manhattan).

He would work hard at developing his professional world. But within a dozen years the was able, at a cost of $100 million, to convert an unprofitable hotel into the fabulous Grand Hyatt on 42nd Street, adjacent to the Grand Central Terminal. And things got only grander after this. By 1979 he built his Trump Tower ($200 million in expenses) on New York City's fashionable 5th Avenue, then went on other projects: a casino in Atlantic City, an Eastern Airlines shuttle service, a skating rink in New York City's Central Park, partial ownership of Miss Universe and Miss USA pageants, a New Jersey football team (briefly), and in 1985 ownership of the Mar-a-Logo estate in Palm Beach Florida, something that became a personal get-away home for him and his family. And along the way, he met and then a year later married (1977) the Czech athlete and model, Ivana Zelnikova, and soon father three children, Don Jr., Ivanka and Eric.

Such a grand success was he that in 1987 he published something of an autobiography, *Trump: The Art of the Deal* (New York: Ballantine Books). It would become a New York Times bestseller for almost a year – and stay of the top of the list for three months – making the fairly young Trump one of Gallup Poll's top-10 best-known Americans at the time.

But ironically that same year financial disaster hit when the stock market crashed, and America slid into deep recession, throwing masses of people in the world of industrial and real-estate development into bankruptcy when the market for their products dried up. Trump himself was deeply invested in his work, owing $billions to banks, and nothing moving on the sales front of his real estate projects. But fortunately, the banks were not interested in another bankruptcy (especially one on this scale) and worked out a program to help him pay out his debts, costing him the loss of a lot of property in order to do so.

And this was accompanied by the news that he was having an affair with a pregnant Georgia model, Marla Maples, shattering his married world as well. He and Ivana would go through a very expensive divorce in 1992, and Trump would then go on the next year to marry Marla after their daughter Tiffany was born. But that marriage was not really headed down a primrose path, an in 1997 they would separate, and then divorce two years later.

But 1997 was the year he published his second book, *The Art of the Comeback* (New York: Times Books). And indeed Trump had slowly achieved just that, a true comeback. In 1994 he had been able to acquire 50 percent ownership of the Empire State Building, and in 1995 finally finish the restoration and then sell the Plaza Hotel (which he renamed the Trump Building).

The following year he met the Slovene model, Melania Knauss, though it would not be until 2005 that they would marry. Attending the wedding were numerous political and media celebrities, including Bill and Hillary Clinton! A little over a year later Melania would give birth to their son,

Barron.

Being the restless soul that he was, in 2003 he turned to the challenge of the world of television, becoming producer and host of the NBC show, *The Apprentice*, the program becoming very popular. Eventually he would take on celebrities as his show's participants, thus in 2008 renaming the program *The Celebrity Apprentice*. He would continue in this role until 2015, when he turned fulltime to his next challenge, national political office. At this point, Trump's personal fortune was in the $3 billion range.

Trump had some earlier thoughts on the matter of politics, back in 1999 trying a run at the U.S. presidency via the Reform Party, then in 2004 even undertaking fundraising for the Democratic Party presidential candidate Kerry. But in 2012 he would return to the Republican Party, thinking of a presidential run himself, before throwing his support to Mitt Romney.

But in June of 2015, Trump announced his candidacy for the Republican Party presidential nomination, running on the challenge to "Make America Great Again" (MAGA). This, unfortunately was a concept in total violation of the moral inclination of America's younger generations, who believed that their "shaming" of America was a sign of personal nobility and that such patriotism as Trump was proclaiming was simply ugly Fascism, which they were personally dedicated to root out at all costs.

Nonetheless, employing the same careful calculation by which he had built up his huge business empire, Trump pulled ahead of his competitors, first of all to gain the Republican Party presidential nomination, and then to conduct a carefully strategized move to win the electoral college votes needed to gain the presidency itself.

No, Trump was no nitwit. Vulgar and abrasive at times, yes. Misleading in his broad public statements about what he planned to do with respect to this issue or that, often yes. But a nitwit. No.

Trump the Christian. Trump was also a dedicated Christian, but in a very Trumpian way. He was raised in a Presbyterian family, but once deeply immersed in the business world, religion seemingly played no particular role in his life. But in later years (around the year 2000?) he seemed to find an interest in Christian televangelism, eventually especially in that of Paula White, an attractive (and very wealthy) White woman leading a largely Black congregation. Her "prosperity gospel" version of the Christian faith, popular among many Evangelicals, touched Trump deeply (she is said to have finally "led him to the Lord" in 2011), and he found himself taking advice from her on matters of Christian faith, both before and then during his tenure in the White House. Thus it was that he was identified fairly closely with the American Evangelical community.

His political opponents accused him of course of taking on these Christian loyalties for purely political reasons. But then Trump was accused of a lot of things, which Trump was always quick to argue back in his own way. In any case, it will always be hard for anyone else to assess the reality of another person's spiritual life. Indeed, religion can be a matter of much show. But privately, it can also be very sincere in a most individualistic way.

In any case, as President he would work closely with the Christian pastoral world (as had Presidents before him), but especially with the various members of his evangelical advisory council, and join them in attempting to free public Christian prayer from governmental prohibition (placed there by the courts), only minorly successful in the effort. And he would push (again only slightly successfully) to allow people whose faith did not put them in accord with the legal requirements of "political correctness" not to be punished by the courts for failing to obey the courts' official social-moral directives.

He was accused of politicizing the Presidential prayer breakfast in February of 2020,* commenting on the religious hypocrisy of individuals "who use their faith as justification for doing what they know is wrong," "nor do I like people who say, 'I pray for you' when you know that is not so." It was generally understood that he was referring to political opponents, Mitt Romney who had just cited his Mormon faith as to why he, as a Republican, had voted for Trump's conviction, and Nancy Pelosi, who had announced that she prayed regularly for the supposedly deeply misguided President ("He really needs our prayers"), while directing the ongoing effort to remove Trump from office. Trump apologized for his comments at the end of his speech "I'm sorry. I apologize. I'm trying to learn. It's not easy. When they impeach you for nothing and then you're supposed to like them, it's not easy folks. I do my best."

And indeed his Good Friday Message that April – and accompanying prayer by Pentecostal bishop Harry Jackson, who also praised Trump for his Christian work – was a deeply moving event calling for peace, reconciliation and deliverance in this time of national troubles, brought on especially by the Covid-19 pandemic. There were no Trumpian swipes at his Washington opponents in the message! And it was also another indicator of the very high standing that Trump had within key parts of the Black as well as White

---

*But this breakfast was taking place the very next day after the Senate had dismissed the impeachment charges delivered to it from the Democrat-controlled House, and just after the mainline Christian journal *Christianity Today* had strongly denounced the president. But it was also three days after Trump had been prayed for in the launch of the bi-racial organization, Evangelicals for Trump Coalition.

Evangelical community.

Special Counsel Mueller investigates the "Russian connection." Once in office as President, by May of 2017 the Steele-inspired rumors of "Trump collusion with the Russians" had mounted so high – thanks to the scandal-hungry media and his dedicated opponents on Capitol Hill – that Congress called for the creation of a special counsel to look into these rumors. Soon former FBI director Robert Mueller was assigned the task, given wide authority to find out whatever he could on the matter.

Then for the next two years, the world had to wait while Mueller's investigation was conducted behind closed doors. This, however, did not keep the news media from speculating wildly about what certainly Mueller must be finding out about the criminal president. But weren't they horrified when finally in March of 2019 – after much federal expense in time and money – Mueller came up with the conclusion that though he did not approve of some of the things Trump did, he could find no basis for criminal charges to be brought against the president.

That was not what so many on Capitol Hill and the national press wanted to hear. Impeachment therefore would have to go down a different road than the much hoped-for Russian connection. They were not going to give up on this all-important crusade against the evil president.

Trump's Federal Court appointments. In the last year of Obama's presidency, Conservative Supreme Court Antonin Scalia died. Obama naturally sought to fill that appointment, but obviously not with a similarly Conservative individual. He proposed a "centrist" Merrick Garland, which simply would have cut further the Conservative voices countering the small but very Liberal Supreme Court majority. The Republican-dominated Senate let Obama know that they would hold up any replacement appointment until a new president was installed as a result of the elections coming up that fall. Thus no action was taken on the Obama appointment.

Then with Trump taking office, not surprisingly he appointed Neil Gorsuch, a judicial Conservative or judicial "originalist," one that insists on a very limited role for federal judges in how federal law is applied. The appointment was ultimately approved in the Senate, 54-45, not surprisingly along purely Republican-Democratic Party lines. Okay, a conservative to replace a conservative.

But then the next year, "centrist" Anthony Kennedy (originally a conservative, who like so many, over the years had moved to the Left to become more "activist" in his judicial philosophy) announced that he would be retiring in July (2018).

When it became apparent that Trump was going to nominate another

Conservative or "originalist" to that spot, the battle was on. The Supreme Court was, after all, the supreme legislative body in the land. And the idea that it would take a more Conservative view on legal matters was totally unacceptable to the Democrats, who looked for their ideological agenda to be enacted through the Supreme Court if they could not get it enacted through Congress. That's how Congress's strongly supported Defense of Marriage Act (DOMA) was overturned during the Obama years.

So they did what they attempted to do years earlier with the Conservative Justice Clarence Thomas, by bringing forward a female "victim," Christine Blasey Ford, who narrated an incident that happened back in her high school days (36 years earlier) when she was accosted ("feared for her personal safety") by a group of drunk teenage boys at a party. And she was sure that one of them was Trump's new appointee, Brett Kavanaugh, although she did not know him personally at the time. But the victim card the Democrats played did not work very well when a friend of hers who was with her at that party remembered no such event having taken place. And Kavanaugh's friends attested to the fact the picture Ford painted was not possible of the Kavanaugh they had known in high school. And his record since then as a judge was spotless, though, yes, conservative. And that was the best the Democrats could offer in their attempt to destroy the character of Kavanaugh.

The news media however spun as negative a picture as possible in support of the victim narrative. Thus the hearings dragged on, until finally in October the Senate approved his appointment 50-48.

Then there was the matter of the Ninth Circuit Court – always reliably Liberal – and therefore the court that the ACLU and other "progressive" groups brought their cases to with the expectation of a very favorable decision in their litigation. But vacancies were occurring, and Trump was appointing more Conservatives, although the Democrats were doing everything possible to hold up the appointments. But even then, the Liberals needed not to worry, as only nine of the twenty-five Circuit Court judges had been appointed by Republican presidents. Trump had a very long way to go to get the Ninth Circuit Court out of Left field, so that he could shut down legislation through judicial decree.

Then in 2020, just a month (October) before the scheduled November elections, Trump was able to appoint yet a third individual to the Supreme Court, replacing Ruth Bader Ginsburg, who had died the previous month (September). The Democrats were furious, remembering how the Republicans had stalled Obama's intended appointment in the last months of his presidency. But the Republicans, possessing a majority in the Senate, pushed ahead with hearings on the Trump appointment of Amy Coney Barrett to the position, a judicial "originalist" or conservative (and a

Catholic) – replacing a very Liberal (and Jewish) Ginsburg. Needless to say, Barrett's Christian loyalties ("dogma" it was termed by Democratic Senator Feinstein) came under considerable questioning by the Democrats (where did she stand on the matter of abortion and gay rights?). In the process the American Bar Association (which usually is listened to in such matters) gave her its highest recommendation, for "integrity, professional competence and judicial temperament." But this did not bring on any support from the Democrats. In any case, in the end, the Republican majority was able to confirm her appointment 52-49, with none of the Democrats in favor and even one Republican (Susan Collins of Maine) voting in the negative.

Thus her appointment probably heightened the fear considerably of the Democrats that the Supreme Court would be even less likely than ever to be the ultimate recourse to put their "progressive reforms" into place by decree.

But they had not yet had the opportunity to see what a Democratic White House (soon-to-be-President Joe Biden) would be able to achieve simply through issuing multitudes of executive orders (presidential decrees) as the law of the land.

The 2018 Congressional elections. By long-standing political habit of the American voter, the mid-term elections of Congressmen (all members of the House and one-third of the Senators) have typically produced a major setback for the party previously in power, especially if it is the party of the individual in the White House. Thus the Democrats were looking forward to some major electoral victories, ones that would finally give them the leverage to do what they wanted most of all to do: get rid of Trump. And indeed that is how the elections for the House seats went: the Democrats were able to regain their majority position, and all the political benefits that went with that. But the elections for the Senate proved to be a shocker: the Republicans actually picked up more seats, thus increasing the size of their majority in the Senate. Congress would thus be divided deeply along party lines separating the agenda of the House (to impeach Trump) and the Senate (to move on to other things).

But most interesting, three new female House members – two Muslims and one Hispanic – received the political spotlight that freshmen Congressmen otherwise never get until they have accumulated some years of experience on Capitol Hill. But not these three members of the "Squad," as they were termed by an adoring press. They held press conferences in which their very words carried the weight of long-established Congressional leaders, even more so. This was another indicator of how media interest – not actual political experience – had moved into position to shape the country's political narrative. Where was that dynamic likely to take the country?

Impeachment, round two. Now with a majority in the House, the Democrats were ready to make the long-awaited move: impeach Trump. They, of course would need some kind of legal grounds to do so. The Mueller investigation had failed to come up with anything they could go with. So they would have to find some new Trump action they could use to justify their actions.

And Ukraine, not Russia, would seemingly offer them what they wanted so badly. An unidentified "whistleblower" inside the Washington Establishment passed information to Democrat Adam Schiff's House Intelligence Committee that in a phone conversation Trump had on July 25th (2019) with Ukrainian President Volodymyr Zelensky, Trump had requested help in getting information concerning corruption rampant in the Ukrainian business world, indicating they he would not release American assistance funds (which would typically end up in the pockets of Ukrainian officials) until this matter was cleared up. The "issue" in all this was that the Ukrainian gas company Burisma Holdings, one of the most corrupt of the organizations, had Hunter Biden, Joe Biden's son, serving on the company's board of directors, for which he received a monthly salary of $50,000. Bringing Hunter Biden into the matter was what the Democrats were hoping to get Trump on, because they could claim that Trump was violating the federal law making it illegal to involve foreign influence in the conduct of American electoral campaigns. And as Joe Biden (former Vice President during the Obama years) was running as a strong Democratic Party presidential candidate, Trump's request (which Trump did not deny that he in fact had made to the Ukrainian president) was an illegal effort to involve Ukrainian influence in the elections. But Trump countered that looking into corruption in Ukraine before he released funding was an important responsibility he had as president, especially as Americans themselves were involved. It was unfortunate that the person involved was the son of Joe Biden. But Trump had a job to do.

So at this point, whether a Trump crime had been committed – or not – involved simply the matter of which ideological version of the event you wanted to go with.

Trump was in no mood to be dragged before Congress to be interrogated by a hostile Schiff and his Democrats – and simply refused to appear on Capitol Hill. So now the issue for the committee became one of Trump's "obstruction of Congress" and "abuse of power." So those two very vague procedural matters were what the Democrat-controlled House finally decided to impeach Trump over. The Ukrainian issue was dropped because it had become increasingly clear that pushing on that issue was not going to work well for the Democrats, and in fact might actually do some considerable damage to Biden if there was too much digging into the details of the event. So that part got dropped.

Thus on December 18th (2019) the House passed impeachment charges against Trump, almost completely along party lines, again, making the matter one of pure politics rather than the law. But then on February 5 (2020) it was dismissed by the Senate. There was no way that any Democrat-dominated House impeachment was going to get even close to a 2/3s vote needed to convict in the Republican-dominated Senate, although the "abuse of power" article did get the support of Republican Mitt Romney, another Republican whom the Trump mouth had succeeded in converting into a dedicated political opponent.

This was clearly a case of partisan politics, not the law, as indeed the impeachment urge had been since its origins in early 2017, in fact every time it had been brought into play since the 1970s. And unfortunately, what the American public would be forced to make of this now on-going event would be shaped (as always) entirely by the way the media wanted to present the "facts" of the case itself.

In any case, it appeared that "impeachment" was now going to serve as a regular instrument of American politics, to be called on to cripple the White House by a hostile Congress, even though the 2/3's Senate vote requirement was going to make it difficult to ever get a conviction. But the impeachment proceedings would of themselves offer all sorts of political opportunity for an anti-White-House congressional opposition, not to mention a scandal-hungry national press.

This was a very bad policy to be bringing into America's national political arena. But it was there, fully supported by Congressional leaders who should have known how dangerous such a new political procedure could make America's national political life. This was nothing more than sleezy Third-World political antics, used regularly to negate national elections that did not go in the direction that certain politicians were wanting them to go. That is to say, elections themselves would no longer be treated as final in their outcomes. There would no longer be any graceful concessions by the defeated contestant, but instead simply an on-going contest of the election decision.

Coronavirus. While all this Democrat-Republican animosity was going on, a horrible pandemic caused by a new coronavirus hit the world. It seemed to have its origins in a Chinese food market in late 2019, spread rapidly across China, then hit Europe – finally moving on to America by January of 2020. No one was quite certain what to do, or what this disease meant for the safety and strength of American society. Fearing a social and economic panic, Trump tried to play down the threat the disease posed to American life – but did attempt to restrict travel coming into America from China, being accused by his opponents of anti-Asian racism in the process! But watching things develop in Italy and Spain, hit especially hard by the disease, by early March it was apparent that something very serious was happening here. Seeing Italy and Spain respond to the disease by instituting the policy of "lockdown" (keeping people in their homes, allowing them out only for such "essential services" as food shopping), a similar lockdown began to be taken up at the state level by America's governors. Thus shops, restaurants, schools, churches, etc. were closed down, and the American streets emptied. But the American economy also went into lockdown mode. How long America would have to remain under such economy-crushing measures was completely unknown.

Trump's federal response was in early-March to authorize $8.3 billion in emergency funding for medical research and hospital care – quickly realizing that this hardly met the severity of the crisis. By mid-March he put before Congress a request for $1.2 trillion in federal assistance, not only for medical assistance but also in support for struggling businesses and support for state unemployment insurance programs. Republican Senate Majority Leader Mitch McConnell was about to bring support to the request when Democratic House Speaker Pelosi entered the dynamic, demanding instead a $2.5 trillion, with a much wider range of financial support involved (education programming, environmental support, and other funding of Democratic Party goals) – including a cutback in the financial support Trump originally wanted for corporate America. This was to be more than an economic measure. It was to be a full social programming venture. And it would also be a huge addition to the national debt.

But in the end a "compromise" was required to get any action at all on the matter, and the net result was a $2.2 trillion program – which included a $1200 or $2400 grant to every American household (depending on single or double adult status). But this was politics rather than economics. Of course. It's what Washington does!*

---

*The U.S. government has come to feel that it has the right (even some kind of duty) to run up a virtually unlimited debt, such as the astronomically high one it has accumulated today, totaling around $28.6 trillion (as of mid-2021) and still rising rapidly. That's approximately $86,000 per person or $270,000 per the average American family of 3.14 members. Who (or what future generation) is ever going to be able to pay that off – or even cover the interest on that debt if it were allowed to move to a more realistic 6% interest rate, rather than the politically set rate today (thanks to policies of the Federal Reserve) which has been held below even 1%? A normal interest rate would consume all of Washington's discretionary/non-mandatory spending, bankrupting the federal government. But it appears that nobody in Washington thinks much about

Meanwhile the virus lockdown was having its own impact – social and psychological – as March turned into April and April turned into May. How long was this lockdown going to last? Tempers began to heat up as debate, even street protests, began to break out over the ongoing restrictions.

"Black Lives Matter." Then in Minneapolis on May 25 occurred the arrest and death of a Black man, George Floyd, by a White cop, Derek Chauvin, involving Chauvin's holding a resistant Floyd to the ground by keeping his knee on Floyd's neck – as Floyd protested "I can't breathe." Indeed he could not, and died as a result. All of this was caught on video and shown repeatedly across all the media, Facebook and YouTube as well as the national news media.

Black fury exploded in Minneapolis – where the incident took place – and Minneapolis quickly began to look like Los Angeles during the Rodney King riots, and Fergusson, Missouri, during the Michael Brown riots. Shops were broken into, then burned to the ground, with whole neighborhoods coming to look like bombed out war zones.

But the action did not stop there. It soon spread to city after city across America as Blacks (and Whites) turned out for "peaceful" protest on behalf of the cause, "Black Lives Matter." Unfortunately, these peaceful protests were also soon accompanied by the looting and burning in city after city across America, similar to those continuing day after day in Minneapolis. Tragically, in St. Louis, Black retired police captain David Dom was killed defending a friend's store, and many police (Blacks among them) were wounded (some killed) during the riots. At this point even some prominent Blacks came out in opposition to the way the demonstrations were developing, complaining that this was not the way to improve race relations in America.

Antifa takes charge. Meanwhile, the cause was joined by angry, mostly-White, Antifa ("Anti-Fascist") youth who turned the matter into a grand assault on all social authority – the pandemic restrictions being big contributors to the anti-authority mood. And the dynamic became one of physical attack on the police (called out, of course, to contain the damage caused by the rioting) – characterized by Antifa rioters (and minority voices as well) as Fascist devils. So this dynamic became more than just one of racial tensions. It began to look like wholesale social revolution, especially in early June when Antifa youth took control of downtown Seattle and

---

this pending financial disaster. Instead Washington seems very willing to add even another $trillion or two onto the debt, if it is perceived as advancing the interests of this group or that group.

turned six city blocks into their police-free "Capitol Hill Autonomous Zone," defended by fully-armed youth.

At this point, a number of big-city mayors (Liberal Democrats) came out with the announcement that they would be cutting back funding on their police budgets, to relocate that money into more "socially sensitive" minority-support programming. Soon this was becoming a refrain heard even more widely among America's state and urban public authorities. Defunding the police was becoming the new thing in the world of "political correctness," which a lot of local officials wanted to get on board with. Needless to say, with the police on the defensive as "fascists," urban crime skyrocketed.

The Supreme Court expands the legal support of LGBTQ dynamics. In the meantime, America was so caught up in the street rioting occurring across the American political map, that it almost missed the importance of the decision that the Supreme Court came to in the case of *Harris Funeral Homes v. Equal Employment Opportunity Commission* (2020). On June 15th the Supreme Court announced that the 1965 Civil Rights Act included also protection of transgender sex, in deciding 6-3 that the Michigan Funeral Home had violated the law when it refused to allow one of its employees to cross-dress when meeting with grieving family members – in violation of the business's dress standards. Interestingly, on the majority side was the supposedly conservative "originalist" Justice Gorsuch, who explained that Title VII of the 1965 Act did not include exactly the wording of transgender rights, but it certainly could be understood to have intended that in the category of "sex" discrimination outlawed by the Act.

What was this? Was Gorsuch sliding Leftward ideologically? Furthermore, although Kavanaugh joined Thomas and Samuel Alito in dissenting, he did so only out of the strictest of originalist principles. Personally, he expressed himself extensively in favor of all the progress happening elsewhere in LGBTQ rights.

But the Left paid no attention to his efforts to put himself on the Progressive side of politics, and attacked him for his vote nonetheless.

And so the politics of the highest court in the land continues to develop.

✳ ✳ ✳

AMERICA AND THE WORLD IN THE AGE OF TRUMP

Trump's wall. Trump had made it a central campaign theme of his that he was going to build a wall to stop the invasion of American territory by throngs of Central Americans (joined by others from different countries and with different agendas) fleeing the anarchy that reigned in Guatemala and El Salvador, but especially in Honduras.

Liberals called Trump's blocking of this massive influx of huge caravans of refugees "inhumane." Some even called for an end altogether of the U.S. Immigration and Customs Enforcement (ICE), though it is doubtful that these same voices would have been willing to give permanent residency to these foreign refugees in their own homes. But it made for a very Liberal narrative, despite the fact that ICE had been just as active in protecting the U.S. border from invasion under Obama's presidency.

But as the Democratic Party knows well, it gets the support of social classes that have come to expect those in authority to take care of them – such as the way things were supposed to work in Central America. But, as happens regularly, those countries had run out of economic assets they could continue to seize and redistribute to their supporters, and thus simply had failed as societies. Consequently, the mass exodus from Central America. And thus also, seeing potential votes (even if not yet citizens) in these government-dependent refugees, Liberals were very upset at Trump's effort to block or just slow up the invasion.

Although Trump did not get Mexico to pay for the border wall (a rather ridiculous idea), he did get Mexican cooperation in slowing up and stalling the caravans passing through Mexico on their way to the United States. And he would indeed add (even though only slightly) to the reach of the border wall – or at least upgrade portions already in existence – a matter in which he took great pride.

A new trade pact with Canada and Mexico. Part of this Mexican cooperation was in response to the trade deals that Trump meanwhile had worked out with not only Mexico to the South but also Canada to the North. That in itself was a major Trump achievement, in an effort to get something of a balance in the trade between America and its neighbors. It had taken some Trump toughness economically to get economic talks underway – new tariffs on Canadian and Mexican steel and aluminum, and his threat to pull out of the North American Free Trade Area (NAFTA) altogether. NAFTA was the result of an agreement put in place back in 1994 to help Mexico get going economically – but which over time had come to disadvantage greatly America trade with Mexico (and to a lesser extent Canada). It took a whole year to reach a settlement. But it did cut back considerably the barriers Mexico had placed on American imports (through the mechanics of its own Valued-Added-Tax or VAT program) and provided a more equal flow of goods and services from country to country.

But at the time of the signing (November 2018) the Democrats had just been voted into a majority position in the House and were not in a very cooperative mood – until some additional provisions favorable to American labor and environmentalist groups were added, allowing finally at the very end of 2019 the new United States Mexico Canada Agreement (USMCA) to go into effect.

Venezuela. Further to the South, in Venezuela, similar problems had been developing with the putting in place there in 1999 of a strongly Socialist regime under Hugo Chavez (nationalizing Venezuela's rich oil industry), a program then passed on to Nicolás Maduro with Chavez's death in 2013. The Socialist government hoped to use oil assets to reward its supporters among Venezuela's lower social classes. But the international pricing of oil had dropped considerably – cutting back severely that Socialist payoff. Now Venezuela found itself sinking rapidly into national poverty. Consequently, there was also a mass exodus of those able to escape the country (about 4 million or 12 percent of the population), headed mostly to other parts of South America and the Caribbean islands.

In 2017 Trump placed an embargo on Venezuelan oil* – but also exports of food and medicine to Venezuela. Then in 2018, Trump was joined by numerous European leaders hoping that Venezuelan elections that year would bring to power the more politically centralist Juan Guaidó, pledged to open the country's economy internationally. But confusion, corruption – but most importantly, the support of Maduro by the Venezuelan military – foiled the effort.

But this in turn offered China, Russia, Cuba, Iran and even Syria and Bolivia opportunity to come to the aid of what was the strongly anti-American Maduro regime – with the intent not only of embarrassing Trump politically, but putting these "assisting" powers in a very strong position to influence political developments in the Western Hemisphere. And as long as Maduro remained in power so too would they remain as part of the political and economic dynamic in that part of the world. Especially for China and Russia, this was a big win.

Confronting China. China seems to be going down the same road as North Korea, strengthening the role of the Great Leader in society. Chinese President Xi Jinping had been making his firm grip on affairs both at home and abroad very attractive to the Chinese mind – that sees this strength only in a Tianzi or "Son of Heaven." Thus in March of 2018, the Chinese National People's Congress voted 2,964 to 2 to end the Chinese Constitution's two-term limit on the presidency – put in place back in the 1990s by Chinese

---

*Anyway, America really did not need Venezuelan oil as it was basically oil-self-sufficient by this point thanks to American shale-oil production.

reformer Deng Xiaoping, to ensure the "collective" rather than personal rule of the Chinese Communist Party (such as had been the disastrous case under Mao Zedong). So, the Chinese found themselves heading down the road of unlimited personal rule again. That seemed to work best for them in their understanding of political dynamics.

And indeed, the Chinese have reasons to be well pleased by the service Xi has been offering the country. He is a skilled player of political Weiqi, a Chinese boardgame where a player wins by the careful placement of numerous checker-like pieces on the grid, and succeeds in finally isolating the opponent, who cannot make any further moves. The Chinese government has been carefully sending out technical advisors to numerous Third World countries, to help them develop their economies, in the process making the Chinese economic – and thus also political – position indispensable in their countries.

But China has also been taking an ever-stronger position in the West's world as well. America (and many other Western countries) find their industries deeply dependent on governmentally subsidized and thus cheap Chinese labor to make their products inexpensive and thus marketable. At the same time, China has skillfully developed its electronic communications industry, financed also by extensive government subsidy – plus a lot of disregard of the World Trade Organization's (WTO) international patent rights (just plain technology theft) – in order to advance China's own technological position. China has been helping its 4G telecommunications giant Huawei now move into dominance in the 5G telecommunications sector, hoping to make as much of the world as possible China-dependent in the telecommunications field. Also, Chinese companies such as Alibaba and Tencent have grown to enormous size, both in China (near monopolies in their respective realms), but also to positions of dominance abroad by buying out foreign companies.

As a sign of the success so far in this venture, in April of 2019 the leaders of some 40 countries gathered in Beijing to celebrate the success so far of China's "Belt and Road Initiative" (started up in 2013) designed to integrate closely the economies of these countries with the Chinese economy. Needless to say, America did not participate – nor did China's Asian archrival India. But Putin did, as well as a lot of African and Middle Eastern leaders, and some European leaders (Poland, Hungary, Serbia, Greece, Italy, Spain. Czech Republic, Switzerland), even NATO ally Turkey, and some Latin American countries (Chile, Argentina). That was quite a show of Chinese support!

Trump responded in March of 2018 by putting in place tariffs amounting to $250 billion on Chinese goods seeking entry into American markets, in order to bring them closer in line with the pricing of unsubsidized international goods. China retaliated with $100 billion aimed at American goods coming to China (but the Chinese actually already import much less of the more expensive Western products). Efforts between Trump and Xi to renegotiate trade relations were attempted in 2019, but with little by way of results. But other Western countries joined the effort to not have Chinese products dumped into their economies, or have their companies bought out by Chinese profits gained in the government-subsidized economic competition.

The coronavirus outbreak however could be quite damaging to Xi's political position. Heaven's withdrawal of its endorsement of the Tianzi is easily understood by the Chinese when some devastating event, such as a plague, occurs. Westerners do not fully appreciate the pressure Xi is under in China itself over this dramatic event. The virus is a very bad thing for Western societies (not just economically but also politically). But for China this can be totally devastating politically to the individual in power at the time. The world needs to watch to see how Xi handles this political challenge. Of course, he will attempt to hide the extent of the damage it is causing, or shift the blame elsewhere. But it is still there as a very serious threat to his personal rule.

And Trump's pressuring the World Health Organization (he announced a pending withdrawal in May of 2020) to look into the origins of the pandemic and, as Trump saw things, stop protecting China, may have been done so, at least in part, for the very purpose of weakening Xi's regime.[*]

Putin's Russia. Russia's "President-for-Life" Putin has been doing everything he can to bring Russia out of the Third-World status it fell into when it attempted "democracy" under Yeltsin – and return the country to the status of being something resembling more closely the superpower it once was. After all, it still holds an amazing quantity of nuclear weapons and possesses a well-developed military machine.

And, like Xi, Putin has been very aggressive in putting his country into the middle of global dynamics again, having Russia act exactly like the major power it once was. In fact the two, Putin and Xi, have been working closely together because they share the same goal: bring down America from its superpower status and have it join the company of the former international greats, Spain, Portugal, France, Britain, Germany, the Netherlands, etc., who now occupy at best only a secondary level of importance in the international scheme of things.

Thus it was that Putin was quick to come to Assad's aid in Syria

---

[*]Biden has since reversed Trump's decision, announcing that the U.S. will not be withdrawing from the organization.

when Obama tried to weaken and then topple Assad's government, merely undercutting America's diplomatic position there, and advancing Russia's at the same time. And thus it was that Putin was also quick to come to Iran's aid when Trump attempted the same thing against Iran, in rejecting Obama's treaty with the Muslim government and then deepening the boycott of Iranian oil. And thus also Putin jumped to the opportunity to be of help to Maduro's government in Venezuela that Trump was trying to bring down. And so it goes, counter-moves (in alliance with China and others) whenever America attempts to exert influence over developments abroad.

Indeed, Putin and Xi's cooperation has been extensive, developing China's Maritime Silk Road access to Europe across the newly open waters of the Arctic above Russia's Siberia, at the same time working to complete the Russian pipeline with the goal of sending much-needed natural gas to the vast Chinese market. And the two countries are working together in the development of the new 5G network, as well as in other infrastructure and technology development.

And then there is also the matter of Russia's natural gas pipeline to Europe, notably to Germany which also is deeply dependent on that Russian gas. This has helped put Russia in a pivotal economic position in Europe that America is finding it hard to compete with.

And thus it seems that the Russians in are no hurry to replace Putin with any other individual. The Russians are not as wed to the idea of "democracy" as America and the rest of the West. They had not fared well in the 1990s with their democratic experiment under Yeltsin. They have been very happy to have a strongman lead them, and – like the Chinese – see no need to turn over leadership on a regular basis. Indeed, a 2019 poll taken by the Levada Center* revealed even that 70 percent of the Russians believed that (what we consider a monster) Stalin played a completely or relatively positive role in the life of the country!

The world of Islam. It seems almost impossible for Americans to understand the world of Islam. When Sunni and Shi'ite Muslims are not fighting each other (their mutual hatred is ancient and deep, something along the lines of the Catholic-Protestant rivalry of the 1500s and 1600s in Christian Europe), they find the one thing they do agree on to be the danger that Western Secular-Humanism poses to their world. Unlike the Westerners themselves, they understand Secular-Humanism to be simply another religion, one which as Muslims, whether Sunni or Shi'ite, they deeply oppose, simply for the way it has placed Human Reason at the head

---

*FP Morning Brief (*Foreign Policy*), January 12, 2021.

of human life, not the God or Allah that created and directs all life. In this they share parts of the same worldview as Christians, although they are as anti-Christian as they are anti-Sunni or Shi'ite in their own world. It's confusing. But not beyond understanding, if Western leaders – such as American presidents – would simply take the time to learn about these things. It would have saved America a lot of trouble in Iraq, Afghanistan, Libya, and Syria. And it was only the intervention of the Egyptian military in Egypt that spared America from making the same mistake in Egypt.

Bush never really caught on to this all-important dynamic. But Obama seemed to understand this dynamic no better than Bush, supposing that "democratic" Secular-Humanism would inevitably rise to dominance in the Muslim Middle East if we simply got rid of other Arab dictators, like we did with Saddam. Libya, Egypt and Syria became test cases for the Obama (and Bush, Jr.) idea that "democratic progress" would be the inevitable result.

And of course, as in Iraq and Afghanistan, such intervention merely spun these societies into a horribly cruel state of civil war, from which millions of people were displaced from their homes and thrust into refugee status. And in the end, this merely gave opportunity for fiercely anti-Western Sunni Muslims to advance the cause of jihad, even to the point of succeeding in establishing a new Sunni Caliphate (the Islamic State) in the war-torn zone of Western Iraq and Eastern Syria.

But Obama did feel that he had achieved at least one foreign policy success (in addition to the taking out of Osama bin Laden in Pakistan) with his appeasement rather than confrontational approach to Iran, with the signing of the nuclear development agreement that would open the West (Europe as well as America) to Iran again.

But Trump didn't see things in Iran the Obama way, claiming that a country whose motto was "Death to America" was not one to be trusted to keep its word on the agreement (there was already way too much secret activity going on in that part of the world concerning nuclear development) and he thus terminated Obama's agreement with Iran.

Whether confrontation rather than appeasement will prove more effective in keeping an Iran determined to bring the West's – and most notably America's – Secular-Humanist cultural dominance in the world to an end remains to be seen. But Iran has been very busy allying with the Russians and Chinese wherever possible in undercutting the American-led Western position in the larger international realm. Would continuing appeasement have changed the direction of Iranian politics? Certainly not, at least as long as militant Shi'a Islam continues to dominate Iran.

Of course, there are still many Secular-Humanists in Iran, but they have been deeply undercut politically by the Muslim militants and the

Iranian Muslim leadership in Iran. And American toughness does nothing to help the political position in Iran of these Iranian Secularists, who appear to other Iranians as highly treasonous in the way they seem to share the same values as the hated American enemy, an enemy under Trump clearly out to destroy Iran's economy and thus society itself.

On the other hand, Trump also made the decision to start withdrawing American ground troops from other positions in the Muslim world, at the same time beefing up the American naval presence in the Middle East, especially in the vital Persian Gulf region where Saudi Sunni and Iranian Shi'ite oil interests are in direct conflict.

Sadly, it was the U.S. withdrawal from Syria that finally severed Trump's stressful relationship with his Secretary of Defense Jim Mattis, who disagreed strongly with the move. But it was part of Trump's effort to get the country out of the business of "nation-building" abroad, and instead finding other ways of working with the world of Islam. Indeed, Trump went on to actually hold diplomatic talks with the Taliban, which in turn opened the way for broader political negotiations among all the Afghan political parties. The Democrats, however, were not impressed (naturally), but said little about the matter. There was little interest in bringing attention to any diplomatic breakthroughs that Trump might have secured for the country.

The general withdrawal of American ground-troop involvement in the Middle East did not mean the withdrawal of American involvement in the region, as Trump demonstrated when he ordered a temporary beefing up of the American air and ground offense against the Islamic Caliphate at Baghouz, which Americans brought to collapse with the massive bombing in early January of 2019. This did put an end to the Islamic State. But of course it did not end the Islamic spirit of jihadism, although it certainly put something of a damper on that spirit.

At the same time, Trump worked very hard to strengthen relations with America's old Arab ally, Saudi Arabia – plus others of the Arab Gulf states. But, for instance, his agreement to sell arms to Saudi Arabia drew a lot of opposition from the Democrats, for no particular strategic reason other than it was Trump who put the deal together. It seems that the Democrats instead would rather have him punish the Saudis for their involvement in the assassination of the Saudi journalist Jamal Khashoggi. Likewise the diplomatic agreement that Trump led the Arab States of Bahrain and the United Arab Emirates to enter into with their old enemy Israel received no acclaim from the Democrats, in fact very little mention at all by the American press corps of the enormous significance of this diplomatic breakthrough.

Trump's relations with Europe. The Trump mouth has been as big a problem in Europe as it has been in America. Trump finds it easy to offend people, especially those that political necessity normally requires a strong working relationship. It makes little sense. And it offers the "never-Trump" groups in Europe plenty of ammunition for their crusades. Thus it was no secret how much Germany's long-time chancellor Angela Merkel disliked Trump, although she and others tried to warm up the relationship as much as possible.

Of course Trump's "hit hard and then negotiate a compromise" strategy (presumably developed during his many years in the business world) did have its positive results, in that his pressure did get some of America's allies moving up to meet their full national financial responsibilities as members of NATO.

But the world of politics is as much a matter of visible symbolism as it is behind-the-scenes deal-making, something that obviously Trump failed to understand. Thus his threat in June of 2020 to withdraw American NATO troops stationed in Germany tended to result merely in deepening the anti-Trump mood in Germany, and elsewhere in Europe.

* * *

THE CHAOTIC 2020 ELECTIONS

Not surprisingly, the Covid-19 pandemic impacted the electoral process deeply, with both the Democratic and Republican parties having to hold mostly virtual (online) conventions, with few delegates able to attend physically, because of the new public participation restrictions.

In the process, the Republicans reconfirmed the Trump-Pence ticket. And the Democrats chose Washington veteran Joe Biden, who had served in the U.S. Senate from 1973 until his move to the position as Obama's Vice President in 2009, also an unprecedently elderly 78 at the time of his selection as the Democrat's presidential candidate! And out of the pre-determined category of a "woman of color" to be chosen as his vice-presidential running mate – a bold act of politically-correct racism/sexism actually – Biden finally chose Kamala Harris, U.S. Senator representing California since 2017 and California attorney General prior to that (2011-2017).

The critical role of the pandemic. The pandemic would also reshape deeply the way the November voting itself went, with the majority of the vote by way of mail-in voting rather than personal presence at a voting station. The latter in fact became itself a major campaign issue, with the Republicans claiming that mail-in voting could easily lead to massive fraud (it is after all easier to check on the authenticity of a registered voter at a polling station), and with the Democrats supporting mail-in voting as a matter of justice as well as convenience.

Then President Trump contracted (a fairly mild) case of the virus in early October, and had to be quarantined, keeping him from attending rallies during this important month leading up to the elections. This did further damage to his presidential credentials, which were already suffering from voter discouragement over the whole pandemic issue. Being the president, he was subtly expected to have solutions to the crisis. He was working on the matter, but not as fast as much of the public expected, an expectation now heightened greatly by the Democrats.

A shameful political debate. But the real problem facing Trump going into this election was the behavior that went on during the first presidential debate held at the end of September. It was a repeat of Trump's performance four years earlier when he constantly interrupted his opponents, in this case Joe Biden, during his presentation. Insults were sent back and forth dominating the conversation, rather than in-depth policy clarification. And the moderator, Mike Wallace, merely added to the confusion with his own frequent interruptions in the discussions. All in all, it was a bad scene – especially for Trump, whose rating suffered the worse of the two candidates, according to the media polls, which of course, varied substantially in their measurement on the basis of their own ideological preferences.

A second debate had to be called off, because of Trump's illness. So only one more debate was conducted (October 22nd), much calmer and more to the policy point this time. But it seemingly changed little in the political standing of either candidate. Trump's terrible first performance had pretty much decided the "undecideds" against him. Thus, according to the various polls, Biden was running well ahead of Trump at that the approach of the elections.

Biden wins. On November 3rd the nation "went to the polls" (the group that had not already voted by mail before that date). Because of the new voting dynamics, it would take several days before a fully clear picture of the outcome could be discerned, and that only when the close Pennsylvania vote was finally confirmed.

Ultimately, over 81 million votes went to Biden and over 74 million votes went to Trump. This was the largest number ever of votes cast in an American presidential election, with both candidates (even Trump) receiving more votes than any previous candidate. Both won 25 states each in the electoral college vote (Biden naturally also winning unfailingly Democratic D.C.'s 3 electoral votes), though Biden's strength in both New England and the Pacific Coast put the actual electoral vote strongly in his favor, 306 to

232. And surprisingly Biden's vote included (very narrowly) Georgia and Arizona, both Republican-leaning since the 1990s, and a matter of great interest to Trump.

A graceless political transition. There had been much previous speculation as to whether or not Trump would offer a graceful turnover of power to his opponent, should he lose the election. As it turned out, the transition was indeed far from graceful.

Rather than concede when it was clear to all (including even the conservative Fox News) that Biden had won the election fairly enough, Trump claimed that Biden had done so only through extensive voter fraud, illegal ballots having given Biden his victory. Trump – despite Attorney General William Barr's announcement that an extensive FBI inquiry into the matter found no evidence pointing to extensive fraud – was going to challenge the results in court in a number of instances (a strategy he had learned years earlier as a businessman).

Despite the assurance of the state authorities that the voting had been amazingly clean, Trump pressed his case (most notably in Georgia, Michigan, Nevada and Pennsylvania), not able to actually demonstrate any true amount of fraud he assured everyone was key to the illegal outcome. It was simply Trump being Trump, using his own reasoning (notably with the help of a band of lawyers) to press his case, by whatever means possible. Ultimately the day of the vote of the Electoral College arrived (December 14th) and the earlier count in favor of Biden was reaffirmed.

Political damage in Georgia. Tragically for the Republican Party, Trump's pressure on Georgia to reexamine the vote (and declare a Republican win) – not once but three times – did not play well in Georgia's runoff elections held on January 5th. In the November elections, Republican incumbent Senator James Perdue had failed to receive the 50% required by the state to be returned to Washington as the state's senatorial representative. Perdue had gained only 49.4% of the vote, with his Democratic opponent Jon Ossoff gaining 47.9% of the vote. But Trump's behavior had created such ill feeling among Georgian independents, that when the runoff was held, the vote switched entirely, even with a smaller turnout: Ossoff with 50.6% and Perdue with 49.4%. Thus the Republicans lost a vital seat (and consequently its majority) in the Senate, largely because of all the Trump antics. The Senate was now tied, 50 Republicans (even some of those rather "independent-leaning") and 50 Democrats, with the new Democrat Vice President Harris able to vote to break any voting ties that might occur.

The assault on Capitol Hill. Then on the following day, just to make the transition even uglier, Trump called for a rally in front of the White House, and challenged a huge and very hyped-up gathering to march on the Capitol Building – and demonstrate to Congress (which had gathered that day to give official authorization to the Electoral College vote) their anger over the supposedly fraudulent elections. This they did, but not stopping merely on the lawn in front of the Capitol Building, but instead storming it, thus producing a very violent confrontation with the Capital police – and the retreat in fear of the gathered Congressional members. In the melee, a female Trump supporter was shot and killed, several protesters died, presumably from medical emergencies, and numerous officers were hurt badly, one dying from his wounds, before they could be cleared out. Many of the participants would later be identified and arrested for what was clearly a federal crime.

Immediately calls were issued for the impeachment of Trump (the third attempt), and indeed on the 13th of the month the House successfully voted exactly that. But of course this action would then have to go to the U.S. Senate, where, even with some Republicans switching to the side to convict, the necessary 2/3rds vote would not be forthcoming. 57 Senators (including 7 Republicans) voted to convict; 43 (all Republicans) voted to acquit. But almost immediately speculation arose as to the possibility of the Democrats finding another way to take Trump down, permanently, so that he would be unable to run again for the presidency.

CHAPTER SIXTEEN

BIDEN TAKES COMMAND

* * *

"UNITY"?

Biden's inauguration day. For a brief but wonderful moment it appeared that America was going to be able to move on past the ugly ideological warfare that had consumed American politics for way too long, when in his inaugural address Biden announced that he intended to serve as president for all Americans, and not just for those (the Democrats) who had voted for him. He wanted unity to be the hallmark of his presidency.
And then, that same afternoon, he headed off to the White House and, with full photographic coverage, proceeded to sign 17 new presidential orders, all of which were designed to undo the Trump legacy and put the Democratic Party's ideological agenda in its place as national policy.

So was all this "unity" just political gloss? Was Biden merely a tool of the ultra-Left wing of the Democratic Party, as some claimed?

* * *

THE MAKING OF JOE BIDEN

Biden's Washington universe. Actually, it must be pointed out that as much as Trump was a total "Washington outsider" – and was hated for it – the new President Joe Biden was a "Washington insider" – and admired by the Washington political Establishment (most notably the Washington press corps) for it. From age 30 on, when he was first elected to the U.S. Senate (as its 6th youngest freshman senator ever!) representing nearby Delaware, Biden had lived for 48 years in a world connecting his relatively nearby Delaware home with his job in Washington. In short, the "universe" that Biden lived in, and had done so for almost half a century, was a very singular universe, one that worked in a very precise, Capitol Hill way, backed up by Washington's huge bureaucratic universe. This was the world such as Biden knew it, from end to end. Indianapolis, Kansas City, Fort Worth, New Orleans, etc. had no personal meaning for Biden. As a

Washingtonian, Middle America was just simply not his world. True, there was Wilmington, the one part of America outside of Washington that Biden was familiar with. But that served him simply as a Washington suburb.

And just as he was a Washington insider, so also was he a solidly Democratic Party veteran. The party too was his world, a force that fed his spirit, shaped his vision, and commanded his total loyalties.

Born into Middle America. Biden was born in November of 1942 – thus qualifying him as a socially compliant "Silent" rather than as a renegade "Boomer" – to an Irish-Catholic family. These two items would also define him deeply as he moved forward in life. His father was a hardworking furnace cleaner in Scranton, Pennsylvania. Then, when Biden was 13, the family moved to Delaware, where the father worked as a successful used-car salesman. In short, Biden was raised in very typical Middle American circumstances. It was a good start.

But he was also a quite ambitious youth, who sought greater things for himself in life. He worked hard to the earn the money so as to be able to attend the prestigious Archmere Academy. Here he performed well as a student and athlete. He then went on to the University of Delaware, ostensibly to major in political science and history, though it would appear that his real major was sports, girls and parties. And that is what led him at spring break first to Florida and then Nassau, where he met Neilia Hunter – and got more serious again about things. He brought up his grades, and was accepted in 1965 to Syracuse University Law School – where he would also live close to Neilia. Indeed, the two would marry the next year.

Unfortunately, try as he might, he was not a great competitor in the world of legal academics, and ranked grade-wise 76 out of his graduating class of 85 students. But in 1969 he passed the bar exam, took a position as a public defender, and subsequently formed a law partnership with a friend. However, he found corporate law to be uninteresting and criminal law poorly paid. Thus the very next year (1970) he ran as the Democratic Party candidate and was elected to the New Castle County Council, beginning his public career.

US Senator (1972-2009). Most amazingly, at only age 29, he decided to run for the U.S. Senate against the veteran Republican Caleb Boggs. Actually Boggs had wanted to step down from the position, and ran again only upon the urging of his fellow Republicans. But Biden was the ambitious one, he and his family working hard to bring him to public notice, and by election time the next November Biden managed to pull ahead of Boggs.

And then, before that month was out, deep tragedy hit Biden and his family, when his wife and daughter were killed in an auto accident, and his two boys Beau (age 3) and Hunter (age 2) hurt badly.

It is easy to understand the anger Biden was feeling against God, and his numbness when he thought of his approaching responsibilities as U.S. Senator. He thought about simply quitting, even life itself.

But Senate leader Mike Mansfield worked hard to get Biden not to quit but instead to take up his calling as U.S. Senator. And so he did. But as it was, Biden would be sworn into office, not in Washington but at the hospital bedside of his son Beau. (Biden would meet three years later in 1975 and marry in 1977 his second wife, Jill Jacobs).

In the Senate his career path was fairly typical, as were also his Democratic Party loyalties, especially during the latter part of the 1970s when he came to work closely with the Carter Administration. During the 1980s he achieved the position as the ranking minority member of the Senate Judiciary Committee, in time to "Bork" Reagan's Supreme Court appointment (Bork was too conservative for Biden's taste), and then in 1991, as that committee's actual chair, he was one of the opposing votes to the Supreme Court appointment of Clarence Thomas.

But he was also active on the Senate Foreign Relations Committee, opposing Bush, Sr.'s. decision to intervene in Kuwait against Saddam Hussein. But he was much more supportive of Clinton's decision to get involved in Yugoslavia, in fact, now as ranking minority member of the committee, he advocated a strong stand in Bosnia even before Clinton himself had decided to do so. He would also be a strong supporter of American intervention in Kosovo.

Then in the years of the Bush, Jr. Administration, Biden served as the Committee's actual chairman, at least during the years 2001-2003 and 2007-2009. Initially he was a strong supporter of Bush's intervention in Afghanistan and Iraq, then backed away from that position, offering the proposal that Iraq be simply federated into three different ethnic regions (Arab Sunni, Arab Shi'ite, and Kurdish Sunni). But he could gather no serious support for the proposal. Then in 2007, he found himself strongly opposed to the "troop surge" in Iraq, which to his surprise (and the surprise of many) actually quieted things down in Iraq.

Presidential runs. Then in 2007, something he had long had his eye on, namely the U.S. presidency, seemed to be a possible goal to be pursued.

Actually he had undertaken just such an effort back in 1987, and had the effort backfire badly when reports came out that he had plagiarized a law school paper and had exaggerated greatly his standing at graduation, the negative publicity being the probable cause of a serious life-threatening brain aneurysms and a pulmonary embolism, which had him hospitalized in February and then again in May. He dropped out of the race, and was even away from the Senate for seven months.

And now he tried again in 2007 as the Bush, Jr. presidency was coming to a close. But he found himself up against strong Democratic Party contenders, Hillary Clinton and Barack Obama. Thus it was that he dropped out of the race early on when the Iowa primary brought him only one percent of the vote!

Vice President (2009-2017). But Obama needed someone to "balance" his ticket, and asked Biden to join him as his running mate. And so Biden was elected Vice President in 2008 and re-elected as such four years later.

However during his second term, Biden found himself to be less strategic to the Obama Administration.

But even more hurtful to Biden was the loss to cancer in 2015 of his 46-year-old son Beau. Beau had conducted himself most admirably in the field of law, military service and presently as Delaware's Attorney General, earlier turning down the idea of running for the US Senate – because he did not want such a gain simply because of his family "legacy." The death of Beau came as a huge, crushing blow to everyone. And it was a reason that Biden announced that he would not be running for public office in 2016. He would throw his support to Hillary.

The 2020 presidential campaign. The next couple of years Biden busied himself teaching (University of Pennsylvania), writing a memoir (*Promise Me, Dad*), and doing a lot of public speaking, not only keeping himself visible before the public eye but making him quite rich from speaker's fees and a writing contract.

However, as the 2020 election season came around, he was ready to announce his candidacy (April 2019), even though if elected he would take office at the age of 78 – an unheard-of age to be taking on such a responsibility. And he would be running against the very aggressive Trump, who had the reputation of knocking down anything that got in his way.

But run Biden did, finally securing the Democratic Party presidential candidacy, and then going on to win the election.

INTO THE "BIDEN ERA"

Very quickly a number of public issues pushed forward as America turned in new directions in the new Biden Era.

The rush for the American borders. Not surprisingly, America is a very attractive destination for those Central Americans – and a huge number of Haitians – wanting to escape the poverty, crime, horrible hurricanes, and more recently the Covid-19 pandemic. But is America itself ready to accept a flood of such people, a flood that would certainly change deeply the very social-cultural character of the nation?

Biden, in his run for the presidency, made it very clear that he and the Democratic Party were strongly in favor of opening its doors to just such a flood of people, claiming humanitarian motives in doing so. The Republicans, backed by a strong Trump resolve, were highly opposed, advocating instead more walls and tighter restrictions designed to slow up and possibly even halt an apparent flood.

And of course this supposedly placed Biden and the Democrats on superior moral ground as the more "humane" party, in comparison to the "inhumane" nature of the Republican position. But in fact, those that understood the politics behind both positions in this debate also understood that the Democrats were looking forward to a grand increase in their electoral support by bringing these immigrants into the American political process – probably with quick amnesty for them as "illegals," followed up by an equally speedy naturalization process.

It is well understood by both parties that these immigrants come from a culture that promised welfare (socialism) in return for their support, and that these immigrants, by political instinct, would certainly be receptive to the same offering in their newly adopted homeland. In short, they are likely to vote Democrat if given the choice, and both parties know this.

But one fact is inescapable, namely, that it is the supposed humane character of Central American Socialism that is the reason their economies failed, most cruelly in Honduras ... but bad elsewhere in Central America. And with this economic collapse has gone the collapse of the moral foundations of these societies... as the people scramble for whatever material support they can find, even if it comes violently. Thus an exploding crime rate has also accompanied this economic collapse in those countries.

The rights and duties of the American voter. Another issue which follows the lines of the immigration debate is this matter of how much discipline does the American voting process need in order to maintain its integrity (the Republicans) or the broadness of its reach (the Democrats). It is well-known that many American residents do not vote, for various reasons. The Democrats suspect that those non-voters would likely be Democratic Party voters if they would but just turn out. Therefore it becomes imperative for the Democrats to make the vote as easy as possible for everyone. And Covid-19 certainly strengthened that position, with the sending out of ballots that could simply be mailed in, well ahead of voting day, and even in some cases in an allotted time period after that date. The Republicans fought this move, claiming that mailed-in votes have no way of being authenticated as to who it was that actually voted, and how many times they might have voted, and what ultimately happened to those mailed-in ballots.

Trump even went on to claim that he had lost the vote in a number of states because of the ease by which fraud was brought into the new voting dynamic, although he could offer no actual evidence for this claim. But it did raise the question: what can be done to preserve the integrity of the vote?

Republicans want the vote to be done the old way: at a voting station, by a person on record as eligible to vote in that district, and with proper identification, usually just a driver's license, although identification cards are supposedly available everywhere for non-driving adults. Democrats answer that such restrictions are designed merely to discourage the nervous voter (supposedly a Democratic Party voter) and thus should be disallowed by law, which the Democrats are working on getting put through (again, principally by way of the federal courts).

This became such an emotional issue that even corporate America jumped in on it, with the state of Georgia finding itself at the center of a deeply emotional battle over its tightening the disciplines of voting in that state. Georgia's new standards were actually no more restrictive than, say for instance, New Jersey's, except that New Jersey is generally considered to be a reliably Democratic Party state, whatever the disciplines, and Georgia is something of a critical swing state. Thus there was a call by Democrats to boycott Coca-Cola and Delta Airlines, headquartered in Georgia, in order to bring pressure to bear on Georgia to back down on its new identification requirements for voting in that state. Likewise the All-Star baseball games were pulled out of Georgia as punishment for the state's new rulings, and American Airlines and Dell went on record in their loud opposition to the Georgia voting issue.

Congress of course jumped into the issue with its "For the People Act" (H.R.1), passed in the House along purely party lines, 220-210, but held up in the Senate, not able to secure a majority there, The idea of this bill was to take away from the states their constitutional right to determine their own voting procedures, and give that right over to a federal commission, as if federal commissions were never politically partisan! Also, it eliminated all identity checks, making it possible for even illegal immigrants to vote. It is easily understandable therefore why the Democrats supported this measure and the Republicans opposed it.

And ultimately, it would be yet another step in ending the checks and balances system of the American Constitution, giving federal authorities in Washington yet another major piece of power by which to govern the country.

Making Washington, D.C. a new "state." In early January of 2021, a bill was introduced with 202 co-sponsors (Democrats, naturally) to create a new state entitled, Washington, Douglass Commonwealth (named after Frederick Douglass), with two voting Senators and one Representative allotted it, members of the Democratic Party to be sure. Whether this would require amending the Constitution (changing the provisions of the 23rd Amendment) or not is debatable, and how the American voting public at large stands on this matter also seems debatable – depending of course on whose poll you consult. Of course Biden and Harris are also supporters of this action.

"Reforming" the Supreme Court. There has been much anger among Democrats over the fact that Trump was able to nominate three individuals to the Supreme Court, ending the small majority that the Left-leaning justices once commanded. Consequently, the Democrats have put forward the idea of "reforming" the Supreme Court, by adding four more justices to the bench, that is, "packing" the Court with Biden nominees – something designed to swing the Court back to the Left politically. Roosevelt attempted such a "reform" in 1937, and it backfired greatly – not even Roosevelt's Democratic Party allies willing to go down this road when it appeared clearly that the American people were convinced that such "reform" was merely another form of political authoritarianism that Roosevelt was increasingly being accused of, at a time, the 1930s, when authoritarianism seemed to be a general trend around the world. Remembering the Roosevelt episode, Biden has moved cautiously on the matter, merely setting up a 36-member commission to "study" the issue carefully. What comes of all this will of course depend ultimately on how the winds of politics blow in the days ahead.

The debate over High-tech's censoring of internet communications. Not surprising, considering the cultural power they command, some of internet's biggest communities have jumped into the political arena. A former president of the United States, Trump, has been banned from having any further public voice by Facebook, Google, Apple, Amazon, and a number of other internet biggies, for political-moral reasons of their own. But they do have the power. And they are most willing to use it.

This in turn raises some deeply serious questions. As anyone should know, a person, group, society, or whatever, can easily find any reason it wants – and justify it morally any way it wants – in order to manipulate and control the public voice. In short, these major sources of the public voice are completely free to shape and control that voice any way they want.

But such unlimited power inevitably leads to self-justifying tyranny. And for a free society such as America has proudly seen itself to be (relatively so, anyway), such control raises all kinds of questions, and fears. And questions and fears can go in most any direction.

What can America do to keep the public conversation open – and within bounds – and without the conversation referees (Facebook, etc.) deciding which part of the conversation they are going to allow and which part are they going to shut down?

This is only going to be an even more important matter in the fast-developing world ahead of us. And yet no one seems to have any good ideas on the matter. All that is heard is just more ideology, supported by clever moral argument. But it needs clarification and broad agreement in America, before such unashamedly authoritarian powers as China and Russia take a larger hand in the world of internet communication.

The Federal state's growing share of the American economy. Biden and the Democrats have been pushing hard for a multi-trillion dollar "infrastructure" program put forward by the Democrat-controlled House – which the Senate has done its best (complements of a Democrat and Republican balance in the number of seats each holds in the Senate) to pare down in size, to avoid a further expansion of the government's debt – as of this writing almost $28 trillion and still climbing rapidly.

Biden claims he will bring a $3.5 trillion budget closer to a balance by enacting new corporate taxes, raising the rate from 21% to 28% of corporate earnings, with the Republicans replying, companies will be forced to raise the prices of their goods and services to cover the new tax expenses, thus adding to an inflation rate that is already growing rapidly.

Also, there is much contention over the word "infrastructure," which this new programming is supposedly all about. The Republicans see government infrastructure in traditional terms: mostly just roads and bridges (that indeed to need repair), which the Republicans are willing to support. But the Democrats see infrastructure in far broader terms, everything from a government-supported change in American lifestyles (carbon-free energy and a "greener" approach to domestic development), education of the young, and increase in welfare support, the latter quite urgent because of the flood of immigrants coming to this country. In short, "infrastructure" is about ideology and politics, and not just about material development of the nation by the federal government – which itself had only very limited constitutional support prior to Roosevelt's New Deal and

Johnson's Great Society.

The Afghan catastrophe (August 2021). First of all, it must be noted that Trump, not Biden, was the one who initiated the idea of a full termination of American involvement in Afghanistan, when in February of 2020 Trump negotiated an American pullout with the Taliban, scheduled for May 1st of 2021 – Trump presuming to be reelected in the coming November elections and thus able to preside over this event.

Bush Jr.'s decision in 2001 to send the US military into Afghanistan after al Qaeda – and then resorting to pro-Western nation-building in that country when nothing came of the anti-al-Qaeda effort – was a terrible idea ... on a number of fronts. Billions of dollars would have to be devoted to curbing the Taliban's power ... and building some kind of pro-Western political system in Afghanistan to counter the Taliban. And once the program was put in place, it would take years, even generations, of ongoing American support to lay the cultural groundwork that would give this nation-building effort some degree of sustainability. After all, American troops are still in Germany, Japan, South Korea, Kosovo ... serving just such a purpose: protecting the social groundwork laid out by an America that in the mid-20th-century took up major responsibilities as one of the world's global superpowers.

In short, nation-building is a huge responsibility that should never be undertaken on the basis of a mere political whim. And pulling out abruptly for a mere short-term political gain can have only one result: social catastrophe.

What seems to have inspired Trump to undertake this pullout was that Americans had tired deeply of the country's involvement in an Afghanistan that seemed to have no further relevance to American politics.

But worse, Trump seemed to have believed that the Taliban would of its own hold to the various conditions (support of an orderly American pullout and certain personal freedoms for the Afghans even after the American departure) of the agreement – and thus began to pull American troops out of Afghanistan, with only 2500 still left in the country as of the end of his presidency ... and even those still on schedule for a final pullout in May.

In coming to office as president, Biden, took up the same policy ... although there were advisors who warned him of the dangers of a full pullout. But Biden assured even the press, which now was awakened to the potential problems involved in a full pullout, that he expected the Taliban to respect the terms of the agreement. However, he simply would not face up to the fact that with the removal of the American troops, America would have no means to enforce the terms of that agreement. So, just a few months into his presidency (April), he announced a full American pullout, to be completed by the end of the coming August.

With this announcement, political morale of the pro-American Afghan social-political system began to collapse. Indeed, the speed of the Taliban takeover of regions, towns and villages apparently surprised even the Taliban. And as the end-of-August deadline approached, the country's capital, Kabul, resembled the scene of Saigon when in the mid-1970s Congress terminated American support of the South Vietnamese society and government. It was a horrible scene of people grabbing onto airplanes as they began their takeoff from the country.

However, by the end of the month thousands of people, locals as well as American citizens, were brought out of the country. Yet shamefully, with the last American soldier pulled out, large amounts of military equipment remained left behind (supposedly dismantled ... but also quite able to be repaired by clever hands). And by no means were all the people who would certainly be hunted down by the Taliban airlifted out of the country ... likely including some Americans still remaining in the country.

All in all, it was a grand American disaster. And China had to be loving to watch America sneak off from a serious global responsibility ... quick to bring notice to the rest of the world that it would be wise not to put trust in America's promise of great-power protection. And indeed, America was not looking at all like a great power at that point.

Did the president(s) of the United States not understand any of this dynamic? What did they think they were achieving from this tactical retreat? Was there some hidden strategic advantage to be gained that would compensate for the obvious political loss from this move? If so, it would remain a mystery.

And again, China had to be loving all of this!

CHAPTER SEVENTEEN
THE LESSONS OF HISTORY*

✱ ✱ ✱

THE TWO AMERICAS

The two human "types." From the very beginning of this American history study we have noted that there have always been "Two Americas."

There is nothing unusual about that. Even the Bible, dating back thousands of years, reveals that there have always been two social types, two human types – something of a "pre-Fall" and "post-Fall" quality to humankind.

One type lives in tightly structured world, designed for narrowly-focused service to "self." This type uses the power of human reason to try to bring the surrounding world under personal control. In essence those of such a type attempt to "play God" themselves – to be all the god that they believe is needed for their own success in life. The God of Heaven is of no interest to them. In fact, they don't want to hear about or be bothered by such a God. Such a social type would be our Adam and Eve after the "Fall" (Genesis 3).

The other type lives in full service more broadly to the realm of "other" – such an "other" reaching from the God of heaven above ... to the world immediately around him or her (the land, the seas, the animals and, most of all, the people living in that world). Rather than seeking to control that larger world (using human reason to do so), they seek instead to harmonize themselves with that world, which means approaching that larger life on its terms rather than on the basis of some personal plan that they themselves have designed.

That would be Adam and Eve before the Fall.

The Bible's Old Testament itself is really a narrative of how a constant tension between those two types challenged ancient Israel, always struggling over this matter, from one generation to the next.

---
*This section is so important that it has *not been summarized* from the original 2020 three-volume study but is essentially reproduced in its original form found at the end of the original Volume Three (with a few small additions).

And the New Testament is about how God, through Jesus Christ, showed humankind the way out of that struggle, the way back to the kind of harmony with God and life itself that was lost with the Fall. Jesus is indeed considered a "second" (or "last" or "ultimate") Adam,* reversing the effect of the behavior of the first Adam, the one that created this spiritual "schizophrenia" in the first place.

But whether people want to take that journey with Christ, or simply remain in the carefully contrived world of utopian plans – ones that make them believe that they are in full control of life's outcomes (and make them whine and blame others like Adam and Eve's son Cain when things don't work out for them as planned) – is a matter of their own choosing.

The deep differences between these two types result from the very starting point from which they begin their journey into life. One type insists on seeing Reality merely as the immediate world around him or her, a purely physical or *material* world of things that suposedly work rather *mechanically* (including people in this category of "things"), things that through human Reason are there to be managed or controlled in their mechanics. This type wields human Reason like a weapon, hoping to force life to go the way the individual intends for it to go.

The other type sees Reality more as a world of deep, virtually "mystical," relationships – relationships of the rather emotional, imaginative, and possibilistic type. When individuals of this type confront Reality, they perceive a world that calls them to connect with that world on a deeper, virtually *spiritual* level. They don't seek to control that world. Instead, they seek to find harmony with it – employing Love, not Reason, as the tool they use to arrive at that personal goal.

The key differences between these two types can be summed up:

	Spiritual	Material/Mechanical
Primary Identifier	*Christianity* – in particular the variety that strives truly to follow Christ (even be Christ for others!)	*Secularism* or its subcategories: *Humanism* ("man is naturally good") *Darwinism* ("man is naturally a dominator")
Vision of life	Life as a network of vital inter-personal relationships, offered, encouraged, and supported by a loving God	Life as a perfect mechanical order of material things (other humans as well) functioning precisely according to "natural" design

---

*By the apostle Paul himself in his first letter to the Corinthian congregation, chapter 15, verse 45.

The reach of life	As far or high as our thoughts / dreams / imagination can go	The visible world of material things
Life's goal	*Harmonization* with life through love and the quest for partnership with both God and fellow man – even with the world itself	*Dominance* over life through the mechanical control of both man and the surrounding physical / social environment
Path to the goal	Mystic union with the Supreme Source (God) of all life, which offers man the power to embrace life fully, even in the face of hardship and opposition	Scientific and technological knowledge, which ideally offers man (as his own God!) the power to control life and even eliminate hardship and opposition
Society	A cooperative community (democracy of equals) founded and operating on the basis of well-understood, long-standing values shared by all	A chain-of-command system (status hierarchy) operating according to the "progressive" (rational or utopian) plans and programs of a ruling elite
Leader	A prophet or teacher; a person who *teaches and inspires* right behavior in others	A governor or manager; a person who *commands and enforces* right behavior in others
American examples	Martin Luther King, Jr., who appealed to Americans to do what they well knew was "the right thing" – to get past prejudices and open up our middle-class democracy to all alike, regardless of skin color	Lyndon Johnson, who developed a "Great Society" program, directed from Washington by "scientific" experts (he did not trust Americans, especially fellow Southerners, to do "the right thing" on their own)
"Extreme" examples	Jesus Christ, whose teachings and example led the way to a sense of the unity with God and fellow man	Josef Stalin, whose brutal dictatorship forced industrialism on Russia, executing and starving millions of Russians in the process
Personal goal	To find ways to fit in; to find ways to contribute to the life of the community (to "*keep up with* the Joneses")	To find ways to achieve elite status; to find ways to climb to the top of the social order (to "*get ahead of* the Joneses")
Preparing for success	Studying, learning in order to gain the knowledge vital to being the best possible contributor to the well-being of the surrounding world	Studying, learning in order to qualify for entrance into the elite institutions (such as colleges and professions) that lead to power, fame and great wealth
Social reward	The joy of finding a place of true service to others	The joy of owning, directing, controlling, dominating
Greatest fear	Isolation	Losing possession or control

* * *
THE TWO SOCIETIES DURING COLONIAL TIMES

Feudal America. At the time of the founding of English America (the beginning of the 1600s) most of European society was governed by a handful of individuals – individuals usually born to that position and thus a position not easily open to even the most ambitious social climbers from the lower classes. Kings, emperors, princes, dukes, barons, and even bishops – drawn from society's "first families" – lorded it over the rest of society. This ruling class "owned" everything: the land, the fields, the rivers, the forests – and virtually everything located there.

This hierarchical or "feudal" social setup was morally justified a number of different ways, though usually by explaining that the very powers of Heaven (God himself) had demanded this exact arrangement. Thus the rest of the population outside the ranks of this ruling elite was forced to stay "in its place" – under the threat of everything from imprisonment or execution, to even the ultimate threat, Eternal Hell, awaiting those who failed to live according to the supposedly God-ordained and long-established rules of such a society – rules dating as far back as 800 years, when Charlemagne put this social order in place.

When at the beginning of the 1500s the Spanish, were to "discover" America and then move to bring the New World of America under the Spanish social order, quite naturally this same feudal social order was established there to secure Spanish territorial claims in America. Spanish America belonged to the Spanish King, whose lands in America (as in Spain itself) were governed politically through the agencies of royally-appointed governors, who in turn were supported by a handful of wealthy first families dominating life locally from their manorial estates or haciendas. And the very hierarchical Spanish (Catholic) Christian Church, governed from Spain by bishops and archbishops, was placed alongside this political structure in order to confirm the moral foundations of this quite typical feudal social order.

When the English, a century later, finally got into the act in establishing the colony of Virginia, a social model was put in place there similar to the one in Spanish America. The English who dared to take up life in America (those who survived the high death rate in doing so) were motivated the same way as the young Spanish conquistadores (conquerors) had been. They came to America hoping to gain social status as gentry and thus membership in the ranks of society's ruling elite – through ownership of quite readily-available American property (simply grabbed from the local Indian population). The more property owned by an individual or family, the higher the social status or social rank.

Some of the earlier arrivals to Virginia went on to achieve quite high social status – such as the Byrd family, which came to own 180,000 acres in Virginia ... and a quite fancy manor or plantation home to house the family. Thus a Virginia aristocracy, functioning much like the feudal aristocracy back home in England, came into being.

For those who came later to Virginia, they did so as indentured workers, to work the land of this Virginia aristocracy for the number of years of their indenture (typically seven years) until they were given a small amount of land and some tools to start out life on their own. But very quickly the truly valuable land was grabbed up by the earliest arrivals, and those who came later found little opportunity to duplicate this rise in status through expanded land ownership. Thus a society of poor Whites began to grow up within this Virginia feudal order.

Ultimately, when a revolt against this unfair distribution of the wealth and social privilege of Virginia occurred, the Virginia aristocracy found it safer to switch from the program of indenture to the institution of African slavery in order to protect and sustain this feudal system. The Africans, brought to enslavement through defeat in tribal wars back in Africa, were carried off to America, where as a broken-spirited people, they proved to be more compliant to the harsh disciplines of the Virginia feudal order.

Puritan America. But the English who came a generation later to the lands north of Virginia, to "New England," came under a very different set of social circumstances, shaped by a very different set of social ideals and social norms. They were religious idealists, inspired by their strong Christian belief that they should live as a people as close as possible to the standards of the first century Christian community, as clearly outlined in character in the Christian New Testament. They came to America not just for their own benefit, but with the belief that by striving to live "Biblically," they would serve God well by living as a social example (as Israel of old was supposed to have done, but failed to do so) giving "Light to the Nations," showing the way for others around the world to achieve the same glorious life that a fatherly God himself had wanted for all his human creation. In America, they would establish a "City on a Hill," there for all the world to see how to live successfully God's way (which had little in common with the feudal way practiced widely not only in Europe but through much of the rest of the world as well).

Thus what Puritan America offered the world was the living example of a society where all the people could live comfortably, proudly even – working together and sharing as equals, enjoying the blessings of social life on this basis of social equality. Equality, not hierarchy, was what God wanted for his people – at least that is how the Biblical narrative reaching from the ancient Hebrews down to the formation of the first century Christian church explained things.

According to these Puritans, Christian society was intended to be a community built on a deep sense of interpersonal connections shared equally among the community members themselves. God was not looking for a well-planned organization – a society organized and directed by a privileged group of "enlightened" individuals who had authorized themselves to do the thinking for and managing of the very dependent multitude of the others making up the society.

The Puritan understanding of Godly society of course required the people themselves to take up the responsibilities of self-government, a social mindset cultivated from a child's very early age onward through the careful mentoring on the part of an older generation of parents, teachers and pastors, individuals who themselves had been carefully raised to adulthood through this same process of socially (that is, morally) disciplined development.

In this, the family was of paramount importance – because the family was the key source of the earliest and most enduring of a person's social instruction, social instruction that would shape and guide profoundly the social-moral character of each new rising generation.

True, even in its sense of basic equality, Puritan New England certainly had its leaders, those who exercised certain supervisory powers over the life of Puritan society. But these men did not constitute a social group set apart from and above the rest. They were members of the same social order as the rest of the members of society – and elected on a regular and recurring basis out of that same social order to represent those people in the councils of social policy-making. They did not dictate that policy to those same people but consulted with them regularly on the basis of town meetings.

This was in fact democracy, the self-rule of the common members of society, guided in that self-rule by the moral instructions of the Christian religion. It was indeed true "Christian democracy" that got America up and running – at least in New England and the Middle Colonies.

Deadly conflict between the two social types. Consequently, two very different societies were set out from the very early years of the English colonization of America.

And ultimately, in the mid-1800s, these two societies would fall into the deadliest war America has ever fought, a brutal war to see which path America was to move down in order to go forward into its future. It was a reckoning that the participants themselves understood that God had called them to. The "City on the Hill," as Founding Father Winthrop called this new society, needed to shine forth in glory, not in cruel social blemish arising from the shameful institution of African slavery.

Ultimately a lot of American boys went to their deaths over this issue (something often overlooked in today's recitation about the anti-Black racism that supposedly accompanies naturally the matter of being a White American) ... some 600,000+ young men killed and another million wounded in this battle for the soul of America – more than those killed and wounded in America's other battles from the War of Independence in the 1770s and 1780s to the Korean War in the 1950s.

And so it was also that Lincoln reminded America in his Second Inaugural Address (1865) that God's judgment weighed heavily on America. It was critical for America to get things right with God.

***

WHY THIS MATTER OF GOD IS SO IMPORTANT

Existentialism. As those who chose to live solely by "Human Reason" see things, it is easy enough to view life as simply something that just happens. One minute you are born, another minute you die. And in between those two events you just exist. So it's up to you (or better yet, up to a well-planned social order) to make of life what you can, for as long as you can. It's as simple as that – at least to the many people who believe themselves to be so very wise about life and its ultimate meaning.

We call this philosophy of life "existentialism," although this same understanding of life applies to other closely-related ideologies as well (such as the "Religious Humanism" of the 1933 *Humanist Manifesto* ... or its contemporary cousin, "Secular Humanism") – all of which see life "scientifically," meaning, simply as a mechanical process for which there is ultimately no particularly sentimental purpose behind it all. Life just is. So get over your ridiculously superstitious search for grand purpose and just do the best you can with what is in front of you. Simply being practical about life will save you a lot of unnecessary heartbreak.

Creationism. But for a moment consider the very existence of the universe itself. It is immense beyond human understanding. And yet it works very precisely according to very exact laws such as we find in the field of physics and chemistry. Yes, we do realize that the universe is "in process," expanding, developing, changing constantly. Yet the laws that direct that very dynamic have been there since the beginning of time. They did not themselves just gradually develop or "evolve" so as to finally arrive at the complex existence that we are able to study today. The laws of physics for example have always been the laws of physics, the same at the beginning of time as they are today. The very same laws were literally there at the foundation of the universe.

These laws directing the character and behavior of the universe are awesome beyond belief. Man discovers these universal laws as one of his greatest enterprises ("science"). But he certainly did not create those laws. They were there in operation long, long ago – long before man began to study and understand them.

But where did these laws come from? They obviously were no accident. They are incredibly "rational" – so rational that rational man himself has discovered that by simply employing man's own powers of reasoning these laws are discoverable ... and enormously useful.

You would think therefore that those who focus their lives on these very laws (the scientific community) would be, of all people, the most awestruck about the Source of such rationality that commands this universe, a Source of Reason that stands before and above the universe itself, before and above all existence itself, a Source of creative power simply summed up as "God." Certainly that is exactly what developed among such great thinkers as Einstein, Schrödinger, Bohr. They were awestruck when they considered the very nature of what Einstein called *der Herr Gott* (the Lord God).

So then why does this same thing not happen with the lesser intellectual luminaries, those who nonetheless consider themselves to be "intellectuals"? Why do they spend so much time and effort to disprove the existence of a Great Mind, a Grand Creator, a Sustainer of it all?

On a simpler plane: why have they forbidden the teaching in the public schools of what is known popularly as "creationism"? Our grand universe designed by a supernatural Cosmic Mind should make much more sense to these individuals of "common sense" than the notion that somehow the universe and the laws that direct its very existence just stumbled into place over billions of years as if it all was merely some kind of grand Darwinian accident. Why do the lesser intellectuals hold so dearly, so religiously, to the latter – immensely unsophisticated – explanation of life itself?

The answer today is the same that it always has been: they want to play the role of that very God themselves.

A life of praise and glory to the Creator and his Creation. Consider the other wonder of creation: we humans! Where else in all of Creation have we found creatures able to celebrate – even just be aware of – the existence of this great creation itself. As far as we know, it is only on this tiny, otherwise totally insignificant, planet that such self-awareness of God's Creation exists at all. In other words, Creation itself does not know of its own existence. But we humans do.

It seems that in all creation we are the only audience able to enjoy with the Creator himself the very glory of such an awesome existence. We have the conscious powers, the rational facilities, able to observe, even work with, Creation itself. We are even able to live in loving harmony with its very existence – and in loving harmony with the One behind this glorious creation and on-going existence.

Long-standing Judeo-Christianity has for thousands of years made it very clear that we humans in fact were made for just this very artistic, very emotional, very creative purpose ourselves. We were created to live in praise of the glory of it all, in worship of both Creation and the Creator.

But lesser human souls balk at this calling, this grand opportunity, to rise to such grand purpose. They choose to live with their noses to the ground, going around in life on a basis limited to their ability to "control" the events in their lives. Little wonder that such souls find a rather shallow purpose to their own existence.

Christians have always understood that we humans were called by the Creator himself to join with him in some kind of cosmic dance with our Heavenly Father, finding delight in being alive – alive with God, but also alive with each other. Jesus was clearly placed among us to show the power that we humans had to live to greater purpose and character – if we would just put aside our pretentions to have life under the control of our own plans and laws. Jesus showed us instead the importance of sharing with each other (regardless of our human social status or level of social "perfection") in common love and celebration of God – and each other – and the power God thus also in return granted us to then live this life to the specific purpose that he himself called each and every one of us to take up.

This is what the Puritans understood they were all about – and thus covenanted with God to put into play with their new community in New England. This was the idea on which they planned to construct a new society – one designed to show the world by personal example how it was that our Creator intended for all humans to live.

The Call to be a City on a Hill, a Light to the Nations.* This was why the New England colonies understood themselves to be a City on a Hill / a Light to the Nations. To their clear understanding, Christianity was always more than just a personal path to greatness ... and eternal life for the

---

*Jesus, in his "Sermon on the Mount" told his followers "You are the light of the world. A city set on a hill cannot be hid." He goes on to say (same verse): "Let your light so shine before men, that they may see your good works and give glory to your Father who is in heaven." Matthew 5:14 pretty much sums up the whole deal!

person of faith. For those who had been "elected" by God to a life of such Christian faith, they had also been commissioned by God to show others the way to the same sonship and daughtership that they enjoyed with God as their Father.

Jesus himself made it clear that those so elected or "called" were to serve as apostles (Greek for "ones sent out") or missionaries – to use the more modern term. Christianity was not just a privilege for themselves alone. It was a call to greater service, to help bring all human life to have a successful "internship" in this life – and thus to find "salvation."*

* * *

HUMAN REASON VERSUS GODLY OR DIVINE REASON

Man's insatiable desire to play God. But holding to that critical piece of Puritan wisdom or insight has not been easy for America (much as it was difficult for the ancient Israelites). Since the Fall of Adam and Eve, man has wanted to play God himself, has wanted to plan and control outcomes in life. God's gift of human reason – given to help man not only take joy in life itself but also find ways to greet challenges placed in front of him on a virtually daily basis – man has instead used to try to redesign life itself so that he hopefully did not have to deal with the complexities of the immediate problems he was facing, so that he would not have to leave up to God the matter of determining what life was ultimately all about and where it all was headed.

This tendency to want to plan and control is particularly obsessive among those who have made it their life-work to live by their powers of reason alone: intellectuals, seated at their desks, rationally planning out their lives, and, if possible, the lives of others as well. They not only want to get their own lives planned and controlled by reason (their reason, of course), they typically want to bring the rest of society along in support of this same endeavor: to have others also live by way of their rational planning. Having others following their lead validates everything they see themselves as being: wise, noble, important.

Thus the "man of reason" does not like to hear anything about a God who lives beyond man's measured world, beyond his pleasant intellectual bubble that he has placed himself in – while trying to bring others with him into that same bubble. To him, the very notion of God stands as some kind

---

*Jesus's Great Commission to his followers: "Go therefore and make disciples of all the nations, baptizing them in the name of the Father, and the Son, and the Holy Spirit, teaching them to observe everything I have commanded you. And thus I am with you always, even to the very end of the age." Matthew 28:19-20.

of threat to his well-reasoned plans for life. Thus he wants the idea of a presiding God eliminated from his world.

This tendency is not new. It is certainly not just American. It is a tendency that all of us struggle with. And, if allowed to continue to develop as a rational process, it will always find itself increasingly hard to be put aside (like alcohol and drugs). And ultimately, it will come to curse and destroy such a world – and those who attempted to design it. The 20th century alone has borne witness to this tragic reality, repeatedly.

But God, thankfully (or hopefully), is not done with the human race, and from time to time, through the prophets of old, Jesus himself, the Christian saints of history, the religious reformers, and more recently the voices of the various Awakenings, God has shaken a self-blinded human race to the core, putting it back on the path that he originally destined humankind to go down.

The call for America to understand this was what so strongly motived Lincoln in his Second Inaugural Address.

This is what the ultimate practical-philosopher Franklin understood – as the Framers in 1787 attempted to put together a new Constitution through solely a purely rational process. Franklin reminded them that it was to God that they were to look in overcoming the multiple roadblocks they found themselves facing in the process, not to human reason. He asked them if they had so soon forgotten how it was to God that they looked repeatedly, during the recent war with England when the dark days offered little logic as to how they were to move forward?

Tragically, soon after this (the early 1790s), the French would ultimately prove what should have been understood without a shadow of a doubt because of the American example just put before them – that planning to rebuild society on nothing more that human reason was a program destined for devastating failure.

The challenge over the past fifty years of Human Reason to the Covenant. And so things went, back in the 1960s and 1970s in Vietnam. And so things went, in the early 2000s in Afghanistan and Iraq. And so things went, more recently in Libya and Syria. And so it has also gone on so many of the streets of America itself. Rational (and extremely expensive) social programming by the experts has not made a dent in solving the many social problems facing America since the 1960s, either at home or abroad. Compassion, not plans, should have been employed – a moral challenge that moral leadership should have focused on instead of all that ideologically-inspired "rational" social planning.

It has been a long and disappointing fifty years since Rational (or Secular) America began to move away from the longer Christian moral-spiritual tradition – the very moral-spiritual tradition that had just brought the country to unprecedented greatness. Almost immediately after having in the late 1940s and 1950s achieved superpower status – and a highly respected Christian model to place before much of the democracy-aspiring world – America began in the 1960s its move away from that very traditional Christian moral-spiritual order ... in order to head down the alluring but highly deceptive Secular road of Human Reason.

America was not quite perfect. But there were those power-brokers and their intellectual advisors who were certain they understood the rational process by which to bring America to perfection. Indeed, it was this very idea of rational social engineering that formed the core of Johnson's Great Society Program. It was also the basis for the Vietnam program Johnson attempted to put into play at the same time.

Evaluating the grand engineers of Human Reason. Not surprisingly, behind this new momentum were those with the highest and most prestigious educations, especially in the legal field.

Lawyers are, by training and professional calling, defenders of someone's need for reason, that is, reason in support of their client's personal and social interests. Lawyers are hired to develop reasonable lines of personal or social defense, ones then presented usually in a court of law – against someone else's interests, the adversaries also reasonably defended by a countering lawyer! How a judge or jury is supposed to find the Truth behind very skilled but intensely conflicting rational arguments offered by opposing lawyers is always a wonder. Legal skill rather than simple truth is designed to always be the winner in a dynamic such as this!

In short, reason and truth are not the same things. Anyone can reason – and we all do, constantly. But finding truth is actually a very different endeavor. But try to get the world to understand that! Try just to get a clever six-year-old to understand that! We start to use reason rather skillfully in support of self-interest at a very early age!

This beautiful world of human reason can be found especially at the pinnacle of America's legal world. No, not Congress. The federal courts! And at the summit of that world of federal courts is found the ultimate citadel of Reason, the U.S. Supreme Court. Americans presume that black-robed Supreme Court justices see truth above mere personal political interest. Actually, these justices are just as political, just as ideological, in their reasoned approach to the law as any other American lawyer. And they are highly political, because they are highly powerful. It is no wonder that life-time appointments to this small but unrestricted or absolute source of American political authority are now fought over with such intensity.

In short, the Supreme Court has made itself the Central Committee, the Politburo* of American democracy.

* * *

THE ROLE OF PERSONAL AND SOCIAL MORALS IN GUIDING AND STRENGTHENING A SOCIETY

It is social morality that defines, and gives strength, to society. The study of social dynamics is not a new thing. Since man himself set out to find answers to why his social world was shaped and acted the way it did, he actually has been asking the great moral question: is this the way society is supposed to work?

And there is an amazing agreement among those that since even ancient times have taken up that question. The Greeks left a rich literature to their descendants in dealing with this very issue. Socrates, Plato and Aristotle spent a huge amount of energy trying to answer this question. Unfortunately, Plato fell victim to the tendency to believe that a moral social order could simply be designed by an enlightened individual (such as himself, of course) and was invited to the Greek kingdom of Syracuse to put his "Platonist" ideas into effect. He nearly lost his life in the political mess that followed, and had to be bought (ransomed) out of captivity (actually slavery) by a friend.

However Aristotle, rather than designing a perfect utopia, studied carefully a wide variety of societies existing either currently or historically (thus employing true social science) and came up simply with a very astute observation: the "good society," as opposed to the "bad society," was distinguished not by the number of people involved in governing that society, whether a government of one, the few, or the many. The good society was characterized by the moral character of those, whether one, few or many, called to govern the society. In other words, a government of a single ruling individual could either be good or bad, depending on the moral character that this person brought to his governance. At the other end of the spectrum, rule by the many could be good, if conducted under well-understood and well-respected moral rules, or could be nothing more than a horrible mob led blindly by demagogues able to whip up the emotions of the masses on the basis of "well-reasoned" whims of this nature or that (usually the political interests of those whipping up the emotions of the democratic masses). The critical difference in each case was the moral discipline that those responsible for the governance of society were working

---

*The name of the small group that, from behind the walls of Moscow's Kremlin citadel, "rationally" governed the lives of the citizens of the former Soviet Union – and of the captive countries of Communist Eastern Europe as well.

under.

The Jews of the Bible too had their way of addressing the same issue, using the power of historical narrative (the Biblical story-telling about the many centuries of existence of their leaders and their people) – to highlight the good and the bad of their own social behavior. In virtually every instance the good was identified with Israel's ability to stay on course with God's instructions, through following God's unchanging Word (the same Word that put the universe into existence), but also his ad-hoc counsel given to those in a leadership position, usually one or another of the Hebrew judges or prophets. However, when the Israelites wandered from this Godly social-moral counsel and discipline, and proceeded to "walk in their own counsel" (which they invariably would do over time), they immediately fell into trouble – until God, out of simply the grace of his ever-faithful heart, came to rescue them from their self-inflicted moral folly.

More recently, the British historian Arnold Toynbee, in his twelve-volume *A Study of History** (taking nearly thirty years, 1934-1961, to complete) examined 28 civilizations in order to see what made them strong or weak, rising or falling. What he noted was the inability of the society to stay on course with the moral foundations that originally brought it into existence and growth, instead over time wandering from that moral course because, in the face of new, rising challenges, a closed and detached elite group of leaders tried to follow unrealistic or utopian (but always self-evidently rational, even if socially suicidal) alternate courses. They would simply abandon their precious, well-tested traditional moral legacy – instead of carefully (thus wisely) drawing on that legacy in creative ways in order to meet the new challenges of life as they arose.

A society's sense of "fair play." Judging from the behavior of Washington politicians both in Congress and in the "deep state" or federal bureaucracy, there is today an incredible lack of any sense of proper rules of social behavior. Almost anything that appears that it might advance an individual's personal political ambitions seems to find some rational justification, one pretending to be in accordance with some kind of moral rule – one that is made up as a person goes along. Can you imagine trying to conduct a soccer or tennis match with the rules simply developed to the advantage of this side or the other in the course of the match? It would be a mess. It would look something like a Third World political election!

Indeed, lately, American politics is looking very "Third-Worldish."

In the days when social leadership was entirely a male concern, much

---

*Toynbee, Arnold. *A Study of History*, Vol. 1: Abridgement of Volumes I-VI; Vol 2: Abridgement of Volumes VII-X. New York: Oxford University Press, 1946 (Vol. 1, renewed in 1974) and 1957 (Vol 2, renewed in 1985).

care was given to the social-moral development of male character. Not to do so was to very likely lead to male behavior that can only be classed as "criminal" – and end up a young man in prison. In fact it is the threat of prison that has long been used as the ultimate discipline to male behavior. But an alternative was once also used – of letting a socially rebellious youth chose military service rather than prison (prison, anyway, famous for teaching even worse social habits!). That was actually a wise choice – because it offered the social-moral discipline that was lacking in the young man's earlier development. Little wonder too that the young men who have served in the military have tended to be much more supportive of the idea of the necessary social order – "patriotism" as we know it. We saw this strongly present in the Vet generation – a generation which served sacrificially in World War Two.

Sports and scouting were other, less drastic, ways for a young man to achieve this same path of social-moral discipline as he approached manhood. Sports taught the importance to young men of "fair play" or "good sportsmanship." A "win" in sports was actually dishonorable if it was not achieved in accordance with the rules of the game. But sadly, sports today is considered merely a game, something for pleasure. Thus the original social purpose for sports is missing entirely. Missing also is the critical role that scouting offered a young man. In fact it has been considered to be highly "progressive" today to take away this very key and very traditional function of boy scouting's focusing on bringing boys into manhood. According to such "progressive" minds, not giving any particular focus on male development will now result in less toxic manhood. Actually, the results are guaranteed to be quite the opposite.

* * *

LEADERSHIP IS KEY TO THE STRENGTHENING OR WEAKENING OF A SOCIETY'S MORAL ORDER

Leaders, not social designs, shape the moral-social order. Modern writers of American civics textbooks typically present the general character and specific features of a social order, or in our case the American social-political order, as the product of a vast amount of legal engineering. The social order is presented as the sum total of well-designed legal structures, laws, political offices, civil and social institutions, that direct the behavior of the members of a society. In other words, it is good laws and good political structuring that make the good society. It is all very mechanical, all very personality-neutral in its operation.

Understanding social dynamics from this viewpoint, it becomes imperative for those involved in social engineering (social-political reformers found in public office, in academia, in the press, even in the field of entertainment, etc.) to lay out on paper and in their public proposals the blueprints for a truly great society, one whose political offices are designed to work along highly rational lines.

We saw how the social commentator John Locke, for instance, was invited in the 1600s to set out a rational social-governmental plan by which to direct the development of the new Carolina colony. But so perfect was it in design that it was quite useless in dealing with the messy circumstances which this new society faced in actually getting up and running. Then also, we saw how the highly academic President Wilson had precise plans for democratizing global society – which tragically fell apart in the face of political reality. More recently, President Johnson and his advisors had beautiful plans and programs to bring America to perfection as the "Great Society," all of which crumbled in the face of unanticipated social dynamics. And then there was the American effort to rebuild a war-torn Afghanistan and a post-Saddam Iraq through implementing constitutional reform.

Beautiful social plans did not automatically make for beautiful social results. But this is a hard reality almost impossible to get the world of intellectual and bureaucratic social planners to understand.

Thus unfortunately, Americans have been taught that "the office makes the man." Political office supposedly empowers, directs and limits the behavior of anyone filling that office. If the office is well-designed, then anyone holding that office and operating under its directives should fulfill quite nicely the responsibilities society has conferred on him or her.

That principle perhaps holds true at the lower, more bureaucratic level, of the social order (whether a nation, a corporation, a military organization, a university, etc.). But it is not bureaucrats that inspire or direct the behavior of larger society.

Indeed, as has been very clear from the American example itself, societies are actually highly leader-dependent in who or what they happen to be. Sadly, Americans – so enraptured with the rather mechanical idea (even ideal) of legal-mechanical constitutional-democracy – find it almost impossible to acknowledge the key role that individual leaders play in the successes (and failures) of societies. Tragically, Americans love to overthrow authoritarian leaders in the name of promoting their ideal of legal-mechanical constitutional-democracy – then always shocked and confused to see how, instead, their efforts to do so typically throw a society into violent social disarray.

But to anyone who has looked seriously at how human history has worked over the countless generations of human life on this planet, it is always very clear how a single individual can shape the character and operation of society.

History is full of such examples. Chinese history, for instance, is really the study of personal dynasties, ones that have arisen out of a period of confusion when the Chinese society is torn apart by warring warlords, until one of these warlords is able to establish ascendancy over the others, and thus begin a new dynasty, and a new period of peace and social development.

The Hebrew Bible is really a story of ancient Hebrew patriarchs and prophets, Abraham, Moses, Joshua, David, Nathan, Elijah, Elisha, and the huge impact they personally had on the shaping of the Hebrew nation.

Western history is filled with the stories of how such individuals as Alexander the Great, Julius Caesar, Constantine, Charlemagne, Luther, Calvin, Louis XIV, Napoleon, etc., had a huge impact on the defining of the social order of their days.

More recently we have also seen how Hitler, Stalin, Gandhi, Churchill, Mao shaped our world (in ways good or bad) in their days.

And certainly in American history, note the enormous impact that Washington, Jackson, Lincoln, Wilson, the Roosevelts, Truman, Johnson, Reagan, Obama, or for that matter virtually every American President in one way or another, each had in shaping American society.

Leaders stand as living-breathing examples of the moral ideals that the people need to embrace in order for their society to succeed. Society's best leaders actually serve society as the very living symbol, even reality, of the moral order and its particular social design. These leaders are not political dictators forcing the people to adhere to strict social policy that they are imposing on society (though some will certainly try to lead this way).

Great leaders do not dictate. They inspire. They themselves become the visible idea, the very embodiment of the ideal features of that society – from the lofty goals or social ideals that the leader represents personally, to the choices to be made or the procedures to be followed which the leader inspires the society to embrace in order for it to be able to reach those lofty goals. This is what brings a society to success, even grand success (or tragically also, massive disaster if wrongly directed), because such leadership is not just accepted. It is followed enthusiastically by the rest of society.

Thus it is that truly "the man makes the office" – not the reverse. We have seen how the office of U.S. president changes in character and political effect as it changes hands, from one individual to the next. True, the office empowers an individual legally. But how (and if) that power is used depends entirely on the personal makeup of the individual holding that office.

This idea that the greatness (or failure) of any society is determined heavily by the personal character of the person acting as society's leader is illustrated very clearly in history.

Alexander the Great was no holder of any particular imperial office (though he was the son of the conquering Macedonian King Philip II), but the one himself who defined by his enormous activity what his huge empire was to become.

Hitler was brought to power as Germany's Chancellor in 1933. But what happened next to Germany had little to do with the mechanics of the German Weimar Republic or the office of Chancellor. In fact, that German constitutional order was quickly put aside by the German people themselves in order to build a German Third Reich or Empire around the very person of their Führer (Leader) Hitler. For better or worse (in this case horribly worse) the German nation redefined itself around the personality of a single individual. The same can also be said of Stalin's Russia and Mao's China. And we must add, this is exactly what is happening today under Xi Jinping's leadership in China and Putin's leadership in Russia.

With respect to America, in the break with King George III's royal rule in 1776 there really was at that point no precise social or political order presiding over or unifying the thirteen different colonies (now new states) as a whole, because the thirteen colonies had for so long simply and ably looked after themselves. But with rebellion against George III underway, these new states would have to find for themselves a higher path, one that could bring them together for success in this Herculean task. Thankfully, there were a number of old well-established social habits that they shared mutually, ones built on America's long-standing moral order, ones that allowed the Continental Congress to function (even though not yet officially approved by all the states).

But the ultimate dynamic that moved America forward from its status as a group of thirteen English colonies to the status of thirteen newly independent but united states was importantly found above even that. It was in America's actual leadership. And here is where George Washington looms large as the foundation on which the independence movement relied for its existence and its durability. As Washington stood firm and unbending before the huge challenge of breaking the determination of the British to force the American states back into submission, so also did these states find inspiration not to bend or yield.

Then not only did he lead the country through the dark days of the rebellion, Washington went on after that to shape greatly what the "United States" was to look like in the way he went at the role of serving as the republic's first president.

That's how social orders are put into place, and thrive (or not).

* * *

GOD'S HAND IN HUMAN HISTORY

We cannot emphasize enough the fact that those who had the greatest influence on society, on history itself, were not bureaucratic *fonctionnaires*,* but instead dynamic individuals of great charismatic character, able to inspire others – many others – to follow them step by step as they led ... even if the path they were taking the people down was highly dangerous.   And the word charismatic is key here. Charisma is an old Greek word χάρισμα (*khárisma*) implying a special anointing, a heavenly or divine grace placed upon a person, such as makes that person unusually gifted as a leader. That divine grace as a gifting comes not from another person or social institution or material or physical property. It has long been understood as coming from above, above as in Heaven, the gods, or God himself (but possibly also Satan as well, if care is not taken in measuring or judging by ancient spiritual standards the voice of such a non-worldly or supernatural source).

The Chinese, for instance, have understood for thousands of years this phenomenon in the form of what they called since ancient times the *Tianming* (Mandate of Heaven). Chinese Emperors gained the necessary respect and support from the Chinese nation in being able to demonstrate the many ways that Heaven had smiled on their rule. Visible social success indicated clearly the approval and support of Heaven. But the downside of that same idea was that when floods, famines, diseases or enemy raiders attacked Chinese society, that same respect and support among the people would melt away. To the people this was a clear sign that the *Tian* (Heaven) had obviously withdrawn that special favor that Chinese society depended on so greatly. And this change in political climate would be the signal to Chinese warlords to put forth their candidacy as the new Emperor. And a violent round of civil war (often lasting centuries) would result, until it was clear that Heaven had once again made its choice: a victor, a *Tianzi* (Son of Heaven) would finally emerge to take charge of China.

But other examples abound. Alexander the Great believed that he was actually the son of a God (or at least that's how he presented himself to the society that supported him) and went to the Siwa Oasis in the middle of the Libyan Desert to have the Amonite priests there attest to this fact.

Likewise, David was anointed at a very early age by Samuel as God's

---
*French for those who govern from their chairs behind desks in governmental office buildings.

chosen leader of Israel, and David was willing to wait through very troubled times, even passing up opportunities to launch his own career, as he waited for God (and only God) to bring his kingship into being.

So also the Roman imperial candidate Constantine was vitally aware of God's appointment of him as future Emperor, moving against a much larger enemy candidate under the sign God had given him to conquer with: the Chi-Rho sign of Jesus the Christ.

And closer to home, we know that both Washington and Lincoln were men of immense Christian faith, drawing on that faith to keep them moving forward during very dark times, when others would have quit.

Of course there have been rulers who have operated apart from just such a sense of divine appointment. But lacking such higher "legitimacy" they are driven to rule by force, often by sheer terror inflicted on a subject people – as paranoia and fear of losing their position (never really quite "legitimate" in the eyes of the people) drives them forward. Certainly Stalin and Mao fit this description. And the manner and ultimately durability of the societies that they ruled over attest to the problems that soon enough develop for a society when it lacks a "higher" hand supporting it.

To be sure, such a "higher hand" is historically defined in different ways, with different versions of Heaven, different versions of God. Or are they all that different? What we humans can understand about the Realm of God can come only through human interpretation, and thus is going to come to us through different cultural versions. But they all point to the same higher source of power, one existing above all human capability itself.

Christianity itself is built entirely on that understanding, not just through the life, death and Resurrection of Jesus but through the empowerment of the Holy Spirit (and in the case of the Apostle Paul, a post-resurrection encounter with Jesus himself), God's very hand in getting Jesus's early followers up and running as a powerful people.

One thing also is clear about these key historical examples: Heaven's call on them to the task of leadership was always quite real to the leaders themselves.

Others, such as intellectuals, who operate only from their self-conceived world of pure reason (thus needing no God beyond their own personal intelligence), will mock those who put forward the claim of divine calling. Why not? No such calling ever came to them – and never will come to them, as long as they put huge material boundaries around their personal sense of reality.

As the opening chapters of the Bible put things, such scoffers have chosen to do what Adam and Eve did in cutting themselves off from God and his counsel (and provision). They have eaten from the Tree of the Knowledge of Good and Evil – so as to be themselves like God ... as the

Deceiver himself beguiled them into believing would be the grand result of this act of disobedience to God. Such individuals can scoff all they want. But they will never find the social significance that they so greatly crave in trying to be so reasonable.

Why is this connection with the higher power of Heaven or God thus so important to social leadership? Leaders are not your average person. Your average person naturally wants to fit in, be an integral part of society. There is absolutely nothing wrong with those instincts. A strong society depends on exactly that very instinct being found widely among its people.

But leaders (at whatever level of society, all the way from the White House, to moms and dads at the family dinner tables) – in any circumstance in which they assume the responsibilities of leadership – must answer to a different voice than that of the immediately approving world around them. Presidents and parents push ahead because they see in their respective world of great moral (and loving/caring) responsibility, whether to the many or the few under their care, something higher or more noble, something not yet attained, something that not even the society they are dealing with can yet see or understand. And by answering to that higher vision, that higher calling placed on their hearts, they do not pull back from a social responsibility simply because the society they are supervising (from little children to jealous rivals) does not see things their way – although it does become an accompanying responsibility to help those in their care to see and understand exactly what the leaders require of them.

Thus it is that true leaders (and not just those occupying high political office) are designed to draw others forward to a higher task, even when the society itself is afraid or confused ... especially when it is afraid or confused. Leaders must lead the people to a higher call, a call that those under their care do not yet see or understand, yet one that is vital to the survival and growth of that society. Leaders must lead.

Lincoln. For instance, Lincoln was so brave as to actually undertake the crushing responsibility of breaking the intention of the Southern states to abandon and thus cripple the American Union. Presidents before him had seen the difficulty of trying to keep the Union together in the face of this horrible question of slavery, and had simply looked the other way, kicking the can of slavery down the road for someone else after them to deal with.

But Lincoln, in assuming the American Presidency, understood that the burden of leading the Union through this deadly challenge was his, by literally Divine appointment. And to God, and God alone, did he increasingly look for comfort and support as he put the nation through this terrible crisis – in order to finally get this matter settled once and for all.

Keeping people with him tested every ounce of Lincoln's personal strength as a leader. Yes, he had his supporters. Great leaders do. But he had also a huge number of whiners who complained about how all this killing of America's young men was way beyond the nation's ability to sustain. They were ready to quit, to let the South be on its way with its slaves and all, and leave what was left of America to get on with things as best it could. Even on his home front, with his wife, he faced the constant demand to "give it up" so that the Lincoln family could just get things back to normal. But "normal" was not an option for America, and Lincoln knew this. God himself had called America to greater things than just letting matters go. America, after all was a covenant nation, commissioned by God to give hope to the world by setting before the world the living, breathing human example of how the little people of the world no longer needed to live in bondage to the powerful of this world. America had to live on as a light to the world showing the way to something we call true democracy.

As Lincoln himself put the matter at the memorial service for those tens of thousands of young men who had died in this horrible 3-day battle on the fields of Gettysburg, Pennsylvania:

It is rather for us to be here dedicated to the great task remaining before us – that from these honored dead we take increased devotion to that cause for which they gave the last full measure of devotion – that we here highly resolve that these dead shall not have died in vain – that this nation, under God, shall have a new birth of freedom – and that government of the people, by the people, for the people, shall not perish from the earth.

It is little wonder that for generations after this speech in 1863, it and the opening lines of America's 1776 Declaration of Independence would be the most memorized words in American history. Lincoln, leading this nation, under God, was determined that this country would not quit in the face of the horrible sacrifice required of those answering the noble call that God himself had placed on the American nation.

And thus America answered its president's reminder of this high calling with a huge "yes! Yes, we will so commit ourselves and our sacred honor to this most noble, this Divine, cause."

That is what Divinely inspired leadership achieves. This is not what ordinary office-holders do. They simply follow plans and programs placed before them. Leaders however inspire others to take action, to take up the hard, even sacrificial, work together so that their society may move forward. It is after all, the effort of the masses of "little people," not the fancy ideas of bureaucratic social planners, that bring societies their grand successes.

God's call on very ordinary individuals. But the Puritans also realized that God's hand was just as available to those same ordinary individuals, doing the ordinary things that human life ultimately depends on. That was the whole point of the Puritan experiment in America. At a time when European kings were defending their positions against a rising middle class, the kings claiming special divine appointment, the Puritans answered back that the same God is just as much interested in and supportive of the "little people" – as clearly was Jesus in his time. They claimed that what God truly wanted to see come to pass was a people who lived and worked together in harmony as equals before God. And equals before God also meant equals before man. And thus the democracy concept was brought front and central in the Puritan experiment. It provided a powerful moral legacy for a new America, one that carried the nation forward for nearly four centuries.

In America, this social dynamic actually has always found its foundation in the American home. Family goals and social discipline – but ultimately the way the family looked above to God – developed repeatedly among the rising generations because of the moral-spiritual leadership the parents provided their children. Parents were/are the rising generation's first encounter with inspiring leadership. Children develop social instincts and social trust at a very early age, because of the leadership their parents provide.

From there, such social inspiration was/is cultivated further through inspiring classroom teachers and inspiring pastors. The high quality of the classroom, and the high quality of the pulpit, was always the key to American democratic success.

That social pattern must never be replaced by the domination, even dictatorship, of the "enlightened ones" found in bureaucratic office or seated behind high judicial benches – or even in front of TV cameras offering 24-hour wisdom or comments on how they believe life should take shape in America – willing to assume, even to take away, such local responsibility from the community's families, schools and churches or synagogues. In America, those in such high social position were long-expected to be there to inspire such grass roots development of the American family, school and church/synagogue – not replace it.

The Humanist challenge.   History reveals again and again that substituting Humanist or Rationalist directives in place of Divine directives has consistently demonstrated what a disaster it could be to America, individually or corporately. Humanism as a religion has done nothing to improve moral or social conditions in America, but instead left them to be merely "whatever" Americans as individuals and groups have decided they would like them to be, for the moment and in this or that particular situation, always highly justified with the latest and loftiest of Reasons. But history makes it tragically clear that societies do not survive the effect of "whatever" ethics.

✳ ✳ ✳

INSPIRING THE WORLD, RATHER THAN TRYING TO FIX IT

It is important to bring back God's covenant with America, for America to get back to serving as "The Light of the World," giving hope to the little people of the world that their God of Heaven, the Creator and Judge of all that has and will happen on earth, wants to show them the path to greater glory, both for themselves, their families and the societies that surround them. America was supposed to exemplify that divine covenant – not force some version of a well-engineered program (engineered by clever human design) on the other tribes and nations of the world.

Looking back in history it is easy to see how America has performed much more effectively in simply acting to inspire and assist other nations – to the extent that these nations themselves have called for such assistance. Truman, taking his cues from his own deep Christian understanding of life and its dynamics was very circumspect in this regard and played the situation in post-war Western Europe masterfully (aid to Greece and Turkey, the Marshall Plan, relief to blockaded Berlin, and the creation of NATO). Kennedy's Peace Corps was set up along these same lines.

And yes, this means even assuming a political toughness at times, if it is done in cooperation of others seeking such assistance – such as was the case of Truman's decision to come to the aid of the South Koreans in warding off the aggression of the North Koreans. Bush, Sr's action against Saddam in Kuwait was built on extensive international support – and most importantly the support of the Kuwaitis themselves – as were Clinton's actions in Yugoslavia against the ethnic cleansing going on there. In each case the goal was not to remake the societies along supposedly improved social lines, but simply to support the peace and prosperity of societies experiencing deep social trauma. Clinton had no desire to remake Serbia, only to back it out of its attacks on its neighboring societies.

Even here, caution and restraint – rather than moral crusading inspired by some plan to perform a makeover of some other society – has characterized America's finest moments. And when bringing peace and prosperity clearly seemed to be beyond America's powers to bring to a specific situation, wise American presidents stayed out of the chaos. Such was Clinton's decision not to save Rwanda from its self-inflicted genocide.

This included Reagan's decision to pull out of Lebanon and Clinton's similar decision in Somalia when it became apparent that American involvement was not inspiring local support. And it included Bush, Sr.'s decision not to go charging into an Iraqi quagmire in an effort to take out Iraq's leader, Saddam Hussein. There were situations that properly called for American action; there were situations where no such calling was there for America. Wise American leaders knew the difference.

Disasters in trying to "free up" the world. Tragically, such wisdom has not always directed America's relations with the larger world. At the end of the 1800s America chose to involve itself in a rebellion of the Cubans against their Spanish lords, and not only took the sides of the rebels in Cuba but also spread that sense of involvement to the Spanish Philippines, where having helped bring down 300 years of Spanish rule there, Americans decided to put themselves in charge of further Philippine development. This then turned the Filipinos against the newly occupying American authorities. In short, America acted no more Liberal than the Spanish in the way they conducted themselves in the life of the Philippine nation.

Then there was soon after that Wilson's decision in 1917 that American boys should go off to Europe to kill German boys, to bring glorious democracy to the world by participating in "the war to end all wars." Only meaningless and deeply tragic death and destruction resulted for everyone involved in this senseless nationalist conflict.

Then there was Kennedy's decision to take down the heavy-handed regime of Diem in Vietnam in 1963, which threw the southern half of the country into political confusion. This was quickly followed up by Johnson's decision to send a few American soldiers to Vietnam to restore that country's broken sense of order – lest the Communist North Vietnam should take advantage of this American-caused situation in the southern half of the country. When that did not suffice to restore a pro-Western social order in South Vietnam, Johnson sent a few more troops, then a few more, until by the last year of his presidency in 1968, he had over a half-million American troops in Vietnam trying to make things go the way he thought they should.

The very exhausting Vietnam venture became a huge disaster for everyone involved, particularly when a Democratic Congress then in the early 1970s decided to undercut a Republican Nixon White House, which was wisely withdrawing American troops from this mess – while at the same time offering a small amount of, yet very vital, financial support to our South Vietnamese allies. Congress simply cut off all further support of the Vietnamese – even mere financial support – allowing the North Vietnamese to be easily able to fill the political vacuum our abrupt departure had created. This in turn left thousands of pro-American Vietnamese to be slaughtered by Soviet Russian-supported North Vietnamese troops who filled that vacuum. And the chaos caused by the collapsing political status quo did not end there, but spilled over even more horribly to the killing fields of neighboring Cambodia.

And Congress never understood, or at least never took responsibility for, the tragedy that mere political ambition at home brought on those dear people abroad.

And equally tragic, entry into the 21st century saw America apparently having learned nothing from the grand tragedy of Vietnam. The horribly failed Vietnam example did not stop Bush Jr. from attempting to "free up" Iraq the way Kennedy had once freed up South Vietnam. Thus Bush decided to "liberate" Iraq in bringing down Saddam Hussein's government in that country. Unsurprisingly – and most tragically, – Bush's massive military effort (Shock and Awe) did not lead to a Humanist's democratic utopia for that country but instead, horrible infighting.

And Bush's similar effort to undercut Afghanistan's Pashto tribesmen in their support of the Taliban did nothing but throw Afghanistan into ever-deeper chaos and violence.

And how exactly was our effort to undercut Syria's President Assad such a "humanitarian" venture? He was simply trying to hold a multi-ethnic country together in the face of Syria's fall into social disintegration. And the same held true for Gaddafi in Libya.

How would we have felt if France or Britain (or both) had decided that it was the "humanitarian" thing to do to undercut Lincoln in the same way we undercut Assad and Gaddafi, because Lincoln's effort to keep the Union together in one piece through military means was in violation of every precept that all Humanists find themselves living and dying for? Thank God (literally) that the leaders of France and Britain did not decide to "go Humanist" on us in the 1860s.

What is truly amazing is how it seems always the case that "going Humanist" (undercutting social authority) ends up with the necessity of having to "go Darwinian" (restoring order by the use of domineering means)!

Where is the wisdom in all this? What does it take to hold a multi-ethnic, multi-sectarian, multi-class society (as all societies at some point tend to be) in a state of peace ... where the streets are safe, homes are secure, and the people able to enjoy the simple prosperity that makes for human happiness?

Christianity has always had a powerful answer to that question: let God direct, inspire, provide ... through similar actions that we sons and daughters of his do on his behalf. He has made very clear in the Bible's instructions as to how life itself is to be understood and addressed. The Bible is like a science textbook on social dynamics. We need to pay attention to what God himself has shown us there, as countless generations before us have done, most wisely.

And God, as always, will prove very faithful in his generous support of those who choose to live the Biblical way, at the same time in providing them with the means to be so generous and supportive of others.

Indeed, America was originally set up for just that purpose, namely, to illustrate as the City on a Hill, a Light to the Nations, how God wants all of us humans to live. And America has clearly succeeded marvelously when it went at things in this manner.

So why then are Humanism and Darwinism so set on bringing down the Christian worldview and the Christian constitutional foundations that have served both America itself and the surrounding world so well?

Somehow Humanism still feels the strong need to prove itself, against Christianity. And Darwinism is totally scornful of Christianity.

* * *

DEFENDING WESTERN/CHRISTIAN CIVILIZATION

The English political leader, but also the author of volumes of Western history, Winston Churchill, referred to Western Civilization as "Christian Civilization." And rightly so. The Christian worldview officially shaped the European (and later, American) Western world since the early 300s, over 1700 years ago (but beginning its influence well before even then). Christianity was central to the understanding of what society was all about, what its purpose was, and how life was to be moved forward to higher things. Until 50 years ago this same Christian understanding about life was also the mainstay of the American idea, giving the country three and a half centuries of national vision and social purpose during its development from a European backwater to its position at the head of the Christian world as its primary defender. Christianity was a central element in America's rise to its status as the world's sole Superpower.

Meanwhile, as a slow but gathering process occurring over the last half-century, all of that cultural-spiritual dynamic has been pushed aside step by step by federal judicial decree, in the effort to replace the Christian legacy with Secular Humanism. The results of that substitution both at home and abroad have been dramatically much less than excellent.

The 2019 Pew Report. On October 17, 2019, the Pew Research Center released a 26-page report which clearly demonstrated how badly that

Christian character of America had declined – in just the last ten years alone. The Center had just completed a statistical analysis comparing changes occurring in America's Christian profile between the years 2009 and 2019, a time-period coinciding with the presidencies of Obama and Trump. The report was appropriately entitled "In U.S., Decline of Christianity Continues at Rapid Pace: An update on America's changing religious landscape."* The title speaks for itself.

The study found that in 2019, only 65% of Americans still described themselves as Christians, down 12 percent over the previous ten years. At the same time, those that claimed no religious affiliation (from atheists to simply "nothing in particular") rose to 26% of the population, up from 17% in 2009 (page 3).

The age of the Americans being surveyed was even more skewed against Christianity. Of the oldest group, the Silents, the decline in Christian affiliation was only 2 percent; for the Boomers it was 6%; and Gen-X 8 percent. But the percentage drop among the Millennials (born in the 1981-1996 period) was a huge 16 percent (page 7). This left 84% of the older Silents still standing in 2019 as Christians – whereas only 49% of the Millennials still identified themselves as Christians (page 8). That is a terrible indicator as to where America is headed into the future morally and spiritually as a nation.

Not surprisingly also, political party affiliation made a big difference. For those that identified themselves politically as Republican, or leaned in that direction, the ten-year decline was 7 percent. But the Democrats marked a 17 percent decline in Christian identity (page 7). As a consequence, in 2019, 79 percent of the Republicans still identified themselves as Christians, whereas the figure stood at 55% for the Democrats (page 19). That is a very significant political difference, pointing further to the likely moral and spiritual direction in which the country is headed, depending upon which of the two political parties is in power in Washington.

Christianity and society. Christianity at its heart (as set forth by Jesus himself) was about Godly empowerment of the individual, in the face of life's many and often quite difficult challenges. Christianity supported human life with the understanding that with simple faith in God alone, these challenges could be met and conquered by even the least socially significant of individuals – because God himself offered his powerful support to those who simply trusted him as their Heavenly Father. God was not interested in a person's social status, as societies tend to do.

---

*https://www.pewforum.org/2019/10/17/in-u-s-decline-of-christianity-continues-at-rapid-pace/

Christianity also demonstrated clearly (during the worst of times of Roman persecution) that individual strengthening through Divine empowerment also worked awesomely well in producing the right structuring for social as well as personal life. In fact, it was the witness of the Christians in their immense personal and social strength that impressed a morally decadent Rome to begin to look to Christianity as the solution to the decay that infected Roman life in every imaginable social area possible.

Admittedly, Christianity has been used as a civic formula for autocracy. But that was never its original nature. And from time to time reforms have swept the Christian world in order to bring the people back to the original character of the Christian faith. The Protestant Reformation of the 1500s and 1600s, during which English Puritanism was founded, was just such an early example – and a critical social foundation for New England and all it stood for. Also, the Great Awakenings were key to keeping Christianity on course in the face of the natural instinct of man to want to displace Divine guidance and support with personal autonomy: the ever-present temptation to want to play God himself.

The Decline of the Christian West. For the past 70 years, since the end of World War Two, Europe has looked to America to play the leading role in defending Western civilization – allowing Europeans to look after their own material development in the meantime. As they lost their leading position in world events, so also they lost interest in the moral-spiritual order that once had made Europe itself the center of global affairs. They were content to live to some kind of grand material, but not grand spiritual, purpose. This moral-spiritual decline, as philosophers ranging from Aristotle to Toynbee have observed, was an indication of Europe's overall political-social decline as well.

America's own self-imposed spiritual decline. But America too now finds itself headed down the same moral-spiritual road as Europe. Worse, many American leaders themselves have called on Americans to take a strong stand against the supposed tyranny of Middle America. These post-modern crusaders feel the need to attack a traditional America still possessing the strong and well-tested and well-proven social standards that for generations America has faithfully lived by. They treat not only such social tradition but even patriotism itself as some kind of disease. Instead, these "progressive" crusaders even consider those who stand publicly against the symbols of American patriotism as the nation's true heroes.

But what do they actually stand for? We know what they stand against. They have made it quite clear that their highest call is to "shame" America, for being whatever it has, over the centuries, become. But a society cannot survive simply on the basis of its people being against its very existence. Where is the unifying idea that will pull America together, and Western civilization with it? Who today is offering strong moral guidance to our great Western or Christian civilization?

In all of this, America seems to be asleep at the wheel, its leading political voices in Washington more intent in playing the game of crippling each other, as if Washington politics were merely a TV game show for wannabe celebrities. True moral leadership all around the political table seems to be in short supply.

The critical need for another "Great Awakening." We have arrived at the same point in which if our civilization is to be saved from its own self-inflicted folly, we are going to need another Divine intervention. Or else the days of American global leadership, as well as the modern Western or Christian Civilization's social-moral-spiritual leadership in the world's development, are over.

China can hardly wait for this to happen!

* * *

A CALL TO RENEW THE COVENANT WITH GOD
EXTENDED TO US THROUGH JESUS CHRIST

So ... at this point it is of critical importance that America finds its way back to the original Covenant with God, similar to the one presented by Moses as the Hebrews were about to enter the Promised Land, and exactly the same one that Winthrop referred to in delivering his famous sermon, "City on a Hill," as the Puritans were about to depart in their ships in order to begin their great Christian experiment in America:

> . . .   *Thus stands the cause between God and us. We are entered into covenant with Him for this work. We have taken out a commission.*
>
> . . .   *if we shall neglect the observation of these articles, [and] embrace this present world and prosecute our carnal intentions, seeking great things for ourselves and our posterity, the Lord will surely break out in wrath against us, and be revenged of such a people, and make us know the price of the breach of such a covenant.*
>
> . . .   *Now the only way to avoid this shipwreck [of God's wrath], and to provide for our posterity, is to follow the counsel of Micah,*

to do justly, to love mercy, to walk humbly with our God. For this end, we must be knit together, in this work, as one man. We must entertain each other in brotherly affection. We must be willing to abridge ourselves of our superfluities, for the supply of others' necessities. We must delight in each other; make others' conditions our own; rejoice together, mourn together, labor and suffer together, always having before our eyes our commission and community in the work, as members of the same body.

. . . Beloved, there is now set before us life and death, good and evil, in that we are commanded this day to love the Lord our God, and to love one another, to walk in his ways and to keep his Commandments and his ordinance and his laws, and the articles of our Covenant with Him, that we may live and be multiplied, and that the Lord our God may bless us in the land whither we go to possess it.

But if our hearts shall turn away, so that we will not obey, but shall be seduced, and worship other Gods, our pleasure and profits, and serve them; it is propounded unto us this day, we shall surely perish out of the good land whither we pass over this vast sea to possess it.

Therefore let us choose life, that we and our seed may live, by obeying His voice and cleaving to Him, for He is our life and our prosperity.

Maranatha ("may our Lord come"). We are way beyond the possibility of human self-help. As a fully-confused and wandering Fourth-Generation people, our help at this point can come only from the intervention of God. And so we pray that God might come and free us from our self-inflicted folly.

But we might also add: "However, dear Lord, please do not make it hurt too much." The Great Depression of the 1930s cured us of our 1920s silliness. The toughness required of human life during the Depression got America smart real fast, and prepared the country for the enormous task of fighting both the German and the Japanese Empires at the same time. Thankfully God had intervened in order to toughen up America, or a still-silly America would have failed horribly to meet successfully the challenge of a war placed before it in 1941.

But today we have over a half-century of silliness to get over, not just ten years, as was the case following the Roaring Twenties. Thus it might take much more "toughening up" of our character than even another ten-year Great Depression to get us back to being a First-Generation people, a people once again able to take on the huge challenges that await us.

We are saddled with an enormous national debt and a Secular-Socialist moral-spiritual dependency we have fallen under at home, and we face the amazing inability to focus on, or even understand, much less answer, the monumental challenges to America rising abroad.

But we are hoping that God will honor the Covenant that our ancestors once signed onto, for themselves and for the future generations to come after them. That is our fondest hope. It is, in fact, our only hope.

Maranatha!

BIBLIOGRAPHY

AMERICA – THE COVENANT NATION

It is important to note that this particular volume is derived greatly from the three-volume series:

Hodges, Miles Huntley. *Securing America's Covenant with God: From America's Foundation in the Early 1600s to America's Post-Civil-War Recovery in the Late 1800s*. Indianapolis: Westbow Press, 2020.

Hodges, Miles Huntley. *America's Rise to Greatness under God's Covenant: From the Late 1880s to the End of the 1950s*. Indianapolis: Westbow Press, 2020.

Hodges, Miles Huntley. *The Dismissing of America's Covenant with God: From the Early 1960s to the Present*. Indianapolis: Westbow Press, 2020.

WORKS OF A GENERAL, BUT RELIGIOUS, HISTORICAL NATURE

Bennett, William J. *America: The Last Best Hope*; Volume I: *From the Age of Discovery to a World at War, 1492-1914*. Nashville, TN: Nelson Current, 2006.

Bennett, William J. *America: The Last Best Hope*. Volume II. *From a World at War to the Triumph of Freedom, 1914–1989*. Nashville, TN: Thomas Nelson, 2007.

Corrigan, John and Hudson, Winthrop S. *Religion in America*. 9th Edition. New York: Routledge, 2018.

Gaustad, Edwin S. and Noll, Mark A., eds. *A Documentary History of Religion in America to 1877*. 3rd Edition. Grand Rapids, Michigan: Wm. B. Eerdmans, 2003.

Holmes, David L. *Faiths of the Postwar Presidents: From Truman to Obama*. Athens: University of Georgia Press, 2012.

Hudson, Winthrop S. *Religion in America: An Historical Account of the Development of American Religious Life*. 3rd Edition. New York: Charles Scribner's Sons, 1981.

Noll, Mark A. *A History of Christianity in the United States and Canada*. Grand Rapids, Michigan: Wm. B. Eerdmans, 1992.

Noll, Mark A. *America's God: From Jonathan Edwards to Abraham Lincoln*. New York: Oxford University Press, 2002.

Marshall, Peter and Manuel, David. *The Light and the Glory: Did God Have a Plan for America?* Old Tappan, NJ: Fleming H. Revell Company, 1977. (basically covering the period 1492 to 1793)

Marshall, Peter and Manuel, David. *From Sea to Shining Sea: God's Plan for America Unfolds.* Grand Rapids, MI: Fleming H. Revell, 1986. (basically covering the period 1787 to 1837).

Marshall, Peter and Manuel, David. *Sounding Forth the Trumpet: God's Plan for America in Peril – 1837-1860.* Grand Rapids, MI: Revell, 1998.

Marty, Martin E. *Pilgrims in Their Own Land: 500 Years of Religion in America.* New York: Penguin Books, 1984.

Meacham, Jon. *American Gospel: God, The Founding Fathers, and the Making of a Nation.* New York: Random House, 2006.

Meacham, Jon. *The Soul of America.* New York: Random House, 2018.

Sidwell, Mark. ed. *Faith of Our Fathers: Scenes from American Church History.* Greenville, SC: BJU Press, 1991.

Smith, Gary Scott. *Faith & the Presidency: From George Washington to George W. Bush.* New York: Oxford University Press, 2006.

Smith, Gary Scott. *Religion in the Oval Office: The Religious Lives of American Presidents.* New York: Oxford University Press, 2015.

THE OXFORD HISTORY OF THE UNITED STATES SERIES

Middlekauff, Robert. *The Glorious Cause: The American Revolution, 1763-1789.* Oxford History of the United States. New York: Oxford University Press, 2007.

Wood, Gordon S. *Empire of Liberty: A History of the Early Republic, 1789-1815.* Oxford History of the United States. New York: Oxford University Press, 2009.

Howe, Daniel Walker. *What Hath God Wrought: The Transformation of America, 1815-1848.* Oxford History of the United States. New York: Oxford University Press, 2007.

McPherson, James M. *Battle Cry of Freedom: The Civil War Era, 1848- 1865.* Oxford History of the United States. New York: Oxford University Press, 1988.

White, Richard. *The Republic for Which It Stands: The United States during Reconstruction and the Gilded Age, 1865-1896.* Oxford History of the United States. New York: Oxford University Press, 2017.

Kennedy, David M. *Freedom from Fear: The American People in the Great Depression and War, 1929-1945.* Oxford History of the United States. New York: Oxford University Press, 2001.

Patterson, James T. *Grand Expectations: The United States, 1945-1974*. Oxford History of the United States. New York: Oxford University Press, 1996.

Patterson, James T. *Restless Giant: The United States from Watergate to Bush v. Gore*. The Oxford History of the United States. New York: Oxford University Press, 2005.

Herring, George. *Years of Peril and Ambition: U.S. Foreign Relations, 1776-1921*. Oxford History of the United States. New York: Oxford University Press, 2007.

Herring, George C. *The American Century and Beyond: U.S. Foreign Relations, 1893-2014*. 2nd ed. Oxford History of the United States. New York: Oxford University Press, 2017.

OTHER KEY WORKS OF A GENERAL NATURE

Carson, Clarence B. *A Basic History of the United States* (in six volumes), Greenville, AL: American Textbook Committee, 1983-1986 and 2004.

Furnas, J.C. *The Americans: A Social History of the United States, 1587-1914*. New York: B.P. Putnam's Sons, 1969.

James, Edward T., ed. *The American Plutarch: 18 Lives Selected from the Dictionary of American Biography, with an Introduction by Howard Mumford Jones*. New York: Charles Scribner's Sons, for American Council for Learned Societies, 1964, renewing numerous copyrights going back to 1929.

McGreal, Ian P. *Great Thinkers of the Western World*. New York: Harper Collins, 1992.

Morison, Samuel Eliot. *The Oxford History of the American People*. New York: Oxford University Press, 1965.

Morison, Samuel Eliot and Commager, Henry Steele. *The Growth of the American Republic*. 5th edition, Volume One. New York: Oxford University Press, 1962.

Russell, Bertrand. *A History of Western Philosophy: And Its Connection with Political and Social Circumstances from the Earliest Times to the Present Day*. New York: Simon and Schuster, 1945.
Sabine, George H. and Thorson, Thomas L. *A History of Political Theory*. 4th edition. Hinsdale, IL: Dryden Press, 1973.

Schweikart, Larry and Allen, Michael. *A Patriot's History of the United States: From Columbus's Great Discovery to the War on Terror*. New York: Penguin Sentinel, 2007.

Tindall, George Brown. *America: A Narrative History*. New York: W.W. Norton & Company, 1984.

AMERICA'S MORAL-SPIRITUAL INHERITANCE

Calvin, John. *Institutes of the Christian Religion.* Translated from the 1541 French edition by Elsie Anne McKee. Grand Rapids, Michigan, William B. Eerdmans, 2009.

Locke, John. *Two Treatises of Government. Treatise II: An Essay Concerning the Original, Extent, and End, of Civil Government.* From the Works of John Locke, A New Edition, Corrected. Vol. V. London: Thomas Tegg, 1823.

Woolhouse, Roger. *John Locke: An Essay Concerning Human Understanding.* Penguin Classic. London: Penguin Books, 1997.

GETTING STARTED

Billings, Warren M. *Sir William Berkeley and the Forging of Colonial Virginia.* Baton Rouge: Louisiana State University Press, 2004.

Bremer, Francis J. *John Winthrop: America's Forgotten Founding Father.* Oxford University Press, 2003.

Brown, John. *The Pilgrim Fathers of New England and the Puritan Successors.* (London: The Religious Tract Society, 1906) reprinted by Pilgrim Publications, Pasadena, Texas, 1970.

Carden, Allen. *Puritan Christianity in America: Religion and Life in Seventeenth-Century Massachusetts.* Grand Rapids, MI: Baker Book House, 1990.

Dallimore, Arnold A. *George Whitefield: God's Anointed Servant in the Great Revival of the Eighteenth Century.* Wheaton, Illinois: Crossway Books, 1990.

Fantel, Hans. *William Penn: Apostle of Dissent.* William Morrow & Co. New York, 1974.

Heimart, Alan and Delbanco, Andrew, eds. *The Puritans in America: A Narrative Anthology.* Cambridge, Massachusetts: Harvard University Press, 1985.

Miller, Perry and Johnson, Thomas H. *The Puritans: A Sourcebook of Their Writings.* 2 Volumes Bound as One. Mineola, NY: Dover Publications, Inc., 2001.

Murray, Iain H. *Johnathan Edwards: A New Biography.* Edinburgh: The Banner of Truth Trust, 1987.

INDEPENDENCE – AND THE NEW REPUBLIC

Beeman, Richard R. *Perspective on the Constitution: "A Republic, If You Can Keep It,"* Philadelphia, National Constitutional Center [no date].

Chernow, Ron. *Washington: A Life.* New York: Penguin Press, 2010.

Cousins, Norman. *"In God We Trust": The Religious Beliefs and Ideas of the American Founding Fathers.* Kingsport, TN: Kingsport Press, 1958.

Faÿ, Bernard. *Franklin, The Apostle of Modern Times*, With Illustrations. Boston: Little, Brown and Company, 1929.

Jensen, Merrill. *The Founding of a Nation: A History of the American Revolution, 1763-1776*. New York: Oxford University Press, 1968.

Lewis, Thomas A. *For King and Country: The Maturing of George Washington 1748-1760*. Edison, NJ: Castle Books, 2006.

O'Reilly, Bill and Dugard, Martin. *Killing England: The Brutal Struggle for American Independence*. New York: Henry Holt and Company, 2017.

Palmer, Dave R. *George Washington and Benedict Arnold: A Tale of Two Patriots* [with a subheading: "One became the father of our country; the other became a man without a country"]. Washington, D.C.: Regnery Publishing, Inc., 2006.

Smith, Page. *A New Age Now Begins: A People's History of the American Revolution*. 2 vols. New York: McGraw Hill Book Company, 1976.

THE AMERICAN REPUBLIC GETS UP AND RUNNING

Barnes, Howard A. *Horace Bushnell and the Virtuous Republic*. ATLA Monograph Series, No. 27. Metuchen, NJ: The American Theological Library Association, 1991.

Chernow, Ron. *Alexander Hamilton*. New York: The Penguin Press, 2004.

Ehle, John. *Trail of Tears: The Rise and Fall of the Cherokee Nation*. New York: Random House, 1988.

Eisenhower, John S.D. *So Far From God: The U.S. War with Mexico, 1846-1848*. New York: Random House, 1989.

Ellis, Joseph J. *American Sphinx: The Character of Thomas Jefferson*. New York: Alfred A. Knopf, 1997.

Goldhammer, Arthur, trans. *Tocqueville: Democracy in America*. New York: Literary Classics of the United States, Inc./Penguin Putnam Inc., 2004.

Hankins, Barry. *The Second Great Awakening and the Transcendentalists*. Greenwood Guides to Historic Events 1500-1900. Westport, CT: Greenwood Press, 2004.

Hardin, Stephen L. *Lust for Glory: An Epic Story of Early Texas and the Sacrifice That Defined a Nation*. Oxford: Osprey Publishing, 2005.

McCullough, David. *John Adams*. New York: Simon & Schuster, 2001.

McNeese, Tim. *The Abolitionist Movement: Ending Slavery. Reform Movements in American History*. New York: Chelsea House Publishers, 2008.

Meacham, Jon. *American Lion: Andrew Jackson in the White House*. New York: Random House, 2008.

Nagel, Paul C. *John Quincy Adams: A Public Life, A Private Life*. New York: Alfred A. Knopf, 1997.

Peterson, Merrill D. *The Great Triumvirate: Webster, Clay, and Calhoun*. New York: Oxford University Press, 1987.

Rudolph, L.C. *Francis Asbury: The Apostle Whose Only Home Was His Saddle, His Parish – The Continent*. Ashville, TN: Abingdon Press, 1966.

Schlesinger, Arthur M., Jr. *The Age of Jackson*. Boston: Little, Brown and Company, 1945.

Wessel, Helen, ed. *The Autobiography of Charles G. Finney: The Life Story of America's Greatest Evangelist in His Own Words*. Minneapolis, MN: Bethany House, 1977.

Wigger, John. *American Saint: Francis Asbury and the Methodists*. New York: Oxford University Press, 2012.

Wills, Garry. *James Madison.* Part of Schlesinger's "American President Series." New York: Henry Holt and Company, 2002.

Wilson, Gay Allen. Waldo Emerson. New York: Viking Press, 1981.

CIVIL WAR (1861-1865) AND RECOVERY

Axelrod, Alan. *Generals South, Generals North: The Commanders of the Civil War Reconsidered*. Guilford, CT: Globe Pequot Press, 2011.

Brand, H.W. *The Man Who Saved the Union: Ulysses Grant in War and Peace*. New York: Doubleday, 2012.

Catton, Bruce. *This Hallowed Ground: The Story of the Union Side of the Civil War*. Garden City, New York: Doubleday & Company, 1956.

Davis, William C. *Crucible of Command: Ulysses S. Grant and Robert E. Lee – The War They Fought, the Peace They Forged*. Philadelphia: Da Capo Press, 2014.

Etcheson, Nicole. *Bleeding Kansas: Contested Liberty in the Civil War Era*. Lawrence: The University Press of Kansas, 2004.

Finkelman, Paul. *Dred Scott v. Sandford: A Brief History with Documents*. Boston: Bedford, 1997.

Foner, Eric. *Reconstruction: America's Unfinished Revolution, 1863-1877*. Updated Edition. New York: Harper Perennial, 2014.

Foote, Shelby. *Vol. 1: Fort Sumter to Perryville; Vol. 2: Fredericksburg to Meridian; Vol. 3: Red River to Appomattox*. New York: Random House Vintage Books, 1986.

Goodwin, *Doris Kearns. Team of Rivals: The Political Genius of Abraham Lincoln*. New York: Simon & Schuster, 2005.

Longacre, Edward G. *General Ulysses S. Grant: The Soldier and the Man.* Cambridge, Mass.: Da Capo Press, 2006.

Miller, William Lee. *Lincoln's Virtues: An Ethical Biography.* New York: Alfred A. Knopf, 2002.

Miller, William Lee. *President Lincoln: The Duty of a Statesman.* New York: Alfred A. Knopf, 2008.

Milton, George Fort. *The Age of Hate: Andrew Johnson and the Radicals.* New York: Coward-McCann Company, 1930.

Robertson, James. *After the Civil War: The Heroes, Villains, Soldiers, and Civilians Who Changed America.* Washington, DC: The National Geographic Society, 2015.

Sandburg, Carl. *Abraham Lincoln: The Prairie Years & the War Years.* New York: Charles Scribner's Sons, 1939.

Smith, Jean Edward. *Grant.* New York: Simon & Schuster, 2001.

Sutton, Robert K. *Stark Mad Abolitionists: Lawrence, Kansas, and the Battle over Slavery in the Civil War Era.* Foreword by Bob Dole. New York: Skyhorse Publishing, 2017.

AMERICA COMES OF AGE

Bannister, Robert C. *Social Darwinism: Science and Myth in Anglo-American Social Thought.* Philadelphia: Temple University Press, 1988.

Brand, H.W. *American Colossus: The Triumph of Capitalism, 1865-1900.* New York: Doubleday, 2010.

Bromley, Michael L. *William Howard Taft and the First Motoring Presidency, 1909-1913.* Jefferson, NC: McFarland & Company, 2003.

Brown, Dee. *The American West.* New York: Touchstone, 1994.

Carnegie, Andrew. *Autobiography of Andrew Carnegie.* Boston: Northeastern University Press, 1986.

Chernow, Ron. *The House of Morgan: An American Banking Dynasty and the Rise of Modern Finance.* New York: Simon & Schuster, 1990.

Chernow, Ron. *Titan: The Life of John D. Rockefeller, Sr.* New York: Random House, 1998.

Cherny, Robert W. *American Politics in the Gilded Age, 1868-1900.* Wheeling, IL: Harlan-Davidson, 1997.

Farrell, John C. *Beloved Lady: A History of Jane Addams' Ideas on Reform and Peace.* Baltimore: Johns Hopkins University Press, 1967.

Gould, Lewis L. *The Presidency of William McKinley.* Lawrence: Regents Press of Kansas, 1980.

Hawley, Joshua David. *Theodore Roosevelt: Preacher of Righteousness.* Foreword by David M. Kennedy. New Haven, CT: Yale University Press, 2008.

Hofstadter, Richard. *Social Darwinism in American Thought.* Boston: Beacon Press, 1992.

Hofstadter, Richard, ed., *The Progressive Movement, 1900-1913.* Englewood Cliffs, N.J.: Prentice-Hall, 1963.

Josephson, Matthew. *The Robber Barons: The Great American Capitalists: 1861-1901.* New York: Harcourt, Brace, 1934.

Kazin, Michael. *A Godly Hero: The Life of William Jennings Bryan.* New York: Alfred A. Knopf, 2006.

McCullough, David. *Mornings on Horseback: The Story of an Extraordinary Family, a Vanished Way of Life and the Unique Child Who Became Theodore Roosevelt.* New York: Simon & Schuster, 2001.
McGerr, Michael. *A Fierce Discontent: The Rise and Fall of the Progressive Movement in America.* New York: Oxford University Press, 2003.

Mowry, George E. *The Era of Theodore Roosevelt and the Birth of Modern America, 1900-1912.* New York: Harper Torchbooks, 1958.

Nevins, Alan. *Grover Cleveland: A Study in Courage.* New York: Dodd, Mead, 1966.

Owens, Robert R. *Speak to the Rock: The Asuza Street Revival and Its Message.* Lanham, MD: University Press of America, 1998.

Pestritto, Ronald J. and Atto, William J., eds. *American Progressivism: A Reader.* Lanham, MD: Lexington Books, 2008.

Rove, Karl. *The Triumph of William McKinley: Why the Election of 1896 Still Matters.* New York: Simon & Schuster, 2015.

Spencer, Herbert. *Social Statistics; Or The Conditions Essential to Human Happiness Specified and the First of Them Developed.* New York: A.M. Kelley, 1969.
Yenne, Bill. *Indian Wars: The Campaign for the Indian West.* Yardley, PA: Westholme Publishing, 2006.

AMERICA ENTERS THE WORLD STAGE

May, Ernest R. *Imperial Democracy: The Emergence of America as a Great Power.* New York: Harcourt, Brace & World, 1961.

The Age of Imperialism

Eby, Cecil D. B*etween the Bullet and the Lie: American Volunteers in the Spanish Civil War.* New York: Holt, Rinehart and Winston, 1969.

Gould, Lewis L. *The Spanish-American War and President McKinley.* Lawrence: University Press of Kansas, 1982.

Hobsbawm, E.J. *The Age of Empire, 1875-1914*. New York: Vintage Books, 1989.

Musicant, Ivan. *Empire by Default: The Spanish-American War and the Dawn of the American Century*. New York: Henry Holt, 1998.

Reckner, James R. *Teddy Roosevelt's Great White Fleet.* Annapolis: Naval Institute Press, 1988.

Wilson and World War One

Bailey, Thomas A. *Woodrow Wilson and the Lost Peace*. New York: Macmillan, 1944.
Brands, H.W. *Woodrow Wilson*. Henry Holt and Co., 2003.

Churchill, Winston. *The Great War.* London: G. Newnes, 1934.

Esposito, Vincent J., ed. *A Concise History of World War I.* New York: Praeger, 1964.

Fleming, Thomas. *The Illusion of Victory: America in World War I.* New York: Basic Books, 2003.

Knock, Thomas J. *To End All Wars: Woodrow Wilson and the Quest for a New World Order*. New York: Oxford University Press, 1992.

Link, Arthur S. *Woodrow Wilson: A Brief Biography.* Cleveland: World Publishing, 1963.

Marshall, S.L.A. *American Heritage History of World War One*. New York: Simon and Schuster, 1964.

May, Ernest R. *The World War and American Isolation, 1914-1917*. Cambridge: Harvard University Press, 1959.

Pestritto, Ronald J. *Woodrow Wilson and the Roots of Modern Liberalism.* Lanham, MD: Rowan & Littlefield Publishers, Inc., 2005.

Pipes, Richard. *The Russian Revolution*. New York: Alfred A. Knopf, 1990.

Smith, Gene. *When the Cheering Stopped: The Last Years of Woodrow Wilson*. New York: Simon and Schuster, 1968.

Tuchman, Barbara W. *The Guns of August*. New York: Macmillan, 1962.

Walworth, Arthur. *Wilson and His Peacemakers: American Diplomacy at the Paris Peace Conference, 1919*. New York: Norton, 1986.

The Roaring Twenties

Allen, Frederick Lewis. *Only Yesterday: An Informal History of the Nineteen-Twenties*. New York: Harper & Row, 1964.

Allsop, Kenneth. *The Bootleggers: The Story of Chicago's Prohibition Era*. New Rochelle, NY: Arlington House, 1968.

Behr, Edward. *Prohibition: Thirteen Years That Changed America*. New York: Arcade Publishers, 1996.

Felix, David *Protest: Sacco-Vanzetti and the Intellectuals*. Bloomington: Indiana University Press, 1965.

Galbraith, John Kenneth. *The Great Crash – 1929*. Boston: Houghton Mifflin Company, 1961.
Leuchtenburg, William E. *The Perils of Prosperity - 1914-1932*. Chicago: The University of Chicago Press, 1958.

Levine, Lawrence. *Defender of the Faith: William Jennings Bryan, the Last Decade, 1915-1925*. Cambridge: Harvard University Press, 1987.

Murray, Robert K. *The Politics of Normalcy: Governmental Theory and Practice in the Harding-Coolidge Era*. New York: Norton, 1973.

Perrett, Geoffrey. *America in the Twenties: A History*. New York: Simon and Schuster, 1982.

Smith, Richard Norton. *An Uncommon Man: The Triumph of Herbert Hoover*. New York: Simon and Schuster, 1984.

Sobel, Robert. *The Great Bull Market: Wall Street in the 1920s*. New York: W.W. Norton, 1968.

White, William Allen. *A Puritan in Babylon: The Story of Calvin Coolidge*. New York: Capricorn Books, 1965.

The Great Depression

Bernstein, Irving. *Turbulent Years: A History of the American Worker, 1933-1941*. Boston: Houghton Mifflin, 1970.

Brinkley, Alan. *Voices of Protest: Huey Long, Father Coughlin and the Great Depression*. New York: Vintage Books, 1983.

Burns, James MacGregor. *Roosevelt: The Lion and the Fox*. New York: Harcourt Brace Jovanovich, 1984.

Conkin, Paul K. *FDR and the Origins of the Welfare State*. New York: Crowell, 1967.

Dewey, John. *A Common Faith*. New Haven: Yale University Press, 1934.

Dewey, John. *Liberalism and Social Action*. New York: Capricorn Books, 1935.

Dickinson, Matthew J. *Bitter Harvest: FDR, Presidential Power, and the Growth of the Presidential Branch*. New York: Cambridge University Press, 1997.

Hurt, R. Douglas. *The Dust Bowl: An Agricultural and Social History*. Chicago: Nelson-Hall, 1981.

Folsom, Burton, Jr. *New Deal or Raw Deal? How FDR's Economic Legacy Has Damaged America*. New York: Simon and Schuster, 2008.

Freidel, Frank. *Franklin D. Roosevelt: A Rendez-Vous with Destiny*. Boston: Little, Brown, 1990.

Kindleberger, Charles P. *The World in Depression, 1929-1939*. Berkeley, University of California Press, 1986.

McElvaine, Robert S. *The Great Depression: America, 1929-1941*. New York: Times Books, 1993.

Smith, Jean Edward. *FDR*. New York: Random House, 2008.

The dictators, and path to World War Two

Bullock, Alan. *Hitler and Stalin: Parallel Lives*. New York: Alfred A. Knopf, 1992.

Butow, Robert J.C. *Tojo and the Coming of the War*. Stanford: Stanford University Press, 1969.

Dallek, Robert. *Franklin Roosevelt and American Foreign Policy, 1932-1945*. New York: Oxford University Press, 1979.

Kennedy, John F. *Why England Slept*. Garden City, NY: Doubleday, 1962.

Large, Stephen S. *Emperor Hirohito and Showa Japan: A Political Biography*. London: Routledge, 1992.

Manchester, William. *The Last Lion: Winston Spencer Churchill Alone - 1932-1940*. Boston: Little, Brown, 1988.

McDonough, Frank. *Chamberlain, Appeasement, and the Road to War*. New York: Manchester University Press, 1998.

Medvedev, Roy A. *Let History Judge: The Origins and Consequences of Stalinism*. New York: Vintage Books, 1973.

Shirer, William L. *The Rise and Fall of the Third Reich: A History of Nazi Germany*. New York: Simon and Schuster, 1960.

Ulam, Adam B. *Stalin: The Man and His Era*. New York: The Viking Press, 1973.

WORLD WAR TWO AND THE START OF THE COLD WAR

Baime, A.J. *The Accidental President: Harry S. Truman and the Four Months That Changed the World.* Boston: Houghton Mifflin Harcourt, 2017.

Calvocoressi, Peter. *Fall Out: World War II and the Shaping of Postwar Europe.* New York: Longman, 1997.

Conot, Robert E. *Justice at Nuremberg.* New York: Carroll & Graf, 1983.
Cray, Ed. *General of the Army: George C. Marshall, Soldier and Statesman.* New York: W.W. Norton & Co., 1990.

McCullough, David. *Truman.* New York: Simon and Schuster, 1992.

Mee, Charles L., Jr. *Meeting at Potsdam.* New York: M. Evans, 1973.

World War Two

Alperovitz, Gar. *The Decision to Use the Atomic Bomb.* New York: Alfred A. Knopf, 1995.

Ambrose, Stephen E. *Band of Brothers: E Company, 506th Regiment, 101st Airborne from Normandy to Hitler's Eagle's Nest.* New York: Simon and Schuster, 1992.

Ambrose, Stephen E. *The Supreme Commander: The War Years of General Dwight D. Eisenhower.* Garden City, NY: Doubleday, 1970.

Beevor, Antony. *Stalingrad: The Fateful Siege: 1942-1943.* New York: Viking Penguin, 1998.

Brinkley, Douglas and Facey-Crowther, David R., eds. *The Atlantic Charter.* New York: St. Martin's Press, 1994.

Burns, James MacGregor. *Roosevelt: The Soldier of Freedom, 1940-1945.* New York: Harcourt, Brace & World, 1970.
Churchill, Winston. *The Second World War.* Boston: Houghton Mifflin Co., 1948. Vol. 1, *The Gathering Storm*; Vol. 2, *Their Finest Hour*; Vol. 3, *The Grand Alliance*; Vol. 4, *The Hinge of Fate*; Vol. 5, *Triumph and Tragedy*; Vol. 6, *Closing the Ring.*

D'Este, Carlo. *Fatal Decision: Anzio and the Battle for Rome.* New York: Harper Collins, 1991.

Dunnigan, James F. *Victory at Sea: World War II in the Pacific.* New York: Morrow, 1995.

Fehrenbach, T.R. *F.D.R.'s Undeclared War, 1939-1941.* New York: David McKay, 1967.

Folsom, Burton W., Jr., and Anita. *FDR Goes to War: How Expanded Executive*

Power, Spiraling National Debt, and Restricted Civil Liberties Shaped Wartime America. New York: Simon and Schuster, 2011.

Gailey, Harry A. *The War in the Pacific: From Pearl Harbor to Tokyo Bay*. Novato CA: Presidion Press, 1995.

Harper, Stephen. *Miracle of Deliverance: The Case for the Bombing of Hiroshima and Nagasaki*. London: Sidgwick & Jackson, 1985.
Hastings, Max. *Overlord: D-Day, June 6, 1944*. New York: Simon and Schuster, 1984.

Heinrichs, Waldo H. *Threshold of War: Franklin D. Roosevelt and American Entry into World War II*. New York: Oxford University Press, 1988.

Hoopes, Townsend and Brinkley, Douglas. *FDR and the Creation of the U.N.* New Haven: Yale University Press, 1997.

Hoyt, Edwin Palmer. *Yamamoto: The Man Who Planned Pearl Harbor*. New York: McGraw-Hill, 1990.

Jackson, W.G.F. *The Battle for Italy*. New York: Harper & Row, 1967.

Keegan, John. *Six Armies in Normandy: From D-Day to the Liberation of Paris*. New York: Penguin Books, 1983.

Kerr, E. Bartlett. *Flames over Tokyo: The U.S. Army Air Force's Incendiary Campaign Against Japan, 1944-45*. New York: Donald I. Fine, 1991.

LaFeber, Walter. *The Clash: A History of U.S.-Japan Relations*. New York: W.W. Norton, 1997.

Lash, Joseph R. *Roosevelt and Churchill, 1939-1941: The Partnership That Saved the World*. New York, Norton, 1976.

Manchester, William. *American Caesar: Douglas MacArthur, 1880-1964*. Boston: Little, Brown, 1978.
Polenberg, Richard. *America at War: The Home Front, 1941-1945*. Englewood Cliffs, NJ: Prentice-Hall, 1968.

Ryan, Cornelius. *A Bridge Too Far*. New York: Simon and Schuster, 1974.

Shirley, Craig. *December 1941: 31 Days That Changed America and Saved the World*. Nashville: Thomas Nelson, 2011.

Spector, Ronald H. *Eagle Against the Sun: The American War with Japan*. New York: The Free Press, 1985.

Taylor, A.J.P. *The Origins of the Second World War*. New York: Atheneum, 1983 [1961].

The start of the Cold War

Acheson, Dean. *The Struggle for a Free Europe*. New York: W.W. Norton, 1971.

Cook, Don. *Forging the Alliance: NATO 1945 to 1950*. London: Secker & Warburg, 1989.

Finn, Richard B. *Winners in Peace: MacArthur, Yoshida, and Postwar Japan*. Berkeley: University of California Press, 1992.

Fossedal, Gregory A. *Our Finest Hour: Will Clayton, the Marshall Plan, and the Triumph of Democracy*. Stanford: Hoover Institution Press, 1993.

Harbutt, Frank J. *The Iron Curtain: Churchill, America and the Origins of the Cold War*. New York: Oxford University Press, 1986.

Hoffman, Stanley and Maier, Charles. *The Marshall Plan: A Retrospective*. Boulder, CO: Westview Press, 1984.

Jackson, Robert. *The Berlin Airlift*. Wellinborough, England: Patrick Stephens, 1988.

LaFeber, Walter. *America, Russia and the Cold War, 1945-1990*. New York: McGraw-Hill, 1991.

Mee, Charles L., Jr. *The Marshall Plan: The Launching of the Pax Americana*. New York: Simon and Schuster, 1984.

Messer, Robert L. *The End of an Alliance: James F. Byrnes, Roosevelt, Truman, and the Origins of the Cold War*. Chapel Hill: University of North Carolina Press, 1982.

Morwood, William. *Duel for the Middle Kingdom: The Struggle Between Chiang Kai-shek and Mao Tse-Tung for Control of China*. New York: Everest House, 1980.

Pogue, Forrest C. *George C. Marshall: Statesman*. New York: Viking, 1987.
Walker, Martin. *The Cold War: A History*. New York: Henry Holt, 1994.

MIDDLE CLASS AMERICA TRIUMPHANT

Acheson, Dean. *The Korean War*. New York: W.W. Norton, 1971.

Albert, Peter J. and Hoffman, Ronald, eds. *We Shall Overcome: Martin Luther King and the Black Freedom Struggle*. New York: Pantheon, 1990.

Ambrose, Stephen E. *Eisenhower: Soldier and President*. New York: Simon and Schuster, 1990.

Beschloss. Michael R. *The Crisis Years: Kennedy and Khrushchev, 1960-1963*. New York: Harper Collins, 1991.

Blair, Clay. *The Forgotten War: America in Korea, 1950-1953*. New York: Times Books, 1987.

Brinkley, Douglas. *Dean Acheson: The Cold War Years, 1953-1971*. New Haven: Yale University Press, 1992.

Buckley, William, Jr. and Brent Bozell, L. Brent. *McCarthy and His enemies: The Record and Its Meaning*. Chicago: Henry Regnery Co., 1954.

Cook, Fred J. *The Nightmare Decade: The Life and Times of Senator Joe McCarthy*. New York: Random House, 1971.

Dallek, Robert. *An Unfinished Life: John F. Kennedy, 1917–1963*. Boston: Little, Brown and Company, 2003.

Freedman, Lawrence. *Kennedy's Wars: Berlin, Cuba, Laos, and Vietnam*. New York: Oxford University Press, 2000.

Gibbs, Nancy and Michael Duffy, *The Preacher and the Presidents: Billy Graham in the White House*. New York: Hachette, 2007.

Goldman, Eric F. *The Crucial Decade - and After: America, 1945-1960*. New York: Vintage Books, 1960.

Goodman, Walter. *The Committee: The Extraordinary Career of the House Committee on Un-American Activities.* New York: Farrar, Straus and Giroux, 1968.

Griffith, Robert. *The Politics of Fear: Joseph R. McCarthy and the Senate.* Amherst: University of Massachusetts Press, 1987.

Halberstam, David. *The Fifties.* New York: Villard Books, 1993.

Herzog, Jonathan. *The Spiritual-Industrial Complex: America's Religious Battle Against Communism in the Early Cold War*. New York: Oxford University Press, 2011.

Hitchcock, William I. *The Age of Eisenhower: America and the World in the 1950s.* New York: Simon and Schuster, 2018.

Hughes, Emmet John. *The Ordeal of Power: A Political Memoire of the Eisenhower Years*. New York: Atheneum, 1963.

Inboden, William. *Religion and American Foreign Policy, 1945-1960: The Soul of Containment.* New York: Cambridge University Press, 2008.

Jones, Howard. *The Bay of Pigs*. New York: Oxford University Press, 2008.

Kahn, Gordon. *Hollywood on Trial: The Story of the Ten Who Were Indicted.* New York: Arno Press, 1972.

Kennedy, Robert F. *Thirteen Days: A Memoir of the Cuban Missile Crisis.* New York: W.W. Norton & Company, 1971.

Khrushchev, Nikita with Talbott, Strobe, ed. & trans. *Khrushchev Remembers*. Boston: Little, Brown, 1970.

Kluger, Richard. *Simple Justice: The History of Brown v. Board of Education and Black America's Struggle for Justice*. New York: Vintage Books, 1977.

Marks, Frederick W., III. *Power and Peace: The Diplomacy of John Foster Dulles*. Westport, CT: Praeger, 1993.

McLoughlin, William G., Jr. *Billy Graham: Revivalist in a Secular Age*. New York: Ronald Press, 1960.

Miller, William Lee. *Piety along the Potomac: Notes on Politics and Morals in the Fifties*. Boston: Houghton Mifflin, 1964.

Oates, Stephen B. *Let the Trumpet Sound: The Life of Martin Luther King, Jr.* New York: Harper & Row, 1982.

Paige, Glenn. *1950: Truman's Decision: The United States Enters the Korean War*. New York, Chelsea House, 1970.

Perrett, Geoffrey. *A Dream of Greatness: The American People, 1945-1963*. New York: Coward, McCann & Geoghegan, 1979.

Purifoy, Lewis McCarroll. *Harry Truman's China Policy: McCarthyism and the Diplomacy of Hysteria, 1947-1951*. New York: New Viewpoints, 1976.

Reeves, Thomas. *President Kennedy: Profile of Power*. New York: Simon & Schuster, 1993.

Stone, I.F. *The Haunted Fifties: A Non-Conformist History of Our Times, 1951-1963*. Boston: Little, Brown, 1963.

Thompson, Robert Smith. *The Missiles of October: The Declassified Story of John F. Kennedy and the Cuban Missile Crisis*. New York: Simon & Schuster, 1992.

Toland, John. *In Mortal Combat: Korea, 1950-1953*. New York: Morrow, 1991.

Williams, Juan. *Eyes on the Prize: American Civil Rights Years, 1954-1965*. New York: Viking, 1987.

Wyden, Peter. *Wall: The Inside Story of Divided Berlin*. New York: Simon & Schuster, 1989.

AMERICA SHIFTS TO THE SECULAR-HUMANIST LEFT

Alley, Robert S. *Without a Prayer: Religious Expression in Public Schools*. Amherst, NY: Prometheus Books, 1996.

Ball, Howard and Cooper, Phillip J. *Of Power and Right: Hugo Black, William O. Douglas, and America's Constitutional Revolution*. New York: Oxford University Press, 1992.

Brands, H.W. *The Wages of Globalism: Lyndon Johnson and the Limits of American Power*. New York: Oxford University Press, 1995.

Bukszpan, Daniel. *Woodstock: 50 Years of Peace and Music*. Watertown, MA: Hourglass Press, 2019.

Chester, Lewis, Hodgson, Godfrey and Page, Bruce. *An American Melodrama: The Presidential Campaign of 1968*. New York: Viking, 1969

Dikötter, Frank. *Mao's Great Famine: A History of China's Most Devastating Catastrophe, 1958-1962*. London: Bloomsbury, 2010.

Dunne, Gerald T. *Hugo Black and the Judicial Revolution*. New York: Simon & Schuster, 1977.

Dallek, Robert. *Lyndon B. Johnson: Portrait of a President*. Oxford: Oxford University Press, 2004.

Friedan, Betty. *The Feminine Mystique*. New York: Norton, 1963.

Gardner, Lloyd C. *Pay Any Price: Lyndon Johnson and the Wars for Vietnam*. Chicago: I.R. Dee, 1995.

Gitlin, Todd. *The Sixties: Years of Hope, Days of Rage.* New York: Bantam Books, 1987.

Hamby, Alonzo. *Liberalism and Its Challengers: From F.D.R. to Bush*. New York: Oxford University Press, 1992

Kahlenberg, Richard D. *The Remedy: Class, Race, and Affirmative Action*. New York: Basic Books, 1996.

Kaiser, Charles. *1968 in America: Music, Politics, Chaos, Counterculture, and the Shaping of a Generation*. New York: Grove Atlantic, 1988.

Karnow, Stanley. *Vietnam: A History, The First Complete Account of Vietnam at War*. New York: Penguin Books, 1984.

Kearns, Doris. *Lyndon Johnson and the American Dream*. New York: Harper & Row, 1976.

Kunz, Diane B., ed. *The Diplomacy of the Crucial Decade: American Foreign Relations During the 1960s*. New York: Columbia University Press, 1994.

Kurlansky, Mark. *1968: The Year That Rocked the World*. New York: Random House, 2005.

Laron, Guy. *The Six-Day War: The Breaking of the Middle East*. New Haven: Yale University Press, 2017.

Lerner, Mitchell B. *Looking Back at LBJ: White House Politics in a New Light*. Lawrence: The University Press of Kansas, 2005.

Logevall, Fredrik. *Choosing War: The Lost Chance for Peace and Escalation of the War in Vietnam*. Berkeley: University of California Press, 1999.

Magnet, Myron. *The Dream & the Nightmare: The Sixties Legacy to the Underclass.* New York: William Morrow and Company, 1993.

McKnight, Gerald D. *The Last Crusade: Martin Luther King, Jr., the FBI, and the Poor People's Campaign.* Boulder: Westview Press, 1998.

McNamara, Robert S. *In Retrospect: The Tragedy and Lessons of Vietnam.* New York: Times Books, 1995.

Oberdorfer, Don. *Tet!* New York: Doubleday, 1971.

Oren, Michael B. *Six Days of War: June 1967 and the Making of the Modern Middle East.* New York: Presidio Press, 2003.

Pearson, Hugh. *The Shadow of the Panther: Huey Newton and the Price of Black Power in America.* New York: Addison-Wesley, 1994.

Pollack, Jack Harrison. *Earl Warren: The Judge Who Changed America.* Englewood Cliffs, NJ: Prentice-Hall, 1979.

Salisbury, Harrison E. *Vietnam Reconsidered: Lessons from a War.* New York: Harper & Row, 1984.

Schwartz, Thomas Alan. *Lyndon Johnson and Europe: In the Shadow of Vietnam.* Cambridge: Harvard University Press, 2003.

Sheehan, Neil, ed. *The Pentagon Papers.* New York: Quadrangle Books, 1971.

Vinen, Richard. *1968: Radical Protest and Its Enemies.* New York: HarperCollins, 2018.

Viorst, Milton. *Fire in the Streets: America in the 1960s.* New York: Simon & Schuster, 1979.

Walder, Andrew G. *China Under Mao: A Revolution Derailed.* Cambridge, MA: Harvard University Press, 2017.

Woods, Randall B. *Lyndon Johnson: Architect of American Ambition.* New York: Free Press, 2006.

AMERICA DIVIDED

Craig, Barbara Hinkson and O'Brien, David M. *Abortion and American Politics.* Chatham, NJ: Chatham House Publishers, 1993.
Davis, Flora. *Moving the Mountain: The Women's Movement in America Since 1960.* New York: Simon & Schuster, 1991.

Franck, Thomas and Weisband, Edward. *Foreign Policy by Congress.* New York: Oxford University Press, 1979.

Garrow, David J. *Liberty and Sexuality: The Right to Privacy and the Making of "Roe v. Wade."* New York: Macmillan, 1994.

Marcus, Eric. *Making History: The Struggle for Gay and Lesbian Equal Rights: 1945-1990*. New York: Harper-Collins, 1992.

Quandt, William. *Peace Process: American Diplomacy and the Arab Israeli Conflict Since 1967*. 3rd ed. Berkeley: University of California Press, 2005.

Steinem, Gloria. *Outrageous Acts and Everyday Rebellions*. New York: Holt, Rinehart and Winston, 1983.

Tribe, Laurence H. *Abortion: The Clash of Absolutes*. New York: W.W. Norton, 1990.

Vogelgesang, Sandy. *American Dream, Global Nightmare: The Dilemma of Human Rights Policy*. New York: W.W. Norton & Company, 1980.

The Nixon Years

Ambrose, Stephen E. *Nixon*. Vol. 2: *The Triumph of a Politician, 1962-1972*. New York: Simon & Schuster, 1989.

Ambrose, Stephen E. *Nixon*. Vol. 3: *Ruin and Recovery, 1973-1990*. New York: Simon & Schuster, 1991.

Bernstein, Carl and Woodward, Bob. *All the President's Men*. New York: Simon & Schuster, 1974.

Blum, Howard. *The Eve of Destruction: The Untold Story of the Yom Kippur War*. HarperCollins Publishers, 2003.

Brodie, Fawn M. *Richard Nixon: The Shaping of His Character*. New York: W.W. Norton, 1981.

Dalek, Robert. *Nixon and Kissinger: Partners in Power*. New York: HarperCollins, 2007.

Emery, Fred. *Watergate: The Corruption of American Politics and the Fall of Richard Nixon*. New York: Times Books, 1994.

Erlichman, John. *Witness to Power: The Nixon Years*. New York: Simon & Schuster, 1982.

Haldeman, H.R. *The Haldeman Diaries: Inside the Nixon White House*. New York: G.P. Putnam's Sons, 1994.

Hersh, Seymour M. *The Price of Power: Kissinger in the Nixon White House*. New York: Summit Books, 1983.

Hunt, Andrew E. *The Turning: A History of Vietnam Veterans Against the War*. New York: New York University Press, 1999.

Jaworski, Leon. *The Right and the Power: The Prosecution of Watergate*. New York: Reader's Digest Press, 1976.

Kissinger, Henry. *White House Years*. Boston: Little, Brown and Company, 1979.

Lang, Gladys Engel and Land, Kurt. *The Battle for Public Opinion: The President, the Press, and the Polls During Watergate*. New York: Columbia University Press, 1983.

McQuaid, Kim. *The Anxious Years: American in the Vietnam-Watergate Era*. New York: Basic Books, 1989.

Nixon, Richard. *In the Arena: A Memoir of Victory, Defeat, and Renewal*. New York: Simon & Schuster, 1990.

Rabinovich, Abraham. *The Yom Kippur War: The Epic Encounter that Transformed the Middle East*. New York: Schocken Books, 2004.

The Ford Years

Cannon, James. *Time and Chance: Gerald Ford's Appointment with History*. New York: Harper Collins, 1994.

Mieczkowski, Yanek. *Gerald Ford and the Challenges of the 1970s*. Lexington: The University Press of Kentucky, 2005.

Murphy, MH. *The Ashes of War: The plight of the Vietnamese people at the end of and after the Vietnam War*. Urbana, IL: Tales Press, 2017.

Ngor, Haing and Warner, Roger. *Survival in the Killing Fields*. New York: Carroll & Graf Publishers, 2003.

The Carter Years

Bourne, Peter G. *Jimmy Carter: A Comprehensive Biography from Plains to Post-Presidency*. New York: Scribner, 1997.

Carter, Jimmy, *Keeping Faith: Memoirs of a President*. Fayetteville: The University of Arkansas Press, 1995.

Eizenstat, Stuart E. *President Carter: The White House Years*. Foreword by Madeleine Albright. New York: Thomas Dunne Books, 2018.

Hadjimichalakis, Michael G. *The Federal Reserve, Money, and Interest Rates: The Volcker Years and Beyond*. New York: Praeger, 1984.

Kaufman, Burton I. and Scott. *The Presidency of James Earl Carter*. 2nd ed. Lawrence: University Press of Kansas, 2006.

Kyle, James H. with Eidson, John Robert. *The Guts to Try: The Untold Story of the Iran Hostage Rescue Mission by the On-Scene Desert Commander*. New York: Orion Books, 1990.

Muravchik, Joshua. *The Uncertain Crusade: Jimmy Carter and the Dilemmas of Human Rights*. Lanham, MD: Hamilton Press, 1986.

Pilevsky, Philip. *I Accuse: Jimmy Carter and the Rise of Militant Islam.* Dallas: Durban House Publishing Company, 2007.

Pollack, Kenneth M. *The Persian Puzzle: The Conflict Between Iran and America.* New York: Random House, 2004.

Sick, Gary. *All Fall Down: America's Tragic Encounter with Iran.* New York: Random House, 1985.

Smith, Gaddis. *Morality, Reason, and Power: American Diplomacy in the Carter Years.* New York: Hill and Wang, 1986.

Wells, Tim. *444 Days: The Hostages Remember.* San Diego: Harcourt Brace Jovanovich, 1985.

Westad, Odd Arne, ed. *The Fall of Détente: Soviet-American Relations During the Carter Years.* Oslo: Scandinavian University Press, 1997.

THE WORLD'S SOLE SUPERPOWER

Albright, Madeleine. *The Mighty & the Almighty: Reflections on America, God, and World Affairs.* Introduction by President Bill Clinton. New York: Harper Collins, 2006.

Beschloss, Michael R. and Talbott, Strobe. *At the Highest Levels: The Inside Story of the End of the Cold War.* Boston: Little, Brown, 1993.

Braithwaite, Rodric. *Afgantsy: The Russians in Afghanistan 1979-89.* New York: Oxford University Press, 2011.

Garthoff, Raymond L. *The Great Transition: American-Soviet Relations and the End of the Cold War.* Washington, D.C.: Brookings Institution Press, 1994.

Halberstam, David. *War in a Time of Peace: Bush, Clinton, and the Generals.* New York: Scribner, 2001.

Magnet, Myron. *Clarence Thomas and the Lost Constitution.* New York: Encounter Books, 2019.

Oberdorfer, Don. *From the Cold War to a New Era: The United States and the End of the Soviet Union, 1983-1991.* Baltimore: Johns Hopkins University Press, 1998.

Samuelson, Robert J. *The Good Life and Its Discontents: The American Dream in the Age of Entitlement.* New York: Times Books, 1995.

Vogel, Ezra F. *Deng Xiaoping and the Transformation of China.* Cambridge, MA: Belknap Press, 2011.

The Reagan years

Brands, H.W. *Reagan: The Life.* New York: Doubleday, 2015.

Burns, E. Bradford. *At War in Nicaragua: The Reagan Doctrine and the Politics of Nostalgia*. New York: Harper & Row, 1987.

Cannon, Lou. *President Reagan: The Role of a Lifetime*. New York: Simon & Schuster, 1991.

Djilas, Milovan. *The Fall of the New Class: A History of Communism's Self-Destruction*. New York: Alfred A. Knopf, 1988.

Draper, Theodore. *A Very Thin Line: The Iran-Contra Affairs*. New York: Hill and Wang, 1991.

Ehrman, John. *The Eighties: America in the Age of Reagan*. New Haven: Yale University Press, 2005.

FitzGerald, Frances. *Way Out There in the Blue: Reagan, Star Wars, and the End of the Cold War*. New York: Simon & Schuster, 2001.

Reagan, Ronald. *An American Life*. New York: Simon & Schuster, 1990.

Schweizer, Peter. *Reagan's War—The Epic Story of his Forty Year Struggle and Final Triumph over Communism*. New York: Anchor Books, 2002.

The Bush Sr. years

Bush, George and Scowcroft, Brent. *A World Transformed: The Collapse of the Soviet Empire, the Unification of Germany, Tiananmen Square, the Gulf War*. New York: Alfred A. Knopf, 1998.

Charles River Editors. *Tiananmen Square Massacre: The History and Legacy of the Chinese Government's Crackdown on the 1989 Protests*. Kindle (no date).

Greene, John Robert. *The Presidency of George Bush*. Lawrence: University Press of Kansas, 2000.

Meacham, Jon. *Destiny and Power: The American Odyssey of George Herbert Walker Bush*. New York: Random House, 2015.

The Clinton years

Cannon, Lou. *Official Negligence: How Rodney King and the Riots Changed Los Angeles and the LAPD*. Boulder, CO: Westview Press, 1999.

Clinton, Bill. *My Life*. New York: Alfred A. Knopf, 2004.

Gingrich, Newt and Armey, Dick. *Contract with America: The Bold Plan by Rep. Newt Gingrich, Rep. Dick Armey, and the House Republicans to Change the Nation*. New York: Times Books, 1994.

Gingrich, Newt. *To Renew America*. New York: Harper Collins, 1995.

Harris, John F. *The Survivor: Bill Clinton in the White House*. New York: Random House, 2006.

Maney, Patrick J. *Bill Clinton: New Gilded Age President*. Lawrence: The University Press of Kansas, 2016.

Rashid, Ahmed. *Taliban: Militant Islam, Oil and Fundamentalism in Central Asia*. 2nd edition. New Haven: Yale University Press, 2000.

Woodward, Bob. *The Agenda: Inside the Clinton White House*. New York: Simon & Schuster, 1994.

AMERICA STUMBLES

Clinton, Bill. *Back to Work: Why We Need Smart Government for a Strong Economy*. New York: Alfred A. Knopf, 2011.

Gingrich, Newt. *Breakout: Pioneers of the Future, Prison Guards of the Past, and the Epic Battle That Will Decide America's Fate*. Washington, D.C.: Regnery Publishing, 2013.

Gordon, Michael and Trainor, General Bernard E. *The Endgame: The Inside Story of the Struggle for Iraq, from George W. Bush to Barack Obama*. New York: Vintage Books, 2013.

McFaul, Michael. *From Cold War to Hot Peace: An American Ambassador in Putin's Russia*. New York: Houghton Mifflin Harcourt, 2018.
Rashid, Ahmed. *Pakistan on the Brink: The Future of America, Pakistan, and Afghanistan*. New York: Penguin Group, 2013.

The Bush Jr. years

Anderson, Terry H. *Bush's Wars*. New York: Oxford University Press, 2013.

Baker, Peter. *Days of Fire: Bush and Cheney in the White House*. New York: Anchor Books, 2014.

Basile, Tom. *Tough Sell: Fighting the Media War in Iraq*. Lincoln, NE: Potomac Books, 2017.

Bernanke, Ben S., Geithner, Timothy F. et al. *First Responders: Inside the U.S. Strategy for Fighting the 2007-2009 Global Financial Crisis*. New Haven: Yale University Press, 2020.

Bush, George W. *Decision Points*. New York: Crown Publishers, 2010.

Byman, Daniel. *Al-Qaeda, the Islamic State, and the Global Jihadist Movement: What Everyone Needs to Know*. New York: Oxford University Press, 2015.

Mann, James. *The Rise of the Vulcans: The History of Bush's War Cabinet*. New York: Penguin Books, 2004.

Mello, Patrick A. *Democratic Participation in Armed Conflict: Military Involvement in Kosovo, Afghanistan, and Iraq.* Palgrave Studies in International Relations. New York: Palgrave Macmillan, 2014.

Record, Jeffrey. *Wanting War: Why the Bush Administration Invaded Iraq.* Dulles, VA: Potomac Books, Inc., 2010.

Sayle, Timothy Andrews, Engel, Jeffrey A., Brands Hal and Inboden, William, eds. *The Last Card: Inside George W. Bush's Decision to Surge in Iraq.* Ithaca, NY: Cornell University Press, 2019.

Smith, Jean Edward. *Bush.* New York: Simon & Schuster, 2016.

Soufan, Ali. *The Black Banners: The Inside Story of 9/11 and the War Against al-Qaeda.* New York: W.W. Norton, 2011.

Sorkin, Andrew Ross. *Too Big to Fail: The Inside Story of How Wall Street and Washington Fought to Save the Financial System—and Themselves.* New York: Viking Penguin, 2009.

Woods, Thomas E. and Paul, Ron. *Meltdown: A Free-Market Look at Why the Stock Market Collapsed, the Economy Tanked, and Government Bailouts Will Make Things Worse.* Washington, D.C.: Regnery Publishing Inc., 2009.

Woodward, Bob. *The War Within: Secret White House History, 2006–2008.* New York: Simon & Schuster, 2008.

Wright, Lawrence. *The Looming Tower: Al-Qaeda and the Road to 9/11.* New York: Alfred A. Knopf, 2006.

Zakaria, Fareed. *The Post-American World.* New York: W.W. Norton & Company, 2008.

OBAMA STRIVES TO "CHANGE" AMERICA

Abrams, Elliott. *Realism and Democracy: American Foreign Policy after the Arab Spring.* New York: Cambridge University Press, 2019.

Baker, Peter. *Obama: The Call of History.* New York: Callaway Arts & Entertainment, 2019.

Brown, Kerry. *CEO, China: The Rise of Xi Jinping.* London, I.B. Tauris & Company, 2016.

Burton, Fred and Katz, Samuel M. *Under Fire: The Untold Story of the Attack in Benghazi.* New York: St. Martin's Press, 2013.

Conlan, Timothy J., Posner, Paul L., and Regan, Priscilla, eds. *Governing under Stress: The Implementation of Obama's Economic Stimulus Program.* [Public Management and Change]. Washington, D.C.: Georgetown University Press, 2017.

Gabriel, Mark A. *Islam and Terrorism: The Truth about ISIS, the Middle East and Islamic Jihad*. Revised and Updated. Lake Mary, FL: Charisma House Book Group, 2015.

Greenberg, Mark. *Obama: The Historic Presidency of Barack Obama—2,920 Days*. New York: Sterling Publishing Co., 2017.

Jackson, Thomas. *Policing Ferguson, Policing America; What Really Happened—and What the Country Can Learn from It*. Skyhorse Publishing, 2017.

Lister, Charles R. *The Syrian Jihad: Al-Qaeda, the Islamic State and the Evolution of an Insurgency*. New York: Oxford University Press, 2016.

Lynch, Marc. *The New Arab Wars: Uprisings and Anarchy in the Middle East*. New York: PublicAffairs (Perseus Group), 2016.

McCain, John and Salter, Mark. *The Restless Wave: Good Times, Just Causes, Great Fights, and Other Appreciations*. New York: Simon & Schuster, 2018.

Obama, Barack. *Dreams from My Father: A Story of Race and Inheritance*. New York: Broadway Books, 2004.
Obama, Barack. *The Audacity of Hope: Thoughts on Reclaiming the American Dream*. New York: Broadway Books, 2007.

O'Connell, Kevin B. *The Case for Probable Cause: A Study of the Darren Wilson Michael Brown Grand Jury Decision*. (Kindle Edition), 2014.

Rockman, Bert A. and Rudalevige, Andrew, eds. *Obama Legacy*. [Presidential Appraisals and Legacies]. Lawrence, KS: University Press of Kansas, 2019.

Souza, Pete. *Obama: An Intimate Portrait*. New York: Little, Brown and Company, 2017.

Woodward, Bob. *Obama's Wars*. New York: Simon & Schuster, 2010.

INTO THE AGE OF TRUMP

Ahmad, Aisha. *Jihad & Co.: Black Markets and Islamist Power*. New York: Oxford University Press, 2019.

Allen, Jonathan and Amie Parnes. *Shattered: Inside Hillary Clinton's Doomed Campaign*. New York: Crown Books, 2017.

Allison, Graham. *Destined for War: Can America and China Escape Thucydides's Trap?* Boston: Houghton Mifflin Harcourt, 2017.

Cohen, Stephen F. *War with Russia? From Putin & Ukraine to Trump & Russiagate*. New York: Hot Books (Skyhorse Publishing), 2019.

Economy, Elizabeth C. *The Third Revolution: Xi Jinping and the New Chinese State*. New York: Oxford University Press, 2018.

Hemmingway, Mollie and Severino, Carrie. *Justice on Trial: The Kavanaugh Confirmation and the Future of the Supreme Court*. Washington, D.C.: Regnery Publishing, 2019.

Katyal, Neal and Koppelman, Sam. *Impeach: The Case Against Donald Trump*. New York: Morgan Legal Consulting (Houghton Mifflin Harcourt), 2019.

O'Reilly, Bill. T*he United States of Trump: How the President Really Sees America.* New York: Henry Holt and Company, 2019.

Rachman, Gideon. *Easternization: Asia's Rise and America's Decline From Obama to Trump and Beyond*. New York: Other Press, 2017.

Shapiro, Ben. *The Establishment Is Dead: The Rise and Election of Donald Trump*. Hermosa Beach, CA: Creators Publishing, 2017.

Smith, Lee. *The Plot Against the President: The True Story of How Congressman Devin Nunes Uncovered the Biggest Political Scandal in U.S. History*. New York: Center Street (Hachette), 2019.
Trump, Donald. *The Art of the Comeback*. New York: Times Books, 1997.

Trump, Donald Jr., *Triggered: How the Left Thrives on Hate and Wants to Silence Us.* New York: Center Street (Hachette), 2019.

Wead, Doug. *Inside Trump's White House: The Real Story of His Presidency*. New York: Hachette Book Group, 2019.

Wegren, Stephen K. *Putin's Russia: Past Imperfect, Future Uncertain*. Lanham, MD: The Rowman & Littlefield Publishing Group, 2019.

BIDEN TAKES COMMAND

Biden, Joe. *Promises to Keep: On Life and Politics*. New York: Random House, 2008.

Biden, Joe. *Promise Me, Dad: A Year of Hope, Hardship, and Purpose*. New York: Flatiron Books, 2018.

Harris, Kamala. *The Truths We Hold: An American Journey*. New York: Penguin, 2020.

Osnos, Evan. *Joe Biden: The Life, the Run, and What Matters Now*. New York: Scribner, 2020.

INDEX

A

Abolitionists/Abolitionist/Abolitionism 136, 137, 138, 145, 530
Acheson, Dean 266
Adam and Eve 129, 312, 492, 493, 501, 511, 550
Adams, John 76, 86, 104, 106, 107, 108, 109, 111, 121
Adams, John Quincy 119, 121
Addams, Jane 183, 184, 191
Affirmative action 318
Age of Reason 46, 64
Agnew, Spiro 345
Alexander the Great 5, 22, 39, 86, 95, 102, 144, 159, 324, 510
Algerian Crisis (1956-1962) 290
Alito, Samuel 470
Allen, Ethan 79
Al-Qaeda 396, 397, 413, 414, 415, 418, 420
Amendments to the Constitution
 First 313, 314, 364, 365, 407, 427
 Ninth 91
 Tenth 92, 303
 Fourteenth 148
 Fifteenth 152
 Sixteenth 197
 Seventeenth 197
American Civil Liberties Union (ACLU) 222, 313, 314, 317, 362, 363, 426, 435, 438, 464
American embassies bombing (1998) 397
American Recovery and Reinvestment Act - $787 billion (2009) 440
Ancien Régime of France 99
Antietam, Battle of (1862) 146
Antifa 469
Anzio, Battle of (1944) 250
Apollo 11 Moon Landing (1969) 333
Arab Spring (2011) 445, 446, 447, 448, 451
 Egypt 446
 Libya 447, 450
 Syria 447, 448, 449
 Tunisia 445
Aristotle 5, 21, 22, 504
Arnold, Benedict 79, 81, 84, 85, 104

Arthur, Chester A. 168
Asbury, Francis 131, 132, 529
Assault on Capitol Hill (2021) 481
Athens/Athenian 18, 19, 20, 24, 26, 98, 192
Atlantic Charter (1941) 247
Attlee, Clement 258
Austin, Stephen 123

B

Ba'athist Party (Iraq) 383, 419
Bacon, Nathaniel 69
Bacon's Rebellion (1676) 70, 87
Barrett, Amy Coney 464
Battle of the Bulge 254
Bay of Pigs operation (1961) 296
Beatles 326, 336
Beecher, Henry Ward 199
Begin, Menachem 357, 358
Behaviorist/Behaviorism 316
Bell, Alexander Graham 159
Belt and Road Initiative (China: 2013-today) 473
Benghazi killings (2012) 449
Berkeley, John 65
Berkeley, William 52, 63, 69
Berlin Wall installed (1961) 296
Bernstein, Carl 343
Bi-Centennial (American - 1976) 352
Biden, Hunter 466
Biden, Joe 373, 428, 465, 466, 467, 474, 478, 479, 480, 482, 483, 484, 485, 486, 488, 489, 549
Bin Laden, Osama 396, 414, 415, 416, 445, 476
Bismarck, Otto von 204, 205
Black Hawk down (Somalia - 1993) 391
Black Hawk (Indian chief) 122
Black Hawk War (1832) 141
Black Lives Matter (BLM) 437, 469
Black Panthers 318, 327, 329, 363, 400
Blair, Tony 418
Bleeding Kansas 138, 139, 529
Blitzkrieg (Lightning War) 246, 254
Boat people (Vietnamese) 351
Boer War (1900-1902) 205
Bohr, Niels 8, 13, 499
Bolshevik 181
Bolsheviks/Bolshevik/Bolshevist 193, 216

Index 551

Bonus Army (1932) 227
Boomer Generation 271, 272, 281, 282, 283, 325, 326, 327, 328, 331, 335, 336, 337, 338, 339, 342, 362, 388, 389, 405, 406, 409, 415, 519
Booth, John Wilkes 150
Bork, Robert 345, 404
Bosnia intervention (1995) 392, 393
Boxer Rebellion (1899-1901) 208
Brezhnev, Leonid 325, 341, 359, 374
Briggs, Charles 200
Brown, H. Rap 319
Bryan, William Jennings 172, 184, 185, 186, 190, 207, 213, 223
Brzezinski, Zbigniew 358
Buchanan, James 139
Buddhists, Buddhist/Buddhism 14, 15, 201
Buddhists/Buddhist/Buddhism 300, 319
Bull Run, Battles of (1861 and 1862) 146
Bunker and Breeds Hill, Battle of (1775) 79
Burgesses, House of 52, 104
Burke, Edmund 179
Burr, Aaron 107
Bush Doctrine 414, 416, 418
Bush, George H.W. (Sr.) 378, 380, 382, 383, 384, 385, 390, 391, 515, 516
Bush, George W. (Jr.) 409, 414, 415, 416, 417, 418, 419, 420, 421, 422, 424, 425, 426, 439, 441, 443, 444, 445, 452, 456, 476, 517
Bushido 253
Bush, Jeb 456

C

Caesar, Julius 25
Caesar, Julius and Octavian 268
Caesar, Octavian "Augustus" 25
Calhoun, John C. 115, 120, 124
Calvert, George and Cecil (Baltimore) 62
Calvinists/Calvinist/Calvinism 9, 26, 42, 43, 44, 65, 129, 130
Calvin, John 41, 42, 46, 57, 129, 224
Camp David Accords (1978) 357, 358

Carnegie, Andrew 161, 162
Carpetbaggers 152
Carson, Kit 155
Carteret, George 65
Carter, James E. (Jimmy) 177, 352, 353, 355, 356, 357, 358, 359, 360, 361, 367, 373, 375, 392, 443, 445
Cash for Clunkers (2009) 440
Castro, Fidel (Cuban dictator) 292, 296, 298, 299
Catherine de Medicis (French queen) 43
Celler, Emanuel 317
Central Intelligence Agency (CIA) 292, 296, 376, 395, 415, 416
Chamberlain, Neville 244, 245, 246, 247, 534
Chappaquiddick incident (1969) 334
Charismatic Movement 355, 366, 407
Charlemagne 35, 36, 37
Charles I (English king) 44, 55, 62
Charles II (English king) 45, 63
Charles I of Habsburg (Spanish king) 40, 43
Chase, Salmon 141, 142
Chavez, Hugo 472
Cheney, Dick 383, 417
Cherokee Indians 122
Chiang Kai-shek 243, 244, 264, 265, 267, 289, 322
Chick-fil-A under attack 435
Chosin Reservoir, Battle at (1950) 268
Churchill, Winston 246, 247, 255, 258, 260
Cicero 25
City on a Hill 10, 55, 67, 496, 500, 518, 521
Civil Right Act of 1964 308
Clark, William 110
Clay, Henry 115, 118, 121, 137, 162
Cleveland, Grover 162, 168, 169, 170, 171, 172
Clinton, Bill 384, 385, 387, 388, 389, 390, 391, 392, 393, 394, 395, 396, 397, 401, 402, 409, 417, 515, 516
Clinton, Hillary 387, 450, 455, 456, 457, 458
Cold War 260, 263, 264, 265, 275, 287, 288, 290, 292, 296, 297,

298, 306, 321, 341, 359, 367, 375, 377
Columbine High School Massacre (1999) 402
Columbus, Christopher 39
Comanche Indians 122
Congo Crisis (1960-1965) 291
Connecticut Compromise (July 1787) 91
Constantine (Roman Emperor) 32, 33, 511
Constitutional Convention (summer 1787) 88
Continental Congress 77, 82, 84, 88, 104, 114
Coolidge, Calvin 224
Cornwallis, General Charles 85, 86
Coronavirus / Covid-19 pandemic 462, 467, 478, 479
Covenant with God 524
Creationism 498
Cromwell, Charles 45, 63, 66
Cruz, Ted 456
Cuban Missile Crisis (1962) 298

D

Darrow, Clarence 222
Darwin, Charles 179, 181
Darwinists/Darwinist/Darwinism 12, 160, 178, 185, 199, 222, 407, 426, 493, 518
David (King of Israel) 511
Davis, Jefferson 143
Days of Rage (1969) 335
D-Day 252
Dean, John 344
Debs, Eugene 171
Declaration of Independence (1776) 80, 97, 104, 107, 352
Defense of Marriage Act of 1996 (DOMA) 434, 464
De Gaulle, Charles 290, 291, 293, 321, 322
Deism 71
Democracy "from above" 307, 310
Deng Xiaoping 358, 359, 376, 382, 473
Depression in rural America (1920s) 219
Descartes, René 176
Détente 341, 367
Dewey, John 193, 194, 198, 232
Dolchstoss - German "Stab in the Back" 218, 239
Dominic/Dominicans 38, 47
Domino theory (Vietnam) 309
Douglas, Stephen 139, 141
Dukakis, Michael 378
Dust Bowl in the Midwest (1930s) 234

E

Eagle Claw, Operation (1980) 360
Edict of Nantes 65
Edison, Thomas Alva 164, 165, 166
Edwards, Jonathan 72
Einstein, Albert 8, 13, 499, 552
Eisenhower, Dwight D. 251, 278, 279, 280, 281, 287, 289, 292, 293, 334
Elizabeth I (English queen) 43
Emerson, Ralph Waldo 130
Entitlement mentality 272, 318, 457
Era of Good Feelings 117, 235
European Union 394
Evangelicals/Evangelical/ Evangelicalism 324, 366, 407, 408, 461, 463
Existentialism 498

F

Facebook 469, 488, 489
Faubus, Orville 287
Federal Home Loan Mortgage Corporation (Freddie Mac) 391, 424
Federalist Papers 95, 96, 102, 114
Federal National Mortgage Association (Fannie Mae) 391, 424
Ferguson, Missouri crisis (2014) Policeman Darren Wilson shoots Michael Brown 436, 437
Fifield, James W., Jr. 236
Fillmore, Millard 139
Finney, Charles Grandison 132
Fisk, James 152, 153, 161
Fitzgerald F. Scott 222
Ford, Christine Blasey 464
Ford, Gerald R. 345, 352, 353, 367, 425, 439, 464
Ford, Henry 166, 167
Fourteen Points (Wilson's) 216
Fox, George 65
Francis/Franciscans 38, 47
Franklin, Benjamin 86, 88, 89, 91,

Index   553

97, 100, 104, 107, 137, 227, 312, 502
Franklin's call for prayer (1787) 89
Fredericksburg, Battles of (1862-1863) 146
Frémont, General John C. 125, 139
French Revolution (1789-1795) 98, 99, 105, 232
Friedan, Betty 327

G

Gaddafi, Muammar 373, 374, 380, 448, 449, 517
Gandhi, Mohandas (Mahatma) 242
Garfield, James A. 167
Garland, Merrick 463
Gates, General Horatio 81, 84, 85
Generation-X 430, 519
Geneva (Switzerland) 1, 41, 42, 57, 300
George III (British king) 76, 82, 206, 509
George VI (British king) 247
Geronimo 155
Gettysburg, Battle of (1863) 147
Ghost Dance craze 157
G.I. Bill 270
Gingrich, Newt 389, 390, 391, 401, 402
Ginsburg, Ruth Bader 464, 465
Glorious Revolution 45
Goldwater, Barry 310, 311
Gompers, Samuel 174
Google 488
Gorbachev, Mikhail 375, 377, 380, 381
  Glasnost 375, 380
  Perestroika 375, 380
Gore, Al 409
Gorsuch, Neil 463, 470
Gould, Jay 152, 153, 161, 532
Graham, Billy 159, 274, 306, 350, 391
Grant, Ulysses S. 146, 147, 149, 150, 151, 152, 153, 154, 167, 169
Great Awakening (First) 72, 74
Great Awakening (Second) 132
Greatest Generation 248
Great Society (Johnson Program) 2, 306, 307, 308, 310, 312, 315, 317, 328, 330, 490
Greece/Greek 2, 5, 12, 16, 18, 19, 20, 21, 22, 26, 30, 31, 32, 34, 205, 261, 263, 473
Grenada intervention (1983) 370
Guaidó, Juan 472
Gulf of Tonkin Resolution (1964) 309
Gulf War or "Desert Storm" (1990-1991) 382, 383

H

Haiti intervention (1994) 392
Halfway Covenant 70
Hamas 374
Hamilton, Alexander 86, 95, 102, 103, 105, 106, 107, 108, 109, 113, 114, 115
Harding, Warren G. 223, 224
Harris, Kamala 478, 480, 488
Harrison, Benjamin 170
Harrison, William Henry 127
Hawthorne, Nathaniel 131
Hayes, Rutherford B. 154, 167
Hegel, Georg Wilhelm Friedrich 178
Hemingway, Ernest 222
Hezbollah 374, 376
Hindenburg, Paul von 239
Hindu 13, 14, 15, 242
Hippie communes 298, 326
Hiss, Alger 276
Hitler, Adolf 218, 228, 232, 233, 239, 240, 241, 242, 244, 245, 246, 247, 248, 251, 253, 254, 255, 257, 260, 261, 264, 272, 282, 323, 509
Hodge, Charles 199
Holder, Eric 437
Homophobia 433, 434, 435, 459
Hooker, Thomas 59, 70
Hoover, Herbert 224, 225, 226, 227
House Un-American Activities Committee (HUAC) 276, 277, 278
Huguenot/Huguenots 43, 65
Human Enlightenment 45, 71, 312
Humanist Manifesto (1933) 194, 198, 232, 313, 315, 365
Humanist Manifesto II (1973) 365
Humanists/Humanist/Humanism 8, 11, 12, 39, 46, 87, 104, 111, 128, 129, 130, 131, 177, 179, 183, 191, 192, 193, 194, 198, 201, 202, 210, 217, 222, 231, 232, 233, 235, 282, 283, 313, 314, 315, 365, 366, 475, 476,

493, 498, 514, 518
Human Reason 71, 129, 475
Hume, David 178
Hungarian Revolt (1956) 289
Hutchinson, Anne 59

I

Identity politics 118, 124, 137, 436, 437
Ignatius of Loyola 43
Immigration and Customs Enforcement (ICE) 471
Inchon, Landing at (1950) 267
Indenture 50, 51, 62, 63, 69
Indian Removal (1830s) 122
Internal Combustion Engine - ICE 165, 166
Iran-Contra Affair (1986-1987) 376, 377
Iron Curtain 260, 263, 297, 376
Islamic Jihad 395
Islamic Republic of Iran 357, 453
Islam/Muslim 16, 35, 37, 202, 374, 415, 420, 447, 449, 450, 475, 476, 477
Israelites 70, 125

J

Jackson, Andrew 116, 117, 120, 121, 122, 126, 127
James I (English king) 44
James II (Duke of York and English king) 65
James ll (Duke of York and English king) 65
Jamestown 49, 50, 51, 52, 69
Jay, John 86, 105, 106, 152
Jefferson, Thomas 80, 97, 103, 104, 105, 106, 107, 108, 109, 110, 111, 113, 114, 115, 119, 121, 129, 130, 139, 143, 235, 313, 316, 348
Jesuit/Jesuits 43, 48
Jesus of Nazareth, the Christ 12, 16, 18, 22, 28, 29, 30, 31, 33, 43, 65, 71, 72, 75, 91, 128, 130, 134, 135, 191, 200, 201, 235, 385, 408, 493, 494, 500, 501, 502, 511, 514, 519
Jew/Jewish/Judaism 10, 12, 16, 17, 18, 26, 28, 29, 31, 200, 239, 323, 346, 374, 408, 417, 433, 465

Johnson, Andrew 151, 152
Johnson, Lyndon 302, 303, 304, 305, 306, 307, 308, 309, 310, 311, 312, 315, 317, 318, 319, 320, 322, 327, 328, 329, 334, 337, 340, 416, 437, 440, 445, 494, 507
Joint Comprehensive Plan of Action (JCPOA) with Iran 454

K

Kagan, Elena 433
Karzai, Hamid 444, 445
Kavanaugh, Brett 464, 470, 549
Kefauver, Estes 278
Kennan, George 261
Kennedy, Anthony 463
Kennedy, John F. 294, 296, 297, 298, 300, 515, 516
Kennedy, Robert (Bobby) 330
Kennedy, Ted 334, 339
Kent State Massacre (1970) 338
Kerry, John 339, 340, 405, 417, 420, 450, 453
Key, Francis Scott 116
Khashoggi, Jamal 477
Khmer Rouge 351
Khrushchev, Nikita 287, 288, 289, 293, 296, 298, 299
Killing Fields of Cambodia 351
Kim Il-sung 266
King, Rev. Dr. Martin Luther, Jr. 11, 285, 286, 299, 311, 312, 329, 330, 494
Kissinger, Dr. Henry 341
Kitzmiller v. Dover Area School District case - 2005 426
Knights of Labor 173, 174
Kosovo 393, 394
Kosovo Crisis (1999) 393
Ku Klux Klan 152

L

Lafayette, Marquis de 86
Lamarck, Jean-Baptiste 179
League of Nations 216, 218, 238
Lebanon crisis (1982-1984) 370
Lee, General Charles 84, 85
Lee, Robert E. 140, 144, 147, 149
Leibniz, Gottfried Wilhelm 176
Lend-Lease (1940-1941) 247
Lenin, Vladimir Ilyich Ulyanov 181, 182, 195, 210, 216, 240

Index

Lewis, Meriwether 110
Lexington and Concord, Battle of (1775) 77
LGBTQ 470
Liberalism 194, 195, 366, 532, 534, 540
Light to the Nations 10, 18, 55, 67, 75, 133, 496, 500, 515, 518
Lincoln, Abraham 122, 140, 141, 142, 143, 144, 145, 146, 147, 148, 149, 150, 151, 152, 154, 278, 284, 299, 419, 498, 511, 512, 513
Little Bighorn, Battle of (1876) 157
Locke, John 46, 64, 104, 177, 507
Lockerbie bombing (1988) 380
Lost Generation (1920s) 222
Louis XIV (French king) 45, 65
Louis XVI (French king) 82
Lusitania sunk (1915) 213
Luther, Martin 40, 41, 46, 285

M

MacArthur, Douglas 264, 267, 268
Machen, John Gresham 235
Machiavelli, Niccolo 39, 40
Madison, James 95, 96, 102, 105, 114, 115, 121, 529
Maduro, Nicolás 472, 475
Maliki, Nouri al- 444
Manifest Destiny 124
Manson murders (1969) 334
Mao, Tse-Tung (Zedong) 194, 243, 264, 265, 267, 268, 288, 289, 321, 322, 323, 341, 351, 358, 373, 473
Maritime Silk Road 475
Market Garden plan 253
Market saturation 225, 234, 423
Marshall, George 251, 262, 264
Marshall, John 111, 112, 122, 313
Marshall Plan (1948-1952) 262, 263, 271, 515
Marx, Karl 181, 240
Mason-Dixon Line 137
Mason, George 137, 312
Massachusetts Bay Colony 58, 59
Massoud, Ahmed Shah 395, 414
Mattis, Jim 477
Mayflower 54
Mayflower Compact 54
McCain, John 456, 458

McCarthy, Joseph 226, 277, 278, 280, 281
McClellan, George 146, 148
McGovern, George 342
McKinley, William 170, 171, 172, 185
Meade, George 147
Meese, Edwin 377
Meiji (Japanese emperor) 207
Merkel, Angela 478
Mexican-American War (1846-1848) 125, 145
Middle America 272, 273, 275, 276, 277, 278, 283, 285, 287, 300, 317, 331, 342, 429, 433, 438, 440, 457, 483, 520
Midway, Battle of (1942) 249
Millennial Generation 519
Miller, Arthur 277
Miller, William and Seventh-Day Adventists 134
Million-Man March (1995) 400
Missouri Compromise (1820) 118, 136, 138
Monica Lewinsky affair (1998-1999) 401
Monitor and Merrimac, Battle (1862) 146
Monroe Doctrine (1823) 119, 206
Montgomery, Bernard 143, 250, 253, 254, 285, 286, 287, 311, 363
Moody, Dwight L. 200
Morgan, John Pierpoint (J.P.) 162, 171
Mormons 135, 155
Mormons/Mormon/Mormonism 135, 462
Mueller investigation (2017-2019) 463
Mueller, Robert 463, 466
Mussolini, Benito 228, 233, 238, 239, 242, 248, 250

N

Napoleon Bonaparte 100, 109, 110, 116, 179, 205
Napoleon, Louis (Napoleon III) 205
Nasser, Gamal Abdel 288, 289, 290, 292, 323, 346
National Association for the Advancement of Colored People (NAACP) 285, 405, 436
National debt 422, 440, 441, 442, 443, 468

National Socialism (German Fascism) 232
Nation-building 383, 415, 416, 417, 444, 445, 477
Navajo Indians 155
New Deal 227, 228, 230, 233, 234, 270, 303, 304, 306, 440
New Frontier (Kennedy program) 293
New Orleans, Battle of (1815) 116
Newton, Isaac 46, 176
Ngo Dinh Diem 300
Niebuhr, H. Richard 235
Ninth Circuit Court 464
Nixon, Richard M. 265, 276, 278, 293, 294, 295, 296, 331, 334, 337, 338, 340, 341, 342, 343, 344, 345, 346, 347, 348, 349, 350, 358, 516
Nobel Peace Prize 184, 245, 358, 443
North American Free Trade Agreement (NAFTA) 390, 471
North Atlantic Treaty Organization (NATO) 264, 290, 296, 320, 321, 375, 393, 394, 415, 417, 418, 445, 448, 450, 473, 478
Northern Alliance (Afghanistan) 395, 396, 415
North, Oliver 377

O

Obama, Barack 178, 340, 389, 390, 426, 429, 430, 432, 433, 434, 435, 436, 437, 438, 439, 440, 441, 442, 443, 444, 445, 447, 448, 449, 450, 451, 452, 453, 454, 455, 457, 459, 463, 464, 466, 471, 475, 476, 478, 485, 508, 519
Obamacare 441, 442
Oglethorpe, General James 68
O.J. Simpson murder case (1994-1995) 400
Oklahoma City bombing (1995) 399
Opechancanough 51
Open Door Policy in China 208
Organization of Petroleum Exporting Countries (OPEC) 371, 372
Orwell, George 275
Oswald, Lee Harvey 301

P

Pahlavi, Shah Mohammed Reza 347, 353, 355, 356, 357, 360, 396, 453
Palestinian Liberation Organization (PLO) 374
Palmer, Mitchell 219
Panama Canal 209, 355, 370
Panic (financial) of 2008 424
Paris Peace Accords of 1973 342
Park Chung-hee 353
Parks, Rosa 285
Patrick, Saint 35
Patton, George 250, 254
Peace Corps 297, 326
Pearl Harbor, Bombing of (1941) 248
Pelosi, Nancy 442, 462, 468
Penn, William 65, 66, 67
Pentagon Papers (1971) 340, 341
Pentecostals/Pentecostal/ Pentecostalism 366, 462
Pequot 60, 529
Perot, Ross 384, 385
Petersburg, Battle of (1864) 147
Philip II, Macedonian king 5, 22
Philip II, Spanish king 43
Pike, Zebulon 110
Pilgrims 53, 55
Plato 20, 21, 130, 504
Pledge of Allegiance 426
Plymouth Plantation 53
Poe, Edgar Allan 131
Polkinghorne, John 8, 13
Polk, James 124, 125
Poor People's March (1968) 330
Potsdam Conference (1945) 258
Powell, Colin 392, 418, 421
Prague Spring (or Czechoslovakian Crisis - 1968) 324, 325
Praying Indians 60
Progressivists/Progressivist/ Progressivism 175, 182, 183, 184, 185, 186, 193, 197, 200, 206, 209, 222, 226, 231, 308, 325, 336, 408
Prohibition (1920s - early 1930s) 221
Puritan/Puritans/Puritanism 44, 45, 53, 55, 57, 58, 62, 63, 70, 71, 72, 106, 121, 224, 231, 277, 333, 496, 497, 501, 514, 520
Putin, Vladimir 448, 449, 450, 451, 473, 474, 475, 546, 548, 549

Index 557

Q

Quagmire in Iraq 374, 383, 417, 418, 419
Quaker/Quakers 62, 65, 66, 67
Quasi War of 1799 108

R

Rather, Dan 421
Reagan, Ronald 6, 352, 367, 368, 369, 370, 371, 373, 374, 375, 376, 377, 379, 380, 384, 391, 392, 407, 412, 484, 544, 545
Realpolitik 2, 332, 341, 343, 346, 391
Reconstruction 151, 154, 167
Red Scare 219, 277
Red Stick Creek Indians 115, 116
Reign of Terror in France (1793-1794) 99
Re-Imagining Conference (1993) 404
Renaissance 38, 39, 40
Revolution of Rising Expectations 317
Richardson, Elliot 344
Roanoke, Lost English colony 48, 49
Rockefeller, John D. 161, 163, 164
Rodney King incident (1991-1992) 397
Rolfe, John 50
Rome/Roman 10, 12, 16, 18, 22, 23, 24, 25, 26, 28, 29, 30, 31, 32, 33, 34, 35, 36, 37, 38, 39, 40, 43, 98, 197, 250, 252, 367, 393, 535
Romney, Mitt 319, 462, 467
Roosevelt, Franklin Delano (FDR) 227, 228, 231, 233, 247, 251, 252, 255, 303
Roosevelt's prayer 252
Roosevelt, Theodore (Teddy) 155, 172, 186, 209
Rousseau, Jean-Jacques 177, 178, 193
Rubio, Marco 456
Ruby Ridge incident (1992) 398
Rumsfeld, Donald 416, 417, 419, 420, 421
Russian Revolution (1917) 212, 213
Rwanda tribal genocide (1994) 392

S

Sacajawea 110
Sacco and Vanzetti trial 219
Sadat, Anwar 345, 346, 357, 358, 373
Saddam Hussein 382, 383, 394, 395, 417, 418, 419, 420, 476, 484, 507, 515, 516, 517
Salem witch-scare (1692-1693) 71
Samuel (Israelite Prophet) 511
Sanders, Bernie 195, 456, 457
Sandinistas (Nicaragua) 376
Santa Anna, Antonio López de 123, 125
Saratoga, Battle of (1777) 81
Scalia, Antonin 463
Schiff, Adam 466
Schrödinger, Erwin 8, 13, 499
Scopes Monkey Trial (1925) 222, 223
Scott, Winfield 122, 143, 145
Second Continental Congress 77, 104
Secular/Secularist/Secularists/ Secularism 11, 27, 28, 32, 46, 183, 190, 194, 201, 206, 222, 223, 231, 282, 306, 314, 315, 316, 317, 354, 356, 357, 364, 365, 366, 373, 374, 380, 402, 426, 427, 433, 447, 475, 476, 477, 493
Seminole Indians 117, 122
Separatists (English) 53, 55
Seward, William 141, 142, 150
Shaftesbury, Anthony Ashley Cooper, Earl of 63, 64
Shay's Rebellion (1786-1787) 87
Sheridan, Philip 146, 157
Sherman, William Tecumseh 148
Shi'ite/Shi'ites/Shi'a Islam 374, 382, 383, 396, 418, 420, 421, 444, 447, 448, 449, 453, 475, 476, 477
Shinto 243
Silent Generation 326, 327, 519
Sioux Indians 154, 157, 158
Sitting Bull (Sioux/Lakota chief) 157
Sitzkrieg (Sitting War) or Phony War 246
Six-Day War (Arabs vs. Israel - 1967) 323, 324
Slater, Samuel 112
Slavery 21, 69, 70, 118, 119, 124, 134, 136, 137, 138, 139, 140,

141, 142, 144, 145, 148, 150, 169, 351
Smith, Adam 179
Smith, John 49
Smith, Joseph 135
Social Gospel 227, 235
Social Security 231, 303, 304, 372, 422
Socrates 20, 504
Solidarność (Solidarity) 380
Sotomayor, Sonia 433
South China Sea standoff (2014-?) 452, 453
Soviet Empire collapse (1989) 380
Soviet Union disintegrates (1989-1991) 381
Spanish-American War (1898) 207
Spanish Flu pandemic (1918) 219
Spoils system 121, 168
Sputnik (1957) 290
Stalingrad, Battle of (1942-1943) 250
Stalin, Joseph 226, 228, 233, 240, 241, 242, 243, 245, 246, 250, 254, 255, 258, 260, 261, 262, 263, 264, 265, 266, 275, 276, 287, 475, 494
Stanley Steamer 165
Stanley twins (Francis and Freelan) 165
Star-Spangled Banner 116
Steele dossier 458
Stein, Gertrude 222
Stowe, Harriet Beecher 137, 199
Sturm und Drang Movement 180
Subprime home mortgages (2000s) 231, 423
Suez Crisis (1956) 288, 289
Sukarno (Indonesian dictator) 284
Sunnis/Sunni Islam 374, 383, 396, 418, 420, 421, 444, 447, 449, 475, 476, 477
Sun Yat-sen 243
Supreme Court cases
  1857 - *Dred Scott v. Sandford* 139
  1962 - *Engle v. Vitale* 313
  1963 - *Abington Township School District v. Schempp* 314
  1963 - *Murray v. Curlett* 314
  1968 - *Green v. County School Board* 363
  1969 - *U.S. v. Montgomery County Board of Education* 363
  1971 - *Lemon v. Kurtzman* 364, 365
  1971 - *Swann v. Charlotte Mecklenburg Board of Education* 363
  1973 - *Roe v. Wade* 363
  1987 - *Edwards v. Aguillard* 407, 426
  2013 - *United States v. Windsor* 434
  2015 - *Obergefell v. Hodges* 434
  2020 - *Harris Funeral Homes v. Equal Employment Opportunity Commission* 470
Surge (troops) in Afghanistan (2009) 444
Surge (troops) in Iraq (2007) 421
Syngman Rhee 266

T

Taft, William Howard 185, 188, 189, 191, 192
Taliban 395, 396, 415, 444, 445, 477, 490, 491, 517, 546, 558
Tammany Hall 153, 170
Taney, Roger B. 139, 140
Taylor, Zachary 125, 139
Tecumseh 114, 115
Tet Offensive (Jan-Feb 1968) 328, 329, 541
Texas Independence (1836) 123
Thomas, Clarence 404, 405, 464
Thoreau, Henry David 130
Tiananmen Square tragedy (1989) 381
Tianming (Mandate of Heaven) 510
Tianzi (Son of Heaven) 472, 474, 510
Tillotson, Archbishop John 71
Tito, Josip Broz 261, 263, 264, 392
Tocqueville, Alexis de 121, 175
Tories 45, 64, 83, 84, 85, 102
Tower, John
  Tower Report - 1987 377
Toynbee, Arnold 505
Trail of Tears 122
Transcendentalists 130, 131
Treaty of Ghent (1814) 116
Treaty of Paris (1783) 86
Trinitarian/Trinitarianism 30, 31
Tripoli, Battle of 110, 111
Troubled Assets Relief Program (TARP) 425

Index 559

Truman Doctrine (1947) 261
Truman, Harry S. 6, 255, 256, 257, 258, 260, 261, 262, 263, 264, 266, 267, 268, 270, 274, 278, 279, 280, 305, 309, 310, 350, 515
Trump, Donald 373, 455, 456, 457, 458, 459, 460, 461, 462, 463, 464, 465, 466, 467, 468, 470, 471, 472, 473, 474, 475, 476, 477, 478, 479, 480, 481, 482, 485, 486, 487, 488, 519
Tuskegee Airmen 285
Tweed, William "Boss" 153, 154
Twin Towers 397, 413, 414, 417
Twitter 455

U

U-2 incident (1960) 292
Ukraine crisis (2010-2015)
  Euromaidan Revolution (2014) 451
  Putin siezes Crimea (2014) 451
  Tymoshenko, Yulia 450
  Yanukovych, Victor 451
Underground Railroad 138
Unitarian/Unitarianism 30, 31, 33, 34, 71, 129, 130, 232
United States Mexico Canada Agreement (USMCA) 472

V

Vallandigham, Clement 146
Valley Forge, winter at (1777-1778) 82
Van Buren, Martin 120, 121, 124, 127
Vanderbilt, Cornelius 153, 160, 161, 164
Varick, James 132
Vereide, Abraham 236, 237, 274
Versailles Treaty (1919) 217, 239, 240
Vets - World War Two Veteran Generation 259, 272, 277, 282, 283, 297, 315, 328, 337, 403, 406
Vicksburg, Battle of (1863) 147
Victoria (British queen) 204
Vietnam 205, 284, 300, 301, 309, 310, 311, 319, 320, 327, 328, 329, 335, 337, 338, 339, 340, 341, 342, 343, 347, 350, 351, 360, 370, 383, 384, 416, 420, 444, 445
Vietnam Veterans against the War March (1971) 339
Vikings 36, 37
Volcker, Paul 8, 360, 361, 371, 372
Voting Rights Act of 1965 311

W

Waco Siege (1993) 399
Wallace, Mike 479
Wall of separation 313, 314
War on Poverty (Johnson program) 308, 309
Washington, George 77, 82, 83, 84, 86, 97, 101, 102, 103, 105, 106, 509, 511
Watergate (1973-1974) 343, 344, 345, 348, 350
Weapons of Mass Destruction (WMDs) 395, 418, 419
Weimar Republic 239, 240
Whigs 45, 64, 79, 122, 124, 125, 127, 138
Whiskey Rebellion 103
Whitefield, George 72, 527
White, Harry Dexter 276
White, Paula 461
Williams, Roger 58, 59, 66, 539
Wilson, Woodrow 6, 177, 180, 181, 184, 186, 189, 209, 210, 213, 214, 215, 216, 217, 218, 229, 238, 272, 436, 437, 516
Winfrey, Oprah 455
Winthrop, John 55, 57, 58, 59, 60, 498, 521
Witchcraft 72
Women's Christian Temperance Union (WCTU) 174
Woodstock Music Festival (1969) 335
Woodward, Bob 343
World Health Organization (WHO) 474
World Trade Center bombing (1993) 396
World Trade Center destruction - 9/11 (2001) 413, 417
World Trade Organization's (WTO) 473
Wounded Knee Creek, Battle of (1890) 158
Wright brothers (Orville and Wilbur) 165

X

Xi Jinping 451, 452, 453, 472, 473, 474, 475
XYZ Affair 108

Y

Yahweh 17
Yalta Conference (1945) 255
Yeltsin, Boris 381, 394, 474, 475
Yippie 330
Yom Kippur (or October) War (1973) 345, 346
Yorktown, Battle of (1781) 86
Young, Brigham 135, 155

Z

Zbigniew, Brzezinski 358
Zimmerman, George shoots Trayvon Martin (2012) 436